A HISTORY OF THE CANADIAN PEOPLES

Second Edition

J. M. Bumsted

OXFORD
UNIVERSITY PRESS

70 Wynford Drive, Don Mills, Ontario M3C 1J9
www.oup.com/ca

Oxford University Press is a department of the University of Oxford.
It furthers the University's objective of excellence in research, scholarship,
and education by publishing worldwide in

Oxford New York
Auckland Bangkok Buenos Aires Cape Town Chennai
Dar es Salaam Delhi Hong Kong Istanbul Karachi Kolkata
Kuala Lumpur Madrid Melbourne Mexico City Mumbai Nairobi
São Paulo Shanghai Taipei Tokyo Toronto

Published in Canada by Oxford University Press

First published 2003

National Library of Canada Cataloguing in Publication

Bumsted, J. M., 1938–

A history of the Canadian peoples / J.M. Bumsted. — 2nd ed.

Includes bibliographical references and index.

ISBN 0-19-541688-0

1. Canada—History. I. Title.

FC164.B862 2003 971 C2003-901106-2

F1026.B9515 2003

Cover & Text design: Brett J. Miller

This book is printed on permanent (acid-free) paper ♾.
Printed in Canada

CONTENTS

MAPS

□ Understanding History

■ Every experienced historian has at some point encountered someone from a totally different background who assumes that 'anyone can do history'. In the sense that anyone can research, write, and even publish historical work without specialized training, that assumption is correct. History is one of those fields—creative writing is another—where the standards of achievement can be flexible and intuitive, and where much of the methodology is based on plain common sense. History's accessibility to almost all of us, not simply as readers but as actual researchers, is one of its great charms and greater merits. And many people do engage in historical research without calling it by that name. Everyone who tries to trace her ancestry through the labyrinth of historical records (often called 'genealogy') is involved in a form of historical research. Everyone who tries to research the background to a business project as part of a report on its present status, or to explain how a sports team achieved a championship season, is in a sense 'doing history'. Every criminal trial (and almost every civil one) is at some level a historical reconstruction. The historical mode is one of the most common ways through which we attempt to understand the world we live in.

To say that nearly all of us engage in some form of historical reconstruction, often unconsciously, is not to say that are no fundamental rules to such activity. Most of us know instinctively that witnesses can be biased or mistaken, that human motivation is complex, and that in the chronological sequence of events—the establishment of which many non-professional historians regard as the centre of the enterprise—the cause must precede the effect. But history is not a laboratory science. Even the simplest rules of evidence and argument can be difficult to apply in specific situations, particularly if the researcher is operating intuitively. Understanding what causes these difficulties is important, and becoming sensitive to the problems of history is one of the chief benefits of formal historical study.

A good many Canadians (probably nearly as many as commonly read fiction or poetry) read history, for recreation and for information. Unfortunately, general readers often approach historical writing in much the same way they approach fiction, judging a work's value by its success in telling 'a good story'. But of course story-telling is only one of numerous ways in which history can be written. Although, as with fiction, there is great pleasure to be had from reading history simply at the level of entertainment, to remain at that level would be to miss much of the best modern historical writing. It is possible without training or formal critical tools to recognize that a Harlequin romance offers a far less complex view of the world than a Margaret Atwood novel; it is somewhat more difficult to appreciate a parallel difference in history. Readers who expect writers of fiction to have distinctive voices and world-views still often assume that all historians participate equally in the effort to recover the truth of the past through application of some unspecified 'scientific' method: if history is about truth, then all historical writing must be more or less equally true, at least if the historian has 'the facts' right. The ordinary reader is frequently unable to distinguish between 'facts' and 'truth', failing to appreciate on one level that factual accuracy is in itself a complex issue and on another level that it has limited value as a critical test.

In addition, many readers fail to distinguish between history as everything that has happened before the present moment (also commonly known as 'the past') and history as the record (usually written) of the unfolding of some event(s) in that past. Yet that past can never be recovered, for reasons I shall discuss. All we can do is attempt to recreate and analyze discrete parts of that past, refracted through the historian's prism. Only this history can be studied and investigated. As a further confusion, history can mean not only the historian's account of the past, but the systematic study of the past as a discipline or a craft. The study of either the work of individual historians or the discipline itself is often known as historiography. Just as filmmakers make a surprising number of movies about the process of making movies, so historians devote more of their energy to examining the making of history than they do to any other single project.

The processes of both reading and researching history can obviously be greatly enhanced by some understanding of the problems that engage historians as they pursue their craft. Before we turn to some of those problems, however, it might be well to consider the question of the value of history.

THE VALUE OF HISTORY

Once upon a time, especially in the nineteenth and earlier twentieth centuries, most people did not question the value of historical study or wonder how it was relevant to their lives. They did not doubt the value of the liberal arts or the humanities, much less debate the benefits of studying languages like Greek or Latin. There are really two separate but related issues inherent in the 'value of history' question. One is whether or not historical study has a sufficient grip on truth and meaning in our modern world to have any value at all, intrinsic or extrinsic. Ultimately, this question involves us in high philosophy and theory, but it also has a particular Canadian edge. The other question is whether or not historical work has a sufficiently attractive vocational payoff to justify its study at the university. Perhaps we should turn to the latter question first, since it is easier to answer and may be of more interest to the beginning historian.

For many centuries, the opportunity to attend a university was available only to those of outstanding intellectual abilities or privileged socio-economic standing. In a world that did not question the importance of religion, the original purpose of universities was to educate clerics. The university gradually became the centre of humanistic scholarship and enterprise generally, but so long as society valued education for its own sake—chiefly because it was something available only to the privileged few—its specific vocational role was quite insignificant. Universities turned out educated and 'cultured' men (not women until well into the nineteenth century) into a world that took it for granted that such people were important to the society. Specific occupational training was not part of the university's function, and preparation even for such elevated professions as law or medicine was done outside its doors. Yet gradually the notion of vocational training did enter the cloistered world of the university, particularly in North America, and by 1940 it was possible to prepare for nearly any occupation through specialized studies at a university, although such opportunities were still limited to members of the élites. Despite the new vocational bent of the university, occupational studies were largely confined to the post-graduate level; most undergraduate students at universities (as opposed to acknowledged vocational centres such as teacher's training colleges) still expected An Education rather than A Vocation.

The great change in the nature of the university really came after 1945, when the idea took hold that all Canadians were entitled to attend university, and the number of university places was greatly expanded. A dynamic relationship has existed between the democratization of the university and the introduction of the idea that there should be some demonstrable economic value to a university degree. Thus specific occupational training now starts at the undergraduate rather than the graduate level. Today at many universities it is likely that the majority of students are enrolled in such programs, and even those who are not in such programs themselves commonly expect a university education to provide some kind of occupational entrée or advantage. In the new occupational sweepstakes, a field like history is of less obvious relevance than one like management or accounting or pharmacy or computers. Some historians would prefer to ignore the question of occupational relevance altogether, but the days of a simple liberal arts education for most university students are probably gone forever. History may not ever compete with accounting or pharmacy or medical school as preparation for employment, but it is still superb preparation for many professional programs (assuming that they do not insist on specialization from day one). And one can do more in the work force with a history specialization than most students might at first think.

There are any number of history-related occupations besides teaching. They include work in archives, libraries, and museums, as well as in government service. 'Heritage' in itself is a major industry in Canada. Other occupations, such as law, journalism, and some branches of the civil service (the diplomatic corps, for example) have traditionally recruited heavily among history graduates, but any job requiring the ability to gather and analyze evidence and then communicate the findings is ideally suited to someone with a background in history. One individual with a graduate degree in history, Mike Smith, has become the general manager of several National Hockey League teams. What students have to do is learn to translate their historical training into the jargon of the contemporary job market. 'Researching term essays in history', for example, can be translated into 'using documentary resources to abstract and analyze complex information'. (At one recent 'interview' for a summer job with a government department, the student applicant was simply asked to summarize a complex document quickly and accurately.) To the extent that history is a discipline that teaches students both to think and to communicate, it should improve their qualifications for almost any job.

Beyond developing essential skills in research, analysis, and communication, what are the uses of history? Certainly few historians today believe—if they ever did—in the use of historical 'laws' of human conduct for predictive purposes. Most historians who have employed historical laws, such as Arnold Toynbee in *A Study in History*, Oswald Spengler in *The Decline of the West*, or Karl Marx in *Capital*, have done so on such an abstract level that it is difficult to translate those laws into specific terms. Toynbee's notion that civilizations pass through recognizable stages paralleling the human life cycle is attractive, but it does not tell us when our civilization will die. Employing the insights of Karl Marx, no reader could have concluded that the 'dictatorship of the proletariat' would come first in Russia, or that it would eventually lead not to a classless society but to the collapse of the Soviet Union. No discipline has worked harder than economics to achieve scientific status, but the whole world has come to appreciate that economists constantly disagree on even the most general level of prediction and analysis.

Yet if history cannot predict, it can help us to understand the difficulty of prediction. In the same way it can help us to recognize the recurrent and ongoing nature of many of society's problems. By and large, historians were far more sanguine about the outcome of the 1992 referendum on the Charlottetown constitutional accord than were the scaremongers on either side of the debate or many of the journalists covering the 'crisis'. Indeed, those with an understanding of Canadian history, constitutional and otherwise, were bound to find the very concept of a 'crisis' suspect, just as they would any other popular journalistic concept, such as 'conspiracy'. The historical record tells us that there have been crises and conspiracies, but equally that these terms have so often been used without justification that they have lost any real meaning.

History provides us not only with a social context but with a personal one as well. The genealogical search for 'roots' has become important for many Canadians seeking to trace their family backgrounds and to understand the circumstances that drove their ancestors across the ocean, or the ways their ancestors' lives changed as a result of the newcomers' arrival. Nor is the question of personal identity merely an individual matter. It is no accident that as minority groups in Canada work to develop themselves as collectivities, they need to establish and assert their historical experience. Over the past thirty years some Canadians have lost interest in the historical mode, adopting what we might call the 'irrelevance of history' position. But this has not been the case with collective 'minorities' such as women, Native peoples, blacks, and ethnic minorities. For these groups, establishing their rightful place in Canadian history has been an absolutely primary function. That these groups' interpretations of their histories have often run counter to the traditional versions of Canadian history does not render them any less consequential—or less historical.

THE ELUSIVE FACT

More than forty years ago, a television series called 'Dragnet' became famous for a catchphrase used by one of its characters, a police detective named Sergeant Joe Friday. When questioning witnesses, Friday always repeated the same request, delivered in an emotionless monotone: 'All I want is the facts, just give me the facts.' The monotone was intended to indicate Friday's objectivity and to extract from his witness a response devoid of personal bias and colouration. Of course he seldom got 'just the facts'—which from our perspective is exactly the point. Somehow, just as the popular mind in the 1950s associated Joe Friday with facts, so it has more recently come to think of historians as dealing in the same coin. The equation of facts and history has doubtless been assisted by the traditional way of teaching history in the schools, by marching out one name, date, event after another for students to commit to memory and regurgitate at the appropriate time in the course of an examination. Of course historians do rely on facts as their basic building blocks; but they do not think of them the way Sergeant Friday did, nor do they use them the way common opinion believes they do.

The *Canadian Oxford Dictionary* offers several meanings for 'fact'. The most familiar is probably number 1: 'a thing that is known to have occurred, to exist, or to be true,' although number 4—'truth, reality'—is also very common. Facts, as 'Dragnet' suggested, are true things, unsullied by any process of interpretation or conclusion. Such things may exist, but they are much harder to come by than one might expect, for several reasons. One problem is the language in which 'facts' must be stated. Another is the context in which they become significant.

Over the last century we have become increasingly aware that language is not a neutral instrument, but one that carries with it a heavy freight of cultural experience and usage. 'John Cabot discovered Newfoundland in 1497' may seem a straightforward statement of fact, but at least half of the words in it conjure up a whole host of meanings. One of those words is 'discovered'. The implication is that what Cabot found was previously unknown—but of course an Aboriginal population had been living in the area for millennia. Even qualifying the word 'discovered' with the phrase 'by Europeans' doesn't help much, since we now know that the Vikings had settled at L'Anse aux Meadows in the eleventh century, and even they may not have been the first Europeans to cross the Atlantic. 'Discovery' is a complex concept. The term 'Newfoundland' is equally problematic, since in modern geographic terms Cabot was not at all precise about his movements, and the land he sighted may not have been part of the island that we know as Newfoundland today. Indeed, Cabot called the land he saw 'the New-Founde Land', and it was only later that the label was applied to the island. Moreover, Cabot's sightings were not confirmed by anything other than vague self-declarations. To top matters off, there are questions about the identity of John Cabot himself, who started in Italy as Giovanni (or Zuan) Caboto and became John Cabot Montecalunya, a resident of Valencia, in the early 1490s, before he called himself John Cabot of Bristol. Almost all but the most simplistic statements are subject to the same difficulties. Philosophers have spent thousands of years trying to formulate 'true' statements, with very little success, and historians are unlikely to do much better. Almost any 'factual' statement worth making has to be expressed in a language heavily weighted with values and contexts. Language is only one of the challenges in the quest for the fact.

Even if facts could be expressed in a neutral language, such as numbers, we would still need to decide which facts are important. At any given moment there exists a virtual infinity of pieces of information that could be isolated and stated. Most 'historical facts' are simply labels of events and dates, names and movements, which by themselves do not tell us very much. They are not statements in which anything is asserted, and therefore they have no standing as facts. Only when their significance is implicitly or explicitly understood do they acquire any utility or susceptibility to truth. 'The Battle of Vimy Ridge' is not a fact, since it does not assert anything capable of being either true or false. 'The Battle of Vimy Ridge in 1917 was won by the Canadian army' is an assertion the validity of which can be assessed. Whether it is false or true (and hence 'a fact') is another matter entirely. The validity of the statement requires a detailed account of the battle in the context of the war.

One of the chief benefits of modern historical study is that it promotes a healthy skepticism about the neutrality and ultimate truth of the notorious fact. Taken by itself, in isolation, the fact has little meaning. It is only when facts are arranged into some larger picture—some sort of interpretive account—that they acquire significance. Those interpretive pictures themselves are subject to change over time. Anyone today who reads a Canadian history textbook written thirty years ago will be struck by the almost complete absence of any reference to women as important historical figures. Yet thirty years ago the majority of readers—even female readers—took that absence for granted. The absence of women does not mean that women were not present. It simply means that historians of that generation did not regard their activities as worthy of attention. The historian can uncover whole constellations of new facts simply by asking a new question of the historical record, as happened when some scholar asked: 'What about the women?' History is not the study of something eternally fixed, of something that can be 'discovered', but rather the continual dynamic re-investigation and re-evaluation of the past.

If historians can recover new facts, however, they are still limited to those facts that have been recorded in some way. The records need not be in written form; sometimes they take the form of oral history, sometimes of artifacts. Whatever form the evidence takes, it has to have been preserved. Preservation may be deliberate or serendipitous, but in either case certain biases may be observed. If we think about our own personal history, we realize that not every part of it has been recorded, let alone recorded with equal care; and much of the individual record that does exist has been preserved not through personal choice but to serve bureaucratic purposes. Not every society keeps public records, however, and even in the record-keeping societies, not everyone produces an equal quantity of evidence. Only a relative handful of historical actors, for example, have left behind their own written accounts. Personal evidence tends to be limited to those involved in self-consciously important activity, as defined by any particular society. Such recorders usually represent that society's élite, and what they record represents what the élites think needs recording. We know far more about taxation in the middle ages than we do about sexual behaviour, for example. Whatever their limitations, it is with the records that historians must start. They are the primary sources for historical investigation, as distinguished from secondary sources (usually other historians' research gleanings and interpretations). In working with primary sources, historians face two problems: the first one of authenticity, the second one of credibility.

For understandable reasons, historians have to be certain that the records they study are genuine. Historians thus prefer to work with original documents, the so-called 'manuscript' sources (although not all manuscripts are necessarily hand-written). The republication of such material often raises questions of accuracy, which become even more problematic when the documents have been translated from one language to another. Even the most scrupulous of editors may subtly alter the meaning of a document through changes in punctuation or spelling, and until our own time the editors of historical documents often intervened in other ways as well. A famous editor of Shakespeare named Thomas Bowdler expurgated material that he considered to be in bad taste (his name is now commemorated in the verb 'to bowdlerize'). Other editors silently rewrote texts to what they regarded as the advantage of their authors. Even the appearance of authenticity is no guarantee; many skilful forgeries have been designed to pass close inspection. The famous Shroud of Turin (supposedly showing the imprint of the body of Christ) is not necessarily a deliberate forgery, but recent scientific investigation has found that it could not be authentically associated with the crucifixion. As for the supposedly fifteenth-century 'Vinland Map', discovered in the 1960s, it still has not been satisfactorily authenticated, and many scholars think it is a forgery.

Even if we are dealing with an 'authentic' document, there are still many potential problems to face before we can use it as evidence. Many documents cannot be precisely dated or attributed to a specific author. But these questions must be addressed before the historian—acting all the parts in a court of law except that of witness—can determine the document's credibility. Was the author in a position to be authoritative? Are there reasons, obvious or subtle, for suspecting bias of some kind? Bias may appear in many forms. Authors may seek to justify themselves; they may place their interpretation of events in a context resulting from their place in society or from their ideological assumptions; they may report hearsay; they may adjust their accounts for literary reasons, or simply to tell 'a good story'. Evidence is best if it can be corroborated by more than one source; but supporting evidence is not always available, particularly for specific details. Like the 'facts' derived from them, the documents themselves are seldom unassailable as sources. Historians work with probabilities rather than certainties, and the more evidence is available, the more likely it is that there will be complications. In any event, students of history need to be both skeptical and critical of what they read, whether documentary evidence itself or interpretations of such material.

THE CONVENTIONS OF HISTORY

Historians have developed a series of conventions for dealing with their raw data. Historical information presented in its unexplicated form—

as a series of unrelated facts—is not history as historians understand it, and insufficient attention to interpretation and context is one of the most common faults of beginning historians. Traditionally, the chief mode for historians has been narrative, the recounting of past events in the sequence in which they occurred. Like all aspects of historical work, narrative requires selection—cutting into the seamless web of the past to isolate a particular sequence of events involving a limited number of characters. Narrative deals with the passage of time, and—since it is axiomatic that cause and effect must be in the right sequence—chronology is critical to historical understanding. Many great historians of the past concentrated almost exclusively on narrative, appropriately embellished with description and context; an example is Francis Parkman, who wrote extensively on the early conflict of the French and British in North America. But most modern historians would agree with Arthur Marwick (1970: 144) that 'the historian must achieve a balance between narrative and analysis, between a chronological approach and an approach by topic, and, it should be added, a balance between both of these, and, as necessary, passages of pure *description* "setting the scene", providing routine but essential information, conveying the texture of life in any particular age and environment.' Some historians have even dropped narrative entirely, although the sequence of events remains implicitly crucial to their work.

Despite the common use of the term 'causation' in historical writing, particularly among beginners, philosophers of history have long emphasized that historians really do not deal much in the sort of cause-and-effect relationships usually associated with scientific work. The past is too complex to isolate factors in this way. Instead, historians talk about 'explanation', which is not quite the same as scientific causation. Explanation requires the inclusion of enough context and relevant factors to make it clear that the events in question were neither totally predetermined nor utterly capricious. As E.H. Carr (1964: 103–4) has observed,

> . . . no sane historian pretends to do anything so fantastic as to embrace 'the whole of experience'; he cannot embrace more than a minute fraction of the facts even of his chosen sector or aspect of history. The world of the historian, like the world of the scientist, is not a photographic copy of the real world, but rather a working model which enables him more or less effectively to understand it and to master it. The historian distils from the experience of the past, or from so much of the experience of the past as is accessible to him, that part which he recognizes as amenable to rational explanation and interpretation, and from it draws conclusions.

In their efforts at narrative and/or explanation, historians also use many other conventions. Among them, let us focus on periodization. The division of the past into historical 'periods' serves purposes beyond the organization of a teaching curriculum. By focusing attention on larger units of time, periodization serves to narrow and limit the range of material to be considered and helps to provide a structure for what would otherwise be a meaningless jumble of events and dates. The choice of beginning and end dates for larger historical sequences is hardly arbitrary, but it is still a matter of interpretation. Take, for example, the standard decision to divide Canadian history at 1867, the year of Confederation. This fundamental periodization reflects the assumption not only that political and constitutional development shaped everything else, but also that the creation of a national state called the Dominion of Canada was the critical point in that development. However, it makes little sense for many other themes in Canadian history. Historians of Canada continually debate the question of relevant periods. The authors of the first survey of the history of women in Canada, for example, were forced to find a new way of periodizing their account, since the standard political and constitutional periodization reflected a chronology that was mainly masculine in emphasis.

NEW INTERPRETATIONS

Like all academic disciplines, history is constantly reinterpreting its subject matter. Some of the pressure for reinterpretation is a simple matter of growth: within the past quarter-century, the number of academic positions for historians in Canada has more than quadrupled, with the result that more individuals are now researching and writing within the field. At the same time, technological advances (in computers and photocopiers, for example) and the advent of the relatively inexpensive airline ticket have made it possible for historians to examine and process documentary materials in ways and quantities that would have been unthinkable at the beginning of the 1960s. Other pressures for revision, of course, come from changes in the social context, which is continually raising new questions for historians to explore, and shifts in the climate of opinion.

In history, revisionist movements usually arise out of new developments in three (often related) areas: subject matter, conceptual frameworks, and methodologies. A new development in any one of these areas may be enough on its own to provoke significant revision. When two or three come together (as is often the case), they can completely alter our understanding of the past.

Addressing new subject matter involves asking new questions about hitherto neglected aspects of the past. In Canadian history, with its traditional focus on the political and constitutional ways in which a national state was created, the opportunities for new questions have been quite substantial. Out of a variety of new subjects, we can perhaps offer three examples: women, Aboriginal peoples, and ethnic groups. While each of these subjects would today be regarded as central to any contemporary understanding of Canadian history, they were virtually neglected until recent years. As we have seen, lack of attention to women in the past did not reflect lack of information, but lack of interest on the part of historians. With the simple act of focusing attention on women, a new field of study was opened. In the case of Aboriginal peoples, the subject had not been entirely neglected, but it had virtually always been approached from the perspective of the developing national state. Thus many of the new questions raised today are aimed at understanding the First Nations' perspectives. As for ethnic groups, research has tended to involve scholars from a variety of disciplines, such as sociology and geography, and has been encouraged by the availability of grant money from governmental agencies at both the federal and provincial levels. Ethnic studies have proved to be politically popular within Canada.

New areas of study often suggest—if not require—new conceptual contexts. In general, all three of the new areas noted above fall under the rubric of 'social history'. As early as 1924, an article on 'The Teaching of Canadian History' advocated the study of the 'actual life of the Canadian people' in 'their efforts to secure a livelihood and then to provide for the higher demands of mind and spirit' (McArthur 1924: 207). Until recent years, however, much of the research in the social history area concentrated on the upper echelons of society in Canada, the so-called 'élites'. Broadening the social base to include individuals outside the ranks of those whose lives were normally documented (women, Aboriginal people, racial and ethnic minorities, ordinary working men) involved a substantial reconceptualization of the nature of Canada's past.

Studying those 'inarticulate' groups often required new methodologies as well. Perhaps the most important methodological innovation was quantification: generating new data sets by processing existing information not previously practicable for historical purposes out of data such as name-by-name census returns. At its worst, quantification could be little more than mindless number-crunching, but at its best it enabled historians to open up whole categories of hitherto unusable documentation. The information collected by the Dominion Bureau of the Census or the various provincial departments of Vital Statistics has provided much new insight into the way ordinary Canadians have lived (and loved) in the past. Computers have made it easier for historians to process large amounts of aggregate information—although the axiom 'Garbage In, Garbage Out' continues to apply. The complex processes of collecting and analyzing new categories of data has been contentious, and beginning historians should understand that the apparently simple act of producing a new set of information involves many steps and many disagreements. 'Hard' numbers and percentages are no more sacrosanct than information that appears 'softer'. Moreover, quantified data still require interpretation, and are subject to all the standard rules that apply to historical explanation.

Although explicit controversies do arise within the field of Canadian history, they are probably less common than controversies among historians of other nations, notably the United States and Great Britain. To some extent the profession has avoided confrontations by allowing each practitioner his or her own area of specialization (or 'turf'). This has made good sense because the number of questions not yet adequately explored in the history of Canada is considerable. Whatever the reasons for the muting of controversy, disagreements in Canadian historiography have had less to do with specific points and interpretations within a single tradition than with first principles and underlying assumptions. Thus Canadian historians tend to disagree only at the mega-level, as in the current debate over Canadian 'national history', which is really a debate among scholars with two totally different sets of assumptions about the role of narrative in the past. Those on the moving frontier of scholarship are in some ways far less embattled than those still working in older traditions, since they can simply add their 'new' interpretations on to the old ones.

Because history is a cumulative subject, students should not think that the latest books and journal articles are necessarily better simply by virtue of their dates of publication. Many older works of historical scholarship can still be regarded as the best treatments of their topics. This is particularly true in traditional areas of study that have not attracted much attention from modern scholars, such as the military history of the War of 1812. Earlier generations were fond of publishing editions of documents, which if well-transcribed, translated, and edited are just as valuable today as they were a century ago. The complete (and most commonly used) edition of the *Jesuit Relations* in English was published between 1896 and 1901. On some topics our only sources are earlier documents; for example, Richard Hakluyt's sixteenth-century accounts are still essential for any study of English overseas voyages.

By now it should be clear that both the writing and the reading of history are extremely complicated enterprises. Whole books with titles like *Understanding History* or *The Nature of History* have been devoted to introducing students to the complexities of the craft, and in the space of a few pages it is impossible to explore all the potential dimensions. In any case, readers of this book should understand that every work of history involves a series of decisions to hold various contradictions in dynamic tension. Among the most important issues held in tension in this book are the following:

1. *Interpretive complexity versus authority.* Virtually every sentence in this work (or any other work of history) could be hedged in with conflicting evidence and interpretation. The result would almost certainly be incomprehensible. I have chosen to favour readability over total academic accuracy. This is not to say that I do not recognize the issues of interpretive complexity. Rather, I have consciously addressed them in two ways: by introducing questions of interpretation into the text on a regular basis, and by including three essays on historiography (one for each of the book's three sections).

2. *Individual biography versus groups and forces.* One problem that all historians face (or ought to face) is how to make the material interesting to readers. As any newspaper editor will tell you, readers like their stories to have people in them. This work uses the experiences of individual people to represent and suggest the complex groups and forces that lie behind them. I do not subscribe to the Great Person theory of history, but I do believe in personalizing history as much as possible.

3. *Overarching master narrative versus the complex voices of social and cultural history.* Whether or not Canadian history has a single narrative is a hotly debated issue today, sometimes posed in the form of the question 'Is there a national history?' The single narrative is also related to the problem of authority, although the two are not the same. A coherent and connected single narrative could be based on the concept of the development of the nation, or on viewing events from the perspective of that nation, or on something quite different. The point is that any such narrative line represents an abstraction. Critics of the abstract, single-narrative approach associate it with the imposition of a hegemonic 'master principle' that in turn is often taken to represent the sequence of events preferred by the 'men in suits' or the 'ruling class' or the 'politicians in Ottawa'. Many groups are commonly left outside such a master narrative: workers, racial and cultural minorities, women, inhabitants of marginalized regions, inhabitants of alienated regions (e.g., Quebec for much of the twentieth century). Over the past thirty years, Canadian historians have concentrated on recovering the voices of these groups. But if those voices were all we heard, telling their own stories in their own tongues, the resulting cacophony would be unintelligible; and to establish chronology and meaningful periodization, we need a structure that will provide some common reference points. Hence a master narrative of some kind is still essential.

The master narrative around which this book is structured, into which all the other stories are woven, is a highly abstract one that may be labelled 'the history of Canada'. I hope this discussion will help readers to understand the chapters that follow.

J.M. Bumsted
Winnipeg, 2002

CHAPTER ONE

□ The Beginnings

■ Once upon a time, a history of Canada would typically begin with the arrival of the European 'discoverers' at the end of the fifteenth century. These events at best mark only the moment at which the land and its people enter the European historical record, not the beginning of its history. Thousands of years of human development had preceded the appearance of the Europeans. The First Nations of North America have their own history. The work of countless modern specialists, chiefly linguistic scholars and archaeologists, has only begun to uncover the barest outlines of the pre-European period. The record of human settlement clearly does not begin with the Europeans.

The First Immigrants

Unlike other continents on planet Earth, North America did not produce indigenous archaic human forms going back thousands of generations. No evidence suggests that any of the many ancestors of *Homo sapiens* developed on this continent. There was no Old Stone Age as in Africa, Asia, or Europe. Instead, the first humanlike inhabitant of North America was *Homo sapiens*, probably arriving as an immigrant in the New World during the last Great Ice Age—which ended 10,000 years ago—perhaps across a land bridge stretching between what is now Siberia and Alaska.

The 30,000 years or more of the human occupation of the North American continent before the arrival of the Europeans were, until very recently, usually labelled 'prehistoric'. That term has now fallen out of common usage, however, because it produces so many misconceptions. No written record of North American development may have existed before the Europeans, but to assume that 'history' begins only with writing is totally misleading. Plenty of earlier records of human activity exist, including oral traditions of the First Nations. From them a fascinating picture of the early history of what is now Canada can be reconstructed. That picture is hardly a static one. Instead, it displays constant movement, adaptation, and change. These early people did not attempt to modify their environment so much as adapt to it. That environment was itself continually shifting, perhaps not over a single season but over several generations.

One of the chief factors influencing the early inhabitants of North America was climate. Until very recently—as the history of the planet goes—most of what is now Canada was covered with glacial ice, which began retreating about 10,000 years ago. Several ice-free corridors ran from Alaska south, through which the first immigrants from Asia probably travelled into the warmer regions of the continent. While some inhabitants adapted to ice and snow, most people began moving northward only as the ice began to melt. By the time of Christ, around 2,000 years ago, most of Canada had acquired a natural environment recognizable to us today. The land had also acquired permanent inhabitants. What we know

TIMELINE

MAJOR EVENTS IN THE EARLY HISTORY OF THE FIRST NATIONS

12,000 BCE (BEFORE COMMON ERA)
Mammal retaining stone weapon killed in New Mexico.

11,000 BCE
Glacial retreat escalates with warming trend.

10,000 BCE
Continued warming alters physical environment as ice retreats.

9000 BCE
Fluted Point people spread across North America.

7000 BCE
Maritime Archaic culture develops the harpoon.

5500 BCE
Maritime Archaic culture develops burial mounds. Notched projectile points appear in British Columbia.

3000 BCE
Forest reaches its northernmost extension.

2000 BCE
Palaeo-Eskimos and other Archaics begin displacing Maritime Archaics on eastern seaboard and in Arctic regions.

1000 BCE
Ceramic pottery appears in Great Lakes area and spreads east.

500 BCE
Dorset people appear in Arctic Canada. Climate deteriorates.

500 CE (COMMON ERA)
Maize cultivation begins in southern Ontario. Climate begins improving.

600
Beothuk culture replaces the Dorset Eskimos in Newfoundland.

1000
Norse settle briefly in eastern North America.

1150
Dorset culture is replaced by Thule culture among Inuit.

1350
Squash and bean cultivation appear in southern Ontario.

1497
First recorded European arrival in North America since Norse.

1634
Beginning of the destruction of Huronia.

about these people comes to us in the form of physical artefacts.

Because of the limited nature of the evidence, the early history of humankind in Canada is often described in terms of surviving tools and weapons, especially projectile points. Archaeologists can infer much from tool-making technology and its geographical spread across the continent. Using various dating techniques, including laboratory testing of organic substances to determine what remains of a radioactive isotope called carbon-14, it has been possible to provide some overall sense of chronological development. The first incontestable evidence of human habitation in northern North America comes in the form of fluted projectile points chipped from various rocks by taking long flakes (or flutes) from the base to the tip. Evidence from other parts of the Americas suggests that habitation occurred long before 9500–8000 BCE, when people using these points spread from Alaska through the central plains and eastern woodlands. They were hunters and gatherers who lived in small units, although not in total isola-

TIMELINE

Major Events in the Early European History in Northern North America

982–5 CE
Eric the Red explores Greenland.

c. 1000
L'Anse aux Meadows is established by the Norse.

1497
John Cabot reaches Newfoundland.

1500
Gaspar Corte-Real lands at Tierra Verde (Newfoundland).

1501
Gaspar Corte-Real brings the first Aboriginals to Europe.

1534
Jacques Cartier erects cross at Gaspé Harbour.

1576
First voyage of Martin Frobisher to Baffin Island.

1585
John Davis enters Davis Strait.

1605
Port-Royal established.

1608
Champlain builds habitation at Quebec.

1610
First English settlers arrive in Newfoundland.

1615
Étienne Brûlé investigates New York and Pennsylvania.

1616
Robert Bylot sails through Davis Strait.

1618
Champlain proposes major French colony on St Lawrence.

1628
Scottish settlement expedition arrives in Maritime region.

tion from neighbours. Evidence survives of trade and exchange of goods.

As the ice melted and the glaciers moved northward, the hunters who made the fluted points spread more widely across the continent. These people have come to be known by archaeologists as the Plano People because of their distinctive projectile-point technology. They flourished from 8000 to 6000 BCE. By 4000 BCE a number of regional offshoots of the Plano People had developed. Over the next 3,000 years these cultures stabilized to some extent, although there was still substantial physical movement. On the western plains, a culture organized around communal bison-hunting emerged, perhaps as early as 3000 BCE. The High Arctic was occupied by Palaeo-Eskimos, who gradually moved to the south into the Barren Lands west of Hudson Bay. The northeastern seaboard was occupied between 2000 and 1000 BCE. On the West Coast, a semi-sedentary lifestyle based on the salmon had developed by 2000 BCE.

From 1000 BCE to 500 CE, substantial cultural changes occurred across North America. Once we stop trying to compare these developments with what was going on in Europe and see them instead in their own terms, we can appreciate how substantial the technological innovations of this period were. The bow and arrow spread rapidly, for example, completely altering hunting techniques. In the same years, pottery-making moved from the Yukon to eastern districts. The introduction of the pot changed food preparation substantially, but pottery also provides evidence of rapidly changing aesthetic sensibilities, as ornamentation was added to design.

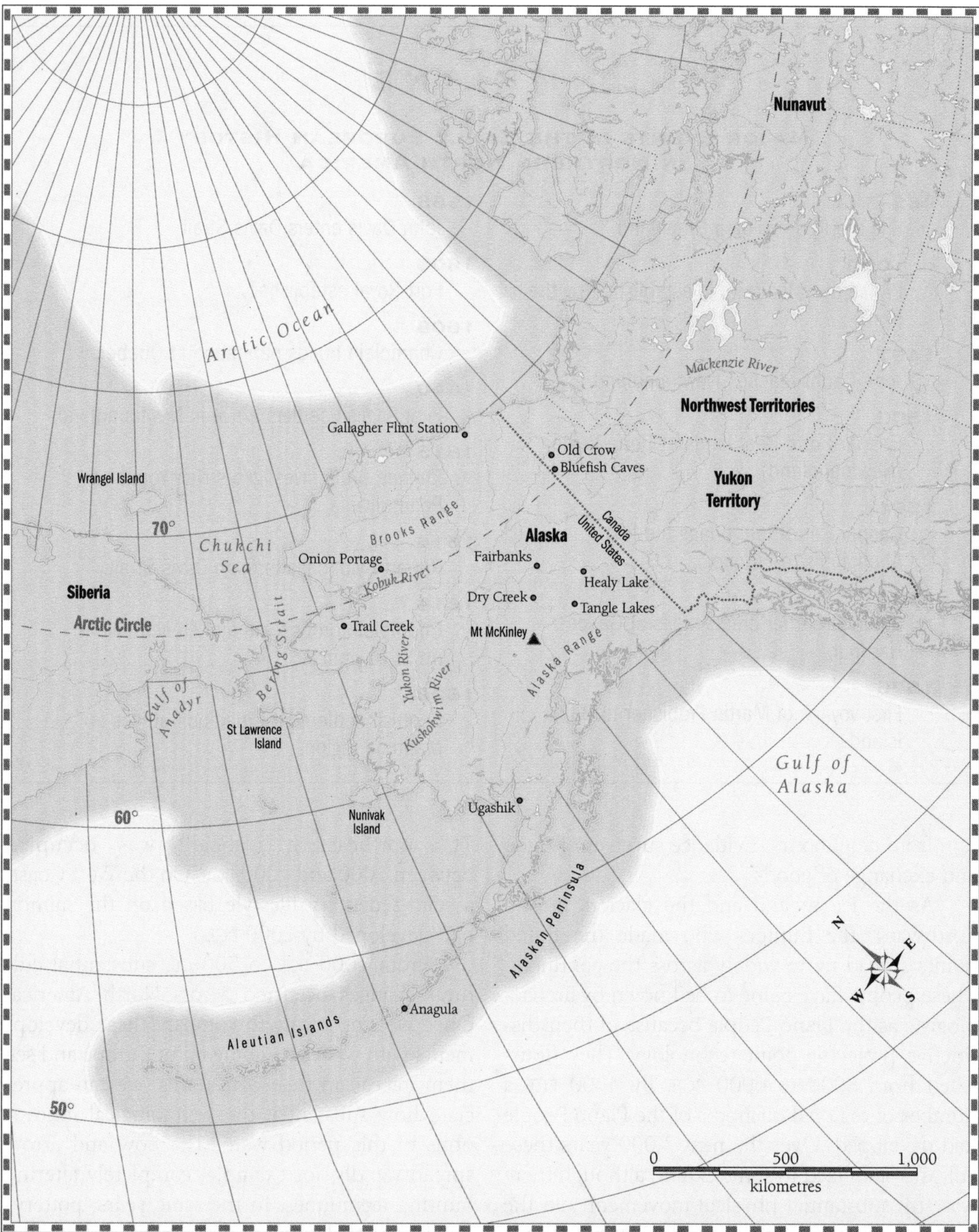

Beringia: The shaded area shows the 'land bridge' at its greatest extent, approximately 20,000 years ago. Adapted from Brian M. Fagan, *The Great Journey: The Peopling of Ancient North America* (London: Thames and Hudson, 1987), 100.

Archaeologists have shifted their classification systems from the projectile point to the pot to characterize peoples of this era. Another new development was the rapid expansion from the south of new funeral practices, chiefly burial in large mounds. This, of course, helped provide a new self-consciously created richness of physical evidence.

THE FIRST NATIONS POPULATION AROUND 1500

Although on the eve of European intrusion all Aboriginal peoples lived in a reciprocal relationship with nature, not all experienced the same relationship. Much depended on the resources of the region in which they lived and the precise combination of survival skills they possessed. Most of the many groups were hunters and gatherers, organized into mobile bands that followed the seasons and the cycles of the game. On the coasts, fishing replaced hunting as the principal means of collecting a food supply. In the north, as in many other areas, whether one fished or hunted depended on the season. On the Pacific Slope, the rich resource base of salmon and cedar made possible considerable accumulations of wealth and social gradation. These Pacific peoples demonstrated that it was not essential to farm in order to prosper. Only one group of people, those living in the area of the Great Lakes, pursued horticulture. This activity, involving the planting of corn, tobacco, beans, squash, and sunflowers, led to the establishment of semi-permanent villages.

Despite the differences in their lifestyles, all First Nations were singularly adept and ingenious at adapting to their environment. None were

☐ Sadlermiut man paddling an inflated walrus-skin boat, watercolour, c. 1830, artist unknown. NAC (Peter Winkworth Collection of Canadiana), W304.

more successful at adaptation than the Inuit, who inhabited an ice-bound world in the north. At sea they used the speedy kayak and on land the dogsled. They lived in a domed snow-hut (the igloo) in winter and in skin tents in summer. Caribou hides served as the basic clothing material and provided much protection from the inclement weather. The Inuit were extremely skilful at making tools and weapons. Their use of bone and ivory for such equipment was extensive, and their aesthetic sense highly developed.

With the possible exceptions of the horticulturalists of south-central Canada and the fisherfolk of the Pacific Slope, the economies of the First Nations were quite simple ones. They were organized around the food supply, offering semi-nomadic people little scope for the acquisition of material possessions that would only have to be abandoned at the next—and imminent—move. Nevertheless, these *were* economies, and those within them functioned according to their inner logic. Food was not cultivated but pursued. The movement of fish and game had certain rhythms, but was at least potentially capricious. When food was available, the population was galvanized into action, gathering as much as possible and consuming it almost immediately. When food ran out, energetic questing for new sources did not necessarily begin at once. The people knew the general patterns of the wildlife and vegetation they sought, and hurry often did little good. It was, for example, useless to hunt for berries in February. Such economies put little premium on the disciplined pursuit of goals, or on the deferral of expectations. Nor did they encourage the sort of unremitting hard labour familiar to the European newcomers.

The numbers of First Nations living in Canada on the eve of European intrusion has become the subject of debate. One point seems clear. The Aboriginal population, lacking immunities to a variety of European diseases, was quickly decimated by epidemics, which spread silently across the land, often in advance of the actual appearance of a European carrier. The size of the population observed by the first European arrivals may have already been modified by disease brought by the earliest fishermen, who may well have preceded the recorded explorers. The indigenous pre-contact population of Canada was probably substantially larger than the most generous estimates of first-contact observers.

The First Intruders

As every schoolchild now knows, Norsemen made the first documented European visitations to North America. Contemporary evidence of these visits is contained in the great Icelandic epic sagas, confirmed in our own time by archaeological excavations near L'Anse aux Meadows on the northern tip of Newfoundland. The sagas describe the landings to the west of Greenland made by Leif Ericsson and his brother Thorvald. They also relate Thorfinn Karlsefni's colonization attempt at a place Leif had called Vinland, an attempt that was thwarted by hostile residents labelled in the sagas as 'Skraelings'. It is tempting to equate Vinland with the archaeological discoveries, although there is no real evidence for doing so.

Later Greenlanders may have timbered on Baffin Island. They may also have intermarried with the Inuit. Attempts have been made to attribute the Thule culture of the Inuit to such relationships. But Greenland gradually lost contact with Europe, and the Icelandic settlement there died away in the fifteenth century. For all intents and purposes, the Norse activities became at best part of the murky geographical knowledge of the late Middle Ages.

In our own time the uncovering of a world map executed in the mid-fifteenth century, showing a realistic Greenland and westward islands including inscriptions referring to Vinland, created much speculation about Europe's geographical knowledge before Columbus. This Vinland map has never been definitively authenticated, and many experts have regarded it with scepticism. The current scholarly view, however, has turned back to a positive evaluation of the map.

KARLSEFNI AND THE SKRAELINGS

The Norse sagas began as manuscripts of the history of the Icelandic Norsemen collected in the thirteenth century. The following selection is from a manuscript called in English 'Eirik the Red's Saga', which is a reworking of original material in agreement with well-established rules of saga-making. Despite its title, 'Eirik the Red's Saga' is much more interested in the Icelanders Gudrid and Karlsefni than in the family of Eirik the Red.

Karlsefni sailed south along the land with Snorri and Bjarni and the rest of their company. They journeyed a long time till they reached a river which flowed down from the land into a lake and so on to the sea. There were such extensive bars off the mouth of the estuary that they were unable to get into the river except at full flood. Karlsefni and his men sailed into the estuary, and called the place Hop, Landlock Bay. There they found self-sown fields of wheat where the ground was low-lying, and vines wherever it was hilly. Every brook there was full of fish. They dug trenches at the meeting point of land and high water, and when the tide went out there were halibut in the trenches. There were vast numbers of animals of every kind in the forest. They were there for a fortnight enjoying themselves and saw nothing and nobody. They had their cattle with them.

Then early one morning when they looked about them they saw nine skin-boats, on board which staves were being swung which sounded just like flails threshing—and their motion was sunwise.

'What can this mean?' asked Karlsefni.

'Perhaps it is a token of peace,' replied Snorri. 'So let us take a white shield and hold it out towards them.'

They did so, and those others rowed towards them, showing their astonishment, then came ashore. They were small, ill-favoured men, and had ugly hair on their heads. They had big eyes and were broad in the cheeks. For a while they remained there, astonished, and afterwards rowed off south past the headlands.

Karlsefni and his men built themselves dwellings up above the lake; some of their houses stood near the mainland, and some near the lake. They now spent the winter there. No snow fell, and their entire stock found its food grazing in the open. But once spring came in they chanced early one morning to see how a multitude of skin-boats came rowing from the south round the headland, so many that the bay appeared sown with coals, and even so staves were being swung on every boat. Karlsefni and his men raised their shields, and they began trading together. Above all these people wanted to buy red cloth in return for which they had furs to offer and grey pelts. They also wanted to buy swords and spears, but this Karlsefni and Snorri would not allow. They had dark unblemished skins to exchange for the cloth, and were taking a span's length of cloth for a skin, and this they tied round their heads. So it continued for a while, then when the cloth began to run short they cut it up so that it was no broader than a fingerbreadth, but the Skraelings gave just as much for it, or more.

The next thing was that the bull belonging to Karlsefni and his mates ran out of the forest bellowing loudly. The Skraelings were terrified by this, raced to their boats and rowed south past the headland, and for three weeks running there was neither sight nor sound of them. But at the end of that period they saw a great multitude of Skraeling boats coming up from the south like a streaming torrent. This time all the staves were being swung anti-sunwise, and the Skraelings were all yelling aloud, so they took red shields and held them out against them. They clashed together and fought. There was a heavy shower of missiles, for the Skraelings had war-slings too. Karlsefni and Snorri could see the Skraelings hoisting up on poles a huge ball-shaped object, more or less the size of a sheep's paunch, and blue-black in colour, which they sent flying inland over Karlsefni's troop, and it made a hideous noise when it came down. Great fear now struck into Karlsefni and all his following, so that there was no other thought in their heads than to run away up along the river to some steep rocks, and there put up a strong resistance.

SOURCE: Gwyn Jones, *The Norse Atlantic Saga: Being the Norse Voyages of Discovery and Settlement to Iceland, Greenland, America* (London: Oxford University Press, 1964), 181–3.

☐ The Oseberg ship, built c. 815-820 CE and used as a burial ship for a prominent woman who died in 834. Constructed of oak, 22 metres long and 5 metres wide, it was designed for rowing as well as sailing and could reach speeds of over 10 knots. Photo by Eirik Irgens Johnsen. © University Museum of Cultural Heritage–University of Oslo, Norway.

Like the Vinland map, none of the various candidates for North American landfalls before Columbus—except for the Norse in Newfoundland—can be indisputably documented. In the fifteenth century, Portuguese and possibly English fishermen may have discovered the rich fishing grounds off the Grand Banks. An occasional vessel may even have made a landfall. The fishermen did not publicize their knowledge, although many scholars insist that awareness of lands in the western Atlantic was probably in common circulation in maritime circles by the end of the fifteenth century.

EUROPE AROUND 1500

The arrival of Europeans in the Americas at the end of the fifteenth century was a collaborative effort by mariners and contemporary scholars of many nations, behind which were profound changes in economies and polities. The ambition to visit new lands was fuelled by the surge of intellectual confidence and the explosion of knowledge associated with the Renaissance. By the end of the fifteenth century, geographers—led by Paolo dal Pozzo Toscanelli, an Italian cosmographer in Portuguese service—were convinced that Europe and Asia were closer than the ancients had conjectured. The schemes of Christopher Columbus were influenced both by Toscanelli and by Portuguese notions of oceanic islands. Geographical speculation and ship

Reconstructed Norse dwellings at L'Anse aux Meadows, near the eleventh-century ruins discovered by Helge and Anne Stine Ingstad in 1960. Eight structures—houses, workshops, and a forge—of the same kind built in Iceland and Greenland were made of sods laid over a frame. Photo J. Steeves, Parks Canada, Department of Canadian Heritage.

design pointed towards transatlantic voyages. Some time in the twelfth century, the Germans developed the cog, a single-masted ship decked over and fitted with rudder and tiller. In the early fifteenth century the cog's hull was lengthened and the vessel was given two additional masts, becoming the carvel (or caravel). Early explorers found smaller ships more manoeuvrable than larger ones and came to prefer them on their voyages. Rigging also improved, particularly with the addition of the square sail to the earlier lateen (triangular) variety.

The art of navigation showed parallel development to ship design, a gradual result of trial and error by countless mariners. The greatest advance was in written sailing directions based on taking latitudes in relation to Polaris and the sun. Longitudes were still based largely on guesswork, mainly on a mariner's estimates of his vessel's speed. In addition to the compass, seamen used quadrants and astrolabes to determine latitude, and were familiar with the need to transfer their data on latitude and longitude onto charts ruled for these variables. *Routiers*—coastal pilot charts of European waters—were readily available, but none of the early explorers who reached North America had the faintest idea of the hazards he was risking. The most remarkable feature of the first known voyages was the infrequency with which mariners ran into serious problems with rocks, shoals, and tides. Such master mariners had an instinctive 'feel' for the sea. They were able to read and deduce much from its colour and surface patterns.

☐ An astrolabe. By turning the sighting rod to point at the sun or a bright star, a mariner could estimate its altitude above the horizon and use that information as an aid to navigation. Negative no. 77-401 © Canadian Museum of Civilization.

Though the early explorers had their blind spots, they were without exception skilled sailors, suitably cautious in uncharted waters, which may explain many glaring failures to uncover rivers and bays obvious on any modern map. Once ashore, however, the first Europeans to reach North America threw caution to the winds, particularly in collecting rumours of rich mineral deposits or routes to Asia. Neither they nor their sponsors were at all interested in the scientific accumulation of knowledge. What they sought was wealth, equivalent to the riches the Spaniards were already taking out their territories to the south. While other motives—such as national advantage and missionary fervour directed against the resident inhabitants—also entered the picture, the easy and rapid exploitation of the resources of the New World long remained the principal attraction.

THE EUROPEAN ENTRY INTO NORTH AMERICA

John Cabot went briefly ashore at the 'newfoundland'. Cabot, originally an Italian, had convinced Henry VII of England to finance one small ship of 50 tons and a crew of eighteen to sail west

JOHN CABOT REACHES LAND ACROSS THE ATLANTIC, 1497

Over the winter of 1497-8, the English merchant John Day wrote a letter to 'El Gran Almirante' (probably Christopher Columbus), giving him an account of a recent voyage by John Cabot. This account provides some of our best evidence for Cabot's landfall.

From the said copy [of 'the land which has been found', which is no longer extant] your Lordship will learn what you wish to know, for in it are named the capes of the mainland and the islands, and thus you will see where land was first sighted, since most of them was discovered after turning back. Thus your Lordship will know that the cape nearest to Ireland is 1800 miles west of Dursey Head which is in Ireland, and the southernmost part of the Island of the Seven Cities is west of Bordeaux River, and your Lordship will know that he [Cabot] landed at only one spot of the mainland, near the place where land was first sighted, and they disembarked there with a crucifix and raised banners with the arms of the Holy Father and those of the King of England, my master; and they found tall trees of the kind masts are made, and other smaller trees, and the country is very rich in grass. In that particular spot, as I told your Lordship, they found a trail that went inland, they saw a site where a fire had been made, they saw manure of animals which they thought to be farm animals, and they saw a stick half a yard long pierced at both ends, carved and painted with brazil, and by such things they believe the land to be inhabited. Since he was with just a few people, he did not dare advance inland beyond the shooting distance of a cross-bow, and after taking in fresh water he returned to his ship. All along the coast they found many fish like those which in Iceland are dried in the open and sold in England and other countries, and these fish are called in English 'stockfish'; and thus following the shore they saw two forms running on land one after the other, but they could not tell if they were human beings or animals; and it seemed to them that there were fields where they thought might also be villages, and they saw a forest whose foliage looked beautiful. They left England toward the end of May, and must have been on the way 35 days before sighting land; the wind was east-north-east and the sea calm going and coming back, except for one day when he ran into a storm two or three days before finding land; and going so far out, his compass needle failed to point north and marked two rhumbs below. They spent about one month discovering the coast and from the above mentioned cape of the mainland which is nearest to Ireland, they returned to the coast of Europe in fifteen days. They had the wind behind them, and he reached Brittany because the sailors confused him, saying that he was heading too far north. From there he came to Bristol, and he went to see the King to report to him all the above mentioned; and the King granted him an annual pension of twenty pounds sterling to sustain himself until the time comes when more will be known of this business, since with God's help it is hoped to push through plans for exploring the said land more thoroughly next year with ten or twelve vessels—because in his voyage he had only one ship of fifty 'tonnes' and twenty men and food for seven or eight months—and they want to carry out this new project. It is considered certain that the cape of the said land was found and discovered in the past by the men from Bristol who found 'Brasil' as your Lordship well knows. It was called the Island of Brasil, and it is assumed and believed to be the mainland that the men from Bristol found.

Since your Lordship wants information relating to the first voyage, here is what happened: he went with one ship, his crew confused him, he was short of supplies and ran into bad weather, and he decided to turn back.

SOURCE: J.A. Williamson, ed., *The Cabot Voyages and British Discoveries under Henry VII* (Cambridge: Hakluyt Society of the University Press, 1962): 211-14.

and find a short route to Asia. Cabot was lost at sea on a second voyage, and his mantle fell to a number of Portuguese mariners, some in English service, who produced a more clearly defined Newfoundland. Most of the sixteenth-century place names in Newfoundland were Portuguese rather than English. Portugal actually attempted to settle a colony on the Newfoundland coast under the leadership of Juan Fagundes, who had earlier sailed as far as the Gulf of St Lawrence. Fagundes ended up on Cape Breton Island, where his little settlement was apparently destroyed by the local residents, who 'killed all those who came there'. Nevertheless, by 1536 Newfoundland was sufficiently familiar, if exotic, to Europeans that a tourist voyage to the island

Jacques Cartier Meets with Aboriginal People, 1534

In the summer of 1534, the French mariner Jacques Cartier cruised along the northern coast and St Lawrence region of North America. His original journal or log of this expedition does not survive, but a printed version appeared in Italian in 1565. Various versions of the journal were collated and translated by Henry Percival Biggar and published in 1924.

On Thursday the eighth of the said month [of July] as the wind was favourable for getting under way with our ships, we fitted up our long-boats to go and explore this [Chaleur] bay; and we ran up it that day about twenty-five leagues. The next day, at daybreak, we had fine weather and sailed on until about ten o'clock in the morning, at which hour we caught sight of the head of the bay, whereat we were grieved and displeased. At the head of this bay, beyond the low shore, were several high mountains. And seeing there was no passage, we proceeded to turn back. While making our way along the shore, we caught sight of the Indians on the side of a lagoon and low beach, who were making many fires that smoked. We rowed over to the spot, and finding there was an entrance from the sea into the lagoon, we placed our long-boats on one side of the entrance. The savages came over in one of their canoes and brought us some strips of cooked seal, which they placed on bits of wood and then withdrew, making signs to us that they were making us a present of them. We sent two men on shore with hatchets, knives, beads, and other wares, at which the Indians showed great pleasure. And at once they came over in a crowd in their canoes to the side where we were, bringing furs and whatever else they possessed, in order to obtain some of our wares. They numbered, both men, women, and children, more than 300 persons. Some of their women, who did not come over, danced and sang, standing in the water up to their knees. The other women, who had come over to the side where we were, advanced freely towards us and rubbed our arms with their hands. Then they joined their hands together and raised them to heaven, exhibiting many signs of joy. And so much at ease did the savages feel in our presence, that at length we bartered with them, hand to hand, for everything they possessed, so that nothing was left to them but their naked bodies; for they offered us everything they owned, which was, all told, of little value. We perceived that they are people who would be easy to convert, who go from place to place maintaining themselves and catching fish in the fishing-season for food. Their country is more temperate than Spain and the finest it is possible to see, and as level as the surface of a pond. There is not the smallest plot of ground bare of wood, and even on sandy soil, but is full of wild wheat, that has an ear like barley and the grain like oats, as well as of pease, as thick as if they had been sown and hoed; of white and red currant-bushes, of strawberries, of raspberries, of white and red roses and of other plants of a strong, pleasant odour. Likewise there are many fine meadows with useful herbs, and a pond where there are many salmon. I am more than ever of opinion that these people would be easy to convert to our holy faith.

SOURCE: H.P. Biggar, ed., *The Voyages of Jacques Cartier: Published from the originals with translations, notes and appendices* (Ottawa: F. Acland, 1924): 54–7.

was organized. London merchant Richard Hore (fl. 1507–40) signed 120 passengers, 'whereof thirty were gentlemen'. When provisions ran short on the Newfoundland coast, some participants allegedly resorted to eating their compatriots. Those surviving were understandably relieved to get back to England.

In 1523 the French entered the picture through the activities of Italian master mariner Giovanni da Verrazzano (c. 1485–c. 1528). Of high birth, Verrazzano persuaded Francis I to sponsor a voyage of exploration. He made three voyages in all, opening a French trade with Brazil and convincing himself that what he was investigating was not Asia but a totally new continent. Verrazzano was succeeded by Jacques Cartier (1491–1557), who had allegedly been to Brazil and Newfoundland. In 1534 Francis I ordered him to uncover new lands, 'where it is said that a great quantity of gold, and other precious things, are to be found.' Little concern was given to the conversion of Aboriginal peoples in Cartier's efforts. He too made three voyages: the first to make a great 'discovery', a second to locate some mineral resource there that would attract investors and the royal court, and a final large-scale effort that failed to produce any profit.

On his first voyage in 1534 Cartier explored the Gulf of St Lawrence. His second voyage in 1535 took him up-river as far as Mont Royal. He visited several First Nations villages and wintered at one of them, Stadacona. Here he heard about the fabulous kingdom of the Saguenay, somewhere farther west. A third voyage was actually headed by a great nobleman, the Sieur de Roberval (c. 1500–60). It was a disaster, finding little wealth to exploit and accomplishing nothing. The gold and diamonds Cartier brought back turned out to be iron pyrites and quartz. 'False as Canadian diamonds' became a common French expression of the time. Despite the lack of accomplishment, a French claim to the St Lawrence region had been established, and the French would ultimately return there.

☐ The frontispiece to *The Voyages of Jacques Cartier*, edited by H.P. Biggar. This portrait of Cartier—if such it is—is imaginary, since we do not have a likeness. Thomas Fisher Rare Book Library.

The next major adventurer to what is now Canada was the Englishman Martin Frobisher (1539?–94), who spent several years searching for the Northwest Passage and great wealth in the

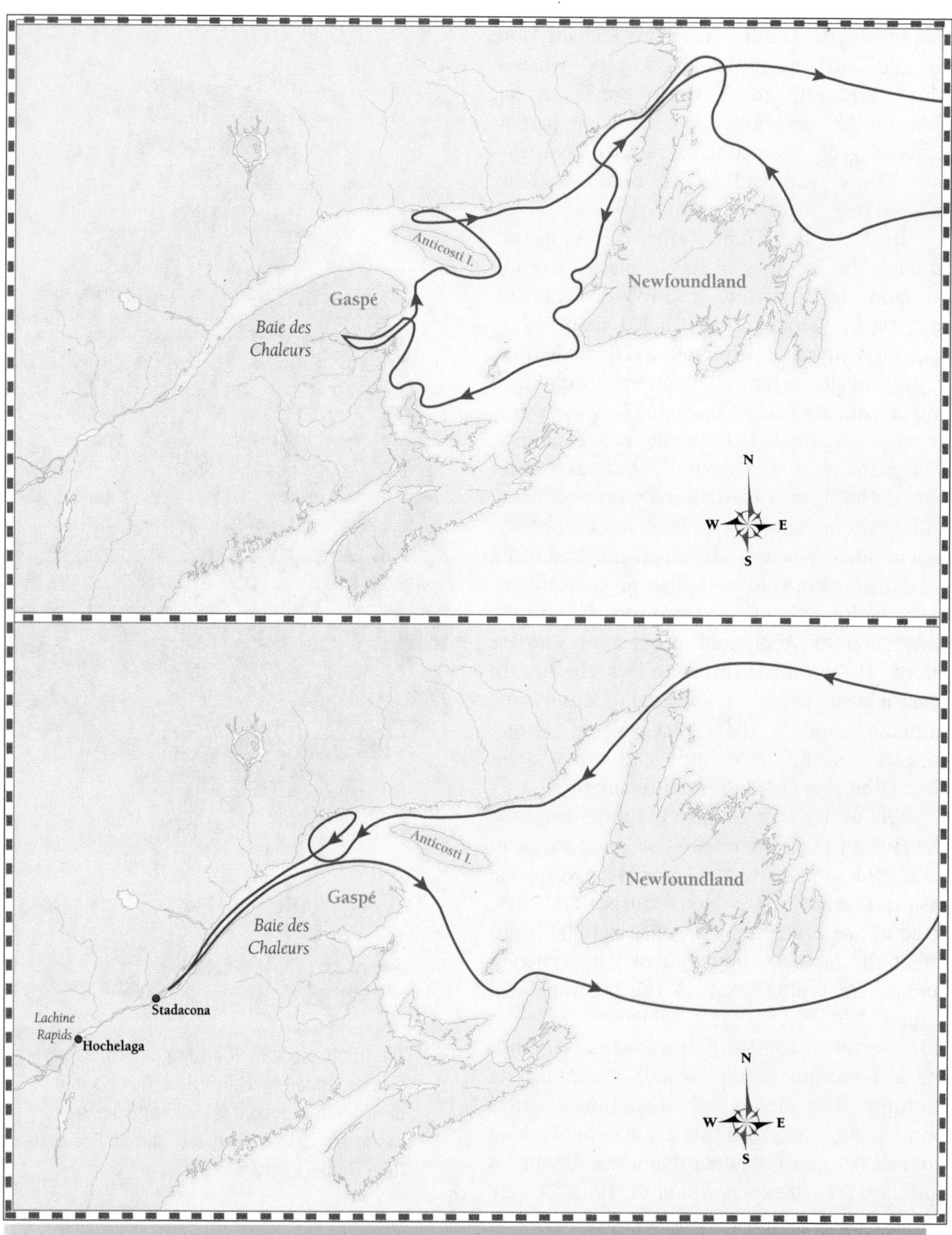

Cartier's first voyage, 1534.
Cartier's second voyage, 1535–6.

AUTOPSY REPORT ON AN INUIT CAPTIVE, 1577

In 1577, Martin Frobisher brought back to England an Inuit man and his kayak. The man created a stir, but he soon contracted some disease and died. An autopsy was conducted on the body by a London doctor. His report follows.

Dr Edward Dodding's 'Reporte of the Sicknesse and Death of the Man at Bristoll which Captain Furbisher brought from the North-West'

On the left side of the dissected cadaver, the first thing which offered itself for my inspection were two ribs, broken by the force of the accident and the blow when he was captured: they were gaping, not stuck together, the care of them had either been neglected as often happens in these most turbulent times and in the narrow confines of naval affairs or, what I rather suspect, had been aroused to inflammation by a disease perceived by no one; and a contusion of the lung in the advance of time had contracted putridity from the same source. Those disorders, creeping freely onwards day by day, had been both stirred up by the ill effect of the external cold, and increased through bad diet, they had not been mended in the meantime from the outside by the surgeon's art, nor struck back from the inside through drugs, and proceeded to an incurable ulcer of the lung. On top of the evil, putrid pus rushed and piled up a very great flow toward the same, composed of a viscid and sticky material, and the left part of the lung so teemed everywhere that it spat out absolutely nothing through the whole time of the disease, and breathing was held in and constricted.

In addition to this his nature was weakened by the raging of the threatening disease: our diet was more generous than either the evil of this disease can bear or perhaps than the man's daily habit allowed, something which had been effected by the highest concern of the supreme commander and the great generosity of those among whom he was living, everyone having been deceived in their opinion more by the hidden nature of the disease and by stupid indulgence than by malevolence, but that disease clearly expressed by the shortness of breath shortly before his death and he was not completely free of dropsy. For in the space of the thorax a quantity and abundance of water of a kind that is rarely seen by observant and industrious anatomists was observed to flow. This was shaken about by the movement of the body as the outcome of the affair assured us, and impeded the breathing out of the lung, and finally the lung itself stuck to the ribs more firmly than anyone would think. . . .

The quantity of due weight which Nature had subtracted from his spleen, leaving it very small, she seems to have added with interest to his extremely capacious stomach, which, packed and distended with water, appeared much greater than those of our men, on account of his incurable, I believe, gluttony. In other parts you would say there was a fear of the English which, from his first arrival, although his face was quite cheerful and cleverly simulated, he concealed and lied about, yet his gesture (as I considered the individual features more deeply one by one within myself, suspecting everything), either they openly betrayed and uncovered the same, or as I often maintained, but to our deaf ears they forebode an impending lethal disease. These things came to our notice and were confirmed more clearly from his pulse than from himself, for his pulses were always smaller, slower and weaker than they were less frequent, and yet they were less frequent than either his youth or his choleric temperament demanded.

At the first attack of the disease, when his strength was still intact, I was summoned, and with great force urged bloodletting, so that the stings of the inflammation would lie deadened and the matter would be lessened and overcome. But it was forbidden by the barbarous man's stupid, excessively barbarous timidity, and the advice of those with whom he was sailing prevailed with me.

Finally, having been called at the hour which immediately preceded the hour in which he departed this life, I found everything threatening death in a short time: his power of speech interrupted, almost completely cut off; his appetite lowered, no pulse; in a word, all his strength and faculties completely prostrated. Having been refreshed a little, he returned to himself as if from a deep sleep and recognised us, his friends. I turned to medicine and he uttered those few of our words which he had learned, in so far as he could, and responded in turn to questions fairly appositely, he sang forth clearly that same song (as they tell who had heard both) which, standing on the shore, his companions of the same place and rank used to lament or celebrate his final departure, like swans who, foreseeing what good there is in death, die with singing and pleasure. But I had hardly left when he exchanged life for death, breaking forth into these final words, uttered in our tonge: 'The Lord be with you.'

SOURCE: Sir James Watt and Ann Savours, 'The Captured 'Countrey People': Their Depiction and Medical History', in Thomas H.B. Symons, ed., *Meta Incognita: A Discourse of Discovery: Martin Frobisher's Arctic Expeditions, 1576–1578* (Hull: Canadian Museum of Civilization, 1999), 556–8.

Three Baffin Island Inuit—a man, a woman, and her child—who were taken prisoner by Frobisher on his expedition to the Arctic in 1577. All three died a month or so after arriving in England. The man was the subject of the autopsy report reprinted above. Copyright © The British Museum 205220 and 234062.

Arctic region. Frobisher was a leading English 'sea dog', part pirate and part merchant. In 1576 he raised the funds for an expedition to sail west to Asia through northern waters. He did not find the passageway, but did bring back mineral samples from Baffin Island. These were pronounced to be gold-bearing, leading to a second expedition in 1577, which brought back 200 tons of ore. About the first of October in 1578, a third fleet returned to England from the land called 'Meta Incognita'. Its principal cargo consisted of 1,350 tons of rocks, collected with great effort and at considerable expense on Baffin Island. Accounts of the return appeared in print before the experts had a chance to examine the cargo. Everyone was demanding to be paid. The owner of one vessel wrote desperately to the government for money to pay his crew, noting, 'Chrystmas beynge so nere, every man cryythe out for mony' (Stefansson, 1938). No money was forthcoming and for five years the sponsors of the expedition tried without success to find evidence of value in the cargo. The rock proved to be nothing more than sandstone flecked with mica. The business degenerated into an unseemly exchange of recriminations and accusations among the investors, and the rock itself was eventually used in Elizabethan road construction.

Map of the North Pole, 1595, by Gerardus Mercator. NAC, NMC-016097.

Frobisher's quest for the Northwest Passage in Arctic waters inspired a series of explorers, mainly Englishmen backed by English capital, over the next fifty years. The best-known of these adventurers was Henry Hudson (d. 1611), who sailed under both English and Dutch auspices. On his last voyage in 1610 he entered Hudson Bay and navigated its eastern coastal waters southward to James Bay before his crew mutinied against him and cast him adrift on a small boat, never to be seen again.

The great voyages of discovery were largely completed by the end of the sixteenth century, even though much of the North American continent remained to be mapped and charted. They occurred against a complex European backdrop of dynastic manoeuvring, the rise of the modern nation-state, the religious disputes of the Protestant Reformation and Catholic Counter-Reformation, and the growth of capitalistic enterprise fuelled by the infusion of new wealth in the form of gold and silver bullion from the Indies. In the sixteenth century Henry VII and Elizabeth I of England joined Francis I of France as important patrons of master mariners who set sail for the West hoping to obtain wealth and national advantage from the voyages they sponsored. The dissolution of an earlier alliance between Spain and England in the wake of the latter nation's becom-

Henry Hudson

Like many another early European explorer, Hudson has left no paper trail beyond the events of the years at the high point of his reputation. We do not know where he was born or when, except that he was apparently an Englishman. In 1607 he was employed by the Muscovy Company (an English company trading with Russia) to seek a Northeast Passage to China across the North Pole, and he followed this voyage up with another in 1608, which sailed to the Russian Arctic but found nothing. This employment has been taken to mean that, whatever his background, he was regarded as highly competent. The Dutch East India Company hired him in 1609 to continuing searching for the Northeast Passage in the *Half Moon*. His crew mutinied near Norway, and he changed his course as a result, crossing the Atlantic to search instead for the Northwest Passage and sailing up the Hudson River, which still bears his name.

Hudson was subsequently hired by a consortium of English merchants to search for a route to Asia through North America. His ship *Discovery* was manned by a number of experienced seamen, including Robert Bylot, who had earlier sailed with William Baffin. The crew was also quite quarrelsome, and the voyage was replete with open conflict and at least one mutiny in which the mutineers backed down only at the last minute. As was the case with the notorious Captain Bligh less than two centuries later, Hudson was a better mariner than a manager of men. He took reprisals against the mutineers. For reasons unknown, he exhibited blatant and continual favouritism to one young man, who eventually turned against him in consort with several others. Hudson refused to pause to replenish provisions at Digges Island, apparently expecting to be in China very shortly. On 23 June 1611, shortly after beginning the voyage back from a winter on Hudson Bay and desperately short of food, the conspirators, led by the former favourite, cast Hudson, his son, and seven other men into a small shallop and cut it adrift. They persuaded Robert Bylot (if his story is to be believed) to pilot the ship back to England. Nothing more is known of the passengers on the shallop, but Bylot brought the *Discovery* back to England after a desperate battle with the Inuit at Digges Island in which several mutineers were killed. Most of what we know about the post-mutiny adventures of the *Discovery* comes to us via a narrative by one of the participants, the curiously named Abacuk Pricket. Bylot was pardoned by a court and went on to a distinguished Arctic career; the other mutineers were eventually tried on a charge of murder and acquitted. Hudson's widow, Katherine, impoverished by her husband's disappearance, had to fight hard to receive compensation from the East India Company, which called her 'that troublesome and impatient woman'. But it finally allowed her to trade in India on her own account. She returned in 1622 with considerable wealth. Given the discontent aboard the *Discovery*, Hudson's accomplishment in navigating through Hudson Strait and hundreds of miles into Hudson Bay was outstanding, although his leadership skills left much to be desired.

A confrontation between Inuit and English sailors, 1577. The artist, John White, was a member of Martin Frobisher's second expedition in search of a Northwest Passage. Copyright © The British Museum.

SEBASTIAN CABOT

Sebastian Cabot (c. 1484–1557) was born in Venice, the son of John Cabot. He would later claim he went with his father on the 1497 voyage to the New World, but he was an inveterate liar and boaster, and no scholar believes his assertions. His career is shrouded in mystery and contradiction. He did receive a royal annuity of £20 in 1505 'in consideration of the diligent service and attendaunce' he had rendered in the port of Bristol. He probably commanded an expedition to America in 1508–9 for which there is no contemporary documentation but a good deal of notice in later sixteenth-century European accounts of discovery. If his own account is to be believed, he sailed on this occasion to the mouth of Hudson Bay, believing this to be the opening of the Northwest Passage to Asia. Like most of the early mariners, including his father, Sebastian was a transnational mercenary. In 1512 he was appointed a naval captain in the Spanish service, and he moved to Seville. In 1518 he was appointed to the office of pilot-major in Spain. The English government sought to entice him back into its service, but the English mercantile community was quite suspicious of Sebastian. The Company of Drapers, a craft guild, was not keen to entrust an American expedition to a man who 'was never in that land hym self, all if he makes reporte of many thinges as he hath hard his ffather and other men speke in tymes past.' He remained as pilot-major in Spain, the major consultant for the government on overseas voyages, and was appointed captain-general of a Seville expedition to South America in 1525. This expedition sailed in early 1526, and eventually made its way in 1527 to the Rio de la Plata searching for gold.

After suppressing a series of mutinies, Sebastian returned to Spain in 1530, where he was charged by the Crown and relatives of his sailors with ignoring instructions, behaving arbitrarily, and endangering the lives of those under his command. Found guilty by the Council of the Indies, he was banished to Africa but never actually went there. He was later rehabilitated by the emperor Charles V, who apparently liked Sebastian's work in the Rio de la Plata. He resumed his post as pilot-major, and over the next few years he came into constant conflict with Spanish cosmographers over technical questions. Sebastian returned to England in 1548 or 1549, receiving an annuity from King Edward VI. He was subsequently consulted by the English Crown on the Northwest Passage, and he drew up the 1553 instructions for the Muscovy Company's first voyage. Although he wrote extensively and supposedly produced many maps and charts, few have survived. The general impression Sebastian leaves is that of a man exploiting his father's reputation and generally operating beyond his capabilities. At the same time, there are suggestions that Sebastian was plausible and knew how to ingratiate himself with the rich and powerful.

ing Protestant, as well as the complex relationships between the ruling houses of the two countries, encouraged Elizabeth to turn her 'sea dogs' (like Frobisher) loose upon the Spanish empire. English exploration was inextricably bound up with 'singeing the Spanish beard' and with politi-

HENRI MEMBERTOU

Membertou claimed to have been a grown man when he met Jacques Cartier, which would mean that he had been born in the early years of the sixteenth century. Regardless of his exact birthdate, Membertou was a venerable old man when the French appeared at Port-Royal in 1605. He was the leader of a small band of Mi'kmaq whose hunting and fishing territory included Port-Royal. The opportunities afforded his band by the arrival of the Europeans were the envy of other Aboriginal leaders, and Membertou was a firm friend of the newcomers. He certainly looked like a leader. Father Biard described him as being taller and larger limbed than his colleagues, and he apparently sported a beard. Much of what has been written about Membertou by the early chroniclers falls properly into the category of legend, but it was true that he was the first Aboriginal to be baptized in New France itself, as opposed to being carried to France and baptized there. The ceremony was performed by the newly arrived priest Jessé Fléché on 24 June 1610. All of Membertou's immediate family were baptized as well, without any proper preparation because the missionary could not speak the Algonquian language and the Aboriginals could not speak enough French. Membertou was given the European name of the king, Henri. After his baptism Membertou appeared eager to become a proper Christian. He wanted the missionaries to learn Algonquian so that he could be properly educated. By 1611 he had contracted dysentery, however, one of the many infectious diseases brought by the Europeans, and by September of that year he was clearly very ill. He insisted on being buried among his ancestors, which annoyed the missionaries, but they gave him extreme unction anyway, and at the end he apparently requested burial among the French. He died on 18 September 1611. The closing year of his life illustrates a pattern often repeated among the indigenous people who were 'Christianized' by the first European missionaries. Unable to understand properly the precepts of Christianity, they could hardly have been said to be converted, and they often died shortly after baptism, succumbing to contagious diseases probably introduced by the missionaries themselves.

cal hostility to Spain heightened by religious grievances. English adventurers often combined the roles of explorer, pirate, and even colonizer. The French had entered the American sweepstakes in the hopes of competing with the Spaniards and Portuguese. After Cartier's pioneering (and unsuccessful) voyages of 1534, 1535–6, and 1541–2, France found itself wrapped up more in its own internal dynastic struggles than in overseas adventuring. The country did not show much state interest in North America until the end of the century, by which time Henry IV had stabilized the monarchy.

In both France and England, overseas investment by an emerging mercantile class took over gradually from the earlier efforts of intrepid mariners backed by the Crown. Cartier's third voyage marked for France the transition from public to private enterprise, and the 1576 voyage of Martin Frobisher in search of the Northwest

Passage to the East demonstrated the new importance of mercantile investment to the English.

By the end of the sixteenth century Europe had established that there were no wealthy Aboriginal civilizations to be conquered on the eastern seaboard, nor any readily apparent sources of rich mineral wealth to be exploited. When it was clear that what the continent had in abundance were fish and furs, a more complex pattern of exploitation had to be developed that required the year-round presence of settlers. Both France and England shifted their energies from maritime thrusts to colonization.

THE IMPACT OF DISEASE ON THE ABORIGINAL PEOPLES

However rapidly European artefacts and animals (such as the horse) may have spread ahead of the newcomers, what dispersed across the continent with even greater rapidity was disease. North America in the sixteenth century was relatively isolated in a geographical sense. A host of communicable diseases common to the 'known world' of international trade and commerce either did not exist or were not so virulent on the American continent, and the population had few immunities to them. Measles, smallpox, typhus, typhoid, mumps, and venereal disease—the last perhaps first contracted by Europeans in the Caribbean region—were as much European introductions as the gun and the horse. Although these diseases spread unusually quickly among an Aboriginal population that had no immunities to them, we must not think that communicable disease was totally unknown in early North America or that the pre-contact population lived in an Edenic state of robust health. In any case, trade and war, including the Aboriginal custom of replenishing population losses by adopting captive women and children, spread new and virulent disease far beyond points of actual European contact. In fairness to the newcomers, they simply did not understand that their sexual promiscuity with First Nations women, or their taking Aboriginals back to Europe as prize specimens or informants, would be devastating to the Native populations. Europeans themselves had become callous about epidemic disease; it was part of life, and they did not understand the concept of immunity. They had no reason to view the Aboriginal propensity for dying in captivity as something resulting from European intervention. For their part, the Aboriginals did not understand that crowding around a sick person to offer affection only spread disease, or that sitting in a sweatlodge and then plunging into cold water was not an effective remedy for a disease like smallpox.

As James Axtell points out, the Aboriginal peoples used three techniques to respond to the demographic disaster. The first, the employment of warfare to replenish the population through captivity and adoption, was of mixed success, particularly when extended to the Europeans themselves. While the process worked well in some ways, it also helped to spread disease, and it certainly increased the hostility of European settlers to the First Nations. The second strategy was intermarriage, which ignored colour bars and many of the social assumptions of European society. The third strategy was to move after depopulation, often joining with other tribes and peoples. The attraction of the Catholic reserves around Montreal and Quebec after the 1640s was in large part a result of the population devastations of the preceding period throughout the Northeast region of the continent.

The introduction of new diseases renders all attempts to estimate the size of the indigenous population at the time of contact totally useless. We have already noted that the indigenous pre-contact population of Canada was substantially larger than the most generous estimates of all the first-contact observers. The east coast population had probably been seriously reduced by epidemic disease during the sixteenth century, and demographic disaster preceded the Europeans right across the country. At the same time, this inadvertent introduction of the early pandemics

FATHER BIARD ON THE MI'KMAQ, 1616

In 1616 the Jesuit missionary Pierre Biard (c. 1567-1622), who had been at Port-Royal since 1611, wrote a 'Relation', which was published in France, describing his experiences with the Aboriginals of the region. It was subsequently translated and republished by Reuben Gold Thwaites.

They are astonished and often complain that, since the French mingle with and carry on trade with them, they are dying fast and the population is thinning out. For they assert that, before this association and intercourse, all their countries were very populous and they tell how one by one the different coasts, according as they have begun to traffic with us, have been more reduced by disease; adding, that why the Armouchiquois do not diminish in population is because they are not at all careless. Thereupon they often puzzle their brains, and sometimes think that the French poison them, which is not true; at other times that they give poisons to the wicked and vicious of their nation to help them vent their spite upon some one. This last supposition is not without foundation; for we have seen them have some arsenic and sublimate which they say they bought from certain French Surgeons, in order to kill whomsoever they wished, and boasted that they had already experimented upon a captive, who (they said) died the day after taking it. Others complain that the merchandise is often counterfeited and adulterated, and that peas, beans, bread, and other things that are spoiled are sold them; and that it is that which corrupts the body and gives rise to the dysentery and other diseases which always attack them in Autumn. This theory is likewise not offered without citing instances, for which they have often been upon the point of breaking with us, and making war upon us. Indeed there would be need of providing against these detestable murders by some suitable remedy if one could be found.

Nevertheless the principal cause of all these deaths and diseases is not what they say it is, but it is something to their shame; in the Summer time, when our ships come, they never stop gorging themselves excessively during weeks with various kinds of food not suitable to the inactivity of their lives; they get drunk, not only on wine but on brandy; so it is no wonder that they are obliged to endure some gripes of the stomach in the following Autumn. . . . These are their storehouses. Who is to take care of them when they go away? For, if they stay, their stores would soon be consumed; so they go somewhere else until the time of famine. Such are the only guards they leave. For in truth this is not a nation of thieves. Would to God that the Christians who go among them would not set them a bad example in this respect. But as it is now, if a certain Savage is suspected of having stolen anything he will immediately throw this fine defense in your teeth, *We are not thieves, like you.*

SOURCE: Reuben Gold Thwaites, ed., *The Jesuit Relations and Allied Documents: Travels and Explanations 1610–1791*, 73 vols (Cleveland, 1896–1901), III, 105–9.

should not be allowed to dominate completely the story of North America in the immediate pre-contact and early contact periods. In the first place, there was no 'Golden Age' in pre-European America in which contagious disease did not exist at all. In the second, 'germs' were not the sole cause of the ultimate reduction (in size and power) of the Aboriginal population. Europeans took actions much more deliberate than introducing epidemics, actions that led to significant reductions in indigenous populations.

EUROPEAN CONTACT AND THE DEVELOPMENT OF CULTURAL CONFLICT

The intrusion of Europeans greatly altered the dynamics of First Nations development, while providing us with a somewhat misleading version of the nature of the population at the moment of contact and beyond. Recorded history was, after all, monopolized by those who had written languages and could make records. In the centuries following European arrival, virtually everything written about the indigenous population of Canada was produced from the European perspective. That perspective, moreover, tended to involve considerable misunderstanding of First Nations culture and behaviour.

In many ways, there was no justification to the assumption of superiority over the indigenous population, which was the common response of the European observer. The visitors' veneer of civilization was a thin one at best, and often wore away quite quickly. What it left behind was evidence of a nasty, brutish, and violent age. Most Europeans still ate with their fingers, bathed as seldom as possible, and enjoyed such amusements as bear-baiting, in which dogs were pitted against captive bears in fights to the death. The institutions of the ruling classes allowed heretics to be tortured in the name of Jesus Christ, witches to be burnt at the stake, and thousands—of different beliefs or backgrounds from those in charge of church and state—to be executed. Public executions were guaranteed crowd-pleasers, especially if the victim could be drawn and quartered while still alive. In some parts of Europe a popular entertainment at fairs was watching blind men in pens attempt to beat each other to death with clubs. Garbage and animal excrement were piled high in the streets of European cities, 'piss-pots' were still emptied into the streets, and one of the major motivations behind European expansion was the search for new and more powerful scents to help disguise the stench of daily life. The term *sauvages* (savages) which the Europeans often used to refer to the First Nations people of North America, is to the modern mind, ironic and insulting.

Whatever technological glitter Europe had (the extent of its actual superiority is debatable), it would prove relatively useless in the wilderness of the New World. Successful Europeans in Canada would for several centuries survive by adopting First Nations technology. European inventions may have helped give the intruders a sense of superiority, as did their emerging capitalist economic order, their new political organization into nation-states, and especially their Christian system of values and beliefs. These pronounced differences between Europeans and indigenous Canadians prevented the visitors from fully comprehending the people they encountered. The Europeans quite unconsciously, often quite subtly, judged First Nations by their own standards.

At the same time, the process of early communication between Europeans and the Aboriginal peoples was a much more difficult business than we might think, or than the contemporary documents would suggest. Europeans and Aboriginals spoke different languages, a good many of them. In Europe, most countries lacked a single national language that was understood in every part of the country. Dialects had both regional and class origins. The great European sea captains, many of whom had connections at the royal court, were likely to have a different pronunciation and vocabulary than the common sailors, although technically both groups spoke the same language. The First Nations spoke several hundred different local languages in a myriad of dialects. Fifty different languages were spoken in what is now Canada, although most of these fell into a few language families. In what is now

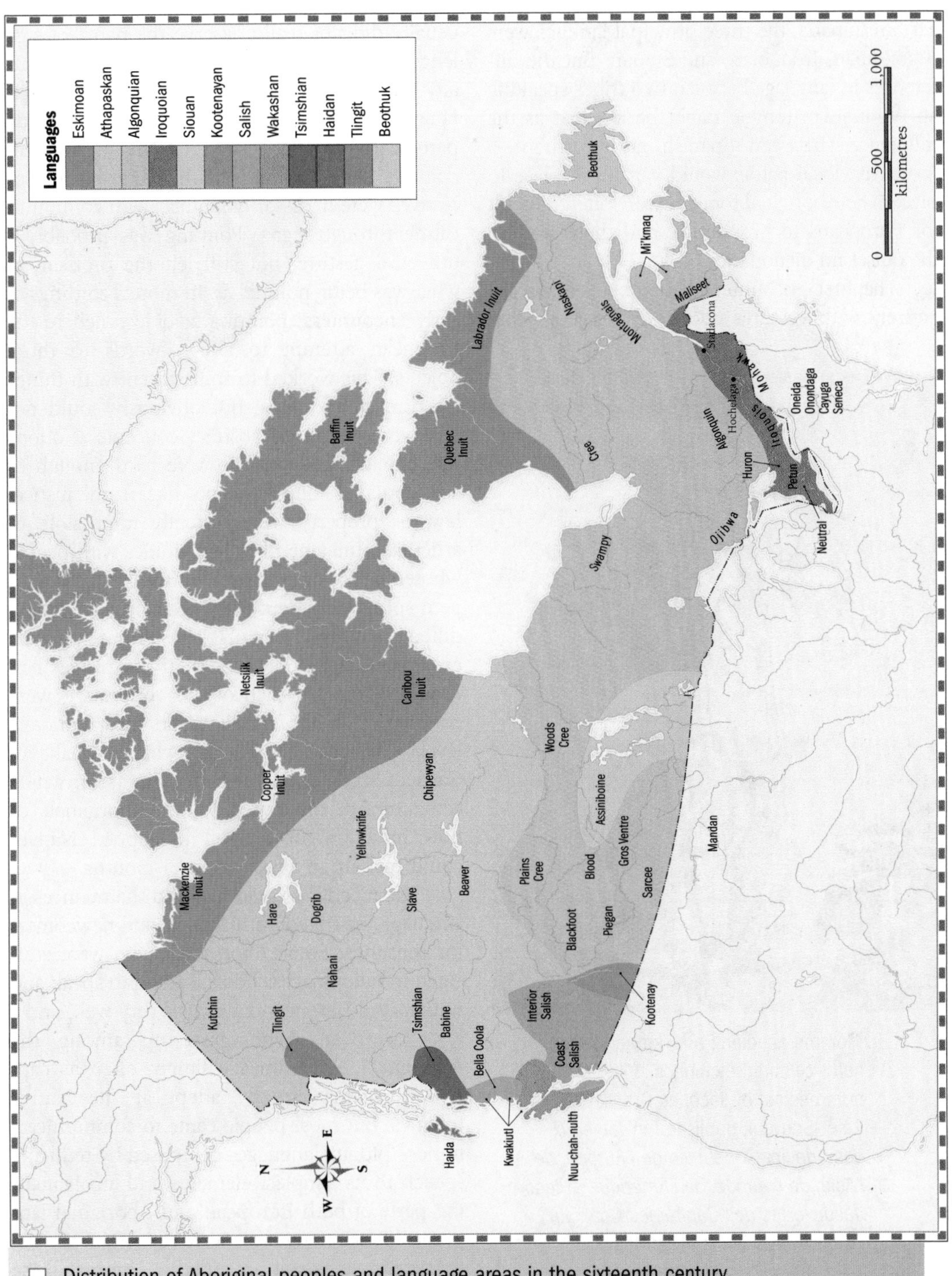

Distribution of Aboriginal peoples and language areas in the sixteenth century.

eastern Canada, the three principal families were Algonquian, Iroquoian, and Siouan. But the differences in language between two tribes speaking an Algonquian tongue might be as great as the differences between Spanish and Portuguese. Moreover, local patois would vary from place to place. The Aboriginal tongues were often difficult for Europeans to pronounce, and there were at the outset no dictionaries.

The first encounters had to be conducted entirely with gestures and body language that usually did not really deserve the name of sign language. Gestures are to a large extent as culturally determined as any other form of language. Hugging, kissing, and touching various body parts carry different connotations in different cultures, for example. Neither Europeans nor Natives were necessarily familiar with communicating through signs. Pointing was probably a universal gesture, but still left the problem of what was being pointed at. In most recordings of early encounters, pointing at objects led to the European attempt to assign words to those objects. This worked to some extent with things like knives and fires, but obviously could not deal very well with abstract concepts. Notions like climate and weather were hard enough to conceptualize, and concepts like truth, justice, law, or property were virtually impossible to articulate. Imagine playing charades with people who come from an entirely different world than you, speak a different language, and have totally different cultural referents! The earliest linguistic exchanges, therefore, even after the parties had acquired some of each other's vocabulary, were conducted on the simplest and most concrete levels. We have to wonder what to make of Cartier's accounts of his first contacts, in which actual motives are imputed to the Aboriginals, or how much linguistic skill kidnapped Natives could pick up in a few weeks or months.

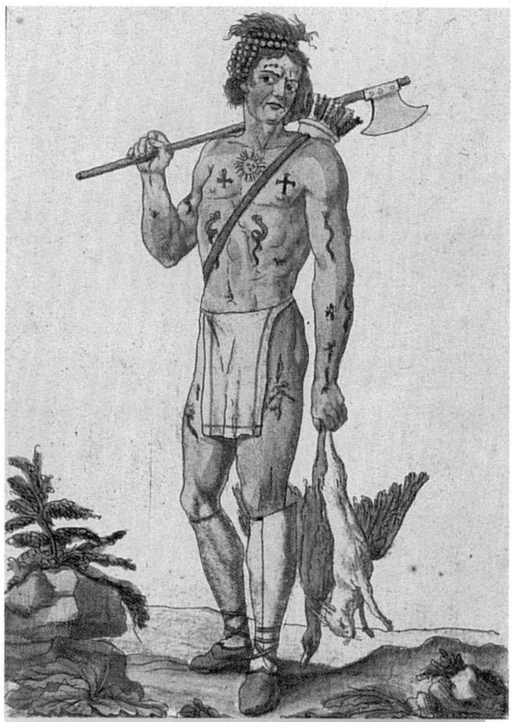

☐ 'Homme acadien': a Mi'kmaq hunter, hand-coloured etching, c. 1788-96, from original by Jacques Grasset de Saint-Sauveur, published in *Tableaux des principaux peuples de l'Europe, de l'Asie, de l'Afrique, de l'Amérique et les découvertes des Capitaines Cook, La Pérouse, etc.* (Paris et Bordeaux, 1796-8). NAC, C-21112.

The niceties of grammar and the nuances of language frustrated both Natives and newcomers for centuries. Some Aboriginals who were educated in missionary schools learned to speak and understand European languages very well, and a few Europeans who grew up among the Aboriginals (sometimes willingly, often as captives) became equally adept at the Native tongues. But most people came to communicate in new 'pidgin' languages composed by reducing speech to its simplest elements and amalgamating parts of both European and Aboriginal languages. Pidgin languages were capable of sophistication as time went on, and they eliminated the potentially inflammatory business of preferring one people's language over another. One very venerable pidgin language was spoken on the coasts of the Gulf of St Lawrence, where Basque fishermen had traded with local Natives from the early sixteenth century. 'Since their languages were completely different,' wrote one observer in 1710, 'they created a form of lingua franca composed of Basque and two different languages of the Indians, by means of which they could understand each other very well' (Bakker 1989: 259). Marc Lescarbot in the early seventeenth century recorded that the Mi'kmaq spoke to the French in a simplified version of their language mixed with 'much Basque'. In the later fur trade in the interior of the continent, pidgin tongues were a complex amalgam of French, Gaelic, English, Cree, and Assiniboine.

Not surprisingly, as relations between Europeans and Aboriginal peoples became more formalized, the need for skilled official interpreters acquired a new urgency. An interpreter who was trusted by both sides in complex negotiations to translate accurately the meaning and nuances of language was a rare commodity and highly prized. As late as 1873, when Treaty No. 6 was being negotiated between the Canadian government and the Saskatchewan Cree, the question of interpreters remained a critical issue. The government had brought two interpreters of its own, and argued it was unnecessary to add another brought by the Cree. The Cree chief answered, 'Very good. You keep your interpreters and we will keep ours. We will pay our own man and I already see that it will be well for us to do so' (Christensen 2001: 229).

The First Nations economies did not produce political institutions on a European scale. Semi-sedentary people had no need for political organizations larger than the band, which was based on the consolidation of a few family units. Even where horticulture was developed, with its large semi-permanent villages, political structure was not complex by European standards. 'Chiefs' were not kings. They may not even have been 'head men' in any European sense. Such a concept of rulership was in most places introduced and imposed on the indigenous population by the newcomers. As is now well known, the Aboriginal notion of property, especially involving land, was well beyond the comprehension of the European. While some First Nations groups could conceive of territory as 'belonging' to them, the concept was one of usage rather than ownership. The indigenous people erroneously identified as kings were quite happy to 'sell' to the European newcomers land that neither they nor their people owned, at least as Europeans understood ownership.

Lacking much inclination to create hierarchical political organizations, the First Nations practised war according to different rules than those employed in Europe, where institutions of church and state went to war for 'reasons of state'. Aboriginal wars were mainly raids by a few warriors, conducted partly because success in battle was an important test of manhood. They were often used to capture women and children to replace those lost within the band. Individual prowess in battle was valued, while long-term military strategy and objectives were not. First Nations had their own military agendas, and were notoriously fickle allies from the European perspective. Only the Iroquois—who in the seventeenth century may have developed a militarily viable form of political organization partly based on European models—were able to compete with the newcomers and withstand their military power.

Nowhere was the gulf between First Nations and newcomers more apparent than in the spiritual realm. Aboriginal religious beliefs were complex, although not readily apparent to the outside observer. They were part of an intricate religio-magical world that the First Nations inhabited and shared with the flora and fauna. Given the hunting orientation of most groups, it is hardly surprising that animals were endowed with spiritual significance. The very act of food consumption often acquired deep religious meaning, becoming a form of worship of the spirit world through everyday activity. Many peoples had legends about the origins of the

THE TRADITION OF THE FLOOD

Antoine Lamothe Cadillac (1658-1730) was one of those immigrants to Canada who arrived with no previous history. He proved to be a wily if unscrupulous fur trader, operating mainly in the Michilimackinac and Detroit areas. At the end of the seventeenth century he prepared a manuscript memoir describing the Native peoples of the region. Are there alternative explanations to his for the flood traditions he discusses?

All these tribes, without exception, have a tradition of the Flood; we shall see what their ideas are on this subject. They say that such a great quantity of snow and rain fell that all the waters, being gathered together, rose higher than the highest mountains, so that people went about everywhere in canoes and the earth was changed into a vast lake. But they maintain that in this universal flood, in which everyone perished, an old man in each tribe was saved, with all his family, because they had the sense when they saw the waters rising to build a very big canoe in which they put provisions and animals of all kinds, and after spending many days in great discomfort they threw an otter out of the boat to see whether he could not get to land somewhere; but they say the otter was drowned, for after some days he was seen floating on the water, on his back. After some time the old man sent a beaver in the opposite direction to see whether he could not find land. They say he found a sort of dam of dry wood, but because he was hungry he returned to the canoe, bringing back a big stump, which made the old man conclude that the waters were beginning to fall; then they turned their canoes toward the spot from which they had seen the beaver returning and at length they saw in the distance a great pile of wood, which had collected in the following manner:

They say that an enormous turtle fell from the sky and floated under water; and as there was a quantity of dry wood around, and other trees with their roots and branches carried hither and thither by the wind and the water, those which came against the turtle fastened to him and remained there, so that in a short time such a large quantity accumulated that one could walk on it as on a raft. When the old man saw this, he landed on it, and finding a little earth on the roots of the trees he collected it and offered it as a sacrifice to the sun, which dried it. Then the old man, after reducing it to dust, sowed it broadcast over the waters, so that it drank up the water with which the earth was covered. Each tribe maintains that the turtle which fell from the sky stopped on the highest mountain in their part of the country, so that there is no agreement where the place was.

If the statements set forth in this chapter are considered attentively the reader may think, as I do, that all these tribes are descended from the Hebrews and were originally Jews, which may also be observed from the terms they use in conversation and in their speeches and customs. . . .

It may be thought that if the Indians are really descended from the Jews they would at least have retained their language, since it is not natural that children should forget what their fathers and mothers have taught them from the time they began to lisp; and it is much more probable that habits, manners, and customs should pass away than the operations of the mind, which cannot be expressed nor known except by means of signs and words, which are lost only by the decay of the organs of the human body.

It seems to me that we may reply to this objection, that a language that is badly taught rusts and perishes completely, as everything else does in the course of time. Reason and experience teach us that a language becomes disfigured and weakened in proportion to its neglect and use. . . . Nor is it surprising that a people who have been wanderers and vagrants for so many centuries, and never accustomed to writing or reading—which are the foster-mothers of a language—should have so corrupted and debased it that scarcely any trace of it now remains.

SOURCE: M.M. Quaife, ed., *The Western Country in the 17th Century: The Memoires of Antoine Lamothe Cadillac and Pierre Liette* (New York: The Citadel Press, 1962): 52-60.

world, and some may have believed in a single Creator. The mixture of authentic Aboriginal lore with European thought and missionary teaching has coloured First Nations legends and tales over the last 350 years. It has made it difficult—perhaps even impossible—to separate one from the other. Formal religious ceremonies were not readily apparent to the visitors, except for the activities of the shamans, who claimed supernatural powers and engaged in several kinds of folk medicine ranging from herbal treatment to exorcism. Shamans were no more priests than other leaders were kings, but Europeans tended to consider their activities to be at the core of First Nations religion. The newcomers found it impossible to grasp that inanimate objects in nature could be alive and have their own powers, or that rituals connected with the ordinary round of daily life could have deep spiritual significance. That First Nations religion had no buildings, no clerical hierarchy, and no institutional presence thoroughly disoriented the Europeans.

Tolerance for alternative spiritual values and belief systems was hardly one of Europe's strong suits in the Age of Discovery. The period of European arrival in North America coincided with the Protestant Reformation and the Catholic Counter-Reformation. Christianity was undergoing profound alteration, with traditional Catholicism subjected to reform from both within and without. Protestants and Catholics alike were quite capable of fierce persecution of any deviation from official belief and practice. Both could agree that what was being encountered in Canada was pagan supernaturalism that needed to be uprooted as quickly as possible and replaced with a 'true faith'. That Europeans themselves could not agree on the truth perplexed some First Nations people, such as the Iroquois, who were exposed to competing French, English, and Dutch missionaries.

The European intruders could not grasp the notion that Christianity was embedded in a well-developed European value system, or that indigenous religious beliefs and practices were integral to First Nations existence. Views of the world and of one's place in it were as integral to life for Aboriginals as they were for Europeans, and the way in which First Nations related spiritually to their environment was a critical part of their culture. Europe could not convert First Nations to Christianity without undermining the very basis of their existence. Naturally the First Nations resisted.

The almost total absence of a quest for complex long-term goals through deferral of expectations was easily one of the most marked features of First Nations society from the European perspective. Europeans believed that goals had to be inculcated at an early age through a series of repressive tactics that included heavy reliance on corporal punishment, although monastic orders proved that the same results could be achieved without the overt use of force. European children were treated like adults and put to work at an early age. First Nations parents, on the other hand, treated their children with affectionate indulgence, seldom inflicting reprimands and totally eschewing corporal punishment. Young warriors learned stoic self-control and an ability to endure hardship and physical pain, but such self-control was more the ability to bear than the capacity to obey. Though circumscribed, controlled, and regulated by ritual, tradition, and custom (what we today would call 'socialization'), most First Nations hated taking orders, particularly from Europeans.

While commenting on the freedom that children were allowed, European observers of every First Nations group in northern North America from coast to coast also wrote that women were badly exploited. European society at the time could hardly be called liberal in its treatment of women. What the newcomers saw as exploitation reflected their inability to comprehend the divisions of labour within a warrior society. Men hunted and fought, while women were responsible for just about everything else. Interestingly enough, when European women were captured by raiding parties and integrated into Aboriginal life, many chose to remain with their captors instead of accepting repatriation back into colonial society. Those captives who were brought home and who wrote about their experiences emphasized that the Aboriginals had a strong sense of love and community and offered—as one set of repatriates acknowledged—'The most perfect freedom, the ease of living, [and] the absence of those cares and corroding solicitudes which so often prevail with us' (Axtell 2001: 213).

As for morality, particularly sexual, the two peoples seemed about equally matched. The generosity of the males in some tribes in permitting their women to bestow sexual favours on the newcomers speaks volumes about the male prerogative in these societies. While some observers felt obliged to comment on First Nations promiscuity, a few had the decency to recognize that Europeans were hardly blameless in this regard. In the saga of European intrusion around the world over the centuries, Europe sent only males, particularly as exploiters and traders in the early period, so local females were employed for sexual purposes. The pattern in the Canadian fur-trade of European males coupling with First Nations females produced a mixed-blood society that had its parallels in other parts of the world.

Almost from the outset, European newcomers to Canada had two contradictory responses to the peoples they were contacting and describing. On the one hand, much of what they saw in First Nations life, particularly beyond mere superficial observation, struck them as admirable. The First Nations exhibited none of the negative features of capitalistic society. On the other hand, there was the equally powerful image of the First Nations as brutal savages and barbarians, particularly in the context of war. This dichotomy of response was particularly keen among the missionaries, who kept trying to 'civilize' the First Nations by converting them to Christianity and forcibly educating them in European ways. Mère Marie de l'Incarnation, the head of the Ursuline School for girls at Quebec, wrote of her charges in 1668 that there was 'docility and intelligence in these girls, but when we are least expecting it, they clamber over our wall and go off to run with their kinsmen in the woods, finding more to please them there than in all the amenities of our French houses' (Marshall 1967: 341).

In the eighteenth century, an idealized and romanticized view of Aboriginal society was used by many European philosophers as a literary convention and fictional device for criticizing contemporary European society. As Peter Moogk has pointed out, conditions of press censorship, particularly in France, made it advisable to use fictitious foreigners, including Amerindians, to express negative opinions about church and state (Moogk 2000: 48–9). The first such character was probably Baron de Lahontan's 'Huron' named Adario, who in 1703 observed that the Ten Commandments were routinely ignored in France, while the Aboriginals practised innocence, love, and tranquillity of mind. Lahontan's books went through numerous editions, and led in the hands of Voltaire and Rousseau to the Enlightenment notion of the *bon sauvage*. The First Nations possessed none of the worst traits of European capitalistic society, such as covetousness and rapaciousness; and they revered freedom, while eschewing private property. What relationship the 'noble savage' bore to the realities of existence in North America is another matter entirely.

Europeans would blunder on for centuries in their attempts to come to terms with the indigenous peoples of North America. The First Nations would prove tenacious in maintaining their own identity and culture in the face of much effort to Europeanize them, but they lacked the physical power to prevent either constant encroachment on their territory, or the continual undermining of the basic physical and spiritual substance of their way of life. The cultural contact between Native and newcomer was a true tragedy. Reconciliation of the two cultures was quite impossible, and the failure of reconciliation resounds still today.

THE FIRST EUROPEAN COMMUNITIES

When generations of painful experience taught Europeans that there was no quick road to wealth by exploiting the indigenous peoples or the resource base of North America, hopes turned to transplanting Europeans who could take advantage of fish and furs. The shift occurred at the beginning of the seventeenth century. A variety of motives jostled in the minds of the early promoters of settlement, few of whom ever planned to set foot on North American soil. National advantage, religion, humanitarianism, greed, personal ambition, and sheer fantasy were all present in various combinations. European monarchs and their supporters were flattered by the 'enlarging of Dominions'. Missions to the First Nations and the possibilities of refuge from religious persecution at home excited the pious. Many a promoter saw colonization as a way to rid Europe of unwanted paupers and petty criminals. Investors were tempted with talk of titles and large land grants. In the pursuit of great profits, common sense was easily lost. Although large-scale colonization activities were begun by the English in Virginia in 1607, the ventures undertaken in the northern latitudes were typically more modest. They consisted mainly of trading posts and fishing settlements.

English familiarity with Newfoundland led London merchants to attempt colonization there beginning in 1610. The London and Bristol Company for the Colonization of Newfoundland (usually known as the Newfoundland Company) was organized by forty-eight subscribers who invested £25 each. The plan was that permanent settlers employed by the company would quickly dominate the fishery over those who came in the spring and went home in the autumn. Europe was desperately short of a protein food for the poor, and dried cod found a ready market, especially in Catholic countries. The first settlement of the company was established by John Guy (d. 1629), who led forty colonists from Bristol to Cupid's Cove on Conception Bay in July 1610, only months after the company was granted the entire island. The venture was funded by sale of stock. The company did not appreciate how difficult local agriculture would be, given the soil and the climate, or how unlikely it was in the vast expanses of the New World that settlers could be kept permanently as landless employees labouring solely for the profit of their masters.

The Newfoundland Company's fishing settlements prospered no more than did those of courtiers like George Calvert, First Baron Baltimore (1579/80–1632), who began a plantation at Avalon in 1623. Calvert discovered to his surprise, as he wrote his monarch in 1629, that 'from the middest of October, to the middest of May there is a sadd face of wynter upon all this land, both sea and land so frozen for the great part of the tyme that they are not penetrable, no plant or vegetable thing appearing out of the earth untill it be about the beginning of May nor fish in the sea besides the ayre so intolerable cold, as it is hardly to be endured' (Cell 1982: 295–6). Not long after penning this complaint, he left for Virginia. In 1632 Calvert was granted

Champlain's drawing of the habitation at Port-Royal, built in 1605 on the north shore of the Annapolis Basin. The parts of the complex are identified in an accompanying key. For example, building 'A' was the artisans' quarters, and 'B' was a platform for cannon. Champlain's own quarters were in building D. NAC, C-7033.

the land north of the Potomac River that would become Maryland.

The French were marginally more successful than the English at establishing colonies in the northern regions, both in Acadia (the region vaguely bounded by the St Lawrence to the north, the Atlantic Ocean to the east and south, and the St Croix River to the west) and in Canada (the St Lawrence Valley). An early effort by the Marquis de La Roche de Mesgouez (c. 1540–1606) on Sable Island failed dismally, with rebellious settlers murdering their local leaders over the winter of 1602–3. The island was subsequently evacuated. A similar result occurred at a settlement at the mouth of the Saguenay River. In May 1604 Pierre Du Gua de Monts (1558?–1628) arrived on the Nova Scotia coast with a young draftsman named Samuel de Champlain (c. 1570–1635). The two men were searching for a suitable site to establish a settlement, a condition of de Monts's grant of a trading monopoly in the region. They tried first on an island in the St Croix River. In 1605 the settlement was moved to Port-Royal in the Annapolis Basin, where de Monts built a habitation, a supposed replica of which still exists today as a historic site. In 1606 the Paris lawyer Marc Lescarbot (c. 1570–1642) joined the colony and wrote a narrative of its development, published in 1609 as *Histoire de la Nouvelle France*. In this work Lescarbot noted the foundation of L'Ordre de Bon Temps in 1607, a sort of dining club with extemporaneous entertainment. He also described the masque he wrote for it (the first stage play composed and performed in North America). The colonists were obliged to leave in 1607 when de Monts was forced to relinquish his monopoly, but a French presence would continue in Acadia from the first establishment of Port-Royal, usually in the form of a handful of individuals trading with the First Nations.

As for Samuel de Champlain, he headed up the St Lawrence in 1608 to found a new trading post for de Monts at Stadacona. Another habitation was erected, this one including three buildings of two storeys—connected by a gallery around the outside, 'which proved very conven-

POUTRINCOURT IS OBLIGED TO ABANDON PORT-ROYAL

Marc Lescarbot was a young lawyer in Paris who associated with 'men of letters'. When he lost a case because of a judge's venality, he agreed to accompany one of his clients, Jean de Biencourt de Poutrincourt, to Acadia in 1606. On his return a year later, Lescarbot published an epic poem, *La Défaite des sauvages armouchiquois*, and then began the composition of a vast history of French America, *Histoire de la Nouvelle-France*. Most of this was dependent on the writings of others, but his account of early Acadia was based on his own adventures.

The sun did but begin to cheer the earth and to behold his mistress with an amorous aspect, when the Sagamos Membertou (after our prayers solemnly made to God and the breakfast distributed to the people, according to the custom) came to give us advertisment that he had seen a sail upon the lake which came towards our fort. At this joyful news everyone went out to see, but none was found that had so good a sight as he, though he be above 100 years old; nevertheless, we spied very soon what it was. Monsieur de Poutrincourt caused in all diligence the small barque to be made ready for to go to view further. Monsieur de Champdoré and Daniel Hay went in her, and, by the sign that had been told them being certain that they were friends, they made presently to be charged four cannons and twelve falconets, to salute them that came so far to see us. They on their part did not fail in beginning the joy, and to discharge their pieces, to whom they rendered the like with usury. It was only a small barque under the charge of a young man of Saint Malo, named Chevalier, who, being arrived at the fort, delivered his letters to Monsieur de Poutrincourt, which were read publicly. They did write unto him that, for to help to save the charges of the voyage, the ship (being yet the *Jonas*) should stay at Campseau Port, there to fish for cod, by reason that the merchants associated with Monsieur de Monts knew not that there was any fishing farther than that place: notwithstanding, if it were necessary, he should cause the ship to come to Port-Royal. Moreover, that the Society was broken, because that, contrary to the King his edict, the Hollanders, conducted by a traitorous Frenchman called La Jeunesse, had the year before taken up the beavers and other furs, of the great river of Canada—a thing which did turn to the great damage of the Society, which for that cause could no longer furnish the charges of the inhabiting in these parts, as it had done in times past. And therefore did send nobody for to remain there after us. As we received joy to see our assured succour, we felt also great grief to see so fair and so holy an enterprise broken; that so many labours and perils past should serve to no effect; and that the hope of planting the name of God and the Catholic faith should vanish away. Notwithstanding, after that Monsieur de Poutrincourt had a long while mused hereupon, he said that, although he should have nobody to come with him but only his family, he would not forsake the enterprise.

It was great grief unto us to abandon (without hope of return) a land that had produced unto us so fair corn and so many fair adorned gardens. All that could be done until that time was to find a place fit to make a settled dwelling and a land of good fertility. And, that being done, it was great want of courage to give over the enterprise, for, another year being passed, the necessity of maintaining an habitation there should be taken away, for the land was sufficient to yield things necessary for life. This was the cause of that grief which pierceth the hearts of them which were desirous to see the Christian religion established in that country. But, on the contrary, Monsieur de Monts and his associates reaping no benefit but loss, and having no help from the King, it was a thing which they could not do but with much difficulty to maintain an habitation in those parts.

SOURCE: Marc Lescarbot, *Nova Francia: A Description of Acadia, 1606*, translated by P. Erondelle, 1609, with an Introduction by H.P. Biggar (New York and London, 1928), 125–6.

ient', wrote Champlain—surrounded by a moat and palisades. Champlain provided a careful drawing of this habitation in his *Voyages*. He was forced to put down a conspiracy and face a devastating attack of scurvy in the first year. The post survived, however, and Champlain gradually allied himself with the local First Nations, who supplied him with furs and drew the French into war against the Iroquois. Champlain had little alternative to an alliance against the Iroquois, and they became mortal enemies of the French.

Only about fifty Frenchmen resided on the St Lawrence by 1615. Among the early settlers, only Louis Hébert (1595?–1627), who came to Quebec in 1617 after lengthy service as a surgeon at Port-Royal, showed an interest in cultivating the land. But Hébert was most useful for his medical and apothecary skills; the trading company actually attempted to discourage him from agriculture. Not until 1618—when Champlain outlined a grand scheme for the colonization of New France in reports to the king and the French Chamber of Commerce—did anything approaching the plans of the Newfoundland Company enter the French vision. Earlier French activities, including those of Champlain himself, had been underfinanced by a succession of individual entrepreneurs and small syndicates. Trading posts, rather than settlement colonies, were the goal.

Until 1618, Champlain had served as an agent for others rather than as a colonial promoter in his own right. In that year, however, he combined arguments for major investment with a scheme designed to appeal to the imperial pretensions of the Crown. New France and the St Lawrence not only held the possibility of a short route to Asia but could produce 'a great and permanent trade' in such items as fish, timber, whale oil, and furs. The annual income was projected at 5,400,000 livres, virtually none of it coming from agriculture and less than 10 per cent coming from furs. Champlain requested that priests, 300 families of four people each, and 300 soldiers be sent to his base on the St Lawrence. Amazingly enough, the French response was enthusiastic, and Louis XIII instructed the syndicate employing Champlain to expedite his plans. The partners and Champlain, however, were unable to agree upon terms or make any progress in establishing the colony. Not until 1627, when Cardinal Richelieu assumed supervision of New

France and established the Company of One Hundred Associates, did Champlain's grandiose schemes receive substantial backing.

THE BEGINNINGS OF OVERLAND EXPLORATION

The geographical shakedown of European colonization activity in the late sixteenth and early seventeenth centuries determined that it would be the French who would take the lead in exploring the northern interior of the continent, and that their activities would extend far beyond the boundaries of what is now Canada. While the English, Scots, Dutch, and Swedes established settlements along the eastern seaboard, the French founded their settlements on the St Lawrence River, in the interior of the continent. Providing access to the Great Lakes and to most of the major river systems of North America, this river would confer enormous power and influence on the nation that controlled it. The St Lawrence focused the French need for new sources of furs to supply the major export commodity of New France. The river's access to the interior ensured that most of the great feats of inland exploration would be executed by the French. The ability of young Frenchmen to adapt themselves to the ways of the First Nations was also critical.

Champlain himself was active in moving inland to investigate territory previously unknown to Europe, but he was not a typical figure. The first major French overland explorer, in many ways quintessential, was Étienne Brûlé (c. 1592–1633), who lived with the Huron near Georgian Bay, Lake Huron, in 1612, and may have been the first European to sight lakes Superior and Erie. A shadowy, elusive figure, Brûlé, like many early explorers, left no written accounts of his life or adventures. It is likely that he had volunteered in 1610 to live with the First Nations and learn their language. He was probably the young man to whom Champlain referred in 1611 as 'my French boy who came dressed like an Indian' (*DCB* 1966 I: 131). In 1615 Brûlé accompanied a party of Huron braves into the territory of the Susquehanna to the south of the Iroquois, in what is now southwestern New York state. He took advantage of the opportunity to investigate the neighbouring regions, perhaps reaching Chesapeake Bay, and certainly tramping around modern Pennsylvania. Brûlé subsequently journeyed to the north shore of Georgian Bay, and then in the early 1620s along the St Mary's River to Lake Superior. Like many Europeans who 'went native', Brûlé was respected by his compatriots as an interpreter, although they were intensely suspicious of his new persona. In Brûlé's case, his moral character and behaviour were criticized by Champlain even before his final 'treachery' in 1629 when he entered the employment of the Kirke brothers after they successfully captured the tiny French colony at Quebec. By pursuing his own agenda rather than observing the abstract national loyalties dear to European hearts and values, he established what would become a familiar pattern among Europeans coming to terms with North America. By 1633 Brûlé was dead, reportedly killed and eaten by the Huron.

Over the course of the seventeenth century, the interpreters, as represented by Brûlé, would be transformed into the coureurs de bois—the 'runners of the woods' or 'bushlopers'—as the English often called them. These men would be responsible for most of the constantly broadening geographical knowledge of the North American continent. Their desire was less to improve cartography than to exploit new sources of wealth, particularly furs, and above all to enjoy an adventurous life in the woods. Whether or not these wilderness bravoes became completely assimilated into First Nations life and culture (some did), they all learned skills from the Aboriginals that made them crucial figures in the economy of New France. Marine skills like sighting latitude or reading the surface of the water were replaced by the ability to live off the land, to paddle a canoe for long distances with few breaks, to hunt animals for food, and of course to communicate successfully with a local First

Nations population, not merely at the level of language but at one of genuine empathy. These inland explorers travelled in exposed parties and had no defensive structure such as a ship to protect them from attack. They lived by their wits and had to be constantly adaptable. They would

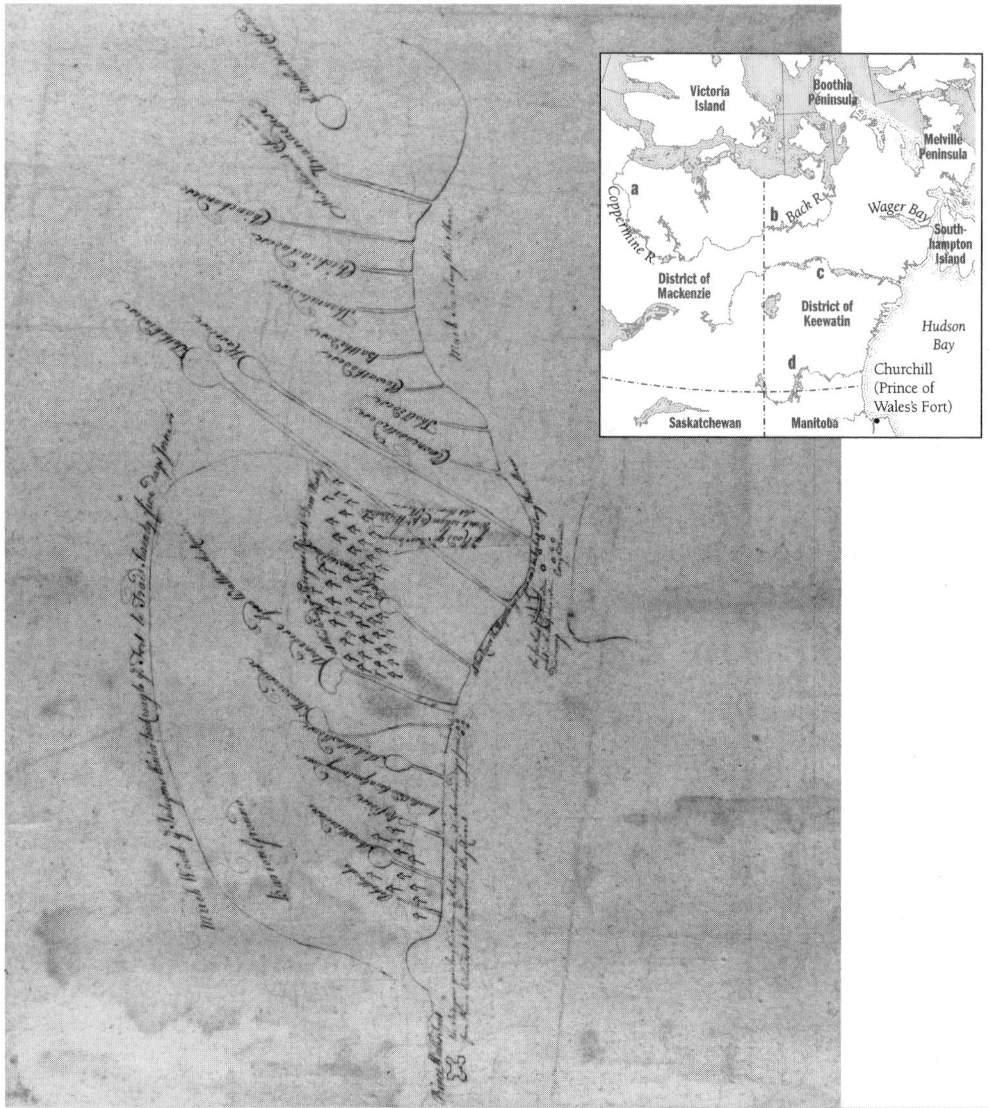

☐ Early untitled map showing rivers flowing into marine waters north of Churchill Fort; drawn c. 1716-17 either by Chipewyan informants themselves or from their reports by James Knight of the HBC. Inset is a modern map of the same territory (based on June Helm, 'Matonabbee's Map', *Arctic Anthropology* 26:2 [1989]). River A is the Coppermine; B is the Back; C is probably the Thelon; and D is the Thlewiaze. Hudson's Bay Company Archives G.1/19.

make splendid guerrilla warriors as Europe moved into warfare for control of the continent.

As Canadian schoolchildren are only too painfully aware, there were a good many overland explorers in the seventeenth and eighteenth centuries, some of whom had automobiles and hotel chains named after them. While most Canadians could, if pressed, name one or two of these explorers, it is very doubtful whether they could offer the name of a single comparable First Nations explorer. Does this mean that the First Nations did not do any travelling in North America? Of course not. What it means is that the Native geographical knowledge of the continent—much of which predated the arrival of the Europeans, who relied very heavily on it—has been ignored by most writers on exploration. The First Nations became part of the fuzzy background rather than the sharply focused foreground. Historians of exploration have long known of the great assistance provided by the First Nations in the 'discoveries' of the Europeans. The Aboriginals provided much geographical information—often even maps—and typically served as guides, interpreters, and canoe paddlers.

CONCLUSION

By the mid-1620s the first period of European intrusion into what is now Canada had been completed. Exploration of the new continent's eastern seaboard was done, and Europe could construct a fairly decent map of its coastline. What lay beyond was beginning to be investigated. Europe was on the verge of deciding that major transplantations of people were going to be necessary if this new northern land were to be exploited. As for the indigenous population, they had been buffeted by epidemic disease, the causes of which were beyond their comprehension, but they had not yet been marginalized. The First Nations could still meet the newcomers on something approximating equal terms. In retrospect, we can see how ephemeral this equality really was.

HOW HISTORY HAS CHANGED

EUROPEAN ARRIVAL IN NORTH AMERICA

Perhaps no better example exists of the ways in which the interpretation of history can change than the treatment of the European arrival in North America. At one point not so many years ago, the common perception of this event was of a bunch of larger-than-life explorer-heroes swaggering onto an underpopulated and underutilized continent, bringing to it the blessings of European civilization and culture. After the Europeans arrived, North American history became an overseas extension of the European story, a story of European settlement spreading rapidly across the continent. If the original inhabitants figured at all in this picture, it was either as obstacles to settlement or, more frequently, as part of the environmental background, much like the trees and the animals and the Canadian Shield.

The picture changed because of a variety of factors. One was a growing political recognition around the world of other cultures besides the European, which in turn led to an appreciation that the European attitude of superiority was ethnocentric. This idea probably reached its high point when the five hundredth anniversary of the arrival of Christopher Columbus in 1492 gave scholars in all fields an opportunity to question the Eurocentric version of 'discovery' that had flourished for centuries. In Canada, the First Nations began to assert their political power. This was accompanied by the development of Canada's

North (where most First Nations people resided); by the growth of an ethos of cultural pluralism in Canada; and especially by extensive litigation over Aboriginal land claims. The result was an explosion of First Nations studies, right across Canada.

The shift in historical interpretation of Europeans' arrival in North America was certainly encouraged by the entrance of historians around 1970 into the field of ethnohistory, previously the exclusive stamping ground of the anthropologists. Ethnohistorians have long understood the need to get behind the traditional documents—all generated by Europeans—and to take advantage of other kinds of evidence. As First Nations studies developed, not only the arrival of the Europeans but the subsequent development of the continent came under new scrutiny. Once historians recognized that what was occurring was a conflict of cultures, they began examining that relationship in its own right, rather than as an exercise in the imposition of European standards on native inhabitants. The very notion of cultural contact as a major theme in early Canadian history would have been virtually unthinkable a generation ago, but contact has now become a central event.

SHORT BIBLIOGRAPHY

Axtell, James. *Natives and Newcomers: The Cultural Origins of North America.* New York, 2001. A series of penetrating essays by North America's leading historian of cultural contact.

Bailey, A.G. *The Conflict of European and Eastern Algonkin Cultures, 1534–1700: A Study in Civilization.* 2nd ed. Toronto, 1969. First produced as a doctoral dissertation in 1934, this pioneering study is one of the classics of the field, still as relevant as ever.

Cell, Gillian. *English Enterprise in Newfoundland, 1577–1660.* Toronto, 1969. Still the standard account of early settlement in Newfoundland and its mercantile connections.

Dickason, Olive Patricia. *Canada's First Nations: A History of Founding Peoples from Earliest Times.* 3rd ed. Toronto, 2002. Easily the best general survey of the history of the First Nations, current and full of detail.

Fagan, Brian. *The Great Journey: The Peopling of Ancient America.* New York, 1987. A bit dated, but still the best account of the prevailing scholarly interpretations of the subject.

Fitzhugh, William and Elizabeth Ward. *Vikings: The North American Saga.* Washington and London, 2000. A splendidly illustrated and authoritative account of the Norse in America.

Harris, R. Cole, ed. *Historical Atlas of Canada.* Volume I. Toronto, 1987. This is one of the great collaborative works of scholarship in Canada, presenting a visual and cartographic record of the period to 1800.

Jaenen, Cornelius. *Friend and Foe: Aspects of French-Amerindian Culture Contact in the Sixteenth and Seventeenth Century.* Toronto, 1976. An early classic, still the best single work on the early contact between the French and the First Nations.

MacDonald, M.A. *Fortune and La Tour: The Civil War in Acadia.* Toronto, 1983. A well-written account of the La Tour family and its vicissitudes.

Nuffield, Edward. *The Discovery of Canada.* Vancouver, 1996. A recent survey.

Paul, Daniel. *We Were Not the Savages: A Micmac Perspective on the Collision of European and Aboriginal Civilization.* Halifax, 1993. Probably the first analysis of early cultural contact in Canada written by a First Nations scholar from a First Nations perspective.

Reid, John. *Acadia, Maine, and New Scotland: Marginal Colonies in the Seventeenth Century*. Toronto, 1981. A stimulating comparative approach to the early settlement of the Maritimes.

Savours, Ann. *The Quest for the North West Passage*. New York, 1999. A recent survey of Arctic exploration.

Trigger, Bruce. *Natives and Newcomers: Canada's 'Heroic Age' Reconsidered*. Montreal and Kingston, 1986. A revisionist account of early Canadian culture contact by Canada's leading expert.

Trudel, Marcel. *The Beginnings of New France 1524-1663*. Toronto, 1975. Still the authoritative account of the early years of New France, written by a scholar who spent his lifetime working on the period.

Wright, J.V. *A History of the Native People of Canada*. 3 vols. Ottawa, 1995–2000. An encyclopaedic survey of Canada's ancient history.

STUDY QUESTIONS

1. Give three examples of ways in which the First Nations lived in a 'reciprocal relationship with nature'.
2. Explain the basic cultural, religious, and political factors behind the European misinterpretation of the First Nations.
3. Comment on the account from Cartier's *Voyages*, 'Jacques Cartier Meets with Aboriginal Peoples, 1534'. Did Cartier make any assumptions about the Aboriginal peoples that would lead to cultural conflicts later? Explain.
4. What can we learn about cultural conflict from Karlsefni's encounter with the Skraelings? What was the principal cause of the conflict between the Norse and the Skraelings?
5. On what grounds could you defend the European intrusion into North America? Identify three grounds and explain each of them.
6. What evidence of Eurocentrism can you find in Dr Dodding's report on the autopsy of 'the Man at Bristol'?

CHAPTER TWO

Struggling for a Continent, 1627–1758

In 1627 Cardinal Richelieu, Louis XIII's 'grey eminence', assumed supervision of New France and established the Company of One Hundred Associates. However, Richelieu's company, unlike the English Newfoundland Company, was organized from the top of the government rather than from grassroots interest in the profits of colonization. It was to be capitalized at 300,000 livres, each participant contributing 3,000, and profits were not to be distributed initially. Of the 107 members listed in May 1629, only twenty-six were merchants and businessmen, mainly from Paris. The remainder were courtiers and state officials. The company's initial venture—at a cost of 164,270 livres—was to send four ships containing 400 people and carrying 'all necessary commodities & quantities of workmen & families coming to inhabit & clear the land and to build & prepare the necessary lodging' to Quebec in 1628 (quoted in Trudel 1973: 118). Unfortunately, England and France had gone to war in 1627, and in July 1628 the company's ships were captured off Gaspé by an Anglo-Scottish armed expedition led by the brothers Kirke. Thus began a military struggle lasting more than a century between France and Britain for control of North America.

The nineteenth-century American historian Francis Parkman wrote of a 'Half Century of Conflict', but in truth the imperial struggle was much more protracted. The conflict would transcend a straightforward European rivalry, increasingly involving as it did both the population of the colonies and the First Nations of the continent—each often fighting with their own agendas—as well as other parts of the world. The French colonies of North America felt the effects of this contest far more than their British counterparts to the south. The much smaller population in New France was more often in the front lines of the fighting, which frequently occurred on French territory. Between 1627 and the final military defeat of New France more than 130 years later, the French experienced only one extended period (from 1713 to the early 1740s) when they were not constantly at war or under severe military pressure, either from Aboriginal peoples or from the British. The pervasiveness of the international rivalry came equally to affect British colonists and British policy in the northern region.

New France Fights for Survival

In July 1629 David Kirke sent his brothers Lewis and Thomas at the head of an Anglo-Scottish armed expedition that forced Champlain's little outpost on the St Lawrence to surrender. Later that same year, an attempt by the Company of One Hundred Associates to reoccupy Quebec failed dismally. The colony was restored to France in 1632 under the Treaty of St-Germain-en-Laye. One of the first French arrivals that year was Father Paul Le Jeune (1591–1664), recently appointed superior-general of the Jesuit

TIMELINE

1627
Cardinal Richelieu establishes the Company of One Hundred Associates.

1628
The Kirke brothers capture Quebec.

1632
Treaty of St-Germain-en-Laye restores Canada and Acadia to France.

1633
Champlain returns to the St Lawrence.

1634
The Jesuits set up permanent missions in Huronia.

1635
Champlain dies.

1639
The Jesuits establish Ste-Marie-aux-Hurons.

1640
The Iroquois begin attacking the Huron.

1642
Montreal is established.

1645
Company of One Hundred Associates surrenders its monopoly to local interests. Madame de la Tour surrenders Fort La Tour.

1747
Canada adopts government by central council.

1649
Iroquois destroy St-Louis and St-Ignace. Martyrdom of Jean de Brébeuf and Gabriel Lalemant.

1654
English capture Acadia.

1659
Bishop Laval arrives in Canada.

1662
French establish first Newfoundland colony at Placentia Bay.

1663
Earthquake strikes Canada. French royal government takes over New France and institutes the Coutume de Paris.

1664
Carignan-Salières regiment arrives in New France. Jean Talon arrives as first intendant.

1667
English return Acadia to France.

1670
Hudson's Bay Company is granted a charter by Charles II.

1689
War of the League of Augsburg begins.

1690
Port-Royal captured by the English; Quebec is unsuccessfully invaded.

1697
Treaty of Ryswick ends War of the League of Augsburg.

1702
War of Spanish Succession begins.

1713
By the Treaty of Utrecht, which ends the War of the Spanish Succession, France surrenders Nova Scotia, Newfoundland, and Hudson Bay claims to Great Britain.

1720
Establishment of Louisbourg.

1737
First iron forge at St Maurice is established.

1744
War of the Austrian Succession begins.

1745
Louisbourg is captured by joint Anglo-American military force.

1748
Treaty of Aix-la-Chapelle ends the War of the Austrian Succession.

1749
Halifax established.

1755
General Braddock is defeated on the Monongahela River; Acadians are expelled from Nova Scotia.

1756
Seven Years' War officially begins.

1758
Louisbourg taken by force under General James Wolfe; Acadians are rounded up and again expelled from the Maritime region; Nova Scotia's first elected assembly meets. Nova Scotia's government advertises for settlers in New England.

missions in Canada. The Jesuits were to be the principal missionary order in the colony. Le Jeune soon began sending the first of the annual reports, the famous *Jesuit Relations*, which were forwarded to the provincial father of the Society of Jesus in Paris to explain and promote in the mother country the missionaries' efforts. They combine a wealth of detail about life in New France, the First Nations, Iroquois warfare, the Huron missions, exploration and travel, as well

CHAMPLAIN'S NEW FRANCE

In 1603 Pierre Du Gua de Monts (1558?–1628) was granted a trading monopoly in northeastern North America in return for an obligation to settle sixty colonists each year and to establish missions among the Aboriginals. Among the first settlers he recruited was a young draftsman, Samuel de Champlain (*c.* 1570–1635), who had been to Tadoussac in 1603 and would serve as geographer and cartographer for de Monts's expedition. Thus Champlain continued a commitment to explore and colonize the New World that would end only with his death (on Christmas Day). Unlike his English contemporaries, William Bradford at Plymouth Plantation or John Winthrop at Boston, Champlain had not been able to lead a prospering colony through the problems of internal growth and the establishment of permanent institutions. Instead, much of his career was spent dealing with the preliminaries of settlement, in the interests of which he sailed to France nine times to further his plans for colonization or to resist attempts to negate them.

As a successful geographer and intrepid explorer who was equal to the most arduous demands of wilderness life, and who was capable in complex dealings with Native peoples, Champlain also left a literary legacy. The three volumes of his *Voyages* (published in Paris in 1613, 1619, and 1632) provide much of what we know about New France during this period. Champlain's map of New France (facing page) appeared in the last volume of his *Voyages*. It includes the territories he explored, which are rendered quite accurately, along with inevitably inaccurate renderings of regions for which he had only second-hand information.

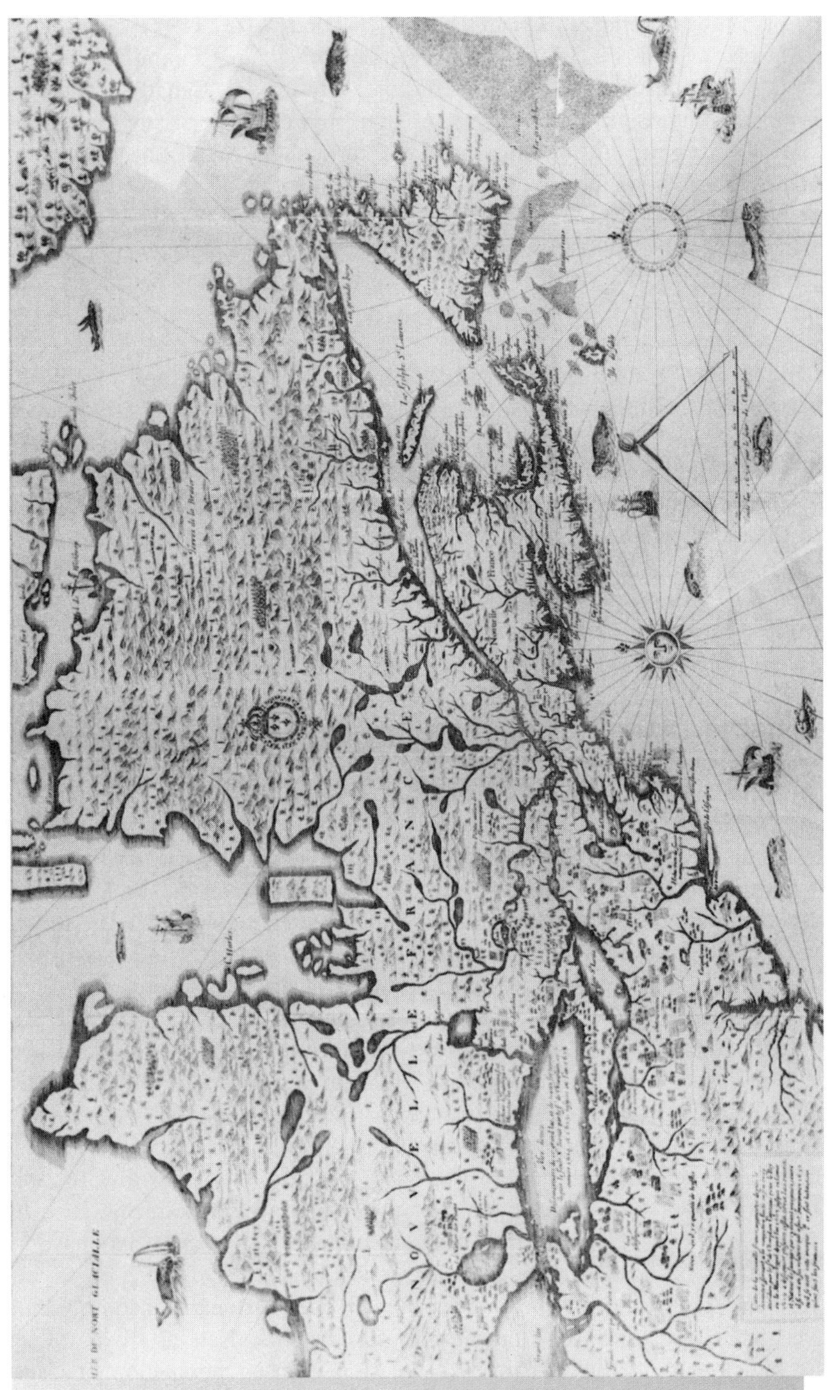

Champlain's map of New France, 1632. NAC, NMC-15661.

as accounts of various miracles. Champlain returned to Quebec in May 1633 after a four-year exile, tired but optimistic. He would die on Christmas Day 1635, his vision of a prosperous colony still beyond his grasp. At the time there were but 150 settlers along the St Lawrence.

Over the next few decades, the forces along the St Lawrence that met in bitter rivalry were less France and Britain and more Catholic evangelical energy on the one hand and resistance from the indigenous population on the other. The prize was control of the fur trade. Conflict along the Atlantic seaboard had more traditional European overtones, while in Canada the long rivalry between the Iroquois and the Algonquian trading allies of the French created much fear and havoc, with disastrous consequences for the Huron people caught in the middle.

The Huron had access to a seemingly inexhaustible supply of furs from the northwest, and the French were determined to keep the flow moving to Montreal and Quebec. The Huron had once outnumbered the Iroquois, but in the 1630s their numbers were greatly reduced by diseases contracted from the French missionaries who lived among them. In 1634, the year the Jesuits set up permanent missions in Huronia, the Huron suffered an epidemic of measles. In 1639 the Jesuits oversaw the building of an elaborate fortified headquarters, Ste-Marie-aux-Hurons, on the Wye River. It eventually comprised twenty buildings, including a residence for priests, a church, a hospital, outbuildings for farming, and residences for lay workers and Huron converts, as well as a canal with three locks.

The Iroquois—supplied by the Dutch with firearms, which the French were reluctant to give to their First Nations allies—were equally determined to control the flow of furs. They ambushed the Huron fur-fleets on the Ottawa River, and between 1640 and 1645 they blockaded the river, while also from 1643 onwards attacking the settlements on the St Lawrence. Under the force of the assault, the Company of One Hundred Associates virtually withdrew from New France in 1645, giving its fur-trading monopoly to the Communauté des Habitants, an organization of Canadian merchants, which agreed to continue to pay for the administration of the colony. While the devolution of the fur trade to local interests was probably a positive move for the colony, the new company soon felt the effects of Iroquois hostility, which limited the fur trade for an entire decade.

The Iroquois soon turned their full attention to Huronia. In July 1648 Senecas destroyed the mission of St-Joseph and killed 700 Huron. In March 1649 a party of 1,200 Iroquois destroyed St-Louis and St-Ignace, where the priests Jean de Brébeuf (1593–1649) and Gabriel Lalemant (1610–49) were tortured to death. The weakened Huron surrendered, fled, or were killed. Before the Iroquois could reach Ste-Marie, the Jesuits there 'applied the torch to the work of our own hands' and fled with some 300 families to Christian Island in Georgian Bay. Most died of starvation or malnutrition. The next year the missionaries returned to Quebec with a few hundred Huron, the pathetic remnant of a once-powerful nation.

The Huron were early victims of European ethnocentrism. As for the missionaries themselves, only the Jesuits' profound faith and misguided intentions—to educate the First Nations in French ways and induct them into a completely alien form of religion—kept them on their indomitable rounds of travel and life under extremely harsh and tense conditions. Many of the Huron turned against the missionaries, blaming their problems with disease and with the Iroquois on the Christian interlopers. Indeed, in exposing the Huron to disease and weakening their culture by introducing alien religious elements, the missionaries may have inadvertently contributed to the destruction of Huronia.

If the missionaries had only limited success with the First Nations, their influence on the early European population of Canada was far more successful. The missionary enterprise in Canada had two basic wings, often only loosely

FATHER LE JEUNE ON THE CONVERSION OF THE 'SAVAGES', 1634

This selection by Father Paul le Jeune (1591-1664), the founding editor of the *Jesuit Relations*, offers some insight into the thinking of the fathers regarding their mission in the early 1630s.

The great show of power made at first by the Portuguese in the East and West Indies inspired profound admiration in the minds of the Indians, so that these people embraced, without any contradiction, the belief of those whom they admired. Now the following is, it seems to me, the way in which to acquire an ascendency over our Savages.

First, to check the progress of those who overthrow Religion, and to make ourselves feared by the Iroquois, who have killed some of our men, as every one knows, and who recently massacred two hundred Hurons, and took more than one hundred prisoners. This is, in my opinion, the only door through which we can escape the contempt into which the negligence of those who have hitherto held the trade of this country has thrown us, through their avarice.

The second means of commending ourselves to the Savages would be to send a number of capable men to clear and cultivate the land, who, joining themselves with others who know the language, would work for the Savages, on condition that they would settle down, and put their hands to the work, living in houses that would be built for their use. . . . I may be mistaken but if I can draw any conclusion from the things I see, it seems to me that not much ought to be hoped from the Savages as long as they are wanderers; you will instruct them today, tomorrow hunger snatches your hearers away, forcing them to go and seek their food in the rivers and woods. Last year I stammered out the Catechism to a goodly number of children; as soon as the ships departed, my birds flew away. . . . To try and follow them, as many Religious would be needed as there are cabins, and still we would not attain our object; for they are so occupied in seeking their livelihood in these woods, that they have not the time, so to speak, to save themselves. . . .

The third means of making ourselves welcome to these people, would be to erect here a seminary for little boys, and in time one for girls, under the direction of some brave mistress, whom zeal for the glory of God and a desire for the salvation of these people, will bring over here, with a few Companions animated by the same courage. May it please his divine Majesty to inspire some to so noble an enterprise, and to divest them of any fear that the weakness of their sex might induce in them at the thought of crossing so many seas and of living among Barbarians.

SOURCE: Reuben Gold Thwaites, ed., *The Jesuit Relations and Allied Documents: Travels and Explorations of the Jesuit Missionaries in New France 1610–1791* (New York, 1959), vol. VI, 145-53.

connected: that of the Jesuits and that of the lay missionaries.

The Society of Jesus was founded by Ignatius Loyola in 1540 as a militant (and militarily organized) order devoted largely to missionary activity around the world. The Jesuits travelled around the globe, especially in the period 1550–1650, preaching and teaching among indigenous people ranging from the Aztecs to the Japanese. They developed a reputation for being able to adapt

'Mort héroique de quelques pères de la Compagnie de Jésus dans la Nouvelle France', lithograph by Et. David, 1844. NAC, C-4462. This rendering tells us much about how the French interpreted these events.

Christianity to the customs of the local people, and they were probably less rigid in their views of what had to happen for true conversion to take place than most missionaries. Members of the order actually looked forward to martyrdom, although they were not supposed to go out of their way to seek it. As soldiers of Christ, they believed that conversion of pagans occurred only through bloodshed. The Jesuits were obviously highly disciplined and committed; to the usual vows of poverty, chastity, and obedience, they added one of loyalty to the Pope. Despite the suspicions of the Crown, they were given a monopoly of religious service in Canada in 1632. The Jesuits tended to be more involved with missionary outreach than with the European population.

The lay missions were organized as part of the French Counter-Reformation, in which lay people discovered they had enormous depths of piety that they were anxious to share with others, including the First Nations in North America. When the widow Marie-Madeleine de Chauvigny de la Peltrie (1603–71) recovered from a serious illness in 1635, she made a vow to establish a school for Native girls in New France. She persuaded Marie de l'Incarnation to join her, put much of her fortune in trust for the foundation, and even financed a vessel and some immigrants to accompany her. Once in New France, she founded the Ursuline convent in Quebec. Another noblewoman sponsored three nursing sisters of the order of Augustinian

MARIE DE L'INCARNATION

Marie de l'Incarnation, oil portrait attributed to Abbé Hugues Pommier (1637-86). Archives des Ursulines de Québec.

Born in Tours, the daughter of a master baker, Marie Guyart (1599–1672) was a devout child who married at the age of seventeen. Her husband died two years later, leaving her with a son. Soon after, she had a mystical experience of conversion. Taking vows of chastity, poverty, and obedience, she lived for some years with her sister and brother-in-law and worked with them in their business. At the age of twenty-seven, she had another experience of the 'inner paradise' and joined the Ursuline Order of nuns. After taking her vows in 1633, Marie had a dream in which God told her to go to Canada. She sailed there in 1639, founded her school, and spent the remainder of her life running it successfully. Mère Marie had an extraordinary ability to combine her fervent spiritual life with her skills as a competent administrator and perceptive observer of the secular life around her. She wrote extensively, in addition to educating young girls, catechizing the local Native people, learning their languages, and preparing dictionaries in French-Algonquin and French-Iroquois as well as an Iroquois catechism. Her writings include spiritual autobiographies, lectures on faith, notes on prayer, and over 13,000 letters (most of them to her son), of which relatively few survive. In her correspondence, Mère Marie dealt not only in spiritual matters but with the business of the entire colony. Her letters are one of the two best sources, along with the *Jesuit Relations*, for the history of New France in the mid-seventeenth century.

Hospitalières on the same ship as the Ursulines. They founded a hospital at Sillery to care for dozens of Aboriginals, most of whom were Montagnais, Algonquin, and Abenaki, with only a few Huron. The Société Notre-Dame de Montréal organized a missionary effort in 1639 that led to the foundation of Montreal in 1642. This work was financed by donations from wealthy laypeople. Thirty-four of the forty-six members were laypeople, and twelve were women. For much of the mid-seventeenth century, Canada would be largely dominated by the

Paul Chomedey de Maisonneuve

Paul Chomedey de Maisonneuve (1612–76) was a member of a distinguished French seigneurial family. He spent his early years in military service in Holland, and at some point he became quite devout. In the late 1630s, while seeking a new vocation, he came upon the *Jesuit Relations*, and was quite impressed by the activities of Father Charles Lalemant. He went to visit Lalemant, who recognized in him the man to lead a new colonization movement to Canada that was being organized by various private lay spiritual societies in France, including the Compagnie du Saint-Sacrement. Lalemant recommended M. de Maisonneuve as a gentleman who would meet all the requirements, and Jérôme Le Royer de La Dauversière, the layman who was the guiding genius behind the Canadian initiative, quickly agreed.

Maisonneuve was given the power to form and organize the new colony at Montreal, and he set off for Canada on 6 May 1641, arriving later that year after many delays. He served in September as godfather (with Jeanne Mance as godmother) of an Aboriginal girl baptized at Sillery, and set out to deal with the local opposition that had grown up to the new colony, chiefly because its location left it exposed to the hostility of the Iroquois. He was offered a site at the Île d'Orleans instead of the island of Montreal, but responded, 'Sir, what you are saying to me would be good if I had been sent to deliberate and choose a post; but having been instructed to go to Montreal by the Company that sends me, my honour is at stake, and you will agree that I must go up there to start a colony, even if all the trees on that island were to change into so many Iroquois.' His inflexibility won the day, although there were continual struggles with the Canadian administration over such matters as the use of firearms.

In August of 1642 Maisonneuve finally arrived in Montreal and the settlers celebrated. In the years thereafter, there would not be many occasions to celebrate, since in 1643 the Iroquois began a series of attacks that would last for years. Initially Maisonneuve refused to allow his people outside of the fort, but in March 1644 he led a party against the Iroquois attackers, ultimately engaging himself in hand-to-hand combat with the Iroquois chief. He made several journeys back to France to deal with administrative and financial affairs relating to the settlement. In 1651 he vowed not to return without at least 100 soldiers. Two years later he was able to honour that vow, sailing for Canada with 120 new recruits, privately funded by Madame de Bullion, and accompanied by Marguerite Bourgeoys. This injection of military might assisted the settlement to survive through the 1650s. In 1665, Maisonneuve—who was not popular with the new royal administration in New France—was recalled to Paris. His return to France symbolized the close of an era in the history of New France; state initiative now succeeded private benevolence as the determining force in the colony.

energy of its leading women missionaries: Marie de l'Incarnation, Jeanne Mance (founder of the Hôtel-Dieu hospital), and Marguerite Bourgeoys (founder of the Congrégation de Notre-Dame).

In 1647 Canada adopted government by a central council, with elected representatives of the districts of Quebec, Trois-Rivières, and Montreal employed for consultative purposes. Such a government was both responsive to the wishes of the inhabitants and autonomous of the mother country, but the arrangement was more a result of emergency conditions than a genuine reform. With the Huron destroyed, the Iroquois turned the full brunt of their fury on the French at Montreal. François Dollier de Casson (1928: 155) observed that 'not a month of this summer [1651] passed without our roll of slain being marked in red at the hands of the Iroquois'. The attacks subsided over the course of the decade, but the menace never entirely disappeared.

The period of the Iroquois wars was a difficult one for the French fur traders, and many headed northwestward to avoid the enemy. Among these adventurers were Pierre Radisson (c. 1640–1710) and his brother-in-law Médard Chouart Des Groseilliers (c. 1618–96?). Radisson was born in France, but had been captured by Mohawks in 1651; adopted by a prominent family, he was forced to learn Aboriginal ways in order to survive. In 1659 the brothers-in-law took a journey to Lake Superior that excited their interest in exploring the fur-bearing region that they knew extended as far north as Hudson Bay. They returned to Montreal in 1660 with a vast haul of beaver skins, which was seen as the colony's salvation. The two fur traders were not well received, however; their furs were confiscated and both men were prosecuted for trading without official permission. Not surprisingly, they wound up in Boston in 1664, where the English were quite enthusiastic about the Hudson Bay fur trade. Eventually the pair would head for London, where their enthusiastic reports about conditions at the Bay led in 1670 to the establishment by the English of the Hudson's Bay Company, which would contend with the French for control of the region until the French conceded it to the English in 1713.

☐ Marguerite Bourgeoys, 'Le Vrai Portrait', painted the day after her death in January 1700 by Pierre Le Ber. This work was not discovered until the mid-twentieth century, when x-rays of a work believed to be an authentic likeness revealed the 'true portrait' under several layers of paint. Musée Marguerite-Bourgeoys, Montreal.

By the early 1660s the tensions within the colony on the St Lawrence seemed to be manifesting themselves in strange forms. A general state of panic was produced by an incident of alleged witchcraft, and in the midst of carnival season in February 1663 the colony was struck by a serious earthquake. Mère Marie de l'Incarnation noted, 'we were all so frightened we believed it was the eve of Judgement, since all the portents were to be seen' (Marshall 1967: 288–9). About this time the French Crown formally withdrew trading privileges and land ownership from the Company of One Hundred Associates and made New France a Crown colony. Given the anxieties and problems of the colony, most of its 3,035 inhabitants were happy to trade autonomy for French financial and military assistance.

In June 1665 four companies of the Carignan-Salières regiment arrived to quell the Iroquois. In September of that year an intendant (or chief administrative officer)—Jean Talon (1626–94)—arrived to revitalize the colony. One of the royal government's first aims was to increase the population, and the filles du roi (orphan girls raised at the king's expense) were sent over for that purpose. Mère Marie reported that 100 girls had arrived in 1665, and more would come later. How long the French Crown would continue such support was uncertain, but it certainly rejuvenated the colony. The government had begun making a concerted effort to deal with the Iroquois menace and to reform both the administrative and economic structure of New France. It would shortly attempt to establish a foothold in Newfoundland and later regain control over Acadia. Although success would hold within it the seeds of destruction, the French in 1665 were on the eve of almost a century of expansion and dominance in North America.

THE MARITIME REGION TO 1667

In the Atlantic region, overtones of European imperial rivalries could be detected in the complex conflicts of the seventeenth century, although local factors were equally important. Much of the confusing history of Acadia after 1624 is wrapped up in the activities of the La Tour family, which illustrate the fluid and violent nature of the period. In 1629, when Quebec was captured by the Kirkes, a tiny trading post on Cape Sable (at the southwestern tip of present-day Nova Scotia) was all that was left of the French presence in North America. It was headed by Charles de Saint-Étienne de La Tour (1598–1666). His father, Claude de La Tour (c. 1570–after 1636) had already returned to France to plead for assistance, but on the return voyage was captured and taken to England, where he quickly made himself at home. Accepted at court, he married one of the Queen's ladies-in-waiting. (The English Queen Henrietta was a French princess and surrounded by women from France.) Claude also accepted Nova Scotia baronetcies for himself and his son from Sir William Alexander, a Scottish courtier, who had been granted Nova Scotia in 1621 by James VI of Scotland (also James I of England).

Returning with his bride to Acadia in May 1630 as part of a Scots-English expedition, Claude stopped at Cape Sable to persuade his son to join him. Charles replied that 'he would rather have died than consent to such baseness as to betray his King' (MacBeath 1966: 593). Declaring his son an enemy, Claude led an unsuccessful attack on the fort at Cape Sable and retreated to Port-Royal, only to discover that the English planned to abandon it. He was forced to throw himself on his son's mercy and confess to his wife that he could not return to Europe. Acadia, like Canada, was returned to France by the English with the Treaty of St-Germain-en-Laye in 1632. The English monarch Charles I needed French financial subsidies as he attempted to govern without meeting Parliament, a policy that led to the English Civil War.

In Acadia, Charles de La Tour continued to lead an embattled life, coming into conflict with others who claimed royal authority in the region. In 1642 his chief rival, Charles de Menou d'Aulnay (c. 1604–50), returned to Acadia with an official order that La Tour appear before the French king to answer charges of treason. La Tour decided to send his wife, Françoise-Marie, to represent him at the royal court. She

TIMOTHÉE SILVAIN

Timothée Silvain (1796–49, born Timothy Sullivan in Ireland) was one of a substantial number of people who were not French but somehow ended up in New France. He was the son of an Irish doctor. At some point he was captured by privateers and carried to New England. From there he fled to Canada in order to practice his Catholic religion. In Canada, he secretly married a poor but well-connected widow with six children and set up a medical practice in Montreal. In 1724 Silvain became a naturalized citizen and received an unremunerated appointment as physician of Montreal Island. He would subsequently inflate this appointment into 'king's physician'. He had many supporters and not a few critics. One of the critics complained that Silvain was unorthodox in practice and as an apothecary gave 'remedies that no one recognizes'. By 1734 he was feared to be angling for the post of king's physician in Quebec, and the local authorities warned the minister that he was a 'charlatan'. After 1740, Silvain claimed to be 'sieur O'Sullivan, Médicin du Roi', and began wearing a sword.

A series of incidents revealed that Silvain had a violent temper. He beat his wife so badly in 1737 that she petitioned for a legal separation, but the couple were eventually reconciled. In 1742 he became involved in an altercation with the lieutenant general for civil and criminal affairs in Montreal, Jacques-Joseph Guiton de Monrepos. This magistrate ordered the evacuation of one of Silvain's houses because it presented a fire hazard. In the course of protesting this action, Silvain poked the magistrate in the chest with his cane. He managed to flee the city with the assistance of his relations, chiefly Jacques-René Gaultier de Varennes, who was the officer on duty at the garrison when Monrepos made his complaint. Monrepos had made himself unpopular with the officers of the garrison over other officiousness, and some of Silvain's relations claimed as well that the authorities were badgering and persecuting him.

When the whole story reached the ear of the minister of marine in 1744, that worthy threw Varennes out of the service and reprimanded the governor of Canada in the process. As for Sullivan, he died in 1749, leaving his estate to his wife's family. His story demonstrates that in Canada, as elsewhere, con men were able to flourish at the fringes of society if their backgrounds were sufficiently exotic and they carried off their pretensions with sufficient aplomb.

successfully argued her husband's case in 1642, then returned in a French warship carrying supplies for La Tour. In 1644 Françoise-Marie again went to France, but this time was unable to protect her husband's interests. Early in 1645, with her husband off in Boston negotiating with the New Englanders, Madame de La Tour commanded the defence of Fort La Tour against an attack by Charles d'Aulnay. Her forty-five defenders held out for four days against an invading force of 200, but she eventually surrendered. All the captives were hanged in Madame La Tour's presence despite conditions of clemency attached to the surrender, and she

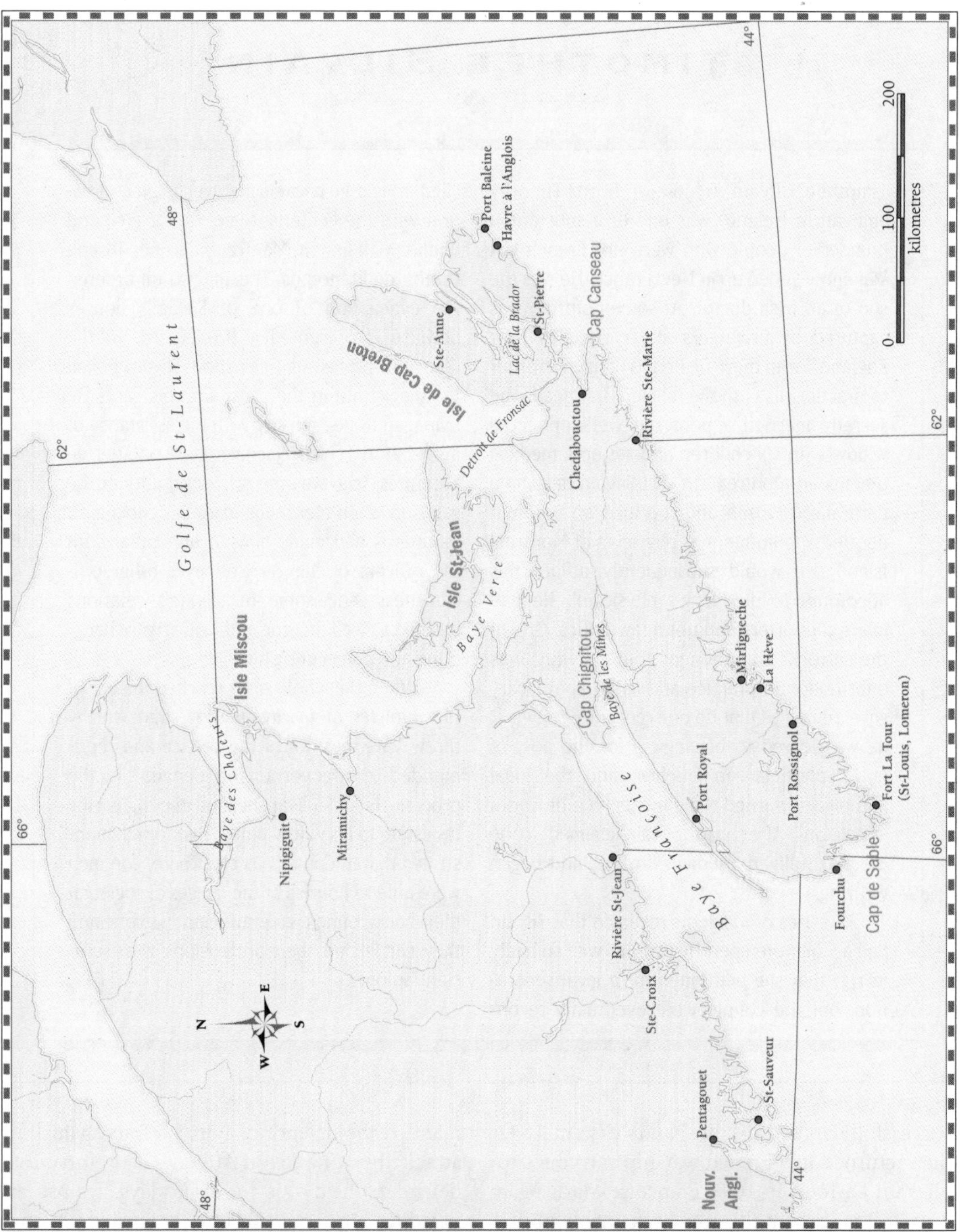

Acadia and environs to 1670. Adapted from A.H. Clark, *Acadia: The Geography of Early Nova Scotia to 1760* (Madison: University of Wisconsin Press, 1968), 76.

died scant weeks later. Charles de La Tour sought refuge in Canada, and d'Aulnay controlled Acadia until his death in 1650.

Charles de la Tour returned to France after d'Aulnay's death to demand an enquiry into his case. He was completely vindicated and again received into royal favour. Returning to Port-Royal with a few new settlers in 1653, he successfully courted d'Aulnay's widow. Pursued by creditors, he was forced in 1654 to surrender his garrison of seventy at Fort La Tour to an invading English expedition of 500 men. La Tour was taken to England, where Oliver Cromwell (by now head of the English state) refused to restore his Acadian property but did agree to recognize the long-dormant baronetcy of Nova Scotia (negotiated earlier by Claude) if Charles would accept English allegiance and pay his English debts. Twenty-five years after denying his father and asserting his loyalty to the French Crown, Charles de la Tour accepted Cromwell's terms. He eventually sold out his rights in Acadia to English partners, and retired to Cape Sable with his wife and family.

For more than forty years La Tour and his family had kept French interests alive in Acadia, but he was at best a trader and not a colonizer. The few settlers he brought to the New World were only incidental to his economic and military activities. Unlike Champlain in Canada, La Tour had no vision of a settled agricultural presence in Acadia, perhaps because he had to contend with the spill-over from complex European rivalries. After his surrender to the English in 1654, the scattered few hundred Acadian residents were very much on their own until formal French occupation was restored in 1667. While the period of English control from 1654 to 1667 left little internal impress on the region, it did isolate Acadia from the French court's rethinking of its American empire in the early 1660s. Thus Acadia was not initially part of the Crown's decision in 1663 to take a more active interest in its American colonies. As a result, its subsequent status was never properly clarified, leading to an administrative weakness that encouraged its population to have an autonomous outlook and encouraged France (in 1713) to surrender under pressure large parts of the region to the English.

NEWFOUNDLAND

As for Newfoundland, neither John Guy's settlement in 1610 nor a series of successors sponsored by both the Newfoundland Company and private promoters were spectacularly successful. But by the 1660s several communities of permanent settlers numbering 1,500 had taken hold on a year-round basis along the rocky coast of the 'English Shore'. The society of these settlements was considerably more elaborate than historians once assumed, consisting of servants, planter employers, and a planter gentry of literate merchants. Incomes from fishing were reasonably good, and the local communities were no less stable than comparable ones in New England. The élite was dominated by the Kirke family, which was active in the Canadian trade (and buccaneering in the 1620s) and in the Newfoundland sack trade of the 1630s and 1640s, later becoming original investors in the Hudson's Bay Company. In 1675 the widow of Sir David Kirke and her son operated ten fishing boats, and the Kirke family had seventeen boats, employing eighty-one crew members. Indeed, on the English Shore of Newfoundland as in many other early communities of North America, widows found opportunities for autonomy in business enterprise that they would not have enjoyed at home. Although Newfoundland had been one of the earliest sites in the New World for English colonization, the focus had quickly shifted south to New England, where the English by 1650 had developed a number of successful colonies with a population in excess of 100,000. The 'new-found' land continued to provide enormous wealth to the British Empire in the form of fish, however, while remaining an unorganized jurisdiction and a marginal area of English settlement.

In the seventeenth century, almost all the

SIR DAVID KIRKE

Sir David Kirke (c. 1597–1654) was one of the notorious Kirke brothers who captured Quebec in 1629. This incident is probably the only one for which most Canadians remember him—if they remember at all. But there was more to his complex North American career than one buccaneering expedition. Kirke was the son of an English merchant who worked out of the French port of Dieppe, and David was apparently born in the French town. In 1627 Kirke's father was one of a consortium of English merchants who financed an expedition, led by David, to drive the French from Canada. David commanded a fleet of three vessels and was accompanied by several of his brothers; hence the common reference to the 'Kirke Brothers' seizing Quebec. He apparently sailed with a fleet carrying Scottish settlers to Nova Scotia. In 1627 Champlain refused to surrender and Kirke did not press the issue. In the Gulf of St Lawrence, however, his ships met and defeated a French fleet, and Kirke returned to Europe with considerable booty.

The French in Paris protested because they regarded the Kirkes as French citizens. Kirke was rewarded with the exclusive right to trade and settle in Canada, to which Sir William Alexander objected. Kirke and Alexander negotiated a compromise to establish an Anglo-Scots colony at Tadoussac. The fleet sent out for this purpose (six ships, three pinnaces) also carried Claude La Tour back to Nova Scotia. Kirke learned from a French deserter of the parlous state of the French garrison in Quebec, and this time Champlain surrendered. The Kirkes not only evacuated the colony but seized all the furs stored in Quebec. They subsequently attempted to work the fur trade with the assistance of a number of bushlopers, including Étienne Brûlé. Quebec was returned to the French by the Treaty of Saint-Germain-en-Laye in 1632, but Kirke was knighted a year later for his services to the Crown.

His North American activities had made Kirke aware of Newfoundland, and in 1637 he was part of a consortium (The Company of Adventurers to Newfoundland) which was made proprietor of that island. In 1639 he became first governor of Newfoundland and moved into Lord Baltimore's house at Ferryland. The four Kirke brothers were at about the same time made English citizens. Sir David began to re-colonize Newfoundland, particularly Ferryland, and he attempted to control summer visiting along the island's coasts. He became one of the principal leaders of the Planters on the island, although his political actions were always controversial. In 1651 he was called home and charged with withholding taxes. Throughout the early 1650s he was under a cloud until his death in 1654, although his family continued to live in Newfoundland and to act as merchants there. Kirke's heirs, led by Lady Kirke, fought a number of legal battles for compensation (partly for the return of Quebec) after his death. Kirke was a good example of the extremely fluid situation among explorers and adventurers in northern North America in the first half of the seventeenth century.

year-round residents were of English origin, chiefly from the West Country counties of Cornwall, Devon, and Dorset. As late as 1732, 90 per cent of the permanent population was still English; but most of the eighteenth-century additions came from southern Ireland through the increasing links between Newfoundland and the Irish ports of Waterford and Cork. One census of wintering inhabitants in 1753 showed 2,668 Irish and 1,916 English. The Irish were being pushed out of Ireland by famine and unemployment, and were attracted to Newfoundland by the cheap fare over combined with work prospects. By 1750 Newfoundland had become a conduit by which Irish Catholics made their way to North America, and it remained so until 1815. Not all who jumped ship on the island remained in residence there.

Parallel to the increase of permanent population in Newfoundland came a shift in fishing practice. After 1714 the English summer visitors abandoned the inshore fishery and turned instead to fishing directly from the offshore banks. By 1750 the inshore fishery was controlled by local residents, but by this time there were already signs of depletion of the inshore fish stocks. The result was not conservation but diversification, with many Newfoundlanders moving into the seal fishery.

CANADA, 1665–1760

That part of New France along the St Lawrence known as 'Canada' mixed French origins and North American environment in a way that defied easy characterization. The French background provided institutions, a terminology with which to express them, and a set of assumptions about how society ought to be organized and operated. The French assumed an ordered and hierarchical society in which the various social orders stayed in their places and duly subordinated themselves to the good of the whole, as defined by the Crown. As a complication, the French Crown was not satisfied simply to replicate the familiar institutions of the Old World in North America, but sought to reform them by stripping them of centuries of European tradition that had decentralized power and limited royal authority. At the same time, the environment provided a set of daily realities that worked against European institutions and assumptions, modifying and altering—while never totally negating—efforts to imitate the mother country. The result was a society that refracted the metropolis in France through the dual prisms of royal reform and North American experience. The external observer was often struck at first glance by the presence of familiar European patterns and terminology, while beneath the surface different designs were constantly evolving.

The royal take-over of 1663 put French administrative policy for the colonies and its execution in the hands of two men, the governor, Jean-Baptiste Colbert, and the intendant, Jean Talon. Colbert was Louis XIV's chief bureaucrat, a highly experienced civil servant. His major tasks both at home and abroad were to strengthen royal government and expand the French economy. As minister of marine, he served as the seventeenth-century equivalent of colonial secretary, in addition to a myriad of other responsibilities. To implement policy in America, Colbert decided to establish the position of intendant, a royal official who, in France, had been developed to cut through the accretion of centuries of devolution of royal power and to act decisively on behalf of the state. Beginning with Talon's first appointment as intendant in 1665, the colony's administration was greatly reorganized and centralized. The governor, though the titular head, was responsible for military affairs, external relations, and the colony's connections with the Church (including education). Over the years the governor would invariably be a member of the French aristocracy and an experienced military man, but routine administration was in the hands of the intendant, a career civil servant whose social origins were in the middle class. There would be some classic

Jean Talon, intendant of New France. This portrait is a nineteenth-century copy, attributed to Théophile Hamel, of a seventeenth-century painting by Frère Luc. NAC, C-7100.

confrontations between intendants and governors, particularly during the regime of Louis Buade de Frontenac (1620–98, governor 1672–82 and 1689–98). But the royal regime consistently backed the intendant.

Colbert and Talon not only managed to put the colony on its feet, but established its administrative and institutional structure for the entire century of French royal control. Their task was no easy one. Political institutions had to be established that were simultaneously responsive to the royal will and satisfactory to the populace. External threats had to be confronted. Population growth had to be stimulated. Some kind of economic viability had to be developed that would not endanger the mother country. Out of all of these factors would emerge a society and culture of enormous tenacity, possessing many resources for regeneration and change.

Canada was ruled by the Sovereign Council, made up mainly of the colony's élite and presided over by the intendant. No regularly elected political body represented the inhabitants. Instead the colony used informal means to test public opinion, including the public protest (or 'riot'), which was a typical feature of life in both Europe and America at the time. Most Canadian riots were over food shortages, to which the government usually responded favourably. The Church was a major component of the government. Its main political task was to help establish, within the ranks of its communicants, due subordination to spiritual and secular authority. During the French regime the Church often found this job beyond its capabilities, partly because it was chronically understaffed. In 1759, for example, there were only seventy-three parish priests among 200 clergymen, hardly enough to provide religious services for everyone in the colony, especially outside the towns. In the symbiotic relationship between church and state, moreover, the state dominated. It appointed bishops, granted seigneuries, and provided most of the revenue for religion. At the same time, the subordinate role of the Church did not mean that Canada was irreligious or secular, or that Catholicism did not permeate the lives of most of its inhabitants. Canada had been born in deep Catholic piety, and Catholic orthodoxy remained the norm.

Because Canada spent most of its existence in a state of siege, the role of the military was crucial. France was prepared to spend money on the military that it would not have allowed for civilian matters. The soldiers' pay was an important source of money for the Canadian economy, and the army was the best local customer for Canadian merchants. Regular soldiers served as a source of labour and as potential additions to the civilian population, which they were encouraged to join at the expiration of their enlistments. Regular troops were not regarded as a sufficient military force, however, and from 1669 the entire adult male population of the colony between the ages of sixteen and sixty was required to serve in the militia, locally commanded by *capitaines de milice* chosen democratically from the ranks of the inhabitants. After 1684 the militia was employed in every war. Much of this militia service was in collaboration with the First Nations in the form of raiding parties, designed to keep the English colonies off balance and prevent them from using their superior numbers to invade the St Lawrence. Foreign observers were always impressed with the martial spirit of the Canadians. For many Canadian élite families, military service in an officer class was preferable to entrance into commerce and industry, just as in France itself. By the eighteenth century, the Canadian élite provided most of the officers for the Troupes de la Marine, and even expected commissions to be reserved for the sons of serving officers.

One of Canada's major disadvantages in its constant wars against the English was the small size of its population. After 1660 French Canada matched the English colonies by doubling in population every twenty-five years, but it could never keep pace numerically. In 1715 the population of New France was 20,000, while that of the English colonies was 434,000. By 1754 the gap had widened, with 70,000 in New France and 1,485,000 in the American colonies to the south. After 1672 few French immigrants arrived in the colony, either publicly sponsored or privately motivated. The reasons for the lack of immigration have been much debated among scholars. One whole constellation of reasons revolves around the unfavourable publicity that Canada—despite or perhaps because of the *Jesuit Relations*—continually received in France. The colony had a reputation for a harsh climate and an absence of amenities, which did not dispose the French to emigrate. Another set of reasons involved conditions in France itself. The absence of agrarian dislocation and the insatiable demands of the French military for manpower both prevented the development of a discontented and displaced population available for colonial migration on a massive scale. At the same time, the traditional juxtaposition of the French and British colonial experiences is in many ways misleading. In relation to the colonies of most European nations in America—those of the Dutch Republic, Sweden, Scotland—New France was successful. The British colonies were unusual in their numbers and dynamism. Unfortunately for the French, the British did not have a handful of colonies in America, but a large number on the mainland and more in the Caribbean, which were both economically vibrant and located on the exposed flanks of New France and Louisiana. In the imperial rivalries that inevitably ensued, the French were at a substantial disadvantage.

At the time of the royal take-over in 1663, both Colbert and Talon had attempted to diversify the economy. They were especially concerned about the colony's heavy dependence on the fur trade. Colbert even saw the fur trade as a menace. 'It is to be feared,' he wrote, 'that by means of this trade, the habitants will remain idle a good part of the year, whereas if they were not allowed to engage in it they would be obliged to apply themselves to cultivating their land' (quoted in Eccles 1983: 104). What the French authorities wanted was an agricultural surplus and the exploitation of timber resources, which would enable the colony to supply the French West Indies with goods currently being obtained from the English. But the economy was slow to diversify. Part of the problem was that the fur trade kept expanding, contributing to a circular effect. The successful French quest for furs not only deflected attention from other enterprises but brought Canada into conflict with the English to the south. The ensuing struggle made it virtually impossible to limit the fur traders, since they were the ideal shock troops for engaging the enemy.

The numbers involved in the fur trade (the voyageurs and *engagés*) grew in number from 200 at the end of the seventeenth century to nearly 1,000 by the mid-eighteenth century. The work was both physically and emotionally demanding. Perhaps as many as one-quarter of able-bodied Canadian males were involved in the fur trade at some point in their lives, usually in their younger years before they settled down with a wife and family in sedentary occupations along the St Lawrence. Many left First Nations wives and mixed-blood families behind when they retired. A few rose to be specialists in the trade, some remaining in the West throughout their lives. A few became *marchands équipeurs* (outfitters), organizing the parties and providing the credit. Unlike the colony's transatlantic merchants, the fur trade merchants were almost exclusively Canadian-born.

The constant quest for furs also drove Canada inexorably westward into the *pays d'en haut*, where some sort of satisfactory relationship had to be worked out with the First Nations. The upper country was the territory upriver from Montreal, beginning beyond Huronia and stretching through the Great Lakes and then on to Louisiana. This territory was claimed by the French by right of exploration and usage. It was originally an important fur-trading region, inhabited almost exclusively by Aboriginals who were mainly Algonquian speakers. Many of the traditional Native groups of the region had been joined by those fleeing westward from the Iroquois in the seventeenth century. These refugees re-established themselves in the country between the Ohio River and the Great Lakes to the west of Lake Michigan. This was an area that had been reduced in population by the Iroquois. The expansion of the fur trade could continue only as far as the western country of the Sioux, another military people. Gradually some of the fur traders, especially those who had married Native women and started families, began to establish themselves in settlements along the river systems. A series of forts and towns, the former deliberately constructed by French policy, the latter mostly accidental creations, grew up in the region. The most prominent were Detroit, Michilimackinac, Green Bay, Cahokia, and Kaskaskia. French fur traders travelled as far west as the Rocky Mountains in the first half of the eighteenth century.

A complex commercial and small-scale artisanal life did develop in New France. There was a small merchant class, particularly at the transatlantic level. Overseas trade was complex and dangerous, and most merchants operated through family and clan connections. Marriage alliances established new branches of family firms in distant ports, and after the deaths of their husbands, women frequently took over the local enterprise. The trading economy over which the merchants presided required peace and stability to perform at its best. It also suffered from a chronic shortage of a medium of exchange, which led the colony to produce its own paper money by using decks of playing cards inscribed in various denominations and signed by the intendant. Officially the cards were promissory notes, but they and the military *ordonnances* that circulated as legal tender after 1735 were both inflationary. A constant demand existed for the local productions of skilled artisans, particularly those master craftsmen who worked for the Church, providing the furniture, ornaments, and decorations for the many church buildings in the colony. Artisans also made many things that would have been too bulky and expensive to import. Two major attempts to industrialize New France were made, both in the 1730s. One was an ironworks near Trois-Rivières (the 'forges du St-Maurice'), the other a shipyard at Quebec. Both required large amounts of state subsidy to survive, but both demonstrated that Canadian workmen could be mobilized for industrial activity and could manufacture serviceable goods on a large scale.

Despite the growth of trade and industry, agriculture was always the dominant form of economic activity along the St Lawrence, functioning around the seigneurial system brought to the valley in 1627 and governed after 1663 by the Coutume de Paris. Seigneurialism in New France probably worked less to order society than to

INTENDANT RAUDOT ON THE CARD MONEY, 1706

Beginning in 1685, New France dealt with its shortage of metallic coins by issuing decks of cards signed by the intendant and inscribed in various denominations. In 1706 Jacques Raudot, who was intendant of New France from 1705 to 1711, wrote a memorandum justifying the practice. It offers a little lesson in mercantilist monetary policy.

Memorandum on the Cards of Canada, Quebec, September 30, 1706

The cards which are issued in Canada serve as money just as coin does in France.

The Kingdom of France derives a certain utility from these cards, since, by this means, the King is not obliged to send funds in coined money for the expenditures which he has the goodness to incur. If it were necessary to send this, it would withdraw from the Kingdom annually 100,000 écus. Consequently this currency leaving the country would render money scarcer. It is true one would not appreciate this disadvantage during the abundance of money, nevertheless it is certain that it would effect a diminution. Moreover, France, by this device, not sending coined money, runs no risk as to it either from the sea or from enemies.

If coined money were sent to Canada, it would afterwards leave the country by two avenues, one part would return to France, the other would go to New England to purchase certain merchandise, which may be had cheaper there than from France. The part of this money returning to France would run the risks of the sea and enemies. The vessels may be taken or lost, and consequently the money they carry is lost to France, and there can be no greater injury to the Kingdom than the loss of its money.

The other part of this money being carried to New England for the purchase of merchandize, results in a considerable injury to France in the loss of its coinage and the advantage which it would produce among her enemies. . . .

Furthermore, there is no fear that money may be carried to New England, which would be very difficult to prevent if there were any in the colony, there being as in France persons who to gain something would risk much.

It is even a matter of policy for kings to attach the prosperity of their subjects to their own persons, in order to render the former more submissive and to take care that all the means which the colonies may have in money are always in the kingdom on which they are dependent. Canada, having nothing but cards, which are secured only on the word of the King, and seeing no other resource except in the good faith of the sovereign, will be still more submissive to him and still more attached to France for the reason that all the supply it can have in money depends on it. Hence, it appears to me that one cannot do better than to permit the continuation of the card money in Canada.

There may arise great abuses regarding these cards; they may be counterfeited in the country; this, however, can be prevented by a close attention, the easier bestowed as the as the resources of every person are known. Counterfeits may also be sent from France and so exactly imitated that one cannot distinguish the true from the false. That is almost impossible to do here, there not being clever people enough of that type. But even if there were some counterfeits they could not remain long without being recognised. To prevent this abuse one has only to change the dies, and shape of the cards every year after the departure of the vessels for France.

It is true that the colony of Canada will suffer somewhat by these cards, it being quite certain that it will buy French merchandise cheaper if it pays for them in coined money and not in cards, for which the merchants receive only bills of exchange which for the most part are not met at maturity. But it is proper that the colony of Canada suffer for the sake of the kingdom from which it receives its benefits, and it is only fair that this kingdom should run no risk of losing its money by the possible loss of its vessels bound for it. . . .

RAUDOT

SOURCE: Adam Shortt, ed., *Documents Relating to Canadian Currency, Exchange and Finance during the French Period* (Ottawa: F.A. Acland, 1925), vol. I, 157–9.

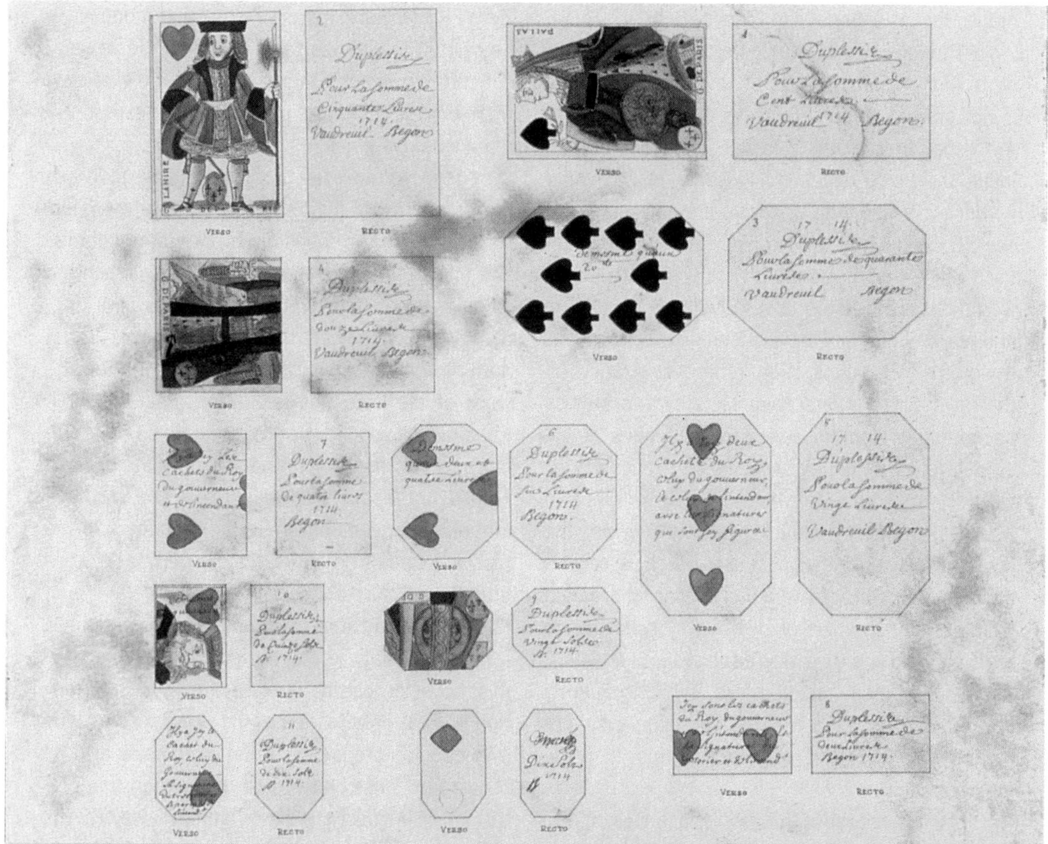

'Playing Card Money', pen with black ink with watercolour by Henri Beau (1863-1949), an employee of the Public Archives of Canada who was employed in the Paris office specifically to copy views, portraits, etc., and to carry out iconographic research. NAC, C-17059.

The iron forges on the St-Maurice, by Joseph Bouchette from his book *The British Dominion in North America* (London, 1832). NAC, C-4356

provide a means of settlement. The state made property concessions to landlords, who were supposed to find settlers to serve as tenants. Although the *censitaire* (tenant) owed various rents and feudal dues to his seigneur, these amounted to very little so long as there was more land than settlers. After the Edict of Marly in 1711, the seigneur could no longer withhold land from settlement in anticipation of price increases if there were settlers demanding it. Since they did not own the means of production, the *censitaires* seldom treated agriculture as a long-term business enterprise. The seigneurial system did not tie settlers to the soil and did not encourage large-scale, staple-crop farming so much as family farms on small holdings. The system was not really feudal, since military obligation in the colony was not tied to land occupation or tenure. Not until the end of the French regime was there sufficient pressure on the land to benefit the seigneur economically. He did acquire social status, however, and by the mid-eighteenth century the typical seigneur was an absentee landlord who lived in town and was involved in a variety of economic and political activities. A seigneury became part of a diversified portfolio of investment for an élite within whose ranks little specialization of function had yet occurred.

By the mid-eighteenth century, Swedish visitor Peter Kalm could describe the heartland of French Canada along the St Lawrence as 'a village beginning at Montreal and ending at Quebec, which is a distance of more than one hundred and eight miles, for the farmhouses are never above five arpents [293 metres] and sometimes but three apart, a few places excepted' (Benson, 1937, II: 416–17). Each farmhouse, usually of three or four rooms built of stone and timber, stood alone. Tiny villages only occasionally developed, usually around churches. Three towns punctuated this continuous settlement:

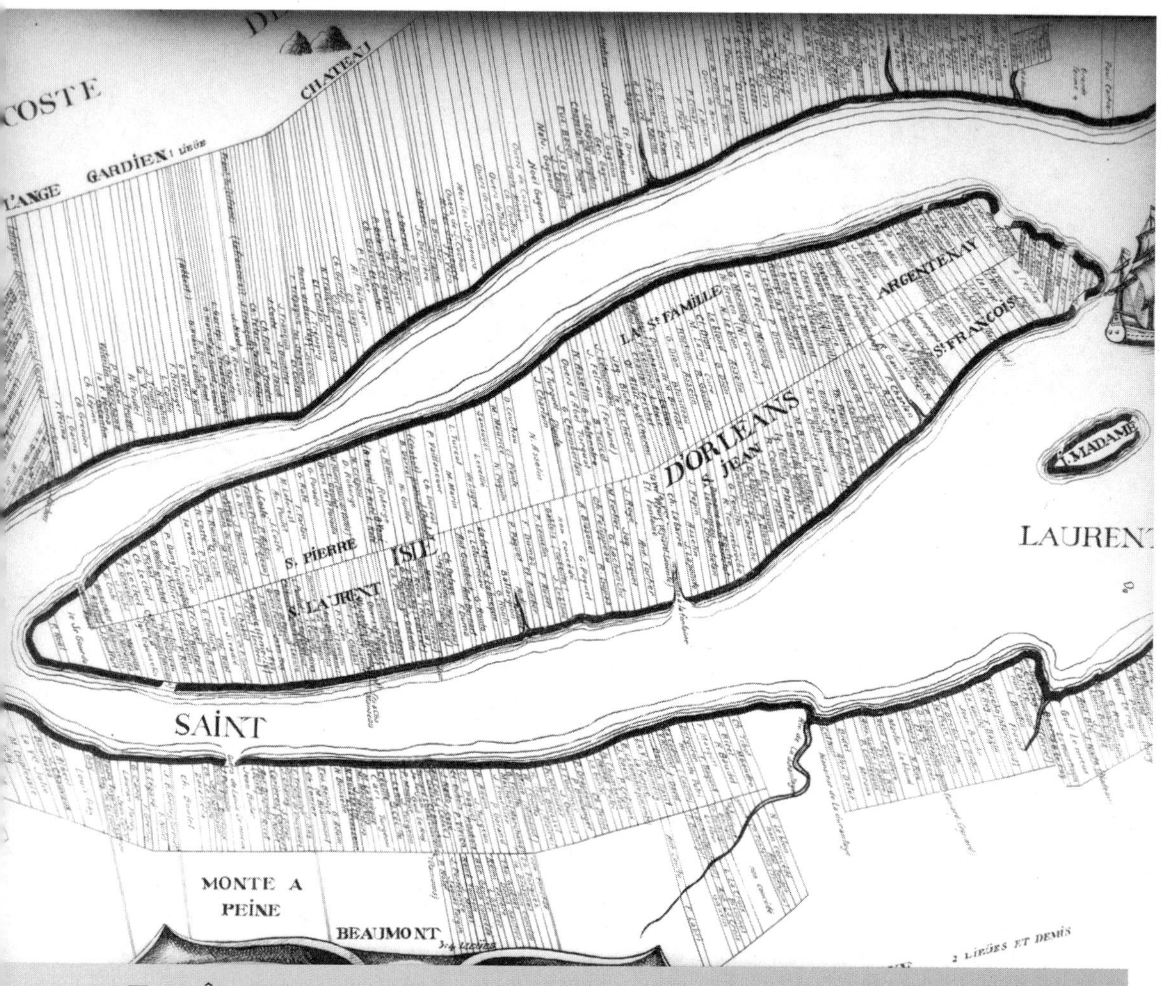

The Île d'Orléans and north and south shores of the St Lawrence, showing the boundaries of the land grants with the names of the seigneurial families in 1709; detail from a larger map of the Quebec region by Gédéon Catalogne and Jean-Baptiste de Couagne. NAC, NMC-0048248.

Quebec towards the eastern end, Trois-Rivières in the middle, and Montreal towards the west. Quebec and Montreal contained impressive and concentrated public and private buildings, often built of stone, but by our standards, both towns were quite small in population and area. On their peripheries, the dominant landscape pattern of the separate but contiguous farmstead was quickly resumed. Narrow lots ran back for long distances from the river, and while there were new rows (*rangs*) of lots available behind the riverfront ones, population was low to move inland. Thus French Canada replicated neither the French medieval village, whence many of its rural settlers had come, nor the English colonial tendency towards isolated farmsteads in the middle of large holdings separated from one another by considerable distances. Instead Canada tried to make its limited population cover as much territory as possible.

☐ The village of Château-Richer (on the north shore of the St Lawrence northeast of Quebec City), 1787, watercolour by Thomas Davies. Included in this pastoral scene are whitewashed stone farmhouses, wooden barns, and eel traps in the river. National Gallery of Canada, 6275.

Although Montreal and Quebec were not large, they did give Canada an urban life and a proportionately larger urban population than in most North American colonies. These towns were the centres of government, of the direction of economic activity, and of the Church and its social services, such as health care and education. They inevitably included a heavy concentration of the upper classes of French Canada, and had an impressive polite society. While there were, doubtless, graduations of wealth and status, French North America was fundamentally divided into two orders: those with, and those without, access to government largesse and patronage. The law was available to all, but only some could expect public and military appointments, government contracts, and seigneurial grants. Upward mobility was a possibility, but most observers agreed that the typical Canadien worked no harder than was necessary, spent a disproportionate amount of time pursuing his own pleasures and interests (which included racing horses and disappearing into the bush), was far more prosperous than his European counterpart, and enjoyed a good deal more liberty.

Slavery was never prohibited in Canada, but it never flourished because there were no large plantations to employ a slave work force. What slaves existed were mainly domestic servants. Not all were Blacks, although 540 Blacks have been identified in Canada. Aboriginal prisoners (*panis*) sold to the French were also kept in bondage. The colonial New Englander John Gyles was technically a slave when he was trans-

☐ New France in 1688. The cartographer, Jean-Baptiste-Louis Franquelin, worked at Quebec from 1671 to 1692 as both geographer and hydrographer to the king. NAC, Cartographic and Architectural Archives Division PH/1000/1688.

ferred from his Aboriginal captor to a French merchant on the Saint John River at the beginning of the eighteenth century. The image of plantation slavery in the American South or in the Caribbean bears no relationship to the slave situation in French America, where many levels of bondage were possible.

As for the roles and status of women, they did not undergo any remarkable transformation in the New World, although some modification of dependence may have occurred for some women, especially widows. The organization of society continued to be fundamentally patriarchal, with the woman in the traditional role of helpmate and child bearer. Both the shortage of marriageable women and the frequent absence of men away on the frontier or in the military somewhat moderated the oppression. There was some limited protection for the property rights of married women, and the autonomous rights of widows were well safeguarded by law and custom. In truth, however, historians do not know very much about the ordinary lives of ordinary women in early Canada, chiefly because of the male orientation of the available documentation. While Canada always had a substantial number of women in holy orders, most women in the colony married (at the average age of twenty-two) and raised a family. If marriage and remarriage rates were high, so too were birth rates and the number of children. Throughout the eighteenth century, raw birth rates ran over fifty per 1,000 inhabitants per annum, and women on average bore seven children. These demographic characteristics were typical of all colonial and frontier societies, however. Childbirth was cer-

KASKASKIA ESTATE INVENTORY

One of the places where it is possible to obtain some evidence about the lives of ordinary people is in the inventories made of their possessions when they die. Such inventories tend, of course, to be biased toward those who possess property, probably not the poorest members of society. In the case of Kaskaskia, we are dealing with a merchant community trading with Aboriginal peoples.

Inventory of Estate of Jacques Bourdon, made 1–5 July 1723

1 walnut wardrobe
8 walnut chairs and 1 armchair
1 dresser with a buffet upon it
1 cot (couchette)
14 plates and 2 pewter dishes
17 glass bottles
1 copper candlestick and 1 pair of snuffers
1 pepper mill
1 pewter saltcellar
1 old salting tub
2 frying pans
1 grill
1 pair of andirons
1 iron shovel
1 old hunting horn
1 spit
2 poor lanterns
3 trunks full of clothes and other merchandise
1 small box full of paper
1 pair of tailor's shears
1 bullet mold
1 pewter (or tin) syringe
1 iron ladle
14 guns and 1 musket
2 miserable scythes
4 hatchets
2 adzes
3 plates and 2 spoons of Spanish silver
2 razor boxes with 3 razors in each and 2 hones
200 gun flints
9 dozen and 8 knives à Chien de Corne, 10 Flemish knives, 2 woodcutter's knives
40 pounds of lead balls
20 pewter spoons
1 comb
10 large diaper linen napkins and 4 large tablecloths of the same
4 old napkins
1 box of grain leather decorated with silver nails with 3 pairs of spectacles, and another box also with 3 pairs of spectacles
1 letter case
1 dice box and 3 dice
1 old four-legged table of black poplar
2 silver cups
2 cupboards of black walnut with 36 shelves, some 8 feet long and some 10 feet
1 pair of pocket pistols
1 old coarse blanket
3 cauldrons of red copper weighing 18 pounds
2 yellow copper cauldrons weighing 3 1/2 pounds
1 cauldron weighing 14 1/2 pounds
1 cauldron weighing 12 pounds
2 iron cooking pans
4 Spanish vases full of oil
2 Natchez earthenware jugs full of oil
2 red copper cauldrons with lids, weighing 24 1/2 pounds, full of bear oil
2 old copper cauldrons
2 old covered cauldrons
1 old salting tub
1 ladle
3 chests
2 barrels of powder weighing 100 pounds each

tainly difficult and dangerous. Canada's menfolk were constantly exposed to the dangers of wartime battle, but their wives faced equal or greater danger every time they gave birth.

In many ways the most difficult feature of New France to comprehend is its culture. In Canada, language came to be the French of the Paris region, spoken extremely well, although with a modified accent and a wonderful new vocabulary adopted from the indigenous people. The French spoken by Acadians was far more archaic and regionalized, coming mainly from the west of France. The French spoken in the interior was heavily laced with words taken over from Aboriginal languages. Emphasizing the spoken language rather than the written word is important, for New France never had either a printing press or a newspaper. The culture was, as was the case among peasants in France of the same period, oral and visual rather than one based on print.

The locus of much of the formal artistic and aesthetic life of Canada was largely in the ritualistic requirements of the Church, appealing to the visual and aural senses of the people. A great emphasis was placed on music, both within the Church and among the people, who brought with them to the New World a rich heritage of song, dance, and music for dance. A literary culture was expressed through folk-tales, fairy stories, and songs, but it too was oral rather than written. Most expressions of culture among ordinary Canadiens were part of the business of everyday life and experience in habitant households in rural parishes. Much was imported from France. Sometimes the North American environment changed the culture, but in many cases—such as the use of swear-words and pejorative slang—French usage still prevailed. Both the decoration of churches and the few examples of early wooden house furnishings that survive point to a strong aesthetic sense. The churches employed the baroque art of the French seventeenth and eighteenth centuries, while the everyday furniture featured simple, elegant, and functional creations of wood.

THE FIRST THREE ANGLO-FRENCH WARS

Although sporadic warfare had occurred in North America since the earliest settlements, a protracted struggle for the continent between the European imperial powers—in which the First Nations were important players—began only in 1689. North American hostilities had their own dynamic, although they were always associated with the larger international rivalries of the mother countries. There were four wars. The first three were the War of the League of Augsburg (1689–97), settled by the Treaty of Ryswick; the War of the Spanish Succession (1702–13), settled by the Treaty of Utrecht; and the War of the Austrian Succession (1744–8), settled by the Treaty of Aix-la-Chapelle. The North American aspects of these first three wars shared a good deal in common. The American fighting in these first conflicts was conducted mainly by the colonists themselves employing their own military methods. Occasionally the mother country would undertake a brief initiative, usually disastrous. Much of the fighting occurred in the backcountry and along the frontier. Such conflict involved the First Nations, who joined the battles for reasons of their own.

The strategy of the French was to send out raiding parties on land and sea to keep the British colonies disunited and off balance. The French hoped that the British would not be able to utilize their superior manpower, resources, and command of the sea (the British controlled the Atlantic for all but brief periods throughout these wars) to invade and capture French territory. The British unsuccessfully—and disastrously—attempted to invade the St Lawrence in the first two wars. In the third, New England troops and British naval forces captured Louisbourg in 1745, leading to the dispatch of a major French fleet to North America in 1746. The fleet met bad weather and experienced epidemic disease, limping back to France without ever engaging the enemy. France itself hoped to

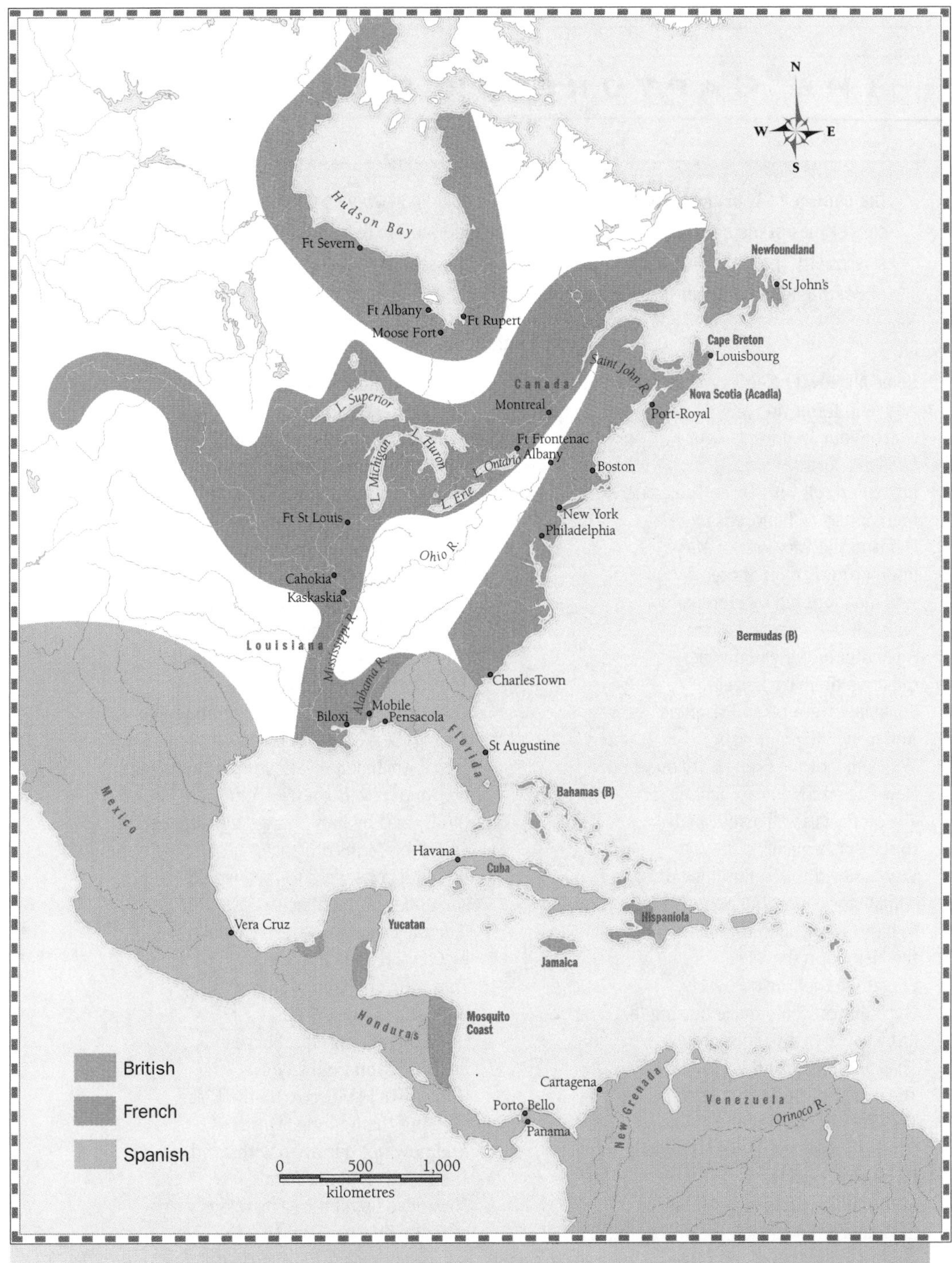

European possessions in North America after the peace of Utrecht (1713).

THE CAPTURE OF LOUISBOURG, 1745

The capture of Louisbourg by New England militiamen in 1745 was one of the great military success stories of the colonial wars. The Americans celebrated in thanksgiving sermons and in broadside poetry (probably intended to be sung) that was sold in single printed sheets on the streets of Boston. Here is one of those broadsides.

New England Bravery

Come all New England's gallant Lads,
And lend to me an Ear,
And of your Brethren's Acts
I will in short declare.
Brave Pep'rell with Three Thousand Men,
(perhaps some hundreds more)
Did land the very first of *May*,
upon *Cape Breton* Shore:
And tho' opposed by Morepang
with full two hundred Men,
A handful of our gallant Lads
did drive them back again.
Some few were taken Prisoners,
And many kill'd out-right
Which taught the *French* at *Louisbourg*
New England Men can fight.
The *Monsieurs* all astonished
to see our Armament,
Were griev'd to see that they must be
within Stone Walls all pent.
In haste they call in to their Aid
the Men upon the Isle
Forgetting their own Poverty,
(such things would make one smile)
But what is vastly more absurd
Than anything like this,
They quitted the *Grand Battery*,
The Glory of the Place.
Of which our *English* Lads did take
Possession quietly,
And with the Guns did ever since
the Enemy annoy.
They also did with mighty Toil
their Batteries erect,
Against the Town and Citadel
which play'd with good Effect.
They sent such Showers of Bombs and Balls
as made the *Frenchmen* quake,
And sputter out such words as these,
Those Dogs the Place will take.
Our men did also batter down
The West Gate and the Wall,
And made therein so large a Breach
That to the French they'd call,
Come out, Jack Frenchmen, come to us,
And drink a Bowl of Punch.
Jack Frenchman *cries, you English Dogs,*
come, here's a pretty Wench,
But by and by they change their Tones,
and after Terms of Peace,
Which if consented to they would
surrender up the Place.
(For they were so severely maul'd
by Cannon Shot and Shells,
That they no Place of Safety found
on Platforms or in Cells. . . .)
Our Gen'ral upon this Success
did send *Monsieurs* Words,
If they would not give up the Place,
He'd put them to the Sword.
And now not daring to withstand
The Force of all our Bands,
They gave up all their Fortresses
into our *English Hands*.

SOURCE: 'New England Bravery', broadside (1745), American Antiquarian Society, Worcester, Massachusetts.

make sufficient military gains around the world so that any territory lost in North America would be returned in the peace treaty. In this it was not always entirely successful. In 1713 it was forced to give up Acadia and its claims to Newfoundland, although in 1697 and 1748 it surrendered nothing of substance in North America. Neither mother country considered the North American theatre anything but a sideshow until the 1750s, when the British, after settling Nova Scotia at government expense, decided to take the New World seriously.

ACADIA AND NOVA SCOTIA

Acadia, that ill-defined geographical region that included more than peninsular Nova Scotia, had been contested ground between the British and the French since the early days of European settlement. Returned to France in 1670, Acadia and especially the village of Port-Royal were often attacked by the New Englanders. Port-Royal was captured in 1690 but returned to France by the Treaty of Ryswick in 1697. New England failed to take Port-Royal in 1707, but succeeded in 1710. Port-Royal was not typical of Acadia, however. The period between 1760 and 1713 saw considerable Acadian expansion, in terms both of numbers and of territory cultivated. A population of about 500 in 1760 had grown to more than 1,500 in 1710, mostly through natural increase, and had planted settlements along the Minas Basin, Cobequid, and Chignecto Bay. Most of Acadia's people came from a relatively small area of southwestern France. Younger members of families moved to new communities, which featured dykes that controlled the inundation of lowland areas by the high tides of the Bay of Fundy. Marsh was drained to allow it to be used for farming. Farms were small but extremely prosperous. Livestock, especially cattle, was the chief produce, traded illegally by the Acadians with New Englanders. A few outlying fishing communities existed on the southwest coast. Acadia had few roads and little overland transportation. Movement was by canoe and small boat.

Government sat fairly lightly upon this population. The French never really asserted tight administrative control over the region, and the Church operated solely through missionaries who provided some contact with Canada. Culturally and politically, the Acadians remained isolated from French Canada. The family (*clan*) and the local community were the important units for a closely knit peasant society. Acadia had developed an inherent sense of autonomy when—in the chess game that imperial warfare represented in the eighteenth century—France found itself obliged to surrender territory in North America with the Treaty of Utrecht (1713). Acadia was one of the pawns given up to the British that year. The *anciennes limites* of Acadia mentioned in the treaty were not defined, and the French subsequently insisted that they had surrendered only peninsular Nova Scotia, informally retaining northern Maine and New Brunswick, and formally retaining the two islands of Île Royale (Cape Breton) and Île St-Jean (Prince Edward Island). As for the population of the ceded territory, which the British called Nova Scotia to emphasize Britain's historic claims there, the inhabitants were given one year to remove to French territory or to remain as subjects of their new masters.

Nobody except the French wanted the Acadians removed, so they were tacitly allowed to remain in Nova Scotia on sufferance. Questions such as their land, language, and religious rights, as well as their political and military obligations to the new rulers, went essentially unresolved. The government of Nova Scotia dealt with the Acadians on an ad hoc basis, accepting their insistence on political neutrality and failing to exercise much authority within the Acadian community. The Acadians were not the first nor would they be the last group to translate unofficial tolerance, born of irresolution, into enshrined 'rights'. The dealings of the Nova Scotian authorities with the Acadians on the

The Porte Dauphine, the entrance to the reconstructed Louisbourg, with the clock-tower of the King's Bastion and barracks in the distance. Parks Canada, Fortress of Louisbourg National Historic Site of Canada, 01 A 339.

question of loyalty before 1740 were never authorized in London, but they led the Acadians to believe that they had an understanding.

Unfortunately for the French population of Nova Scotia, their loyalties were being constantly tested by the French, who had begun after 1720 to construct a fortress at Louisbourg on the southeastern coast. The French fortified the town, garrisoned it, and employed it as the military and economic nerve-centre of the Atlantic region. By 1734 the town site—four east-west streets on about 100 acres (40 ha)—was surrounded by walls on three sides with impressive gates. As well as a civilian population of 2,000 by the 1740s, Louisbourg contained a garrison of 600 soldiers (which in the 1750s would be increased to 3,500). The fortifications, poorly located and badly built, were never completed. Captured by New Englanders in 1745, Louisbourg was exchanged for Madras (in India) at the Treaty of Aix-la-Chapelle in1748. The capture and return of Louisbourg had several important effects in Nova Scotia. One was to encourage the British to do some military settling of their own as a counterweight to Louisbourg. Another was to turn the attention of the local authorities to the Acadians. The Nova Scotia Council in 1745 declared of the Acadians that 'if they are

JODOCUS KOLLER

Jodocus Koller (c. 1700–49) was born in Switzerland. In 1719 he enlisted in a Swiss regiment of the French army, which was organized to serve in colonial garrisons. In the early 1720s, Koller was posted to Louisbourg, where he was put to work on the walls of the fortress, a construction that was based on the treatises of the great military engineer Sebastien de Vauban. In Louisbourg, Koller appears both to have saved money and acquired the skill of the stonemason. He was promoted to sergeant, and in 1729 he married a local girl, Marie-Catherine Auger, the daughter of a French soldier who had opened an inn in the town. Koller retired from the military in the early 1730s. He collected his pay for three years after discharge, and obtained a grant of land. While Koller worked as a stonemason, he and his family lived in a house on Rue Dauphine which he had purchased in 1728. He appears to have become thoroughly integrated into the life of his community.

By 1735 Koller was raising animals on his grant, and by 1740 he was selling livestock to a butcher in the town. In 1738 he acquired a boat. Over the next few years, he would become a small merchant, selling firewood, hay, and livestock. He began to employ his old comrades. In 1745 when the Yankees camped outside Louisbourg and began to lay siege to the fortress, Koller was away on business. On his return, he found his farm being used by the invaders, and he managed to spy on them before returning to the town, where he became second-in-command of the local militia company. The militia engaged in guerilla harassment in May of 1745, but the fortress soon capitulated. Koller lost everything he possessed. He and his family were deported from Louisbourg back to France by the Americans. Koller, his wife, and four of their children died in an epidemic in Rochefort in 1749. Two of the children returned to Louisbourg as wards of their grandmother. Despite its sad ending, Jodocus Koller's life in Louisbourg before the fall of the fortress had been as successful as anyone in his situation could possibly expect.

not absolutely to be regarded as utter Enemies to His Majesty's Government they cannot be accounted less than unprofitable Inhabitants for their conditional Oath of Allegiance will not entitle them to the Confidence and Privileges of Natural British Subjects . . .' (National Archives of Canada 1745:A27). British settlement and Acadian removal were commonly coupled in the minds of British officials on both sides of the Atlantic. With the founding of Halifax, an almost inexorable sequence of events was set in motion that would result in the forcible expulsion of 6,000 Acadian residents from the colony.

The decision of the British government to use the public purse to populate a British colony—the first time Britain had done so in America, at a cost of more than £600,000 between 1749 and 1764—marked a new British interest in the Atlantic region. In 1749 Britain recruited some 2,500 people, including soldiers and sailors recently disbanded and some London artisans, and shipped them to Nova Scotia. They arrived to find huts, tents, and primitive conditions. The new governor, Lord Edward

Cornwallis (1713–76), complained that most of the new arrivals were 'poor idle worthless vagabonds' (quoted in Bell 1990: 344n). The British government soon sought a new source of more reliable settlers, turning to 'foreign Protestants' from Switzerland, France, and Germany. It employed as recruiting agent the young Scotsman John Dick (d. 1804), who was empowered by the Board of Trade over the winter of 1749–50 to recruit up to 1,500 'foreign Protestants', who would receive land, a year's subsistence, arms and tools, but not free transportation. Dick protested that free passage would be the main inducement, but he managed to fill the order. There were again complaints about the recruits, who were labelled 'in general old miserable wretches' (Bell 1990: 344n). In the end Dick sent over 2,700 Germans and Swiss, many of the latter actually French Huguenots from Lorraine. These immigrants were mainly farmers and skilled labourers. Uncertainty over land titles confined them to shanty-town Halifax until the Nova Scotia government determined to remove them to a site 50 miles (80 km) west of Halifax, renamed Lunenburg. There they resettled, an unhappy crew that was 'inconceivably turbulent, I might have said mutinous', according to the officer in charge of the relocation, Major Charles Lawrence (c. 1709–60) (Bell 1990: 435).

The settlement of Halifax was only one of a series of new pressures brought upon the province's Acadians. The French were reinforcing Louisbourg and constructing new forts (Fort Beauséjour and Fort Gaspéreau) on the disputed Chignecto peninsula. The French also began encouraging the Acadians in Nova Scotia to remove to French territory, especially the previously neglected Île St-Jean, which grew to more than 2,000 residents by 1752. The bulk of Nova Scotia's Acadians remained where they were, but after the renewal of undeclared war in North America in 1754, the government of the colony decided to settle the question. In July 1755 the Executive Council of Nova Scotia summoned Acadian deputies into a meeting room in Halifax and informed them that conditional fealty was impossible. The Acadians must immediately take the oath of allegiance in its common form. The Acadian representatives temporized overnight. When they were told that if they refused to take an unconditional oath, 'effectual Measures' would be taken 'to remove all such Recusants out of the Province', some offered to concede (Akins 1869: 259–60). The council then refused to administer the oath, however, saying 'that as there was no reason to hope their proposed Compliance proceeded from an honest Mind, and could be esteemed only the Effect of Compulsion and Force, they could not now be indulged with such Permission' (Akins 1869: 259–60). A classic confrontation between the civic inflexibility of the state and a collective minority demanding special treatment was in the closing stages of resolution. The council decided not only to expel the Acadians but to distribute them to several British colonies in the south.

More than 6,000 Acadians were summarily rounded up in the late summer and early autumn of 1755 by the British military and transported by ship to the south. There was little resistance, although many escaped to the woods and headed for French territory or to the inhabited north. The Acadians were not received with great enthusiasm in the British colonies, which had not been warned to expect them, and many eventually returned to the province. The British government never commented on the action of the Nova Scotia government, which it had never authorized, except to note that the colony had regarded it as an 'indispensably necessary for the Security and protection of the Province' (quoted in Brebner 1927: 230). As for those who did escape to the French, after the British forced the surrender of Louisbourg in July 1758, another expulsion began. A further 6,000 Acadians, including 3,500 on Île St-Jean, were summarily rounded up by the British military and sent back to France. A storm at sea destroyed many of the vessels carrying the Acadians, and perhaps as many as half of them drowned. The British never

Halifax in Nova Scotia 11th August 1755.

Sir

The success that has attended his Majesty's Arms in driving the French from the encroachments they had made in this Province furnished me with a favorable Opportunity of reducing the French Inhabitants of this Colony to a proper obedience to his Majesty's Government, or forcing them to quit the Country. These Inhabitants were permitted to remain in quiet possession of their Lands, upon condition they should take the Oath of Allegiance to the King within one Year after the Treaty of Utrecht, by which this Province was ceded to Great Britain; with this condition they have ever refused to comply, without having at the same time from

were pleased to allow me to extend still further his Royal Grace to such as would return to their Duty, I offered such of them as had not been openly in Arms against us, a continuance of the possession of their Lands, if they would take the Oath of Allegiance unqualified with any Reservation whatsoever, but this they have most audaciously, as well as unanimously refused; and if they would presume to do this when there is a large fleet of Ships of War in the Harbour, and a considerable Land force in the Province, what might not we expect from them when the approaching Winter deprives us of the former, and when the Troops which are only hired from New England occasionally and for a small time, have returned home.

As by this behaviour the Inhabitants have forfeited all title to their Lands

☐ Letter from Charles Lawrence regarding the expulsion of the Acadians, 11 August 1755. NAC, MG53, No. 71 2-4.

succeeded in eliminating the French presence from the region, however. Many Acadians escaped into the bush, others returned from their exile. What the expulsion did accomplish was to remove the Acadians from their traditional lands and force them to the unsettled margins of the Maritime colonies.

The founding of Halifax also had a substantial impact on the First Nations of Nova Scotia, especially the 1,000 Mi'kmaq remaining in the colony. The Mi'kmaq had attempted to pursue their own best interests during the years of warfare between the French and the English. They understood that British concepts of land ownership and settlement were disastrous to them. As a result they declared war against the British in 1749, and were met with a policy of extermination ordered by Lord Cornwallis. A final peace treaty with the Mi'kmaq in 1761 did not deal with land rights. No longer a military threat, the First Nations would soon cease to be regarded as important in the colony.

In the wake of the conquest of Louisbourg, the Nova Scotia government in October 1758

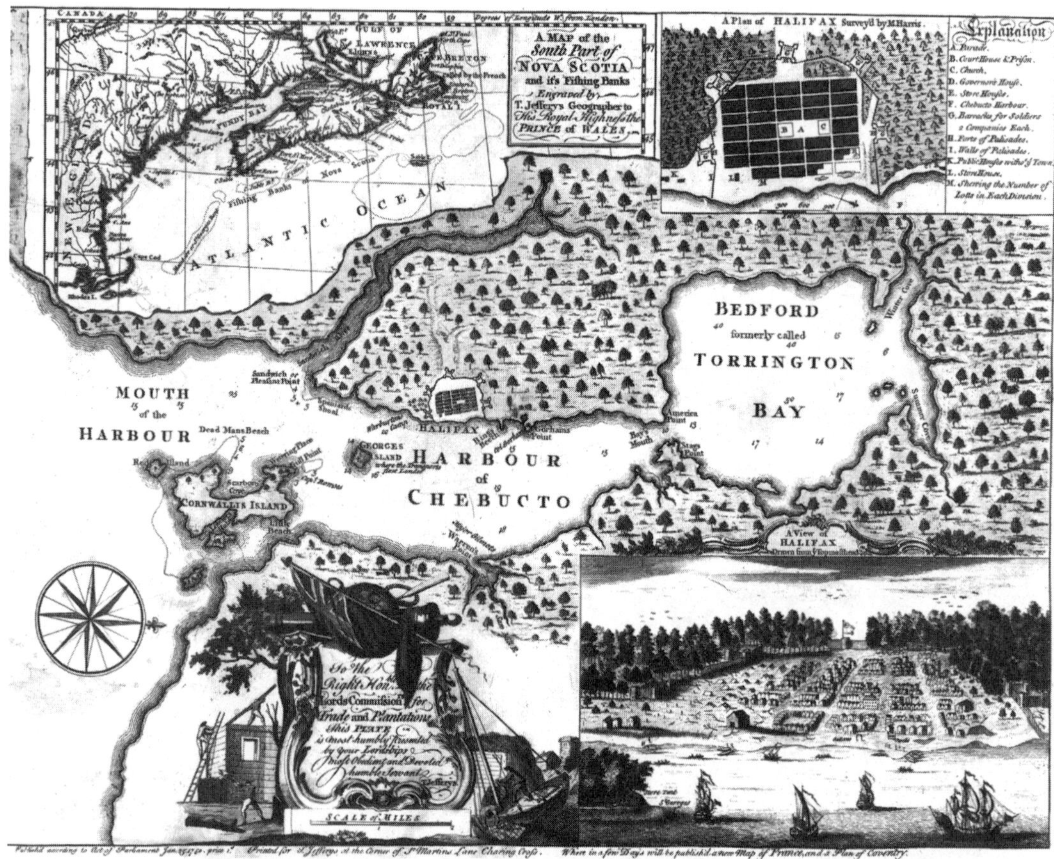

'A Map of the South Part of Nova Scotia and its Fishing Banks', by Thomas Jefferys, 1750. Inset at the upper right is 'A Plan of the new town of Halifax Surveyed by M. Harris'; at the lower right, 'A View of Halifax drawn from ye top masthead'. NAC, NMC 1012.

sent out advertisements to New England, offering to those who would settle in the colony free land, free transportation to it, and initial assistance in the form of food and tools. A few days before these advertisements were published, a legislative assembly—the first widely elected governing body in what is now Canada—met in Halifax. Nova Scotia was now a full-fledged British colony, the fourteenth mainland colony in Britain's North American Empire. This point had been reached with brutal measures that were characteristic of the age.

The Seven Years War

Officially this war began in 1756 in Europe, although the North American contestants had been engaged in open conflict for several years. In 1754, a desperate struggle between the British and the French for the allegiance of the Aboriginal peoples in the Ohio country and for sovereignty over the region came to a head. The French had tried to assert their claim in 1749 by sending a military expedition, led by Pierre-Joseph Céleron de Blainville (1693–1759), that

A map by Thomas Jefferys showing the British claims to Acadia. Library of Congress, Prints and Photographs Division, 705008.

planted lead tablets all along the Ohio and Allegheny Rivers stating the French claims to the region. The French in 1752 and 1753 built military posts in the area. In the latter year the British sent George Washington with a small party to deliver a letter to the French commandant at one of the French posts, Fort Le Boeuf, claiming the Ohio Valley and requesting the French to leave. They refused. In turn, the British governor of Virginia was authorized to use force to expel the French. He sent Washington back a year later with a force of 159 men, backed by a party of Aboriginals, to establish a fort on the Ohio. On the way, the expedition confronted a small French party of 30 men commanded by Joseph Coulon de Villiers de Jumonville (1718–54), who were travelling east to see whether Washington had entered what the French regarded as their territory. If he had, he was to be ordered formally to withdraw. Jumonville's party

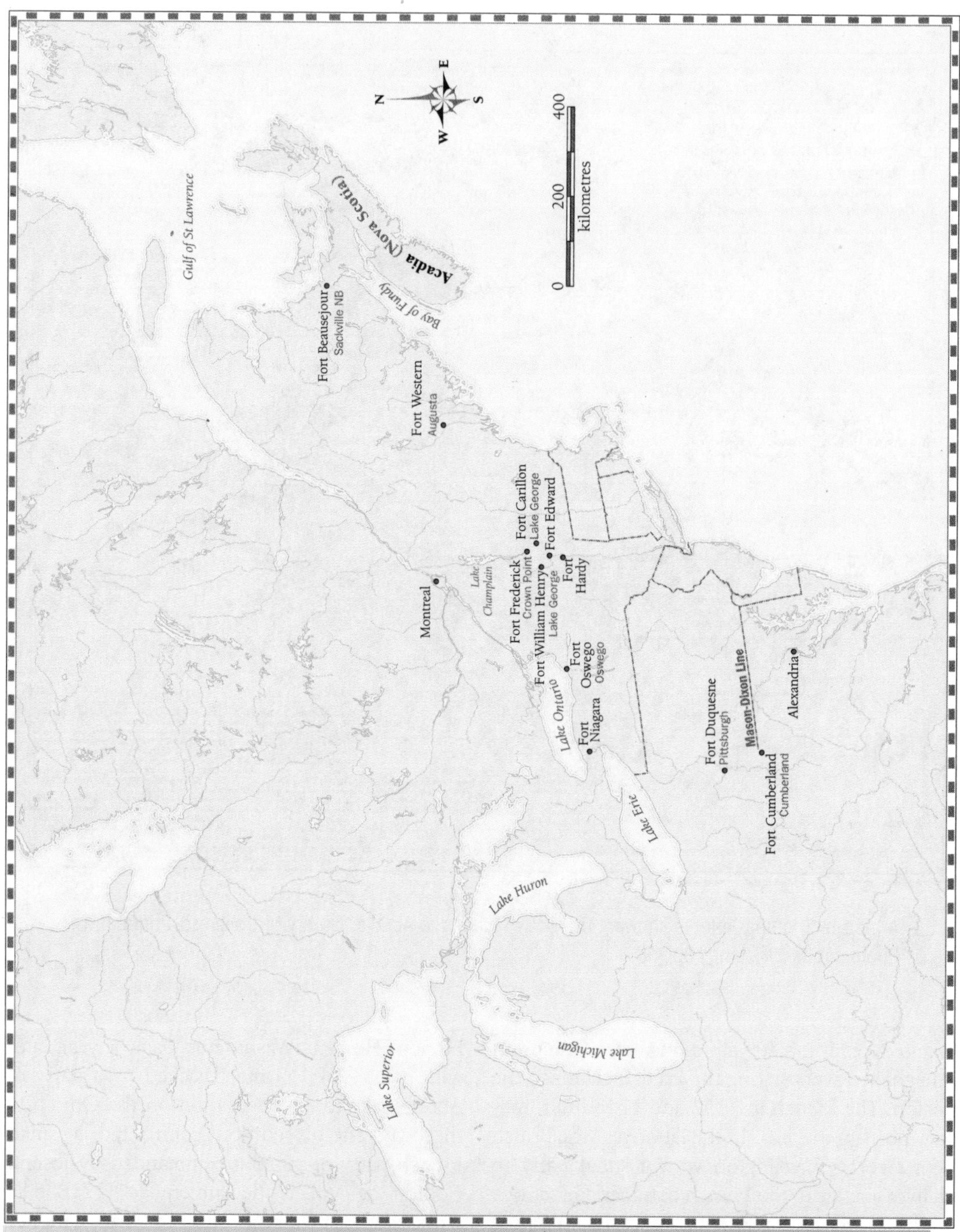

☐ The war in 1755. Adapted from Seymour Schwartz, *The French and Indian War 1754-1763: The Imperial Struggle for North America* (New York: Simon and Schuster, 1994), 37.

was specifically ordered not to provoke trouble; he was on a diplomatic not a military mission.

On 28 May 1754, Washington and some of his men entered the French camp, which was not well guarded. In the course of the ensuing melee, Jumonville (who had been wounded) was dispatched in traditional Aboriginal fashion with a tomahawk by one of the warriors. 'You are not yet dead, my father,' Tanacharison said to the wounded Frenchman in the ritual language of the time, and so he killed him (White, 1991: 241). Washington subsequently did his best to deny that Jumonville had been murdered, arguing that the French had hostile intentions—putting his reputation for never telling a lie in jeopardy. The incident led the French to send out a much larger force from Fort Duquesne, which in early July forced the Virginians to surrender. This surrender in turn led the British to dispatch two regiments under General Edward Braddock to America, and they were devastated at the Monongahela River in the early summer of 1755. News of this defeat—war still not having formally been declared—contributed to the British decision in Nova Scotia to expel the neutral Acadians from their province. Thus did the imperial struggle in the west have impact in the maritime region, demonstrating that however marginal these regions were, their domestic development was still affected by larger events.

In the beginning, the French seemed to be doing well. They had destroyed General Braddock's army of British regulars in 1755. On this occasion, the French tactics of ambush and guerrilla warfare easily triumphed over professional soldiers. A year later, under General Montcalm, they took 1,700 prisoners at the surrender of the three forts of Chouaguen headed by Fort George. Hit-and-run raiders kept the American backcountry in a constant uproar along the Ohio frontier. General Montcalm and other French officers were not happy with the brutality of these military actions. Given their naval weaknesses, however, the French needed to keep the British off balance to prevent a build-up of forces that would lead to an invasion.

In 1757 the French concentrated on New York as the major battlefield. Montcalm won several more notable victories, putting the French in control of the lake route into Canada. But the British continued to pour men and supplies into North America. A year later, the British managed to force the surrender of the garrison at Fort Frontenac on the north shore of Lake Ontario. A sideshow in the Ohio region saw the British capture Fort Duquesne on the Ohio River. The British further increased the number of troops at their disposal, employing their naval superiority to besiege successfully the exposed French fortress at Louisbourg in 1758. The French garrison held out just long enough to prevent the enemy from continuing on to an invasion of Quebec that same year, but the French were pulling back militarily. The situation in New France itself was becoming desperate. The government was unable to get reinforcements of men or fresh supplies, especially of arms and munitions, because the British controlled the sea. Moreover, the colony was in terrible shape financially, with runaway inflation. The civilian government and the military leadership were at constant loggerheads, and morale was very low.

CONCLUSION

At the beginning of 1759, the situation was very grave for New France. After more than a century and a half of successful struggle against environment, First Nations enemies, French neglect, and British hostility, the Canadians had their backs to the wall. The Acadians had been forcibly removed from Nova Scotia and Louisbourg captured. A series of powerful British armies, backed by a wealthy government determined to win, was gathering for the invasion of the St Lawrence. The locus of power was about to shift, to the detriment of the French in North America.

HOW HISTORY HAS CHANGED

MILITARY HISTORY

The colonial wars in North America are a topic that clearly transcends Canadian history to involve American and European history as well; and perhaps more than most subjects from this time and place, these wars have been the focus of international scholarship. They were also the subject of the American historian Francis Parkman's (1823–93) classic books, a perfect topic for his heroic and romantic narrative approach—often known as 'drums and trumpets' history—which was accepted in Canada by historians before 1900 as readily as in the United States. Parkman's work (and his generalizations) remained much more widely known than the later studies of succeeding generations of professional historians, such as L. H. Gipson in the United States and Guy Frégault in Canada. Frégault to some extent emulated Parkman more than Gipson, especially in his biographical approach to much of the material.

In contrast to Parkman, what the professional scholars demonstrated quite clearly from the beginning was that warfare in this period was a pretty hit-or-miss kind of business. Getting an army to the right place at the right time—and being able to supply it—were not easy matters, and the few occasions when they were accomplished (Louisbourg, Quebec) were followed by military success. The first professional historians also established the overall framework of the wars. They were both European and colonial struggles, often not well coordinated. The French were on the defensive from the beginning, but were able to survive because the British could not for a variety of reasons mount a decent invasion. The French were also overextended from the beginning, having to defend a frontier that stretched across nearly 3,000 miles (4,800 km). Again, the French were saved by the incompetence of the opposition. In treating these conflicts, American historians liked to home in on the constant jousting between the British and the colonists, which could be seen as foreshadowing the later American Revolution.

Although the colonial wars are obviously crucial to understanding the development of Canada, they have been relatively neglected in recent Canadian scholarship, mainly because military history became so unfashionable in this country in the last third of the twentieth century. With the exception of Ian Steele, few Canadian scholars have worked consistently over the last thirty years on the history of the actual warfare of the colonial period. What Steele insisted on was the irregular nature of most of the forces and much of the conflict. On the other hand, a good deal of work has been done on the bureaucratic and social context of the contending armies and navies. James Pritchard has specialized in the French navy, for example, and in several major works has demonstrated that the navy had many of the same problems of administration and organization as did the army. We also know significantly more about the soldiers (less about the sailors) who did the actual fighting. As a result, we have come to recognize just how polyglot the military forces of this period were, how badly they were treated, and how frequently they resisted or mutinied. We appreciate the internal rivalries among the officers, especially between the colonials and the Europeans, and the hostility between the regular soldiers and the militia. These conflicts were endemic to both sides. Both Americans and Canadians have for centuries liked to believe in the importance of the militia, often even mythologizing it, and despite the tendency of the professional historians to prefer the regulars, the militia myth in the colonial period has never really been demolished. Because of the new interest in Aboriginal history, we also have a much clearer picture of the First Nations allies of both sides, and especially of the independent agenda of the Aboriginals.

Military history—even in its broadest rather than narrower contexts—has been one of the most neglected areas of Canadian history in recent years, but it is now beginning to make something of a comeback.

Short Bibliography

Blackburn, Carole. *The Jesuit Missions and Colonialism in North America, 1632–1650.* Montreal and Kingston, 2000. A recent study of the missionary activities of the Jesuits with the Huron, placed in a contemporary context of colonialism.

Dechêne, Louise. *Habitants and Merchants in Seventeenth-Century Montreal*. Kingston and Montreal, 1992. An award-winning study of the development of early Montreal.

Delâge, Denys. *Bitter Feast: Amerindians and Europeans in Northeastern North America 1600–1664*. Trans. Jane Brierly. Vancouver, 1993. An analysis of the early relationships between First Nations and European intruders.

Eccles, W. J., *France in America*. Markham, ON, 1990. The best overview of the French Empire in North America.

Griffiths, Naomi. *The Contexts of Acadian History, 1587–1781*. Montreal, 1992. A series of fascinating essays by the leading specialist on early Acadia.

Handcock, Gordon *'So Longe As There Comes Noe Women': Origins of English Settlement in Newfoundland*. St John's, 1989. The story of early English settlement in Newfoundland.

Harris, R. C. *The Seigneurial System in Early Canada: A Geographical Study*. Madison, 1966. The classic revisionist text on the subject, not yet superseded.

Head, C. Grant. *Eighteenth-Century Newfoundland: A Geographer's Perspective*. Toronto, 1976. An interesting example of what the historical geographer has to contribute to Canadian historical analysis.

MacDonald, M.A. *Fortune and La Tour: The Civil War in Acadia*. Toronto, 1983. A well-written account of the La Tour family and its vicissitudes.

Mahaffie, Charles D. *A Land of Discord Always: Acadia from Its Beginnings to the Expulsion of Its People 1604–1755*. Camden, ME, 1995. A recent synthesis of the story of Acadia.

Moogk, Peter. *La Nouvelle France: The Making of New France—A Cultural History*. East Lansing, MI, 2000. A fascinating new analysis made from the standpoint of culture and cultural studies.

Moore, Christopher. *Louisbourg Portait: Life in an Eighteenth-Century Garrison Town*. Toronto, 1982. An award-winning book based on early court records, demonstrating how much fascinating material can be teased out of such sources.

Pritchard, J. S. *Anatomy of a Naval Disaster: The 1746 French Expedition to North America*. Montreal and Kingston, 1998. A wonderful account of the French navy in a time of crisis, demonstrating how difficult it was to coordinate military activities in the eighteenth century.

Simpson, Patricia. *Marguerite Bourgeoys and Montreal, 1640–1665*. Montreal and Kingston, 1997. A sympathetic account of one of the leading female figures of seventeenth-century Canada.

Steele, Ian. *Guerillas and Grenadiers, The Struggle for*

Canada, 1689–1760. Toronto, 1969. A useful short history of the Canadian wars, emphasizing the roles of both the regular and irregular forces.

Trudel, Marcel. *Introduction to New France*. Toronto, 1968. A textbook summary of New France by its leading modern historian.

White, Richard. *The Middle Ground: Indians, Empire and Republics in the Great Lakes Region 1650–1815*. Cambridge, 1991. A revisionist work that takes the First Nations seriously in strategic and cultural terms.

STUDY QUESTIONS

1. Reread the excerpt from Father Le Jeune's *Relation*. Identify and explain the three techniques he recommends for converting the Aboriginal people. By what means did the missionaries hope to sell themselves to the Huron?
2. What were the advantages and disadvantages of card money?
3. Reread the poem 'New England Bravery'. How did the New England poet interpret the victory at Louisbourg?
4. What do the careers of Kirke, Silvain, and Koller have in common?
5. Briefly explain why the Maritime region was such a scene of violence in the seventeenth century.
6. In the matter of its economic development, did Canada owe more to its European origins or to its North American location? Explain.
7. What were the three chief differences between the earlier colonial wars and the Seven Years' War?
8. How does Intendant Raudot justify the use of card money?
9. What can we deduce from the inventory of Jacques Bourdon's estate?

CHAPTER THREE

Becoming and Remaining British, 1759–1815

The British established a foothold in Canada with their victory at the Battle of Quebec in 1759. They consolidated their position in 1760, and kept the conquest at the peace treaty in 1763. The theory was that eliminating the French would stabilize North America. It did not work out that way. Within a few years of the conquest, the American colonists had begun an armed rebellion and attempted unsuccessful invasions of Quebec and Nova Scotia. The British reorganized their North American empire after the Americans left it, taking advantage of the thousands of exiles and refugees called Loyalists whom the war had produced. Within a generation, in 1812, the Americans declared war on Great Britain and attempted another round of invasions of Canada, but were beaten back by British regulars and colonial militia with considerable difficulty. The period from 1759 to 1815 was thus one of great turmoil and change. British North America would settle down only after 1815.

The Conquest and Its Aftermath

The series of abortive and aborted British attempts to seize Quebec, the administrative capital of New France (in 1690, 1711, and 1746), did not prevent another major expedition under General James Wolfe (1727–59) from trying again. The largest and best-equipped military force that North America had ever known assembled at Louisbourg over the winter of 1758–9, while the frozen ice of the St Lawrence isolated the French. The British force consisted of 8,600 troops, most of them regulars, and 13,500 sailors aboard 119 vessels, including twenty-two ships of the line and five frigates. This great armada required six days simply to clear Louisbourg harbour in early June 1759. On 27 June, Wolfe landed his army on the Île d'Orléans without serious French opposition. There followed over two months of skirmishing, as Wolfe attempted to land his army closer to the French forces, and the French commander-in-chief, the Marquis de Montcalm (1712–59), sought to prevent such a move. Meanwhile, Wolfe and the British admiral, Sir Charles Saunders (1713?–75), were at constant loggerheads, and Montcalm found evidence that his forces, mainly French-Canadian militiamen, would not stand up to offensive action.

Wolfe tried a number of plans, all without success. He was becoming desperate. As the end of summer approached, there was less time for the massive British fleet to remain in the St Lawrence, and its commanders were pressing for a final confrontation. Finally, after partially recovering from a fever, Wolfe made a final effort. His troops found a path up the cliffs to the plain above at the Anse au Foulon, and managed to pass the French sentries unmolested. The British drew their battle lines covering the plain above the cliffs. Inexplicably, Montcalm decided to attack the British army without waiting for reinforcements. The French ranks broke first, both

TIMELINE

1759
Battle of Quebec.

1760
Final French surrender.

1763
Treaty of Paris transfers New France and Acadia to Great Britain; the British king issues the Proclamation of 1763.

1773
The Island of Saint John calls its first assembly.

1774
Parliament passes the Quebec Act. It also passes Palliser's Act to regulate the Newfoundland fishery.

1775
The Americans invade Canada.

1776
An American party invades Nova Scotia.

1778
Peter Pond reaches the rich Athabasca country; James Cook arrives at Nootka Sound.

1781
The British surrender at Yorktown; a smallpox epidemic decimates the First Nations around Hudson Bay.

1782
The first Loyalist fleet departs for Nova Scotia.

1783
Treaty of Paris ends the War of the American Revolution by recognizing American independence.

1784
British North America is reorganized; New Brunswick is separated from Nova Scotia and given a separate government; Cape Breton gets a government but no assembly.

1786
Guy Carleton (now Lord Dorchester) is appointed governor-general of British North America.

1787
Charles Inglis, the first Anglican bishop in North America, arrives at Halifax.

1788
King's College is established by the Nova Scotia assembly (it actually opens in 1790 in Windsor).

1789
The British and Spanish spar at Nootka Sound.

1791
Upper and Lower Canada are separated by the British Parliament's passage of the Constitutional Act of 1791.

1792
First legislature in Upper Canada is convened at Newark (Niagara-on-the Lake). Captain George Vancouver begins his survey of the BC coast.

1793
Alexander Mackenzie of the North West Company reaches the Pacific Ocean via an overland route from Montreal.

1800
King's College (now the University of New Brunswick) is founded at Fredericton.

1806
Le Canadien, the first French-language newspaper, is published in Quebec.

1808
Simon Fraser reaches the Pacific via the Fraser River.

1809
First steam vessel (the *Accommodation*) begins service between Montreal and Quebec.

1811
Hudson's Bay Company makes a land grant of 116,000 square miles (300,429 km^2) to Lord Selkirk.

1812
Americans declare war on Great Britain and invade Canada; the first settlers arrive at Red River.

1813
York (Toronto) is sacked by the Americans.

1814
Treaty of Ghent inconclusively ends the War of 1812.

Wolfe and Montcalm were mortally wounded, and the British possessed Quebec. The war was not ended, for the bulk of the French army escaped and would fight on valiantly for another year. The Battle of Quebec (or of the Plains of Abraham) was probably the first military engagement in North America that was fought almost entirely on European rather than American terms. A fully professional army, well disciplined and on the day well led, defeated a partly untrained one. Backed by a government at home with regular troops and naval support, the British finally breached the defensive position that the French had enjoyed for over a century.

British reinforcements and supplies arrived first on the St Lawrence in 1760, and a traditional three-pronged attack on Montreal—anchored by a large army led by General Jeffrey Amherst (1717–97) from New York—forced the surrender of that town, the final French stronghold, in early September. The fifty-five articles of capitulation would govern the British occupation of Canada until the governments in Europe finally settled matters by the Treaty of Paris in

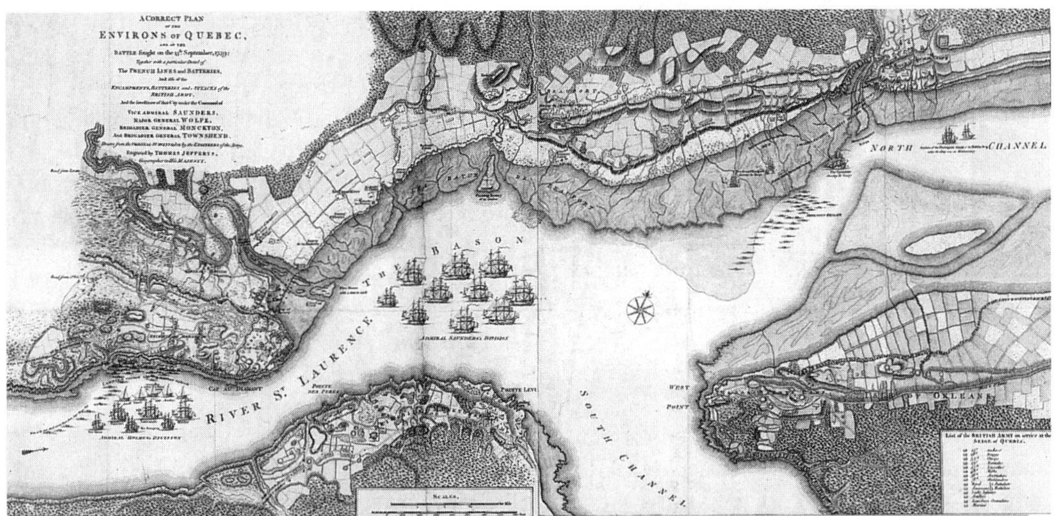

☐ This 1760 map by Thomas Jefferys, who was then geographer to George III, illustrates the Quebec campaign in 1759. Wolfe set up camp on the Île d'Orléans (lower right); tried and failed to land at Montmorency, on the north shore (above the North Channel), in July; moved his fleet upriver past Quebec in September; and landed at l'Anse au Foulon (extreme left) to wage the brief battles on the plains of Abraham (above). NAC, C-128079.

Preparatory drawing for the engraved print 'The Death of Wolfe' by James Barry, watercolour, c. 1763. NAC (Peter Winkworth Collection of Canadiana), P3253.

1763. Until Europe made a final determination, Britain dealt with the colony with a fairly light hand. Canada was governed by military administrators who spoke French and accepted it as the 'language of the country'. A few of the French-Canadian élite departed for France, while a number of new suppliers (mainly American colonials tied to British and American trading patterns) made their inevitable appearance.

Peace negotiations in 1761 proved unsuccessful, not because the French had balked at sacrificing North American territory, but because war minister William Pitt had wanted more concessions around the world. When the French West Indies fell totally and the British began an assault on Spanish Havana—Spain had earlier foolishly entered the war on the side of France—the French and Spanish had their backs to the wall. The French offered to sacrifice more continental American territory. Louisiana east of the Mississippi was surrendered for Martinique and Guadeloupe. The French were granted fishing rights in Newfoundland and the tiny islands of St Pierre and Miquelon in exchange for the surrender of all other claims to territory in the northern part of the American continent. The Spanish proved no problem after the fall of Havana. In a complicated arrangement, Britain returned Havana and Puerto Rico and kept Spain's Florida, while France compensated Spain for its losses by ceding it the western half of Louisiana and the port of New Orleans.

The final arrangement was sold to the British public by emphasizing the great gains made in North America. Having stressed the security won for the American colonies as a result of the war—at monumental expense to the British people in manpower and money—the government needed an American policy. Its first effort at creating one was the notorious Proclamation of 1763. Like most British policy for its northern possessions produced over the next few years, the Proclamation of 1763 was not directly intended to effect fundamental changes for Britain's older seaboard colonies. Four new governments were created out of the American acquisitions, including Quebec, which was limited to its St Lawrence settlements. This truncated province was to be governed by British law and, as soon as possible, an elected assembly. The Island of Saint John and Cape Breton were attached to Nova Scotia. Land grants to retired officers and disbanded servicemen were to be readily available. In the west, beyond the river systems of the Atlantic coast, no land grants were to be made. This territory was to be reserved for the First Nations, and any trading in it was to be regulated by the imperial government.

☐ Quebec: 'View of the Bishop's house with the ruins as they appear in going down the Hill from the Upper to the Lower Town', by Richard Short from a drawing made at the siege in 1759. NAC, C-000352.

The Proclamation had ramifications beyond the territory ceded by the French. It was preceded by the beginning of a major Aboriginal uprising in the interior, known as Pontiac's Rebellion. Both the declaration of limits for American westward expansion and the need to finance Britain's new military responsibilities would enrage the American colonials. They began a series of provocative responses to Britain that would escalate into an organized colonial rebellion or 'revolution'. It became apparent that policy for the new territories could not be executed by Great Britain in isolation.

Although neither the Proclamation of 1763 nor any other British policy document ever elaborated a full settlement policy for what is now Canada, the outlines of that policy were perfectly plain. The British did not wish to populate their northernmost colonies with emigrants from the mother country itself. Great Britain was at the beginning of a major economic shift, usually called the Industrial Revolution. Instead of having excess population, it wanted to retain its people, both as a labour force and for military purposes. The British were, however, prepared to make land grants to disbanded soldiers, who were not regarded as very useful at home in peacetime. They were also willing to accept 'foreign

The Lords of Trade and Policy for the West

In the late spring of 1763, the British government turned its attention to what it should do with the new territories ceded to Britain by the Treaty of Paris. It was easily agreed that most of the territories could be included in old colonies or established in new ones, but one exception was 'that large Tract of Country bounded by the Mississippi and the Limits of the Hudson Bay Company on the one hand and on the other by the Limits of Canada, East and West Florida and His Majesty's ancient Colonies.' The Lords of Trade—the equivalent of a colonial office at the time—offered a different policy for this territory in a report of 5 August 1763. This report led directly to the Proclamation of 1763.

To the King's Most Excellent Majesty. . . .

We have taken this important Subject into our most serious Consideration and do most humbly concur in Your Majesty's Opinion, of the propriety of putting this Country under a particular Government, by a Commission under Your Great Seal, with a most precise Description of its Boundaries, in Order to ascertain the actual possession of its Property, and with such Powers as may be necessary, as well to maintain and secure the free Exercise of the Indian Trade, which it is proposed all Your Majesty's Subjects shall enjoy within it, under proper Regulations, as to prevent its becoming a Refuge to Criminals and Fugitives.—But at the same time, we beg Leave to submit to your Majesty, the following Objections which have occurred to us, against the annexing this Country to any particular Government, especially to that of Canada.

1st We are apprehensive that, should this Country be annexed to the Government of Canada, a Colour might be taken on some future Occasion, for supposing that Your Majesty's Title to it, had taken its Rise, singly from the Cessions made by France, in the late Treaty, whereas Your Majesty's Title to the Lakes and circumjacent Territory as well as to the Sovereignty over the Indian Tribes, particularly of the six Nations, rests on a more solid and even a more equitable Foundation; and perhaps nothing is more necessary than that just Impressions on this Subject should be carefully preserved to the Minds of the Indians, whose Ideas might be blended and confounded if they should be brought to consider themselves as under the Government of Canada—

2d We are apprehensive as the whole of this Country would become subject to the Laws of a particular Government or Province, it would give that Province such superior Advantage in respect to the whole of the Indian Trade, which Your Majesty in Your Justice and Wisdom has determined to leave as open as possible to all Your Subjects, as might controul and obstruct it to the Prejudice of Your other Colonies—

3d If this great Country should be annexed to the Government of Canada, we are apprehensive, that the Powers of such Government could not be carried properly into execution, either in respect to the Indians or British Traders, unless by means of the Garrisons at the different Posts and Forts in that Country, which must contain the greatest Part of Your Majesty's American Forces and consequently the Governor of Canada would become virtually Commander in Chief or constant and inextricable Disputes would arise, between him, and the commanding Officers of Your Majesty's Troops—. . . .

We would further submit, whether the issuing such Commission and Instructions may not be delayed; till by the receipt of such Information, which your Majesty has been graciously pleased to direct, We are enabled to make a full and particular Report on that very important subject.—. . . In the mean time, We humbly propose that a Proclamation be immediately issued by Your Majesty as well on Account of the late Complaint of the Indians, and the actual Disturbances in Consequence, as of Your Majesty's fixed Determination to permit no grant of Lands nor any settlements to be made within certain fixed Bounds, under pretence of Purchase or any other Pretext whatever, leaving all that Territory within it free for the hunting Grounds of those Indian Nations Subjects of Your Majesty, and for the free trade of all your Subjects, to prohibit strictly all infringements or Settlements to be made on such Grounds, and at the same time to declare Your Majesty's Intentions to encourage all such Persons who shall be inclined to commence New Settlements from Your old Colonies, together with all foreign Protestants, coming by themselves or with such Undertakers, in Your new Colonies of East and West Florida or your old Colony of Nova Scotia . . . .

SOURCE: Adam Shortt and Arthur G. Doughty, eds, *Documents Relating to the Constitutional History of Canada 1759–1791* (Ottawa: King's Printer, 1907), 110–12.

Protestants' as settlers, although they hoped that colonial Americans, already acclimated to the New World, would become the principal newcomers. The creation of a First Nations reserve in the west would force land-hungry Americans south and north: south to Florida, north to Quebec and Nova Scotia. The British hoped that new immigration would soon outnumber and overwhelm the French in Quebec, but they were not prepared to subsidize the movement of settlers beyond making land available to them.

From the Proclamation to the Rebellion

In Nova Scotia, a third contingent of subsidized settlers was added to the first group at Halifax and the 'foreign Protestants'. The New England 'Planters' came to the province between 1759 and 1762. Governor Charles Lawrence took advantage of a substantial annual parliamentary grant for Nova Scotia to recruit over 8,000 Yankees. He provided them with land, transportation, and subsidies until the financial tap was turned off in 1762. The New Englanders came mainly from land-hungry areas of Rhode Island, Connecticut, and southeastern Massachusetts. They saw migration to Nova Scotia—which was an alternative to movement to northern areas of New England—as particularly attractive because it was financed by the government. The migrants tended to move in kinship groups, often as entire communities. Most were farmers, although others were fishermen seeking improved access to superior fishing grounds. The farmers settled on Acadian land in the Minas Basin, while the fishermen moved to south-shore outports they named Yarmouth and Barrington after their New England counterparts.

The Planters had been promised not only cheap land but liberty of conscience and a government 'like those of neighbouring colonies', a guarantee they took to mean that they could replicate the participatory local democracy of their former homes (quoted in Bumsted 1971: 8). They soon found that Nova Scotia had no intention of permitting strong local government. Political disillusionment was added to disappointment over the climate and the absence of markets. Perhaps half the newcomers left within a few years of the termination of subsidies, complaining of 'Nova Scarcity'. While Yankee farmers wheeled and dealed in small parcels of land, the élite office-holding classes (both within and without the colony) acquired large grants of wilderness land—3 million acres (1,214,100 ha)

'Part of the Town and Harbour of Halifax in Nova Scotia, looking down Prince Street to the Opposite Shore', one of six prints of drawings of Halifax made by Richard Short in 1759. NAC, C-4294.

in the last few days before the Stamp Act became effective in 1765; having to buy stamped paper would greatly increase the cost of obtaining the grants. Only a handful of these speculators became active in either settlement ventures or commercial development.

By 1767, when a detailed census of Nova Scotia was taken, the colony was well-populated, with 11,072 people in Nova Scotia proper, another 707 in Cape Breton, 1,196 in the northern section (now New Brunswick) and 519 on the Island of Saint John. The census also demonstrated what a heterogeneous population was already in place, consisting of 11,228 Protestants and 2,246 Catholics, and several ethnic groups (see Table 3.1). In addition, the returns showed 95 'Negroes' and a scattering of 'Indians' (apparently no serious attempt was made to count them). Within a few years, substantial numbers of Scots would come to the region from both the Lowlands and especially the Highlands, adding Gaelic to the English, German, French, and Mi'kmaq already freely spoken throughout the region.

Land speculation also dominated the development of the Island of Saint John. The entire land surface of the island was distributed to absentee owners (mainly British office holders and military men) by lottery in 1767. These proprietors were supposed to settle the land in return for their grants, but most would merely hold it in the hopes that it would become more valuable. The British allowed the proprietors on the Island of Saint John, which was initially attached to Nova Scotia, to petition for a separate

TABLE 3.1
POPULATION OF NOVA SCOTIA IN 1767 BY ETHNICITY

Place	English	Irish	Scotch	Americans	Germans	Acadians
Nova Scotia	686	1831	143	5799	1862	650
Cape Breton	70	169	6	170	21	271
North (NB)	25	53	17	874	60	147
Saint John	130	112	7	70	3	197
Totals	912	2165	173	6913	1936	1265

MARY CANNON

Mary Cannon (*c.* 1751–1827) was born in Halifax after the middle of the eighteenth century, her origins quite obscure. At a fairly early age she became the housekeeper of J.F.W. DesBarres, who was engaged in surveying the coast of Nova Scotia and establishing himself as a major proprietor on lands that had for the most part been inhabited by Acadians. At some point she became the mistress of DesBarres, and ultimately bore him five daughters and a son. Gradually Mary assumed direction of DesBarres's Nova Scotia estates, and was left in charge of them when he returned to England (and his legal wife and children) in 1774. She acquired full power of attorney in 1776 and spent the remainder of her life managing the properties, apparently with the expectation that she and her children would inherit them.

DesBarres returned to British North America as lieutenant-governor of Cape Breton Island in 1784, and Mary continued as his estate manager, although the two seldom met. During this period, Mary and DesBarres became increasingly estranged, and Mary gradually ceased attempting to work with him, operating instead on her own. DesBarres ultimately sent an agent to report to him on her administration. The agent, John MacDonald of Glenaladale, was critical of Mary's performance as agent, but insisted that she was entitled to some portion of the estate. The situation was not resolved, however. DesBarres was replaced in Cape Breton and returned home to England, but in 1805 (at the age of 83!) he was appointed lieutenant-governor of Prince Edward Island. During this governorship, which lasted until 1812, the two parties engaged in extensive litigation. Although Mary preserved the estate, it did not prosper, partly because of Desbarres's absence, partly because of lack of capital. When DesBarres finally agreed to deed to Mary's children that portion of his lands on which Mary lived, the estate was only a shell of its earlier self. Mary was not the only woman who administered estates in British North America for an absent male, but her problems were rendered more difficult by the nature of the relationship between herself and DesBarres.

government in 1769, on the understanding that it would not cost the mother country a penny.

In Quebec, a number of military officers (and sometimes their men) took advantage of the British offer of land grants. The anticipated stampede of American settlers to Quebec did not occur, however. The Americans were put off partly by the presence of thousands of francophone Roman Catholics and the absence of familiar institutions such as representative government and universal freehold tenure. In a classic vicious circle, the laws, government, and culture of Quebec could not very well be reconstructed until large numbers of anglophones arrived, and this immigration was not likely to happen until change had occurred. Moreover, Americans did not move north into any of the British colonies after 1763. Most of the newcomers were British, mainly Scots, who began leaving their homes in the mid-1760s. The Scottish influx had only begun to gain momentum when it was closed down by the warfare of the American rebellion.

Everywhere in the northernmost colonies in these years, freehold land tenure and the concept of the yeoman farmer fought an uphill battle. The seigneurial system still controlled land in Quebec, the Island of Saint John had been distributed to proprietors who were expected to settle as tenant farmers did in Europe, and much of Nova Scotia was held by large landholders. In the absence of aggressive government settlement activity, those who acquired grants of land in North America in order to settle them were committed to replicating a European pattern of landholding, with aristocratic landlords and peasant tenants.

The administration of the new province of Quebec was greatly complicated not only by the small number of anglophones but by the emerging political turmoil to the south. The colonial authorities in Quebec began by introducing some British elements into the system, but ended up confirming many French ones. English criminal law was put into effect, but the French civil law was largely retained. The British in London agreed that British laws against Catholics did not extend to Quebec. Grand-Vicar Jean-Olivier Briand (1715–94) was chosen by his Canadian colleagues to head the Church in Quebec, and was consecrated bishop near Paris on 16 March 1766. Officially he would be only 'superintendant' of the Quebec Church, but in practice he was accepted as its bishop and the collection of tithes was officially supported. There could be no elected assembly until there were more Protestants. The process of confirmation of the institutions of the Old Regime gained a real boost from Governor Guy Carleton (1724–1808). An Anglo-Irishman, Carleton was a firm believer in a landed aristocracy, the subordination of a tenant class, and a close connection between church and state. He came to see that, with adjustments to circumstance, his overall vision for society was quite compatible with that of the Old Regime of New France. As the Americans to the south became increasingly restive and turbulent, Carleton became less eager for reform and more interested in pacification. Inevitably he turned to the handiest instruments at his disposal.

Instinctively grasping the need for collaborators to rule an 'alien' population, Carleton recognized the clergy and the seigneurs as natural leaders who could be won over if their rights and privileges were protected. In the process some of the economic damage to the economy resulting from the geographical dismemberment of Quebec in 1763 could be undone. The result was the Quebec Act of 1774. Most of the ancient boundaries of Quebec were restored to the colony. His Majesty's subjects in Quebec 'professing the Religion of the Church of Rome' were granted free exercise of their religion and exempted from the traditional oaths of supremacy (a new one was supplied). The Catholic clergy were allowed 'their accustomed Dues and Rights, with respect to such Persons only as shall profess the said Religion'. Provision was also made for the support of a Protestant clergy. All matters relating to property and civil rights were to be decided by the traditional laws of Canada. This clause, in effect, preserved the seigneurial system. English criminal law was continued, and the province was to be governed by a newly structured legislative council; there was no provision for an elected assembly.

Parliamentary critics of the administration that introduced this measure complained of its 'sowing the seeds of despotism in Canada' (Edmund Burke, quoted in Neatby 1972: 38–9). The Americans assumed a direct connection between it and their own situation, including the Quebec Act as one of the 'Intolerable Acts' passed by the British Parliament at this time to punish the Americans for the Boston Tea Party. The legislation was certainly influenced by the need to pacify Quebec, but it was not intended to aggravate the Americans. If the act was supposed to secure the loyalty of the Canadians, however, the strategy was not entirely successful.

Implementing British policy in the old *pays d'en haut* was, if anything, even more difficult than coming to terms with the old and new subjects of Quebec. Part of the problem was that the British army, which was responsible for administering this region, did not really appreciate the extent to which the French and the Aboriginals

☐ Governor Guy Carleton, painted in 1923 by Mabel B. Messer 'from a copy that hung in Rideau Hall' ; original artist unknown. NAC, C-002833.

FRANCES BROOKE

Frances Moore (1724–89) was born in Lincolnshire, the daughter of an Anglican curate. She grew up in Anglican rectories and later moved to London, where in 1755 and 1756 she edited a weekly periodical, *The Old Maid*, under the name of 'Mary Singleton, Spinster'. While she was not the first woman in England to become a professional writer and journalist, she was one of the most successful of the type in her time. In 1756, she married an Anglican clergyman named John Brooke, who soon after was appointed acting chaplain to the British army in America. Brooke sailed for the New World late in 1757, served as chaplain at Louisbourg from 1758 to 1760, and then moved to Quebec. Meanwhile, Frances remained in London, publishing several novels and achieving a literary reputation in the literary set headed by Samuel Johnson. In company with her sister Sarah, she finally joined her husband in Quebec in 1763, and resided in that colony for most of the time until the couple returned to England in 1767.

John Brooke was regarded as a troublemaker in Quebec. He was too friendly with the merchants and hence was unpopular with the garrison. Moreover, he spoke no French and was anti-Catholic. Frances was even more meddlesome, although she was fairly popular in official circles in the colony. According to Fanny Burney, she was short and fat, and squinted, but she also had 'the art of showing agreeable ugliness'. While in Quebec, Frances wrote *The History of Emily Montague*, the first novel written in what is now Canada. She brought the manuscript back to London, where it was published in 1769. *Emily Montague* was cast in the form of a series of letters, mainly from Quebec to recipients in London. While some of the letters develop a romantic plot, many of them present the correspondents' feelings about being in North America, with descriptions of the province of Quebec. One of the characters declared that Quebec was lovely 'and the mode of amusements makes us taste those scenes in full perfection.' A subseries of letters offers a commentary on the French population of Quebec and advocates a British policy of assimilation. The novel probably had more influence on Canadian affairs in Britain than did a number of pamphlets published around the same time.

Frances returned to London in 1768, continuing her literary career, which included the libretti for several comic operas. Just before the American Revolution she and a female friend ran the Haymarket Opera House. She may have written at least one other novel about British official society in Montreal, *All's Right at Last; or, the History of Miss West*, published pseudonymously in 1774.

Frances Brooke was an important figure in Quebec on two counts. In the first place, she offered an example of the new independent woman, with a successful creative career. In the second place, she demonstrated how the British ruled an empire: by successfully recreating the agreeable élite society of home in the colonies.

had become connected with one another, by trade and by marriage. One soldier commented of the French residents of the region—the British called them the 'Interior French'—that 'they have been in these upper Countrys for these twelve, twenty, or thirty years, [and] have adopted the very principles and ideas of Indians, and differ little from them only a little in colour.' The return of British persons who had been taken prisoner by the Aboriginals would not be easy, since many had become thoroughly integrated into their adoptive tribes. The British did not trust these people, who often took Aboriginal names, and thus did not treat them with the same kindness that the people of Canada received. The British army had expected to be able to employ the sort of imperialistic policies that it thought proper to use with 'heathen savages'. The army did not understand the system by which the fur-trading country had long been governed. General Jeffrey Amherst, who was responsible for the west in the early 1760s, saw the region in the simple terms of British conquest and Native subjects. He sought to eliminate the whole mediation process that had governed the 'middle ground' under the French, including the gift-giving relationship. 'Purchasing the good behaviour, either of Indians or any others is what I do not understand,' he wrote. 'When men of what race soever behave ill, they must be punished but not bribed' (Gage 1772). As British fur trader George Croghan observed, 'The British and French Colonies since the first Settling America . . . have adopted the Indian Customs and manners by indulging them in Treaties and renewing friendships making them large Presents which I fear won't be so easey to break them of as the General may imagine' (quoted in White 1991: 258).

Further complicating matters for the British conquerors was the emergence of an insurgency among the Aboriginal population of the Great Lakes region. This began in the prophetic teachings of Native leaders like Neolin, but soon became a general war against the British when they tried to fill the policy vacuum between the conquest of Canada and its actual cession in 1763. Amherst had no compunctions about suggesting in response that the Aboriginal people be given blankets infected with smallpox. But the uprising quickly burnt itself out. The ostensible leader, the Ottawa chief Pontiac, was unable to unite the many factions, and Amherst's successor, Thomas Gage, decided to try to mend some fences. Gage also determined to take advantage of Pontiac, and offered to treat him as if he really were an Aboriginal leader. In 1765 Pontiac accepted George III as his father and formally made peace. He would die in 1769 in the streets of the French village of Cahokia, clubbed from behind. Some Aboriginal leaders fought on, including Charlot Kaské, a Shawnee leader whose father was German and whose wife was a British captive adopted by the Shawnees since childhood. Kaské insisted that the British would strip his people of their land:

> The English come there and say that the land is theirs and that the French have sold it to them. You know well our fathers have always told us that the land was ours, that we were free there, that the French came to settle there only to protect us and defend us as a good father protects and defends his children. (White 1991: 307)

Despite the Proclamation of 1763, the British army administrators on the spot were prepared to tolerate European settlement in the region, and the Algonquians knew it.

The British administration also attempted to resurrect the old alliance of the region between the Whites and Aboriginals, with the British in place of the French. This policy was limited by the failure of London to provide the money for presents. But its adoption meant that the British began to discourage their fur traders from moving into the lower Great Lakes. Instead, the British used forts to distribute trade goods to the Interior French, who continued to dominate the trade. British traders would have far more success in the Northwest, where trading networks had not yet been established.

THE FIRST AMERICAN CIVIL WAR

In early April 1775 British troops, attempting to raid clandestine colonial arms depots in Massachusetts, were fired upon by the Americans. A long-festering imperial political crisis turned into a shooting war. From the vantage point of the American leadership, they were involved in a 'revolution' to secure their rights against the arbitrary authority of the British Crown. From the vantage point of the British government, the Americans were engaged in a 'rebellion' against duly constituted authority. Whatever its label, for many of the inhabitants in British North America the event meant involvement in an extended civil war in which brother fought brother, friend opposed friend, and many were eventually pushed into exile. Indeed, the proportion of exiles from the new United States (relative to population) exceeded that from France after 1789, from Russia after 1917, and from Cuba after 1955. Instead of seeing the people of the northernmost colonies as impotent victims of the American Revolution taking place to the south, it makes far more sense to view them as participants (although often at a distance) in a great civil war that affected the whole transatlantic region of Britain's vast empire.

The Americans moved quickly in 1775 to organize an alternative government and raise an army, under the command of George Washington of Virginia. While that force was still in embryo, the Second Continental Congress authorized an invasion of Quebec as a move to give 'the coup de grace to the hellish junto' governing Great Britain (quoted in Stanley 1977: 27). Washington was somewhat more enthusiastic about this plan than he was about subsequent proposals to invade Nova Scotia. One army was ordered to proceed to Quebec by way of Lake Champlain and the Richelieu River. Another was authorized to travel across northern Maine and along the Chaudière River to the St Lawrence.

The sudden turn of events found the government of Quebec in a state of shock and confusion. Governor Carleton, only recently returned from London with the Quebec Act in his dispatch case, complained he had insufficient military force to withstand an invasion. A public *mandement* from Bishop Briand, ordering the population to ignore American propaganda under threat of denial of the sacraments, had little effect. The seigneurs appointed to raise a militia found it difficult to do so. Carleton's alliance with Quebec's traditional leaders proved useless, largely because he misunderstood the dynamics of the Old Regime. The Church never had much influence on habitant behaviour, and the seigneurs had never much to do with the militia. The British merchants of Quebec had never been cultivated by Carleton and proved singularly uncooperative. Not even the First Nations leapt into action on Britain's behalf; most of the Iroquois would remain neutral until they were forced to side with the British later in the war.

Fortunately for the British, the Americans were neither as well organized nor as lucky as Wolfe's expedition had been in 1758–9, and the Québécois were not as enthusiastic about 'liberation from tyranny' as the invaders had hoped (Hatch 1970: 60). General Richard Montgomery (1736–75), struggling to bring an invading army up the Lake Champlain route, wrote that 'the privates are all generals' and that those from different colonies did not get along together (quoted in Hatch 1970: 60). Benedict Arnold (1741–1801), bringing his army across what is now Maine under horrendous late autumn conditions, lost nearly half his troops in the process. On 11 November, Montgomery and his troops arrived near Montreal and pressed on to Quebec, although his soldiers were constantly deserting. At the same time, the habitants were hardly rushing to enlist in the American army. In Quebec, Colonel Allan Maclean (1725–84), who had earlier organized two battalions of disbanded Highland soldiers, had stiffened resistance. Montgomery joined Arnold at Pointe-aux-Trembles on 3 December. He quickly determined that he lacked the force and the supplies to besiege Quebec. Instead, he decided to storm the town. The assault on 31 December was a desperate move by the Americans, who were suffering from smallpox as well as problems of logistics and morale.

The garrison held. The result, wrote one British officer, was 'A glorious day for us, as compleat a little victory as ever was gained' (quoted in Stanley 1977: 27). General Montgomery's frozen body was found not far from the barricade against which he had led the charge. He was subsequently buried with military honours, with Guy Carleton, who had known him from earlier campaigns, as chief mourner. General Arnold took a ball through the left leg at the first battery, and over 300 Americans were taken prisoner. The American forces, now under Arnold's command, remained in military occupation of more than fifty parishes over the winter of 1775–6. Their desperate seizure of foodstuffs, sometimes paid for with worthless Continental currency, according to one American, cost the occupying army 'the affections of the people in general' (quoted in Dyer and Viljoen 1990: 49). A commission from the Continental Congress, headed by Benjamin Franklin, pronounced from Montreal, 'Till the arrival of money, it seems improper to propose the Federal union of this Province with the others' (quoted in Dyer and Viljoen 1990: 49). In May 1776 British reinforcements arrived at Quebec, and by mid-June the Americans had completely

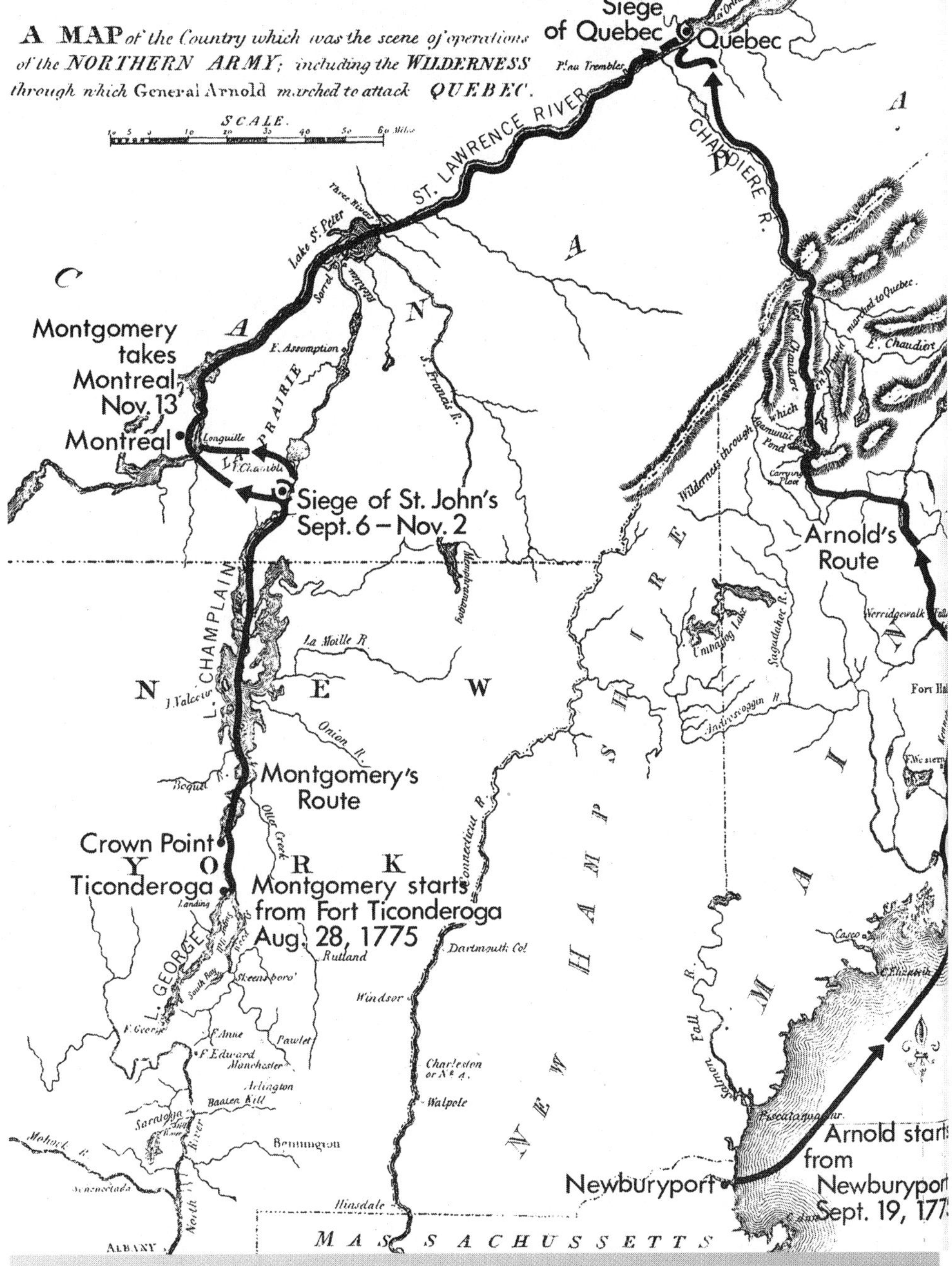

'A Map of the Country which was the scene of operations of the Northern Army; including the Wilderness through which General Arnold marched to attack Quebec'. Metropolitan Toronto Reference Library.

THE AMERICANS ATTACK QUEBEC, 1776

The following account of the assault on Quebec is from the diary of Captain Thomas Ainslie.

December 31st 1775:
It snow'd all night, it was dark, the wind was strong at N.E. About 4 o'clock in the Morning Capt: Malcom Fraser of the Royal Emigrants being on his rounds, saw many flashes of fire without hearing any reports; the sentries inform'd him that they had perceived them for some time on the heights of Abraham, the sentinels between Port Louis & Cape Diamond had seen fix'd lights like lamps in a street—these appearances being very uncommon & the night favouring the designs of the enemy, Capt: Fraser order'd the Guard and Pickets on the ramparts to stand to their arms. The drums beat, the bells rang the alarum, & in a few minutes the whole Garrison was under arms—even old men of seventy were forward to oppose the attackers.

Two Rockets sent by the enemy from the foot of Cape Diamond were immediately followed by a heavy & hot fire from a body of men posted behind a rising ground within eighty yards of the wall, at Cape Diamond, the flashes from their muskets made their heads visible—their bodies were cover'd: we briskly return'd the fire directed by theirs.

. . . Arnold's party was obliged to pass close under the pickets behind the Hotel Dieu & Montcalms house, where they were exposed to a dreadful fire of small arms which the Sailors pour'd down on them, as they passed. Arnold was here wounded in the leg & carried off:—his men proceeded, forced our guard, & got possession of our battery at Saut au Matelot.

Every power of Col: McLean was exerted on this occasion, he had his eye everywhere to prevent the progress of the attackers; his activity gave life to all who saw him—he follow'd the Gens: orders with military judgment. The Canadian militia shew'd no kind of backwardness,—a few of them stood to the last at a little breastwork near the battery at Saut au Matelot; when they were in the greatest danger of being surrounded, they retreated to the barrier.

The Flower of the rebel army fell into our hands. We have reason to think that many of Arnold's party were killed in advancing, & many killed & wounded in endeavouring to get back. Our fire from the Pickets gall'd them exceedingly.

SOURCE: Sheldon S. Cohen, ed., *Canada Preserved: The Journal of Captain Thomas Ainslie* (Toronto: Copp Clark, 1968), 33–7.

retreated, never to return. Quebec became an important centre for the British army, later serving as the staging point for a counterinvasion of the United States (equally unsuccessful) in 1778, led by General John Burgoyne.

The Americans had desperately wanted Quebec. George Washington wrote to Benedict Arnold early in 1776: 'To whomsoever it belongs, in their favour, probably will the balance turn. If it is ours, success, I think, will most certainly crown our virtuous struggles; if it is theirs, the contest, at least, will be doubtful, hazardous and bloody' (quoted in Dyer and Viljoen 1990: 49). The Rebel leaders did not feel the same way about Nova Scotia, partly because of its protection by the British navy, partly because there was not enough visible evidence of enthusiastic residents ready to support an invading army. Some American sympathizers like Jonathan Eddy (1726/7–1804) and John Allan (1747–1805)

AN AMERICAN PRIVATEERING RAID

Simeon Perkins (1734/5-1812) was born in Norwich, Connecticut, and migrated to Liverpool, Nova Scotia, in 1762. When the American Rebellion began, Perkins remained loyal to the Crown. As lieutenant-colonel of the Queen's County militia, he was responsible for the defence of Liverpool.

Thursday, April 9th, [1778]—Pleasent [*sic*] day. Wind N.W. Capt. Hopkins, and Capt. Gorham, Capt. Dean, B. Harrington, are about going to Halifax. Some of them get to the mouth of the Harbour and discover a privateer sloop at anchor back of the Island. . . . She continues at anchor till towards night she came into the Harbour, and the wind being small, rowed up into Herring Cove and sent a boat almost up to the Bar. I went on the Point to hail them but she tacked about and returned on board the sloop. Seeing a sloop full of men come into the Harbour it was truly alarming in our defenceless condition. . . . I had some men under arms, and kept a sentry on the Point, relieved every half hour. Soon after Mr Collins return I found that the sentry, Robert Bramham, was deserted. Had left his musket, and taken a skiff from shore, and no doubt remained but he was gone on board the privateer. This put us in some Consternation, as this Bramham . . . had heard all our Council. The sloop soon got under way, and stood athwart the Harbour, and finally went out of sight. I then ordered a guard of one sergeant and four privates dismissed the remainder of the People, and went home. In less than two hours I was informed that the Privateer was coming in again. I immediately alarmed the People from one end of the street to the other, and mustered about 15 under arms. The sloop came in with Drum and fife going, and whuzzaing, etc. They anchored a little above the Bar, and sent a boat on board Mr Gorham's schooner, and Mr Hopkins schr. I gave orders not to speak to them or fire upon, except they offered to come on shore to rob the stores, etc. If they made any such attempt to engage them. They searched the two schrs. mentioned, and returned on board the Privateer, and hove up their anchor, and went out after daylight. They had boarded a sloop in Herring Cove, Benjamin Harrington, master, and demanded a hhd. of Rum, which was landed as she was coming in, but finally took up with 40 gallons, which Harrington produced. . . .

It is now Fryday morning, April 10th,—The Privateer is gone out. Wind S.E. All is quiet. A small schr., Prince Doan, Master, arrives from Barrington. The Privateer put a man on board her in the night, but released her this morning. I am mutch fatigued, and sleep a sound nap. In the afternoon I hear the Privateer is gone into Portmatoon.

SOURCE: Harold A. Innis, ed., *The Diary of Simeon Perkins, 1766–1780*, vol. 1 (Toronto: Champlain Society, 1948): 139–41.

recruited a private army in Machias and Maugerville, consisting of eighty men, who marched overland from the Saint John River towards the British outpost at Fort Cumberland in late October and early November 1776. This 'invasion' was joined by a few residents from the area, but was quickly suppressed by British reinforcements, leaving those Nova Scotians who had supported the Americans either abjectly explaining away their actions or quickly departing for American lines, leaving behind their wives and families to be sworn at and 'often kicked when met in the street' (quoted in Clark 1988: 49). Civil wars were truly nasty ones.

The affair at Fort Cumberland was more typical of this war than was the earlier invasion of Quebec. Away from the armies, the opposing parties—Rebel and Loyalist—fought vicious little battles with one another for control of the uncommitted local population, often paying back old scores along the way. On the high seas, legalized pirates (called privateers) captured unarmed ships and attacked unprotected settlements along the coasts. Between 1775 and 1781 the privateers literally brought commerce to a halt in the Atlantic region, causing a number of food shortages, particularly in Newfoundland and the Island of Saint John. Both these colonies went for long periods without the arrival of a single vessel from overseas. On the borders between Loyalist and Rebel territory, guerrilla raiders (often including Native allies) attacked farms and villages. Since most of the population of the northernmost provinces lived on the coast or near an American border, everyone lived in constant fear of attack.

Given the insecurity of the times, it is hardly surprising that the radical preacher Henry Alline (1748–84) had considerable success in the Maritime region in introducing a movement of Christian pietism and rejuvenation often called The Great Awakening. Alline rejected secular affairs in favour of the self-government of the godly, emphasizing that Christ had commanded his followers 'to salute no man by the way' (quoted in Bumsted 1971: 93). He travelled the countryside, composing and singing hymns, regarding music both as a way to attract and hold an audience and as a useful vehicle on the road to salvation. At his death he left a legacy of evangelism and revivalism among his followers, who were called New Lights. In a period of confusion, Alline offered an alternative path to public involvement.

Not all residents of the northernmost colonies who did make a conscious choice selected the British side. One who did not was Moses Hazen (1733–1803), a native of Massachusetts, who had settled in the Richelieu Valley of Quebec after the Conquest. After a period of fence-sitting in 1775, Hazen committed himself to the United States and was appointed by the Continental Congress to command a regiment he was to raise in Canada. Hazen successfully recruited several hundred habitants, many of whom retreated with him from Canada in June 1776 and stayed together as a unit throughout most of the war. His men (and the Nova Scotia refugees) were ultimately compensated by the American Congress with land and financial assistance.

Like many other North Americans, most Native people attempted to remain out of the conflict. For the Iroquois, neutrality proved impossible. One of the Mohawk leaders, Joseph Brant (Thayendanegea, 1742–1807) became persuaded that only continued active alliance with the British could protect the interests of Native people by preserving ther land from the encroachment of European settlement. Brant was unable to convince the Iroquois councils, but he recruited a force of about 300 Aboriginal warriors and 100 Loyalist settlers, which was active in scouting and raiding operations, and in 1778 collaborated with Butler's Rangers (a Loyalist regiment) in guerrilla raids in the Mohawk Valley of New York. The Americans responded to such activity in 1779 with a major expedition into the land of the Iroquois, laying waste the country. The Iroquois, including Brant, were forced to retreat to Fort Niagara, where they became supplicants for British aid.

Farther west in the fur-trading country, Native peoples were better able to ignore the war. The western fur trade was relatively unaffected by the American Revolution. The western movement of the Montreal-based fur trade, now dominated by English-speaking traders, continued unabated. By the time of Lexington and Concord, they were pressing up the Saskatchewan River into the basin of the Churchhill River. In 1778 Peter Pond (1740–1807?) broke through into the richest fur trade country of the continent: the Athabasca region. The competi-

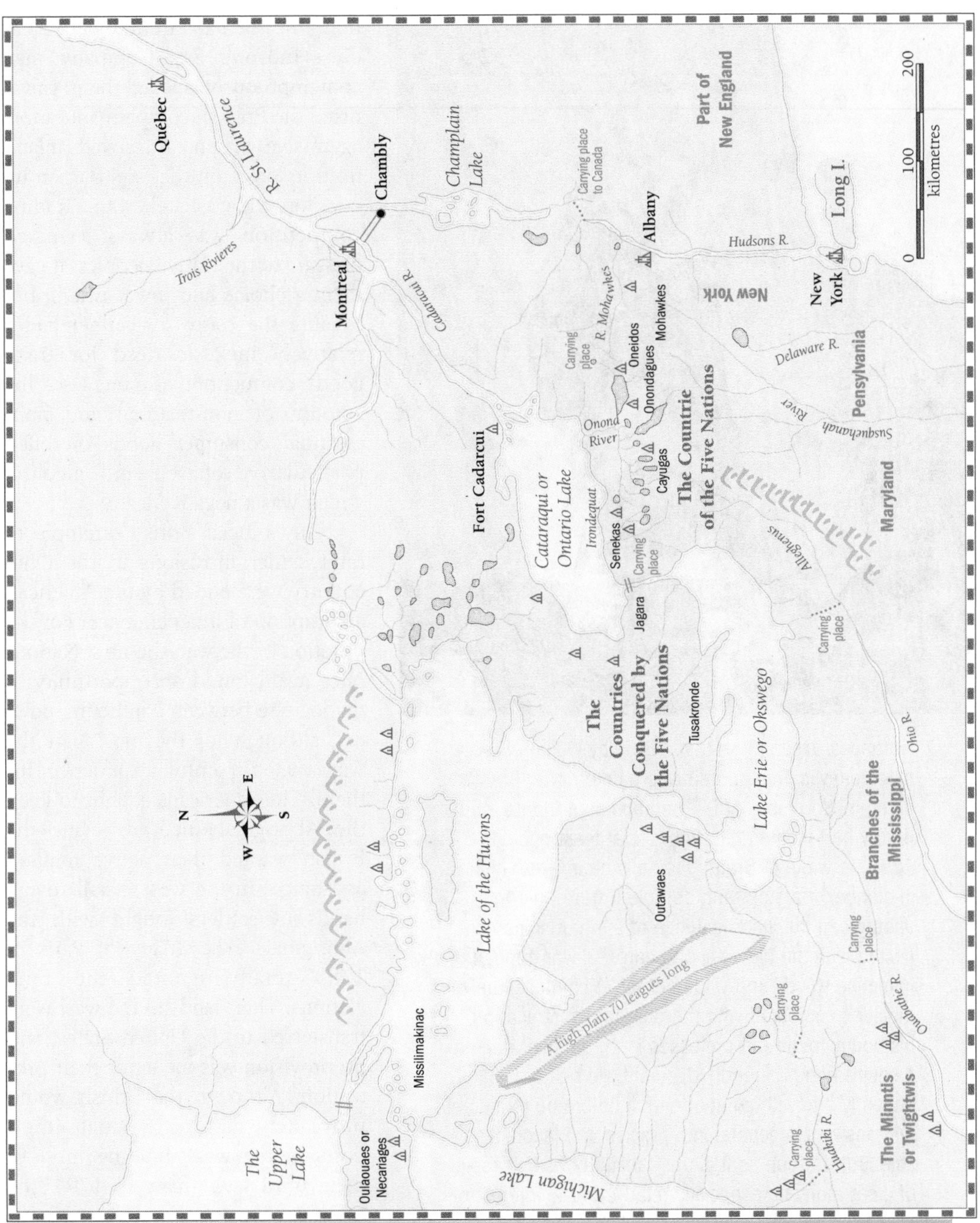

'The country of the Five Nations', based on the frontispiece to vol. II of *The History of the Five Indian Nations of Canada* (New York, 1902) by Cadwallader Colden (1688–1766), surveyor-general (1720) and lieutenant-governor (1761) of colonial New York.

'Portrait of Joseph Brant', c. 1807, by William Berczy, oil on canvas. This portrait was painted after Brant's death in November 1807, perhaps as a tribute, but Berczy had painted him from life at least once. In 1799 he wrote of Brant: '. . . he is near 6 feet high in stance, of a stout and durable texture able to undergo all the inconvenience of the hardships connected with the difficulties to carry on war through immense woods and wildernesses–His intellectual qualities compared with the phisical construction of his bodily frame–he professes in an eminent degree a sound and profound judgement. He hears patiently and with great attention before he replies and answers in general in a precise and laconic stile. But as soon as it is the question of some topic of great moment, especially relative to the interest of his nation he speaks with a peculiar dignity–his speech is exalted energy and endowed with all the charm of complete Retorick.' National Gallery of Canada, 5777. Purchased 1951.

tion, the 'Pedlars from Quebec', as one Hudson's Bay Company man contemptuously labelled them, galvanized the English company into more aggressive action. It moved inland from its posts on the Bay to open up ones on the Saskatchewan. Trading competition was always a mixed blessing to the Native peoples. It gave them a choice and lower prices, but because the Native consumer had a relatively inelastic need for trade goods, competition also increased the amount of non-material and non-essential consumer goods on offer, particularly tobacco and alcohol, which was a negative feature.

Any official British attempts to limit settler intrusions in the Ohio country were ended by the American assumption of independence. For the duration of the war, the First Nations once again found an opportunity to manoeuvre between conflicting powers, although for the most part the war was a painful experience for them. The Americans sought to keep the Aboriginals neutral, while the British wanted their active military assistance. In the west, small roving bands of settlers fought with the Aboriginals. The Treaty of Paris in 1783 totally ignored the First Nations. Their lands in the west were transferred to the United States, and no provision was made for their protection. Although the British would prove reluctant to evacuate their posts in the west, holding most of them until Jay's Treaty in 1794, the Aboriginals were now at the mercy of punitive American military expeditions and advancing settlement. Many of the more militant First Nations leaders (such as Tecumseh)

JOHN STUART TO THE SOCIETY FOR THE PROPAGATION OF THE GOSPEL, 1781

John Stuart (1740/1-1811) was a Pennsylvania-born clergyman of the Church of England, posted in 1771 to Fort Hunter in New York, where he ministered chiefly to a congregation of Mohawks.

Montreal, October 13th, 1781

Sir,

No doubt but the venerable Society is surprised that they have not heard from me during the four years past; yet I flatter myself the following Narrative of my Situation will sufficiently apologise for my Silence.

At the Commencement of the unhappy Contest betwixt Great Britain & her Colonies, I acquainted the Society of the firm Reliance I had on the Fidelity and Loyalty of my Congregation; which has justified my Opinion:—For the faithful Mohawks, rather than swerve from their Allegiance, chose rather to abandon their Dwellings & Property; and accordingly went in a Body to Genl. Burgoyne, & afterwards were obliged to take Shelter in Canada. While they remained at Fort Hunter I continued to officiate as usual, performing the public Service intire, even after the Declaration of Independence, notwithstanding by so doing I incurred the Penalty of High-Treason, by the new Laws.

As soon as my Protectors i.e. the Mohawks were fled, I was made a Prisoner, within the Space of four Days, or be put into close Confinement; and this only upon Suspicion that I was a loyal Subject of the King of Great Britain. Upon this, I was admitted to Parole, and confined to the Limits of the Town of Schenectady, in which Situation I remained for upwards of three years. My House has been frequently broken open by Mobs;—my Property plundered, and indeed every Kind of Indignity offered to my Person by the Lowest of the Populace;—At length my Farm and the Produce of it was formally taken from me in May last, as forfeited to the State, and as a last Resource I proposed to open a Latin School for the Support of my Family; But this Privilege was denied, on pretence that as a Prisoner of War, I was not intitled to exercise any lucrative Occupation in the State. I then applied for Permission to remove to Canada, which after much Difficulty & Expence I obtained. . . .

I cannot omit to mention that my Church was plundered by the Rebels, & the Pulpit Cloth taken away from the Pulpit—it was afterwards imployed as a Tavern, the Barrel of Rum placed in the Reading Desk,—the succeeding Season it was used as a Stable—And now serves as a Fort to protect a Set of as great Villains as ever disgraced Humanity. . . . My Papers being mislaid, I cannot send the Notitia parochialis at present altho the Number of Baptisms has been comparatively small, none applying to me except a few distressed Loyalists. I have not preached a Sermon since the Declaration of Independence. . . .

With great Respect, Sir,
your very huml. Servant
John Stuart

SOURCE: James J. Talman, ed., *Loyalist Narratives from Upper Canada* (Toronto: Champlain Society, 1946), 341–4.

Tecumseh

Tecumseh (the name means 'shooting star') was born around 1768 in present-day Ohio. He first distinguished himself at the Battle of Falling Timbers in 1794, and subsequently helped translate the prophetic teachings of his brother Tenskwatawa ('the Prophet') into a movement devoted to holding onto First Nations land. As he told one American 'Indian agent' in Ohio, 'The Great Spirit above has appointed this place for us, on which to light our fires, and here we will remain. As to boundaries, the Great Spirit above knows no boundaries, nor will his red people acknowledge any.'

Although the Americans blamed this resistance on the British, it is clear that the Natives had their own agenda. Tecumseh and his brother were active after 1808 in an effort to unite all the First Nations under one banner, but both 'the Prophet' and the movement lost credibility when they failed to halt the Americans and were badly beaten in battle by Governor William Henry Harrison at Vincennes late in 1811. When Tecumseh returned to his village from the Vincennes defeat, he found it devastated, and although he rebuilt, he was obviously determined to join the British in an effort of resistance against the Americans.

He led a war party into Upper Canada in June of 1812. At the head of 600 First Nations, Tecumseh helped cut General William Hull's supply lines and eagerly supported Isaac Brock's aggressive scheme to attack Detroit. Brock would later comment that he never met 'a more sagacious or a more gallant Warrior' than Tecumseh. In 1813, Tecumseh was at the head of an even larger party of First Nations that helped attack Fort Meigs. He stepped in to prevent his warriors from completing a slaughter of prisoners at this point and became known as a humane leader. Later in 1813, at the battle of Moraviantown, Tecumseh was killed. His body disappeared. The man himself quickly passed into myth and legend, one of the most popular figures of nineteenth-century Canadian verse and story, most of which attempted erroneously to make him out to be a Canadian patriot rather than a First Nations leader.

would support the British in the War of 1812, finding little joy in the eventual military stalemate.

Outside of the trans-Appalachian west, the British assumed after 1763 that in most eastern places the First Nations were a declining people who needed to be integrated into the European population as quickly as possible. Those Aboriginals who insisted on maintaining their old ways were quickly shoved to the margins of society and, at least in Newfoundland, driven to extinction. The situation was different in Upper Canada and in the vast northwestern regions of the continent. The core of British policy in this region since 1763 had consisted of maintaining an orderly frontier. In theory this involved a legal procedure for the orderly purchase of lands, the reservation to the Aboriginals of sufficient land on which to make a living, and, in Upper Canada, the full application of legal rights under the law wherever possible. This approach was taken partly to distinguish Canada symbolically from the United States. It involved the application of the common law to everybody, including the Aboriginals, both because the common law was a bulwark of Tory ideology and because it provided a framework for good government. The law-centred approach was meant to avoid unnecessary violence and warfare and to re-educate Aboriginal people into the new order. It worked better in theory than in practice. The law-centred approach assumed that the First Nations did not become a part of society until they were thoroughly integrated into Europe's hierarchies and authority structures.

The revolutionary period did see one curious development in Hudson Bay. A great French fleet had been beaten by the British off Jamaica in 1781, and three of the dispersed vessels ended up in the Bay, where they did significant damage to Hudson's Bay Company posts before returning to France. Far more serious than the French depredations, however, was the appearance in this region in 1781 and 1782 of a major epidemic of smallpox among the Native peoples, who lacked European immunities and suffered heavy mortalities.

On the Pacific coast, the American Revolution was even more remote than on Hudson Bay. From the European perspective, the major event was the appearance in March 1778 of Captain James Cook (1728–79) in Resolution Cove, Nootka Sound, off the western coast of Vancouver Island. Cook was on another quest for the Northwest Passage, spurred by new information that suggested one might exist. In Nootka Sound, he and his crews observed the Nuu-chah-nulth people. The visitors were much impressed with their trading acumen and especially their principal trading commodity: the sleek, thick fur pelt of the sea otter. Cook was killed on the return voyage through the Pacific to England. An impressive account of the voyage in 1784 included descriptions of the sea otter pelts. Soon there was a rush to cash in on their obvious value, for they offered something to trade in the otherwise difficult Chinese market.

'A Man of Nootka Sound', drawing by John Webber, c. 1778. The artist was a member of Captain Cook's expedition to the west coast of North America. NAC, C-013415.

While James Cook's crews were still on the high seas returning to England, the British lost the war of the American Revolution. Whether they could ever have won it remains an open question. Military suppression of movements of national liberation has never been a very successful strategy. The Americans managed to hold on, assisted by considerable British military stupidity and inefficiency, and they found allies in Europe. France joined the war in 1778. Unable to defeat the Americans with regular troops, the British turned increasingly to provincial Loyalist units to do the actual fighting, thus further enhancing the civil war aspect of the conflict. On the New York and Carolina frontiers, Loyalists and Rebels fought fierce battles in which no quarter was asked or given.

With the help of the French navy, the Americans finally succeeded in 1781 in trapping a large British army under Lord Cornwallis in Virginia. The surrender of Cornwallis was really the end of the line for the British. The ministry could no longer pretend that victory was just around the corner. It surrendered, allowing its critics to negotiate the peace. The final agreement worked out with the Americans, signed on 30 November 1782, gave the Rebels most of what they wanted. It recognized the independence of the United States, and allowed the new nation fishing rights in the Atlantic and gave to it the entire Ohio Valley. Equally important, the British negotiators failed to insist on any real security for either their Aboriginal allies or the Loyalists.

ACCOMMODATING THE LOYALISTS

From the beginning of the revolutionary conflict, some colonials had supported the British. As the war continued, many more were pressured by events into choosing sides and ended up with Great Britain. The struggle had been a bitter one, and officers of the provincial Loyalist regiments insisted that they be included in any Loyalist resettlement scheme, since 'The personal animosities that arose from civil dissension have been so heightened by the Blood that has been shed in the Contest, that the Parties can never be reconciled' (quoted in Wright 1955: 41–2). The British authorities in New York, where most of the Loyalists had gathered, accepted this argument. They were allowed to join the contingents of Loyalists that departed by ship for Nova Scotia in 1782 and 1783. Other Loyalist regiments already in Quebec joined British regulars in settling there at the close of the hostilities. The British were prepared to make extensive grants of land to these new arrivals, and to support them with supplies while they remade their lives. Perhaps 40,000 people received land grants and assistance as Loyalists, with about 30,000 settling in Nova Scotia (part of which would become the province of New Brunswick in 1784), 750 on the Island of Saint John, 1,000 on Cape Breton, and the remainder in Quebec—mainly in what would become Upper Canada.

The Loyalists were quite a disparate group of newcomers. Of the total of 40,000, well over 3,000 were Blacks who settled in Nova Scotia, and almost 2,000 were Aboriginals who settled in Upper Canada. Over half of the 40,000 were civilian refugees and their families; the remainder were officers and men either from former Loyalist regiments or from British regiments disbanded in America. A large proportion of both groups were neither American nor English in origin. Quite apart from the Blacks and the Aboriginals, a disproportionate number of the new settlers came from Scotland, Ireland, or various German principalities. Anglican clergyman Jacob Bailey (1731–1808) characterized his new neighbours in the Annapolis Valley of Nova Scotia as 'a collection of all nations, kindreds, complexions and tongues assembled from every quarter of the globe and till lately equally strangers to me and each other' (quoted in Bumsted 1986: 34).

Some unknown number of the Loyalist settlers were women. Most of the records of the Loyalists list only the males, who got land grants, served in the military, and received stores. But of the 3,225 individuals who presented claims to the British government for compensation of losses during the war, 468 (or about 14 per cent) were women. Only a small percentage of these women had worked outside the home, and most of them were obviously most familiar with their immediate households. Many other women and their families accompanied their husbands into their new surroundings. The loss of homes and cherished contents was probably more traumatic for Loyalist women than were property losses for men. Certainly the gradual re-creation of stability was much more difficult. Men could re-establish friendships and relationships in meeting places outside the home, but women usually could not. Women—who were often not consulted about the decision to support the king or to emigrate—

'Encampment of the Loyalists at Johnston, a New Settlement on the banks of the St Lawrence River in Canada', watercolour by James Peachey, 6 June 1784. An officer in the 60th Regiment, Peachey was deputy surveyor-general at the time, surveying lots for disbanded troops and Loyalist refugees. 'Johnston' was the future Cornwall, Ontario. NAC, C-2001.

had sacrificed a great deal for a principle. They had every right to be bitter about their fate.

From the first days of the war, the British military authorities in America had attempted to enlist some of the half-million slaves to fight against their masters, chiefly by promising them their freedom. Thousands of Blacks found their way to British lines by whatever means possible, drawn by promises only the British could possibly honour. Loyal Blacks were usually evacuated when the British withdrew from an American district. Most of them ended up in New York with the other Loyalists and the British army. More than 3,000 were transported to Nova Scotia. Although they were free, they were not well treated. Only 1,155 of the Black Loyalists in the province actually received land grants, which averaged less than 11 acres (4.5 ha) per grant. Blacks became part of the mobile population of the region, taking up whatever employment was available. They suffered many disabilities. In Nova Scotia they were not entitled to trial by jury. In New Brunswick they were not allowed to vote. Freed Blacks were treated more harshly in the courts than White people convicted of the same or similar crimes. An unknown number of Blacks, who were brought to British North America as slaves by Loyalist masters, continued in that status until the early years of the nineteenth century, when local courts ruled slavery out of existence in the colonies by extending English laws. Not surprisingly, nearly half of the Nova Scotia Black Loyalists would accept with alacrity in 1791 a chance to immigrate to the African colony of Sierra Leone.

Throughout the war the British had played on the First Nations' fear that the Americans intended to settle in large numbers on their ancestral lands, which had never been recognized as belonging to them. Some Natives had joined the British, and all were punished for this choice by both sides. The Iroquois were driven from their lands in New York state. The First Nations were abandoned by the British in the rush for extrication from an unpopular and expensive war. Britain transferred to the Americans sovereignty over land south of the Great Lakes and as far west as the Mississippi River, totally ignoring the fact that most of that land was claimed by its Aboriginal allies, who

TABLE 3.2
CANADA CENSUS OF 1784

POPULATION, SEXES, CONJUGAL CONDITION

Districts	Population	Sexes: Male	Sexes: Female	Married and Widowed: Male	Married and Widowed: Female	Married and Widowed: Total	Children & Unmarried: Male	Children & Unmarried: Female	Total
Québec	44,760	22,064	20,570	7,911	7,280	15,291	14,153	13,190	27,347
Trois-Rivières	12,618	5,806	5,850	2,080	2,247	4,327	3,786	3,603	7,389
Montréal	55,634	26,134	24,339	10,140	9,272	19,867	15,994	14,612	30,606
Total	113,012	54,064	50,759	20,131	19,354	39,485	33,933	31,405	65,338

APPORTIONMENT BY AGES &C.

Districts	Male	Female	Males: Under 15	Males: Over 15	Females: Under 14	Females: Over 14	Servants	Slaves	Infirm	Temporarily absent	Total
Québec	7,911	7,380	10,041	4,112	8,984	4,206	1,795	88	150	93	44,760
Trois-Rivières	2,080	2,247	2,874	912	2,726	877	676	4	118	104	12,618
Montréal	10,140	9,727	11,637	4,357	10,803	3,809	4,020	212	625	304	55,634
Total	20,131	19,354	24,552	9,381	22,513	8,892	6,491	304	893	501	113,012

BUILDINGS, LANDS, CROPS, AND CATTLE

Districts	Houses	Agriculture: Arpents under culture	Agriculture: Bushels sown	Cattle: Horses	Cattle: Oxen	Cattle: Young Cattle	Cattle: Cows	Cattle: Sheep	Cattle: Swine
Québec	7,157	628,240	126,318	9,166	8,456	12,439	16,344	41,252	22,202
Trois-Rivières	1,973	214,875	39,349	3,155	1,602	3,147	5,368	10,206	6,458
Montréal	9,794	726,703	217,682	17,825	12,036	16,620	22,579	33,238	41,805
Total	18,924	1,569,818	383,349	30,146	22,094	32,206	44,291	84,696	70,465

would insist they had never surrendered it to the Americans. The Native refugees were given a grant of land along the Grand River in what would become Upper Canada. Here a 1785 census showed 1,843 Native residents, including more than 400 Mohawks.

Few of the Loyalists stayed where they were initially settled. The town of Port Roseway (or Shelburne), on the southwest coast of the Nova Scotia peninsula, became notorious as a place where almost all of the 10,000 people who had been transported there left within ten years. The decade of the 1780s saw continual Loyalist relocation, sometimes within the colony of original settlement, sometimes in another colony of greater promise, and often eventually back to the United States after subsidies ran out and the initial American hostility had died down. Much of the land initially granted to the Loyalists had only limited agricultural potential, and everywhere homes had to be hewn out of a wilderness. The Loyalist settlement did reassert the principle of freehold tenure in all the colonies. The most stable newcomers were members of the office-holding élite, who tended to cluster in the provincial capitals.

If the Loyalists were a restless population physically, they were also a discontented and highly vocal one politically. Only a small fraction would receive formal compensation for property lost in the United States. All felt that they had suffered for their allegiance to the Crown, and that this made them deserving of both land and government assistance. Since many of the Loyalists were former American colonials, they were accustomed to certain levels of political participation. They also shared many political assumptions with their former neighbours. Loyalists may have supported George III, but they expected to be admitted to full participation in the political process for which they had fought. Quebec Loyalists thus complained bitterly about the absence of a representative assembly in the province. Nova Scotia and Island of Saint John Loyalists were unhappy about the domination of government by earlier inhabitants. Loyalists were also divided among themselves,

A LOYALIST PETITION OF 1786

The instant town of Saint John, New Brunswick, was inhabited by hundreds of Loyalists who had been farmers, tradespeople, and artisans in the American colonies. They were no friends of the pretensions of the Loyalist elite and the government of the province of Nova Scotia. Most of this petition survives in original manuscripts and various copies in the court files of the Public Archives of New Brunswick. One incomplete original manuscript contains 297 of the original signatures. The copy used by New Brunswick Loyalist historians, however, was badly done, and led these historians to believe mistakenly that the petitioners were only semi-literate. The original makes clear this was hardly the case.

To His Excellency Thomas Carleton [etc.]
The Humble Petition of the Subscribers Electors of the City and County of St. John—

Sir

We His Majestys dutiful and Affectionate Subjects, Electors of the City & County of St. John, After having suffered every Evil which could be inflicted upon Loyal Subjects by the cruel hand of usurpation, for an Adherence to the Person of our King and his Government, and a most oppressive Tyranny since our Arrival in this place, patiently have born those Hardships from a due Regard to the British Constitution under the firm Persuasion of being relieved from our Bondage upon Your Excellencies arrival, cannot now sit Silent under the complicated grievances we suffer & the fearful apprehension of what this infant Settlement must undergo, if such dangerous measures are persisted in, which threaten no less than a speedy dissolution of the same or a Revolution to us no less dreadful;

particularly the most daring, violent & alarming Invasion of our Liberties striking directly at the Vitals of our most excellent Constitution.

We have proved ourselves to be the most faithful and Loyal Subjects to the best of Governments by the Sacrifice of all that can be near & dear to us, & have joyfully Emigrated to an uninhabited Corner, in order to preserve that warm Attachment to our glorious Constitution & the best of Kings which penetrates & pervades our Hearts, & expected to have experienced its Blessings & His Fatherly Care in our New Situation, instead of which we are made the laughing Stock of our Neighbours, and the boasted Privileges of Britons are turned into Redicule, by their most bitter Enemies late their fellow Subjects.

For we have publicly seen British Subjects confined in Irons, Carried into a Garrison and there examined under the authority of a Military Guard, & Prosecutions still hanging over their heads, for supposed offences—One of our legal Representatives confined in a Sentry Box, at the discretion & by the order of a Private Soldier—the Military introduced & unnecessarily & unlawfully patrolling the streets, during an Election, to the Terror & Alarm of the peaceable inoffensive inhabitants—Taxes levied by the Incorporation Contrary to Law—These Taxes unaccounted for to the People—Crown Officers neglecting and refusing to discharge their Duty . . . .

We most positively affirm these proceedings to be unjust, Injurious to the Freedom of Election, manifest Violations of the Rights of the People, & Subversive of the first Privileges of the British Constitution, and . . . producing an extraordinary Situation, viz, the Representatives of the People in Opposition to the People. . . . And . . . . assure You that as we by no means think We are represented in the present House of Assembly, we can on no Account conceive ourselves bound by any Laws made by them so unconstitutionally composed.

Signed this 3d Day of March, 1786 [326 signatures follow]

SOURCE: D.G. Bell, *Early Loyalist Saint John: The Origin of New Brunswick Politics 1783–1786* (Fredericton: New Ireland Press, 1983), 150–4.

with the chief divisions being between the old élite, who sought to re-establish themselves as the natural leaders of society, and the more articulate among the rank and file, who sought a more democratic and open future. The coming of the Loyalists finally provided the cadre of articulate anglophone settlers that the British had hoped for in 1763. The new settlers not only spoke English, but did so with an American accent. Patrick Campbell, on the Grand River in Upper Canada in 1792, was answered by a man 'in a twang peculiar to the New Englanders': 'I viow niew you may depen I's just a-comin.' When asked how far, the response was, 'I viow niew I guess I do'no,—I guess niew I do'no—I sear niew I guess it is three miles' (Campbell 1837: 157). In most respects—except for loyalty to George III—the Loyalists were thoroughly Americanized.

REINVENTING BRITISH NORTH AMERICA

The loss of the American colonies, combined with pressure from the Loyalist leadership, gradually produced a political reorganization of British North America. It is at least arguable that since the Americans were the ones who had separated, what remained of British North America carried on the imperial continuity in the New World. Stage one came in 1784, after the Treaty of Paris of 1783, when a governor-generalship was established to administer Britain's remaining North American colonies. Sir Guy Carleton, now

Lord Dorchester, was the first appointee to this post in 1786. Britain also created two new provinces in 1784. New Brunswick was hived off from Nova Scotia and given a set of political officials chosen from the 'needy' Loyalist élite. The capital, Fredericton, was laid out in 1785, the year the first governor, Thomas Carleton (brother of Guy) arrived. Cape Breton was also given a separate government, administered by a lieutenant-governor and council without an assembly until it was reunited with Nova Scotia in 1820. No changes were made in the government of Newfoundland, which was still being administered by officials resident in St John's only during the summer months; there was still no assembly. There was now a court system operating on the island, however. Nor were alterations made immediately in Quebec, although Dorchester arrived in 1786 with a new chief justice in the person of William Smith (1728–93) of New York. Smith's political views were distinctly Anglo-American. He was known to have little sympathy for the Old Regime.

In 1787 a former Loyalist pamphleteer, the Reverend Charles Inglis (1734–1816), arrived in Halifax as the first North American bishop of the Church of England. Although most Loyalists were not Anglicans, the British government wished to establish a close connection between church and state. The new bishop was also initially responsible for Quebec. Inglis worked uphill for years to bring Anglicanism to a level worthy of state support. The Loyalists pressed hard for institutions of higher learning in the colonies. William Smith of Quebec advocated a secular university for his province, Inglis helped establish King's College in Windsor, and Benedict Arnold (who lived in Saint John as an unpopular Loyalist refugee from 1786–91) spearheaded a movement for a university in New Brunswick, which did not take root at that time.

In the western part of Quebec, demands for British institutions, particularly an assembly, produced the second stage of political reorganization: the Constitutional Act of 1791. This parliamentary legislation split Quebec into Upper and Lower Canada, giving the former a lieutenant-governor—the first one was John Graves Simcoe (1752–1806)—both an executive and a legislative council, and an assembly. In theory, Upper Canada's lieutenant-governor would be responsible to the governor of Quebec, and all the chief officials in the various colonies to the governor-general, but Britain's efforts to create an administrative hierarchy was not very effective. Each colony of British North America continued to turn directly to the British government as the source of real authority.

Despite self-denying legislation by Parliament in 1777 that no direct taxes would be collected in British North America without the consent of the governed in a legislative assembly, and however much eighteenth-century British statesmen were still committed to the principle of colonial assemblies, Great Britain was reluctant to universalize these institutions. French Canada got an assembly in 1791 less because Britain felt it was entitled to one than because the Loyalist settlers up-country insisted on having one, and symmetry between Upper and Lower Canada needed to be maintained. For the British, assemblies implied that colonies had come to full maturity, including the possession of a decent revenue to control. Cape Breton, because of its small size and remote location, would have to grow into an assembly; it never did. As for Newfoundland, Britain still hesitated to grant it full colonial status, partly because of its large population of Roman Catholics. The Loyalist period, however, saw the achievement of full political privileges for Roman Catholics in most of British North America, both through local legislative initiative and parliamentary fiat (for Quebec). Only on the Island of Saint John (which in 1786 passed laws permitting Catholics to own land but not to vote) and in New Brunswick until 1810 were Catholics still disenfranchised politically.

A less publicized development than the introduction of assemblies and the expansion of voting franchises was the elaboration of the legal system of the various colonies. This system was based chiefly upon English law and English models except in Quebec, where English criminal law was joined to most aspects of French civil law. The establishment of colonial courts and assemblies meant that new English statute law extended to British North America only where specifically authorized, but the colonial legal system took over earlier English statute law and the whole body of the common law, including its patriarchal treatment of women. The introduction of the law was necessary both to good government and especially to business, which would have been lost without the adjudication of the complex system of credit employed in commerce. While the law in British North America would develop its own characteristics over time, it was always closely linked to its English origins. Here was the origin of what Lord Macaulay would later describe for England as a system where 'the authority of law and security of property were found to be compatible with a liberty of discussion and individual action'.

The Loyalist migration was ended by 1786, when compensatory land grants and provisioning virtually ceased everywhere in British North America. In one decade the loyal provinces of British North America had received a substantial contingent of American settlers, well subsidized by the British government, that they had not previously been able to attract. So-called 'late Loyalists' would continue to come to Upper and Lower Canada, drawn by offers of land. The Atlantic region would never again experience a substantial American influx. For all colonies of British North America, immigration and settlement would long have crucial importance, but the post-Loyalist wave would have to be managed under quite different circumstances.

IMMIGRATION AND SETTLEMENT, 1790–1815

Between 1790 and 1815 immigration to British North America came from two major sources: the British Isles (mainly the Scottish Highlands and Ireland) and the United States (mainly upper New York state, Pennsylvania, and New England). The British newcomers settled everywhere, while the Americans were almost entirely confined to the Canadas. Most of the Scots were drawn to the Maritime region, where they had already established beachheads of settlement, but some went to Lower Canada and eastern Upper Canada to join Scottish communities there. The major movement from Britain occurred in a brief interlude of European peace between 1801 and 1803, chiefly to the northeast shore of Nova Scotia, to Cape Breton, and to Prince Edward Island. Prosperity in Newfoundland and New Brunswick during the period 1812–15 drew many Irish to these colonies. More Protestant than Catholic, many came from northern Ireland.

Some of the American arrivals were Quakers and Mennonites encouraged by offers of exemption from military service in Upper Canada, but they were soon joined by a large influx of settlers who took up readily available land from government or private entrepreneurs. Some of these newcomers were fleeing American policies they disliked, including the new Constitution of 1789 and the severe repression of Pennsylvania whisky distillers in the 1790s, but most were simply part of the North American moving frontier. Until 1798 the Upper Canadian government treated these arrivals as Loyalists. Between 1791 and 1812 the English-speaking population of Lower Canada (mainly American) tripled from 10,000 to 30,000 and represented 10 per cent of the province's population. The Americans were located mainly in the Ottawa Valley and the Eastern townships. In Upper Canada, by the time of the War of 1812, Americans made up as much as 80 per cent of a population estimated by one contemporary at 136,000. As tensions grew between Britain and the United States after 1807, the British began to be worried by the predominance of Americans in Upper Canada. In both Canadas, Americans tended to recreate their own local culture and institutions rather than insist

☐ 'Part of York the Capital of Upper Canada on the Bay of Toronto in Lake Ontario', 1804, by Elizabeth F. Hale. Looking east along Palace (now Front) Street, this view shows Cooper's Tavern (at left, facing what is now Jarvis Street) and the houses of Duncan Cameron (a merchant), William Warren Baldwin, and William Allan. In the distance are the government buildings and blockhouse (with flag). NAC, C-34334.

on political and legal reform of provincial political systems they regarded as oligarchical and repressive.

Another distinctive population emerged from obscurity in the Maritime region in this period. Despite the best efforts of the British to eliminate the Acadians in the 1750s, the campaign had not been completely effective. We do not understand very well the process by which the Acadians regrouped in the region, since most of the movement occurred outside record-keeping and beyond the reach of central authority. After the Treaty of Paris of 1763, British policy permitted Acadian resettlement, provided that oaths of allegiance were taken and that the population moved to designated places in small numbers. Acadians gradually returned the Maritime region to farm and fish, usually in remote districts far from existing settlement and often on marginal land. The governments of the region made no attempt to assist or accept them, but they were tolerated and left to create their own institutions.

Those institutions were dominated, as they always had been, by the nuclear family, kinship, and to a much lesser extent by the Church. The scattered Acadians had great difficulty in obtaining priests, especially French-language ones, from the Quebec Church, which claimed it had few priests to spare for missionary service. As a result, the Acadians became accustomed to a religion dominated by laymen and supplemented by the arrival of occasional missionaries. Many of the regulations of the Church, including those on marriage, were not enforced, and parochial organizations were slow to develop. Despite the problems, by 1803 a religious census showed nearly 4,000 Acadians in Nova Scotia, nearly 4,000 in New Brunswick, and nearly 700 in Prince Edward Island.

It was certainly the case that government and politics everywhere in British North America were, to say the least, cosy. The governments of the various provinces were dominated by a small cadre of well-paid office holders appointed chiefly in England, in collaboration with local élites represented on the councils. While serious political conflict between the elected assemblies and the provincial oligarchies that governed British North America was almost inevitable, it was slow to develop. The oligarchy associated the aspirations of the assemblies with the worst aspects of levelling republicanism—after 1789 the French Revolution succeeded the American as the chief example. Criticism of government was immediately rejected and critics were silenced by any means necessary, including violence.

In most provinces, early political opposition was sporadic and usually conducted within the ranks of the élite according to well-defined rules. Many of the early opponents of government—men like James Glenie (1750–1817) in New Brunswick, William Cottnam Tonge (1764–1832) in Nova Scotia, Robert Thorpe in Upper Canada (1764–1836), and William Carson (1770–1843) in Newfoundland—were outspoken political gadflies who received very little consistent support from their colleagues. Only in Prince Edward Island (which the Island of Saint John became in 1799) and Lower Canada did anything resembling political parties develop before the War of 1812.

Lower Canada started its separate legislative existence with politics divided along class lines. The 'French Party' consisted chiefly of Canadian seigneurs, supported by the clergy and a few English officials. They wanted all the French civil law restored and retained. The bulk of the French-Canadian population were not yet integrated into the political system. The opposition, mainly English merchants, wanted the introduction of English commercial law, radical constitutional changes, and the right of habeas corpus. Over the next few years, the ideas and controversies of the French Revolution gradually made their way to Canada, often assisted by deliberate propaganda and subversion from France via the United States. In 1796–7, the French government actually developed a plan for the invasion of Canada from Vermont, although it had little public support.

The English official élite in Lower Canada over-reacted to the French threat, exaggerating the colony's importance to France and the disloyalty (or potential disloyalty) of the Canadian people. The élite acted as though the colony was constantly faced with insurrection, and then engaged in repressive tactics. In 1794, the assembly, opposed by only a few Canadian members, passed an Alien Act that suspended habeas corpus not only in cases of treason but also in cases of sedition. The legislation was used to conduct a witch-hunt and jail many without recourse to bail.

As the French-Canadian population became more experienced at electoral politics—and their experience grew rapidly—they inevitably reacted to the suspicions and repressive tactics of the official élite. By 1796, the Canadians won a majority of seats in the assembly. Official Lower Canada saw this election as a victory for treason and the revolt of the Canadian lower orders. The new ethnic division was quickly made more permanent by the authorities' insistence on viewing the French Canadians as determined to turn the colony over to the French

LOUIS DULONGPRÉ

Louis Dulongpré (1759–1843) was born in Paris. He came to America with a French naval squadron during the American Revolutionary War, and drifted up to Canada by 1785. He made a great impression in Quebec, and ran a music and dancing school in Montreal from 1787 to 1792, adding a boarding school for young ladies in 1791. In 1789 he was associated with a number of local residents in the establishment of the Théâtre de Société in Montreal, and managed it briefly until the local curé opposed it. The clerical opposition apparently drove Dulongpré from the public world of the arts.

He decided to become a painter, and went to the United States to improve his technique. In 1794 he returned from Maryland to advertise his technical proficiency in 'Miniature and in Crayons, Pastels'. For the next few decades he was the most important painter in Montreal. Much of his work was in portraits, which were of course the most lucrative part of a painter's output. He is said to have painted more than 3,000 portraits over the 25 years between 1795 and 1820. He also found a market for historical and religious paintings in the Catholic Church, and he did other work for various churches ranging from gilding to architecture to interior decoration. He did the vault of the church of Notre-Dame in Montreal in 1809. In much of his religious art he used his family, especially his wife, as models, and he once joked that his wife 'had her portrait in all the churches'. The artist understood very well that public visibility and acquaintanceship with potential patrons was an important part of his marketing. He thus became a member of the Agriculture Society in Montreal, he served as a fireman, and he was captain in a militia battalion at the outbreak of the War of 1812. His unit allowed regular troops to leave their garrisons to repel enemy invasions, and as a major he participated in the battle of Plattsburgh in 1813. On retirement in 1828 from the militia, he was made a lieutenant-colonel. Dulongpré dabbled in mass art, opening a shop in 1812 for manufacturing oiled floor-cloths, but he was apparently unable to compete with European products.

In later years, Dulongpré and his wife invested heavily in a warehouse scheme for supplying small merchants (the Maison Canadienne de Commerce), apparently attempting to secure an annuity for their old age, but between the depression of 1836 and the rebellions of 1837, the company failed and left them practically destitute. Louis went to the States to live with his daughters around 1840 after the death of his wife—the couple had 13 children, four of whom grew to adulthood—but was soon back in Montreal. He died in the home of a friend. Dulongpré was the classic Canadian artist of his time, versatile, self-advertising, and commercially inept, constantly teetering on the edge of poverty.

sans-culottes. The ethnic division also ended any possibility of reform of the government created by the Constitutional Act of 1791. The Canadians continued to favour reform, while the former anglophone reformers now allied themselves with the English officials to form the 'English Party', which was devoted to preservation of the status quo. The French-Canadian

☐ Thomas Douglas, Earl of Selkirk. This painting was supposedly based on a portrait by the Scottish artist Henry Raeburn. The location of the original is unknown. NAC, C-1346.

reformers received little support from the Catholic Church, either. Virtually the only emigrants from France to Lower Canada during this period were clergymen, refugees from the anticlericalism of the Revolution who were hardly likely to preach revolution to their flocks.

By the end of the eighteenth century, the ethnic division was probably irreparable and it only got more entrenched in the years before the War of 1812. The English party in the assembly and the 'Château Clique', the anglophone oligarchy that ran the government, continued to fear an imminent French invasion, one that would be warmly supported by the Canadiens. Such fears were encouraged by the deterioration of relations between the United States and Great Britain and by the increased pressure of the 'Parti Canadien' (as it came to be called) for a constitutional change that the English élite was certain represented the start of rebellion. Partisanship reached a new height during the 1810 elections, in which Governor Lieutenant-General Sir James Henry Craig seized newspaper printing presses and jailed both printers and leaders of the Parti Canadien, thus producing a symbol of British tyranny. The French Canadians had quickly adopted the tactics of a popular party in a British-style legislature. But they had been forced to do more. They had also turned their popular party into one committed to the preservation of French-Canadian values and even the perpetuation of French-Canadian nationalism.

The period before 1815 also saw the beginnings of the settlement of the west. In 1811 the Earl of Selkirk (1772–1820) received from the Hudson's Bay Company a grant of 116,000 sq. mi. (300,417 km^2) covering parts of present-day Manitoba, North Dakota, and Minnesota. In return for this grant Selkirk was to supply the HBC with employees to aid it in its bitter struggle with the North West Company for control of the western fur trade. Selkirk hoped to be able to keep the colony he intended to establish at the forks of the Red and Assiniboine rivers separate from the fur trade rivalry, but this would prove impossible. Miles Macdonell (c. 1767–1828) was named the first governor of Assiniboia, as the territory was called in June 1811. On 26 July he and the first contingent of colonists left for Hudson Bay, arriving two months later at York Factory. After wintering on the Nelson River until the breakup of ice (at the end of June), they did not arrive at the junction of the Red and Assiniboine rivers until 30 August 1812. The colony soon ran afoul of the North West Company, which used the Red River region as the source of pemmican for provisioning its traders on the vast inland canoe routes it had established.

THE WAR OF 1812

After some years of worsening relations, the Americans declared war on Great Britain on 18 June 1812. There were several factors behind the war. One was Britain's high–handedness in searching American ships on the high seas during the Napoleonic blockade, removing British subjects aboard them and recruiting them into her navy. Another was the British failure to abandon the Ohio Valley, where military posts continued to monitor the fur trade. Most of all, the Americans coveted Canada, which they proceeded again to invade in 1812 and 1813. A succession of invading armies were thrust back through the major entry points: the Detroit–Windsor corridor, the Niagara peninsula, and Lake Champlain. A relatively small number of British regulars, assisted by colonial militia and Native peoples, held the province against American armies, which were neither well trained nor well led. A number of Canadian heroes emerged from the war, their reputations to be further mythologized after it was over: General Isaac Brock, Tecumseh, and Laura Secord.

The appearance of invading American armies posed a crisis of allegiance for many of the American settlers in Upper Canada. Most remained silently on their farms, although some supported their countrymen and retreated across the border with them. A handful of Americans were arrested and tried for treason at Ancaster in 1814. Before the war had ended, York (Toronto)

☐ 'The Battle of Queenston. October 18th, 1813 [*sic*]', by Major James B. Dennis, coloured lithograph, c. 1866, after the original print published in 1836 by J.W. Laird & Co. in London. The battle of Queenston Heights actually took place on 13 October 1812. NAC, C-276.

was burnt, the American capital at Washington was sacked in retaliation, and Fort Michilimackinac (on western Lake Huron) was captured and held by Canadian voyageurs. The final struggle for naval control of the Great Lakes took place in 1814; the Americans appeared to be winning. The last battle of the war, at New Orleans, was actually fought after a peace of stalemate had been signed at Ghent on 24 December 1814.

The Americans treated the War of 1812 as a second War of Independence, a necessary struggle to complete the process of separation from the mother country. National survival was taken as victory. From the British perspective, the war had been little more than a sideshow to the major struggle, which was against Napoleon in Europe. As for British North America, in the lower provinces (as the Maritime region was coming to be called), the War of 1812 mainly represented an opportunity to serve as a conduit for illicit trade between Britain and the United States; the region was never actively involved in the military struggle. Only in the Canadas did the War of 1812 have any great impact. In Lower Canada, the support the French Canadians gave the British demonstrated their loyalty. In Upper Canada, the war provided a demarcation point between the loyal and the disloyal, the latter composed almost entirely of Americans. During and after the fighting, the Canadian oligarchies (especially in Upper Canada) were able to appropriate Loyalism as their monopoly and use it against their American opponents. The great struggle between British and American allegiance was played out internally in Upper Canada between 1812 and 1815, and the British won. After 1815 the overt American influence on Upper Canada would gradually decline.

Despite the return to the status quo *ante bellum*, the War of 1812 had considerable impact upon British North America in several areas. One was in the domestic politics of Upper Canada. To earlier notions of loyalty to the British Crown inherited from the period of the American Revolution was added a new ideological stream born of the War of 1812. The Upper Canadian Tory elite became convinced that the province had been in great danger, as much from the internal menace of American residents as from the

A COMMON SOLDIER FIGHTS IN THE WAR OF 1812

Shadrach Byfield was born near Bradford, England, in 1789, and joined the British army in 1807. By 1812 he was serving in Canada as a private in the 41st Foot. In the following account, written years later, he describes a battle at Brown's Town in January 1813. The account was originally published in 1828.

Orders were given to cross the river St Lawrence. We landed at a place called Brown's Town, and then proceeded for the river Reasin, with about 500 of our troops and a few Indians. We had to contend with about 1400 of the enemy, under the command of General Winchester. When within about two miles of the enemy, we encamped for part of the night; early in the morning, we proceeded to meet them, and under cover of a wood, we approached near to them, unperceived; we formed the line, and had a view of them as they surrounded their fires. While we were forming, the Indians marched so as to get round their right flank. We had six field pieces, which led on in front of the line. We were then discovered by one of their sentries, who challenged and discharged his piece, which killed one of our grenadiers; we then gave three cheers, and the Indians followed with a war whoop; the fight then commenced very warmly. It was on the 22nd of January, 1813. . . . As the day approached, we discovered that what had been supposed to have been the enemy's line was a made fence behind which they were sheltered, with holes in it through which they fired at us. About this time my comrade on my left hand was killed. It being now light, I saw a man come from the fence when I said to my comrade, 'There is a man, I'll have a shot at him.' Just as I said these words and pulled my trigger, I received a ball under my left ear and fell immediately; in falling I cut my comrade's leg with my bayonet. He exclaimed, 'Byfield is dead.' To which I replied, 'I believe I be,' and I thought to myself, is this death, or how do men die? As soon as I had recovered so as to raise my head from the ground, I crept away upon my hands and knees and saw a sergeant in the rear, who said, 'Byfield, shall I take you to the doctor?' I said, 'Never mind me, go and help the men.' I got to the place where the doctor was, who, when it came to my turn to be dressed, put a plaister to my neck and ordered me to go to a barn which was appointed for the reception of the wounded. As I was going, the blood flowed so freely as to force off the plaister. I now saw a man between the woods, and asked him what he did there. He told me he was wounded in the leg. I observed to him that if I had not been wounded worse than he was, I should be back, helping the men. I then asked him to give me a pocket handkerchief to tie round my neck, to stop the blood. He replied, 'I have not got one.' I said, 'If I do not get something, I shall bleed to death.' He immediately tore off the tail of his shirt, and wound it round my neck. I then got to the barn, and laid down with my fellow sufferers. I had not been there long before the doctor came and said, 'My dear fellows, you that can had better get away, for our men are terribly cut up, and I fear we shall be all taken.' He rode away, but soon returned saying, 'My dear fellows, we have taken all of them prisoners.' At which news I exclaimed (being quite overjoyed), 'I don't mind about my wound, since that is the case.' While in the barn, I was much affected by seeing and hearing a lad, about 11 or 12 years of age, who was wounded in one of his knees. The little fellow's cries from the pain of his wound; his crying after his dear mother; and saying he should die, were so affecting that it was not soon forgotten by me. He was a midshipman, belonging to one of the gunboats; I think his name was Dickenson.

SOURCE: *Recollections of the War of 1812: Three Eyewitnesses' Accounts* (Toronto: Baxter Publishing, 1964): 15–18.

external one of American troops. That elite carried over into the postwar period its beliefs in the necessity of the simultaneous suppression of political opposition and the maintenance of social harmony, by force if necessary. These twin beliefs served as the basis for Upper Canadian Toryism for several generations (Mills 1988).

Another important effect of the War of 1812 was upon the Aboriginal people, many of whom had supported the British. It was never quite clear how a British victory would contribute to the cause of Aboriginal unity or the dream of a First Nations state, but it was certainly plain that the maintenance of the status quo was—from the Aboriginal perspective—a victory for the American expansionists. The United States had used the war to solidify its control of the 'Middle Ground' in the Ohio Valley and to push the Aboriginals farther towards the margins. One of the articles of the Treaty of Ghent stipulated that both the United States and Great Britain would endeavour not only to end hostilities with the Native peoples, but 'forthwith to restore to such tribes or nations respectively all possessions, right and privileges which they may have enjoyed or been entitled to in one thousand eight hundred and eleven, previous to such hostilities' (quoted in Allen 1992: 169). This clause remained a dead letter. As it became clear that the British sought détente with the Americans in the wake of the war, many of the tribes near the border sullenly came to terms with the American government after the Treaty of Ghent, while others retreated farther west to continue a resistance they understood full well was doomed.

In the northwest, a little war between the Hudson's Bay Company and the North West Company ran its own course, occasionally touching on the larger Anglo–American conflict. In 1813, for example, Lord Selkirk very nearly succeeded in persuading the British government to finance the recruiting, equipping, and transporting to the Red River of a Highland regiment to be commanded by himself. The purpose of the unit was to protect the west from an American take-over. The scheme won ministerial approval, but was vetoed at the last moment by the commander-in-chief, the Duke of York, not because it would have crushed the North West Company but because it involved Highlanders. In 1816 Selkirk recruited as soldier/settlers a number of disbanded troops from several Swiss regiments that had fought for the British in North America, leading them to the Red River. As in the War of 1812, the western fur trade war was fought to an expensive draw. The two rival companies would settle matters by merging in 1821, shortly after Selkirk's death.

CONCLUSION

By a diplomatic convention in 1818, Great Britain and the United States would agree to declare the Great Lakes an unarmed zone and the 49th parallel to be the Anglo–American border from the Lake of the Woods to the Rocky Mountains. British policy after the war would consistently be to seek entente rather than trouble with the Americans, so in a sense the Americans had won. The final defeat of Napoleon at Waterloo in 1815, rather than the Treaty of Ghent, marked the major watershed for Britain and her North American colonies, however. After 1815 the shift from an overheated war economy to a peacetime one in the British Isles produced substantial unemployment. Even after the postwar depression had ended, a new round of industrialization and agricultural rationalization left many without work in their traditional occupations and places of residence. The result was a new era of emigration and immigration. Between 1815 and 1860 more than a million Britons would leave their homes and come to British North America. In the process they would help bring the colonies into maturity.

HOW HISTORY HAS CHANGED

LOYALIST LEGENDS

The Loyalists are one of the few subjects that are as important in American as in Canadian history. For the Americans, the Loyalists are part of the opposition in the American Revolution, and American historians have always lost interest in them in the period after the States achieved independence in 1783. Canadian historians become interested in the Loyalists as they leave the United States. There are no clear definitions of what constitutes a Loyalist, but the traditional assumption has always been that Loyalists have to be American refugees. This poses several problems. One is what to do with those resident in the northern colonies (Upper and lower Canada, etc.) who remained loyal. Another is to determine when American refugees ceased to be Loyalists and became merely immigrants. Research and writing about Canadian Loyalists has passed through several stages over the centuries.

In the first stage, which began at the time of the American Revolution and continued until well into the twentieth century, the Loyalists were viewed as the founders of Anglo Canada and given a special hagiographic cachet. The high point of Loyalist enthusiasm probably occurred in the 1870s and early 1880s, when the various centennials of the larger Loyalist migrations and settlements were celebrated. The key work was Egerton Ryerson's *The Loyalists of America and Their Times*, published in 1880. Loyalists naturally appeared in a favourable light in the dominant imperial and WASPish ideologies of the time.

In the second stage, which began about the middle of the twentieth century, Canadian historians reconsidered the questions of both the composition of the Loyalists and their importance in Canadian development. The aim was to recover a reasonably accurate picture of who the Loyalists actually were by freeing them from the legends and hagiography of the nineteenth century. The pioneer work was Esther Clark Wright's *The Loyalists of New Brunswick*, which in 1955 relied on land settlement records to reconstruct the story of the Loyalists in the province. A series of works since have demonstrated that the Loyalists were an interesting if not completely representative cross-section of colonial American society. They included several racial minorities (Blacks, Aboriginals), a number of ethnic groups, and a substantial minority of women. Many of the Loyalist settlers in British North America were disbanded soldiers rather than civilian refugees. Not all Loyalists were political conservatives. The multi-racial and multi-ethnic composition of the Loyalists was well suited for Canadians of the last decades of the twentieth century, who were busy establishing a multi-ethnic society in the nation. One unresolved question of Loyalist composition remained, and that was the extent to which the Loyalists were actually Americans, who brought American culture and American assumptions to Canada.

A third stage of Loyalist historiography began in the early 1970s. Instead of seeking to uncover the 'real Loyalists', it deliberately set out to explore and understand the Loyalist myths and legends that have developed in Canada, on the grounds that what people thought the Loyalists were was probably as important as their actual composition. The net result has been studies that examine the Loyalist celebrations in the 1870s, the merger of Loyalist legend into imperialist ideology, the Loyalist literary tradition, and the use of Loyalism by politicians, especially in the nineteenth century. This sort of analysis increasingly has taken on post-modernist overtones.

SHORT BIBLIOGRAPHY

Brown, Wallace and Hereward Senior. *Victorious in Defeat: The Loyalists in Canada*. Toronto, 1984. Somewhat dated, but still the best survey of the Loyalists.

Bumsted, J.M. *The Peoples' Clearance: Highland Emigration to British North America 1770–1815*. Edinburgh and Winnipeg, 1982. A revisionist work which argues that the early Scots came to British North America of their own volition.

Clarke, Ernest. *The Siege of Fort Cumberland: An Episode in the American Revolution*. Montreal and Kingston, 1996. A recent study that emphasizes that being loyal in revolutionary Nova Scotia was no easy matter.

Dowd, Gregory. *A Spirited Resistance: The North American Indian Struggle for Unity 1745–1815*. Baltimore and London, 1992. A book focusing on the conflicts in the Ohio country from the

First Nations perspective.

Greenwood, F. Murray. *Legacies of Fear: Law and Politics in the Era of the French Revolution*. Toronto, 1993. A work making the point that British officialdom and its anglophone allies in Lower Canada helped create the province's ethnic division through their paranoid politics.

Greer, Allan. *Peasant, Lord and Merchant: Rural Society in Three Quebec Parishes 1740–1840*. Toronto, 1985. A detailed localized study of rural French Canada.

Knowles, Norman. *Inventing the Loyalists: The Ontario Loyalist Experience and the Creation of Usable Pasts*. Toronto, 1997. A postmodern work more interested in Loyalist mythology than Loyalist actuality.

Lawson, Philip. *The Imperial Challenge: Quebec and Britain in the Age of the American Revolution*. Kingston and Montreal, 1989. A well-researched study of Quebec in the British Empire.

Neatby, Hilda. *Quebec: The Revolutionary Age 1760–91*. Toronto, 1966. Old but still the standard study.

Potter-MacKinnon, Janice. *While the Women Only Wept: Loyalist Refugee Women*. Montreal and Kingston, 1993. A pioneer work focusing on Loyalist women in Canada.

Sheppard, George. *Plunder, Profit and Paroles: A Social History of the War of 1812 in Upper Canada*. Montreal and Kingston, 1994. A revisionist study concentrating on the internal struggle in Upper Canada during the War of 1812.

Walker, James St G. *The Black Loyalists: The Search for a Promised Land in Nova Scotia and Sierra Leone, 1778–1870*. Halifax, 1976. The pioneering study of the Black Loyalists and their fate.

STUDY QUESTIONS

1. How did the Proclamation of 1763 respond to the problems of the British in North America at the time? Why did it fail to avert the American Revolution?
2. What was the political effect of the American invasions of Canada in 1775–6?
3. Who were the Loyalists?
4. Were the Loyalists the 'founders' of English-speaking Canada? Explain your answer.
5. What can you deduce about Canadian society in 1784 from the census data in Table 3.2? How does the colony compare with Nova Scotia in 1767 (Table 3.1)?
6. Identify three reasons to explain why the War of 1812 was so crucial to British North America.
7. Define the term 'oligarchy'. Explain how this concept operated in British North America, especially in Lower Canada, during this period.

CHAPTER FOUR

Relying on Resources, 1815–1840

Not until after the end of the War of 1812 did the various provinces of British North America really begin to develop their economies. Not surprisingly, those economies were based almost exclusively on exploitation of the rich natural resource base of the country, with a rising merchant group providing commercial links to the outside world. In this period, the resource economy relied heavily on transatlantic (chiefly British) markets and took full advantage of imperial trade advantages whenever they could be found. Overseas trade to the Caribbean also expanded. While there was some trade with the United States, few in British North America concentrated on the American market. The economies of the United States and British North America were still too similar in their reliance on primary resources to develop much interdependence. The society that took shape within the resource economy depended heavily on immigration from the British Isles to fuel its growth. Like the economy, it had a fairly simple structure, dominated by a self-conscious élite, which was challenged politically towards the end of the period. In cultural terms, French Canada continued to survive and even flourished. In many of the English-speaking provinces, there was a subtle but significant movement away from a highly derivative Americanized culture (chiefly attributable to the Loyalists) to a more hybrid culture that consciously looked to Great Britain for its priorities.

The Resource Economy

British North America began the postwar period of peace after 1815 with an extremely limited economy, heavily dependent upon British financial aid. By the 1840s it could boast a very active, even vibrant, commercial economy based on its rich inheritance of natural resources and a growing transatlantic carrying trade. The economic growth worked together with the appearance of new immigrants who flocked into its seaports and made their way onto its wilderness lands. Economic development was always complex, never straightforward. In most regions of European settlement it was anchored from the outset by natural resources. Fish, furs, timber, and grain—along with their ancillary industries—represented well over 90 per cent of all economic activity in British North America during this period.

Natural resources required a market, and before the 1840s Britain's colonies found the market chiefly in the United Kingdom and within the British empire, where trade policies tended to remain favourable to colonial raw materials. In the 1840s, when Britain shifted to a policy of international free trade, British North America had significant adjustments to make to fit into the new economic and commercial patterns. But for infant colonies rapidly expanding in population, British preferential treatment for colonial raw materials constituted a major boost. The mother country provided not only the market but also much of the capital with which British North

TIMELINE

1816
Métis and Selkirk settlers clash at Seven Oaks.

1817
Bank of Montreal founded.

1818
Britain agrees to allow France to carry on a dry fishery on Newfoundland's west coast. Britain and the United States agree in principle to extend their boundary across the 49th parallel from Lake of the Woods to the Rocky Mountains. Dalhousie University is founded in Halifax.

1820
Cape Breton is annexed to Nova Scotia.

1821
Hudson's Bay Company and the North West Company merge as the Hudson's Bay Company. Bank of Canada is chartered. Contract is let for the first Lachine Canal.

1824
Founding of Canada Company.

1825
Lachine Canal completed.

1826
Canada Company is chartered and purchases most of the Crown reserves and half of the clergy reserves of Upper Canada. Rideau Canal is begun.

1827
British Parliament rejects major government resettlement scheme for Canada brought forward by Robert John Wilmot-Horton. Hudson's Bay Company establishes Fort Langley on the Fraser River.

1829
First Welland Canal is opened. King's College is founded in Toronto.

1832
John Richardson publishes *Wacousta*. Newfoundland establishes its first assembly.

1833
Slavery is abolished by the British Parliament in the British Empire. First crossing of the Atlantic by a steamship (the *Royal William*). Cholera epidemic in Lower Canada.

1834
Village of York is incorporated as Toronto. The Rideau Canal is completed. Assembly of Lower Canada passes the Ninety-two Resolutions.

1835
The Selkirk family's interests in Red River are sold to the Hudson's Bay Company and the General Quarterly Court of Assiniboia is established.

1836
T.C. Haliburton publishes *The Clockmaker* as a book. New Brunswick legislature gains control of Crown lands in the province. The first railway in Canada is completed, running 16 miles (26 km) from La Prairie to St John's, Quebec.

1837
Rebellions erupt in Upper and Lower Canada.

1838
Lord Durham is appointed governor-general to investigate colonial grievances. A second uprising in Lower Canada is brutally suppressed.

1839
Durham submits his report on British North America. The Hudson's Bay Company establishes the office of Recorder of Rupert's Land.

Americans developed their resource base. British capital was never very adventurous. It preferred known industries and may well have constricted colonial diversification. But for a people desperately short of capital, no real alternative to British investment seemed possible. The Americans were

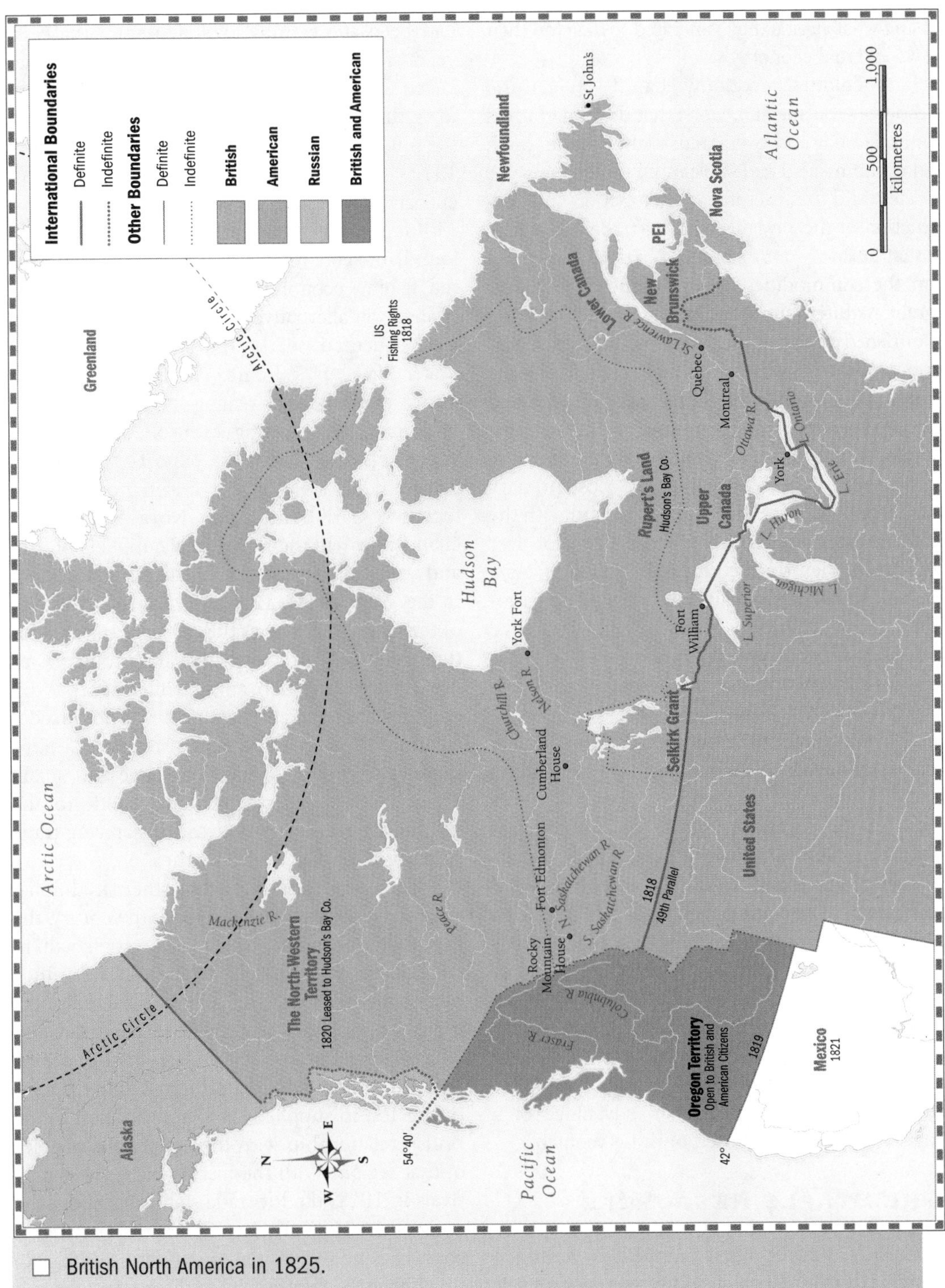

International Boundaries
Definite
Indefinite
Other Boundaries
Definite
Indefinite
British
American
Russian
British and American
Greenland
Newfoundland
St John's
Arctic Ocean
Arctic Circle
US Fishing Rights 1818
Lower Canada
New Brunswick
PEI
Nova Scotia
Atlantic Ocean
0
500
1,000
kilometres
St Lawrence R.
Quebec
Montreal
Ottawa R.
L. Ontario
York
L. Erie
Upper Canada
L. Huron
L. Michigan
L. Superior
Rupert's Land
Hudson's Bay Co.
Hudson Bay
York Fort
Fort William
Selkirk Grant
Churchill R.
Nelson R.
Cumberland House
Fort Edmonton
N. Saskatchewan R.
S. Saskatchewan R.
Rocky Mountain House
Peace R.
Mackenzie R.
The North-Western Territory
1820 Leased to Hudson's Bay Co.
1818
49th Parallel
United States
Columbia R.
Fraser R.
Oregon Territory
Open to British and American Citizens
1819
Mexico
1821
Alaska
Pacific Ocean
54°40′
42°
N
E
S
W

British North America in 1825.

using what capital they generated to develop their own internal economy.

A colonial economy based on natural resources was inevitably one that depended upon international and even transatlantic trade. Such an economy also had substantial implications for society and its structure. The extraction and production of the raw materials of trade was a seasonal business, for example. Rhythms depended on the commodities being produced. Fish and grain required summer labour, while timbering flourished in the winter months. Moreover, initial production was in the hands of small-scale commodity producers. These people exploited those working for them and were in turn exploited by the merchants who handled the commercial system of marketing. Most primary resource producers had little connection with the international market. They had no control over the prices they received for their products. As a result, they tended to attempt to maximize production by ruthlessly exploiting the resource regardless of economic conditions.

As a small capitalist, the typical primary producer—whether boat owner, farmer, or lumberer—identified with the commercial system rather than with his labour force, thus impeding the development of any working-class consciousness or the formation of an articulated class structure. Merchants had to be successful entrepreneurs, but found it difficult to move beyond their immediate commercial horizons. They were prepared to invest in processing raw materials within their own sphere of interest, but not outside it. The result was a highly exploitative and unadventurous economy, with a fluid and fuzzy social structure. It was an economy that could celebrate the values of an independent yeomanry at the same time that it took advantage of a labour force not composed of those yeomen.

THE STAPLE RESOURCES

The fishery was the oldest and most rewarding of British North America's resource commodities. It had been successfully exploited since the early years of the sixteenth century. Traditionally associated with Newfoundland, it continued to dominate that colony's economic picture throughout the nineteenth century. By the end of the War of 1812, the actual production of fish was almost entirely in the hands of Newfoundland residents. Although after 1815 the market for Newfoundland cod remained stagnant for decades, the fishing economy experienced considerable change. Smaller buyers of fish in the outports were squeezed out by the larger merchants of Water Street in St John's. The fishery expanded into Labrador, and sealing became far more important, representing over one-third of the value of the fishery's exports by 1831. Newfoundland was unable to gain ground in the lucrative Caribbean trade. Nova Scotia merchants now had their own local suppliers of fish, and were able to carry more diversified cargoes to the West Indies. The Lower Canadian fishery of the Gaspé region was the object of the agricultural interests' disdain. While the industry was not a particularly buoyant one after 1815, it did employ a considerable workforce. It produced a significant export trade, and it required a large number of sailing vessels both large and small. These characteristics contributed both to the shipbuilding industry and to the carrying-trade capacity of British North America.

The fur trade was the other traditional resource industry. By the nineteenth century, the fur trade's economic value was very small in comparison with that of other resources. In a non-economic sense the fur trade was of enormous importance. It provided the means by which Great Britain retained its claim to sovereignty over much of the northern half of the continent. It also supplied the administration of the British relationship with the indigenous peoples of that region. With the merger of the two great rivals in 1821, the fur trade stabilized under the aegis of the Hudson's Bay Company. The Pacific coast became increasingly important to the HBC. It deliberately overtrapped in the far west since it

SEALING IN NEWFOUNDLAND

Joseph Jukes was an Englishman employed on a geological survey of Newfoundland in 1839. In a book about his experiences published in 1842, he recorded the following from his diary.

March 12th: Again foggy, with a southeast wind. As we stood on deck this morning before breakfast, we heard a cry down to leeward, like the cry of a gull, which some of the men said it was. It became, however, so loud and continued, that both Stuwitz and I doubted its being the cry of any bird, and one of the men took a gaff and went to look. We watched him for some distance with our glasses as he proceeded slowly through the fog till he suddenly began to run, and then struck at something, and presently returned dragging a young seal alive over the ice, and brought it on deck. It was of a dirty white colour, with short close fur, large expressive eyes, and it paddled and walloped about the deck fierce and bawling. A Newfoundland dog called Nestor, belonging to the captain, approached it, but it snapped at his nose and bit him, though its teeth were just beginning to appear. After taking it down below to show the captain and demand the usual quart of rum for the first man who caught a seal, one of the men knocked it on its head and skinned it. Stuwitz then cut off its 'flippers' or paws and its head, and after breakfast we took it into the 'after-hatch' or steerage where he drew and dissected it. In the middle of the day we heard from some of the men who had been out on the ice, that a vessel a few miles ahead of us had already 2500 seals on board, so we pushed on through the ice, and shortly came into a lake of water. On the borders of this many young seals were lying and two or three punts were hoisted out to despatch and collect them. I shot one through the head that was scuffling off a pan of ice, but the crew begged me to desist, as they said the balls might glance from the ice and injure some of the men who were about. Having picked up the few which were immediately about us, we hoisted in our punts again, as there were several vessels near us, and more coming up, and bore away farther north through an open pool of water. In passing through a thin skirt of ice, one of the men hooked up a young seal with his gaff. Its cries were precisely like those of a young child in the extremity of agony and distress, something between shrieks and convulsive sobbings. . . . We soon afterwards passed through some loose ice on which the young seals were scattered, and nearly all hands were overboard slaying, skinning and hauling. We then got into another lake of water and sent our five punts. The crews of these joined those already on the ice, and dragging either the whole seals or their 'pelts' to the edge of the water, collected them in the punts, and when one of these was full brought them on board.

SOURCE: J.B. Jukes, *Excursions in and about Newfoundland*, 2 vols (London, 1842) as reprinted in Peter Neary and Patrick O'Flaherty, eds, *By Great Waters: A Newfoundland and Labrador Anthology* (Toronto: University of Toronto Press, 1974), 82–3.

assumed that it would eventually lose out to the Americans. Indeed, the company was able to hold its own against fur competitors, but not against the constant stream of American settlers into the Willamette Valley. The fur trade had a remarkable influence in the west, chiefly because furs were its only export commodity. The entire region was organized politically and economically around the trade.

The old staples of fish and fur were replaced by timber and grain in primary economic importance in the nineteenth century. Both these com-

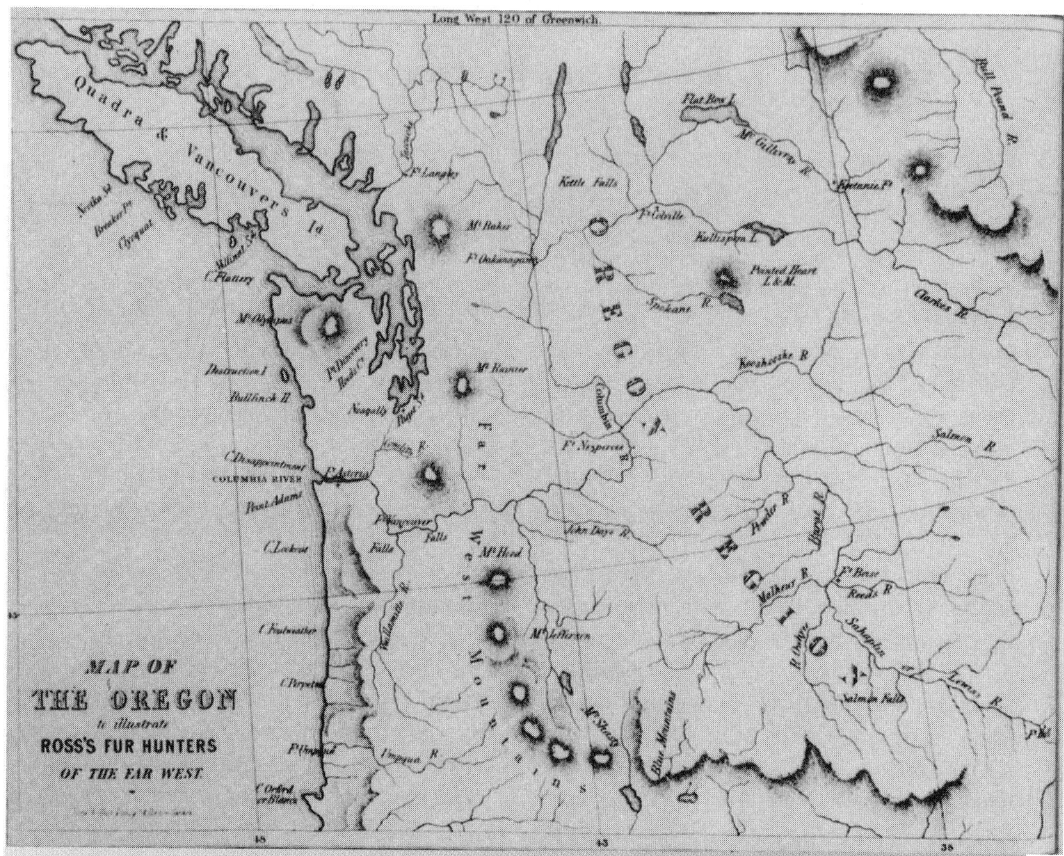

☐ One of the best accounts of the Oregon territory was written by the fur-trader Alexander Ross after he retired to Red River with his Okanagan wife and their children. *Fur-Hunters of the Far West* was first published in 1853. This map is from the 1855 edition. Metropolitan Toronto Reference Library.

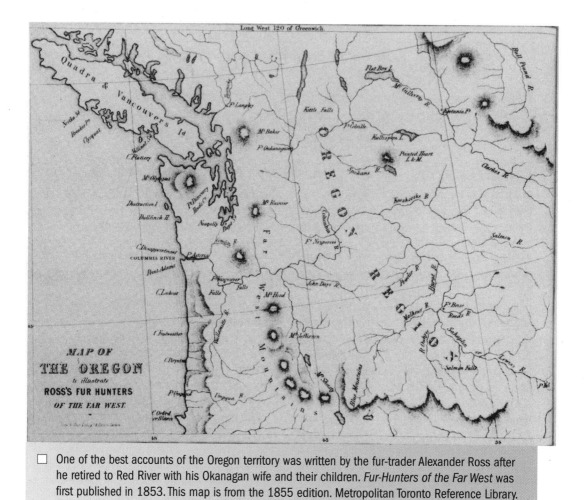

modities benefited from imperial preference, which gave them considerable advantage in the large and lucrative British market during their start-up years. Not until the 1840s did Britain begin seriously to eliminate the differential duty scales that the Corn Laws and the Timber Laws had created during the Napoleonic Wars. Every hint of change in imperial regulations brought a chorus of fears of economic disaster from the colonial mercantile community. While colonials may have been chained economically to the mother country, they revelled in the chains and were loath to break them.

Every province of British North America except Newfoundland quickly became involved in the timber trade after Napoleon closed the Baltic (the traditional source of British supply) in 1807. Even tiny Prince Edward Island enjoyed a considerable boom from cutting down its trees, most of which were relatively accessible to open water. Primary-growth forest was cut as quickly as possible with no thought for either conservation or oversupplying the market. In no province was the industry more important than in New Brunswick. Its dependence on timber as an export commodity had become almost complete

The forts of the recently merged Hudson's Bay and North West companies at Pembina on the Red River, 1822, watercolour by Peter Rindisbacher. The NWC post, Fort Gibraltar, is on the left, the HBC post, Fort Douglas, on the right. NAC, C-001934.

by the mid-1820s. The needs of the industry controlled every aspect of the province's life. Settlement was closely connected to the opening of new timber territory. It was no accident that the handful of timber princes who controlled the licences to cut on Crown land were also the leading politicians of the province. Under the large entrepreneurs was a variety of local businessmen—storekeepers, brokers, and sawmill operators—who actually organized and dealt with the hundreds of small parties that wintered in the woods. The industry preferred to do as much processing of the timber on the spot as possible, moving inexorably in that direction. As early as 1837 the sawmills of Samuel Cunard, on the Miramichi River in northeastern New Brunswick, were capable of cutting 42,471 ft (12,945 m) of boards per day, 'the produce of 320 logs and 50 workmen' (quoted in Wynn 1980). Much timber was also processed into wooden sailing-ships.

In the extensive agricultural lands of the St Lawrence Valley and Upper Canada, wheat quickly became the dominant crop. It met a growing demand abroad and it transported well as either grain or flour. Wheat quickly turned farmers into agricultural specialists, who exploited their soil much as did the timbermen the forest. Lower Canada's wheat yields on rapidly exhausted soil often cropped for decades were frequently inadequate for home consumption. While Upper Canada was able to transform its wheat profits from great surpluses into non-

These two photos from the New Brunswick lumber camps obviously post-date 1840 and the invention of the camera, but there is no reason to think that conditions in the timber trade changed much in the course of the nineteenth century. From Adam Shortt and A.G. Doughty, eds, *Canada and Its Provinces* (Edinburgh, 1914), vol. 14. Metropolitan Toronto Reference Library.

agricultural investment, by the 1850s it too had exhausted its best soils and was looking westward. Most farmers also produced for their own consumption, of course, and some (such as those on Prince Edward Island) produced livestock and potatoes for export or supplied a local market with produce. Even Maritime farmers grew more wheat than was good for them, however.

THE MERCANTILE SYSTEM

The resource economy worked only because of its capacity to deal with the international market. The merchant capitalist looked after transportation and marketing in a world of totally unsophisticated credit and banking. Merchants operated at all levels of volume and capital investment. Some placed goods in a number of vessels and invested small amounts in other ships and voyages, as had been done in the colonies since the earliest days. The growing extent of the resource trade demanded larger entrepreneurs, however. Whether the merchant was large or small, international mercantile activity in the first half of the nineteenth century was extremely dangerous. Financial disaster lurked everywhere. Ships could be lost at sea, markets could be miscalculated, debtors could be unable to pay. Communications were incredibly slow. Because of the difficulties in finding trustworthy partners and agents abroad, the extensive family network was still the international basis of much mercantile activity. Few of the large merchant princes of this period avoided at least one bankruptcy, and fewer still left fortunes to their heirs. The sailing-ship, filled with outgoing cargoes of resource commodities and incoming ones of manufactured goods and new immigrants, remained the backbone of British North America's economic system in this period.

Some manufacturing activity did exist in British North America. It involved relatively small establishments that engaged in two kinds of production. One was by artisans producing for local markets goods and services that either could not be imported profitably or could not be imported at all. Every town had its saddler, every village its blacksmith. The second type of production involved the processing of resource commodities. Grain was distilled into whisky, brewed into beer, and milled into flour. Wood from land being cleared by farmers was burnt into potash, and timber was cut at sawmills into deals. Among many specialized manufacturing enterprises, shipyards that transformed timber into sailing vessels were the most extensive. The small shipyard was to be found wherever there was timber and open water; the commerce of the Great Lakes required as many sailing vessels as the transatlantic trade.

Shipbuilding was the ideal colonial processing industry. It relied primarily on a rich natural resource—timber—that British North America had in abundance. It did not require excessive capital outlay for physical plant or materials, and its end product provided its own transportation to market. On the other hand, even during its heyday it was not an industry with either a future or a capacity to generate industrial development. As early as 1840 wood and sail were already being overtaken by iron and steam. These technologies required an entirely different form of industrial organization than a handful of craftsmen employing hand tools, carefully assembling a wooden ship on the edge of open water. Neither the technology nor the industrial organization flowed logically out of the nature of colonial shipbuilding, which became instead the symbol of the mercantile resource economy's limitations.

Providing the infrastructure for trade and commerce was a gradual business. Banks were slow to develop because most colonials were suspicious of institutions that could, in effect, manufacture money. The Bank of Montreal was founded in 1817, and the Bank of Canada was chartered in 1821, opening at York in 1822. Early banks did not cooperate together and their services were limited. An expanding internal economic system required roads, bridges, and canals

'View in King Street [Toronto], Looking East', hand-coloured lithograph, 1835, by Thomas Young. The buildings on the left (north) are the jail, the courthouse, and St James Church at Church Street. NAC, C-041602.

to connect the population with their markets and sources of supply. Most people wanted such facilities, but did not want to pay for them out of taxes. Much road building was done by labour levies upon the local population. After the American success with the Erie Canal, canal building became the craze in the Canadas. The early Canadian canals—the Lachine Canal, the Welland Canal, the Rideau Canal, and the Chambly Canal—either opened water access into Lake Ontario or improved the St Lawrence River system. Their thrust was to enable the economy to shift from a transatlantic focus to an internal one. This process would really take hold with the introduction of the railroads in the 1850s.

Trade and commerce were the basis of urban growth, although the major cities of the British colonies in North America were centres of political activity as well as commerce. It was easier to flourish, however, without being a capital (Montreal or Hamilton) than without trade (Fredericton). No city dominated more than its immediate region and none was very large. Nonetheless, most urban centres in British North America were growing rapidly. York in 1795 contained twelve cottages. By the time it was incorporated and renamed Toronto in 1834 it had over 1,000 houses, 100 shops, and a population of 9,252. The cities were small in area as well as population, many being collections of tightly packed buildings radiating out from a port facility. Such a city had little concept of zoning and not many amenities, although by the 1830s matters were improving. Toronto was fairly typical for 1830 in lacking sidewalks, drains, sewers, water supply, and street lighting,

PHILEMON WRIGHT

Philemon Wright (1760–1839) was born in Woburn, Massachusetts. He fought with the Americans in the Battle of Bunker Hill in 1775, and subsequently moved to the Vermont frontier. In 1796 Wright bought land in Lower Canada and a year later he petitioned the government there for the township of Hull on behalf of himself and a number of associates (who turned out to be fellow citizens of Woburn). Wright himself led a party of 63 settlers (presumably all Americans like himself) to Hull in March of 1800. Initially he had planned to establish himself as a squire in a new agricultural society, but he soon added timbering to the economic mix. From the beginning Wright took farming seriously, and in 1820 he became one of British North America's first 'Wheat Kings', harvesting nearly 36,000 bushels of wheat on his farms. A few years later, his harvest reached over 71,000 bushels. As well as grain crops, Wright also raised large amounts of cattle.

Whether Wright's lumbering activities were simply offshoots of his agricultural involvement—as was innkeeping, milling, and retailing—or whether timber was from the beginning the fulcrum of the entire enterprise is not entirely clear. In any event, by 1806 Wright was floating rafts of squared timber down the Ottawa River to Quebec. Initially much of the wood came from settlers' land during clearance, but gradually Wright got the wood from land acquired specifically for the purpose. He wa a classic example of economic integration, both horizontal and vertical. He had a piece of virtually every economic enterprise remotely related to Hull Township, and he controlled the production of timber from woodlot to point of sale on the St Lawrence.

Wright showed little interest in provincial politics before 1830, but as a critical member of a regional élite he had a good deal of local power. He was an officer of militia, and justice of the peace, and after 1817 commissioner for the summary trial of small causes. It was Philemon Wright who asked the Royal Institution for Advancement of Learning to begin a school at Hull, and although he began life as a Congregationalist he gradually moved towards the Anglican Church. Wright was master of the first Masonic lodge established in Hull in 1813. He was elected to the assembly in 1830, sat for four years, and went home without having become a member of the legislative council and the Château Clique. Wright was the perfect example of a 'Late Loyalist' who demonstrated how Yankee ambition and ingenuity could work in British North America.

all developments of the 1830s and 1840s. Policing consisted at best of a few ward constables and a night watch. For most urban centres in British North America, 1840 marked the break between remaining an eighteenth-century town and becoming a nineteenth-century city.

IMMIGRATION

After 1815 circumstances combined to alter patterns of immigration, especially from the British Isles. Resistance to emigration from both the British government and the British ruling classes was quickly broken down by unemployment and a new round of industrialization and agricultural rationalization. Pressures on Britain's poor relief system increased, and among those who governed the nation it became common wisdom that Britain was once again overpopulated. The burgeoning of the North American timber trade provided the shipping capacity for the transatlantic movement of immigrants at low cost. Immigrants came to British North America chiefly to obtain access to land, something that was becoming increasingly difficult to obtain in the British Isles. Many Britons had an extremely idealized picture of the wilderness. The essayist Thomas Carlyle wrote in 1839 of the vastness of North America, 'nine-tenths of it yet vacant or tenanted by nomads, . . . still crying, Come and till me, come and reap me!' Despite the best efforts of a number of writers of immigration manuals, many newcomers failed to appreciate the need for capital or the difficulties involved in clearing much of this vacant land of trees and brush. In 1846, in her book *The Backwoods of Canada*, Catharine Parr Traill included 'some official information' 'to render this work of more practical value to persons desiring to emigrate'. Table 4.1 presents two examples: charts on the sale of Crown lands in Lower and Upper Canada, 'abstracted from Parliamentary documents'.

What we know about the numbers departing the British Isles suggests that Scottish emigration remained relatively steady throughout the period at 10–15 per cent of the total flow. A far higher proportion of Highlanders than Lowlanders departed in these years. Irish emigration was more variable, ranging annually from 30 to 70 per cent of the total numbers. Irish movement to North America before the

TABLE 4.1

THE QUANTITY OF CROWN LANDS GRANTED AND THE CONDITIONS ON WHICH THE GRANTS WERE GIVEN FROM 1823 TO 1833

LOWER CANADA

Year	Number of acres granted to militia claimants	Number of acres granted to discharged soldiers and pensioners	Number of acres granted to officers	Number of acres granted, not coming within the previous descriptions	Total number of acres granted
1824	51,810	–	4,100	34,859	90,769
1825	32,620	–	1,000	16,274	49,894
1826	3,525	5,500	–	48,224	57,249
1827	7,640	6,300	800	38,375	53,118
1828	7,300	–	4,504	9,036	20,840
1829	3,200	–	–	5,282	8,482
1830	81,425	–	2,000	10,670	94,095
1831	9,400	8,273	3,408	9,900	30,981
1832	10,116	19,000	4,000	4,000	37,116
1833	5,200	22,500	1,200	–	28,900
Total	212,236	61,573	21,012	176,623	471,444

Settler's Conditions: That he do clear twenty feet of road on his lot within the space of ninety days.

Military and Militia Conditions: That he do, within the space of three years, clear and cultivate four acres of his lot, and build a dwelling-house thereon.

TABLE 4.1 (CONTINUED)

UPPER CANADA

Year	Number of acres granted to militia claimants	Number of acres granted to discharged soldiers and pensioners	Number of acres granted to officers	Number of acres granted, not coming within the previous descriptions	Number of acres granted to UE Loyalists*	Total number of acres granted
1824	11,800	5,800	5,500	134,500	30,200	187,800
1825	20,300	5,700	8,100	149,060	45,000	228,160
1826	16,600	3,100	4,700	19,390	24,800	68,590
1827	10,900	4,200	7,200	33,600	20,200	76,100
1828	10,800	900	3,000	4,304	30,800	49,804
1829	5,300	7,500	8,400	3,230	22,600	47,030
1830	6,400	12,500	12,600	9,336	27,400	68,236
1831	5,500	58,400	7,200	8,000	34,200	113,300
1832	19,300	97,800	7,600	6,100	62,600	193,400
1833	35,200	46,000	–	9,100	135,600	225,900
Total	142,100	241,900	64,300	376,620	433,400	1,258,320

Condition: Actual settlement.

*UE Loyalists means United Empire Loyalists–individuals who fled from the United States on the outbreak of the American war of independence. The grants in this column were mostly to the children of these individuals.

SOURCE: C.P. Traill, *The Backwoods of Canada* (London: M.A. Nattali, 1846).

1840s was dominated by Protestants from northern Ireland. Only in the mid-1840s did the Irish emigrants begin to include huge numbers of Catholic southerners. As a result, the whole nature of Irish emigration to British North America was quite different from Irish emigration to the United States. British America received far more Irish emigrants in the early period than did the United States. The Irish flow to what is now Canada included far more Protestants and Orangists than did that to the United States, where the emigrants were almost exclusively Catholics from the south.

The national and regional complexity of the population in the British Isles at this time produces several interesting questions and problems. It is tempting from a twenty-first-century perspective, for example, to assume that the British emigrants were a relatively homogeneous group of people. Nothing could be further from the truth. Each of the historic nations of Britain continued in the nineteenth century to preserve its own culture and history. There was no homogeneity of either language or religion. Many of the Irish, especially in the south, spoke the Irish tongue. Almost all Scots from north of the Highland fault spoke Gaelic as a first language, while those in the Lowlands spoke a Scottish variant of English. Dialects and linguistic variants were also extensive in England and Wales. In the latter place, there was a north–south division whereby the northerners were more likely to speak Welsh than English. At the same time, the nineteenth century saw a considerable growth of a common 'Britishness' that to various extents overcame regional distinctions. On the

☐ Irish emigrants awaiting departure on the quay at Cork, as depicted in the *Illustrated London News*, 10 May 1851. NAC, C-3904.

other hand, acceptance of the concepts of Great Britain and Britishness was quite variable. Many of the southern Irish, for example, would not have agreed that they were British, or that they were willing subjects of the British Crown.

Another difference between immigration to the United States and to British North America was in the nature of the vessels employed in the transatlantic passage. This had certain ramifications for the sorts of emigrants who departed for each of the countries. Those going to the United States tended to travel in large vessels specifically designed to carry passengers, while those going to British North America usually travelled in smaller vessels designed for the timber trade. These ships carried passengers on the return voyage in makeshift accommodations instead of sailing in ballast. The result of this difference was that the passage to British North America cost significantly less than that to the United States. When this difference in cost is combined with the much shorter duration of the passage from the British Isles to the eastern seaports of British North America (which meant that fewer provisions were required for the journey), it seems likely that far more immigrants to British America sailed on extremely limited budgets and without much capital in reserve than was typically the case for those who went to the United States. It is hard to generalize, because the rates for passengers varied substantially from time to time. One Belfast advertisement from 1820 put the charge for a family of husband, wife, and six children to the United States at 80 guineas, for example, and the cost for the same family to New Brunswick at 24 guineas. Such rates meant that only those with considerable capital—or who were willing to acquire considerable debt—could afford to sail at all. Many of those arriving in British American ports without

ADVICE FOR IMMIGRANTS

Numbers of books and pamphlets were published between 1800 and 1860 devoted exclusively to offering advice for immigrants. Most of the advice was useful, although few authors went into details on how difficult the passage and transition would be.

[Liverpool] is undoubtedly the best port to embark from, as vessels may there be met with at any time during the spring and summer months; and the expense of travelling to that town, even from places at a considerable distance, is not great. . . . In the winter and very early in the spring, there are also vessels constantly going to New York, from whence there are steam-boats to Albany, and a stage to Montreal, or to Sackett's harbour opposite Kingston, by Utica. This would be the best route for persons without families, or who had but little baggage, and who were desirous of leaving England in February or March. A considerable duty or per centage (as much, I believe, as thirty per cent) on the value of their baggage, is paid at New York by persons not intending to settle in the United States, but who were only passing through them in order to proceed to the British colonies. Persons with families, and a considerable quantity of baggage, had therefore better embark for Quebec; and the commencement of April would be soon enough to leave Liverpool, as vessels cannot proceed up the river St. Lawrence to Quebec before the middle of May, on account of the ice. . . .

Coarse warm clothing with flannel shirts, thick worsted or yarn stockings, and strong shoes or half-boots nailed, are most suitable for the climate of Canada in winter; and duck slops, duck trowsers, and calico or homespun linen shirts, for summer wear. Fur caps may also be brought out, as they are expensive here. Any old clothes will serve during the voyage out, and in travelling through the country. Beds may be taken out (without bedsteads). Curtains and curtain-rings, cords, blankets, sheets, warm rugs or coverlets, and several spare bed-ticks. All these latter articles are extremely dear in Canada. Scarcely any thing else need be provided, as all articles of hardware, axes suitable for the country, plough-irons, harrow-teeth, Dutch and tin ovens, tea-kettles, kettles for cooking meat in, &c., &c., &c. may be purchased at Montreal at nearly the same prices as in England.

Every thing should be well packed in strong boxes, cases, or trunks, the more portable they are the better, each not exceeding three feet in length, eighteen inches in breadth, and one foot in depth, made water-tight if possible, or in barrels about the size of flour barrels, also water-tight; and all to be well lashed up or corded. Beds, bedding, curtains, &c. &c., may be sewed up in a wool-sack or very coarse harden, with a strong cord round them; this is the most convenient and best method of taking out beds. China or other earthenware may be packed in tow or the refuse of flax. . . .

All spare money must be brought out in guineas or Spanish dollars, which may be purchased for good bills at any bullion office in Liverpool. Dollars are bought for about 4s. 4d. or 4s. 6d. each.'

SOURCE: 'English Farmer Settled in Upper Canada,' *A few plain directions for persons intending to proceed as settlers to His Majesty's province of Upper Canada, in North America* (London, 1820), as found in Harold Innis and A.R.M. Lower, eds, *Select Documents in Canadian Economic History 1783–1885* (Toronto, 1933), 96–8.

capital may have intended to move on to the United States when they had acquired the means, but how many actually managed to do so is another matter entirely. Large numbers of those arriving with little or no capital were already in debt to friends or relatives at home.

'The Emigrant's Welcome to Canada', c. 1820. W.H. Coverdale Collection of Canadiana, NAC, C-41067.

They had borrowed the price of steerage passage and were bound to repay the debt out of their first earnings.

Costs and geography also meant that British North America rather than the United States throughout the period received the vast bulk of the emigrants from the Highlands of Scotland. Many of these Highlanders arrived virtually destitute in British North America and could not afford to continue on to the United States. Sufficient numbers of Gaelic-speakers from Highland Scotland arrived in various parts of British North America (notably parts of Upper Canada, the eastern townships of Lower Canada, Cape Breton Island, and Prince Edward Island) to make the language an important medium of communication in these areas. This simply did not happen in the United States, where newcomers were strongly encouraged to assimilate to the dominant society.

Four patterns of organized emigration and settlement developed after 1815. The first pattern involved government assistance, which was often a combination of British official recruitment of emigrants and settlement, with public aid, on land made available by the several colonial governments. Such schemes, frequently involving either soldiers disbanded after the wars or excess Irish population, continued sporadically until 1830. What the various schemes best demonstrated was that the financial cost of establishing British emigrants in British North America was high. Even those who argued that the existing operations were unnecessarily profligate estimated £60 for a family of five. In the late 1820s the British government rejected a

'A First Settlement', by W.H. Bartlett, engraved by J.C. Bentley, from N.P. Willis, *Canadian Scenery* (London, 1842), vol. II. NAC, C-2401.

proposal for a major government resettlement scheme to be financed by local authorities as an alternative to poor relief. It was brought forward by the parliamentary undersecretary at the Colonial Office, Robert John Wilmot-Horton. Thereafter government policy abandoned public assistance for emigration.

The other three patterns were not mutually exclusive. Some emigrants could even combine all three. The second pattern emphasized settlement on the land. It involved private proprietors of land, usually large land companies. These occasionally offered financial assistance, but most frequently they made land available to emigrants on affordable terms. This process was intended to appeal to emigrants with some financial resources. There were three large land companies: the Canada Company, the British American Land Company (in the Eastern Townships of Quebec), and the New Brunswick and Nova Scotia Land Company. In 1826 the Canada Company had purchased most of the Crown reserves and half of the clergy reserves of Upper Canada, thus providing a colonial revenue. It settled large number of emigrants on its lands.

A third pattern emphasized transport to North America but not settlement on the land. Private emigrant contractors would offer passage to North America in sailing vessels. The ships involved were usually in the timber trade, temporarily converted to provide accommodation on the outward passage. The contractor provided low rates of passage but as few services as possible. His passengers were frequently deposited at seaports in British North America and left to their own devices. The lucky ones managed to make their way to some destination.

The vast majority of emigrants, whatever their transport and settlement arrangements, fitted into the fourth pattern. They had arranged their own passage, frequently coming to British North America without fixed plans or destination. Sometimes they intended to join relatives or friends who had preceded them. If they had capital, they found land. It was generally estimated that at least £100 (beyond the cost of passage) was required to establish a farm on wilderness land, and even more was required to purchase one already improved. Those who could not afford this expense joined the ranks of the labouring class or, in the case of unattached females, went into domestic service. The transatlantic passage in sailing-ships lasted from six to eight weeks, and was long and arduous even for those who could afford cabin accommodation. For those in steerage (the vast majority), the discomfort and health hazards were high. After 1825 the British government abandoned attempts to regulate the traffic in any serious way.

Aside from the assisted settlement schemes, public policy was never really mobilized to settle British North America. The major shift in policy after the mid-1820s, apart from the ending of assisted settlement, was the abandonment of the practice of giving colonial land away; now a 'sufficient price' was to be charged, to ensure a revenue for colonial improvement, and to guarantee that those acquiring land had some capital. In the end, settlement was achieved out of the trials and tribulations of those who tried their luck. Apart from their physical energy, the immigrants were also a great source of wealth for the colonies they entered. If every immigrant brought on average only £10, between 1815 and 1845 that amount would have injected £10 million into the local economies.

THE RESOURCE SOCIETY

The resource society of the early nineteenth century was dominated by two overlapping élites. One governed, the other controlled international commerce. In most colonies their separate identities were easily confused when they battled politically, employing imported rhetoric that suggested deeper divisions than actually existed. By far the majority of the population was composed of the non-élite: small shopkeepers, artisans, minor civil servants; owners of small industries such as gristmills, tanneries, soap factories, and breweries; and resource workers and farmers. In the British context of distinguishing between those who held land and those who did not, few 'landholders' in British North America possessed anything but land that was in the process of becoming farms. Most landowners were forced to hold multiple employments, often working side by side with the landless. Women in this society acquired the status of their husbands. Those without spouses had some autonomy, but were severely limited in any upward mobility. Finally, the indigenous peoples lived outside the social structure, although the missionaries constantly tried to bring them into it.

The governing élite included the leading appointed colonial officials of government, military officers, church leaders, and the merchants who lived in the capital city. The first three enjoyed the enormous advantage of a substantial guaranteed annual salary, usually paid in London in pounds sterling. This income, the access to credit, and the style of living it encouraged, all enabled colonial officials to emulate the British values of the landed gentry. Their houses reflected their aspirations. The magnificent house of John Strachan (1778–1867) on Front Street in Toronto was popularly known as 'The Palace' even before he became bishop of Toronto in 1839. In 1819, the year after it was built, his brother visiting from Scotland is alleged to have commented, 'I hope it's a' come by honestly, John' (quoted in Arthur 1986: 44). Not surprisingly, colonial officials believed in the balance of interests and order, the maintenance of which John Beverley Robinson (1791–1863) once described as 'the foundation of good government in the social state' (quoted in Brode 1984: 175). Such men were well educated and very able. They governed British North America with an extremely limited vision, usually without soiling themselves in sordid graft and corruption.

The most successful merchants (and a few professional men) shared the lifestyle of the major colonial office-holders, usually without their status. What really limited the social positions of the merchants was the impermanence of their incomes, which could be greatly affected by conditions in the market. The British associated status with land because an income from landed estates was rightly regarded as far more permanent and inheritable than income from trade or industry. British North America was never able to generate a landed aristocracy. The colonial official's income was only for life, although a few offices were passed on from father to son. The typical seigneur in Lower Canada did not have enough income to cut much of a figure. The trouble with land in North America was its sheer availability. An Upper Canadian backwoods farm consisted of a larger acreage than many an English landed estate. Most land was held for speculation rather than status. Lacking an aristocracy based on land, British North America instead began developing a social structure based on wealth and conspicuous consumption. Money might be temporary, but it could be made visible. British North America also had high regard for education, professional training, and the life of the mind. The concentrations of leading professional men in the larger towns were admitted to the ranks of élite society, though in a subordinate position.

While the governing élite and its merchant partners lived mainly in the political capitals that were also the great commercial centres of British North America, a sprinkling of others in the hinterlands also assumed the functions of leadership. Such regional leaders included local merchants and professional men, prominent farmers, and retired half-pay officers. These were the men who were elected to the provincial houses of assembly from the countryside, where they inevitably came to contend with the governing élites for political control of the province. Regional prominence was recognized by election to the assembly and appointment to local civic office. Thus these were also the men who served as local justices of the peace. They tended to be the militia officers as well. Before 1840 most would have described themselves as farmers, although they usually engaged in a variety of occupations, hoping to succeed and survive. One of the most striking feature of the lives of most British North Americans was their lack of occupational specialization. Over the course of a lifetime most colonials would hold many different jobs, both in succession and simultaneously.

Coming to terms with the remainder of society in British North America is more complicated than dealing with the élite. Despite the vaunted availability of land, not everyone was that British (and American) ideal, a land-holding yeoman farmer. In some places (Newfoundland, Prince Edward Island, and Lower Canada), freehold land was not easily available. Moreover, the land that was worth holding was not wilderness but an improved market farm. Cultivating land carved out of primary-growth forest was a tedious process. Such 'improvement' was hampered by the difficulties of finding a market for surplus agricultural products. Farmers inevitably embraced crops such as wheat, which could be transported into a regular market system. Improvement was further hampered by the availability of alternative employment in fishing, timbering, shipbuilding, and construction—which could sustain a farming family before it was plugged into the market—but would also slow down the land-clearing process essential to agrarian success.

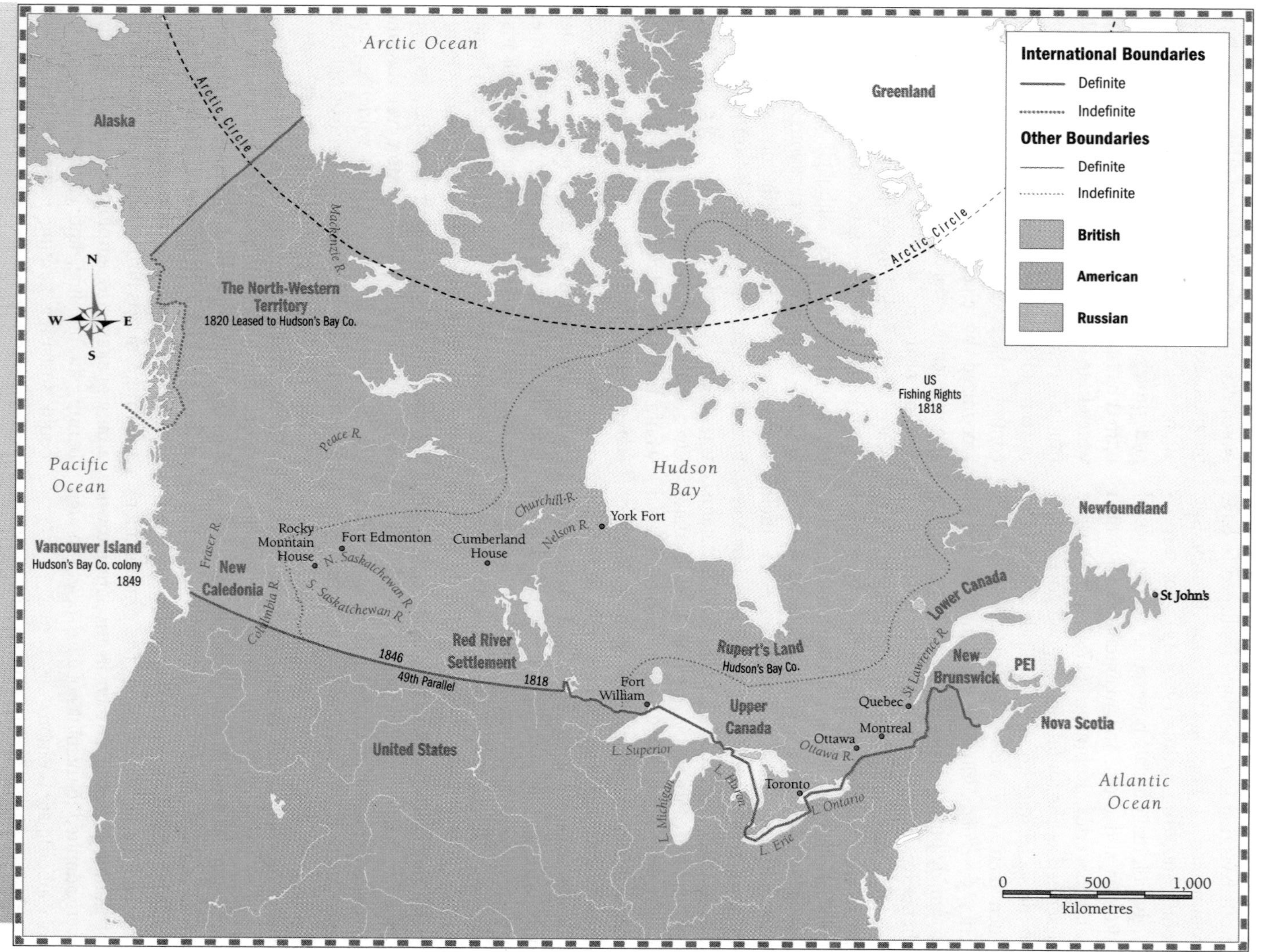
International Boundaries
Definite
Indefinite
Other Boundaries
Definite
Indefinite
British
American
Russian
Arctic Ocean
Greenland
Alaska
Arctic Circle
Mackenzie R.
The North-Western Territory
1820 Leased to Hudson's Bay Co.
N
W
E
S
US Fishing Rights 1818
Peace R.
Pacific Ocean
Hudson Bay
Churchill R.
Nelson R.
York Fort
Newfoundland
Rocky Mountain House
Fort Edmonton
Cumberland House
Vancouver Island
Hudson's Bay Co. colony
1849
Fraser R.
New Caledonia
N. Saskatchewan R.
S. Saskatchewan R.
Columbia R.
Lower Canada
St John's
Red River Settlement
1846
49th Parallel
1818
Rupert's Land
Hudson's Bay Co.
St Lawrence R.
New Brunswick
PEI
Fort William
Upper Canada
Quebec
Nova Scotia
Ottawa
Montreal
Ottawa R.
United States
L. Superior
L. Huron
L. Michigan
Toronto
L. Ontario
L. Erie
Atlantic Ocean
0
500
1,000
kilometres

British North America in 1849.

At the bottom of colonial society were the poor. They fell into three categories: permanent, immigrant, and casual; and into two major groups: those who had relations or friends to look after them and those who did not. While British North America was often spoken of on both sides of the Atlantic as a 'land of opportunity' and a 'good poor man's country', it was absolutely essential to be healthy, or to have kinfolk prepared to help with one's welfare. Those who through disability, incompetence, or misfortune (such as young orphans) could not look after themselves and had no one to do it for them became the objects of charity or lived permanently in squalor. Recent immigrants who arrived in port without capital resources joined the ranks of the poor wherever they disembarked. Unable to move onto the land, these newcomers merged into the third category, the casually employed. Because of the seasonal nature of most Canadian employment, winter saw the largest number of unemployed. Winter was also the worst time to be poor, for food costs increased and the need to keep warm in a Canadian winter was inescapable. Malnutrition and inadequate clothing, combined with underheating, provided a ready-made recipe for the spread of illness and contagious disease. The poor were 'relieved' chiefly to prevent their turning 'by despair to commit depredations' (quoted in Fingard 1988: 197). Contemporary society tended to identify poverty with the city and personal failure. It saw poverty as a moral rather than an economic problem.

Between the poor and the prosperous was a variety of occupational and social groups that defy rational ordering by almost any scheme. An examination of the Newfoundland fishing-boat owner suggests some of the difficulties. A property owner and an employer, the boat owner was probably landless except for a small house lot for which he held no deed. He was usually deeply in debt to the merchant who bought his fish and supplied him with essentials. Forced to contract debt, the fisherman soon found himself in slavish servitude. The fishery's truck system also operated in the timber districts and the fur trade. In another guise it also worked in farming communities, which accumulated large debts to local storekeepers who supplied goods that could not be made at home. Moreover, huge portions of British North America consisted of uneconomic farms that were kept operating on a subsistence level, often by women and children, while the male landholder was off elsewhere working for wages. As with the élites, houses told the tale. Settlers hoped to progress from log hut (or shanty) to log-house to permanent dwelling built of stone or brick or finished lumber in accordance with their prosperity. In 1831 Upper Canada had 36,000 dwellings, of which 75 per cent were constructed of logs and fewer than 1,000 built of brick and stone.

Colonial society also included a number of categories of people who were quite outside the social structure as it was then understood. One such group was women. The law in British North America was quite different for men and for women. Women were citizens only in that they were inhabitants of British North America whose civil rights had yet to be ultimately decided. They were for the most part 'non-legal entities'. A variety of disabilities operated against women. They could not be legislators, or lawyers, judges, magistrates, or members of juries that decided the fate of many women in both civil and criminal actions. Politically disenfranchised—several provinces even passed legislation in this period depriving widows of the vote—women were especially disadvantaged by marriage. As the English jurist Sir William Blackstone put it, 'In law husband and wife are one person and the husband is that person.' All real property passed into the hands of the husband, who was entitled to control his spouse. Women were expected to produce many children in an age when maternal mortality ran very high. Despite the drawbacks, most women preferred marriage to the alternatives.

At least among the élite and the very prosperous, there was the beginning of a process of converting the home into the central social unit for cultural transmission and the pursuit of happiness. As British North American society became more settled, and somewhat more urbanized, within the ranks of the middle and upper classes there emerged a clear separation of

BUILDING A LOG-HOUSE IN UPPER CANADA

Catharine Parr Traill (1802–99) was the youngest of nine Strickland children, seven of whom (including Susanna Strickland Moodie) became published authors. Catharine married a retired army officer in 1832 and the couple headed off to Canada to settle. Her pioneering experiences, originally told in letters sent home, were published anonymously in England.

It was the latter end of October before even the walls of our house were up. To effect this we called 'a bee'. Sixteen of our neighbours cheerfully obeyed our summons; and though the day was far from favourable, so faithfully did our hive perform their tasks, that by night the outer walls were raised. . . . The following day I went to survey the newly raised edifice, but was sorely puzzled, as it presented very little appearance of a house. It was merely an oblong square of logs raised one above the other, with open spaces between every row of logs. The spaces for the doors and windows were not then sawn out, and the rafters were not up. . . . A day or two after this I again visited it. The *sleepers* were laid to support the floors, and the places for the doors and windows cut out of the solid timbers, so that it had not quite so much the look of a bird-cage as before. After the roof was shingled, we were again at a stand, as no boards could be procured nearer than Peterborough, a long day's journey through horrible roads. . . . Well, the boards were at length down, but of course of unseasoned timber: . . . we console ourselves with the prospect that by next summer the boards will all be seasoned, and then the house is to be turned topsy-turvy by having the floors all relaid, joined and smoothed. The next misfortune that happened was that the mixture of clay and lime that was to plaster the inside and outside of the house between the chinks of the logs was one night frozen to stone. Just as the work was about half completed, the frost suddenly settling in, put a stop to our proceeding for some time, as the frozen plaster yielded neither to fire nor to hot water, the latter freezing before it had any effect on the mass, and rather making bad worse. Then the workman that was hewing the inside walls to smooth them wounded himself with the broad axe, and was unable to resume his work for some time. . . . We have now got quite comfortably settled, and I shall give you a description of our little dwelling. . . . A nice small sitting-room with a store closet, a kitchen, a pantry, and bed-chamber form the ground floor; there is a good upper floor that will make three sleeping rooms. . . . Our parlour is warmed by a handsome Franklin stove with brass gallery and fender. Our furniture consists of a brass-railed sofa, which serves upon occasion for a bed; Canadian painted chairs; a stained pine table; green and white muslin curtains; and a handsome Indian mat which covers the floor. One side of the room is filled up with our books. Some large maps and a few good prints nearly conceal the rough walls, and form the decoration of our little dwelling. Our bed-chamber is furnished with equal simplicity. We do not, however, lack comfort in our humble home; and though it is not exactly such as we could wish, it is as good as, under existing circumstances, we could have.

SOURCE: C.P. Traill, *The Backwoods of Canada* (London: M.A. Nattali, 1846): 135–43.

work-life and home-life, and women withdrew into the privacy of the home. This growth of the concept of domesticity began in the ranks of the élite, but gradually made its way down into the middle class as the century went on. It was connected with increasing prosperity and the construction of larger houses, which in turn encouraged new notions of social space. It became possible to conceive of reserving different rooms for different functions (and different people), to distinguish 'public' rooms from 'private' rooms, and to introduce ideas of privacy as well. Instead of spending his life almost entirely in public spaces, the husband and father now came 'home' from work to renew himself. Women were placed on a pedestal as keepers of culture and as civilizing influences.

For most women in British America, struggle with the pioneering conditions of carving farms out of the wilderness was the principal reality of life. An absence of labour-saving devices—except the domestic servant, for those who could afford one—meant that most work associated with the home involved heavy, physical drudgery and long hours. Women were not only responsible for food preparation, but for much food production and most of its preservation. Women made soap and candles, they washed clothes, they tended the fires under the maple syrup. While conditions could become less primitive over time, there was never any appreciable reduction in the amount of a woman's labour required to keep the family going. She was also responsible for bearing and raising children. In a society in which infant mortality was high and labour outside the family hard to come by, a considerable incentive existed for the production of large families. Women were also expected to help their men in work in the male sphere when required. In the resource society of British North America in the first half of the nineteenth century, men were often away from home for long periods. In their absence, their wives had to run households and farms, as well as manage businesses. Although women's work was drudgery never done, they were never properly rewarded. Domestic duties were not regarded as a labour to be remunerated, and women's contributions to the success of the family estate were rarely taken into account in inheritance strategies. The typical pattern was for sons (usually eldest sons) to inherit the property, while the caring patriarch specified that the heir was responsible for the maintenance of his mother. Daughters counted for very little in this pattern.

Other groups almost completely marginalized by colonial society included indigenous peoples and Blacks. In much of the eastern region of British North America, settlement had eliminated hunting grounds, and there was no place for the indigenous peoples to go. They were offered the choice of provisions of land in unsurveyed local reserves or general integration into the farming community. The year 1836 saw several major and contradictory developments in First Nations policy. In that year the first serious British attempt at coordinating policy came with a Parliamentary Enquiry that covered the entire empire. Canada featured prominently in this investigation, with a litany of abuses exposed from one colony to the next. The government of Nova Scotia refused to provide any information. In its 1,000 page report, the committee concluded that First Nations policy should remain under British control. It also recommended against making treaties with local Aboriginals, on the grounds that the treaty process was so heavily weighted in favour of government that it could never produce a satisfactory result. This recommendation was never implemented, and treaty-making was even transferred to colonial governments in ensuing years.

Symptomatic of this transfer were developments in Upper Canada in 1836, when Lieutenant-governor Sir Francis Bond Head decided that attempts at assimilation were a mistake. Instead, he argued that the 'greatest kindness we can perform towards these Intelligent, simple-minded people is to remove and fortify them as much as possible from all Communication with the Whites' (Dickason, 2002: 211). Head subsequently engineered the cession of 3 million acres of land by the Ojibwa in return for a promise that Manitoulin Island and its adjacent islands would be protected as Aboriginal territory. The Ojibwa

ANGÉLIQUE PILOTTE

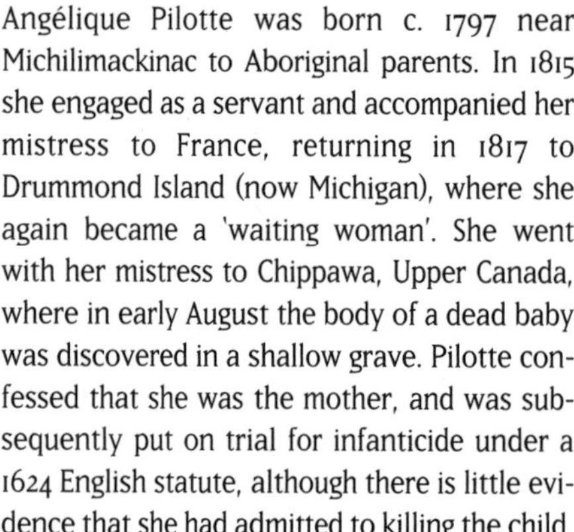

Angélique Pilotte was born c. 1797 near Michilimackinac to Aboriginal parents. In 1815 she engaged as a servant and accompanied her mistress to France, returning in 1817 to Drummond Island (now Michigan), where she again became a 'waiting woman'. She went with her mistress to Chippawa, Upper Canada, where in early August the body of a dead baby was discovered in a shallow grave. Pilotte confessed that she was the mother, and was subsequently put on trial for infanticide under a 1624 English statute, although there is little evidence that she had admitted to killing the child.

Pilotte had spent most of her life in Ojibwa society, and does not appear to have understood much English or most of the legal niceties connected with the charge against her in the Niagara court. Several of the witnesses, including her mistress, thought that she was mentally challenged,although the problem may have been one of language, combined with racial prejudice, rather than mental acuity. In any event, she had admitted to concealing a pregnancy, to bearing a live child, and to burying it when it subsequently died—which were the key points in the law against infanticide. A jury quickly found her guilty but recommended mercy. Nonetheless, the judge—who over the years insisted that Aboriginals should be brought under English justice—sentenced her to be hanged, with the body subsequently given over for dissection.

Pilotte's lawyer, Bartholomew Beardsley, encouraged her to petition for mercy, partly on the grounds of substantial communications problems; Pilotte insisted that she had been misunderstood and misinterpreted. But Beardsley also emphasized that Pilotte was a victim of cultural misunderstanding. In Ojibwa society, the girl had acted perfectly appropriately in the way she had given birth. Pilotte knew only 'the customs and maxims of her own nation', which included 'the invariable custom of Indian women to retire and bring forth their children alone, and in secret'. The jury backed her plea for a pardon. One juror wrote to the local newspaper that the jury had recommended mercy because 'she was a savage and had no knowledge of the usages of the Christians.' A number of prominent citizens of Niagara, many of whom were involved in trade with Aboriginals, also supported her petition, as did Robert Gourlay (the Scots-born opponent of the Upper Canadian government at the time).

The appeal went to Upper Canada's chief executive, colonial administrator Samuel Smith, who sent it to London for a final decision. Pilotte waited in prison while the appeal crossed the Atlantic. The British authorities altered her sentence to one year's imprisonment. She had already served most of that time, and she was apparently released to return to her people. The Pilotte case could be read in a number of ways. It could be seen as an illustration of the harshness of the laws against women, as an example of the way in which minorities were treated (for the successful appeal was not common practice), or as an instance of the ultimate triumph of British justice.

PETER JONES

Peter Jones (Kahkewaquonaby). Peter Jones Collection, Victoria University Library (Toronto).

Peter Jones ('Kahkewaquonaby' or 'sacred feathers' in Ojibwa , 'Desagondensta' or 'he stands people on their feet' in Mohawk, 1802–56) was born near Burlington, Upper Canada, the son of a retired English surveyor and a Mississauga chief's daughter. He was brought up among the Mississaugas, and then sent to school by his father, where he was called Peter Jones and acquired English. His father remarried a prominent Mohawk and Peter was adopted into a Mohawk family. Peter was converted to the Methodist Episcopal Church at a camp meeting in Ancaster in 1823, and he led a group of Mississauga Indians—including many of his own family—to a mission village on the Credit River in 1826. The village began farming successfully and had nearly 1,000 acres cleared by the 1830s.

Peter became a trial preacher in 1827 and in 1829 was elected one of the chiefs of this band. He went on circuit to raise money for mission activities, much of it for his own people. He and his brother John (who was for years his faithful assistant) refused at one point to join the Anglicans, despite a tempting offer to do so from Archdeacon John Strachan. Jones toured the United States in 1829 and in 1831 toured Britain, usually appearing in 'Indian' garb, where he had an audience with the King, and met his future wife, Eliza Field, who came to Canada and assisted her husband in his missionary work. Jones was ordained in the Methodist Church in 1833. Jones and his people successfully refused to join other Ojibwa bands in removing to Manitoulin Island in the late 1830s, but some of the Credit people objected to the complete loss of Native identity that Jones preached. In the 1840s he lost much of his energy, and even confessed to his wife—on his third British missionary tour, in 1845—'I am getting heartily tired of begging.'

Jones also objected to posing as an Indian when at heart he felt himself to be totally Europeanized. Several years later he was able to lead 200 of his people to new land on the Grand River at New Credit. His health continued to deteriorate, but he spent his last years residing in a handsome brick Georgian villa constructed for him not far from Brantford. His funeral was quite spectacular, and after his death his wife edited his diaries and his historical papers for publication. He had published many sermons and speeches during his lifetime. Much of his most important work, however, was done in translating scripture and hymns into Ojibwa. Jones assisted his people to survive by adapting to European ways, but he appears to have paid a heavy psychological price for his own efforts to remain within both the Aboriginal and European worlds.

knew full well that the deal was a bad one, but reasoned that if they did not agree they might lose everything. For all the First Nations, the reverberations of extensive settlement could be felt at long distances from the actual European presence, and settlement was inexorably coming to the west as well as to the east.

As for the Blacks, thousands flocked to Upper Canada between 1820 and 1860. Some were slaves seeking freedom, for it was well known in the United States that slavery was illegal in British North America. By and large, the Upper Canadian authorities protected slaves who made their way into the province. After 1830, an increasing level of organization moved fugitive Blacks from the United States. One key development was that of the 'Underground Railroad'. This was, of course, not a railroad at all, but a complex network of organizations, people—Black and White, male and female—and safe houses through which Black fugitives were smuggled northwards and eventually across the border. Fugitive slaves were joined by thousands of freed northern Blacks seeking a better life in British North America. Many of the freed Blacks were active in abolitionist activities and in the Underground Railroad. Harriet Tubman (1820–1913, known as 'Moses') made a number of trips into slave territory from her home in St Catharines, rescuing as many as 300 slaves over the course of her career. Unfortunately, all Blacks faced prejudice and social disadvantage in their new land. They were granted civil liberty but were never really made to feel at home. Many returned to the United States after the Emancipation Proclamation of 1863.

Religion and Education

The privileged élites were supported by the clergy of the established church, the Church of England, as well as by the Church of Scotland and the Roman Catholic Church. All these churches taught the doctrine of subordination to rightful authority. Those not associated with these churches found the pretensions of the ecclesiastical establishment, particularly in maintaining such traditional monopolies as marriage rites and education, constant irritants that could be associated with the oligarchic constitutional system. Dissenters chafed under arrangements that granted 'liberty of conscience' to all Christians while denying them full powers to act in such matters as the solemnization of marriage. The Church of England fought an unsuccessful rearguard action to maintain its pretence to monopoly.

In Lower Canada, the Catholic Church solidified its position within the political structure, especially under Bishop Joseph-Octave Plessis (1763–1825, bishop and archbishop, 1806–25), who was appointed to the province's legislative council in 1817. Plessis presided over the devolution of the Church in British North America. In 1819 Rome elevated him to an archbishopric at the same time that it created new dioceses in Upper Canada and Prince Edward Island, both headed by Highland Scots. Plessis was not himself an ultramontanist. He did not believe that the Church, although the guardian of moral law, must be heeded in all matters relating to politics. But he did attempt, with some success, to strengthen the structure of his Church by educating more clergy, by obtaining government recognition of its legal position (especially in Lower Canada), and by reforming its far-flung governance. His successors were more sympathetic to the pretensions of Rome than Plessis had been.

Dissenters in every colony not only chafed at the conservative social vision of the established churches and their support of hierarchy and privilege but also objected to the view of God they promulgated. The most numerous dissenters were Methodists and their itinerant preachers, although the Baptists also had a considerable following. Most dissenters were evangelicals who believed that God had to be felt emotionally rather than comprehended rationally. These feelings were 'awakened' at revivals and the Methodist 'camp meetings' which were so com-

HARRIET TUBMAN

Born Araminta Ross to slave parents on a Maryland plantation, Harriet Tubman worked in the fields as a child and was subject to many abuses. On one occasion she was struck in the head by an object thrown by an overseer, and thereafter was subject to seizures. She took her mother's Christian name (Harriet) at an early age, and around 1844 married a freed Black named John Tubman. In 1849 she escaped from the plantation and removed without her husband to Philadelphia, where she worked as a cook and began her activities of slave liberation with the Underground Railroad. She started with members of her own family. Although she was both illiterate and physically handicapped, Tubman never let these obstacles interfere with her activities, and, indeed, they probably served as a persuasive disguise for her many clandestine exploits. Who could be suspicious of such a person?

In 1851, after the passage of the Fugitive Slave Act, Harriet removed to St Catharines, Canada, making a number of journeys back into the United States to lead fugitive slaves to freedom. During these years a reward was offered by slaveholders of $40,000 for her capture, dead or alive. In 1857 she returned to Maryland to lead her parents to Canada, subsequently removing them to a house in Auburn, New York, which she bought with the financial assistance of sympathizers, notably William Seward, later the American secretary of state. Tubman opened a boarding house in St Catharines in 1858, and the notorious abolitionist zealot John Brown stayed there in the early part of that year. Brown described Tubman in a letter to his wife as 'the most of a *man*, naturally, that I *ever met* with.' She soon began employing the Auburn home of her parents as a permanent residence, however, although she continued to retain contacts in Canada and received financial assistance from there for many years.

During the American Civil War she acted for the Union Army in a number of capacities, including that of spy, returning to Auburn after the cessation of hostilities. The American Congress refused to give her a pension in 1868. That same year she married Benjamin Davis, and after his death began receiving his pension. Tubman became a mythical figure in the black community from a relatively early period, especially after a biography published in 1869 by Sarah Elizabeth Hopkins Bradford entitled *Harriet Tubman: The Moses of Her People*, which describes her exploits (which are essentially undocumentable) in considerable detail.

mon in Upper Canada. The evangelicals were not only passionate but also populist in their attitude. For many in the establishment, passionate populism was tantamount to revolution.

Education was another area of conflict between establishment privileges and the needs of an expanding population. The Church of England attempted to insist that it alone was entitled to the revenue from Crown lands set aside for the support of a Protestant clergy. It also tried to maintain close control over the institutions of higher education—universities, colleges, and academies—on the grounds that such education had to involve moral as well as technical knowledge. Only a relative handful of students had places at these institutions. For the authorities, education was seen as necessary for social order. For the common folk, it represented a means of mobility and liberation. Systems of education brought to the colonies after 1815 were based on teaching the older children, who in turn passed their lessons by rote to the younger. Only towards the end of the period was there much demand for broadly based public education. The curricula of such schools as existed were extremely eclectic. Despite the absence of regular schooling in most provinces, the population was surprisingly literate. Immigrants brought with them their educational experiences in England, Ireland, Scotland, or America. These experiences were often coloured by a substantial class bias as well as ethnic and denominational ones.

Colonial Culture

The schools were not yet the bearers of the cultural aspirations of the resource society of British North America. While a common stereotype identifies this period as one of extremely limited and primitive cultural and artistic production—particularly by European or American standards—such a view reflects a particular set of assumptions about culture. Indigenous high culture was understandably rare. Foreign models were usually employed. There was, however, a substantial folk culture, which included a well-established oral tradition, in the form of tales and songs, handed down from generation to generation and from group to group. There was also a tradition of craftsmanship. The simple pine furniture of clean, uncluttered functional lines produced by hundreds of anonymous craftsmen during the colonial period found little favour in succeeding generations, which regarded heavy ornamentation and the use of highly polished wood veneers as exemplary. But today we recognize that the aesthetic values of those anonymous furniture makers were on a level with their high craftsmanship.

Most high culture was produced by people who made their living in some other way, and who often regarded their artistic activity as diversion or by-product rather than conscious art or professional activity. Most of the producers of élite culture—like most of the élite of this period—were born abroad. Of the 538 people given entries in Volume VII of the *Dictionary of Canadian Biography*, covering those who died between 1835 and 1850, fewer than 200 were born in the colonies, and most of these were born in Lower Canada. Young people educated in British North America were usually trained by seniors who were educated abroad, usually with emphasis on slavish reproduction of both form and content. There was some respectable work.

In literature, John Richardson (1796–1852) produced one unusual novel in *Wacousta, or, The Prophecy*, published anonymously in London and Edinburgh in 1832. Thomas McCulloch (1776–1843) had a literary success with short sketches, *The Letters of Mephibosheth Stepsure*, originally published in a newspaper and not collected in book form until 1960. Thomas Chandler Haliburton (1796–1865) wrote twenty-one sketches about Sam Slick in 1835–6, which became *The Clockmaker; or The Sayings and Doings of Samuel Slick, of Slickville*. Haliburton went on to become an international best-selling writer. Both McCulloch and Haliburton produced their best work for a local colonial audience. When they wrote for international markets, they were less imaginative and inventive.

Another interesting development of this period was the emergence of middle-class female authors, often recent immigrants, who portrayed the colonial scene in their works. The first novel by a native British North American—*St Ursula's Convent; or, The Nun in Canada,* published in Kingston in 1824—was written by Julia Catherine Hart (1796–1867)—née Julia Beckwith of Fredericton, New Brunswick. Nearly 150 subscribers paid 9s 4d for copies of the two-volume work. Hart published several other novels, all of which were characterized by unrealistic, often fantastic, plots and settings. In *St Ursula's Convent* she tapped a rich vein of Protestant suspicion of what Catholics 'got up to' in convents, although her tale was more melodramatic than immoral.

The Strickland sisters—Catharine Parr Traill (1802–99) and Susanna Moodie (1803–85)—were more polished, and each sister wrote a classic work based on her experiences as an immigrant in Canada (Gray, 1999).

MEPHIBOSHETH STEPSURE

When the readers of the *Acadian Recorder* opened their newspapers on 22 December 1821, they found the following, the first in what was to become a series of letters to the editor. The anonymous author was Thomas McCulloch, Presbyterian minister of Pictou.

Gentlemen:

Happening one day to call upon Parson Drone, the clergyman of our town, I found him administering his old, standard consolation to my neighbour Solomon Gosling. The parson has been long among us, and is a very good sort of man; but, I believe, he has fared very hardly: for though my townsmen all respect him, and are the most active people in the world at selling watches and swapping horses, they have never made themselves richer and, therefore, have little to give but good wishes. But the parson, except when he is angry, is very good-natured and disposed to bear with a great deal; and, having acquired a large fund of patience himself, he has become a quack at comforting, and prescribes it indiscriminately for all sorts of ills. His own life has been spent between starving and preaching; and having no resources himself, it never occurred to him that, for the wants and troubles of others, there can be any remedy but patience.

My neighbour Gosling is completely an everyday character. His exact likeness may be found at any time, in any part of the Province. About thirty years ago, his father David left him very well to do; and Solomon, who at that time was a brisk young man, had the prospect, by using a little industry, of living as comfortably as any in the town. Soon after the death of old David, he was married and a likelier couple were not often to be seen. But unluckily for them both, when Solomon went to Halifax in the winter, Polly went along with him to sell her turkeys and see the fashions; and from that day the Goslings had never a day to do well. Solomon was never very fond of hard work. At the same time he could not be accused of idleness. He was always a very good neighbour; and at every burial or barn raising, Solomon was set down as one who would be sure to be there. By these means he gradually contracted the habit of running about; which left his own premises in an unpromising plight. Polly, too, by seeing the fashions, had learnt to be genteel; and for the sake of a little show, both lessened the thrift of the family, and added to the outlay; so that, between one thing and another, Solomon began to be hampered, and had more calls than comforters.

When the troubles of life arise out of idleness, a return to industry is usually the last shift. The habits which my neighbour had been gradually contracting, left him little stomach for the patient and persevering toils of a farming life: nor would urgent necessity permit him to wait for the sure but slow returns of agricultural exertion. But necessity is the mother of invention; and though the family of Goslings were never much noted for profundity of intellect, Solomon, by pure dint of scheming, contrived both to relieve himself from his immediate embarrassments and to avoid hard labour. Though Goose Hill farm, from want of industry, had not been productive, it was still a property of considerable value: and it occurred to Solomon, that, converted into goods, it would yield more prompt and lucrative returns than by any mode of agriculture. Full of the idea, accordingly, my neighbour went to town; and by mortgaging his property to Calibogus, the West India merchant, he returned with a general assortment of merchandise, suited to the wants of the town. When I say a general assortment, it is necessary to be a little more explicit. It did not contain any of those articles which are employed in subduing the forest, or in cultivating the soil. These he knew to be not very saleable. He was aware that though old Tubal Thump supplies the whole town with iron work, he is so miserably poor, that he can scarcely keep himself in materials. The only article of the iron kind which he brought was a hogshead of horse shoes, which a blacksmith in Aberdeen, who knew something of America, had sent out upon speculation. From the number of horses and young people in the township, Solomon knew that horse shoes would meet with a ready sale.

SOURCE: Thomas McCulloch, *Letters of Mephibosheth Stepsure* (Halifax, 1862), reprinted as *The Stepsure Letters* (Toronto: McClelland and Stewart, 1960), 11–12.

Traill's *The Backwoods of Canada* (London 1836) is made up of eighteen letters home to family and friends in Suffolk. It is a sensitive early account of the pioneer experience. Never complaining, she left readers with an overall impression of cheerful adaptation to the rigours of life in a previously unsettled area of Upper Canada, where she willingly made do with whatever was at hand. Upper Canada itself, however, is portrayed as a land 'with no historical associations, no legendary tales of those that came before', and the impenetrable forest all around her is 'desolate', 'interminable', 'a maze'. It simultaneously isolates and liberates the author. Susanna Moodie's *Roughing It in the Bush: or, Forest Life in Canada* (1852) is the best known of a number of works by Moodie that offer trenchant (and often discouraging) descriptions of the pioneering experience. Moodie was particularly good at the satirical description of the customs of the average immigrant, customs such as the 'bee' and the 'charivari'.

Another successful writer was Anna Brownell Jameson (1794–1860). More willing to flout the gender rules of her society, Jameson was a well-published author in 1825 when she married the lawyer Robert Jameson. She did not initially accompany her husband to Dominica or to Upper Canada when he received judicial appointments in the colonies, but joined him temporarily in 1836 while she attempted to negotiate a legal separation. While in Canada she travelled extensively, and the result of her journeys was the book *Winter Tales and Summer Rambles in Canada* (1838). Jameson deliberately set out to relate her adventures from both a personal and a feminist point of view. As she records under the date of 13 March 1837, 'In these days when society is becoming every day more artificial and complex, and marriage, as the gentlemen assure us, more and more expensive, hazardous and inexpedient, women *must* find means to fill up the void of existence' (quoted in Gerry 1990/91: 37). Most women from the élite classes did not attempt to publish their literary efforts, but instead composed lengthy and fascinating letters to friends and family or kept diaries which remained in family papers and have only in recent years been published.

In the non-literary arts, the official culture of British North America was derivative and unadventurous. Painters inevitably emphasized Euro-

'The Woolsey Family', William Berczy, 1809, oil on canvas. If the sitters in this portrait look oddly detached from one another, the reason is that the artist drew each one separately. Once all the figures had been transferred to the canvas, he painted in the background around them. National Gallery of Canada, Ottawa, 5875. Gift of Major Edgar C. Woolsey, Ottawa.

pean styles and techniques, which were sometimes acquired from working with established masters, and the market had little interest in anything else. Within this tradition a few fine painters emerged, such as William Berczy (1744–1813), Louis Dulongpré (see p. 113 above), and Joseph Légaré (1796–1855). In architecture, Late Georgian style predominated. It was not only what architects and craftsmen knew, it symbolized British authority and epitomized British standards.

Rather more interesting things were happening in the vernacular culture of the common people, which tended to be oral rather than written, traditional rather than imitative, and often connected either with artisan conventions or religious energy. For all inhabitants of British North America, singing religious hymns and secular songs was an important part of their lives. People sang as they worked in the fields, the voyageurs sang as they paddled their canoes, and fishermen sang as they pulled up their nets. Most of what was sung was inherited from Europe, although both music and lyrics were frequently altered by time and new circumstances. Many pioneers sprang from ethnic backgrounds in which the bard, a combination of poet and songster, represented an important folk memory. Gaelic-speaking bards from the highlands of Scotland not only carried on the tradition in British North America but extended it. A rich heritage of crafting in wood produced not only furniture and useful ornamentation

'Curling on the lake near Halifax', c. 1867, from Lt Henry Buckton Laurence, *Sketches of Canadian Sports and Pastimes* (London, 1870). NAC (W.H. Coverdale Collection of Canadiana), C-041092.

(such as the weather vane), but the sailing-ship itself, a monument to the skills of carpenters and builders. Popular culture suggested some of the rich possibilities for creative adaptation. By 1840, for example, Scottish settlers familiar with the sport of curling had not only imported the game into a climate ideally suited for it but had made great strides forward in its popularization and regularization. So successful was the game that around 1840 the world's first indoor curling facility was constructed in Montreal.

THE POLITICS OF THE ÉLITE

Like the culture, the politics of the resource society were in flux. By 1820 the governments of the various provinces of British North America were becoming well ensconced in power. The pattern was a fairly standard one, even for Newfoundland, which still did not have representative government and would not acquire it until 1832. Each colonial government was headed by a governor (or lieutenant-governor). Appointed in England, he was often a military man. No figureheads, governors of this period had considerable power and autonomy. The governor administered the province in association with the principal office holders—also English appointments, although sometimes colonials were appointed—who, with the prominent merchants, comprised his council or councils. The resultant oligarchies were given various derisive labels. In Upper

Canada there was the 'Family Compact', in Lower Canada the 'Château Clique', in Nova Scotia the 'System', and in Prince Edward Island 'the Cabal'. As administrations, these groups were not necessarily unenlightened Tories. They believed in the need to increase the prosperity of their colonies, and usually attempted to mediate among the conflicting interests that emerged, provided they remained well ordered. Most of the oligarchies favoured government intervention in the economy, particularly through the creation of new infrastructure such as banks, roads, and canals. The popularly elected assembly, which comprised one part of the legislative system that also included the council (or in some provinces, a separate legislative council), had a very limited role in the process of government. In 1820 the assemblies did not yet have control of the revenue or finances of the provinces, much less any real involvement in their administration.

Under this constitutional arrangement, political conflict could take a number of forms. One involved disagreement between the governor and the oligarchy that comprised the provincial administration. This could come about either because the governor was expected to implement unpopular instructions from the mother country, or because he sought to limit the self-perpetuating power of the oligarchs. More frequently after 1820, the conflict involved a fierce struggle between the administration and the leaders of an assembly eager to expand its prerogatives and authority. A new generation of political leaders emerged who were willing to invoke popular support on behalf of their attacks on the prevailing governments. Four reformers stand out in this period: William Lyon Mackenzie (1795–1861) of Upper Canada, Louis-Joseph Papineau (1786–1871) of Lower Canada, Joseph Howe (1804–73) of Nova Scotia, and William Cooper (1786–1867) of Prince Edward Island. None of these men actually overturned the political system, but they did make some inroads against it, anticipating in a variety of ways a gradual democratization of politics in British North America.

☐ William Lyon Mackenzie, 1834, by an unknown artist; lithograph published in *Canadiana Military Events*, III, 337. NAC, C-24937.

All four reformers (and others) sounded radical in their rhetoric. All believed in the importance of the 'independent cultivator of the soil', displaying profound hostility to commerce, the merchant classes, and expensive economic development by the public sector (quoted in Halpenny 1976: 156). Equality of conditions and opportunity was what mattered. William Cooper sought this equality through escheat, a process by which the large landholders of Prince Edward Island would be stripped of their ill-gotten holdings and the land redistributed to those who actually tilled the soil. In the 1830s both Papineau and Mackenzie turned to the American ideas of Jacksonian democracy when they found themselves unable either to persuade

JOSEPH HOWE

Joseph Howe in later life, 1871. NAC, C-22002.

Joseph Howe (1804–73) was the son of a Halifax Loyalist printer, largely self-educated, who had entered the family firm and then began publishing his own newspaper, the *Novascotian*, in 1828. His paper increasingly pressed for political reform, and Howe was acquitted of criminal libel in 1835. This persecution encouraged him to enter politics in 1836 as a Reformer, and it was his government that in 1847 achieved responsible government. In 1855 he helped recruit in the United States for the Crimean War, making comments that cost him the Catholic vote in his province in 1857. He became premier again (1860–3), then imperial fishery commissioner (1863–6).

Although the young Howe had visions of a unified British North America, the mature politician did not want Nova Scotia to become absorbed into Canadian expansion. Thus Howe led the anticonfederate forces in Nova Scotia, focusing in 1866 particularly on the failure of the Tupper government to submit the question to an election. He led an anticonfederate party to success in the first dominion elections, but was unable to effect repeal in Ottawa and entered the federal cabinet in 1869. Howe was famed as one of the great orators of nineteenth-century Canada.

the British government of the inadequacy of existing constitutional arrangements or to alter the system by political activity. These reformers wanted to overturn the corrupt oligarchies that ran their respective provinces, and replace them with administrations that would be responsible to the province as represented in the House of Assembly. They could also agree, as a result of their agrarian and anticommercial assumptions, that public 'improvements' paid for by the public purse or sponsored by the government (such as canals and banks) represented an unnecessary financial burden on the taxpayer, being in effect 'class legislation'. As Mackenzie argued, the 'true source of a country's wealth' was 'labour usefully and prudently applied' (quoted in Fairley 1960: 217). For Papineau in Lower Canada, an active economic state was being dominated not only by a mercantile class but by a British mercantile class, which promoted capitalism.

It is in the context of the struggle between commercial capitalism and agrarian idealism

LOUIS-JOSEPH PAPINEAU

☐ Louis-Joseph Papineau, lithograph by Antoine Maurin. NAC, C-5435.

Louis-Joseph Papineau (1786–1871) was the son of a Montreal notary who purchased the seigneury of Petite-Nation from the Quebec seminary in 1802. He was educated at the Petit Séminaire and then trained as a lawyer.

In 1809 Papineau was first elected to the legislative assembly of Lower Canada, beginning an association of nearly fifty years with that body. He joined the Parti Canadien at the outset, and was chosen speaker of the House in 1815. As leader of that party and its successor, the Parti Patriote, after 1826, he advocated political reform that would leave the traditional social system intact. Papineau was simultaneously a democrat and a social conservative suspicious of the economic and social transformations occurring in his province.

Over the years his commitment to British institutions decreased, and he became more attracted to the American model of Jacksonian democracy, which sought to eliminate political privilege without radical social change. Papineau's commitment to the survival of beleaguered French Canada also increased. He did not instigate the popular rebellion of 1837, but he did try (with limited success) to become its leader. His inability to lead the rebellion was intimately connected with his inability to understand the aspirations of the rebels. When threatened with arrest he fled to the United States, and he played little part in the renewal of insurrection in 1838. He spent some years in exile in France, returning to Canada in 1845 and to politics in 1848.

that we must understand both the Tory commitment to public involvement in economic activity and the reform opposition. These political reformers had no conception that economic development could be directed by government on behalf of the people, any more than they had a general conception of any positive role for the state in ensuring the social well-being of its citizenry. They were typical nineteenth-century liberal democrats who sought to reduce (rather than increase) the influence of government on the lives of the population, as well as to limit the temptation of special privilege. As Mackenzie put it in a broadside entitled 'Independence' in late November 1837, 'We contend, that in all laws made, or to be made, every person shall be bound alike—neither should any tenure, estate, charter, degree, birth or place, confer any exemption from the ordinary course of legal proceedings and responsibilities whereunto others are subjected' (quoted in Fairley 1960: 223).

REFORM AND REBELLION

Eventually in 1837 the frustration of the reformers in the Canadas led to rebellion. Political violence was hardly new in 1837; it was endemic throughout this era. Though sometimes spontaneous, it could also be carefully calculated for partisan purposes. The mob was the political expression of the ordinary inhabitant, who was not usually at the centre of politics in this period. The difference in 1837 was the attempt to coordinate large-scale violence to overthrow the governments of the Canadas by force. The uprisings can be viewed in a variety of ways: as political events, as cultural manifestations, as examples of subterranean pressures resulting from agrarian discontent, or, in Lower Canada, as an expression of Anglo–French animosity. They were a combination of all these things. Had the rebellions not been so quickly and brutally suppressed, similar uprisings might well have broken out in the lower provinces, particularly in Prince Edward Island, where agrarian and political discontents were also strong.

On one level the rebellions of 1837 were unsuccessful challenges to the stability of the élite political cultures of the Canadas. The ostensible leaders, William Lyon Mackenzie and Louis-Joseph Papineau, had become totally frustrated in their attempts to wrest control of the government from the hands of the powerful cliques of Toronto and Quebec and put it in the hands of the popularly elected assemblies. Part of the frustration, particularly for Mackenzie, was that the assemblies themselves could be manipulated by the oligarchy. The so-called 'popular parties' in the assemblies of the colonies were in large part dominated by members of regional élites who were more representative of the grassroots countryside. The regional élites wanted a more open political culture. If home rule was one ambition of the reformers, the expansion of politics beyond the ranks of the governing élite (and their kin) was another. In this sense the rebellions marked the first of a series of movements in Canadian history to decentralize authority and political power.

In Lower Canada, the Parti Canadien and its successor, the Parti Patriote, more consistently dominated the lower house than had the reformers in Upper Canada. The reason was that the party conflict in Lower Canada had long since taken on racial overtones. The Parti Canadien was dominated by French-Canadian professionals who represented the regional élites and who had no hope of gaining admission to the ruling Château Clique. In February 1834, the Ninety-Two Resolutions, prepared by Papineau and three others, were adopted by the assembly of Lower Canada and submitted to London. They catalogued grievances and requests, among them the legislature's control of revenue, the executive's responsibility to the electorate, and the election of legislative councillors. These resolutions were in effect rejected by the British Parliament in March 1837, and the way was opened for rebellion.

Beyond their political and constitutional significance, the rebellions were also manifestations of popular, especially agrarian, discontent. Part of the reason for the ineffectuality of the rebellions was that there was little relationship between the reform leaders—who were operating within the élite system even while trying to change it—and popular opinion, which was responding to the collapse of the international wheat market in the mid-1830s. Both Mackenzie and Papineau persistently denied that they had planned an insurrection, although they were prepared to lead one when it emerged. Rural districts had been restive for several years in both provinces, and some protest meetings held in 1837 were attended by armed farmers. A rural uprising near Brantford,

WILLIAM LYON MACKENZIE DESCRIBES AN ELECTION CAMPAIGN, 1824

On Monday morning we arrived at St Thomas, the place appointed for holding the election for the county of Middlesex, of which I will now give a brief account. The hustings were placed near the church, on a high and well-chosen spot of ground. The village was crowded with people, and the result of a contested election, not yet begun, was joyfully anticipated by the friends of all three of the candidates though, of course, only two could succeed. Groups stood in every direction, some wearing an oak-tree leaf in their hats, which signified 'Mathews and Liberty'; others, ribbons as favours. On one man's hat was tied a broad orange ribbon: the inscription, 'Rolph and Mathews', showed his party; three-fourths of the people had no party emblems about them at all. A little after ten o'clock, Mr Warren, the returning officer, Colonel Talbot, Mr Rolph, Colonel Burwell, Captain Matthews, and Mr Bostwick, mounted the hustings. Mr Warren was dressed in blue, had his sword appended to his side, and cut a fine figure as returning officer. He read the writ, and five or six hundred persons, who were bystanders, were hushed, when the tall figure of Colonel Burwell was extended to its full length, as he arose to address the multitude. He commenced pleading in justification of his past conduct, and parried admirably the thrusts of some teasing electors who were perpetually demanding why he had acted so and so, why did this, and said that? He spoke of the milk of human kindness, of location tickets, of flogging bills, of asking no votes, and read part of the Upper Canada Gazette for the edification of those present. . . . The next speaker after Colonel Burwell was Captain Mathews, of the half-pay (or rather retired allowance) royal artillery; he met a joyful, kind reception. His manly, athletic form and courteous demeanour, added to the independent English principles he professed to espouse, secured to him a distinguished place in the good graces of many a worthy yeoman. . . . This wealthy intelligent, and patriotic Englishman made an excellent speech, remarkable for its brevity, considering the variety of subjects he embraced; as he concluded the people rent the air with their acclamations. . . . His well-wishers have only one fear, namely that he will [act] too independent a part. Mr Rolph (who spoke last) promised to act with independence, and to defend the people's rights; spoke with considerable animation of the fine country in which he that day had the honour to be a candidate; expressed a warm interest in its prosperity and that of the province at large; adverted to the time when it was a desert; reminded them of what had been effected in twenty-one years, and augured well of the future fate of the country, its agriculture, and its infant manufactures. Getting warm, he forgot that he was at a country election, and commenced a sentence in his professional way, 'Gentlemen of the Jury'. . . . It was a cheering spectacle to a friend of Canada to see the happy groups of horsemen from every quarter ride up to the hustings, shouting blithely, 'Rolph and Mathews!'—'Mathews and Liberty!' Even the newly-elected members of Oxford came with their bands of yeomen to vote for the men of the people's choice. Mr Burwell had represented the country for twelve years, and his votes and conduct had so incensed the farmers that they determined to put him out. That precious political selection, the local magistracy, supported him almost to a man.

SOURCE: M. Fairley, ed., *The Selected Writings of William Lyon Mackenzie* (Toronto: Oxford University Press, 1960): 20–2.

THE UPPER CANADIAN REBELLION, 1837

Adam Hope to Robert Hope, 24 December 1837

. . . The St. Thomas Volunteers were called out into active service. Dr Chas Duncombe M.P.P. for Oxford was understood to be posted in the Township of Oakland with 500 men, about 10 miles from Brantford, in a westerly direction, and supposed to be mediating an attack upon that village. After the defeat of MacKenzie & his Brother Rebels at Toronto Col. MacNab of Hamilton was dispatched with 400 men to dislodge the Rebels under Duncombe & scour the London District at the same time despatches were sent to the Clerk of the Peace of this District, an active & determined man—to raise the Militia & effect a junction with MacNab. About 50 or 60 political fanatics, chiefly young men, from the township had gone off in a body to join Duncombe, armed with rifles & toma hawks; this had a corresponding influence upon the loyal disposed inhabitants of St. Thomas who simultaneously resolved to arm themselves & follow the Rebels. It was given out that the only object of our expedition was to overtake the rebels who had gone from Yarmouth & bring them to account for their insolence. The whole company I believe with the exception of one individual was in the dark about the ultimate object of our mission. Waggons were pressed into our service in all directions. Several Barrels of Pork, Beef & Bread followed the army & on the forenoon of the 13th the Volunteers amtg to 50 & the Militia to about as many left St. Thomas. The whole village was in a state of great excitement. I left a few directions with Mr Hodge who stopped at home to look after matters in the event of accident, about my papers &c, & soon found myself in the *ranks* of the Volunteers with a good Yankee rifle on my shoulder & several rounds of ball cartridge in my pocket. One of the waggons carried also a supply of Powder & Ball. It was cheering to see the enthusiasm of the People who turned out to join our ranks as we passed along the road. Our great difficulty was to procure a sufficient supply of firearms & in order to accomplish this the Magistrate authorized our men to seize what arms they could find in the houses on the road in the '*Queen's name*.' Our force amounted to about 150 men bearing arms before we have travelled 20 miles. . . .

SOURCE: Colin Read and Ronald J. Stagg, eds, *The Rebellion of 1837 in Upper Canada* (Toronto: Carleton University Press, 1989), 234.

Upper Canada, led by Dr Charles Duncombe (1792–1867), dispersed on 13 December when he heard of the easy defeat of Mackenzie's motley crew of rebels at Montgomery's Tavern north of Toronto. Certainly the rural districts in Lower Canada provided their own rationale and impetus for rising in arms against the government. When political agitation turned to insurrection, many moderate members of the élite leadership of the reformers fell away, to be replaced by armed farmers.

Unfortunately for the rebels in both the Canadas, their self-declared leaders had a fairly narrow agenda of political change and no notion of how to turn a spontaneous uprising into an organized rebellion. Mackenzie, Papineau, and Duncombe all became caught up in their own hysteria, panicked, and fled to leave others to

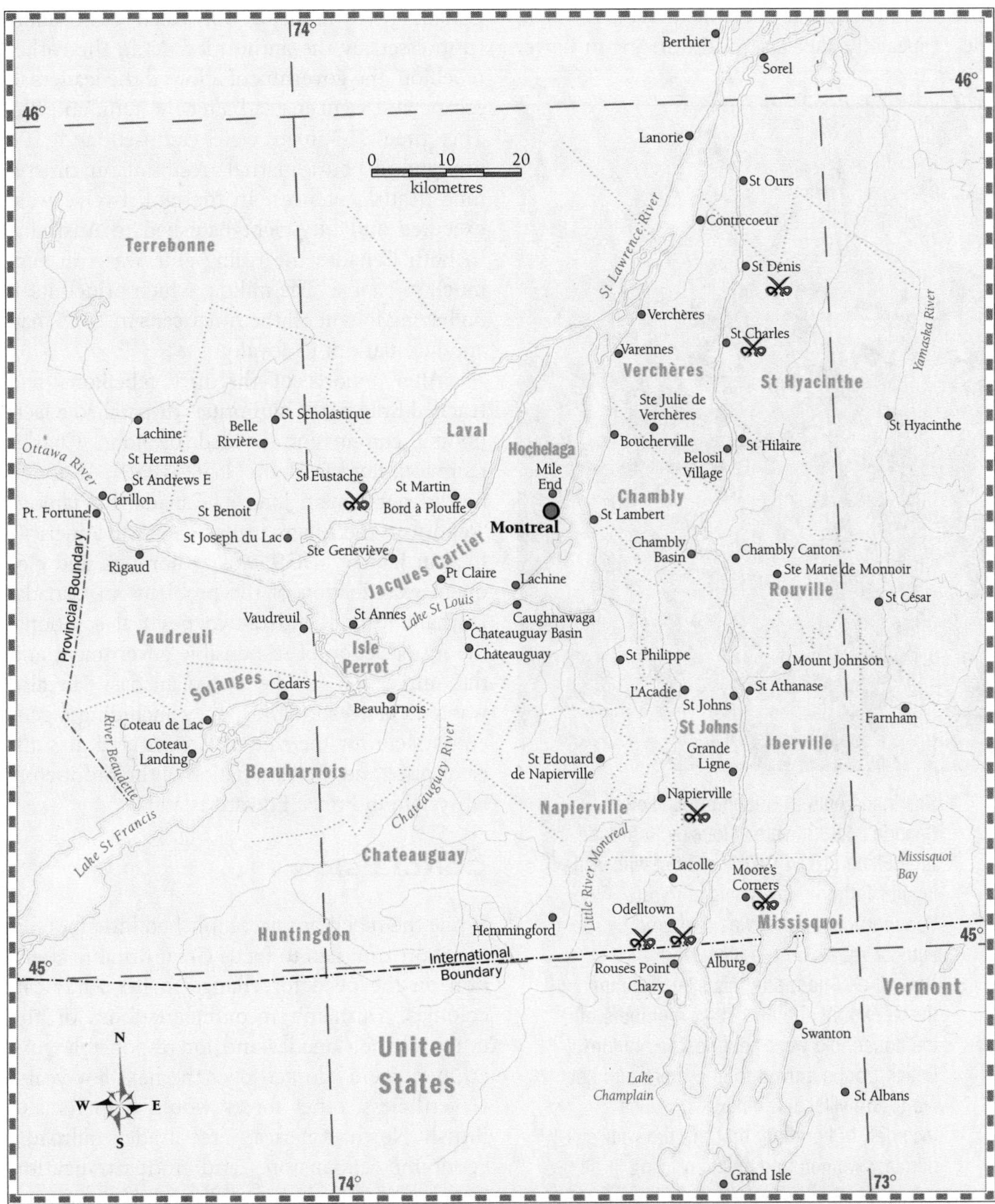

Southwestern Lower Canada in 1837, showing the region of Lower Canada in which the major fighting of the 1837 rebellion occurred. The battles, mainly the result of local rural uprisings, are marked with crossed swords. Based on a map from A.D. Decelles' *The Patriotes of '37: A Chronicle of the Lower Canadian Rebellion* (1916).

face the music. There was considerable music to face, especially after a second uprising in Lower Canada in November 1838, which was brutally suppressed by the authorities. As in the earlier rebellion, the government allowed the leaders to escape and went instead after the rank and file. This time 753 men were captured and 108 brought to court martial, resulting in ninety-nine death sentences. In the end, twelve were executed and fifty-eight banished to Australia. In both Canadas the ruling élite was still very much in charge. The militia, which prided itself on having fought off the Americans in 1815, had another mark of its loyalty.

'The Insurgents at Beauharnois, Lower Canada', 1838, watercolour by Katherine Jane Ellice (1814-64). The artist was visiting her father-in-law's seigneury at Beauharnois when it was captured by Patriote rebels on the night of 4 November. She made this sketch during the week that she and other members of the household were held hostage before British troops arrived to free them and set fire to the village. The next day, Ellice recorded in her diary that the fire was 'still burning; women and children flying in all directions. Such are the melancholy consequences of civil war.' NAC, C-013392.

After reports of the first rebellions had reached Britain, the authorities dispatched a fact-finding commission headed by John Charles Lambton, Lord Durham (1792–1840). Although he did not remain long in Canada, his famous 'Report on the Affairs in British North America', filed in January 1839, was a thorough and eloquent examination of the problems in Canada. Durham recommended two political solutions: the introduction of responsible government and the unification of the two Canadas. He also wanted changes in land policy, including a general system for the sale of Crown land at sufficient price and the elimination of the proprietorial system in Prince Edward Island.

CONCLUSION

While the rebellions accomplished little more in the short run than to focus Great Britain's attention on the need for change in her American colonies, Durham's recommendations for the union of the Canadas and for responsible government were adopted over the next few years. Nevertheless, other forces would help remake British North America. Free trade, railroads, economic expansion, and industrialization were, in the end, more powerful engines of change than either political uprisings or constitutional reform.

HOW HISTORY HAS CHANGED

EMIGRATION AND IMMIGRATION

In some ways, the history of immigration and settlement in early Canada has not changed very much over the years. The overall story told in older works is still recognizable in the twenty-first century, although as in so many other areas, we could use a new synthesis. At the same time that the old works are still relevant, constant revision has occurred in important but scattered parts of the story. The older works are much more important for telling us about government policy than about immigrant decision-making.

One of the most important questions for students of transatlantic movement has always been whether to concentrate on 'emigration'—the process of leaving the homeland—or 'immigration'—the process of coming to a new land and adapting to it. The traditional tendency had been for the British historians to treat the process as emigration, and the North Americans to investigate it as immigration. One set of scholars took the migrants to the boats, another set picked them up at the boats on the other side, and the matter of the transatlantic passage was negotiable for both sets, with a literature of its own. By and large, the view from Europe has always been less favourable to and enthusiastic about the transatlantic movement of population than has been the view from North America.

Developments in funding and technology have made it possible for Canadians to do detailed research in the British archives, including the local study necessary to investigate carefully the origins of immigrants and then to follow them to their Canadian destinations. Along the way, Canadian scholars have made a significant contribution to understanding why it was that people sought to leave—or were pushed from—their homeland. They have also helped us understand how and why these people settled where they did on the other end. The tendency for the research to become much more microscopic in nature has made it possible to understand and highlight new aspects of the process. Modern treatments understand the importance of the communication of information within the population likely to emigrate, particularly letters from North America and word-of-mouth linkages among family and community groups. Modern discussions appreciate the 'chain' nature of most immigration. They also understand the importance of the economic situation of the immigrant, and especially the amount of money he or she is able to bring to the transplantation process.

There has also in recent years been much more concentration on the cultural baggage of the immigrants, and its adaptation in the new homeland. Modern Canadian scholarship on transatlantic movement, with its increasing focus on origins of immigrants as well as on destinations, has had to come to terms with the regional complexities of the British Isles. There were at least three Irelands, at least two Scotlands, at least two distinctive peoples in Wales, and a number of distinctive regions in England itself. In the beginning, not all of these people were first-language English speakers, and religious preferences were complex. The question of the impact of this regionalism on Canadian development has started to be considered in the literature in ways that go beyond the traditional ethnic approach of 'The Scot in Canada' or 'The Irish in Canada'. The question of the cultural identities of the immigrants from the British Isles is a complex one, not least because on one level there was a British identity and on other levels a series of regional and national ones.

More attention is now being paid to the literature of immigration—particularly the substantial number of publications purporting to give advice to prospective immigrants—and to the letters home of immigrants, both those published at the time and those unpublished until recently. Lurking under all the analysis is the question of whether immigration to British North America actually fulfilled the expectations of the immigrants. Scholars are only now turning to examine the return flow of disappointed immigrants to their areas of origin.

Short Bibliography

Brown, Jennifer, *Strangers in Blood: Fur Trade Company Families in Indian Country*. Vancouver, 1980. A fascinating study of family life in the fur trade in the first half of the nineteenth century.

Cadigan, Sean T. *Hope and Deception in Conception Bay: Merchant-Settler Relations in Newfoundland 1785–1855*. Toronto, 1995. A revisionist analysis of socio-economic relations in Newfoundland, based largely on underutilized court records.

Cameron, Wendy, and Mary McDougall Maude. *Assisting Emigration to Upper Canada: The Petworth Project 1832–7*. Montreal and Kingston, 2000. A recent account of one of the largest assisted emigration schemes of the 1830s.

Creighton, Donald, *The Empire of the St Lawrence*. Toronto, 1958. The classic study of the old mercantile system of Canada.

Greer, Allan. *The Patriots and the People: Rebellion of 1837 in Rural Lower Canada*. Toronto, 1994. A recent account of the Lower Canadian rebellion of 1837, focusing on the rural community and popular agitation.

Houston, Cecil, and W.J. Smyth. *Irish Emigration and Canadian Settlement: Patterns, Links, and Letters*. Toronto, 1990. A useful study of the emigration of the Irish—from both North and South—to Canada.

Johnston, Hugh. *British Emigration Policy, 1815–1830: 'Shovelling Out Paupers'*. Oxford, 1972. The standard study of British policy in the era of pauper emigration.

Lower, A.R.M. *Great Britain's Woodyard: British America and the Timber Trade 1763–1867*. Montreal, 1973. An important analysis of British North America's timber trade.

McCallum, John. *Unequal Beginnings: Agriculture and Economic Development in Quebec and Ontario until 1870*. Toronto, 1970. A controversial and revisionist study which argues that Ontario enjoyed advantages over Quebec because of its agricultural beginnings.

Macdonald, Norman. *Immigration and Settlement: The Administration of the Imperial Land Regulations, 1763–1840*. Toronto, 1939. An old but useful study of land policy and immigration.

Ouellet, Fernand. *Economic and Social History of Quebec, 1760–1850: Structures and Conjunctures*. Toronto, 1985. A provocative survey by the leading scholar of French Canada in the early nineteenth century, based on European historical conceptualizations.

Read, Colin. *The Rising in Western Upper Canada, 1837–8: The Duncombe Revolt and After*. Toronto, 1983. A good corrective to the notion that William Lyon Mackenzie led the only rebellion in Upper Canada in 1837.

Sager, Eric, and L. Fischer. *Shipping and Shipbuilding in Atlantic Canada, 1820–1914*. Ottawa, 1986. An innovative study, based on a massive collaborative project funded by the Social Sciences Research Council of Canada.

Stewart, Gordon. *The Origins of Canadian Politics: A Comparative Approach*. Vancouver, 1986. A provocative survey based on American and

British political models.

Warkentin, Germaine, ed. *Canadian Exploration Literature: An Anthology*. Toronto, 1993. A rich collection of what was probably the most robust writing in British America before 1850.

Wilton, Carol. *Popular Politics and Political Culture in Upper Canada, 1800–1850*. Montreal and Kingston, 2000. A recent study focusing on popular politics in Upper Canada.

Wynn, Graeme. *Timber Colony: A Historical Geography of Early Nineteenth Century New Brunswick*. Toronto, 1981. A richly rewarding analysis of timbering in early New Brunswick.

STUDY QUESTIONS

1. Why was the relationship between land policy and immigration so critical?
2. How did the British attitude toward emigration change in the first half of the nineteenth century?
3. If you were contemplating immigration to British North America in the first half of the nineteenth century, what would be the most important questions that you would want answered before you made a decision?
4. How might the data on Crown lands (Table 4.1) have assisted prospective immigrants? What could prospective immigrants have concluded from these charts?
5. Identify the four staple resources in British North America at this time.
6. Identify and explain the most important characteristics of the resource economy of British America between 1815 and 1840.
7. How did élite society operate in British North America in the first half of the nineteenth century?
8. What were the causes of the rebellions of 1837? Were they the same in both Upper and Lower Canada? Would you have supported the rebellions?

CHAPTER FIVE

Becoming a Nation, 1840–1867

A seamless web of political and economic expansion, beginning somewhere around 1840, ended in Canadian Confederation. Between 1840 and 1871, British North America changed from a collection of loosely connected colonies in the northeastern sector of the continent, heavily dependent on the mother country both economically and politically, to a transcontinental nation with a rapidly diversifying internal economy in the early stages of industrialization. Because the province of Canada took the lead in national unification, the beginning of the process can be identified as the Act of Union, which joined Upper and Lower Canada in July 1840.

British North Americans had witnessed many changes over the centuries since first settlement. But in terms of technology, a settler in 1640 would have still been quite at home in the Canada of 1840. The era of political unification was the first period that experienced substantial technological advances, radically altering perceptions of distance and time in a vast domain separated from Europe by thousands of miles of ocean. With the railroad, travel not only sped up substantially, it acquired a predictable timetable. The discovery of telegraphy, and the eventual laying of a transatlantic cable from Newfoundland in 1866, affected the perception of time as well as distance. By 1870 the largest telegraph company in Canada had 20,000 miles (32,000 km) of wire extended across eastern Canada. Communication now could take place in seconds instead of months. The ability to operate to a schedule and communicate instantly completely altered the world and the way people operated within it. These changes were not a necessary prerequisite for union, but they were clearly part of the facilitating background. In many respects, modern Canada began not in 1867 with political unification but in the 1840s, the first era of transforming technological change.

From Imperialism to Free Trade

By 1840 the mercantile economy of British North America had reached its apex, and it began to undergo considerable change. That alteration resulted from a number of factors. The most important was clearly the British government's demolition of the imperial trading system, which had prevailed since the seventeenth century. Instead of mercantilism, Britain moved to free trade. In the process the mother country wiped out protectionist advantages for her colonies. As a result, in place of a transatlantic economy based on the sailing-ship, some of British North America began to think in terms of a continental economy. Fortunately, the railway came along at exactly this time, providing possibilities for internal development and internal markets. Equally fortunately, Britain resolved long-standing differences with the Americans, making possible the negotiation of a trade treaty, which provided some access for British North America to the lucrative American market. An important factor in the reorganization

TIMELINE

1841
Union of Upper and Lower Canada proclaimed.

1842
Webster-Ashburton Treaty resolves the New Brunswick border. Great Britain experiments with partially elected, partially appointed legislature for Newfoundland.

1843
Fort Victoria established on Vancouver Island.

1846
Oregon Boundary Treaty settles western boundary. Corn Laws and Timber duties are repealed by British Parliament. St John's, Newfoundland, is destroyed by fire.

1848
Nova Scotia gets responsible government. Lord Elgin concedes responsible government to Canada. Newfoundland reverts to an elected assembly.

1849
Vancouver Island is leased by the British to the Hudson's Bay Company and becomes a Crown colony. Rebellion Losses bill is enacted, leading to riots in Montreal. Annexation movement flourishes.

1851
James Douglas becomes governor of Vancouver Island. Cable is laid from New Brunswick to Prince Edward Island, which receives responsible government. Colonial government takes over post offices.

1852
Grand Trunk Railway is incorporated.

1854
Reciprocity Treaty with United States is signed, to last ten years.

1855
Petroleum is discovered in southwestern Canada. Newfoundland receives responsible government.

1856
The first legislature meets on Vancouver Island.

1857
British Parliament holds enquiry over the future of the northwest. Palliser and Canadian Exploring Expeditions are sent west to investigate the region. Gold is discovered on the Thompson and Fraser rivers. Ottawa is chosen by Queen Victoria as the site for the capital of the province of Canada. Canadian legislature passes an Act for the Gradual Civilization of the Indian Tribes in the Canadas.

1858
British Columbia becomes a colony.

1859
The first steamer is launched on the Red River. First newspaper is established in Red River.

1860
Cariboo Gold Rush begins in British Columbia. Prince Edward Island Land Commission convenes.

1861
American Civil War begins. Montreal and Toronto introduce horse-drawn cars for public transportation.

1862
Cariboo Road is begun in British Columbia.

1863
First salmon fishery on the Fraser River established.

1864
Reciprocity Treaty is terminated by a vote of the American Senate, to take effect in 1866. Charlottetown and Quebec Conferences are held to discuss union of British North America.

1866	**1867**
Transatlantic cable laid from Newfoundland to Europe. Union of British Columbia and Vancouver Island implemented, with Victoria as capital.	The British North America Act is passed by British Parliament to take effect 1 July 1867. Emily Howard Stowe obtains a medical degree in the United States.

of the commercial economy was the rise of industrialization. Internal markets within the continent required not raw materials but finished goods. Colonial business sought to oblige.

British economists, beginning with Adam Smith in *The Wealth of Nations* (1776), provided a thoroughly reasoned theoretical critique of the old mercantile system. They offered an alternative vision of international expansion based upon free trade. In the years following Smith, a number of classical political economists in Britain—Malthus, Chambers, Ricardo, and Mill—expanded on earlier critiques of mercantilism, always insisting that freedom worked best, especially in the market-place. Despite the intellectual demolition of protectionism in the first quarter of the nineteenth century, the British government found it hard to give up; it artificially assisted influential sectors of the economy, particularly agriculture. Eventually the free traders won out, chiefly because of Britain's industrial successes after 1815. By the 1840s, the British industrial economy could no longer afford the luxury of protectionism, which limited its access to foreign raw materials and protected markets. The ministry, led by Sir Robert Peel, gritted its teeth and systematically removed protection for corn and other raw materials, including timber. The British still sought to emphasize importing cheap raw materials and exporting finished goods overseas. Instead of trading with colonies, however, they sought to trade with the entire world. Most merchants appreciated the nature of the revolution that was occurring in Britain. The *Quebec Gazette* summarized several generations of argument in 1842 when it wrote of the timber trade, 'Our great ground of complaint is that British Acts of Parliament created the trade, caused capital to be invested in the trade, trusting to these acts, which by the uncertain character they now assume may ruin thousands. We never asked for protection; it was given on grounds of national policy' (quoted in Lower 1973: 88). British free-trade policies would have a tremendous psychological impact on colonial merchants.

In the short run, the British North American rush to export wheat and timber under the old system, before the repeal of the Corn Laws and Timber duties of 1846 took effect, resulted in a collapse of prices in 1847 that would last for the remainder of the decade. Further complicating matters for colonial governments was the arrival of thousands of impoverished Irish immigrants, refugees from the Great Famine of the 1840s. They brought sickness and expense to the colonies along with their anguish. The result of these blows was a conviction that the mother country had subverted the old empire. The crisis seemed much worse in the united Province of Canada because of its reliance on wheat exports. Canadian mercantile policy in the later 1840s was to attempt to come to terms with the Americans. The Canadians continued to improve their canal system. They argued for reciprocal free trade between British North America and the United States in the natural products of each.

Britain's industrial needs also contributed to the need for international peace and bilateral understandings. One of the understandings came with the United States. Since 1815 Britain had sought entente with the Americans, a process that gained momentum during the period of free trade. By 1846 most of the outstanding boundary questions between the two nations had been resolved. In 1842 the Webster–Ashburton Treaty had sorted out the complex eastern boundary issues along the Maine–New Brunswick border. The boundary question was even more complex west of the Rocky Mountains, where the two nations had agreed in 1818 to share occupation until there was a need for a decision. Many Americans had settled in the Oregon territory south of the Columbia River, and presidential candidate James K. Polk in 1844 had rattled American sabres with his campaign slogan of '54–40 [the latitude in degrees and minutes of the southernmost Russian boundary on the Pacific Slope] or Fight'. Under the Oregon Boundary Treaty of 1846, the border across the Rockies to the Pacific continued from the Great Lakes at the 49th parallel to the Pacific (excluding Vancouver Island). This 'compromise'

TABLE 5.1

TRADE OF THE PROVINCE OF CANADA WITH THE UNITED STATES

Year	Imports from the United States $	Exports to the United States $	Year	Imports from the United States $	Exports to the United States $
1850	6,594,860	4,951,156	1858	15,635,565	11,930,094
1851	8,365,764	4,071,554	1859	17,592,916	13,922,314
1852	8,477,693	6,284,520	1860	17,273,029	18,427,918
1853	11,782,144	8,936,380	1861	20,206,080	14,261,427
1854	15,533,096	8,649,000	1862	22,624,860	15,063,730
1855	20,828,676	16,737,276	1863	18,457,683	18,426,891
1856	22,704,508	17,979,572	1865	14,820,577	21,340,350
1857	20,224,648	13,206,436	1866	15,242,834	32,587,643

TRADE OF THE UNITED STATES WITH THE BRITISH NORTH AMERICAN PROVINCES

Year Ending June 30	Exports from the United States $	Imports by the United States $	Year Ending June 30	Exports from the United States $	Imports by the United States $
1850	9,515,991	5,179,500	1863	27,619,814	17,484,786
1851	11,770,092	5,279,718	1864	26,574,624	29,608,736
1852	10,229,608	5,469,445	1865	28,829,402	33,264,403
1853	12,432,597	6,527,559	1866	24,828,880	48,528,628
1854	24,073,408	8,784,412	1867	21,020,302	25,044,005
1855	27,741,808	15,118,209	1868	24,080,777	26,361,379
1856	29,025,349	21,276,614	1869	23,381,471	29,293,766
1857	24,138,482	22,108,916	1870	25,339,254	36,265,328
1858	23,604,526	15,784,836	1875	36,225,735	28,271,926
1859	28,109,494	19,287,565	1880	30,775,871	33,214,340
1860	22,695,928	23,572,796	1885	40,124,907	36,960,541
1861	21,676,513	22,724,489	1890	41,503,812	39,396,980
1862	20,573,070	18,511,025			

TABLE 5.1 (CONTINUED)

TRADE OF THE LOWER COLONIES WITH THE UNITED STATES

(Unit £1,000)

	New Brunswick		Nova Scotia		Prince Edward Island		Newfoundland	
	Imp. from the US	Exp. to the US	Imp. from the US	Exp. to the US	Imp. from the US	Exp. to the US	Imp. from the US	Exp. to the US
1850	262	77	322	197	8	11	153	20
1851	330	83	283	151	16	20	201	20
1853	574	121	415	277	37	24	177	41
1854	711	97	575	318	39	16	237	28
1855	782	123	738	481	43	33	354	79
1856	714	173	678	413	52	27	388	109
1858	564	163	583	408	42	63	323	113
1859	675	236	576	456	62	87	361	106
1860	688	248	651	446	56	78	364	81
1862	616	185	605	362	46	43	345	47
1863	739	259	771	373	71	105	344	60
1864	691	263	860	489	83	77	306	41
1865	636	361	865	723	90	120	348	109
1866	779	386	808	645	74	21	291	88

	Imports by the Province of Canada from the United States		Imports by the United States From the Province of Canada	
	Dutiable $	Free $	Free $	Dutiable $
1850	5,803,732	791,128	636,454	3,649,016
1851	6,981,735	1,384,030	1,529,685	3,426,786
1852	7,613,003	864,690	761,571	3,828,398
1853	10,656,582	1,125,565	1,179,682	4,098,434
1854	13,449,341	2,083,757	380,041	6,341,498
1855	11,449,472	9,379,204	6,876,496	5,305,818
1856	12,770,923	9,933,586	16,487,822	640,375
1857	9,966,430	10,258,221	17,600,737	691,097
1858	8,473,607	7,161,958	11,267,618	313,953
1859	9,032,861	8,560,055	13,703,748	504,969
1860	8,526,230	8,746,799	18,427,141	434,532
1861	8,338,620	11,867,460	18,287,217	358,240
1862	6,128,783	16,514,077	15,026,093	227,059
1863	3,974,396	14,483,287	13,358,127	567,677

souce: D.C. Masters, *The Reciprocity Treaty of 1854* (London: Longmans Green & Company, 1936): Appendix B.

allowed the Americans to possess the state of Washington, in which they had virtually no nationals and which had been occupied chiefly by the Hudson's Bay Company. The 49th parallel artificially bisected the Pacific Slope, where mountain ranges and river valleys ran north and south rather than east and west. While the geographical interests of British North America may have been sacrificed by the Oregon settlement, entente was good for business.

Along the way to reciprocity, some Canadians were briefly seduced by the idea of annexation to the United States. Annexationism was a movement that gained support after an intense political debate over compensation for Lower Canadians who had not rebelled but had lost property in 1837. It was a far less important movement than that of reciprocity. Both flourished in the economic and political uncertainties of the late 1840s. Many British North Americans saw annexation as the inevitable result of the failure to achieve reciprocity rather than as a desirable end in itself.

Canadians, especially those dependent on the wheat economy, viewed internal markets—which to them meant the United States—as the only alternative to those lost in Britain. The eastern provinces also saw advantages to gaining access to the American market. The Americans displayed no interest until 1852 when the British government decided to toughen its fishery policy. The resultant Reciprocity Treaty of 1854 was hardly a very broad-reaching free trade agreement. It removed tariff and other barriers on a variety of enumerated goods, chiefly raw materials common to both countries. It did not remove barriers on finished goods, although the Americans hoped that a more prosperous British North America would buy more American manufactures. The treaty was potentially much more beneficial to British North America than to the United States. This helps explain why the Americans were so eager to end it at the expiration of its initial ten-year term. It does not appear to have greatly increased trade in either direction during its lifetime. The Reciprocity Treaty of 1854, nevertheless, was of enormous psychological value to British North America.

The Rise of Industrialism

The Reciprocity Treaty encouraged merchants, entrepreneurs, and politicians (mainly in the Province of Canada) to continue reconceptualizing their economic orientation. They moved from an imperial context, in which the British market was critical, to a continental context, in which internal markets were dominant. Once turned from its traditional transatlantic economy to a continental one, Canada began to industrialize. Indeed, one of the principal reasons why American trade in dutiable items did not expand during the ten years of the agreement was that the manufacturing capacity of British North America—again, particularly in the Province of Canada—grew substantially as well in this period. The internal market permitted agriculture in Canada West to shift partially out of grain cultivation into mixed farming. The concern for modernization led to the elimination of the seigneurial system in the St Lawrence Valley by legislative fiat. A bill replaced traditional seigneurial obligations with a quitrent, which gave tenants the opportunity to purchase their lands.

The process of economic reorientation was not a uniform one. Canada and the Atlantic region moved in somewhat different directions. While the Canadians became immersed in internal development—even territorial expansion into the prairie west—the Atlantic provinces continued to find the older transatlantic economy quite comfortable. They based their prosperity on a shipping industry committed to the wooden sailing-ship, which the region was still successfully producing. The period from 1840 to the early 1870s was the 'Golden Age of Sail' in the Atlantic region. With hindsight, it is possible to recognize the long-term technological weaknesses of the wooden sailing-ship. So long as ves-

TABLE 5.2

RAILWAYS OF CANADA

STATEMENT SHOWING THE COST, STOCK, BONDS, LOANS, FLOATING DEBT, AND DIVIDEND ACCOUNTS, OF CANADIAN RAILWAYS IN 1860
(COMPILED FROM THE REPORT OF THE INSPECTOR OF RAILWAYS)

			Funded Debt						
Corporate name of railway	Cost of road and equipment	Capital stock paid in	1st preference bonds	2d preference bonds	3d preference bonds	Goverment loan	Floating debt	Interest paid on debt in 1860	Dividends paid in 1880
Great Western and its branches	23,000,104.00	16,158,641.00	6,327,640.00	Included in 1st pref. Bds.		2,791,947.00*	–	528,254.00	3 per cent
Grand Trunk and its branches	55,690,039.92	13,524,803.48	9,733,333.33	4,066,262.23	17,096,450.60	15,142,633.33	12,163,213.07	1,039,685.72	for six months
Northern (Toronto to L. Huron)	3,890,778.68	823,818.50	491,046.67	1,092,566.68	287,481.35	2,311,666.67	–	55,545.21	
Buffalo and Lake Huron	6,403,045.86	4,345,701.26	2,433,333.33	811,111.11	–	–	145,999.99	–	
London and Port Stanley	1,017,220.00	935,542.00	399,400.00	120,000.00	–	–	77,770.00	–	
Welland	1,309,209.92	710,299.60	486,666.67	243,333.33	–	–	211,851.93	–	
Erie and Ontario	–	–	–	–	–	–	–	–	
Port Hope, Lindsay and Beaverton, and branch	–	–	–	–	608,333.33	–	–	–	
Cobourg and Peterborough	–	–	–	–	–	–	–	–	
Brockville and Ottawa, and branch	1,901,000.00	207,000.00	–	648,000.00	–	–	280,000.00	4,968.00	
Ottawa and Prescott	1,432,647.21	300,630.35	486,666.67	300,000.00	243,333.34	–	179,332.37	2,321.69	
Montreal and Champlain, and branch	2,485,425.16	1,226,250.00	777,186.66	192,200.00	84,400.00	–	285,525.51	92,451.69	
Carillon and Grenville	–	–	–	–	–	–	–	–	
St Lawrence and Industry	50,171.00	42,300.00	–	–	–	–	909.00	48.00	2 per cent
Stanstead, Shefford, & Chambly	–	–	–	–	–	–	–	–	
Peterborough & Chemung Lake	–	–	–	–	–	–	–	–	
	97,179,641.75	**38,278,986.19**	**21,743,605.66**	**7,473,473.35**	**17,711,165.29**	**20,246,247.00**	**13,344,600.87**	**1,869,224.52**	

*The total amount borrowed from the Province by the Great Western Railway, on account of the Guarantee Law, was $3,755,555.18. In July 1858, this company repaid $957,114.45 of this amount.

Note: The length of roads for which there are no returns of cost in the above table is 172¼ miles, including eleven miles of Preston and Berlin, not running. The cost of these roads cannot be far from $5,000,000, and the total cost of Canadian Railways is over $100,000,000. The expenditure 'on capital account', is much greater than the 'cost of road and equipments'. In the case of the Grand Trunk Railway, the total expenditure is about $70,000,000—the difference representing interest and discount accounts, loss in working, etc. Of the Grand Trunk cost, $1,621,231.69 was on the Portland Division, and therefore not in Canada.

STATEMENT SHOWING THE EARNINGS, EXPENSES, INCOME, MILEAGE, NO. OF EMPLOYEES, AND NO. OF LOCOMOTIVES AND CARS ON CANADIAN RAILWAYS IN 1860
(COMPILED FROM THE REPORT OF THE INSPECTOR OF RAILWAYS)

				Deductions from returns							
Corporate name of railway	Total earnings in 1860	Total expenses in 1860	Net income for 1860	Earnings per mile per week	Expenses per mile per week	% of expenses to earn's	Total miles run exclusive of piloting, shunting & c.	Total persons employed on line	No. of locomotives	No. of carriages: Passengers	No. of carriages: Freight
Great Western and its branches	2,197,943.34	1,993,806.00	204,043.00	122.51	111.13	91	1,261,604	2,049	89	127	1,269
Grand Trunk and its branches	3,349,658.18	2,806,583.17	533,075.01	58.72	49.20	84	8,195,064	3,118	217	135	2,538
Northern	332,967.01	260,466.56	72,500.45	67.40	52.72	78	280,035	370	17	20	801
Buffalo and Lake Huron	315,763.99	264,191.29	51,572.70	37.48	31.36	83	334,457	458	28	24	255
London and Port Stanley	29,385.57	23,256.02	6,129.75	23.55	18.62	78	41,300	38	2	2	50
Welland	64,554.40	51,274.35	13,280.06	49.64	39.44	79	47,810	104	4	4	87
Erie and Ontario	–	–	–	–	–	–	11,220	–	1	4	10
Port Hope, Lindsay and Beaverton, and branch	53,694.04	40,111.01	13,583.08	18.28	18.64	75	73,806	66	5	3	65
Cobourg and Peterborough	–	–	–	–	–	–	–	–	4	2	66
Brockville and Ottawa, and branch	53,801.10	34,427.25	19,373.85	16.30	10.42	64	53,715	74	3	8	79
Ottawa and Prescott	75,362.16	51,465.11	23,897.05	26.83	18.33	68	67,911	92	5	8	79
Montreal and Champlain	232,803.44	136,349.62	105,708.82	53.45	31.31	59	185,633	202	16	15	173
Carillon and Grenville	7,937.25	5,762.18	2,175.06	11.77	8.54	72	6,000	11	2	5	5
St Lawrence and Industry	8,796.00	7,819.00	978.00	14.08	12.50	88	12,440	24	2	5	5
Stanstead, Shefford, & Chambly	–	–	–	–	–	–	43,720		Leased by the Montreal & Champ.		
Peterborough & Chemung Lake	–	–		–	–	–	–		Worked by Cobourg & Peterborough		
	6,722,666.48	**5,675,511.56**	**1,046,316.78**	**63.65**	**53.73**	**84**	**5,614,715**	**6,606**	**395**	**862**	**4,982**

The improvement in the gross receipts of the first three roads since 1860, is as follows:

	1861		1862	
	Gross earnings	Earnings per mile	Gross earnings	Earnings per mile
Great Western	$2,266,864	$6,570	$2,686,060	$7,786
Grand Trunk	3,517,829	3,226	3,975,071	3,647
Northern	414,100	4,359	409,899	4,309

SOURCE: H.Y. Hind, *The Dominion of Canada* (Toronto: L. Stebbins, 1869).

sels that cost less than half as much to produce as iron steamers were more than half as profitable, however, they would flourish. The carrying trade provided employment for thousands. It also produced an outward-looking international orientation rather than one that focused on internal continental development. The Atlantic provinces sought to expand transportation links with Canada (mainly railways) in terms of transatlantic linkages.

The Province of Canada saw railways as a means to continental rather than transatlantic linkages. Canadian railway expansion would not occur in earnest until after 1850, after the complete demolition of the old imperial trade system. By 1850 only 60 mi. (97 km) of track were in operation in Canada. The obstacles had not been technological; the technology had been available since the 1820s. Finance and psychology were the barriers. Railways were expensive capital investments, few routes in British North America promised to be immediately profitable, and investors shied away, at least until the railway boom of the 1850s. In that decade a mania for internal development totally captured the imaginations of Canadian politicians and investors, encouraged by exaggerated promises of profits resulting from railway expansion. Canadian railway trackage had to be well built because of the climate. By 1867 the total cost to Canada of 2,188.25 mi. (3,520 km) of track was $145,794,853, or roughly $66,000 per mile. In order to pay for this construction, the railways borrowed on the British exchanges. Governments had to guarantee the loans and contribute themselves. The Canadian government itself, by 1867, had incurred a provincial debt on railway construction of over $33 million, and its municipalities added considerably more.

Vast expenditures brought out the worst in businessmen and politicians, who commonly served together on interlocking directorates and engaged in the various aspects of railway construction. Allan MacNab (1798–1862), who was seven times chairman of the Canadian assembly's railway committee between 1848 and 1857 and served the province as co-premier in 1854–6, was at various times president of three railway companies, chairman of another, and director of two more. Small wonder he once commented, 'All my politics are railroads.' Bribes to politicians were common. Construction overruns were a way of life. Corruption ran rampant. The most serious problem, however, was that too much construction occurred in advance of a settled population that could sustain a profitable level of traffic. This would always be the Canadian dilemma: trading off development against sustainability.

All railway promoters insisted that their lines would promote manufacturing by reducing transportation costs. Railways not only closed the distance between markets, they also served as a major market for industrial goods, often becoming industrial manufacturers themselves. The Grand Trunk Railway, incorporated in 1852 to build a railway from Toronto to Montreal, began by building its own rolling stock. By 1857 it decided to produce its own rails as well, constructing an iron foundry and rolling mill in Hamilton. This was the heavy-industry section of the economy. As manufacturing grew and required increasing amounts of capital investment, most of the large firms were relatively recent creations. Some of the old entrepreneurs successfully made the shift from the commercial economy. Many others did not.

The growth of industrialization—the introduction of manufacturing and related commerce on a large scale—inevitably made labour relations an increasingly important issue in British North America. The resource economy had employed large numbers of men on a seasonal basis, offering little opportunity for organization. Industrialization rationalized and stabilized the labour market. Manufacturing tended to be more continuous, and much of it was conducted indoors. Overhead costs encouraged employers to seek a stable and experienced labour force. The rise of a capitalistic labour market stabilized and settled the workers, but did little for their

The Great Western Railway station, Hamilton, CW, c. 1850-60. NAC, C-019415.

bargaining position. Those with highly developed skills were in the strongest position, and labour organization first developed in industries employing such workers, such as printing. Early trade unions emerged in certain skilled industries in various cities. Such unions almost never had any contact with one another. They could achieve only immediate and localized gains.

Like organization, labour militancy was local and extremely limited. Most industrial action consisted of unsystematic rioting. Employers responded to industrial action of any kind by calling in the police or the military. Before the 1850s there was a tendency for unions to identify with their particular trades rather than with fellow workers in other trades in other places. The development of industry and the rise of factories employing mechanization brought considerable change to the incipient labour movement. A handful of international unions appeared, either British or American in origin. Unions with several local chapters also organized. Although mechanization encouraged unionization, the impersonality of the factory system created problems for labour, particularly when juveniles and women were drawn into the labour market. These workers were hard to organize.

WESTWARD

By mid-century there were signs that the vast territory west of the Lakehead would not forever remain the monopoly of the fur trade. There were also signs of Canadian interest in the west, beginning with editorials in the Toronto *Globe* in 1850. One key development in western settlement was the establishment in 1848 of Vancouver Island as a British colony. Until then, Britain had been content to allow the Hudson's Bay Company to act as custodian of all British interests in the west. Earlier the HBC had sent James Douglas (1803–77) from Fort Vancouver (now in the state of Washington) to establish Fort Victoria on Vancouver Island. This was a fall-back position if the Oregon Territory were lost, as it was in 1846. In 1849 Vancouver Island was leased to the company for an annual payment of seven shillings. The HBC would organize the colony there. James Douglas returned to Fort Victoria as chief factor of the company, subsequently becoming its governor in 1851. Settlement on the West Coast was slow. Most newcomers came from the British Isles. They sought to reproduce the life of the British gentry on the Pacific Slope. This was not easy. The Colonial Office insisted on encumbering Vancouver Island with unworkable land policies. Land must be high-priced (a pound an acre) and settlement must be led by those who could afford to bring out labourers as settlers to work the lands.

The trouble with such notions was that the

JOHN TOD

John Tod (1794–1882) was born in Dumbartonshire, Scotland, and received a village school education, the advantage in life that the lowlands of Scotland provided for all its sons. After working in Glasgow, in 1811 he signed on with the Hudson's Bay Company, which was trying to beef up its role in the fur trade of the north. Tod was one of the 'Glasgow clerks' who revolted at Stornoway in the summer of 1811, causing Lord Selkirk's first party of settlers to have to winter at York Factory. He finally sailed aboard the *Edward and Ann*. He was initially posted to Severn District on Hudson Bay, served in the Island Lake District (now Manitoba), and in 1823 was sent by the company to New Caledonia. He travelled overland from York Factory to the west coast in the summer of 1823, mainly by York boat in company with several other leading fur traders. The route was via Île-à-la-Crosse to the Athabasca and Peace Rivers, ending up at Fort George (now Prince George). After a year at Fort George, he was posted to Fort McLeod, where he had the time to read deeply in the extensive library that was available at that remote post.

Despite the books, Tod found that wilderness life in New Caledonia was not conducive to his health, and he was sent to Nelson River near York Factory, commissioned as a chief trader, and allowed a year's leave to go back to Britain. On the boat home he met Eliza Waugh, a schoolmistress and governess who had been at Red River, and the two married in England, returning to Rupert's Land via New York and Canada in 1835. At Island Lake in 1837, his wife suffered a nervous breakdown, and Tod took her home to Wales, where she remained until her death. When he returned he was again sent to New Caledonia. He crossed the continent as head of the 1838 annual brigade, starting from Norway House via the Saskatchewan and Athabasca rivers to Jasper House. The brigade travelled by horse across the mountains, and then down the Columbia River in boats. He spent the next few years in charge of posts in the interior of British Columbia. Ill health again forced Tod out of the wilderness, and he was put in charge of Fort Nisqually in 1849. Soon after that, he moved to Fort Victoria, where he acquired land and in 1852 retired with his mixed-blood family to his property at Oak Bay, which is now a heritage site.

Tod had not advanced beyond chief trader in the company partly because of his health problems, but mainly because George Simpson did not like him. Simpson's suspicions of Tod may have been caused by Tod's relative unconventionality. He was described by one contemporary as 'of excellent principle, but vulgar manners', an interesting observation considering his love of books and music—he played both the fiddle and the flute. He was perhaps too 'arty' for many in the fur trade. He was made a member of the Legislative Council of Vancouver Island in 1851, serving until 1858. He did not marry his country-born wife until 1863 because news of Eliza's death in 1857 did not reach Victoria until then. Tod was an example of an HBC trader who decided to retire on the west coast rather than in Red River, and he arrived in Victoria early enough to be co-opted by James Douglas into the early administration of Vancouver Island. His memoir, which he called 'The Career of a Scotch Boy', was eventually edited and published in 1954.

labourers constantly abandoned their masters, as they had done in the early seventeenth century in Newfoundland and in the eighteenth century on Prince Edward Island. Much of the early agricultural activity was conducted by the Puget's Sound Colonization Company, which had been transferred from the Cowlitz Valley and had its own colonization program. There were four farms, each managed by a 'gentleman bailiff' and worked by hired labour imported from Britain (mainly Scotland) for the purpose. A dour Scot, Kenneth McKenzie (1811–74), was put in charge of farming operations, and he found himself constantly struggling with the social pretensions of the bailiffs. '*Balls & parties* every now & then for farmers in a new country will not do,' he admonished one of his underlings, telling another, 'It is profits we want at as little outlay as possible' (Ormsby 1958: 102–3). The HBC was astounded to discover that one of these bailiffs spent eight times his annual salary in 1854 on various expenses and purchases, including 1,606 pounds of sugar and seventy gallons of brandy, rum, whisky, and wine.

In 1838 the British government had extended the Hudson's Bay Company monopoly over the west for twenty-one years. A major parliamentary enquiry took place in 1857 before the government decided its policy. The HBC officials had attempted to argue that the west was inhabitable only in river valleys limited in extent; most of the region was a vast desert too cold and too arid to be settled. The enquiry's report was not very favourable to the HBC. It acknowledged 'the desire of our Canadian fellow-subjects that the means of extension and regular settlement should be afforded to them over a portion of this territory' (quoted in Bumsted 1969: 220). It recommended that the HBC cease to control Vancouver Island. It also encouraged the annexation to Canada of the districts on the Red River and the Saskatchewan River. At the same time, the report maintained that for much of the west, the continuation of the trading monopoly of the company was desirable and appropriate. While the British Parliament was considering the future of the west, two scientific expeditions (one British and one Canadian) set out in 1857 to investigate the region first-hand. The leader of the British expedition was an Irishman, Captain John Palliser (1817–87). The Canadian Exploring Expedition was under the titular command of George Gladman (1800–63), assisted by Simon James Dawson (1820–1902) and Henry

Youle Hind (1823–1908). The findings of these expeditions helped to end the public perception of this vast region as utterly unfit for human habitation. Both published reports acknowledged the great agricultural potential of the west, once opened by a railway.

Meanwhile on the West Coast, sheer serendipity brought the region to the attention of

SARAH LINDLEY CREASE

Sarah Lindley Crease (1826–1922) was born in the London suburb of Acton Green, England, the daughter of an important English botanist who was a fellow of the Royal Society and later a professor at London University. She was raised in an educated household, was well-read, and was taught all the genteel arts appropriate to a woman of her time and station. Her father's continual use of botanical illustrators meant that she learned much about sketching and pictorial reproduction through copper engraving and wood-block printing. The family was sufficiently well connected that Sarah accompanied her father to Westminster Abbey for Queen Victoria's coronation. She subsequently attended Mrs Gee's school at Hendon from 1838 to 1842. After a lengthy engagement, she married a young lawyer, Henry Crease, in 1853. Crease was forced by a financial scandal (in which he was ultimately found innocent) to emigrate to British North America in 1856, and by 1858 he had managed to land on his feet as the first barrister in British Columbia. He rose rapidly to become the province's attorney-general in 1861, and lived with his family in New Westminster from that date to 1868. The family moved to Victoria and Henry subsequently became a supreme court justice in 1870.

The Creases had an extremely amicable marriage. They sketched together on their honeymoon, wrote love letters to one another while separated by the Atlantic from 1856 to 1860, and shared a common social life in Victoria. Both cradle Anglicans, the Creases taught Sunday school, organized charitable events, and continued their interest in sketching and painting. Their home in New Westminster—'Ince Cottage'—had a large garden and a white picket fence. Their house in Victoria—'Pentrelew'—was a three-storey Italianate brick house designed by a team of California architects and completed in 1875; it had a large garden. Typical representatives of the English upper middle classes transported to British North America, the Creases used their houses to establish their credentials as leaders of society in both New Westminster and Victoria, frequently entertaining and allowing thier rooms to be used for meetings. Despite their pretensions and their status, life was not necessarily easy for Sarah Crease, especially in the early years in British Columbia. The couple had seven children, all of whom had to be sent to England for schooling or long visits. Such family expenses, combined with their houses and the costs of servants to look after them, ensured that there would be continual financial worries. One of the characteristics of a middle-class marriage in the nineteenth century was domesticity, which of course meant that Henry was responsible for making the money through his outside employment, and Sarah was responsible for looking after the house and the children. Although there were servants, no woman in Sarah Crease's situation could sit back and rest, at least not while she had her health. Housekeeping on a daily basis was a major occupation, and seven pregnancies and childbirths between 1854 and 1872—plus the subsequent responsibility for the children—were constant drains on her energy. After 1880, Sarah was unable to continue with her sketching because of glaucoma, which resulted in several operations. She devoted much of her time in later years to maintaining a vast family correspondence

the world. In 1857 the discovery of gold on the mainland, along the Thompson and Fraser rivers, attracted fortune-hunters from around the world. The amount of gold easily available was quite small by earlier California standards. The ensuing rush was a pale imitation of the American one. Nevertheless, hundreds of miners, mainly from California, made their way to the Fraser River in the interior of British Columbia in the spring of 1858. The quiet village

The Aurora gold mine, Williams Creek, BC, 15 August 1867, by Frederick Dally. Metropolitan Toronto Reference Library T14321.

of Victoria was transformed overnight into a major port. South of the 49th parallel, talk of American annexation spread rapidly. The British government rushed through legislation putting New Caledonia under the direct jurisdiction of the Crown. The mainland colony of British Columbia came into formal existence on 2 August 1858, with James Douglas as governor. The two colonies were at first administratively separate. The miners, however rough in appearance, were not really badly behaved and accepted British authority readily enough.

Most of the gold required proper machinery and capital expenditure to extract. Many of the gold seekers found employment in other ways, taking advantage of the developmental spin-off from the rush. The discovery of gold irreversibly altered life for the indigenous peoples of the Pacific Slope. Even remote regions could contain great mineral wealth. The settlers and the government ignored the land claims of indigenous peoples in the rush to exploit the land itself. Few settlers disagreed with the view that the 'indolent, contented savage, must give place to the busteling [*sic*] sons of civilization & Toil' (quoted in Fisher 1977: 105). For the Aboriginal peoples the result was a very serious cultural disruption, recovery from which would be extraordinarily difficult, if not even impossible.

The Fraser River gold rush presaged a new element in the resource economy of British North America: exploitation of the rich mineral wealth of the northern part of the continent. New technologies provided a constantly expanding market for British North America's mineral wealth. They also brought new means of extracting it from the ground. By the 1850s copper ore was being mined along Lake Superior, and petroleum was discovered in southwestern Ontario in 1855. Production of crude oil in Canada by 1863 ran to 100,000 barrels a year. Unlike timbering, mineral production tended to be extremely capital intensive, requiring specialized scientific knowledge. Until the twentieth century, production involved only a few minerals well located for outward transportation in bulk. Coal seams on both coasts were obvious targets. The continent's burgeoning industrialization would demand ever larger quantities of minerals, and the future potential was indisputable.

Responsible Government and the Reorientation of Politics

The British government gradually resolved the constitutional problems of the commercial period in British North America over the decade following the unification of Upper and Lower Canada in July 1840. Legislative union did not by itself satisfy Lord Durham's other major recommendation for Canada, the right of the assembly to decide policy and its implementation through control of 'the persons by whom that policy was to be administered' (quoted in Craig 1963: 141). Part of the problem was that nobody at the time understood the importance of political parties or how they could work in responsible government. Colonial governors served as party brokers rather than conceding responsible government. Finally in 1848 the governor of Canada, Lord Elgin (1811–63), called upon the leaders of the Reform parties, recently successful at the polls, to form a ministry. Louis La Fontaine (1807–64) and Robert Baldwin (1804–58) had allied their respective parties in 1842 on a Reform platform. In placing himself, as a representative of the Crown, above party politics and leaving government in the hands of leaders selected by their parties, Lord Elgin inaugurated responsible government in the Province of Canada.

The victory of responsible government in Canada did not begin the story nor end it, however. Nova Scotia—where Joseph Howe had been agitating for responsible government as a Reformer since 1836—finally achieved it after an election on 5 August 1847, which focused on that single issue. The Reformers were victorious, and when a Reform administration took office in late January 1848, the province became the first colony to achieve responsible government. Prince Edward Island acquired responsible government in 1851 and New Brunswick in 1854. A British attempt at alternative constitutional arrangements complicated the situation in Newfoundland. In 1842 Britain gave the colony a legislature composed partly of elected and partly of appointed members, thus amalgamating the old council and assembly into one body. The experiment was not popular and never had a proper chance to work. The older Constitution returned in 1848. Newfoundlanders immediately began agitating for 'a form of Government . . . with a departmental Government and Executive Responsibility similar in character to that form lately yielded to . . . Nova Scotia' (quoted in Gunn 1966: 315). The British reluctantly gave in to this demand in 1855.

☐ George Brown. NAC, PA-6165.

The lower provinces, even including Newfoundland, were sufficiently homogeneous to be able to live with a two-party system. Canada was not so fortunate. It could and did create four parties. The Reform alliance of Baldwin and La Fontaine was largely illusory. It quickly transpired that Canada East (the unofficial designation for the former Lower Canada) had slipped back into old voting patterns removed from Reform. The principle of governing by a coalition from each of the two sections of the united province, was inherently unstable. By the mid-1840s the French had become enamoured of the principle of the 'double majority', in which the province would be governed by an assembly majority in each of its two main sections. Such an arrangement naturally appealed to French Canada's growing sense of nationality. It also required the parallel growth of political parties in the two sections. Two factors emerged to complicate matters for the Province of Canada.

One was the rise of a new political movement in Canada West at the end of the 1840s. A radical Reform group known as the Clear Grits, with whom the moderate Reformers gradually merged, appeared under the leadership of George Brown (1818–80). Centred in the western districts, the Grits were the heirs of William Lyon Mackenzie rather than Robert Baldwin. They were democrats, populists, geographical expansionists, and opponents of close connections between church and state in a Protestant rather than a true secularist sense. Furthermore—and ominously—they were hostile to French Canada in traditional anglophone ways. In 1840, when the population of Canada East had been greater than that of Canada West, each section of united Canada got forty seats in Parliament. When the census of 1851 showed that the population of the anglophone section was growing more rapidly, George Brown adopted 'representation by population'—'rep by pop'—as a campaign slogan when he stood as an independent Reformer in the general election of that year. He won easily. 'Rep by pop' came to epitomize the brassy reformism of the Clear Grits.

The growing pressures of the Grits contributed to, but did not by themselves produce, the second development of the 1850s. This was the gradual withdrawal of French Canada into its own agenda, centred on the development of nationalist aspirations and the preservation of French-Canadian culture and society. The leaders of the Catholic Church took upon themselves the mantle of nationalism. They used the Grits to separate nationalism from reform. In the context of Canada West, the Grit espousal of 'voluntaryism'—the separation of church and state—was directed chiefly against the Anglican Church. Such ultra-Protestantism had even more implications for the Catholic Church. Voluntaryism was not quite the same as secularism. The voluntaryists sought to free the state from 'religious privilege', but could contemplate with equanimity the passage of legislation controlling the availability of alcoholic beverages during the sabbath (which they held sacrosanct). While God might not be eligible to hold land and or be exempt from taxation, he could be used to justify state intrusion in matters of morality. Such ideas were very much at odds with the principles of French-Canadian religious nationalists. The result was an alliance between the latter and the Upper Canadian opponents of the Grits.

TIMOTHY ANGLIN

Timothy Warren Anglin (1822–90) was born in Ireland, his family part of the new Irish Catholic middle class. He left Ireland for British North America in 1849, in the wake of the Great Famine. In Saint John, New Brunswick, he soon established *The Saint John Weekly Freeman*, a weekly newspaper devoted to the interests of the large Catholic community of the city. Anglin campaigned against public hostility to Irish Catholics at the same time that he argued that the Irish must work to improve themselves, both as individuals and as a community. Anglin was a particularly successful exponent of the rough and tumble journalism of his time, and his newspaper broke with the reformers (the 'Smashers') in the mid-1850s when it became clear that they were no particular friends of the Irish. In 1861 he ran successfully as an independent for the provincial assembly. In politics he was a moderate liberal who supported democratic political reform and maintenance of the rights of the individual. 'Where the rights of the individual are trampled upon there is despotism,' he once argued.

Anglin managed not to allow his Irish hostility to Great Britain to control all his opinions, but he was never a warm supporter of the British. It was possible in the 1860s to combine hostility to British policy with support of the British Empire, since it was clear that the British government itself wanted to reduce its commitments to its various settlement colonies, especially those in British North America, which were menaced by the American juggernaut. Anglin disagreed with the British devolution of responsibility for British North America, insisting that Britain foot the bill for imperial defence. To a considerable extent, he saw confederation as another attempt by the British to break the imperial bonds. It was also a Canadian 'conspiracy' that had few advantages for the common people of New Brunswick. In 1864 he opposed the Quebec Resolutions in the *Freeman* because the plan of legislative union offered little to New Brunswick and because there was obviously no intention to consult with the people. Anglin thus joined the anti-confederate government of A. J. Smith.

When the Fenian threat emerged, Anglin found himself regarded as part of the Fenian-loving anti-confederate Catholic Irish, and when confederation triumphed, he was certain that the conspiracy had won. Nevertheless, he tried to work within the new political arrangement, and served a Catholic Acadian constituency in Parliament for fifteen years. Because of his agitation on the New Brunswick Schools Question in 1872–3, he found himself outside the Liberal government of Alexander Mackenzie, although he was made speaker of the House of Commons in 1874. Gradually his power base weakened and his political philosophy became outdated. Defeated in the 1882 election, he moved to Toronto to become a Liberal journalist, receiving several political appointments from the Mowat government. Anglin was often held to be better in political opposition than in supporting the government. No social reformer, he became increasingly reactionary in later years, fearful of socialism, atheism, and new science.

The rise of denominational divisions as major factors in politics was not confined to the Canadas, although the sectional situation—Roman Catholicism in Canada East and evangelical Protestantism in Canada West—gave such matters a special edge in that province. To a considerable extent, denominational politics reflected the growing democratization of the political process. As the interest, involvement, and size of the electorate grew, politicians turned to issues that appealed to the voter. Denominations also reflected ethnic background and regional strengths. Infighting among religious denominations constantly tussling for advantage transferred easily into the political arena. In Nova Scotia such struggles had occurred for years over the creation of institutions of higher learning. No denomination could allow another an educational edge, and the result was the creation of a series of colleges and universities, one for each major denomination (and one for each ethnic branch of Catholicism in the province). By the 1850s the venue for denominational disagreements had shifted to public education. In Prince Edward Island the question began over Bible reading in the schools, a practice pressed by the evangelical Protestants and opposed by the Roman Catholics. The 'Bible Question' helped realign island politics as Catholics and liberal Protestants, backed by the old Tories, joined against evangelical Protestants. By 1858 the principal issue in that year's election was between Protestantism and Romanism, and the result was a Protestant and a Catholic party. In Newfoundland as well, the contending political parties wore denominational as well as ethnic faces, the Liberals backed by the Irish Roman Catholics and the Tories supported by the English Protestants.

In Canada, John A. Macdonald (1815–91), the Scots-born lawyer from Kingston, came gradually to dominate the anglophone Conservatives. Macdonald was not a man to allow abstract principle, such as the double majority, to stand in the way of power. In 1856 he was able to forge a new coalition among the moderate (some said very pragmatic) Tories whom he led and the Bleus of French Canada, led after 1859 by George-Étienne Cartier (1814–73). This alliance enabled the Tories to remain in power despite Grit victories in Canada West. It also led George Brown's *Globe* to comment in August of 1856 that 'If

☐ John A. Macdonald, c. 1883-4, oil portrait by Thomas Horsburgh, from a photograph by William James. NAC, C-097288.

Upper and Lower Canada cannot be made to agree, a federal union of all the provinces will probably be the result.' By 1863 most of Canada's leading politicians had come to concur on the need for some other form of union.

The New Imperial Relationship

The imperial government conceded responsible government in British North America because it had little choice, given its unwillingness in the era of free trade to devote unnecessary amounts of money to colonial administration. There was a feeling in both the Colonial Office and the Parliament that the separation of colonies, particularly colonies populated with large numbers of British emigrants, was inevitable when those colonies had reached a point of sufficient 'maturity'. An equally strong feeling was that the costs of imperial administration were an unnecessary drain on the public purse. A student giving a cursory glance at the literature on the British Empire and British America between 1840 and the early 1860s could be easily forgiven for concluding that once responsible government had been conceded, nothing much happened on the imperial front until the British started pressing seriously for union of the colonies at the end of the 1850s. Such a conclusion would not be correct for a number of reasons.

Even when colonies were given internal self-government, the business of colonial administration continued, albeit in a somewhat different context. Moreover, not every colony in British North America had acquired self-government. The Colonial Office still had enormous power and responsibility in the west, and ultimate authority over Aboriginal policy. It was the imperial administration that created the colony of Vancouver Island in 1849, for example, and the colony of British Columbia in 1857. As well, the British government still appointed colonial governors, and both it and they still had considerable moral authority in the colonies. Some historic issues, such as the clergy reserves in Upper Canada, were fought out in the context of responsible government and were resolved with its achievement. Others, such as the land question on Prince Edward Island, were not settled and continued to fester. Finally, Britain was still in charge of the international situation of the colonies. This included diplomatic relations with the United States, which encompassed such business as the survey of the boundary line beginning in 1857. Britain was also responsible for both the direction and financing of the land and sea defences of British North America. Under free trade and responsible government, Britain reduced its military establishment in British North America and attempted with mixed success to convince the colonials to take up the burden. When the American Civil War endangered the stability of the continent, the imperial authorities would respond by attempting to strengthen colonial defence through political and constitutional revisions.

VICTORIAN SOCIETY

The relationship between political unification and social change was a complicated one. There were some obvious connections, however. A number of major themes dominated the society of these years. First, there was an unmistakable sense of geographical movement, mainly out of the older and more settled rural districts. Second, the class structure of society began to take shape and even solidify. The chief changes were the appearance of a new business class, the emergence of a working class associated with urbanization and industrialization, and the rapid professionalization of certain educated and skilled segments of the middle class. Along with the development of social classes went a strengthening of certain caste lines associated with class but not identical with it. Finally, an enormous expansion of voluntary organizations of all sorts occurred, at least partly to provide some sense of personal identity and belonging in a time of great mobility and social change.

Throughout the 1840s and 1850s British immigration to North America continued at high levels. Driving immigration were the potato famines in Ireland, which peaked in 1846. Between 1840 and 1860 well over 600,000 British immigrants arrived in British North America, most of them seeking land on which to build a new life. Combined with the natural population increase within the colonies, the arrival of this horde of new settlers put enormous pressure on available agricultural land, particularly land suitable for staple crop farming for the market. Second-generation farmers accepted less desirable land or moved to the United States, where a more rapid industrialization than in British North America had created new employment and where the west was open to settlement. Thus, at the same time that thousands of land-hungry immigrants were moving in, thousands of disillusioned members of the younger generation within the colonies were moving out.

The first sign of serious out-migration had come from the seigneurial districts of French Canada, the heartland of French-Canadian culture, language, and religion. Almost any opportunity was superior to a future on a farm of less than 100 acres (40 ha) of worn-out land. Over the course of the 1830s more than 40,000 left Lower Canada for the United States, and that figure jumped to 90,000 in the 1840s and 190,000 in the 1850s. One clergyman called this population loss the cemetery of the race. The visitor to New England can still see standing, usually empty and forlorn, the extensive brick buildings that housed the nineteenth-century factories employing these migrants. Thousands of French Canadians also moved into the Eastern Townships of Canada East, originally intended as anglophone enclaves. In the Upper St Francis district of the Eastern Townships, for example, the francophone population grew from 9.7 per cent of the district in 1844 to 64.1 per cent by 1871. Others continued to fill up unpopulated regions in the Laurentians and around Lac St-Jean. State and church both promoted colonization of these regions as an alternative to migration to the United States. As well as moving out of the country or into new districts, thousands of French Canadians moved into the cities and expanding towns of the province where they often found employment as manufacturing workers. In Montreal especially, many of the newcomers were female. Some found employment as domestic servants, but most worked in a few burgeoning industries, particularly clothing manufacture, textile production, and the making of tobacco products.

In Canada West, most of the movement into the United States before 1870 was into the rich agricultural districts of the American Midwest, and beyond. A constant stream of Canadians made their way across Ohio, Indiana, and Illinois onto the American prairies, contributing to the

'Roxburgh Place, Residence of A. Marshall, Esq.', 1868. The unnamed artist who painted this farmstead—located in Oxford County, in southwestern Ontario—is thought to have been a local schoolteacher. Courtesy Michael S. Bird.

rapid settlement of states such as Minnesota and the Dakotas. A key factor driving the migrants was the ultimate inability of the family farm to accommodate the needs of all family members. Successful farming required numbers of children, but large families also created pressures for the expansion of landholdings and eventually led to the removal of some of the younger generation. In this male-dominated society, only males normally had expectations of inheritance; hence the tendency in all British North American rural society to throw off a disproportionate number of females (usually between the ages of fifteen and twenty-one) into the cities and non-agricultural employment. Some farms in some districts were more divisible than others, but the pressures on the younger members of the next generation to seek their fortunes elsewhere was always strong. Elder sons (and the women they married) could look forward to becoming pillars of and local leaders in their community. For most of the children of most farmers, however, coming of age meant moving on. Some new land within Canada West was available to the north. Settlement after mid-century moved rapidly up to Georgian Bay and into the Muskoka country, heedless of the prominent outcroppings of the Canadian Shield. For most who chose to remain in Canada West, however, cities and towns were the obvious destinations.

The years before 1860 were ones of considerable internal expansion in the Atlantic region. Settlers moved onto less desirable and more remote lands, while others moved into the major urban centres. Population growth rates continued to be extremely high despite decreasing immigration, although they had ominously begun to decline for Nova Scotia as early as the 1850s. By the end of that decade, very few of the older settled districts could support their natural increases in population, much less sustain incoming immigrants. In Newfoundland, for example, there was considerable movement into the largely unsettled western part of the island, and a vast increase in a seasonal migration into the Labrador fisheries; in some outports over two-thirds of the working males became seasonal workers in Labrador. Neither expansion nor seasonal migration could, in the end, accommodate the growing population. Many began to turn to out-migration, often to the United States. By the 1860s over one-third of the counties in the Maritime provinces were experiencing population losses. The correlation between rural counties (with economies largely dependent on fishing and farming) and depopulation was very high. While out-migration was a general phenomenon, Scots and Irish were overrepresented in the exodus and Acadians underrepresented. Most of those departing were between the ages of fifteen and twenty-five.

Most British North Americans uprooted themselves at least once. Many a British North American was constantly on the move. Wilson Benson, an immigrant of the 1830s, tells the story in his autobiography. Beginning in Ireland at age fifteen, Benson changed his district of residence eleven times (six times in Ireland and Scotland between 1836 and 1838 and five times in Canada West between 1838 and 1851) before finally settling on a farm in Grey County in 1851 at age thirty. He bought the farm not with his savings but with an inheritance from Ireland. Benson had changed jobs twenty-nine times in those years, and apprenticed to at least six different trades in the 1830s and 1840s before finally settling down to farming. In his later years, he also kept a store in his community. On the whole, transients like Wilson Benson were not economically successful. In both urban Hamilton and in rural Peel County, Upper Canada, there was a remarkable correlation between transiency and poverty. Whether such people failed because they were continually on the move, or constantly moved in search of a better life they never found, is debatable. So too is the question of whether their failure was so deep-rooted as to be transmittable to their children. In any case, the success stories (at least measured in terms of wealth) usually involved those who remained more or less permanently in one place.

The need for a sense of belonging in an era of change and mobility helps explain the enormous expansion in the number of private associations devoted to non-occupational and non-economic goals. Despite the growth of the state, even in Canada it did not weigh heavily on the lives of British Americans. Political allegiances were not as important to the average person as family, religion, and fraternal commitments. Churches continued to be important. They were increasingly dominated—especially on the Protestant side—by women, who made up the bulk of the attending congregations. Women also supported their own religious organizations with their own money, kept separate from the larger funds of the church, and these organizations offered many women their first glimpse of independent administration. British Americans also found a place in the temperance societies, which had begun in the 1820s but really expanded in the 1840s under the Sons of Temperance, a fraternal organization that served 'no liquor stronger than tea'. The temperance movement crusaded against drunkenness, but it was also a way of reacting against new immigration—mainly Irish—and asserting a sense of Protestant hegemony.

By 1870 few British Americans—whether urban or rural—could be found who did not belong to a good number of voluntary societies beyond their churches. In earlier eras, private fraternal organizations had supplemented or provided public services such as water, light, fire protection, and library facilities. By 1870, many organizations had virtually relinquished charita-

McCARTHY'S SONG

This song is credited to Irish schoolmaster Michael McCarthy of Taylor's Bay Harbour, Nova Scotia. The story is a familiar one.

Long shall I remember one day last December,
My fob lined with silver, my heart full of glee,
Being out on a frolic, determined to travel,
Intending great Halifax city to see.

I crossed Taylor's Bay Harbour in very good order,
From back to Pope's Harbour both up hill and down;
I took into my noddle to get a full bottle,
Oh, at the Brian's tavern, that hole of renown.

At the hotel I arrived; I was kindly invited,
Led into the barroom as you may suppose,
With Brian's ale and water, and wine in the corner
They bid me sweet kindly with a how-do-you-do.

I called for a flagon, all hands then I treated,
All hands then I treated and paid the cash down.
Says this Brian, 'my dear fellow, come let us be mellow,
You have plenty of money, I pray you sit down.'

Being easily persuaded myself then I seated,
All hands again treated with full bumpers round.
Being fond of the cratur [creature?] my head got elated,
On the floor they soon made me a bed of shake-down.

It's there I lay groaning and horrors bemoaning,
Not one to control, not a heed to my call;
They battered and bruised me and sorely abused me,
I'm sure that they broke both my liver and all.

My room then I ordered in very poor quarters,
A chamber more fierce than the frozen north pole.
No friend to come near me, and no one to cheer me
But a bucket of cold water to nourish my soul.

Oh, early next morning the landlord gave warning
To pay for my quarters and what I did call.
I paid to each farthing each treat that was called on,
He swore black and blue I paid nothing at all.

Then my guardian angel cries, 'Flee from the danger,'
He told my heart it was time to begone.
Like Lot leaving Sodom and wicked Gomorrah
For home then I started quite feeble alone.

Each step as I walked I staggered and halted,
My heart's blood been gushing through his mouth and nose,
When Hilshy and Glawson like big kind Samaritans
Conducted me safely to old Mrs Haws.

Next day I was greeted and most kindly treated,
On my wounds that was bleeding she poured oil and wine;
With mother's feeling she nursed and relieved me,
Her words full of sweetness, they seemed divine.

My health being regained I offered her payment,
She freely forgave me her labour and time.
May the great God reward her both here and hereafter
Then in glory eternal I hope she may shine.

Now my frolic is over, no more I'll be rover,
Good-bye to Pope's Harbour and Halifax town.
Here I'll die easy with Henry and Sarah,
A bonnie Scotch laddie that cares not a frown;
And Brian's ale and water I'll ne'er taste hereafter,
But home keep a bottle my sorrows to drown.
My Irish blood would scorn at the name of the informer,
Excise men I'll call on to pull this house down

SOURCE: Helen Creighton, *Songs and Ballads from Nova Scotia* (New York: Dover Publications, 1966), 288-90.

ble and public goals in favour of entertainment and companionship for their members. Some of the new societies were created to provide a framework for sporting activities such as curling, lacrosse, or baseball.

Perhaps the most characteristic Canadian voluntary and fraternal society was the Orange Order, founded in Ulster in 1795 to defend Protestantism and the British monarchy. In Canada the Order added to its original politico-religious aims a strong fraternal aspect, providing social activity and ritual for its local members. At its height, the Orange Order probably never counted more than 50,000 actual members, scattered across the continent and across social classes, but that membership spread out informally. One estimate suggests that one in three Protestant Canadians in the Victorian period had strong Orangist links. The Order unified Protestants of all origins and served as a focal point at the local level for social intercourse and conviviality. It also served as a lightning rod for various hostilities. It was particularly active in organizing demonstrations against the influx of Catholic Irish into Canada in the 1840s and 1850s, and later against the Métis in the Canadian West.

Rural overpopulation produced some migrants who would settle and tame undeveloped regions, and others who would provide a labour force for industrialization. While the farming pioneers remained small-scale commodity producers indeterminately related to the class structure, the urbanized workforce swiftly turned into a landless working class. At the other end of the scale, merchants turned into bankers, financiers, and industrialists, and became far wealthier. Over the middle decades of the nineteenth century, the older social structure of élites and non-élites disappeared, to be replaced by one far more clearly stratified.

Successful businessmen were highly esteemed in the era of economic transformation, achieving their high status partly by self-ascription and partly by their acknowledged economic and political power. Nowhere was the power more evident than at the municipal level, where businessmen formed a mutually supportive coterie that took the lead in all aspects of life in the city, including its development and land market. Most business leaders in this period were self-made men, not in the sense that they had risen from rags to riches, but in that they had achieved their position in the community by their own efforts. Scots were overrepresented in business ranks, where Protestantism predominated. The new wealth was in finance and manufacturing. The wealthier business leaders of Montreal and Toronto began to adopt extravagant lifestyles that were in many respects comparable to those of their American counterparts.

As Canadian cities began the shift from commercial entrepôts to industrial and financial centres, they already contained significant inequalities in terms of wealth and income. In Hamilton, for example, the most affluent 10 per cent of the city held 88 per cent of its propertied wealth, drew nearly half its income, and controlled about 60 per cent of its wealth. On the other hand, the poorest 40 per cent earned only

☐ Orange Order parade along King Street, Toronto. Metropolitan Toronto Library Board, T13222.

about 1 per cent of the city's total income and controlled about 6 per cent of its total wealth. Nevertheless, rich and poor in Hamilton lived in close proximity to each other. Only as cities grew larger and developed an expanding middle class that could afford to move out of the urban centre and a working class desperate for housing would the industrial city emerge with its clear divisions between rich and poor, and between one economic function and another. In the preindustrial city the role of women and children in the labour force was fairly limited. Industry could and did employ both women and children for some of the simple repetitive tasks that supplemented the machines. Factory owners found that children worked for low wages. Families often insisted that employers take on the entire family, so they would earn enough to live. In the last analysis, the major characteristic of families on the unskilled side of industrialization was their vulnerability to poverty. Not all the working-class poor worked in factories. Opportunities for women were strong at the lower end of the labour force in domestic service, as well as in business and clerical occupations. The mid-Victorian Age saw changes in the retail trade as well as in manufacturing. In 1840 retail establishments were relatively small. By

1870 general merchandising had begun to spawn the department store. The T. Eaton Company was founded in Toronto in 1869.

Between rich and poor, the middle class—although it ranged from small urban merchants to small-town industrialists to well-to-do rural farmers—came increasingly to be anchored by members of the educated professional occupations. Professionals' relative dependability of income tended to set them apart. Guaranteeing that dependability through professionalization was the chief development within the middle classes in this period. The numbers of qualified practitioners were increased through formal education, and at the same time stringent licensing requirements were imposed, often set by the occupation itself. The doctors took the lead. An attempt in 1839 to legislate the creation of a College of Physicians and Surgeons of Upper Canada failed in 1840, although another similar attempt in Canada East in 1847 was more successful. Perhaps significantly, doctors were one of the first groups to organize nationally: the Canadian Medical Association formed in the very year of Confederation. Lawyers engaged in a similar policy, with most provincial law societies formed between 1846 and 1877.

The first Eaton catalogue, 1884. According to a prefatory note, it was published in response to 'the immense increase in our Mail Order Department'. Metropolitan Toronto Reference Library.

Outside the class structure entirely were women, Aboriginal peoples, people from Asia, and Blacks (or Negroes, as they were then called). In Victorian Canada women were regarded as the bearers and nurturers of children. Their proper place was to be in the home as wife, helpmate, and mother. Women had few legal rights. A woman could not expect automatically to inherit a deceased husband's property. In most provinces, a husband could sue a wife for divorce on grounds of adultery, but a wife could sue a husband only if he were adulterous and had committed some other heinous offence. The courts expected women to reform violent husbands rather than prosecute them. Mothers had a better chance to rights of guardianship over children if they were unwed. Despite the domestic ideal, many women worked. The most invisible women workers were the domestic servants. The typical domestic servant in the census of 1871 was a single woman in her twenties who lived in the house and could both read and write. The highest occupation to which most women could aspire was that of schoolteacher. Actively recruited into the teaching ranks, they then remained at the lower end in terms of both salary and responsibility. There was little opportunity for entry into the professions. Emily Howard Stowe (1831–1903) obtained a medical degree from the New York Medical College for Women in 1867, but she could not achieve proper

MRS E.J. JARVIS TO MRS WILLIAM JARVIS, 1837

Anna Maria Boyd was born in New Brunswick, and married Edward Jarvis in 1817; the couple had eight children. In 1837 Jarvis was supreme court justice of Prince Edward Island and the owner of an impressive new house. Anna Maria describes the preparations for the housewarming in the following letter.

Charlotte Town, Prince Edward Island
February 13, 1837

My Dear Caroline,

. . . I fear you have thought me negligent about writing to you. I believe my last to St. John & Halifax were dated in November. I had a great deal to attend to in December. The miss Grays came to us on New Years day & remained nearly four weeks & during that time I cut out my two drawing room Curtains & partly made them, assisted in putting them up, in addition to the window curtains of four other rooms each with two windows. The blinds (chintz) were also made & fixed & we had a House warming on the first day of February (Cornelia's birthday), which hurried the Ball & myself as I wished to celebrate it. She has my affectionate good wishes for many happy returns of it. There were eighty-one persons at the Ball including our children. We invited one hundred & ten. The dancing was kept up with great animation until nearly four o'clock in the morning & every one expressed themselves delighted with their entertainment. Sir John & Lady Harvey, Capt. & Miss Harvey and the two young men honoured us. Lady Harvey expressed herself much gratified by our inviting the two Boys. Sir John left us soon after Supper, but her Ladyship remained for the sake of her children. She is a most devoted Mother. The Curtains were much admired & I am told the effect of the two rooms was exceedingly good. I received the Company in the dining room & when Sir John and Lady Harvey were ushered into the Ball rooms by the Chief Justice & myself the music struck up God Save the King, & after walking round the rooms Miss Harvey opened the Ball with Major Lane. The whole thing went off with style & astonished many present. I borrowed a dining table the length of our own & had the two set up for supper in the room that Mary occupies as a bed room. I wish Mary could write a good description of the whole to you, as to myself I was too much fatigued in mind and body to attempt it & even the repetition is painful to me for I was more disposed to cry than to be cheerful & yet I was obliged to force my spirits. After supper my anxiety eased & I danced several quadriles & felt rested towards morning. You will be astonished that I am alive when I tell you that in one week six rooms were furnished with window curtains, three of them & the Hall window with chintz blinds. Pictures were hung round the dining room, Carpets taken up, four room floors cleaned & two put down again, bell ropes put up in the bedrooms & the Clock in the Hall, added to which I stood by while seven hogs were cut up. (Hams & shoulders cut by myself.) I assisted in the salting & packing down, I hired a woman to assist me to prepare the supper & she with the rest of their servants did their duty most faithfully to the last and every individual including the musicians left the house gratified by the attention shown to them by the *Host & Hostess*. One of the Musicians came as a particular favour to us. . . .

I unfortunately broke my spectacles just before Christmas & I cannot read with the pair I am writing with only by putting the reading glass before them. In this stupid place there are none for sale & I am puzzled to know how I am to get such articles to suit my eyes by sending to foreign parts for them. It is only occasionally that I write a decent letter, but for the above mentioned circumstances I am unable to do so & I shall make Mary use her pen oftener than she has done. . . .

Yours very affectionately, A.M. JARVIS

SOURCE: Jarvis Papers, Saint John Museum, Saint John, New Brunswick.

accreditation until 1880. The first woman lawyer would not appear until the next century.

Blacks and Chinese joined the Aboriginal peoples in suffering from widespread racial prejudice and discrimination in British North America. After 1840 governments pressured the indigenous peoples of the settled provinces to become freehold farmers. While governments recognized some Native rights, that alone did not lead to much protection. In 1850 the Canadian

Chinese CPR construction workers in camp at Kamloops, BC. NAC, C-2880C.

Parliament passed legislation that operationally defined who was and who was not an 'Indian' within the meaning of the acts involved. The process of legislating for Aboriginals rapidly escalated after 1850. In 1857 the legislature of Canada passed the Act for the Gradual Civilization of the Indian Tribes in the Canadas. It contained many provisions that ran against the expressed wishes of the Aboriginals. Canadian policy became devoted to removing Natives from the paths of settlement, by coercion and compulsion if necessary. Most of these policies—which defined 'Indians', made them citizens when properly educated, and provided for land grants—passed on to the Dominion of Canada from the Province of Canada in 1867.

Few British North Americans believed that the state would come to their assistance in times of trouble. For some, politics and government were a source of employment or patronage, but for the average person the government (whether local, provincial, or federal) existed mainly to act as an impartial and somewhat distant

A Petition from the Coloured People of Hamilton to the Governor-General, 1843

Hamilton, [Canada West]
October 15, 1843

Dear Sir

We the people of colour in the Town of Hamilton have a right to inform your Excellency of the treatment that we have to undergo. We have paid the taxes and we are denied of the public schools, and we have applied to the Board of the Police and there is no steps taken to change this manner of treatment, and this kind of treatment is not in the United States, for the children of colour go to the Public Schools together with the white children, more especially in Philadelphia, and I thought that there was not a man to be known by his colour under the British flag, and we left the United States because we were in hopes that prejudice was not in this land, and I came to live under your Government if my God would be my helper and to be true to the Government. I am sorry to annoy you by allowing this thing, but we are grieved much, we are imposed upon much, and if it please your Excellency to attend to this grievance, if you please Sir. I have left property in the United States and I have bought property in Canada, and all I want is Justice and I will be satisfied. We are called nigger when we go out in the street, and sometimes brick bats is sent after us as we pass in the street. We are not all absconders[.] Now we brought money into this Province and we hope never to leave it, for we hope to enjoy our rights in this Province, and may my God smile upon your public life and guide you into all truth, which is my prayer and God bless the Queen and Royal Family.

The Coloured People of Hamilton

SOURCE: C. Peter Ripley, ed., *The Black Abolitionist Papers: Volume II: Canada 1830–1865* (Chapel Hill: University of North Carolina Press, 1986), 97–8.

umpire. Government mostly affected events outside the citizen's personal experience. Nevertheless, the exodus from older settled districts, with traditional agrarian and resource-oriented economies, into towns and cities demonstrated two points. First, it showed the

THE TESTIMONY OF MARIA THOMAS, 1863

In 1863 a well-known Anglican clergyman in Red River was put on trial for attempting an abortion on his fifteen-year-old mixed-blood serving girl, who accused him of rape. The transcript of the trial was carried in full in the local newspaper and represents the most detailed account that we have of any such trial in British North America.

Maria Thomas sworn.—I know prisoner have been in his service. Engaged April 1, 1861. Was engaged for one year—was engaged one month more. Wages for year 8 pounds wages for extra month 13s; I engaged then for a second month, at, I think, the same rate of wages. I stayed after the second month as Mr Corbett told me two weeks. I left because Mrs Corbett could not agree with me. Mr Corbett and I were always together at the byres feeding the cattle. Mr Corbett daed [*sic*] always have something to do with me at the byre. He had dealings with me there. He lay with me—he had connections with me, up on the loft of the stable over where his mare was kept. The loft was made of round sticks with hay on them. There was a hole in the wall, which Mr Corbett made after he first had connection with me. He took a broad chisel and hammer and made it. It was mudded up by old Tom Swain. The hole was made for Mr Corbett to watch through. He said he made this hole to watch his wife—that he might see her when she came towards the byre. After it was closed it was re-opened by Mr Corbett with the same chisel. He told me he had re-opened it. Mr Corbett first had connection with me one day last winter, in my bed in the kitchen of his own house, I was washing that day. When I finished, Mr Corbett made up a little wine, put medicine in it, and told me to drink it before anybody would see me. I drank it and when I was kneeling at prayers I fell asleep. Little Polly (a girl employed about the house) pushed me when they were done, and I got up and went into the kitchen. While I was putting away the things I felt as if I would fall asleep; as soon as I had finished I went and laid down and fell fast asleep. When I awoke in the morning it was late and I felt as if I could not move. Little Polly who slept with me that night, pulled me up when I told her. When I got out of bed I felt as if my inside would all fall out. I saw blood lying in the bed and I said what can be the matter with me? I went out to the porch, met Mr. Corbett and told him my troubles were coming on. He smiled and said he had been with me that night, and said it would be all right. I told him I would tell the Bishop. He shed tears, and told me, like a good girl not to do it; he said he would give me money and get me things whenever he went down to the Fort. He gave me a French Merino dress and a black one. I cannot tell how long after he first had connection with me. Afterwards on the stable-loft, more than once, he lay with me, I cannot say how often: but it was nearly every time we went to feed the cattle. He would tell me to go up to the stable-loft to throw down hay, and as soon as I would go up, he would go after me. He also examined me with his fingers in the byre. He did so twice.

SOURCE: 'The Trial of G.O. Corbett', *The Nor'-Wester*, February 1863.

extent to which the older mercantile economy was failing to support the rate of population growth. Second, it showed the extent to which new economic development was essential. By the 1860s politicians were extremely conscious of the movement of depopulation, particularly to the United States. Territorial expansion westward was one solution. A more sophisticated economy was another. Both seemed to many political leaders across British North America to require new political arrangements.

THE CREATION OF CULTURAL INFRASTRUCTURE

The conscious cultivation of mind, creativity, and aesthetic taste—which is what most people have in mind when they think of 'culture'—is obviously something that does not come easily to a pioneer society living on the edge of a vast wilderness and spending most of its energy on survival. Such culture requires a complex infrastructure in order to flourish. While small parts of that infrastructure had been in place almost from the beginning of settlement in North America, the elaboration of substantial institutional support for culture was slow to develop. The years between 1840 and 1870 were important in terms of that elaboration, if only because they witnessed such a striking growth in urban populations. Only a few illustrative examples can be discussed here.

Until the 1830s most newspapers had been published weekly, but bi-weekly editions for papers in the larger cities began in the late 1830s. The Saint John *News* introduced a penny edition in 1839, and dailies started in the 1850s. Most early papers were four page-sheets and had relatively small circulations, printing no more than 1,000 copies, although readership could be far greater. Susanna Moodie described the typical newspaper of her day as 'a strange mélange of politics, religion, abuse, and general information', adding that it 'contains, in a condensed

PROSPECTUS OF THE NOR'-WESTER, 1859

The undersigned have now commenced the publication of a Newspaper in the Red River Settlement, near Fort Garry, entitled *The Nor'-Wester*, and devoted to the varied and rapidly growing interests of that region.

Exploring parties, organized under the direction, respectively, of the Canadian and British Governments, have established the immediate availability for the purpose of colonization of the vast country watered by the Red River, the Assiniboine, and the Saskatchewan; and private parties of American citizens, following Captain Palliser, are engaged in determining the practicability of rendering this great overland region to the gold deposits of British Columbia. The Red River Settlement is the home of a considerable population, hardy, industrious, and thrifty; occupying fine farming estates, with all the advantages of prairie and timber combined. It has Churches many; and educational advantages which will endure comparison with those of more pretentious communities. And for hundreds of miles beyond stretches one of the most magnificent agricultural regions in the world, watered abundantly with Lakes and navigable Rivers, with a sufficiency of timber, with vast prairies of unsurpassed fertility, with mineral resources, in some parts, of no common value, and with a climate as salubrious as it is delightful. Such a country cannot now remained unpeopled. It offers temptations to the emigrant nowhere excelled. It invites alike the mechanic and the farmer. Its river and rolling prairies and accessible mountain-passes secure it the advantages which must belong to a highway to the Pacific. It has communication with Canada via Fort William; and regular communication with the Mississippi, via steamboat and stage to St. Paul. What can impede its development? What can prevent the settlement around Fort Garry from becoming the political and commercial centre of a great and prosperous people?

The printing press will hasten the change, not only by stimulating the industrial life of the Red River Settlement, but by assisting the work of governmental organization, the necessity for which is admitted on all sides not only by cultivating a healthy public sentiment upon the spot, but by converting to more distant observers an accurate knowledge of the position, progress, and prospectus of affairs.

The *Nor'-Wester* starts on an independent commercial basis. Indebted to no special interests for its origin and looking to none for its maintenance, it will rely wholly upon the honest and efficient exercise of its functions as the reflex of the wants and opinions, the rights and interests of the Red River Settlement. Its projectors go thither tied to no set of men, influenced by no narrow preferences, shackled by no mean antipathies. Their journal will be a vehicle of news, and for the pertinent discussion of local questions; governed only by a desire to promote local interests and a determination to keep aloof from every entangling alliance which might mar its usefulness at home or abroad. It will be a faithful chronicler of events—a reporter assiduous and impartial. Especially will it aim to be the medium for communicating facts, calculated to enlighten the non-resident reader with regard to the resources and geography, the life and the sentiment, of the district in which it will be published. Nor will efforts be wanting to make it equal to the tastes of the Red River settlers; arrangements having been made that will assure reliable correspondence from Canada and elsewhere. During the early winter months of its existence, *The Nor'-Wester* will be published fortnightly, to meet the mail arrangements with Canada; next spring it will be published weekly, and will be continued regularly thereafter.

The connection which the subscribers have maintained with the Toronto press, is referred to as evidence of their practical ability to carry out the task they have undertaken.

Price TWO DOLLARS per annum, payable invariably in advance. Letters may be addressed to Box G99, Post Office, Toronto, until the 20th September, proximo; after that date, communications to be addressed to Fort Garry, in all cases prepaid. WILLIAM BUCKINGHAM. WILLIAM COLDWELL. November 22, 1859.

SOURCE: *The Nor'-Wester*, 28 December 1859.

form, all the news of the Old and New World, and informs its readers of what is passing on the great globe, from the North Pole to the Gold Mines of Australia and California' (quoted in Rutherford 1982: 38). One modern content analysis of four papers from this era corroborates this description (Rutherford 1982: 39). George Brown published the first daily in 1853, printing it on a steam-powered cylinder press, and he reached a hitherto-unheard-of circulation of 28,000 by 1861. In British North America Brown was a pioneer in the regular serialization of popular fiction, including the works of Charles Dickens. He also aggressively covered the arts, especially in the local community. All newspapers, especially the dailies, benefited from the introduction of telegraphy to British America in the late 1840s.

In history everything connects. Critical to the emergence of the daily newspaper and the development of a larger and more sophisticated arts community was the introduction of mass education. This began in the 1840s, especially in anglophone British North America. Mass education was a product of the introduction of publicly supported schooling combined with the

JEAN-BAPTISTE MEILLEUR

Jean-Baptiste Meilleur (1796–1878) was born on Montreal Island, and was educated at the college of Montreal. He subsequently studied medicine in Vermont, receiving his doctorate in 1825 from Middlebury College. He also studied at Dartmouth, apparently supporting himself by giving French lessons and writing *A Treatise on the Pronunciation of the French Language* (1825). He returned to medical practice at L'Assomption in 1826, acquiring the usual accoutrements of a successful doctor at the time, including a militia rank of lieutenant and election to the Lower Canadian assembly in 1838. He sympathized with political reform in 1837, but not with violence. He wrote extensively on educational and scientific topics, and began in 1828 a series of letters on education in *La Minerve* which led to the establishment of a college at L'Assomption in 1834.

Meilleur responded to Lord Durham's challenge for educational improvement in Lower Canada in an exchange of letters with Arthur Buller in Montreal's *Le Populaire* in 1838 and with a famous series of letters published in Quebec's *Le Canadien* that same year. These letters outlined a system of public schooling for the province, in which at least the primary grades would be free. He recommended supplementing Jesuit funding, the source for most schooling in the province, with various duties and licences to finance education. He was heavily critical of the existing state of education, and recommended a series of levels ranging from primary school through classical teaching (at the high school level) to academic teaching of practical subjects (also at the high school level) to training at normal schools. When Canada passed an Education Act in 1841, Meilleur applied to be superintendent, and was so appointed—without pay—for Lower Canada. Meilleur served in this onerous post for thirteen years, administering the original Education Act and six subsequent revisions. In 1845 he became superintendent of education for Lower Canada under an act that made the parish the basis of the school system. An 1846 act provided for parish school commissions which were to match educational grants from the province. This act was much opposed by various local districts as an introduction of taxation for education; the rioting went on for years in some places.

Meilleur was a hard man to work with, for he was an intellectual loner rather than a political animal, and he was not happy in his job. In 1853, the report of a committee chaired by Louis-Victor Sicotte called for further reforms in education to provide some energy for the system, and eventually in 1855 Meilleur took the hint and resigned. He subsequently served as director and then inspector of the Montreal post office, then provincial deputy registrar. After he retired Meilleur found more time for intellectual activity, and in 1860 he published *Mémorial de l'éducation du Bas-Canada*, which summarized the educational record of the province. In 1870 he became president of the Natural History Society of Quebec. Meilleur was something of a polymath, and—whatever his flaws—the founder of the educational system in Quebec.

principle of universality. The result was that increasing numbers of people learned to read and write, and this increased the audience and market for the arts and culture. Census data from 1861 suggest that more than ninety per cent of the population of Canada West could read, a tribute to the early introduction of free schooling. The figures were lower in Canada East, where over one-third of the population could not read in 1861, and in the Maritimes, where 22.6 per cent could not read and 32.7 per cent could not write. The 1871 census indicated that only just over 12 per cent of Ontarians could not write; the figure for Quebec was 45.8 per cent and for the Maritimes 23.3 per cent. The data suggest that French Canada remained a much more oral society than English Canada. Naturally, the younger members of society were

The Victorian era was fond of graphic illustrations of progress. Here four schoolhouses illustrate the improvements made from the early days of settlement to the 1860s: 1-2: 'First Settlers' School-houses'; 3 'Country District School-house'; 4 'Village School-house'. From H.Y. Hind, *The Dominion of Canada: Containing a Historical Sketch of the Preliminaries and Organization of Confederation* (1869).

TABLE 5.3

SCHEDULE OF THE COURSE OF STUDY, UNIVERSITY OF TORONTO, 1868

Matriculation

Xenophon's Anabasis, book i.
Sallust's Catilina
Virgil's Aeneid, book ii.
Latin Prose Cosmopolitan
Arithmetic, to end of square root
Algebra, first four rules
Euclid, book i.
English Grammar
Outlines of English History

Not including the honour course, which includes options, etc.

Outlines of Roman History, to death of Nero
Grecian History, to death of Alexander
Ancient and Modern Geography

First year

Homer's Illiad, book vi
Lucian's Vita and Charon
Virgil's Aeneid, book vi.
Cicero, de Amicitia
Latin Prose Composition
Arithmetic
Algebra
Euclid, books i–vi
Plane Trigonometry
English Composition
English Language and Literature
French Grammar
Montesquieu's Grandeur et Décadence des Romaines
Ancient History
British History
Elements of Chemistry
Elements of Physiology
Elements of Botany
Paley's Natural Theology
Paley's Evidences

Second year

Homer's Odyssey, book xi
Demosthene's Olynthiacs
Horace, Odes
Cicero, two orations
Latin Prose Composition
Statics, Dynamics
English Composition
English Literature
French Composition
La Bruyère Caractères
French Literature
German Grammar
Adler's German Reader
German Literature
German Composition
Schiller's William Tell, etc.
German Literature
Medieval History
British History
Chemistry and Chemical Physics
Mineralogy and Geology
Murray's Logic
Wayland's Moral Philosophy
Locke, books ii, iii, and iv.

Third year

Sophocles, Oedipus Rex
Herodotus, book ii
Horace, Satires and Epistles
Livy, book v
Latin Prose Composition
Hydrostatics, Optics
French Composition
Racine's Phèdre and Athalie
Bossuet's Oraisons Funèbres
French Literature
German Grammar, etc.
German Composition
Lessing's Minna von Barnhelm
German Literature
Modern History
British History
Chemistry
Comparative Physiology
Vegetable Physiology, etc.
Ried's Intellectual Powers
Stewart's Moral and Active Powers
Whately's Political Economy

Final examination

Euripides, Medea
Thucydides, book vii
Juvenal, sat. iii, vii, viii, and x
Tacitus, Germania and Agricola
Latin Prose Competition
Acoustics, Astronomy
English Composition
English Language and Literature
French Composition
Corneille's Le Cid
De Staël's De l'Allemagne
French Literature
Chemistry, Mineralogy, Geology, Physical Geography, and Meteorology
Smith's Wealth of Nations

more literate than their elders, and males in most places more literate than females. Raw literacy data do not tell us much about how individual people employed their skills, but combined with increases in the number of libraries and the availability of books and newspapers, the figures suggest a marked increase in the audience for cultural productions.

Higher education is just as important as mass education for the development of culture, since it helps create an interest in the life of the mind and improves aesthetic taste. By 1867 there were seventeen degree-granting institutions in the colonies, as well as a number of colleges that provided some higher education but did not actually give degrees. Virtually every province (and even Red River) had at least a college or two, and several provinces (such as Nova Scotia) had a plethora of them. Colonial institutions of higher learning had their limitations. With few exceptions, they were small, with enrollments of under 100 students. Except for Dalhousie (1818), McGill (1821), New Brunswick (1828, secularized 1859), and the University of Toronto (1827, secularized 1850), all the remaining institutions of higher learning were church-related and church-governed. One of the reasons for a large number of small colleges and universities was that every major denomination insisted on founding a school where its own students could be educated, free from the doctrinal pollution of the competition, and mainly for the ministry. Only a few of these colleges taught science seriously, partly because of the expense of proper laboratories, partly because of the origins of higher learning in the traditional arts curriculum. Most teachers did not have higher degrees and had no pretensions to research or independent scholarship. They taught many hours a week, usually by lecture and with an insistence on rote memorization. But somehow a sense of connection to the wider world of humanistic culture permeated the system, and helped to create an audience for higher thought.

THE ROAD TO CONFEDERATION

The political problems of the Canadas were the immediate stimulus for Canadian politicians to begin to explore the possibility of a larger union with the eastern provinces, beginning at the famous Charlottetown Conference of September 1864. Such a solution did not come out of thin air, however. Politicians had discussed the political unification of the provinces of British North America on and off since the days of the Loyalists. Few of the early proposals were very elaborate. Most gave no consideration to whether the proposed union would result in an independent national state. Most came from Tories concerned with enhancing the power of the Crown or providing a basis for economic development. By the 1850s, however, there was emerging, particularly in the Canadas, some sense of the existence of 'a true Canadian feeling—a feeling of what might be termed Canadian nationality, in contradistinction to a feeling of mere colonial or annexation vassalage', as the Montreal *Pilot* put it on 6 April 1850. Sometimes these sentiments were couched in high-flown rhetoric. Often economic or cultural protectionism dominated the phraseology, but a new Canadian feeling was growing in power after mid-century. It flourished partly on changing communications technology that made it possible to transmit fast-breaking news across the provinces in moments.

Neither the bind of the double majority nor the beginning of national sentiment was alone sufficient to propel British North Americans to national unification. As was so often the case, events in the United States provided the catalyst. The American federal union broke apart with surprising suddenness in 1861. The southern states seceded into their own Confederacy. The American Civil War began. Many Canadians quietly rooted for the Confederacy despite its maintenance of slavery. Britain adopted an official policy of neutrality. The British watched warily while public opinion in the northern states,

The Charlottetown Conference, September 1864. On the left, Charles Tupper is standing against the first pillar and D'Arcy McGee against the second, with George-Étienne Cartier in front of him; seated next to Cartier is John A. Macdonald. NAC, C-733.

whipped up by American newspapers, talked openly of finding compensation for the lost Confederacy by annexing British North America.

Britain could hardly leave her North American colonies unprotected. Defending them at great expense was not something the British faced with relish, however. By the 1860s the British ruling classes believed that colonies like British North America would inevitably separate from the mother country. Why not hasten the process and save money? An independent British North America could organize its own defences. In 1864 the military situation in the United States turned more dangerous for British North America, as the Union forces gained clear victories over the Confederacy. In several respects the efforts of the Canadians to create a larger union fitted very well with British desires for reduced colonial responsibility and expense. The full weight of the still-considerable influence of the British colonial system came down on the side of unification.

In Canada the difficulty of agreeing to military mobilization was one of the many factors that led George Brown to propose a political coalition with his enemies. The understanding rested on a commitment to a British American federal union. This Great Coalition—a ministry formed by a union of the Conservatives under Macdonald and the Bleus under Cartier, with the Grits led by Brown, announced in the Canadian Parliament on 22 June 1864—broke the political deadlock. The new government moved on a variety of fronts over the summer of 1864. Most important was to prepare the outlines of federal union for a conference of Maritime delegates called at Charlottetown in September to discuss Maritime union. The maritime region contained a good deal of abstract support for unification with Canada, tempered by two realities: any

Maritime participation in a larger union must not work to the disadvantage of the provinces, and a strong feeling that the Maritimes were doing pretty well within the existing imperial structure.

Historians sympathetic to central Canada have always tended to view the Maritime defence of local interests as parochial. Such an interpretation misses the point. One problem with the Canadian initiative was that Canada was so much bigger and more powerful than the other provinces that almost any union would seem more like annexation than confederation. The Maritimes, moreover, were already part of a larger political and economic system known as the British empire. Many Maritimers had travelled on sailing-ships to the far corners of the world, and in many ways Maritime voters were far more cosmopolitan than the Canadians themselves. At the time, the case against Confederation was quite reasonable. Unification seemed an impracticable visionary scheme, proposed by politicians in the Province of Canada to meet their needs. It was not necessarily in the best interests of the other colonies.

Considerable ingenuity was required in 1864 to explain to delegates from smaller constituencies how the Canadian proposal really worked to their benefit. The union as finally developed was somewhat different than the one initially proposed. The biggest difference was in the place of the provinces. The Canadians originally intended to create a strong central government by consolidating all the provincial legislatures (and their powers) into one grand Parliament. This procedure of legislative union was how Great Britain had earlier incorporated Scotland and Ireland. The Canadians granted the need for local governments to deal with local matters. They did not intend those local governments to be fully articulated provincial governments, certainly not provincial governments capable of forming a counterweight to the central federal one. Neither Scotland nor Ireland (after union) had separate political administrations based upon legislatures, although both still had local governments. The Maritime delegates at Charlottetown responded to visions of greatness, fuelled by food, drink, and much convivial conversation. They agreed to the Canadian scheme. By the time of the Quebec Conference a month later, many had had sober second thoughts.

Prince Edward Island took the lead at Quebec against the Canadian steamroller. The smallest province of British North America, the island had fought annexation to Nova Scotia for almost a century. It found it hard to give up its autonomy to proposals that reflected Canadian dominance. When John A. Macdonald moved that the three sections of British North America—Canada West, Canada East, and the four Atlantic provinces—each have twenty-four members in the Senate, he gave away the game. In the American Senate, each state had two senators regardless of population; in the Canadian Senate, the four smaller provinces would have only one-third of the senators among them. Eventually the Quebec Conference accepted this arrangement, offering Newfoundland an additional four senators. Prince Edward Island also made a big issue—without any success—over getting one more member of the House of Commons than its population allowed (six instead of five). A further and telling debate came over the power of the local governments. The majority case was that Canada's fundamental principle had always been that 'all the powers not given to Local should be reserved to the Federal Government' (quoted in Waite 1962: 95). But a number of Atlantic delegates were not happy. The subsequent debate over the Quebec resolution was not over the principle of union but over its terms. While it would be convenient to see the matter of terms as a petty haggling over details, some of the details were fairly important.

Another Canadian principle was legislative sovereignty. 'We the People' would not create this union, as in the United States. Instead, an act of the British Parliament would create Canada. Conveniently enough, this denial of popular sovereignty meant that Confederation

Lieutenant-Governor Gordon of New Brunswick on the Charlottetown Conference

In September 1864, several members of the Canadian government (Cartier, Galt, Brown) stayed in Government House with the lieutenant-governor of New Brunswick, Sir Arthur Hamilton Gordon. The Canadians discussed with Gordon the recent conference held at Charlottetown, and Gordon reported on their remarks to the colonial secretary, Edward Caldwell.

. . . . 4. The discussions of the Conference were for the most part conducted in a conversational and informal manner. Two subjects, however, were debated at some length in more elaborately prepared speeches. These were—the Composition and mode of election of the Legislative Council—and the authority from which appointments to the local Judiciary should emanate.

5. With regard to the former subject less difference of opinion was found to exist than I should have anticipated. It was agreed that the Federal Legislative Council should consist of 60 members, 20 from Upper Canada, 20 from Lower Canada, and 20 from the Maritime Provinces. It was generally desired that the members of this body should be nominated for life by the Crown, and with hardly an exception the elective principle as applied to the Legislative Council was decidedly condemned. Mr. Brown, though the leader of the Ultra-democratic party in Canada entirely participated in this disapproval of an elective Upper Chamber and strongly supports the views of those who desire to see a return to the system of nomination abandoned in Canada 8 or 9 years ago. . . .

6. With respect to the appointment of the Judges a very animated discussion took place, and I am informed that the Honourable E. B. Chandler, one of the Delegates from this Province made an extremely effective speech on this subject. . . . He . . . strongly urged that the appointment of Judges should be vested in the Central Government, and he was warmly supported by Mr Tilley, who also urged the adoption of some measure which should entirely remove these appointments from the influence of party politics. . . .

7. With respect to the important question of the attributes to be assigned the respective Legislatures and Governments there was a very great divergence of opinion. The aim of Lower Canada is a local independence as complete as circumstances will permit, and the peculiarities of race, Laws, religion and habits which distinguish its people render their desire respectable and natural. A similar desire, but prompted by less worthy motives, animates the Delegates from Prince Edward Island and some from this Province, who fear the loss of the local importance which attaches to a separate Government. Those on the other hand who look chiefly to the future and desire to see the British North American Provinces forming a strong and united State are desirous, as I before observed in my previous Despatch, to reduce the local Legislatures and Governments to the smallest possible dimensions, to invest them with the smallest possible portion of independent powers, and to obliterate, as far as practicable, existing Provincial boundaries. . . .

SOURCE: Public Record Office, London, Colonial Office 188/141.

did not go before the public in the form of an election, a ratification convention, or a referendum/plebiscite. The public debate on the Quebec Resolutions did not always take into account the niceties of political theory. But critics understood the basic thrust of the proposals well enough, and the debate did affect their interpretation and ultimate implementation. While the Canadians had initially intended to reduce the provincial governments to municipal proportions, both French Canada and the Maritimes made clear that the provinces would have to survive relatively intact. The proponents of union in Canada East emphasized that Confederation meant giving French Canadians their own province, with—as the *Courrier de St-Hyacinthe* put it in September 1864—the two levels of government both 'sovereign, each within its jurisdiction as clearly defined by the constitution'. An informal adjustment addressed this matter. On the other hand, the opposition fulminated unsuccessfully to the end over the refusal of the proponents of Confederation to take the scheme to the people.

Newspapers, pamphlets, and debates held in the legislatures of each of the provinces discussed the Quebec resolutions. What these demonstrated most of all was the success of the proponents of union in capturing most of the positive ground. Critics could reduce the proposals to rubble, but had little to put in their place. For Canada, the absence of alternatives was particularly striking. The debates also demonstrated that the Quebec resolutions were, on the whole, far more acceptable to Tories than they were to Reformers. Although the debates in the Canadian Parliament were lengthy and long-winded, the ultimate result was approval. The eastern provinces could stand pat, however, and some did. Newfoundland—convinced it would be little more than 'the contemptible fag-end of such a compact' with Canada after an election fought on the question in 1869—remained outside Confederation until 1949. Prince Edward Island felt insufficiently compensated for 'the surrender of a separate Government, with the independent powers it now enjoys'. It would not join until 1873.

The situation in New Brunswick and Nova Scotia was more complex. In the former province, a coalition of opponents to union headed by A.J. Smith (1822–83) blew away the pro-Confederation government of Samuel Leonard Tilley (1818–96) in an 1865 election. A year later another election was held against the background of threatened invasion by thousands of Irish nationalists (the Fenians), many of them veterans of the American Union army who had kept their arms when disbanded. The threat was sufficient to return Tilley to office. The new administration moved an address favouring Confederation, not, it must be noted, as embodied in the Quebec resolutions but 'upon such terms as will secure the just rights and interests of New Brunswick, accompanied with provision for the immediate construction of the Intercolonial Railway'. When this motion carried, opposition disappeared.

In Nova Scotia, which owned 1 ton of sailing ship for each of its 350,000 inhabitants, there was much concerted opposition to union. Joseph Howe led the opponents of Confederation. He attacked the union's Canadian origins from the vantage point of someone perfectly content with the British empire. Confederation smacked too much of Canadian self-interest. It gave Upper Canada rep by pop, and Lower Canada provincial autonomy, but offered nothing to Nova Scotia. The Nova Scotia legislature never did approve the Quebec resolutions. The government, led by Charles Tupper (1821–1915), introduced a motion calling for a 'scheme of union' in which 'the rights and interests of Nova Scotia' would be ensured (quoted in Pryke 1979: 27). It passed thirty-one to nineteen. Unlike their counterparts in New Brunswick, the opponents of Confederation in Nova Scotia did not melt away. They eventually went on to elect full slates of candidates provincially and federally that promised to take Nova Scotia out of the union in which it had become involved.

Although neither Nova Scotia nor New Brunswick ever actually approved the Quebec resolutions—which all but the most ardent unionists recognized would consign the smaller provinces to national impotence—the fundamentals laid down at Quebec became the basis of the new Constitution. Small wonder that the region later complained about the deal they had made. In November 1866 delegates from Canada, Nova Scotia, and New Brunswick met in London to work out the final details, essentially the Quebec resolutions with more money for the Maritimes and the Intercolonial Railway. All agreed that the name of the new country should be that of its principal progenitor, thus openly declaring the primacy of Canada in the arrangement and causing confusion ever afterwards for students of Canadian history. The resulting legislation, the British North America Act, passed quickly through the British Parliament in 1867. The MPs barely looked up from the order paper as they voted. The Queen signed the bill into law on 29 March 1867, with the date of proclamation 1 July. Governor-General Lord Monck (1819–94) called upon John A. Macdonald, the man everyone most closely associated with the union, to be the first prime minister.

On the morning of 1 July—a day of celebration and military parades in all four provinces—the new country was proclaimed in the recently completed Parliament buildings in Ottawa. Macdonald received a knighthood. The ceremonial launching of the new nation did not, however, guarantee its success. Much was still needed to make Canada work.

CONCLUSION

The road to Confederation was a complex one, with many paths coming together. The British cut British North America free from their mercantile system. The British North Americans naturally were drawn to the continental economy, and began to build railroads and industrialize. The Province of Canada cast covetous glances westward, where the hold of the Hudson's Bay Company was weakened by the beginnings of settlement. A unified Canada was not only more powerful but also a leader in achieving responsible government and producing a new imperial relationship. Immigration to Britisah North America continued, producing much mobility, which in turn led to a need for roots. Population growth brought a new cultural infrastructure. By the 1860s, the Canadians were ready to take the lead in creating an expanded nation, which they did against the better judgment of many in the Atlantic region.

HOW HISTORY HAS CHANGED

ACHIEVING RESPONSIBLE GOVERNMENT

By and large, Canadian historians are no longer fascinated with politics and constitutional development, in either the domestic or the imperial sense. Nevertheless, the shifting interpretations of British North America's political development between 1840 and 1860 tell us a good deal about changing fashions in Canadian historical writing. The traditional view, which prevailed until well into the twentieth century, saw the colonies (especially Upper and Lower Canada) rebelling against Britain's failure to allow them colonial self-government. Lord Durham recommended responsible government—colonial legislative autonomy—as a solution to the discontent, and this answer was adopted after considerable pressure from colonial reformers in the early 1840s. We can perhaps call this the Whig interpretation. There was always some disagreement over whether responsible government came in 1841 or 1848, chiefly because there were different interpretations of what was required before responsible government was actually in place. Was it legislative autonomy from the Colonial Office or the triumph of party government freed from the governors? Gradually this question of different interpretations became essential for a new interpretation that developed over the period from 1920 to 1950. This interpretation argued that the British had resisted party government throughout the 1840s, and responsible government as party government was won by politicians in British North America only after a hard struggle over the course of that decade. We can label this the neo-Whig interpretation.

After 1950, much more work was done on imperial policy and imperial politics, with the result that the old views of a backward and oppressive British imperial government—against which the colonials had to rebel—became much harder to sustain. On the colonial side, additional research had emphasized that the political situation in the colonies was much more complex than anyone had previously imagined. The colonial reformers were not necessarily the good guys, and the British were not necessarily the bad guys. The move to free trade took on new importance, and British imperial policy (rather than Lord Durham) became the crucial element in the achievement of responsible government. This, of course, produced its own problems (by downgrading the pressures exerted on the imperial system by colonial politicians) and led ultimately to an interpretation that attempts to balance imperial and domestic influence.

Since the 1980s, less and less interest has been shown by Canadian historians in either domestic or imperial political matters. This probably reflects in part the severing of most of Canada's imperial ties, in part a general cynicism about modern politics, and in part the fact that politics, imperial or domestic, in the pre-Confederation era were almost exclusively in the hands of the élite. Instead, there has been a growing focus on other developments that resonate more in the modern world. Perhaps the most important of these developments is the growth of the administrative state, a subject which has increasingly fascinated historians of Europe and North America, as they have come to realize that in many ways the key figures in government were not the politicians at all, but the bureaucrats who administered the day-to-day routine of government. This recognition is perhaps not as fully developed in Canada for the pre-Confederation period as it is in British, German, or American historiography, but it does clearly seem to represent the direction of new interpretation.

SHORT BIBLIOGRAPHY

Bradbury, Bettina. *Working Families: Age, Gender, and Daily Survival in Industrializing Montreal*. Toronto, 1993. An exciting work on early industrialization in Montreal from the twin perspectives of women and the working classes.

Buckner, P.A. *The Transition to Responsible Government: British Policy in British North America 1815–59*. Westport, CT, 1985. Now the standard study, based on detailed research and elegantly argued.

Courville, Serge, and Normand Séguin. *Rural Life in Nineteenth-century Quebec*. Ottawa, 1989. A middle-level synthesis of an important topic.

Curtis, Bruce. *Building the Educational State: Canada West, 1836–1871*. Sussex and London, 1988. A revisionist work that argues the importance of educational policy for state formation in this period.

Gagan, David. *Hopeful Travellers: Families, Land, and Social Change in Mid-Victorian Peel Country, Canada West*. Toronto, 1981. The product of a huge quantification project, this book attempts to explain the relationship between land and mobility in rural English Canada.

Galbraith, John S. *The Hudson's Bay Company as an Imperial Factor*. Toronto, 1957. The classic statement of the imperial role of the Hudson's Bay Company in the nineteenth century.

Greer, Allan, and Ian Radforth, eds. *Colonial Leviathan: State Formation in Mid-Nineteenth Century Canada*. Toronto, 1992. A recent collection of essays, informed by current international thinking about the nineteenth-century state.

Hodgetts, J.E. *Pioneer Public Service: An Administrative History of the United Canadas, 1841–1867*. Toronto, 1955. A pioneer work decades ahead of its time.

Katz, Michael. *The People of Hamilton, Canada West: Family and Class in a Mid-Nineteenth-Century City*. Cambridge, MA, 1975. The first attempt to apply American quantitative methodology on a large scale to a Canadian subject.

Lucas, Sir Charles, ed. *Lord Durham's Report on the Affairs of British North America*. 3 vols. Oxford, 1912; reprinted New York, 1970. The scholarly edition of the complete Durham report.

Masters, D.C. *The Reciprocity Treaty of 1854*. Ottawa, 1963. Still the standard account of this important treaty.

Metcalfe, Alan. *Canada Learns to Play: The Emergence of Organized Sport 1807–1911*. Toronto, 1987. An important work which documents the development in Canada of organized sport in the nineteenth century.

Monet, Jacques. *The Last Cannon Shot: A Study of French-Canadian Nationalism*. Toronto, 1969. The classic study of the emergence of nationalism, under the watchful eye of the Church, in Lower Canada/Canada East.

Saddlemyer, Ann, ed. *Early Stages: Theatre in Ontario 1800–1914*. Toronto, 1990. A collection of pioneering essays which demonstrate how much there is to be learned about Canadian culture in the nineteenth century if one chooses to look.

Shippee, L.B. *Canadian-American Relations 1849–1874*. New Haven, 1939. Still the best overall study of the topic.

Tucker, Gilbert. *The Canadian Commercial Revolution 1845–1851*. Ottawa, 1970. The most useful survey of this question.

Waite, Peter B. *The Life and Times of Confederation, 1864–1867: Politics, Newspapers, and the Union of British North America*. Toronto, 1962. Still the best account of the central period of unification.

Winks, Robin. *Canada and the United States: The Civil War Years*. Montreal, 1971. Old, but still the standard work; a thorough account of Canadian–American relations during the war years.

Zeller, Suzanne. *Inventing Canada: Early Victorian Science and the Idea of a Transcontinental Nation*. Toronto, 1987. A work with a controversial argument—that science helped unite British North America—and a good deal of material on colonial science.

STUDY QUESTIONS

1. Explain how Britain's espousal of the free trade doctrine affected markets for Canadian wheat in the late 1840s.
2. Explain why the free trade doctrine led to the Reciprocity Treaty between British North America and the United States. How did this, in turn, lead to more railway-building and the rise of industrialism in British North America?
3. What can we learn from the trade statistics on pp. 167–8?
4. Write a short essay on Canadian railways in 1860 based on the tables on pp. 170–1.
5. Identify three reasons to explain why people in Canada West were so anxious to move into the Canadian West.
6. Outline the political consequences of the move to responsible government in Canada East.
7. Why did volunteer and fraternal organizations become so popular in British North America?
8. Explain how the infrastructure of an educational system and a publishing industry contributed to Canadian cultural production during this period.
9. Give two reasons to explain why people in the Maritimes might think of Confederation as a 'Canadian Plot'.

CHAPTER SIX

Expanding the Nation, 1867–1885

Although 1 July 1867 would be celebrated a century later as the date for Canada's 100th birthday, it was in the larger sense only an interim point. The new union consisted of four provinces—Ontario, Quebec, Nova Scotia, and New Brunswick—carved from the three that had created it. Sir John A. Macdonald's government was conscious that a lot of British territory on the continent had been excluded. The new government was also quite obviously the old Canadian coalition, with a few Maritime faces. Its organization was the old Canadian departments. It used buildings erected in Ottawa for the old Province of Canada. If the new administration seemed familiar, so did many of its policies. It bought off the malcontents in Nova Scotia with better terms that were entirely financial. It started building the Intercolonial Railway along the eastern coast of New Brunswick. With the prodding of the British, the Hudson's Bay Company would sell Rupert's Land and the Northwest Territory to the new nation. Canada devoted much energy to rounding up the strays and expanding coast to coast.

In many respects, the two decades from 1867 to 1885 would focus on tying up the myriad loose ends created by unification. There was the need to create new policies for the new Canada. In the end, too many policies continued from the older Canada, occasionally writ larger to accommodate the other provinces. The creation of new identities was even more difficult. The easiest identities to accept were the old provincial ones. Collectively, these provincial identities grew to provide one alternative to the national identity envisioned by the founding fathers.

Adding New Territory

One of the earliest legislative actions of the new Canadian government in December 1867 was the passage of resolutions calling for transcontinental expansion. Most of the legislators regarded such expansion as the nation's inevitable right, a sort of Canadian version of manifest destiny. As a result, in 1868 a ministerial delegation went to London to arrange the Hudson's Bay Company's transfer of the northwest to Canada. While complex negotiations continued, the Canadian government began building a road from Fort Garry to Lake of the Woods. This was part of a proposed road and water system linking Red River with Canada. The road builders established informal connections with Dr John Christian Schultz (1840–96), the influential leader of the local faction that had been agitating for Canadian annexation for years. Nobody paid any attention to the Métis who constituted the bulk of the local population of the settlement. The Canadian delegation in London finally worked out a deal for the transfer. The British government received the territory from the Hudson's Bay Company (the Canadians put up £300,000 and agreed to substantial land grants for the company) and subsequently transferred it intact to Canada.

Since the arrangements for the west were

TIMELINE

1867
British Columbia's legislative council resolves to request that the province be allowed eventual admission into Canada, which officially comes into existence on 1 July 1867 under an all-party government headed by Sir John A. Macdonald. Resolutions for territorial expansion are passed by the Canadian Parliament in December. The Americans purchase Alaska from Russia.

1868
Canada First is founded in Ottawa. Five hundred and seven Zouaves are recruited in Quebec for the papal army.

1869
Resistance to Canada, led by Louis Riel, begins in Red River. Newfoundland election produces an anti-confederate assembly.

1870
Louis Riel allows execution of Thomas Scott. The Manitoba Act is passed by the Canadian Parliament. The Wolseley Expedition is sent to Red River. Negotiations are begun with British Columbia for admission to Canada. Dominion Notes Act of 1870 is passed.

1871
British Columbia enters Confederation on 20 July 1871. The Washington Treaty is signed with the United States. The Bank Act of 1871 is passed.

1872
In a federal election, Conservatives win 103 seats to 97 Liberals. Ontario Society of Artists is formed.

1873
Prince Edward Island enters Confederation. The Macdonald government resigns over the Pacific Scandal. Liberals under Alexander Mackenzie take over federal government.

1874
Liberals win a clear majority in Parliament (133 to 73) over Conservatives.

1875
Woman's Christian Temperance Union is founded in Picton, Ontario.

1876
Intercolonial Railway is completed, linking Saint John, Halifax, and Montreal. Alexander Graham Bell invents a workable telephone. The first wheat crop is exported from Manitoba.

1877
Saint John fire leaves 13,000 homeless.

1878
Conservatives returned to power, 137 to 69 Liberals. Sir John A. Macdonald returns to power.

1880
Royal Academy of Arts is formed. Canadian government signs contract with the Canadian Pacific Railway.

1881
CPR reaches Winnipeg. The boundaries of Manitoba are expanded. 15,000 Chinese workers are allowed into Canada.

1882
Royal Society of Canada is formed. Conservatives are re-elected, 139 to 71 Liberals, now led by Edward Blake. Macdonald remains prime minister.

1883
CPR construction crews discover nickel near Sudbury, Ontario. Canadian Labour Congress is founded.

1884
Louis Riel returns to Canada.

1885
The second resistance led by Louis Riel (the North West Rebellion) is crushed. Riel is executed. The last spike is driven in the CPR.

made without bothering to inform the Red River people of their import, it was hardly surprising that the locals were suspicious and easily roused to protest. The Métis were concerned on several counts. The road-building party had been involved in a number of racist incidents. There was transparent haste on the part of the Canadian government to build a road and to send in men to survey land. This rush suggested that Canadian settlement would inundate the existing population without regard for its 'rights'. Canada made clear that it intended to treat the new territory as a colony. Furthermore, some of the road builders bought land cheaply from the Aboriginal peoples—land that the Métis thought was theirs. The Métis quickly perceived the Canadians as a threat to their way of life, perhaps even to their existence. The Canadian government received a number of warnings in 1869 that trouble was brewing. The warnings came from the Anglican archbishop of Rupert's Land, Robert Machray (1831–1904); from the governor of the Hudson's Bay Company, William Mactavish (1815–70); and from Bishop Alexandre Taché (1823–94), the Catholic bishop of St Boniface. Ottawa received all such reports with little or no interest. Subsequent events were largely a consequence of avoidable Canadian blunders and insensitivities. In colonial thralldom itself until only a few years previously, Canada had little experience in managing imperial expansion. It handled the project very clumsily, and the entire nation would pay dearly for its mistakes.

In October 1869 a leader of the Métis

A RED RIVER LETTER

This letter, dated 6 October 1869, represents the earliest written statement of the Métis case for opposition to Canada. The letter was probably drafted by Louis Riel. It claims no authority except 'the people themselves', meeting in an assembly composed of two representatives of each parish. The letter claims 'indisputable rights' that are unspecified.

St. Boniface, 6 Oct., 1869

Dear Mr Editor,

. . . . Several newspapers of Upper and Lower Canada have freely published their views on what inconveniences might arise in the organization . . . [of a territorial government by Canada for Red River]. And now that the Canadian people have heard these different discussions, would they not be glad to know what the people of Red River themselves think of all that? Here it is:

They do not appear to be at all ready to receive a Canadian governor. A Council chosen and constituted outside the country cannot hope, we think, to see its decrees highly respected. One perhaps can judge by the demonstrations which the *Métis* population of Red River has just made. Each parish has elected two representatives in order that they might pronounce in its name on the proceedings of the Canadian government with respect to the people of Red River, and the following are the resolutions that these representatives have passed in their first assembly:

1. These representatives declare in the name of the *Métis* population of Red River that they are loyal subjects of Her Majesty the Queen of England.

2. These representatives acknowledge themselves, in the name of the *Métis* population of Red River, beholden to the Honourable Hudson's Bay

Company for the protection which they have received under the government of that Company whatever the nature of that government may have been.

3. The people of Red River having till now upheld and supported the government of the Honourable Hudson's Bay Company, which has been established in the country by the Crown of England, the said representatives declare, in the name of the *Métis* population of Red River, that Snow and Dennis have disregarded the law of nations in coming to carry out public work here in the name of an alien authority without paying any attention to the authority to-day existing in the country.

4. The Honourable Hudson's Bay Company being about to lay down the government of Red River, the said representatives declare, in the name of the *Métis* population of Red River, that they are ready to submit to that change. But at the same time, being settled, working and living on the lands which they have assisted the Company [to open up, the people] of Red River, having acquired in the above manner [indisputable rights in that country,] the representatives of the *Métis* population of Red River loudly proclaim those rights.

5. The colony of Red River having always been subject to the Crown of England, and having developed in isolation, through all the hazards of its situation, the said representatives declare in the name of the *Métis* population of Red River, that they will do everything necessary to have the privileges accorded so liberally by the Crown of England to every English colony respected on their behalf.

There, Mr Editor, is what we would like to communicate to you. And those who take the liberty to send these things to you will not be the last to ensure that the rights of the people of Red River may be respected.

TWO MÉTIS SETTLERS OF RED RIVER

☐ Louis Riel, a carte-de-visite studio portrait taken in Ottawa following his election as member of Parliament for Provencher, Manitoba, in 1873. NAC 002048.

SOURCE: *Courrier de Saint-Hyacinthe*, 28 Oct. 1869, as translated in W.L. Morton, ed., *Alexander Begg's Red River Journal*, 411-13.

appeared in the person of Louis Riel (1844–85), a member of a leading family in the community. His father, for whom he was named, had successfully led a Métis protest in 1849 against the Hudson's Bay Company, which had won the right to trade freely in furs. The young Riel spoke out publicly against the surveys. He then led a party that stood on the surveyors' chains and ordered them to stop. In the meantime, William McDougall (1822–1905) was on his way from Canada to assume office as lieutenant-governor of the northwest. A newly formed National

This photograph shows Louis Riel at the centre of his provisional government sometime in early 1870. In the top row, left to right, are Bonnet Tromage, Pierre de Lorme, Thomas Bunn, Xavier Page, Baptiste Beauchemin, Baptiste Tournond, and Thomas Spence. In the middle row are Pierre Poitras, John Bruce, Louis Riel, John O'Donoghue, and François Dauphenais. In the front row are Robert O'Lone and Paul Proux. Although Canada had not annexed Red River in December 1869 as planned, it never admitted that the provisional government was legal. NAC, C-12854.

Committee of the Métis resolved that McDougall should not be allowed to enter the country. The Métis made it clear that they would oppose him by force if necessary. Canada responded to the unrest by refusing to take over the territory until it was pacified. Riel escalated the conflict. In early November he and a large band of armed Métis took possession of Upper Fort Garry, the Hudson's Bay Company central headquarters. The Métis then invited the anglophone inhabitants of the settlement, most of whom were mixed bloods themselves, to send delegates to meet and coordinate policy. Riel managed to get tacit consent for the establishment of a provisional government and approval of a 'list of rights'. On 7 December he and his men surrounded Dr Schultz's store, taking Schultz and forty-eight Canadians to Fort Garry as prisoners. The next day Riel issued a 'Declaration of the People', announcing a provisional government. He declared that the people of Red River wanted to be allowed to negotiate their own entry into Confederation on the basis of the 'rights' already agreed to by the residents. William McDougall made a fool of himself with an illegal proclamation of his government—Canada having refused to take possession of the territory—and then returned home.

AMBROISE LÉPINE

Ambroise Lépine (1840–1923) was born in St. Boniface, his father a well-to-do French-Canadian farmer and his mother a Saskatchewan *métisse*. Ambroise was educated at St Boniface College, and so was hardly the illiterate 'savage' he was often made out to be by later Canadians in Manitoba. He married Cécile Marion in 1859; the couple would have fourteen children. The Lépines farmed a riverside lot (number 272) not far from the Riel family, but Ambroise also participated in the buffalo hunt. He was described as 'of magnificent physique, standing fully six foot three and built of splendid proportion, straight as an arrow, with hair of raven blackness, large aquiline nose and eyes of piercing brilliance'. In 1869, Lépine became an important figure in the uprising against the Canadian annexation of Red River, not surprising in view of his family position and his reputation for hunting prowess, as well as his imposing size. He returned to the settlement around the end of October, just in time to be ordered to the border to make sure the Canadian governor, William McDougall, did not cross it to assert Canadian control over the territory. Nobody knew who was in charge of this party, he later remembered, 'and I was made leader.' Lépine very nearly did not get his assignment right. He initially allowed McDougall to cross the border, and then returned the next day to escort him back into the United States.

Lépine continued to be associated with Louis Riel, and was the commander of the Métis who surrounded the house of John Christian Schultz in early December. He later helped Riel and W.B. O'Donoghue raise the flag of the provisional government over Upper Fort Garry on 10 December. On 8 January, Lépine was named adjutant general of the provisional government, given the responsibility for the administration of justice. He was the equivalent of the chief of police in the settlement. He later represented St Boniface in the Convention of Forty which met to formulate the demands to be made of the Canadian government, and chaired the Military Council of the convention. It was Lépine who led the Métis forces out of Upper Fort Garry to confront the men from Portage la Prairie returning from a military gathering at Kildonan. The Métis were on horseback and the Portage boys on foot. The latter surrendered. Their captain, Charles Arkoll Boulton, was initially condemned to death by Riel, but was reprieved. Later, Lépine presided at the hearing that sentenced Thomas Scott to death, casting the deciding vote in favour of execution over the objections of his brother, Baptiste. The next day, he refused to listen to pleas for Scott's life and stood by stoically as the Canadian was shot by a firing squad.

Lépine later had trouble with his men at Upper Fort Garry, and at one point both he and they went home. According to Alexander Begg, he was brought back on the understanding that he would not be so overbearing in his manner. When the Canadians took over Manitoba in late August of 1870, Lépine went on the run with Louis Riel. No amnesty for the leaders of the provisional government had been publicly declared, and the Canadians regarded the death of Scott as a murder, not a political crime. Lépine helped Riel in 1871 to raise a Métis militia force against a possible Fenian invasion, and later that year was paid by the Canadian government to leave Manitoba with Riel. He soon returned from St Paul, Minnesota, and in 1873 was arrested at his home for the death of Scott. His trial, which was really intended to test the government's case against Riel, ended in a conviction for murder by a half English-, half French-speaking jury. Lépine did not testify at the trial, but issued a statement that denied the competence of the court to try him, while insisting that he had acted as a member of a *de facto* government; both assertions were dismissed by the court. He was sentenced to be hanged, but was spared by the Canadian governor-general, who commuted the sentence to two years in prison and permanent loss of civil rights. Lépine declined an amnesty conditional on leaving Manitoba for five years, and decided to serve his sentence. He was released in 1876, spending the remainder of a long life in poverty and obscurity. He was conspicuous by his absence from the rebellion of 1885. In 1909 he helped A.-H. Trémaudan in the writing of a history of the Métis nation.

Louis Riel marshalled his forces brilliantly. A convention of forty representatives, equally divided between the two language groups, debated and approved another 'list of rights'. The convention endorsed Riel's provisional government. It appointed three delegates to go to Ottawa to negotiate with the Macdonald government. So far, so good. But in early March, Thomas Scott, a prisoner who was an Orangeman, got into trouble with Riel and his guards. A Métis court martial condemned Scott to death without offering him a chance to be heard. Riel accepted the sentence, commenting, 'We must make Canada respect us.' The 'murder' of Scott would have enormous repercussions in Orange Ontario, which was looking desperately for an excuse to condemn the Red River uprising. The three-man delegation from Red River, headed by Abbé Noel Ritchot (1825–1905), gained substantial concessions from the Canadian government. If honoured, they would guarantee some protection for the original inhabitants of Red River against the expected later influx of settlers and land speculators. In what the Canadians always regarded as an act of extortion at the point of a gun, the Métis obtained the Manitoba Act of 1870. This legislation granted provincial status to a Manitoba roughly equivalent to the old Red River settlement, with 1,400,000 acres (566,580 ha) set aside for the Métis and bilingual services guaranteed. The remainder of the northwest became a territory of Canada. One of its government's principal tasks was to extinguish Aboriginal title through the negotiation of treaties with the indigenous peoples. These agreements would open the way for settlement by people of European origin.

In May 1870 the Canadian government sent a so-called peaceful military expedition to Red River. The troops occupied the province for Canada in late August, forcing Riel and his associates to flee for their lives. The Scott execution provided the Canadian government with the excuse to deny Riel and his lieutenants an official amnesty for all acts committed during the 'uprising'. Those who negotiated with Canada always insisted that such an amnesty had been unofficially promised. The result was that Louis Riel went into long-term exile instead of becoming

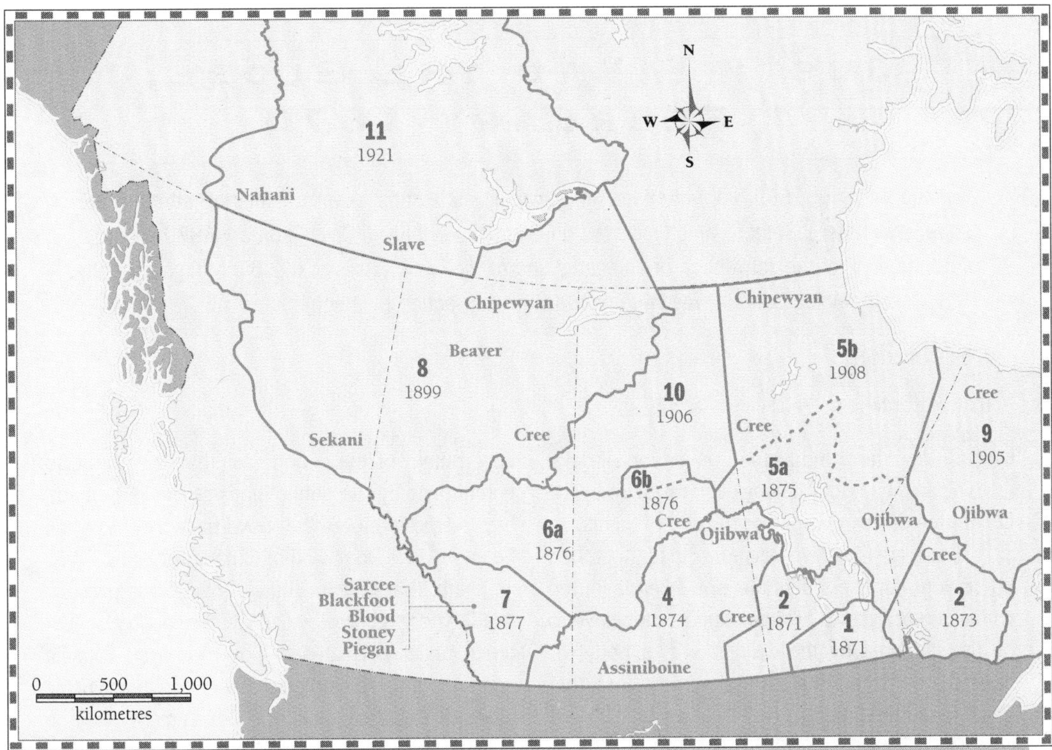

The numbered treaties, 1871-1921. Adapted from J.R. Miller, *Skyscrapers Hide the Heavens: A History of Indian-White Relations in Canada,* rev. edn (Toronto: University of Toronto Press, 1991), 166.

premier of the province he had created. (An amnesty was granted Riel in 1875, on the condition that he be banished from the country for five years.) Whether the government would keep better faith over its land guarantees to the Métis was another matter.

After the postage-stamp province called Manitoba was taken out, the remainder of the territory transferred to Canada by the Hudson's Bay Company—the North-West Territories—was initially administered under the original legislation passed by the Canadian Parliament in 1869 to deal with the west. It clearly envisioned a region held in colonial tutelage, with both government and natural resources under the strict control of Canada. The lieutenant-governor of Manitoba also served as lieutenant-governor of the Territories. The temporary legislation of 1869 was renewed without change in 1871. Not until 1872 were the Territories actually given even an appointed council. It consisted of 11 members, only two of which resided in the region. The other nine lived in or near Winnipeg, and initial meetings of the council were held there. Only in 1905—long after a second rebellion, in 1885—was provincial status finally granted to the Territories, which became Saskatchewan and Alberta.

While the question of Rupert's Land dragged slowly to its conclusion, the Canadian government was presented with an unexpected (although not totally unsolicited) gift. It con-

'JUSTITIA' TO THE GLOBE, 1 FEBRUARY 1870

Over the winter of 1869–70, Alexander Begg—writing as 'Justitia'—sent a series of letters to the *Globe* newspaper in Toronto which reported on events in Red River. On 1 February 1870 he wrote of the meeting of the convention of delegates and of the first clauses of the 'Bill of Rights' (really the terms for joining Canada) recommended to the convention by a committee.

THE BILL OF RIGHTS

Red River Settlement, February 1, [1870]. . . .

On Saturday, the 29th ult, the Convention of delegates again met, Friday having been taken up by the Committee of six in preparing the 'Bill of Rights.'

There are, I believe, 21 clauses in it altogether, but as your correspondent has only been favoured with a cursory glance at them, and as they have to be first adopted by the delegates as a body, or rejected by them, I will only give you those that have passed the ordeal.

On Saturday, therefore, the following four resolutions were adopted by the Convention, being the first four of the list:—

1st. That in view of the present exceptional position of the North-West, duties upon goods imported into the country shall continue as at present (except in the case of spiritous liquors) for three years, and for such further time as may elapse, until there be uninterrupted railroad communication between Red River Settlement and St. Paul, and *also* steam communication between Red River Settlement and Lake Superior;

2nd. That as long as this country remains a territory in the Dominion of Canada, there shall be no direct taxation except such as may be imposed by the Local Legislature, for municipal or other local purposes;

3rd. That during the time this country shall remain in the position of a territory, in the Dominion of Canada, all military, civil, and other public expenses, in connection with the general government of the country, or that have hitherto been borne by the public funds of the Settlement, beyond the receipt of the above-named duties, shall be met by the Dominion of Canada.'

4th. That while the burden of public expense in this Territory is borne by Canada, the country be governed under a Lieutenant-Governor from Canada, and a Legislature, three members of whom, being heads of Departments of the Government, shall be nominated by the Governor General of Canada. . . .

On Monday the Convention met again, and remained sitting till a late hour in the evening. They passed the following resolutions in addition to the four given above:—

5th. That after the expiration of this exceptional period, the country shall be governed, as regards its local affairs, as the Provinces of Ontario and Quebec are now governed, by a Legislature by the people, and a Ministry responsible to it, under a Lieutenant-Governor, appointed by the Governor-General of Canada;

6th. That there shall be no interference by the Dominion Parliament in the local affairs of this Territory, other than is allowed in the Provinces, and that this Territory shall have and enjoy, in all respects, the same privileges, advantages and aids in meeting the public expenses of this Territory, as the Provinces have and enjoy;

7th. That while the North-West remains a Territory, the Legislature have a right to pass all laws, local to the Territory, over the veto of the Lieutenant-Governor, by a two-thirds vote;

8th. A Homestead and Pre-emption law;

9th. That while the North-West remains a Territory, the sum of $25,000 yearly be appropriated for schools, roads and bridges;

10th. That all public buildings be at the cost of the Dominion Treasury;

11th. That there shall be guaranteed uninterrupted steam communication to Lake Superior, within five years; and also the establishment by rail of a connection with the American railway as soon as it reaches the International line;

This is as far as I can give you by this mail. While the last clause (the 11th) was being discussed, Mr [Alfred] Scott, delegate from Winnipeg, wished to have the time allowed for communication with Pembina curtailed to an unreasonable degree. The calculations and figures he gave to the Convention were found to be impracticable, and at last the question was put, 'What would be the use of a railway to Pembina before it is connected with another line further east from that point?' A Mr Cummings rose and said the only use he could see for such a road would be, 'to bring Statesmen to Fort Garry.' This finished the discussion, and the clause passed as I have given it to you. I have not time by this mail to make any remarks on the 'Bill of rights' as far as it has gone, but I hope by next mail to go into the subject fully, when it will have passed the Convention complete.

SOURCE: Toronto *Globe*, 19 February 1870

sisted of a request from British Columbia—to which Vancouver Island had been joined in 1866—for admission into the new union. The initiative from the Pacific colony had originated with the Nova Scotia-born journalist Amor De Cosmos (William Alexander Smith, 1825–97), a member of the colony's legislative council. As early as March 1867 he had introduced a motion that the British North America Act, then about to be passed by the British Parliament, allow for the eventual admission of British Columbia. Entry into Confederation would introduce responsible government and resolve the colony's serious financial difficulties, which resulted partly from the interest on debts incurred for road building during the gold rushes. Union with Canada received an additional impetus when—coterminously with the passage of the British North America Act but quite independent of it—the American government purchased Alaska from the Russians. The purchase touched off demands in the American press for the annexation of British Columbia as well. Officially the British notified the colony in November 1867 that no action would be taken on its relationship with Canada until Rupert's Land had been duly incorporated into the new nation.

Union with Canada was debated by the British Columbia Legislative Council in March 1870. This debate was different from earlier ones in the eastern legislatures, for the British North America Act was already in place and in operation. British Columbia could not hope to influence the shape of Confederation, only to decide whether it would enter the union and upon what terms. The debate was a bit curious. The opponents of Confederation wanted the issues of popular elections (in an elected assembly) and responsible government cleared up in advance of union, while the pro-confederates—the government party—were quite satisfied with the local status quo.

Negotiations between British Columbia and Canada took place in the late spring of 1870. The Canadians were generous to a fault. Of course British Columbia could have responsible government. Of course the debt would be wiped out. Of course there would be subsidies and grants, as

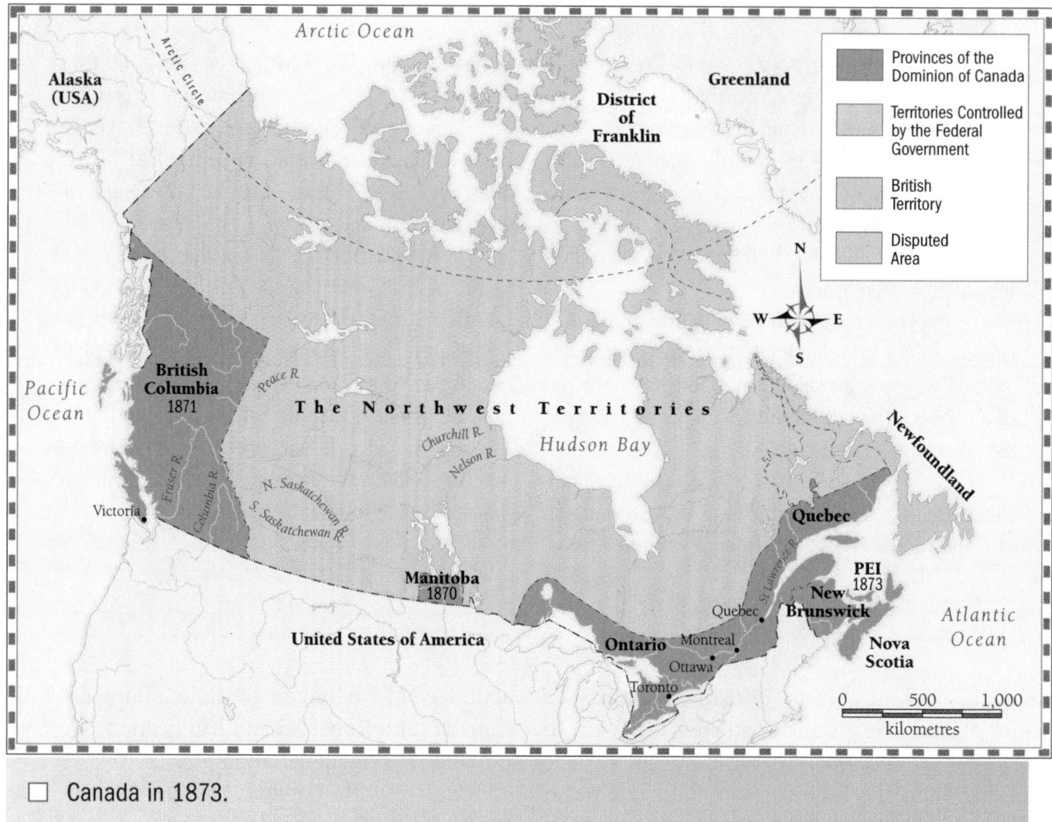

Canada in 1873.

well as federal support for the naval station at Esquimalt. And of course British Columbia could have a rail link with Canada, to be begun within two years and completed within fifteen. The promise was audacious, although Canada obviously needed a transcontinental railroad to match the lines rapidly being constructed across the United States. The terms were far better than expected, and on 20 July 1871 British Columbia entered Confederation as the sixth province. While in most respects the new province remained isolated until the completion of the rail link in 1885, Confederation encouraged the development of a new land policy for the province. The provincial government opened its Crown lands to massive pre-emption and free land grants; the largesse of British Columbia would far exceed that of the federal government.

Prince Edward Island's acceptance of terms in 1873 was almost anticlimactic. The tiny province had tried to survive without much support from the British, who made clear their lack of enthusiasm for a Crown colony. The imperial refusal to pay the salary of the lieutenant-governor was seen as a 'confederate screw unfairly put upon us'. Both the Americans and the Canadians actively wooed the island. In the end, it entered Confederation in the wake of a profligate policy of railway construction, which many saw as a scheme to force it into union. As well as offering to take over the debt and the railway, Canada agreed to guarantee continuous communication with the mainland and to help buy out the last of the old landed proprietors. Only one island MLA, the crusty farmer Cornelius Howatt, refused to vote for the Canadian offer.

Unlike Prince Edward Island, Newfoundland was not persuaded to join the union at all. In 1869 Newfoundland held an election fought on the issue of Confederation with Canada. The economy improved in the period before the election, while the opponents of Confederation employed every argument in their rhetorical arsenal. These included rumours that Canada would use Newfoundland children as wadding for their cannons. The 1869 election went decisively against the pro-confederates. The island's Catholics opposed union. In one Catholic area, a pro-confederate candidate was greeted by priest and populace carrying pots of pitch and bags of feathers. The Protestant vote split equally. In the end the election returned nine confederates and twenty-one antis. The confederates blamed their defeat on the nasty campaign tactics of the opposition, but Newfoundland's union with Canada was not a matter of high priority for anyone. Both the British and Canadian governments acquiesced in Newfoundland's continued autonomy—despite sporadic union discussions as in 1887 and 1895—until 1949.

As well as dealing with the strays, the Canadian government had also to pacify Nova Scotia and New Brunswick. This was especially true of Nova Scotia, where pledged anti-confederates took both federal and provincial seats in the election that accompanied union. The British government refused to allow reconsideration of the initial decision to join Canada,

THE REMINISCENCES OF DR JOHN SEBASTIAN HELMCKEN

In 1892, Dr John Sebastian Helmcken (1824–1920) of British Columbia wrote in manuscript a lengthy collection of his memories. The manuscript ended up in the Provincial Archives of British Columbia in Victoria, and was edited for publication by Dorothy Blakey Smith, appearing in print in 1975. Here Helmcken discusses the election of 1868, fought over the issue of Confederation. His use of what we would regard as racist language was quite common in the nineteenth century.

. . . [A] general election was ordered; Confederation being the burning question, everyone rampant on one side or the other; of course the American element being against the Union. At this time no distinct terms had been proposed, but if I recollect rightly De Cosmos and the colored man Gibbs and [John Norris] had been to the 'Yale Convention'; a Convention for the purpose of an organization for Confederation purposes. The Convention was ridiculed and lambasted by opponents—the colored man [Gibbs] having a good share. By the bye I had been a means of getting the coloured man elected to the House of Assembly and really he was in some measure a superior man and very gentlemanly withal. I think he claimed being a West Indian.

I came out against Confederation distinctly, chiefly because I thought it premature —partly from prejudice—and because no suitable terms could be proposed. The tariff was a sticking point: although we had at this time a tariff but could change it to suit ourselves. Our income too would be diminished and there at this time appeared no means of replenishing it by the [British] North America Act. Our population was too small numerically. Moreover it would only be a confederacy on paper for no means of communication with the Eastern Provinces existed, without which no advantage could possibly ensue. Canada was looked down upon as a poor mean slow people, who had been very commonly designated North American chinamen. This character they had achieved from their necessarily thrifty condition for long years, and indeed they compared unfavourably with the Americans and with our American element, for at this time and previously very many liberal-handed and better class of Americans resided here, many in business—some on account of the Civil War necessitating their remaining even after the frightful internecine killing had ceased. Our trade was either with the U.S. or England—with Canada we had nothing to do. Of course my being an Anti-confederationist, led to my being dubbed an Annexationist, but really I had no idea of annexation, but merely wished the Colony to be let alone under HM Govt and to fight her way unhampered. I had nothing whatever to do with annexation petitions, and do not know who signed them—tho I have heard that some who now hold or have held official positions have done so. This petition doubtless went to the President of the U.S. but no one has ever been able to see a copy of it since, altho it is said to exist in Victoria somewhere. There is no doubt the Americans had a contempt for Canada and this feeling extended to the colonists.

I suppose the election was one of the fiercest ever fought in Victoria, everyone seemed crazy, I among the number – these were the days of great excitements. I had the British and American elements and Jewish element on my side and after a time the election came on. Numberless ladies wore my colours, red, white and blue, in shape according to their taste, the men likewise. Ladies were at the windows waving their handkerchiefs, every hack in the place was frightfully busy. The polling went actively on, but there were no rows, or if there were, they were insignificant. Various committees had districts under control; they had to get the voters up and were responsible therefore. The cry went round that both sides had a number of voters locked up and were feeding them with whisky, to get them into proper trim; altho this accusation was not strictly true, still voters came to the polling place, where the Courts of Justice now stand, in files. Notwithstanding all this there were no rows outside the polling places, the matter was too serious for this. At length 4 o'clock struck – the polls closed; everyone tired – thirsty, hoarse and expectant. The Anti-confederates had won handsomely. . . .

SOURCE: Dorothy Blakey Smith, ed., *The Reminiscences of Doctor John Sebastian Helmcken* (Vancouver: University of British Columbia Press, 1975), 246–8.

chiefly on the grounds that such important political actions should not be taken at the whim of local electorates. The leading anti, Joseph Howe, eventually accepted that there was no alternative to accepting confederation. In February 1869 Howe ran as a pro-confederate in a federal election in Hants County, which was hotly contested. He won with a comfortable majority and headed off to Ottawa, joining the federal cabinet within weeks. In some ways this grudging acquiescence in a situation with which he did not agree may have been the most important political act of his career.

The Development of National Policies

As well as completing the creation of a transcontinental nation, the Macdonald government gradually improvised some national policies with which to govern the new Dominion. Confederation was encouraging to foreign investment. From its inception, Canada was able to import large amounts of capital to help create its infrastructure. Between 1865 and 1869 Canada raised $16.5 million in Great Britain, a figure that rose to $96.4 million in 1870–4, $74.7 million in 1875–9, and $69.8 million in 1880–4.

The government obtained some recognition of Canadian diplomatic autonomy by its acquiescence to the Treaty of Washington in 1871. Outstanding issues with the Americans included the *Alabama* claims. The *Alabama* was a Confederate raider built in Britain for the southern states. The Americans, half-seriously, demanded the cession of British-American territory in compensation for the losses it inflicted on northern shipping. In 1871 the British government made Macdonald a member of an international joint commission set up in 1870 to deal with the fisheries question. The British made clear they were willing to surrender Canadian interests in the fisheries to settle outstanding Anglo–American differences. Macdonald signed the resulting treaty.

On the domestic front, the banking system of the new nation grew rapidly from 123 chartered bank branches in 1869 to 279 in 1879 and 426 by 1890. Two major pieces of national legislation were the Dominion Notes Act of 1870 and the Bank Act of 1871. The former allowed the government to issue circulating notes of small denominations, only partly backed by specie. The latter exerted control over the banking system. The Bank Act specified capital requirements for banks, prohibited new foreign-owned banks, and supplied general regulation. Canada accepted the international gold standard, but the government would share the issuance of currency (and the control of the creation of money) with the banks until well into the twentieth century.

Much capital would be invested in railways. The opportunity for railway expansion was one of the principal arguments for Confederation. Railways were a prime target of foreign investors. The Macdonald government was slow to move on a transcontinental line, chiefly because of the enormous expense involved in building so far ahead of population needs. To some extent, the offer to British Columbia cast the die. There followed an unseemly scuffling over a charter, awarded in 1873 by Parliament to the Canada Pacific Railway Company of Sir Hugh Allan (1810–82). Then the Pacific Scandal broke. Allan had provided the government with money for its 1872 election campaign. Macdonald was unable to steer totally clear of the corrupt dealings. In November 1873 the government resigned. Replacing it was a Liberal government headed by a Scottish-born former stonemason, Alexander Mackenzie (1822–92). He sought to build a transcontinental line more gradually, using public funds. He also encouraged private interests to hook up with American western lines. Trains began running from Minnesota to Winnipeg late in 1878.

Mackenzie's government was also largely responsible for the initial funding of western railway construction. It gave the railway companies large land grants along the right of way. Although Canada developed a seemingly generous homestead policy by which pioneers could receive free land grants in return for developing the land, the generosity was deceptive. Almost no homestead land was available within easy access to the rail lines. Most early settlers ended up purchasing their land, either from the railways or from the Hudson's Bay Company.

Mackenzie's government had a number of positive achievements to its credit. It resolved the Louis Riel question in 1875 by granting the Métis leader an amnesty, conditional on his residence in exile for five years. It established the Supreme Court of Canada that same year, and subsequently created the office of the Auditor General. But the real importance of the Mackenzie government was its demonstration that the nation could be governed by another political party with different policies from the one led by Sir John A. Macdonald. Mackenzie was a man without charisma, however, and many critics thought he spent too much energy micromanaging the budget.

The probity of his government did not save Alexander Mackenzie in 1878. Sir John A. Macdonald returned to power. Recognizing the temper of the times, Macdonald worked hard to restore in the public mind a sense of identification between his party and the process of nation

SIR JOHN A. MACDONALD ON THE NATIONAL POLICY, 1882

Canadian political parties did not adopt official platforms until late in the nineteenth century. In earlier elections, voters could glean some notion of the parties' policies from the speeches of their leaders, which were widely reported in the press. The following excerpts are taken from various campaign speeches made by Sir John A. Macdonald and reported in the Toronto *Mail* in May and June 1882.

WHY THE GOVERNMENT GOES TO THE COUNTRY

Because we thought it was of the greatest consequence to Canada, and to the future prosperity of the manufacturers of Canada, that the people should have an opportunity of expressing their opinion whether our policy is wise or not. A good many manufactures have been commenced, but they would have been quadrupled, four times as many manufactures would have been started in Canada, if it were not for the dread that the policy of 1878 would be destroyed and upset by a free trade Parliament in 1883.

THE ISSUE

We desire that the people may at once declare whether they wish to have fair trade, plenty of work, and prosperity, or free trade, want of labour, and poverty. We place that fairly before the people and say:—If you want to reverse that policy, do; if you want a continuance of prosperity, declare so at the polls, and you will have five years ahead during which that policy cannot be reversed. We have had three years now and at the end of five years more the manufacturing interest will be so strong that, as in the United States, it will be able to fight its own battles, and there is no fear of that policy being reversed to ruin the manufacturer who has put his money, his means, his credit, and his capital into such enterprises.

Why, sir, the true National Policy is this—to find, at all events, a home market for as much as we can, and if in consequence of our industry and of good seasons we raise more in the country than we can consume ourselves, to send the surplus abroad.

building. Decisiveness and flamboyance were part of the image. Even before the election was called, Macdonald had his platform. He introduced into the House of Commons a resolution 'That this House is of the opinion that the welfare of Canada requires the adoption of a National Policy, which, by a judicious readjustment of the Tariff, will benefit and foster the agricultural, the mining, the manufacturing, and other interests of this Dominion' (quoted in Easterbrook and Watkins 1962: 238). The Tory leader invented neither the policy nor the term used to describe it. Both went well back into the history of the Province of Canada, which had begun using a tariff as an instrument of both protection and revenue in the late 1840s. Nor did John A. Macdonald ever articulate the version of the national policy as it was later lovingly described by economic historians and textbook writers. But he certainly recognized some relationship involving tariffs, manufacturing, employment, and national prosperity. He also wanted a transcontinental railway and the accompanying western settlement necessary to make it a reality. All these features had been and remained a traditional part of Canadian economic expansionism.

What Macdonald achieved was masterful in

its own way. He succeeded in persuading a large number of Canadians in all provinces that policies strongly driven by the economic self-interest of some of the people in some of its constituent parts were in the best interest of the nation as a whole. He then persuaded the electorate that his party was the one that had successfully built the nation and would continue to do so. The fact that the opposition party took the lead in developing a different version of nation-building helped in this identification.

The responsibility for immigration policy had been divided between the Dominion and the provinces by the British North America Act. Both the Macdonald governments and the Mackenzie one sought to develop federal supremacy over immigration policy, in large measure to make possible the rapid settlement of the west. The Dominion also began to set rules indicating which immigrants would be acceptable. The federal Parliament passed its first immigration legislation in 1869, and in 1872 prohibited the entry of criminals and other 'vicious classes'. That same year Parliament passed the Dominion Lands Act, which created homesteading privileges on western lands. The Dominion then began extensive advertising in Europe for new settlers. In the mid-1870s Canada also negotiated with several European groups, including the Mennonites and the Icelanders, for group settlement in Manitoba. In 1879, a federal Order-in-Council prohibited the entrance of paupers and destitute immigrants. Not long afterwards, the government began to admit large numbers of Chinese immigrants (up to 15,000) to labour on the transcontinental railroad. In 1882, a contingent of 240 Jews left London for Manitoba and the North-West, and a 'New Jerusalem' was established by Jews in what would become Saskatchewan. By the mid-1880s, a substantial groundswell of public opinion had emerged that wanted to go further in immigration restriction than the existing regulations. This portion of the public was becoming increasingly worried about the admission of 'unassimilable' newcomers.

THE QUEST FOR IDENTITY, REGIONAL AND NATIONAL

The British North America Act had no guarantees that political unification would necessarily create a nation. After 1867 Canadians made various attempts to locate themselves in their world. Some of these attempts were political and constitutional. Others were cultural, with intellectuals and artists playing their part providing rhetorical flourishes as well as creating national institutions in which the arts could operate.

The development of nationhood in the years after 1867 should not obscure the fact that not all Canadians shared in the same vision (or version) of the meaning of the nation. One of the major questions was whether Canada was an indissoluble new creation or the product of a compact among the provinces that they could modify or even leave. Since the time of the debate over Confederation in the 1860s, people had disagreed over the nature of the union. While most Canadians in 1867 saw the British North America Act as creating a strong central government, provincial legislatures still existed. They would quickly assert more than the merely local power accorded them by the Quebec resolutions. One of the arch-critics of Confederation, Christopher Dunkin (1812–81), had prophesied in 1865 that 'In the times to come, when men shall begin to feel strongly on those questions that appeal to national preferences, prejudices and passions, all talk of your new nationality will sound but strangely. Some older nationality will then be found to hold the first place in most people's hearts' (quoted in Waite 1963: 511). Even Sir John A. Macdonald had admitted in Parliament in 1868 that 'a conflict may, ere long, arise between the Dominion and the States Rights people' (quoted in Cook 1969a: 10).

Ontario initially spearheaded the provincial-rights interpretation of the new union. The seeds of this interpretation were inherent in the constitutional arrangements, and the movement could have begun anywhere. As early as 1869 Ontario became distressed at 'the assumption by the Parliament of Canada of the power to disturb the financial relations established by the British North America Act (1867), as between Canada and the several provinces' (quoted in Cook 1969a: 11). Not surprisingly, it was the old Reform Party of Canada West, in the persons of George Brown, Edward Blake (1833–1912), and Oliver Mowat (1820–1903), that took the lead. They demanded—in Blake's phrase of 1871—'that each government [Dominion and provincial] shall be absolutely independent of the other in its management of its own affairs' (quoted in Cook 1969a: 13). The Rouges of Quebec soon joined in the same call, adding the identification of French-Canadian 'national' rights to Ontario's 'provincial' ones. Before long, Liberals in most provinces—many of whom had either opposed Confederation or been lukewarm about it—had embraced provincial rights.

Provincial rights often seemed interchangeable with Ottawa-bashing for local political advantage, lacking in any other principle than the desire to pressure Ottawa into fiscal concessions. In its early years, Quebec did not dominate the movement. There was little insistence upon Confederation as a cultural deal between two distinct societies. In 1884, for example, the Honourable Honoré Mercier (1840–94) tabled resolutions in the Quebec legislature stating merely that 'the frequent encroachments of the Federal Parliament upon the prerogatives of the Provinces are a permanent menace to the latter' (quoted in Cook 1969a: 31). The ensuing debate involved no more cultural nationalism than one back-bencher's assertion that 'le Québec n'est pas une province comme les autres' (quoted in Cook 1969a: 33). Although the Riel affair of 1885 (discussed later in this chapter) pushed Quebec towards the brink of arguments of cultural distinctiveness, when Mercier (by this time premier of Quebec) invited the provinces to the Interprovincial Conference in 1887 to re-examine the federal compact, broad agreement could be reached on demands for better terms and constitutional change by the five provinces attending without the need for such concepts.

Provincial rights involved on one level a political-constitutional struggle over revenue and power. On another level they were a reflection of the continued identification of the people of Canada with their province of residence, as much as, if not more than, with their nation. The educational structure of Canada certainly encouraged this identification. In all provinces education passed from private to public financial support at the same time that schooling became increasingly universal. However, section 92 of the British North America Act left education completely in the hands of the provinces. It is almost impossible to talk about any integrated national movements. Indeed, education would become one of the most divisive issues in the new nation. A major question was whether provinces would have a single public school system for all students, or would support separate religious (and linguistic) education as well. Educational diversity was still the norm after Confederation. There were, at best, provincial educational systems and norms, not national ones.

Although a nationalist movement was beginning to develop, it did not pose a serious challenge to provincial loyalties. The movement calling itself Canada First, for example, did not have a program that was particularly attractive outside Protestant circles in Ontario. Canada First was an exclusive secret society rather than a broad-based organization. It did not help that its vision of Canada was really that of Canada West writ larger. Despite the presence in its ranks of the Nova Scotian Robert G. Haliburton (1831–1901), the son of T.C. Haliburton, most of Canada First's members, including Charles Mair (1838–1927) and George Denison (1839–1925), were from Canada West. The movement's chief accomplishment was to turn the Ontario public against the Métis of Red River by arousing sentiment over the 'murder' of Thomas Scott. Indeed, Canada First's nationalism was, in several senses, racist. Haliburton was one of the earliest exponents of the notion that Canadians were the heirs of the Aryan northmen of the Old World. He told the Montreal Literary Club in March 1869 that the new Canadian nationality comprised 'the Celtic, the Teutonic, and the Scandinavian elements', and embraced 'the Celt, the Norman French, the Saxon and the Swede' (quoted in Berger 1986: 154–60). Canada Firsters looked down their noses at Aboriginal peoples and the Métis. They saw the French as the great 'bar to progress, and to the extension of a great Anglo-Saxon Dominion across the Continent', as the Toronto *Globe* put it on 4 March 1870.

While Canada First's notions were compatible, to some extent, with the westward thrust of Canada West, they were, fortunately, not totally typical of the conscious development of Canadian nationalism. The French-Canadian poet Octave Crémazie (1827–79), for example, lamented ironically that Canada's major literary languages were entirely of European origin. He continued: 'if we spoke Huron or Iroquois, the works of our writers would attract the attention of the old world. . . . One would be overwhelmed by a novel or a poem translated from the Iroquois, while one does not take the trouble to read a book written in French by a native of Quebec or Montreal' (quoted in Raspovich 1969: 225). The search for an essential 'Canadian-ness' went on in many corners of the new Dominion. It was nowhere so successful as in the somewhat remote New Brunswick town of Fredericton, home of the University of New Brunswick. There the rectory of St Anne's Parish (Anglican) produced Charles G.D. Roberts (1860–1943), while not far down the road lived his cousin Bliss Carman (1861–1929). Along with Ottawa's Archibald Lampman (1861–99) and Duncan Campbell Scott (1862–1947), these men comprised the Confederation Poets. Modern literary critics have invented this designation for this first school of Canadian poets who wrestled with Canadian themes, notably the local or regional landscape, with some degree of skill and sensitivity. As Crémazie had suggested, however, the European origins of their language limited their efforts.

While many intellectuals and artists sought ways to articulate Canadian-ness in their work, others took a more prosaic route towards the realization of a Canadian national identity. Curiously enough, it was the painters, not normally known for their political acuity, who took the lead in organizing national groups to maintain professional standards and publicize Canadian achievement. The Ontario Society of Artists, formed in 1872 and incorporated in 1877, was at the forefront of this effort. The OSA was instrumental in the formation of the Royal Canadian Academy of Arts in 1880—in collaboration with the governor-general, Lord Lorne (1845–1914)—and in the establishment that same year of the National Gallery of Canada. One of the founders of this organization wrote, 'We are bound to try to civilize the Dominion a little' (quoted in Williamson 1970: 64). The year 1880 was doubly important in art circles, for in that year the Canadian Society of Graphic Art was also founded.

The first president of the Royal Canadian Academy, the painter Lucius O'Brien (1832–99) was art director of an elaborate literary and artistic celebration of the young nation. *Picturesque Canada* (1882) was based on the highly successful books *Picturesque America* and *Picturesque Europe*. It was the idea of two Americans, the Belden brothers, who had established themselves in Toronto. The editor of the project—George Monro Grant (1835–1902), principal of Queen's University—stated in the preface: 'I believed that a work that would represent its characteristic scenery and history and life of its people would not only make us better known to ours and to strangers, but would also stimulate national sentiment and contribute to the rightful development of the nation.' The two large volumes of *Picturesque Canada*—which can sometimes be found in second-hand bookshops—contain 540 illustrations. They included wood-

CHARLES G.D. ROBERTS' 'CANADA', 1886

In 1886 Charles G.D. Roberts published a small volume of verses in Boston, entitled *Divers Tones*. The following is one of the first poems in the book.

Canada

O Child of Nations, giant-limbed,
Who stand'st among the nations now
Unheeded, unadorned, unhymned,
With unanointed brow,—

How long the ignoble sloth, how long
The trust in greatness not thine own?
Surely the lion's brood is strong
To front the world alone!

How long the indolence, ere thou dare
Achieve thy destiny, seize thy fame –
Ere our proud eyes behold thee bear
A nation's franchise, nation's name?

The Saxon force, the Celtic fire,
These are thy manhood's heritage!
Why rest with babes and slaves? Seek higher
The place of race and age.

I see to every wind unfurled
The flag that bears the Maple-Wreath;
Thy swift keels furrow round the world
Its blood-red folds beneath;

Thy swift keels cleave the furthest seas;
Thy white sails swell with alien gales;
To stream on each remotest breeze
The black smoke of thy pipes exhales.

O Falterer, let thy past convince
Thy future,—all the growth, the gain,
The fame since Cartier knew thee, since
Thy shores beheld Champlain!

Montcalm and Wolfe! Wolfe and Montcalm!
Quebec, thy storied citadel
Attest in burning song and psalm
How here thy heroes fell!

O Thou that bor'st the battle's brunt
At Queenston, and at Lundy's Lane,—
On whose scant ranks but iron front
The battle broke in vain! –

Whose was the danger, whose the day,
From whose triumphant throats the cheers,
At Chrysler's Farm, at Chateauguay,
Storming like clarion-bursts our ears?

On soft Pacific slopes,—beside
Strange floods that northward rave and fall,—
Where chafes Acadia's chainless tide –
Thy sons await thy call.

They wait; but some in exile, some
With strangers housed, in stranger lands;—
And some Canadian lips are dumb
Beneath Egyptian sands.

O mystic Nile! Thy secret yields
Before us; thy most ancient dreams
Are mixed with fresh Canadian fields
And murmur of Canadian streams.

But thou, my Country, dream not thou!
Wake, and behold how night is done,—
How on thy breast, and o'er thy brow,
Bursts the rising sun!

SOURCE: Charles G.D. Roberts, *Divers Tones* (Boston: Lothrop, 1886), 2-5.

☐ 'Lock no. 1, new Welland Canal', from volume I of *Picturesque Canada* (Toronto, 1882), 385. NAC, C-083047.

engravings based on paintings, and, for the West, photo-engravings of photographs, that offered serene vistas fulfilling the promise of the title. The descriptive texts by Grant, Charles G.D. Roberts, and others, presented an idealized, complacent view of the cities, towns and regions of Canada, praising the present and pointing to a glorious future.

The Royal Society of Canada was founded in 1882 to promote research and learning in the arts and sciences. Lord Lorne again provided much of the impetus, replicating a British institution to establish the importance of cultural accomplishments in creating a sense of national pride and self-confidence. The first president, J.W. Dawson (1820–99), principal of McGill University (another Nova Scotian transported to central Canada) emphasized in his presidential address a sense of national purpose. Dawson stressed especially 'the establishment of a bond of union between the scattered workers now widely separated in different parts of the Dominion' (quoted in Royal Society of Canada 1932: 91–2). Thomas Sterry Hunt (1826–92), a charter member and later president, observed that 'The occasion which brings us together is one which should mark a new departure in the intellectual history of Canada' (Royal Society of Canada 1932: 91–2). He added that 'the brightest glories and the most enduring honours of a country are those which come from its thinkers and its scholars' (Royal Society of Canada 1932: 91–2). However romantic that praise might sound, what mattered was Hunt's emphasis on the country as a whole. Like the Royal Canadian Academy, the Royal Society had its headquarters in Ottawa.

OTHER IDENTITIES

We can easily make too much of the political arena. The elaboration of a number of competing and occasionally incompatible identities by and for its citizens characterized the Victorian Age. As well as their national and provincial loyalties, most Canadians had firm allegiances to their ethnic origins, whether these were French Canadian, Acadian, or British. French Canada further elaborated its cultural identity in this period, and the Acadians began consciously to develop one. As for those people whose origins were in the British Isles, they simultaneously thought of themselves as British as well as Welsh, Scotch, Irish, or English. Indeed, British Canadians may well have thought of themselves as more British (as opposed to Welsh or Scottish) than did their compatriots at home.

The state did not weigh heavily on the daily lives of most Canadians in this era, although the administrative state had begun its development before Confederation. Taxation had not yet become ubiquitous and occurred mainly as tariffs and duties. Moreover, the state—as represented by province, nation, or city—did not normally provide social benefits or solace when people got sick, lost jobs, retired, or died. For some, politics and government were a source of employment or patronage. For most Canadians, however, government had very little to do with their lives. For many people, political allegiance to the state was therefore not as important as loyalty to the caring institutions: family, ethnic group, religion, and fraternal organization. Churches and religion were most important. Canada was a Christian country and few of its citizens openly defied Christian norms and values. By the 1880s the mobility of many Canadians contributed to the tendency to belong to a good many other voluntary organizations beyond the church. In an earlier period, voluntary organizations supplemented or provided municipal services such as water, light, fire, and libraries as well as charity. By the 1880s some organizations had begun providing entertainment and companionship for their members.

The mid-Victorian period was a crucial era for Roman Catholicism in Canada. Within French Canada the period witnessed the emergence of the Church as the leading voice of French Canada's national aspirations and the assumption of local leadership by the curé. It also saw the Church take on the ultramontane character that would remain with it for many years. In Quebec, the man who symbolized the ultramontane Church in the mid-Victorian period was Bishop Ignace Bourget (1799–1885). Bourget was consecrated coadjutor to the bishop of Montreal in early 1837, on the very eve of rebellion, and succeeded to the see in 1840. He died in June 1885, on the eve of the second Riel uprising, although he had retired a few years earlier. Bourget was always an active defender of both the papacy and the position of the Church in Canada. He introduced the Roman liturgy and fervently opposed the principles of the European revolutions of 1848. Gradually he became the leading opponent of liberal thinking in the province, particularly as it was represented by the Institut Canadien in Montreal. Bourget carried on a lengthy battle against the Institut and especially its library, which contained many prohibited books. Equally important was his expansion of the ecclesiastical administration of his diocese, so that nearly every parish had a priest and nearly half the priests had an assistant. The clergy were now able to mobilize public opinion, as they did in 1868 when they helped raise 507 Zouaves in Quebec (and over $100,000 to support them) to serve in the papal army. Quebec bishops strongly supported the doctrine of papal infallibility at the Vatican Council.

English-speaking Catholicism had succeeded by 1840 in separating itself from francophone control. At about the same time, the hierarchy had also re-established its control over the laity, which had previously assumed considerable autonomy in the absence of local bishops and clergy. Anglophone bishops from the Maritime region were among those who attempted unsuccessfully to prevent the issue of papal infallibility from being decided at the Vatican Council of 1869–70. Contemporaries often overlooked the importance of anglophone Catholicism in the nineteenth century. Only in Canada West/Ontario were Protestants in such a clear numerical ascendency and position of power that the regional culture assumed obvious Protestant dimensions. This Ontario culture, especially as it expanded westward onto the prairies, began in some circles to be confused with Canadian culture.

By 1840 Protestantism everywhere in British North America had largely cut itself free from its foreign origins in either Great Britain or the United States. The major development of the mid-Victorian period, notably in an Ontario where Protestantism emerged as a distinct and all-embracing culture, was the construction of a broad alliance among the major denominations: Anglican, Presbyterian, and Methodist. The gradual elimination of the major points of public friction between the established churches and the dissenters made this possible. The result was a Victorian Protestant culture in Ontario that emphasized the relationship between social stability and Protestant morality. A firm belief in God and his millennium formed the basis for the latter. Gradual social change was progressive, offering a way of understanding the events and changes that swirled around the individual in the Victorian era. The moral code was strict, but chiefly voluntary and individualistic.

The churches, especially the Protestant ones, were also a key to the growth of a vast network of clubs, societies, and charities. By the mid-nineteenth century women members were implicitly challenging the male governance of the churches. Evangelically oriented churches frequently employed their ladies' aid or women's auxiliary groups to sponsor missionary activity. By 1885 there were over 120 Baptist Women's Missionary Aid Societies scatttered across the Maritimes. Women generally used their own money to support their religious organizations, which kept separate accounts and offered many women their first opportunity at independent administration.

Technically independent of the churches, but closely connected in overlapping membership and social goals, were reform organizations like the Women's Christian Temperance Union. Letitia Youmans (1827–96), a public school and Sunday school teacher in the Methodist Church, founded the first Canadian local of the WCTU in Picton, Ontario. The WCTU spread rapidly across Canada in the 1880s, preaching that alcohol abuse was responsible for many of the social problems of contemporary Canada and campaigning for public prohibition of the sale of alcoholic beverages. Most of its members came from the middle class, and much of its literature was directed at demonstrating that poverty and family problems among the lower orders could be reduced, if not eliminated, by cutting off the availability of alcohol to the male breadwinner.

Canadians have tended to associate Orangism with political matters—organizing parades on 12 July, opposing Roman Catholics, objecting to the 1870 execution of Thomas Scott—and with the Irish. Nevertheless, the order's real importance and influence continued to rest on the twin facts that its membership united British Protestants of all origins and that it served as a

CHARLES CHINIQUY

Charles Chiniquy (1809–99) was born in Kamouraska and studied at the Séminaire de Nicolet. He was ordained to the priesthood in 1833, and was an early exponent of the struggle against the evils of alcohol. He founded a temperance society in his parish in Beauport (near Quebec City) in 1840, and in 1841 carried most of its members into total abstinence. He quickly became a stunning lecturer, and was capable of holding spellbound crowds numbering in the thousands. His techniques were little different from those of the great Protestant evangelists of the eighteenth century. Like them he could describe the evils from which his listeners suffered with graphic conviction. Like them he preached for conversions, inviting his audience to come forward, repent, and sign a temperance pledge.

Chiniquy was required in 1846 by the archbishop of Quebec to enter the Oblate order to atone for an incident of sexual abuse. He did not take well to discipline, however, and soon found himself totally outside the priesthood. When he petitioned for permission to return to priestly duties, he was refused. But Bishop Bourget of Montreal encouraged him to continue his preaching for temperance, which he did between 1848 and 1851. Again there was a sexual transgression, and Chiniquy was seconded to the bishop of Chicago for yet another temperance crusade, chiefly among French-Canadians in the United States. He settled in St Anne, Illinois, and was wildly successful, creating great envy among his colleagues, who objected to his arrogance and censoriousness. In 1856, when ordered transferred from St Anne, he defied his bishop and refused to leave.

Chiniquy was summarily excommunicated in September 1856, spent several years trying to work out a compromise with the aid of the Canadians, but in 1858 was excommunicated again. He responded by leaving the Catholic Church and taking some of his people with him. In 1860 he and 2,000 supporters joined the Presbyterian Church. Within two years the Chicago Presbytery had suspended him, and he joined the Canadian Presbyterian Church. As a Canadian Presbyterian he became a committed enemy of the Catholic Church, denouncing all forms of abuse. Not surprisingly, the Presbyterians loved him, and he found large audiences for his continued preaching tours. He married in 1864. Beginning in 1873 he made the evangelization of French Canadians—and their conversion to Protestantism—his mission in life. He was particularly critical of oral confession, which he claimed exposed the penitent's weaknesses to the priests. In 1878 he began a two-year tour of the Antipodes for his health, and then wrote his memoirs, which were extremely popular, reaching 70 editions in all languages by 1898. He died in Montreal.

focal point on the local level for social intercourse and conviviality. As a 'secret' society, it had elaborate initiation rites and a ritual that appealed to men who spent most of their lives in drudgery. Lodges provided a variety of services for members, including an elaborate funeral. But if local fraternity was the key to Orangism's success, its public influence was enormous. In 1885

John A. Macdonald's government would prefer to risk alienating Quebec by executing Louis Riel than alienating Orange Ontario by sparing him.

The Orange Order was hardly the only fraternal organization that grew and flourished in Canada. Because most of these societies were semi-secret, with rites based on Freemasonry, they appealed mainly to Protestants. The Masons themselves expanded enormously during the mid-nineteenth century. They were joined by a number of other orders, such as the Independent Order of Oddfellows (founded in England in 1813 and brought to Canada by 1845), the Independent Order of Foresters (founded in the United States in 1874 and brought to Canada in 1881), and the Order of Knights of Pythias (founded in Washington, DC, in the early 1860s and brought to Canada in 1870). The Knights of Labour was an all-embracing labour organization that owed much to the lodges. Fellowship and mutual support were the keys to the success of all of these societies. Their success led to the formation in 1882 of the Knights of Columbus as a similar fraternal benefit society for Roman Catholic men, although the first chapters in Canada were probably not founded until the early 1890s. While few of these societies admitted women directly, most had adjunct or parallel organizations for women. By the 1880s many Canadians belonged to one or more of these societies. Membership offered a means of social introduction into a new community, provided status and entertainment to members, and increasingly supplied assurance of assistance in times of economic or emotional crisis.

CULTURAL LIFE

The creation of the nation did not directly affect all aspects of cultural life. Indeed, most culture in Canada existed quite apart from political considerations. Despite their new self-consciousness about the need for cultural achievements to match their political accomplishments, most Canadians probably did not appreciate how much progress was being made in many cultural spheres. Only a brief sampling of cultural activity in Victorian Canada—focusing on painting, theatre, music and organized sports—can be included here.

Painting was the most vibrant and productive of the arts in the era immediately after Confederation, with many artists producing large numbers of canvases, some of them key works in the history of Canadian painting. The beginning of the period coincided roughly with the end of a tradition of landscape painting that had become dominant partly in response to the developing quest for national identity and the topographical beauties of the new country that were just being discovered. Lucius O'Brien (1832–99) and John A. Fraser (1838–98) were two of numerous painters who traveled west in 1880 at the invitation of the Canadian Pacific Railway to paint the Rockies. O'Brien's most famous painting, however, is *Sunrise on the Saguenay* (1880). It is a remarkable depiction of the sublime in nature, while in its poetic, moody treatment of the romantic scene it is also an outstanding Canadian example of a style, popular in the United States, that came to be called 'luminism'. This painting was hung in the inaugural exhibition of the Royal Academy, of which O'Brien was the first president, and deposited in the new National Gallery of Canada.

Homer Watson (1855–1936) and his friend Horatio Walker (1858–1936) both came to concentrate on Canadian landscapes that romanticized rural scenes. Oscar Wilde, after seeing Watson's work in Toronto, called him 'the Canadian Constable'. In fairness to Watson, he was no imitator, since at the time he had never heard of Constable. Walker, who was born in Listowel, Canada West, wintered in New York and summered on the Île d'Orléans. He specialized, with great commercial success, in striking, sentimentalized interpretations of Quebec farm life in the style of the French painter Jean-François Millet. Walker himself described his preoccupations:

> The pastoral life of the people of our countryside, the noble work of the Habitant, the magnificent panoramas which surround him, the different aspects of our seasons, the calm of our mornings and the serenity of our evenings, the movement of ebb and flow of our tides which I have observed on the shores of my island which is truly the sacred temple of the muses and a gift of the gods to men: such are the preferred subjects of my paintings. I have passed the greatest part of my life in trying to paint the poetry, the easy joys, the hard daily work of rural life, the sylvan beauty in which is spent the peaceable life of the habitant, the gesture of the wood cutter and the ploughman, the bright colours of sunrise and sunset, the song of the cock, the daily tasks of the farmyard, all the activity which goes on from morning to evening, in the neighbourhood of the barn.[1]

By 1880 young Canadian painters sought to study in the academies of Paris, the centre of the art world of the time. There they learned to paint large, richly detailed, subtly coloured, naturalistic canvases featuring the human figure and sentimental subtexts. One of the most gifted of these painters was Robert Harris (1849–1919), born in Wales and brought up in Charlottetown, Prince Edward Island. Harris was a sought-after portrait painter. His best-known work is *The Fathers of Confederation,* painted from photographs and based on extensive research (on such matters as eye and hair colouring), but he also occasionally produced paintings that evoked everyday life in Prince Edward Island (or all of Canada), such as *The Chorister* (1880), showing a young man singing in a church choir; *Harmony* (1886), a portrait of a young woman (his wife) playing the harmonium, a popular musical instrument in rural Canada; and *A Meeting of the School Trustees* (1885).

Perhaps the most important development in Canadian theatre in this period was the extension of railroad construction, which would make possible extensive touring across the nation by theatrical and vaudeville companies. By the 1880s, most Canadian cities could look forward to visits by professional performers, which undoubtedly raised the standard of presentation and provided models worthy of emulation. At the same time, the arrival of professionals and the raising of standards could be damaging to local amateurs, who had previously dominated the theatrical scene and occasionally even produced home-grown plays and musicals. The struggle between visiting professionals and local amateurs would continue in Canada for many years.

Although only a few trained musicians existed in British North America, the mid-Victorian era saw the development of a widespread musical life. Garrison bands and choral groups were the chief components. In British Columbia the band of the Royal Engineers brought new standards of musical performance when it arrived in the colony in 1859. From that year until 1863 (when it was reposted to Britain) it entertained as militia band, fire-brigade band, brass band, and even a dance band. In British Columbia, as elsewhere, brass bands were the most common and popular instrumental ensembles throughout the nineteenth century. Few band musicians were professional or professionally trained. A number of brass bands were organized in the province in Aboriginal communities and residential schools. At least thirty-three sprung to life between 1864 (when the Oblates founded the St Mary's Mission Band near Mission City) and the end of the century. In Red River, a brass band from St Boniface played as the Métis provisional government raised its new flag in December 1869.

By the time of Confederation, larger cities were producing substantial numbers of musical societies, chiefly choral in their orientation. In 1864, for example, the Mendelssohn Choir and the Société Musicale des Montagnards Canadiens, as well as Les Orphéonistes de Montréal, joined the Montreal Oratorio Society. Montreal also helped produce the first well-known Canadian composer, Calixa Lavallée (1842–91), best known today for the music to 'O Canada'.

'Sunrise on the Saguenay', oil on canvas, 1880, by Lucius O'Brien. National Gallery of Canada, Ottawa.

He made his debut at the piano in Montreal at age thirteen, spending much time in the United States until he went to Paris in 1873. Returning to settle in Quebec, Lavallée wrote a grand cantata for the reception of Governor-General Lord Lorne and his wife. It concluded with a stirring contrapuntal arrangement of 'God Save the Queen' and 'Comin' thro' the Rye'. Unable to make a living in Canada, the composer spent the last years of his life in exile in the United States. Although Canada was not often generous to its professional musicians, it embraced amateur musical performance with gusto. Most music making occurred in the home, with people gathering around the piano to sing hymns and popular songs of the day.

The mid-Victorian period in Canada saw a continued development of organized sports and games. Most were imported, although some (like lacrosse) had local origins. Lacrosse had begun life as an Aboriginal game called *baggataway* or *tewaarathon*, and was played by many tribes under various rules. In 1833 the First Nations near Montreal played lacrosse, and in 1856 the Montreal Lacrosse Club was organized, to be joined by two others before 1860. A Montreal dentist, William George Beers (1843–1900), codified the game in Montreal and promoted it across the country. Lacrosse flourished between 1868 and 1885, achieving great success as a spectator sport until it was overtaken by baseball and hockey. Snowshoeing, which became very

'A Meeting of the School Trustees', oil on canvas, 1885, by Robert Harris. National Gallery of Canada, Ottawa. Purchased 1886, #6.

popular as an organized winter activity in the 1860s (often among the summer lacrosse crowd) was another obviously Aboriginal development. The Montreal Snow Shoe Club was organized in 1843, and in Winnipeg a snowshoe club, begun in 1878, was the major winter diversion for members of the city's élite by the early 1880s.

The formulation of rules for these and other sports occurred in most cases between 1840 and 1880, which was the great era of codification of sports. Precise dates are very contentious, with many communities advancing their own claims for 'firsts'. Certainly by 1880 most sports and games familiar to us today had reached a stage of rule development that would have made them comprehensible to a modern Canadian. What is important about the development of sports is not simply the introduction of standardized rules, techniques, and equipment, but the sheer scope and ubiquity of sporting activity on the part of both participants and spectators. While many Canadians participated, many more gathered to watch sporting activity. The development of any of the major games followed roughly the same

Caughnawaga (Kahnawake) Mohawks, lacrosse champions of Canada, 1869, James Inglis. NAC, C-001959.

path of regularization, which made it possible for teams from one place to play teams from another.

By 1885 two aspects of sports in Canada had evolved: participation and spectacle. Sports still had not achieved an overt political meaning. There was not yet the creation of either national leagues or national teams to play in international competitions. Expansion, sophistication, and growing organization matched the development of the nation. The mobility of the population moved various sports and games around the country and made the standardization of rules both possible and necessary. Both the development of official rules and growing hierarchies of teams and players pointed to the future.

THE STRUGGLE FOR THE WEST

Sincere efforts were made in the new Dominion to encourage a sense of nationhood transcending the linguistic barriers between French and English and the geographical barriers of the provinces and the regions. Nevertheless, the new Canadian nationality remained fragile, more than a bit artificial, and very racist. In addition, at least outside French Canada, it tended to express the prejudices and values of British Ontario. The crucible for the new Canada, many believed, was in the vast expanse of territory west of the Great Lakes. Here its limitations were most clearly evident.

The interests of the Canadian government in the Northwest Territory, especially under Sir John A. Macdonald, were focused on agricultural settlement. This would provide both an outlet for excess eastern population and the means of encouraging the development of a truly transcontinental nation. The process of settlement pushed the Aboriginal inhabitants of the region out of the way as quickly as possible. The

Canadian government negotiated a number of treaties with the First Nations that extinguished Aboriginal titles in exchange for reserves on the most marginal and least attractive land. In August 1876, for example, the Aboriginal peoples of central Saskatchewan gathered at Fort Carlton to consider the terms of the government's Treaty No. 6. The Plains Cree chief Poundmaker (Pitikwahanapiwiyin, c. 1842–86) objected to the arrangement, saying that the government should be prepared to train his people as farmers and assist them in other ways after the buffalo

WILLIAM GEORGE BEERS

William George Beers (1841–1900) was born in Montreal, educated at Lower Canada College, and after four years' apprenticeship, 1856–60, quickly became one of the premier dentists in British North America. In the process, he became one of the leading spokesmen for the middle class in the colonies and later the dominion. Beers was an active proponent of professionalization, for example. He helped found the Dental Association of the Province of Quebec in 1868 and began the Canada *Journal of Dental Science* in 1871, publishing it until 1879, when he ran out of money. Perhaps even more important than Beers' campaign to make dentists respectable professionals was his successful effort to make the sport of lacrosse not only respectable but a leading sport in British North America/Canada. Beers had played lacrosse for many years and was extremely fond of the game, which was mainly played by Aboriginals in a very free, unstructured, and often brutal manner. At about the same time as dozens of other individuals all across North America who engaged in various sports and games began to structure them, Beers began to rationalize and codify the rules of lacrosse. In 1860 he published a pamphlet that standardized various aspects of the game, including the size of the field, the number of players, and a set of basic rules. As a result of his efforts, lacrosse became increasingly popular among the white middle classes, and in 1867 Beers led in the organization of the National Lacrosse Association. The new association was composed of 29 lacrosse clubs from Ontario and Quebec. His 1869 book, *Lacrosse, the National Game of Canada*, helped popularize the game beyond central Canada. If Beers had not existed, he would have had to be invented by those historians who have seen in 'manly' sports an expression of the dominant values of white middle-class central Canada ultimately writ large by Canadian nationalist/imperialists across the nation. Beers saw lacrosse as a 'manly' game that could be played more scientifically by whites than by Aboriginal people. It was also, he observed, an entirely Canadian game which promoted Canadian patriotism across the entire dominion. Beers also promoted snowshoeing and tobogganing, writing 20 pieces on Canadian sports for a New York journal, and subsequently contributing to a variety of Canadian and American magazines. As well as being an enthusiastic sportsman, Beers would become after Confederation a Canadian Imperialist. He was also a Presbyterian and a Conservative. He would later help found the Montreal Amateur Athletic Association in 1883 and the Canadian National League in 1893.

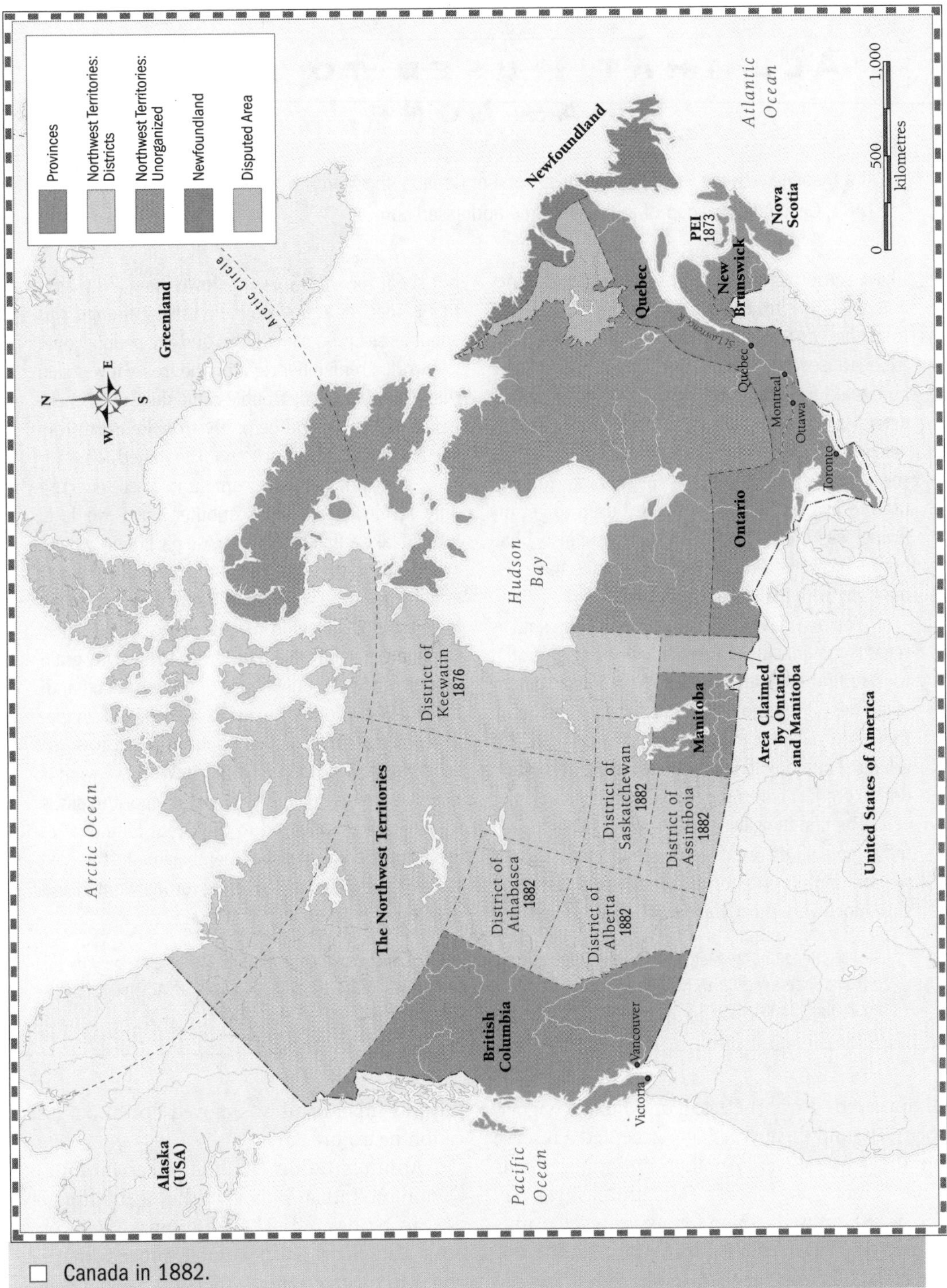
Provinces
Northwest Territories: Districts
Northwest Territories: Unorganized
Newfoundland
Disputed Area
N
E
S
W
Greenland
Arctic Circle
Arctic Ocean
Newfoundland
Atlantic Ocean
Quebec
PEI 1873
Nova Scotia
New Brunswick
St Lawrence R.
Quebec
Montreal
Ottawa
Toronto
Ontario
Hudson Bay
District of Keewatin 1876
Manitoba
Area Claimed by Ontario and Manitoba
United States of America
The Northwest Territories
District of Saskatchewan 1882
District of Assiniboia 1882
District of Athabasca 1882
District of Alberta 1882
British Columbia
Vancouver
Victoria
Alaska (USA)
Pacific Ocean
0
500
1,000
kilometres

☐ Canada in 1882.

'ALL THAT I USED TO LIVE ON HAS GONE.'

At a meeting with the visiting governor-general of Canada, the Marquis of Lorne, at Fort Carlton in 1881, Chief Ahtahkakoop of the Plains Cree addressed Lorne.

I have reason to be thankful to see His Excellency and since this [treaty] medal was put on my neck from the Great Mother I am thankful— & all my tribe—to see the Great Mother's representative here that I will speak for her as I speak for my children. I am a poor man and now will express my views on this subject, but as I look round I do not see anything I could live by. I see nothing, all that I used to live on has gone. Where I used to get my [living] was the animal the buffalo, and also I had horses, now the buffalo and the horses have left me. I say with that I am a poor man.

You may have seen the poverty of the land as regards the animal—that was my hunting ground. I used to find them all I wanted. Now it is a solitary wilderness. I find nothing there, when I look at all this I see but one thing left, that is to work the ground. I am too old to work but I think of my children & grandchildren they may learn.

The first thing [we want] is some strength, i.e., farm implements & cattle—these are necessary. If we don't progress faster than in the past years, we shall move very shortly and my Grandchildren will not see it for we walk very slowly now. Why I say this is that the crops we have raised the half was spoilt as sickness came on us and my people could not work. I remember right on the treaty it was said that if any famine or trouble came the Government would see to us and help. My trouble arose from partly starvation and sickness. The remedy I ask for now. We want nets, we want guns. I ask for these only for living. There is another thing we lack. When I take a flail to thrash I lose part of my wheat. I want a thrashing machine. A thrasher and a reaper and the power to work them. There is no end to my losses. I loose [lose] in the thrashing. I have miles sometimes to go through the snow to have my grain ground, and I am only about to bring back a handful. I make no doubt that his Excellency will sympathize with us, that he will open his heart towards the trouble of his Indian Children. What we want is speedy help on my farms. I have no more to say. I wish to be remembered to the Great Mother & to the Princess and please remember me in the cold winter days & give me covering for my women and children.

SOURCE: 'Report of the Marquis of Lorne's trip', quoted in Deanna Christensen, *Ahtahkakoop: The Epic Account of a Plains Cree Head Chief, His People, and Their Struggle for Survival 1816–1896* (Shell Lake, SK, Ahtahkakoop Publishing, 2000), 422–3.

disappeared. Nevertheless, Poundmaker signed the treaty, and three years later accepted a reserve on the Battle River. Another important Plains Cree chief, Big Bear (Mistahimaskwa, c. 1825–88), refused to sign for six years. He capitulated on 8 December 1882 when his people were starving and needed food. The following July, his small band was moved north to a reservation near Fort Pitt.

Administration of the treaties and of Dominion 'Indian policy' in the west left a good deal to be desired. The Aboriginals were obviously caught in an inexorable process that was going to change forever their traditional way of life. The buffalo were rapidly disappearing, the victims of both over-hunting and the arrival of settlement and new technology. Most Aboriginal leaders saw the handwriting on the wall clearly enough. They did not get anywhere near enough help from the Department of Indian Affairs, however. The government expected the Aboriginals to be able to become self-sufficient virtually overnight. It did not supply the reserves with enough food to prevent starvation and disease, and it complained when the Natives slaughtered their livestock for something to eat. The reserve land tended to be marginal, the assistance supplied was inadequate—often for financial reasons—and the attitude of many of the government's Indian agents was basically unsympathetic. By the early 1880s, the North-West was a virtual powder-keg of Aboriginal discontent. Cree leaders in what is now Alberta sent a letter to John A. Macdonald (who was minister of the interior and head of Indian Affairs as well as prime minister) complaining of destitution and noting that the motto of their people was: 'If we must die by violence let us do it quickly.' The winter of 1883–4 was particularly harsh and severe, and many were starving. Some Indian agents wrote to Ottawa, but nothing was done. In June 1884, Big Bear and his followers, with many others, travelled to Poundmaker's reserve to hold a big meeting. They discussed the serious state of affairs, after which some 2,000 Aboriginals put on a Thirst Dance, a religious ritual.

The Canadian government had established the North-West Mounted Police in 1873 to act as its quasi-military agent in the west. It modelled the NWMP on the Irish constabulary. Its officers, drawn from the élites of eastern Canada, believed in a notion of public stability that associated crime and violence with the 'lower orders' and the Aboriginal peoples. The Mounties kept ahead of settlement and have

SARA RIEL

Sara Riel (1848–83) was born in Red River, the third daughter of Louis Riel and Julie Lagimodière. Because two older sisters died in infancy before she was born, she was always regarded as the eldest daughter in a large family. She and her elder brother Louis grew up together, roaming the woods and fields of the settlement in the summertime. She was always very religious. With her brother she attended the Grey Nuns School in St Boniface. She boarded there from 1858 to 1866, and her school workbooks and letters are in the archives of the Soeurs Grises de Saint-Boniface. She wrote regularly to her siblings about proper behaviour. On 2 September 1865 she entered the Grey Nuns' novitiate and became a professed nun on 8 March 1868, the first St Boniface *métisse* to take such a step. Sara took on the religious vocation that her mother had hoped for Louis. It was Sara who wrote to Montreal in 1866 to find out what was happening to Riel, and she took the lead in family business that one might have expected from Riel's mother, of whom she was very protective, possibly because Julie Riel was not literate.

Sister Sara was teaching school and living at the St Norbert Nunnery in December 1869 when Charles Tupper visited there. She provided Tupper with a letter that enabled him to cross the barricades and meet with her brother.

She and another nun subsequently sang for Tupper in Cree. She made a great impression on Tupper, and according to his memoirs he corresponded with her until her death. In 1871 she was transferred back to St Boniface, where she tended the sick in the hospital and was in charge of mending linen. Later in 1871 she left Winnipeg for the mission at Île-à-la-Crosse in Saskatchewan, the first Red River *métisse* to become a missionary. She nearly died of pneumonia in 1872. Regarding her recovery as a miracle, which she attributed to prayers to a seventeenth-century nun named Marguerite-Marie Alacoque (this experience was offered to Rome as evidence towards beatification), she changed her name to Sister Marguerite-Marie on 27 November 1872. 'I ought to bury my name with my life under the cold snow of the cemetery and ought no longer to be known or to live on except in the memory of a mother, of a brother and of a family who love me tenderly,' she wrote.

Sara wrote Bishop Taché in 1877 that she was so concerned about her brother that her colleagues thought she too might be losing her mind. She lost contact with Riel after his dismissal from confinement in an asylum, and only managed to restore contact with him a few months before her death. He had wilfully ignored her for a lengthy period. She welcomed his new wife into the family in a very supportive letter to Riel in Montana. She died in 1884 of tuberculosis, and while Riel's immediate reaction to her death was calm, he later made disparaging comments about the nuns 'who caused his sister's death'. A collection of her letters to her brother has been published by Mary V. Jordan as *To Louis from your sister who loves you Sara Riel* (Toronto 1974). Suggestions of some sort of incestuous relationship between Sara and Louis have never been proved, and are based on very thin evidence. Few letters from Riel to Sara survive, and not many more from Sara to him. She played an insignificant role in the earlier biographies of Riel and has only gradually become a figure in her own right in the more recent studies.

always been seen as the chief instruments of a more peaceful process of western expansion than occurred in the neighbouring United States. Certainly in Canada there was less overt violence, but this was often owing to the early exertion of state power and control.

Settlement drove the Métis, like the First Nations, to the margins. By 1885 Ontario-born settlers outnumbered the Métis five to one in Manitoba, and only 7 per cent of the population of the province was of mixed-blood origin. Many Métis drifted farther west, to the Saskatchewan Valley, where they formed small mission settlements including Qu'Appelle, Batoche, and Duck Lake. The buffalo were becoming scarce everywhere. Government surveyors caused uncertainty and fear, as they had in Red River a decade earlier. Over the harsh winter of 1883–4, many Métis and Aboriginals starved. The Métis turned in despair to Louis Riel. He had apparently put his life back together after years of exile in the United States and hospitalization for mental disturbance in 1876–8 at Longue Pointe, Quebec. He became an American citizen and was teaching in St Peter's, Montana (where he had married), when a delegation from the Saskatchewan country visited him on 4 June 1884. They told him of the grievances that were burdening the peoples of the region, explained that agitation was developing against the Canadian government, and

Big Bear (centre) trading at Fort Pitt, an HBC post on the North Saskatchewan River, 1884. In the same year the post was taken over by the North-West Mounted Police. In April 1885, in the course of the uprising, Big Bear's band attacked the fort, which they evacuated and then burned. NAC, PA-118768.

pleaded with him to return to Canada to lead them. Why Riel agreed to do so is one of the many mysteries surrounding his life. However, within a month he and his family were in Batoche. By December 1884, Riel and W.H. Jackson (secretary of the Settler's Union) had finished drafting a long petition (with twenty-five sections), which they sent to Ottawa. It concluded by requesting that the petitioners 'be allowed as in [1870] to send Delegates to Ottawa with their Bill of rights; whereby an understanding may be arrived at as to their entry into confederation, with the constitution of a free province'. Ottawa acknowledged the petition, but gave no other response.

In March 1885 events took a menacing turn. Riel's military leader, Gabriel Dumont (1836–1906), intercepted a small NWMP detachment near Duck Lake. The engagement turned into a full-fledged battle in which fatalities occurred on both sides. Riel called upon the First Nations to assist him, and there were incidents of Aboriginal violence connected less to Riel's resistance than to younger warriors' discontent with conditions. Poundmaker's people broke into buildings in Battleford, terrifying settlers. The Cree warrior, Wandering Spirit (Kapapamahchakwew, c. 1845–85), led a band that attacked Frog Lake, killing nine. Prime Minister Macdonald determined to crush this rebellion quickly, sending an armed force under Major-General Frederick Middleton (1825–98) by way of the new Canadian Pacific Railway. The Canadian force of 800 men arrived at Batoche on 9 May. They quickly defeated Riel and about 200 Métis. The uprising was over by 12 May. Dumont and others fled to the United States. The government arrested Riel.

☐ Riel in the prisoner's box. He addressed the court twice during his trial, once after all the evidence had been presented (when he spoke for more than an hour) and once before sentence was pronounced. NAC, C-1879.

A formal charge of high treason, carrying the death penalty, was laid against Riel on 6 July. (Despite the fact that Riel was an American citizen, the Canadian government held with the British government that he was also a British subject, since British citizenship acquired through birth could never be renounced). Even were Riel a foreign national, however, he could still be tried for treason. The government chose to focus responsibility for the rebellion upon Riel, which would allow leniency towards most of his followers. The trial began on 28 July in Regina, where feelings ran high. It was a political trial, infamously coloured in many ways by Macdonald's determination to have Riel found guilty and executed.

Riel passionately denied a plea of insanity introduced by his lawyers, realizing that to be declared insane (i.e., not responsible for his actions) would devastate his reputation and impugn his honour. The six-man jury (operating under the law of the North-West Territories) found him guilty, but recommended mercy. It is not clear whether the jury brought in the mercy recommendation because it felt Riel's resistance was partially justified or because it did not really believe that he was responsible for his behaviour. In any case, because the charge was high treason, a guilty verdict brought a mandatory death sentence. The Canadian government could have heeded the jury's recommendations, but refused to do so. Ottawa dismissed two appeals, and hanged Riel on 16 November.

If Riel was treated without sympathy by the Canadian government, the punishments meted out to the First Nations, who were regarded as having joined Riel's resistance rather than acting on their own initiative, were equally severe. The

'The Surrender of Poundmaker to Major-General Middleton at Battleford, Saskatchewan, on May 26, 1885', oil on canvas, 1887, by R.W. Rutherford. NAC, C-002769.

Macdonald government used the occasion of the rebellion and the violence committed by the leaders of the First Nations to crush the Aboriginal protests against the failure to observe the negotiated treaties. Eight warriors were executed in late November of 1885, and before the courts were finished, more than fifty others had been sentenced to imprisonment. Among the leaders, Poundmaker stood trial for treason and was sentenced to three years in prison. Released after a year, he died four months later. Big Bear received a similar sentence, but was released after a year and a half. Wandering Spirit was hanged. The trials were most improper, conducted without full translation against people who understood little English and less of the law being employed. Few were properly represented in court. Most First Nations leaders and people tried to remain clear of the Métis uprising, but this did not save them from a subsequent campaign of repression by Assistant Indian Commissioner Hayter Reed, who argued that the rebellion had abrogated the treaties and who introduced a series of policies that made the First Nations totally dependent on the largesse of Canada.

The execution of Louis Riel had a lasting impact on Canada. In Quebec it strengthened French-Canadian nationalism and helped turn voters away from the Conservative Party, which they had supported since Confederation. On 22

☐ A CPR construction crew laying track at Malakwa, BC, c. 1881-5. NAC, C-001602.

☐ The first transcontinental passenger train arrives at the foot of Howe Street in Vancouver, 23 May 1887. City of Vancouver Archives, CAN.P.78, N.52.

November 1885, at a huge gathering in the public square in Montreal called the Champ de Mars, Honoré Mercier, the Liberal leader in Quebec, joined Wilfrid Laurier in denouncing the government action. Mercier insisted: 'In killing Riel, Sir John has not only struck at the heart of our race but especially at the cause of justice and humanity which . . . demanded mercy for the prisoner of Regina, our poor friend of the North-West.' Laurier added: 'Had I been born on the banks of the Saskatchewan . . . I would myself have shouldered a musket to fight against the neglect of governments and the shameless greed of speculators.' The two leaders disagreed over Mercier's proposal that French Canadians leave the two major parties and form one of their own. Laurier insisted that Mercier's proposal would destroy Confederation. Symbolically, French Canada took the execution of Riel to represent the final exclusion of the francophone from the west. Few spoke of the symbolic meaning of the execution of Wandering Spirit for the Aboriginal peoples.

The military defeat of the Métis, the humiliation of the First Nations, and the public execution of Louis Riel in November 1885 were only part of the reason why that year (and that month) were so significant, not only in the history of the west but in the history of Canada. In November 1885 workers drove the last spike at Craigellachie in eastern British Columbia, marking the completion of the Canadian Pacific Railway. The CPR had been resurrected in 1881 as a hybrid corporation controlled by private capitalists and financed largely by the state, which, along with public subsidies, gave it about 25 million acres (10,117,500 ha) of land along its right of way. Contemporaries actively debated the question of building in advance of settlement, particularly given the inducements needed to persuade hardheaded businessmen to proceed with construction. The Macdonald government defended the railway on the grounds of national interest. Since this concept is not measurable in dollar amounts, it is impossible to know whether the price was too high. Even before the line was completed, Macdonald used it to send troops west to help suppress the Métis uprising of 1885. The construction of the CPR was a spectacular feat of engineering, partly thanks to the managerial skills of William Van Horne (1843–1915). The CPR was built chiefly on the backs of 6,500 Chinese coolie labourers especially imported for the job. Many died, and those who survived were summarily discharged when the work was completed. With the CPR finished, the Canadian government moved swiftly to limit Chinese immigration. With the Plains peoples and their Métis allies totally subjugated, Canada was open for settlement from coast to coast.

CONCLUSION

The west was to be an anglophone colony of Canada. Not only were First Nations, Métis, and Chinese cast aside as quickly as possible, but French Canadians were not expected to settle there in any substantial numbers. National consolidation was arguably complete in 1885, but much Canadian 'nationalism' still bore the distinctive mark of the Ontario WASP. Two cultures, French and English, were in firm opposition to each other, and other cultures were thoroughly marginalized. Trying to satisfy the nation's two main components would continue to be the most challenging task facing the Canadian government.

HOW HISTORY HAS CHANGED

CANADA'S WESTERN POLICY

Some of the most intense controversy in Canadian historiography has concerned the subject matter of this chapter, most particularly in regard to the western policy of the Canadian government and its treatment of the local inhabitants. To some extent Canada's western policy has been treated as a product of its attempts to create a strong national government. For the most part, though, the government's policy has been seen as separate from the larger debate over national versus provincial rights. The chief issues have revolved around the treatment of the Métis and Louis Riel and the way they got translated into the national political controversies of the day.

The principal debate has been over the treatment of the Métis by the federal government, especially in terms of their land claims. Much of the argument has centred on whether the problems over the distribution of Métis land were a result of deliberate obstructionist policies by the Canadian government or of difficulties beyond the control of the government. Douglas Sprague and others have insisted that the Métis were a stable and persistent population in the Red River period, and that behind their rapid disappearance from Manitoba after 1870—and their problems in their new homes—was a deliberate government policy to dispossess them of their land rights. Thomas Flanagan and Gerhard Ens, on the other hand, have maintained that the government treated the Métis more than fairly, and that most of the problems facing the Métis were essentially of their own making.

The treatment of Louis Riel by historians has shifted substantially over the years since the nineteenth century. In his own lifetime, even people who defended Riel regarded him as cruel and insane. Recent studies have not only made him a more sympathetic character, but have turned him into a true Métis leader. Riel has now to some extent passed beyond biography into the realm of mythology.

Lurking behind the Métis debate itself is another issue, perhaps even more interesting and important. Sprague had raised the land claims issue when he was working as a researcher for the Manitoba Métis Federation. The Federation then used Sprague's research in its legal case against the federal government. Canada, in turn, hired its own historians—most notably Thomas Flanagan and Gerhard Ens—to do research and prepare the documentation for a defence brief. For many historians, this use of subsidized scholarship for litigious purposes subverts the independent scholarly standing of those involved, turning them into what one critic has called 'hired guns'. When Sprague accuses the Canadian government of bad faith, even of provoking the 1885 Rebellion, or when Flanagan insists that Louis Riel received a fair trial in 1885, one may question whether their conclusions are not simply part of their briefs on behalf of their clients. Much recent scholarship in Canada, not only on the Métis, has been conducted on behalf of litigants in complex court cases. Few Canadian historians believe any longer in 'objectivity', or complain about partisanship in historical writing—which has characterized Canadian historiography since its very beginning—but many are still committed to a philosophy of academic independence. It is fair enough to turn one's scholarship to one side or another of a highly charged political issue; but is it equally fair to do so as a subsidized or hired researcher?

Beyond the land claims stands the larger question of federal policy towards and treatment of the west. Most historians would concede that the Canadian government handled the west badly, but whether the treatment was malicious or simply incompetent is another matter, as is the question of whether the government's behaviour justified an armed uprising. One of the problems with viewing Canadian western policy as incompetent blundering, of course, is that the blunderer-in-chief comes to be seen as Prime Minister Macdonald himself.

SHORT BIBLIOGRAPHY

Berger, Carl. *Honour and the Search for Influence; A History of the Royal Society in Canada*. Toronto, 1996. A study by Canada's premier historian of ideas.

Bolger, Francis. *Prince Edward Island and Confederation 1863–1873*. Charlottetown, 1964. The standard work on the subject.

Bumsted, J.M. *The Red River Rebellion*. Winnipeg, 1996. A revisionist account of the insurgency in 1869–70.

Cook, Ramsay. *Provincial Autonomy, Minority Rights and the Compact Theory 1867–1921*. Ottawa, 1969. A detailed investigation of the subject.

Creighton, Donald. *John A. Macdonald: The Old Chieftain*. Boston, 1965. Still the standard biography of the old man.

Ens, Gerhard. *Homeland to Hinterland: The Changing Worlds of the Red River Métis in the Nineteenth Century*. Toronto, 1996. A revisionist study that sees the Métis as responding seriously to the changing economic circumstances of the nineteenth century.

Flanagan, Thomas. *Riel and the Rebellion: 1885 Reconsidered*. Rev. ed. Saskatoon, 1998. A well-researched study which argues that Riel received a fair trial in 1885.

Pryke, Kenneth G. *Nova Scotia and Confederation 1864–1873*. Toronto, 1979. The standard work on the subject.

Reid, Dennis. *Our Own Country Canada: Being an Account of the National Aspirations of the Principal Landscape Artists in Montreal and Toronto 1869–1890*. Ottawa, 1979. A wonderful example of the integration of art history into the larger context.

Shelton, W. George, ed. *British Columbia and Confederation*. Victoria, 1967. A useful collection of essays on the subject.

Sprague, D.N. *Canada and the Métis, 1869–1885*. Waterloo, 1988. The best statement of the case against the government with regard to the Métis and especially the Métis land question.

Stanley, George F.G. *Louis Riel*. Toronto, 1961. The standard biography.

Stonechild, Blair and Bill Waiser. *Loyal till Death: Indians and the North-West Rebellions*. Calgary, 1997. A sympathetic account of the First Nations in the rebellions.

Thomas, L.H. *The Struggle for Responsible Government in the Northwest Territories, 1870–97*. 2nd edn. Toronto, 1978. Somewhat misleadingly titled, a judicious overview of the situation in the prairie west in the last third of the nineteenth century.

Thomson, Dale. *Alexander Mackenzie: Clear Grit*. Toronto, 1960. The only modern full-length study of a complex personality.

Ware, Tracy, ed. *A Northern Romanticism: Poets of the Confederation*. Ottawa, 2000. A representative collection of the works of the Confederation poets.

STUDY QUESTIONS

1. Was the Métis action led by Louis Riel in 1869–70 a true rebellion? Explain why or why not.
2. Identify three ways in which railroads helped to 'complete' Confederation.
3. List the advantages and disadvantages that you would find if you settled on homestead land in the 1870s.
4. Why did Ontario spearhead the provincial rights movement?
5. What effect did the railroads have on the development of theatre arts during this period?
6. Give two reasons to explain why the Canadian nationality was so fragile in the post-Confederation period.
7. What were the main differences between the movements that Louis Riel led in 1869–70 and 1885?
8. What sort of Canada does Charles G.D. Roberts envision in his 1896 poem?

CHAPTER SEVEN

Becoming Modern, 1885–1918

In the years after Confederation, Canada became one of the richest nations in the world in terms of gross national product and per capita income. Given the advantage of hindsight, historians from comparably sized countries—such as Mexico, Brazil, or Argentina—can only envy Canada's privileged position of wealth, if not power, in this critical period. From the late 1870s to the end of the First World War, Canada was in the top ten of the world table of industrial development. Though the country possessed rich agricultural and natural resources, much of the key to its success lay in the exploitation of these advantages by a burgeoning industrial sector. Canadians often saw the weaknesses of the Canadian economy. From the vantage point of most of the world, however, Canada was rich, powerful, highly industrialized, and 'progressive'. It possessed a vibrant labour movement. Before the Great War, Canada had created a self-sustaining internal economy and a dynamic foreign trade. While the nation was transforming its economy, it was also altering its society and culture. There was another round of immigration, much of it drawn from outside the British Isles. Canada became an increasingly urbanized country. This was also the great era of reform, both political and social. As well, there was a great national debate over Canada's place within the British empire. The political system that made all these developments possible operated through the mediating influence of political parties.

The Developing Political and Constitutional System

The Fathers of Confederation had not written political parties into the Canadian Constitution. Nevertheless, by the mid-1880s a two-party system had evolved at both the federal and provincial levels that would remain unchanged until the First World War. Indeed, this period was in many respects the golden age of Canadian party politics. Party affiliations were serious matters. Being a Liberal or a Conservative was a commitment passed on from father to son; small towns had parallel Liberal and Conservative business establishments, including funeral parlours. The seeming vitality of the two-party system disguised, to some degree, the underlying tensions of Canadian federalism. Before 1914, however, the parties seemed flexible enough to contain various currents of conflict and disagreement. Both national parties developed consensual systems capable of holding differing ideologies, sections, and interest groups.

The key to the successful functioning of the national parties—and the allegiances of their adherents—was in large part the power of patronage. Both parties, in office, distributed honours and jobs to their leading supporters, by carefully apportioning rewards to individuals whose qualifications were judged solely in terms of political service and loyalty. The patronage system rewarded chiefly those members of the Canadian professional and business élites (mainly from the

TIMELINE

1886
W.S. Fielding introduces legislation in Nova Scotia calling for secession from the union. The first CPR transcontinental arrives in Manitoba.

1887
Honoré Mercier leads *nationaliste* Liberals to victory in Quebec. St Catharines opens electric street car.

1890
Manitoba government abolishes public funding for Catholic schools. CPR builds rail line through Maine to connect Moncton with Montreal.

1891
Sir John A. Macdonald dies.

1892
A great fire destroys St John's, Newfoundland.

1896
Wilfrid Laurier leads the Liberal Party to a national electoral victory. Gold is discovered in the Klondike. The Manitoba Schools Question becomes a national issue.

1898
A national referendum is held on prohibition of alcoholic beverages. Newfoundland completes a railway across the island.

1899
Canadian Northern Railway is incorporated. Alaska Boundary Dispute is referred to an international tribunal. Canada agrees to send volunteer troops to South Africa.

1900
Art Museum of Toronto is founded. Prohibition legislation is passed on Prince Edward Island.

1901
The first wireless message transmitted across the Atlantic is received on Signal Hill near St John's, Newfoundland.

1902
Ernest Thompson Seton founds Woodcraft Indians.

1905
Saskatchewan and Alberta are created provinces out of the Northwest Territories. Ontario Conservatives finally win political control of the province.

1906
Ontario Hydro-Electric Commission is created.

1907
Development of Marquis wheat. Canadian Department of Interior begins paying bonuses to European immigrant agents for labourers. Canadian Art Club is founded in Toronto.

1910
Steel Company of Canada is created by an amalgamation of smaller firms.

1911
Robert Borden's Conservatives take over federal government in the Reciprocity Election. Marius Barbeau is appointed as anthropologist in the Museum Branch of the Geological Survey of Canada. Noranda gold/copper mine opens in Quebec.

1912
Social Services Council of Canada is organized. Quebec's boundaries are extended to Hudson Bay.

1914
Canada and Newfoundland enter the Great War.

1915
Canadian Expeditionary Force fights in the first Battle of Ypres. Ontario introduces Regulation 17.

1916
Canada introduces a business profits tax. The Newfoundland Regiment is decimated at the Battle of Beaumont Hamel.

1917
Canadian Expeditionary Force suffers heavy losses at Vimy in April. Canada introduces an income tax. Conscription Crisis emerges over introduction of Military Service Act, followed by the Wartime Elections Act. Much of Halifax is destroyed by an explosion.

1918
The Great War ends. Spanish influenza epidemic begins.

so-called middle class) who ran the two parties. The system diminished ideological and regional differences, offering French Canadians their own opportunities for advancement. Patronage thus encouraged a stable party system in which matters of principle were less important than the division of the spoils of victory.

Despite their consensual utility, Canadian political parties had considerable difficulty in mediating the relationships between the federal and provincial levels of government. The rise of a strong movement for provincial rights, initiated by Ontario, joined by Quebec, and supported on occasion by all provinces, was almost inevitable. The chief, although not sole, bone of contention would be economic development. Provinces insisted that they, not the federal government, should control development within their boundaries. What was unexpected was the support for provincial rights provided by the Judicial Committee of the British Privy Council, the court of last resort for federal–provincial disagreements. In a series of landmark decisions stretching from the 1880s to the Great War, the Judicial Committee consistently reduced the power of the federal government and enhanced that of the provinces. Both anglophone and francophone voters tended to support this readjustment of Confederation. They saw the provinces as a check on the federal government's power, and they consistently supported provincial parties that wanted to confront Ottawa. Thus there was nothing unique about the 1887 victory in Quebec of the *nationaliste* Liberal government of Honoré Mercier (1840–94). W.S. Fielding (1848–1929) had won for the Liberals in Nova Scotia in 1884 on a platform of provincial rights. In 1886 Fielding introduced legislation calling for the secession of Nova Scotia from the union. Obviously provincial parties could not afford too close an identification with their federal counterparts, particularly while the latter were in power. Only with the success of Laurier's Liberals in 1896 did the Ontario Tories escape the albatross of a federal Conservative party, for example. By 1905 they won a control of the province that they would seldom relinquish over the next ninety-five years.

A great irony of Confederation was that French Canada continued as the region upon which national political success had to be built. Until the death of Sir John A. Macdonald in 1891, the Conservatives had successfully appealed to Quebec with a judicious combination of local political patronage and national political policies. The execution of Louis Riel late in 1885 threatened that appeal, but the government's Quebec ministers held firm. The Grand Old Man's successors, including J.J. Abbott (1821–93), John S. Thompson (1844–94), and Charles Tupper (1821–1915), simply did not have the magic. In 1896 Wilfrid Laurier (1841–1919) became the national *chef*. He had put together a coalition of provincial Liberal parties by softening the potential issues of division. Laurier's agonizing over the Manitoba Schools Question of the early 1890s, when his distaste for a unilingual policy for Manitoba schools was matched only by his refusal to prevent provinces from running affairs within their own general mandate, was a pure reflection

Wilfrid Laurier, c. 1882. NAC, PA-013133.

of his approach. Laurier saw national unity and national harmony as identical and, not surprisingly, viewed a bicultural state as essential. He was able to survive politically on the strength of Quebec support and a period of great national prosperity until 1911, when the Liberal program of establishing a Canadian navy and limited free trade with the United States brought defeat. Through his compromises, Laurier had managed to blunt to some considerable extent the growing sectional division between Quebec and the remaining provinces of Canada.

The Conservatives of Robert Borden (1854–1937) replaced Laurier's Liberals in 1911. The Tories split the Quebec vote while sweeping Ontario, thanks in large measure to the support of the Ontario provincial party. Key issues in the 1911 election were American reciprocity and imperial naval defence. Borden's victory was a triumph for Canadian imperial sentiment, anticontinentalism, and middle-class reform. Borden had set out his Halifax Platform in 1907, calling for civil service reform, public ownership of telephones and telegraphs, a reformed Senate, and free mail delivery in rural areas. Borden spoke for the 'progressive' forces of Anglo-Canadian society and reform, which had been marshalling strength since the mid-1880s. Laurier had enacted some of Borden's planks, including civil service reform in 1908, but the Conservatives still claimed the imperial mantle. Borden achieved some of his imperial vision only with the beginning of the Great War. The Conscription Crisis of 1917 completed the process, which began in 1911 with the defeat of Laurier, of the political isolation of French Canada. At the same time, neither the west nor the Maritimes were content, as events after the war's end soon demonstrated.

THE ECONOMIC INFRASTRUCTURE

Control of capital through chartered banks headquartered chiefly in central Canada was one of that region's great advantages. Unlike the United States, Canadian banking was always highly centralized. In 1914 in Canada there were only twenty-six banks operating 2,888 branches. Some of the larger banks (the Royal Bank, the Bank of Commerce) had more than 300 branches each. From the beginning, Canadian chartered banks focused less on serving local customers than on facilitating the transfer of commodities and funds. Their credit facilities, especially for outlying districts of the nation, were quite limited. The banking industry itself wrote Canadian banking legislation. The Canadian Bankers' Association was an organization of a few powerful men. The president of the Banque Provinciale complained that it was 'a tool in the hands of three or four men who today control the whole of the finance of the country'.

Although in 1913 Montreal-headquartered banks held almost half of the assets of all Canadian banks ($788 million of $1,551,000,000), Quebec contained considerably fewer branch banks per capita than the remainder of the nation. The result was the founding by Alphonse Desjardins (1854–1920) of the caisses populaires, often run by curés in association with Catholic parishes. Financial institutions to compete locally with the chartered banks did develop, not only in the form of caisses populaires but as government savings banks, local savings banks, and credit unions. Their economic power was limited, however, and the chartered banks continued to grow. Banks with head offices in central Canada refused to make local loans and set local interest rates at high levels. Sir Edmund Walker (1848–1924), president of the Bank of Commerce, labelled regional complaints 'local grievances against what we regard as the interests of the country as a whole' (quoted in Naylor 1975, I: 103).

The Canadian Bank of Commerce building at 25 King Street West, designed by R.A. Waite and erected in 1889-90, was one of several new office buildings in Toronto that had some claim to architectural distinction and even grandeur. At seven-and-a-half storeys, it soared over neighbouring three- and four-storey buildings, and reflected the influence of the first skyscrapers in New York and Chicago. City of Toronto Archives, Micklethwaite Collection SC 497 #21.

Transportation continued to be an essential ingredient of development. As in the age of the first railway boom of the 1850s, railways were both a means of development and a field of investment. Substantial railway construction involved significant public subsidies, often in the form of land grants along the right of way, as well as other boons. The CPR received from the government the completed line from Fort William to Selkirk, as well as the line from Kamloops to Port Moody. Moreover it received a cash payment of $25 million, plus 25 million acres (10,117,500 ha) 'fairly fit for settlement', and various tax exemptions on its land. In addition, it had a monopoly position. Nor was the Canadian Pacific the only railway so favoured. Dozens of railways incorporated in Canada during these years. Local communities fought desperately for railways, seeing them as links to a prosperous future. Sir William Mackenzie (1849–1923) and Sir Donald Mann (1853–1934) constructed a second transcontinental line, the Canadian Northern Railway, which passed considerably to the north of the CPR. Everyone outside central Canada complained about the high costs of freight, but all Canadians relied on the railway. Passenger travel was swift and relatively inexpensive.

Energy was another essential. Canada always possessed rich potential energy resources. Coal never provided much advantage, but abundant water power did. Changing technology at the close of the nineteenth century enabled major nat-

A 1907 poster exhorting immigrants to settle in western Canada. National Library of Canada, C-30621.

ural waterfalls to be harnessed and others to be created through dams. Development for hydroelectric power was substantial in the early years of the twentieth century. No province had greater potential for hydroelectricity generation than Quebec. Unlike Ontario, which established the Ontario Hydro-Electric Commission in 1906, under the chairmanship of Sir Adam Beck (1857–1925), Quebec permitted its hydroelectric development to be carried out by private enterprise. The process of exploiting electricity, both for light and for power, was one of the great unsung technological developments of the age. Industry could use water-power as an alternative to fossil fuel. Cheap hydroelectric power became an advantage for Canadian industry. The manufacturing community saw cheap power as essential to its growth and development. Hydroelectricity lit Canadian homes at relatively low cost. It fostered the growth of electric-powered public transportation, such as the tram and the trolley.

The period between 1880 and 1919 was a great age of science and technology throughout the Western world. Most fields of scientific endeavour transformed out of all recognition the basic theoretical assumptions that had dominated humankind for generations. The number of inventions that altered in practical ways how people lived and worked was astounding. Canada played little role at the frontiers of pure science. Its record in the technical application of science was somewhat better, as the record of the Dominion Experimental Farms system (created by Ottawa in 1886) demonstrated. The great achievement of Canadian agricultural research in this period was the creation of Marquis wheat in 1907 by Charles Edward Saunders (1867–1937). In both science and technology, however, Canada was fortunate to be able to borrow heavily from Great Britain and the United States. Most Canadian technical accomplishment came through adapting imported technology to Canadian conditions.

Population growth was also necessary for economic development. Immigration provided much of that growth for Canada in this period, as in others. Between 1880 and 1920 nearly 4.5 million immigrants arrived in Canada, mainly from Europe and the United States. Beginning in the mid-1890s, the origins of the newcomers shifted perceptibly. Most of the earlier immigrants came from the British Isles, while after 1896 large numbers came from eastern and southern Europe. In addition, Americans again began arriving in Canada in large numbers, their destinations the 'Last Best West' in Alberta and Saskatchewan. By 1901, 34 per cent of the newcomers came from other countries, with 33 per cent from the United States and 22 per cent from Britain. During the peak decade of immigration (1905–14), nearly 2,800,000 immigrated to Canada, with the numbers about equally divided among central and eastern Europe, the United States, and the British Isles. Between 1901 and 1911 alone, the Canadian population grew by 43 per cent. In the 1911 census, over 20 per cent of all Canadians enumerated had been born abroad. While many of the newcomers settled on farms, fully 70 per cent joined the labour force in industry and transportation. Canadian business and government specifically recruited many of the newcomers, often on a contract basis, to provide an industrial workforce. In 1907 the Canadian Department of the Interior began paying bonuses to European immigration agents for people who had labour experience, such as farmers, navvies, or miners. Many other workers arrived as contract labourers. Much of this industrial workforce ended up in Canada's cities.

Another Round of Industrialization

The growth in financial centralization and industrial capacity, particularly the shift from the processing of primary goods into the secondary manufacturing of finished goods, were both major economic developments in Canada in the years 1880–1919. Continued industrialization always involved more than the construction of new and larger factories. Canadians needed to extend and rationalize transportation facilities. They had to mobilize investment, exploit resources, and recruit a labour force. Despite the national policy, Canada did not maintain control over, or ownership in, its economy. Its emergence on the international scene increased its vulnerability to world economic conditions and economic cycles. Moreover, its industrial development was distinctly uneven, with industrial growth well above the national average in Ontario, on the national average in Quebec, and well below the national average in the Maritime and western provinces. Larger urban centres, such as Montreal and Toronto, expanded constantly, while smaller communities fell steadily behind.

One of the keys to Canadian economic growth between 1885 and the Great War was an influx of foreign investment. Few nations depended so heavily on foreign capital in order to fuel economic growth as has Canada throughout its history. Investment in this era—particularly in the boom years 1900–13—was significant. Like other countries, Canada used most of its imported capital to finance large development projects, such as railways and hydroelectric generation. Canada's imports of capital came in the two forms of indirect (portfolio) investment and direct investment. These two types of investment reflected the respective activity of Canada's two largest financial partners. Much of the portfolio investment came from Great Britain. Much of the direct investment came from the United States. In terms of the foreign domination of the economy that resulted, the two types of investment were quite different. Direct investment resulted in far greater control. At the time few Canadians agonized over-much about the extent or the origin of foreign ownership. Foreign control did not become a serious issue in Canadian economic theory or public life before the late 1950s. Until then, almost all Canadians might have agreed with the American entrepreneur Frank Clergue, who declared in 1901 that 'foreign money injected into the circulating medium of Canada' would 'remain forever to the everlasting blessing of thousands of its inhabitants' (quoted in Bliss 1972: 38).

As students now learn routinely in introductory economics courses, portfolio investment represents money borrowed against securities, in this period mainly bonds. Bonds are a relatively safe investment. They do not carry management implications. The British preferred portfolio investment in Canada because their prosperous citizens wanted to clip coupons in their old age. Government (federal, provincial, municipal) and the railways did most of Canada's borrowing in Britain. The money went to finance transportation networks and public works. Little was available for private enterprise, almost none for venture capital. In the first years of the twentieth century, Canadian entrepreneurs exploited the British investment market in new ways. The chief innovation was the promotion of bond issues for giant industrial operations created from the merger of smaller compa-

Workers at looms, c. 1908. City of Toronto Archives, James Collection 137.

nies. Nobody was more successful at merging than William Maxwell Aitken (1879–1964, later Lord Beaverbrook), son of a New Brunswick Presbyterian minister. His great triumph came in 1910 with the creation of the Steel Company of Canada, the bonds for which his Royal Securities firm sold in London. 'I created all the big trusts in Canada', Aitken boasted after he had moved to England in search of greater challenges. He was the most visible and sharpest operator in a movement that saw fifty-eight giant corporations created in Canada between 1909 and 1912.

The United States was an importer of British capital before the First World War and had little available for overseas portfolio investment. The Americans invested directly in Canada to gain access to Canadian raw materials and the Canadian market. They went heavily into the resource sector. They also invested in Canadian manufacturing to gain maximum access to the Canadian market. Less than half of American direct investment was in manufacturing, but the total amount involved was over $100 million by 1910. The protective tariff played an important role in encouraging American branch-plant investment. Early Canadian protectionism sought to foster employment. Canadians did not worry much about the outflow of profits or the influx of foreign managers. Canadians generally accepted that Canadian businessmen and investors were not very adventurous, preferring familiar fields and allowing the Yankees to take the chances. Far from endangering the Canadian identity, American investment fostered it. The

MAX AITKEN

William Maxwell Aitken, first Baron Beaverbrook (1879–1964), was born in Maple, Ontario, the fifth of ten children, nine of whom survived into adulthood. His family moved in 1880 to Newcastle, on the New Brunswick resource frontier, where his father was minister of the Presbyterian church. Young Max (as he was called) grew up in comfortable middle-class surroundings, and although obviously bright, was unable to apply himself at school. At the age of sixteen, he became a clerk in the law firm of Richard B. Bennett in neighbouring Chatham, but he was too impatient to make a career as a lawyer. His obvious métier was in selling and promoting, and before his twenty-first birthday he had become successful as an insurance salesman in Saint John. He soon moved into selling private company bonds, and in 1903 founded the Royal Securities Corporation in Halifax, which he used as a springboard for modernizing and rationalizing a number of business enterprises in the Maritime region, becoming a multimillionaire by 1907.

Aitken was not satisfied in Halifax, and in 1907 he moved to Montreal, where he had purchased the Montreal Trust Company and expanded his business consolidations on the back of a long-lived Canadian boom. He continued to buy small outmoded companies and combine them into larger corporations (with more up-to-date machinery and business practices). His first great success was the consolidation (in 1910) of a number of cement companies into the Canada Cement Company.

He followed this the same year by creating Stelco, which brought together a number of smaller companies responsible for various stages in steel-making into a single, vertically integrated producer of steel. Aitken's operations did add genuine value to the companies he consolidated and modernized, although some of his dealings in the stock and bond markets at the very least sailed close to the edge of illegality. In 1910 he and his family moved to England, where he was convinced by fellow New Brunswicker Andrew Bonar Law (leader of the British Conservative Party) to enter politics, winning a parliamentary seat in the autumn of 1910. Within a year he was knighted, combining continued industrial consolidation in Canada with life as a Tory MP until the Great War.

During the war Aitken served as Canadian Military Representative in England, introducing the Canadian War Artists program in 1916 and, as Lord Beaverbrook, becoming Minister of Information in the war cabinet in 1917. He wrote and published several military histories during the war, one of which—*Canada in Flanders*—was widely circulated and helped publicize the heroic actions of the Canadian Expeditionary Force. He had bought a bankrupt newspaper, the *Express*, in 1917, and after the Armistice he put most of his considerable energy into building a media empire, starting with the *Daily Express*, which reached out to all sectors of English society and became the first popular newspaper in the country. He followed this success with the *Evening Standard* and the *Sunday Express*. During the dark days of the Second World War he served as Churchill's minister of aircraft production, bullying the industry into a greatly increased pace of production that helped save Britain in 1940. After the war he wrote extensively while presiding over his media empire and frequently visiting New Brunswick.

alternative was immigration to the United States.

The Americans preferred to locate their branch plants in southern Ontario. This choice came for a variety of reasons. Americans were active in the heavy industries of Ontario, partly because Ontario was so close to the industrial heartland of the United States south of the Great Lakes. Moreover, Ontario deliberately encouraged Americans to invest in the processing of raw materials by allowing them virtually free access to the province's natural resources. Ontarians believed that they had all the requirements for self-sufficiency within their own borders. The province required that resources taken on Crown land be processed in Canada. 'Debarred from the opportunity of cutting logs for export, it is an absolute certainty that the American lumberman, in default of other sources of supply, will transfer his sawmill enterprises to Canadian soil' (quoted in Nelles 1974: 217). American preference both contributed to and reflected the industrial development of Ontario.

After 1885 manufacturing replaced commerce as the chief propellant of urban growth in Ontario. Much of the new industrial plant involved sophisticated technological applications, often imported from the United States. Ontario became the centre of the Canadian iron and steel industry. The transformation of the older iron industry into the steel industry was symptomatic of the process that was occurring. Coal replaced charcoal as the source of heat. The refining process turned into two steps, first involving open-hearth furnaces and then a steam-driven rolling mill. The result was a product with a slightly higher carbon content. Its name was steel. Mechanization occurred at every step in the manufacturing process. 'Gigantic automation' was the watchword at huge installations like Stelco's Hamilton plant or Algoma's Sault Ste Marie operation. Steel rails were the most common standard product. Ontario's manufacturing grew in a number of smaller urban centres.

Quebec manufacturing relied far less heavily on heavy industry (and vast capitalization) than did Ontario. It depended far more on an industry based on labour and fussy mechanization, such as clothing, wood products, textiles, and food processing. Part of the explanation for the difference may reside in labour availability. Part may have been the availability of cheap hydroelectric power in Quebec after 1900. Quebec had eliminated Ontario's early advantage in secondary over primary manufacturing by 1915. Montreal provided the greatest concentration of Quebec's manufacturing sector. By 1900 workers in that city represented about half the manufacturing labour in the province. It is easy to overemphasize the notorious lag between the two central Canadian provinces. They were more like one another than they were like the remainder of the nation. The industrial disparity between the central provinces and the others grew continually in the years before 1914.

While the absence of industrialization in the Canadian west was a consequence of the recentness of its settlement, this did not apply to the Maritime region. Here rural stagnation joined a crisis in the shipbuilding industry. The growth of new technologies was partly to blame, but the problem was mainly a failure of the Maritime shippers' nerve. The shippers always viewed their ships as instruments of trade. Instead of reinvesting their capital in a modern shipbuilding industry, they and the business community of the region made a desperate effort to exploit the internal market. They accepted the national policy and tried to work within it. The attempts at continentalism seemed initially successful in the 1880s, but rapidly turned to failure.

The reasons for the ultimate Maritime failure remain uncertain. Most Maritime entrepreneurs seemed to lack the financial resources to withstand the ups and downs of the economic cycles. They tended to blame many of their problems on high railway freight rates. At about the same time that the region's business community was moaning about railway rates, outside capital moved in and began buying up locally based companies. Montreal capitalists did most of the damage. They bought up and dismantled many burgeoning industries still servicing the local market.

MANUFACTURING OUTPUT, 1870–1890

One of the developments of the post-Confederation period was the tendency for the industrial output of the Maritime region to lose ground to Ontario and Quebec. The following table documents the change in output by province in various industrial sectors between 1870 and 1890.

PERCENTAGE CHANGE IN MANUFACTURING OUTPUT, 1870–1890

Industry	Nova Scotia	New Brunswick	Quebec	Ontario
All factories	128	42	104	116
Farm production (butter, cheese, and cloth)	60	67	50	34
All manufacturing	120	44	101	113
Consumer goods	160	95	100	119
Durable goods	30	-10	83	61
Intermediate goods	214	50	120	162
Chemical products	210	03	149	410
Clothing	224	49	125	277
Coal & petroleum products	164	321	365	-5
Food & beverages	361	292	122	82
Iron & steel products	142	21	92	90
Leather & fur products	-1	-12	50	41
Nonferric metal products	348	204	191	854
Nonmetallic mineral products	114	121	186	215
Printing	54	111	86	177
Paper products	48	-52	313	254
Rubber goods	na	na	202	4311
Transport equipment	3	-38	154	26
Tobacco products	-78	64	162	263
Textiles	505	443	406	150
Wood products	213	2	64	153

SOURCE: Kris Inwood, 'Maritime Industrialization from 1870 to 1910', *Acadiensis* 21:1 (Autumn, 1991), 147.

'Steel mills at Sydney, Cape Breton', oil on canvas, 1907, by the railway magnate Sir William Cornelius Van Horne. Built between 1900 and 1905, these two plants attracted hundreds of workers, creating an instant city. The Montreal Museum of Fine Arts, gift of the artist's grandson, William C. Van Horne. Photo Brian Merrett.

Maritime entrepreneurs, convinced that they were at a substantial geographical disadvantage in competing with central Canada, ceased trying in most sectors after 1895. Instead, the region turned to the panacea of iron and steel. Surely the presence of local raw materials would make this industry a competitive one. Unfortunately, central Canadian interests soon took over the Maritime steel industry. By 1911 Montreal controlled much of the region's industrial enterprise. Toronto, on the other hand, moved into the region's wholesale and retail marketing sector. Between 1901 and 1921 the number of regional businesses that were branches of central Canadian firms more than doubled, from 416 to 950. The net result of both sorts of take-overs was a regional loss of economic autonomy. Outsiders siphoned capital away from the Maritimes, and when times got tough, they closed stores and factories. The region was systematically deindustrialized and decommercialized. It would never recover its economic vitality.

Most of the businessmen who operated the industrializing economy were immigrants or sons of immigrants, with Scots farmers overrepresented in both categories. Few had begun at the bottom of the social scale. French Canadians were seriously underrepresented among large-scale entrepreneurs and industrialists, even within their own province. Most French-Canadian businesses remained small in scale, family controlled, and confined chiefly to the province of Quebec. These businessmen did share an overall philosophy. They insisted on government involvement in large schemes of public development, such as railways. They accepted government power to grant monopolies of public service through charters or access to Crown lands through advantageous leases. They sought to minimize competition wherever possible, even if public regulation was the price paid for the reduction. Small businessmen who could not combine institutionally to control trade, such as the small retailers, fought hard for early closings and price-fixing. Business rhetoric about competition had less to do with extolling the virtues of free enterprise than with complaining about unfair competition. The business community insisted that what it wanted was a 'living profit', a reasonable return on investment of time and capital.

While few business leaders believed in policies of laissez-faire in the relationship between the state and business, the situation was quite different when it came to labour organizations. Labour organization was an illegitimate combination designed to erode the right of the individual to run his business as he saw fit. Nevertheless, the growth of industrialization was conducive to an expanding worker militancy. The Canadian state proved relatively receptive to the rights of labour to organize. Whereas in the United States public policy was almost universally hostile to labour organization, in Canada laws that legalized union activity were put on the books beginning in the 1880s. Many of the late nineteenth-century labour organizations in

ARTHUR W. PUTTEE

Arthur W. Puttee (1868–1957) was born in Folkestone, England and learned the printing trade in his father's shop. He was raised a Baptist, but turned to liberal Christianity and Unitarianism early in his adult life. He came to North America in 1888, initially establishing himself on a homestead in Portage la Prairie. Finding agricultural labour arduous, he headed to the United States to work as a journeyman printer, eventually returning to Manitoba and the composing staff of the *Manitoba Free Press*. Puttee was soon an active member of the Winnipeg Typographical Union (WTU), an important craft union in the city, and became its president in 1893. As a craft unionist, throughout his career Puttee preferred conciliation and arbitration to labour confrontation, although during his time in the WTU it faced technological threats from new linotyping machinery. The printers responded to the new technology by asserting the prerogatives of their craft, including union control over apprentices and operation of the new machinery. Puttee was serving as secretary of the WTU in 1896, when the union successfully struck the Winnipeg *Tribune* in 1896.

Printers were not only skilled artisans, but had to be literate. Many, including Puttee, went into politics. In Puttee's case, he used the Winnipeg Trades and Labor Council (WTLC) as a springboard, being an early advocate of the organization of a labour party in the city through a labour newspaper, *The People's*

Voice, which he helped to purchase in 1897. Within a year he was editing and managing the paper. Puttee's ideological position of advocacy of independent political action by labour has been described as 'labourism'. In June 1899 he was nominated as an independent labour candidate for a Winnipeg seat in the House of Commons. His campaign appealed not only to organized labour but to 'the people', offering proposals both to expand political democracy and to protect labour against capitalism. Many of his campaign planks were common currency among progressive reformers in the United States and Canada. He advocated universal adult suffrage, proportional representation, initiative and referendum, and a popular veto on all legislation. He also favoured public ownership of all 'natural monopolies', and sought to raise most revenue by taxing 'land values'. He was elected in a close vote in January 1900, becoming both the youngest Member of Parliament at the time and the first MP specifically elected as a labour candidate (although he joined several Ontario 'independents' in the House). He was re-elected in the November 1900 election, receiving much support from the Liberals.

In Parliament, Puttee saw himself as a citizens' representative as much as a labour one. His opposition to the protective tariff, railroad subsidies, and extensive immigration to Canada was particularly noteworthy. He was defeated in the 1904 general election, and returned to Winnipeg to open a new printing company, Winnipeg Printing and Engraving, which took over the publication of *The People's Voice*. Puttee continued to advocate labour unionism, including the organization of the Canadian Labour Party based on the British model, but increasingly in Winnipeg he came to be seen as a conservative influence. In 1918 he opposed a general strike of civic employees, and was pushed out of the WTLC by more radical and militant labour leaders. After 1918 he continued to run his printing company, but was no longer active in politics.

SOURCE: Bryan Dewalt, 'Arthur W. Puttee: Labourism and Working-Class Politics in Winnipeg, 1894–1918', unpublished M.A. thesis, University of Manitoba, 1985.

Canada were foreign imports, chiefly from the United States. If Canadian labour got much of its structure from the Americans, it drew much of its practical experience from Great Britain. For Canada as a whole, the Canadian Labour Congress formed in 1883 as a holding body for local trade councils, and in 1892 became the Trades and Labor Congress of Canada.

In this period most labour conflict revolved around the right to organize and the recognition of unions. Government acceptance of union activity in some ways increased the frequency of conflict. Moreover, the civil authorities frequently intervened in labour conflicts, usually in the name of public order and often on the side of management. Such intervention often produced violence. Strikes were certainly common everywhere in Canada, especially after 1900. In Ontario's ten largest cities, between 1901 and 1914, there were 421 strikes and lockouts involving 60,000 workers. In the Maritimes, 324 strikes occurred between 1901 and 1914. Except in the far west, the majority of the workers involved in these confrontations were skilled rather than unskilled. By 1914 approximately 155,000 Canadians belonged to organized labour unions, many of them affiliated with American internationals.

NATURAL RESOURCES

If Canada was to avoid eternal international balance-of-payment deficits (the plague of Third World countries in our own era) it obviously needed commodities to export. It found many of these in the natural resources sector. To a considerable extent Canada's resources were the old mainstays of the colonial staple economy, now produced under different guises. Resources not only earned money abroad, they encouraged manufacturing at home.

AGRICULTURE

As if on some master schedule, the Canadian wheat economy continued to expand without pause. Fields of operation moved from central Canada to Manitoba and slightly later to the Northwest Territories (which became the provinces of Saskatchewan and Alberta in 1905). Between 1870 and 1890 thousands of farmers, chiefly from Ontario, poured into the west. The number of acres of occupied land went from 2.5 million to over 6 million (1,011,750 to 2,428,200 ha) in the years 1881–91, while the acres of land under cultivation exploded from 279,000 to 1,429,000 (112,911 to 578,316 ha) in the same ten-year period. The opening of the CPR was critical for the production of western wheat. So too was the appearance of new wheat strains capable of maturation in the short prairie growing season.

Before the mid-1890s the typical prairie settler was an Ontario-born farmer who came west to make a new start. Despite the passage of the Dominion Land Act of 1872, which made a fair amount of homestead land available, most farmers preferred to purchase land from companies set up by the great corporate benefactors of government land grants, especially the railways. Farmers believed (with some legitimacy) that homestead land was less likely to acquire rail transportation than was land owned by the railway itself. Although homestead land was free to the male settler (women could not apply for homesteads), successful farming still required substantial capital investment. Conservative estimates of the costs of 'farm-making' ranged from a minimum of $300 (the annual wage for an unskilled labourer) to $1,000. Most farmers brought money with them from the sale of land back east. The western farmer was a market farmer. Although the family grew as much food as possible for personal consumption, the farmer's instinct was to increase constantly his acreage under production. Before the First World War, mechanization was limited mainly to harvesting. Animals (horses and oxen) did most of the ploughing and cultivation. Nevertheless, the individual farmer managed to cultivate considerable quantities of land, limited mainly by the size of his labour force. In 1898 Ontario-born A.J. Cotton (1857–1942) harvested a crop of over 17,000 bushels of top-grade wheat in Treherne, Manitoba.

Beginning in the 1890s an open and aggressive Canadian immigration policy, conducted by both the federal and provincial governments, brought new settlers to the prairies. Many came from the United States, which no longer had an unsettled frontier of its own. Others came from eastern Europe, where a long tradition of grain culture existed. The new immigrants moved onto the great dry-belt area of Saskatchewan and southern Alberta, where they initially experienced some very good luck with rain and moisture. By 1921 over 44 million acres (17,806,800 ha) of the prairies were under cultivation. According to one set of calculations, the wheat economy in 1901–11 contributed over 20 per cent of the growth in per capita income in Canada.

While wheat was the big prairie crop, other crops were possible. Before the arrival of farmers, much of southern Alberta and southwestern Saskatchewan was the domain of ranchers, who grazed their cattle on open range leased from the federal government. At the height of the cattle boom in 1898, Canadian ranchers exported 213,000 live head. Although ranchers insisted that much of the range land was unsuitable for farming because of water shortages, their obvious

A Ukrainian family harvesting wheat, 1918. NAC, PA-88504.

self-interest in an open range negated the force of much of their argument. Nevertheless, water was a major potential problem in much of the west.

MINES AND TIMBER

In 1890 Nova Scotia was the leading mining province in Canada, chiefly because of its rich coal resources. After that year, three factors hastened a great shift in Canadian mineral extraction. One was the development of new technologies to extract ore. Another was the increasing availability of railway transportation to remote areas. Most important of all, the international market created a new demand for metals that Canada had in abundance: copper, nickel, and silver. Almost overnight, Ontario and British Columbia became the leading mineral producers.

Although the most famous mining rush of the period was to the Yukon's Klondike district for gold, the Klondike was hardly typical of the mining industry. More representative were the mining towns that suddenly sprang up and equally rapidly closed down in the mountains of British Columbia and Alberta. Like most Canadian mines, these required considerable machinery and expertise to exploit, well beyond the resources of the individual miner. Well-capitalized corporations opened such mines, employing money and technology often imported from the United States. In Quebec, the most buoyant segment of the mineral industry between 1900 and 1920 was asbestos fibre, used chiefly in construction material consumed in the United States. The Canadian mining industry greatly benefited from the military requirements of the Great War.

In the forest industry, the decline through permanent depletion of the white pine forests of eastern Canada pushed the centre of activity to the west. British Columbia had millions of acres of Douglas fir and cedar. The province started harvesting in the coastal regions close to water, but soon pushed inland. Most of its production went to American markets. The remaining forests of eastern Canada proved valuable for their softwood. The pulp and paper industry expanded rapidly, driven by an insatiable American demand for inexpensive newsprint. By 1915 wood pulp and paper represented one-third of the value of Canadian exports, virtually equal to wheat and grain in the overseas market. Quebec produced nearly one-half of Canada's wood pulp and paper.

The resource sector produced its own version of labour militancy. The sector was difficult to organize by traditional means. In mines and lumber camps, the distinction between skilled and unskilled labout had little meaning. Nevertheless, worker alienation was often extreme. In British Columbia, unrest was particularly strong among miners, who worked for large absentee corporations under difficult conditions. In this kind of environment, syndicalists and radicals (such as the Wobblies or the Impossibilists) did very well. They preached the need for the destruction of capitalism and the organization of all workers into general unions.

URBAN AND RURAL CANADA

In 1881 Canada had a population of 4,325,000, of whom 3,349,000 lived outside urban centres. Forty years later, of the nation's 8,788,000 inhabitants, only 4,811,000 resided in non-urban areas, and 1,659,000 lived in cities with populations over 100,000. While the non-urban population had grown over these years from 3,349,000 to 4,811,000, the number of city dwellers had burgeoned from 974,000 to 3,977,000. Urban growth was obviously a major trend of the period 1880–1918. Canada developed some very large metropolitan centres, but their residents did not constitute the entire urban population. If 1,659,000 Canadians lived in cities of over 100,000 in 1921, another 2.2 million lived in smaller centres, with 1,058,000 in towns of 5,000 to 29,999 people and 765,000 in towns of 1,000 to 4,999. Canadian urban growth in this era produced all sorts of new problems for the nation. At the same time, urban development was not the entire story for these years. As the statistics well demonstrate, before 1921 more Canadians continued to reside in rural than in urban areas. Rural Canada, although its earlier dominance was gradually eroding away, was still very important to the national ethos. Moreover, the very sense of the gradual loss of traditional rural values was critical for the Canadian psyche.

THE CITY

As with most other aspects of Canadian development in this period, urban growth was not even across the regions. Maritime cities grew fairly sluggishly. None could establish regional dominance. Indeed, Halifax lost ground as central Canada siphoned off its financial institutions. In Quebec, Montreal continued its path to the status of the Dominion's premier city, with Quebec City and other towns lagging far behind. In Ontario, Toronto was plainly the 'Queen City', although a number of smaller cities (Hamilton, London, and Kingston) were vibrant. Ottawa inhabited a world of its own as the nation's capital, as it always would. The most spectacular urban growth rates were in the west, which in this era spawned two major cities, Winnipeg and Vancouver, and two contenders for such a rank, Edmonton and Calgary. While western settlement usually suggests farms and agriculture, urban development in the west was strong from the outset. Land speculation drove local pretensions, and many communities aspired to be regional entrepôts. In the prairie provinces the urban population grew from 103,000 to 606,000 between 1900 and 1916. City dwellers, who represented 25 per cent of the region's population in 1901, had increased to 35 per cent only ten years later. By 1921 in British Columbia, Vancouver (117,217) and Victoria (38,727) contained 25 per cent of the population of that Pacific province.

The larger cities of Canada most clearly exposed the social problems of the later Victorian and subsequent Edwardian eras. The greatest problem was poverty. Existing evidence suggests that up to half of the Canadian urban working class lived below, or at best around, the poverty line. Most working-class families were glad to supplement the father's income with the earnings of wife and children in menial occupations. Given the grinding conditions of their lives, it is not surprising that many sought refuge in alcohol. Unbalanced diets and malnutrition were only the start of the problems of the poor. Their housing was typically overcrowded, with poor sanitation and a lack of open yards and spaces. Homeownership was difficult, even for the middle classes, because mortgages were hard to obtain and were only of short duration, often no more than three or four years. Malnutrition and deplorable housing conditions combined to produce high overall death rates and high infant mortality rates in Canada's largest cities. The mortality differentials between the poor and the prosperous were substantial, ranging from 35.51 deaths per 1,000 in 1895 in one working-class ward in Montreal to less than thirteen per 1,000 'above the hill'. Infant mortality rates in Canadian cities were little different from those in places like Calcutta and Bombay. The children of the urban poor often got little schooling. Moreover, the poor resisted pressures for compulsory education.

If the city had social problems, it also made possible a rich and varied cultural life. Before 1918 cultural life maintained an amateur tradition of considerable vitality. The major development in Canadian urban culture in this era was not so much the appearance of first-rate artists as the creation of an institutional infrastructure that might eventually enable them to emerge. The city made possible the development of cultural institutions in the form of both organizations and buildings to house them. The construction of museums, for example, was characteristic of the age. The Art Museum of Toronto appeared in 1900, the Royal Ontario Museum in 1912 (it opened in 1914). Equally characteristic of the era was the formation of artistic organizations. The Canadian Art Club (1907) was organized in Toronto, although its founders had no idea how to achieve their goal of introducing new Canadian painting to the entire nation. Formal art and music schools were organized in most of the larger urban centres, offering regularized instruction to neophyte painters and musicians. Theatrical buildings became a measure of a city's status. As early as 1891 Vancouver had a 1,200-seat opera house. Toronto's Royal Alexandra Theatre (1906–7) seated 1,525, and Winnipeg's Walker Theatre (1907, recently renovated as a theatrical venue) seated 2,000 in splendid comfort. These buildings operated continuously, housing mainly professional touring companies and local amateurs. Indigenous professional theatre emerged first in Montreal. There were ten different professional companies at work in Montreal in the 1890s. In 1899 alone these companies gave 618 performances of 109 plays.

The extent of the growth of urban Canada between 1880 and 1919 was largely unanticipated. The large city cut against most of the dominant ideologies of the time, which were traditional and rural. The institutions of urban government were not well integrated into the overall Canadian political system. The British North America Act did not leave much room for the governance of cities that would have budgets and revenues as large as those of the provinces in which they were located. Urban government and urban politics operated outside the structures of Confederation, with their own agendas and distinct party labels. Most cities were slow to abandon property qualifications for voting. Local merchants and real estate promoters tended to dominate city councils, even in cities with a relatively democratic franchise. The ward system produced municipal politicians who curried favour with the electorate through corrupt practices ranging from the purchasing of votes to offers of 'jobs for the boys'.

No urban centre could expect to prosper in this era if it was not on a main-line railway. Contemporaries clearly recognized this reality. During the several outbursts of railway expansion—particularly between 1906 and 1915, when more than 14,000 new miles (22,530 km) of railway track were laid in Canada—efforts by aspiring communities to become depots and junction

A slum interior, October 1913. A mother, grandmother, and six children share one small space. Presumably the younger woman's husband was out at work—or looking for a job. City of Toronto Archives, DPW 32-243.

points were prodigious. Conversely, rumours of new railway construction were sufficient to create a village where none had existed previously. The extremes to which communities would go to publicize themselves in order to attract railways were occasionally ludicrous and often expensive. Agricultural fairs, as well as the presence of town bands and sports teams, publicized communities. A marching brass band and a baseball team were two of the best advertisements an 'up-and-at-'em' town could enjoy. 'Bonusing'—financial inducements for railways and business entrepreneurs alike—was a way of life in this period.

If urban growth relied upon railway networks, it operated in a context of fairly blatant and open land speculation. The attempted creation of every new city in western Canada began with a land boom. This stage of development usually ended with a collapse in land prices that required years of recovery. Many small businessmen in the west made a decent living selling out in one community just ahead of the bust, and moving to a new town site further down the rail line. The false fronts on western small-town stores were symbolic of the transitory nature of commitment. Speculation in land involved not merely businessmen—or the west. Almost all segments of local communities across Canada joined in real estate speculation whenever they could. Indeed, the attempt to turn a profit by investing in undeveloped land must surely be one of the most enduring features of Canadian life. Speculation was different from development. The former involved the holding of land for future profit, the latter the translation of land—often acquired at bargain prices—into immediate profit as sites for houses or factories.

TOWN AND SUBURB

In the larger urban centres land speculation and development were inseparable from the process of suburbanization. This trend combined with urban expansion away from the commercial core of most cities. There were three distinct motives for suburban expansion. Different types of suburbs were the result. The first motive dominated among the

HERBERT BROWN AMES ON POVERTY IN MONTREAL

In 1897 the Montreal businessman Herbert Brown Ames published a series of articles in the *Montreal Star* that subsequently appeared as a book. The articles were based on his careful survey of social conditions in part of the west side of Montreal. The district he had selected probably offered a fair sample of working-class residences in Montreal at the end of the nineteenth century.

It will be remembered that, according to our industrious census, the total number of poor families was reckoned at 888 in 'the city below the hill'. Half of this number were by the writer selected as material for a second and more searching investigation, with a view of more fully examining the characteristics, conditions and causes of our west end poverty. Four hundred and thirty-six families were sought for, and the first fact that was brought to the notice of the investigator was that 46 families, or 10 1/2 per cent of the above number, had left their former abodes, within the two months between the first and second canvass, drawing attention to one of the sad features of poverty's lot, viz., the constant necessity to move on because of inability to satisfy the claims of the landlord. If this ratio were maintained, and each month saw 5 per cent of the poor evicted, in a year not half these families could be found at the former addresses.

A second fact, made apparent by the special investigation, was that our west-end poverty was not the result of recent immigration. Quite the reverse from what would have been the case in New York or Chicago, hardly a dozen families were discovered that had not been residents of the city for at least three years. The vast majority were old residents who had lived in Montreal for the greater part of their lives. The presence of poverty, then, in the nether city is not chargeable to any considerable influx of foreign elements.

In the case of 323 families inquiries were made as to the causes, assigned by the people themselves, for their indigent condition. With 109 families, or 34 per cent the reply was 'irregularity of work'. The wage-earners were not without vocations but their employment was intermittent and often work ceased altogether for considerable periods. With 87 families or 28 per cent the answer was that the wage-earners had no work whatever, nor did there seem to be any immediate prospect of getting any. With 27 families, or 9 per cent, old age had unfitted and with a like number sickness had prevented the worker from earning the requisite support. Out of these 323 families, among the poorest of the poor, 62 per cent claimed to be able to better their condition were employment regular and abundant. That a certain percentage of the answers given did not state the real facts of the case is quite probable. Few are the families that will admit to a stranger that drink, crime or voluntary idleness is the cause of their misery, though in 7 per cent of the cases visited drunkenness was clearly at the bottom of the trouble. Still it is the belief of the investigator that the undeserving among the poor form a far smaller proportion than is generally imagined.

As to the composition of the family, out of 390 families, 8 were found wherein the head of the household was a widow, and 54 cases where the husband was too old or too ill to work, making in all 140 families, or 36 per cent of the whole, that might be called 'decapitated' family groups. In about two-thirds of the families, or in 64 per cent of the cases examined, there was an able-bodied man in the house, oftimes more than one, a man able to work and professing to be willing to do so. If these proportions may be taken as fairly indicating the average among the families of the poor, it is evident that at least one-third of them are in indigent circumstances through no fault of their own. . . .

SOURCE: Herbert Brown Ames, *The City below the Hill*, ed. Paul Rutherford (Toronto: University of Toronto Press, 1972), 74–6.

prospering business and professional classes, who moved to new residential suburbs to escape the noise, odours, and bustle of the central city. Horse droppings on busy city streets, for example, were a major problem before the Great War. Some of these suburbanites were attempting to separate themselves from the growing slums of the industrializing city. The architectural style most closely associated with the new suburban élites grew out of the English Arts and Crafts movement and became known as the English Domestic Revival. A second motive for suburban growth was the quest for lower land costs and lower taxes outside the central city. The result was the development of a number of industrial suburbs, such as Maisonneuve in Montreal, which flourished outside the city but were still within its orbit. The third motive was proximity to work. As industrial development moved into the cheaper outskirts, workers were forced to follow their jobs into often inadequate new housing. During this period, most large cities in Canada grew by a continuous process of absorbing outlying communities.

The genuine Canadian small town tended to fit one of two models. It was either a community serving a surrounding rural area, sometimes with a manufacturing plant or two, or a single-resource community, often remotely located, that had formed around a mine or mining/smelter operation. The resource town consisted almost exclusively of single males and a handful of women. There were precious few sources of entertainment other than booze and gambling. Many resource towns, though not all, were company towns. Such communities were both violent and restive, often centres of labour unrest.

The service community, on the other hand, was the centre of economic, social, and recreational life for its district. Before the advent of radio and television, the social life of small-town Canada bustled impressively. Organizations of all kinds proliferated and flourished. Most towns had a variety of lodges and an endless round of meetings, dances, and 'occasions'. The last ranged from concerts to plays to sermons by visiting evangelical preachers to lectures on temperance or exotic places. By the end of the Great War, most towns had a 'movie house' or a hall that exhibited motion pictures on a regular basis. Many small towns had exercised the local option permitted by liquor legislation and 'gone dry'. Small-town social relations were often strained, particularly between the middle classes and those who worked in the factories that almost every eastern small town possessed. In the west, class conflict often pitted farmers against hired hands or the crews of threshing contractors. The possibility of outbreaks of violence was never far away.

Even more serious were the gender constraints inherent in the small town structure. Masculinity dominated the life of the town, in terms both of family relationships and especially of extracurricular activity. Local sports were controlled by notions of manliness, and most athletic organizations catered only to men. Local fraternal organizations were equally masculine and exclusionist, although occasionally they had women's auxiliaries. One of the most important underlying tensions in many (although not all) small towns

THE TOWN DIRECTORY OF TREHERNE, MANITOBA, 1895

In 1907 Alan Ross, a local poet in Treherne, Manitoba, published a small volume of his verse. It included the following poem, the subject of which is self-explanatory.

Town Directory 1895

E. Hamilton's our high school master;
D. Hamilton puts on the plaster;
Revds. McClung, Fraser and George Fill
On Sundays do our pulpits fill;
T.J. Lamont's our town M.D.;
One blacksmith's name is Thos. Lee;
Rogers sells dry goods and coffees;
Alexander keeps post office;
D. Williams and J.K. McLennan
Sell dry goods, cod, haddock finnan,
Ben Englewain repairs the clocks;
Our miller's name is Jas A. Cox;
James Telford Reid's our legal light
One retired farmer's called John White;
'Tis G.A. Anderson that carried
The business on for Massey-Harris;
And S. L. Taylor sells the pills,
That sometimes cure and sometimes kill;
C.W. Barkwell is town baker;
Ed Roberts is the undertaker;
Tom Roberts helps his brother Ed.
Sell furniture and house the dead;
Joe Straube is town hardware man;
In athletics Paulin leads the van;
One livery's kept by the Parker Brothers;
And John Perrie keeps the other;
Jas. Stevenson keeps the 'Manitoba',
With parlor, dining-room, and lobby;
Fred Rocket keeps the 'Rocket House';
Our tailor's name is Harry House;
D. Harvie harness makes and collars
Watt Smith irons wagons, sleighs and rollers
And general blacksmith shop controls;
His carriage maker's William Bowles;
Andrew Ross supplies the butcher meat;
Malcolm McClarty shoes the feet;
H. Watson, Senior health inspector;
James McAdam's tax collector;
Claude Somerville's mill engineer;
John Coulter is mill charioteer;
James Emmond sues for delinquent debts,
And William Frame does serve the writs;
Robson deals in lumber, lime, and bricks . . . .

SOURCE: Alan Ross, *Poems* (Treherne: *The Treherne Times*, 1907), 18.

was between church-related and other voluntary organizations. The church organizations were dominated by women and often sought reform, including prohibition of alcohol and elimination of gambling. The masculine-dominated voluntary structure was often, by implication, the chief target of these reformers. The attentive and careful reader can find all these tensions exhibited in the novels of small-town life that dominated Canadian literature in these years.

RURAL CANADA

A number of major changes occurred in Canadian agriculture during the period from 1880 to 1914. The most obvious was the enormous expansion of farming in the prairie west, concentrating singlemindedly on grain cultivation. Elsewhere, the era saw a major shift in eastern Canada towards specialized farming. In central Canada, farmers moved into specialized high-quality consumer production, becoming increasingly dependent on off-farm processing, particularly of cheese, butter, and meat. By 1900 Ontario had over 1,200 cheese factories, which captured over half of the British market. Ontario cheese makers were renowned around the world. Quebec farmers had greater difficulty in making the change because of the marginality of much of their land. Specialty farming was very remunerative for those able to engage in it. The aristocrats of farming were the dairy farmers and the fruit farmers. Along with specialized farming came new technology, although the ubiquitous tractor did not replace the horse until after the Great War. More important were mechanical harvesters, centrifugal cream separators, and the introduction of refrigeration. Technology was essential to specialization. It was also capital-intensive. Not all farmers could make the shift. Those who could not often stagnated or failed absolutely. Between 1891 and 1921 the Maritime region lost 22,000 farms and 1,556,709 acres (630,000 ha) of farm land under cultivation. Unmodernized farms could not continue to support the entire family. By 1911 the Farmer's Advocate could refer to the 'perennial debates as to "Why the Boys Leave the Farm"'. While urban migration was one response, another was for farmers—and farm women—to move into the traditional resource industries of the nation. Males went to sea to fish or into the woods to cut timber. Females worked seasonally in factories, processing farm products or fish.

Contemporaries often blamed the growing rural exodus on the social and cultural attractions of the city. While it might thus be tempting to visualize rural Canada as a vast wasteland of isolated and unlettered country bumpkins, such a view would be most inaccurate. Isolation did exist, as did educational limitations. On the other hand, a relatively efficient and inexpensive postal service provided contact with the wider world. People read books and discussed them at clubs that met in local churches. Clergymen often talked about controversial books and topics from their pulpits. Many farm families received at least one daily newspaper through the mail—seldom on the day of publication, but usually only a day or two later. Canadian dailies in this era provided more substantial fare than today. International coverage was much fuller, and many papers saw themselves as 'papers of record', often reproducing verbatim accounts of court trials and important meetings. In the spring of 1919, for example, the *Winnipeg Tribune* carried a full stenographer's report of the debates at the labour convention in Calgary, which agreed to 'an Industrial Organization of all workers'. Most rural folk also relied heavily for their edification on farm journals such as the *Grain Growers' Guide* (1908–28) and more general magazines like the *Christian Guardian*, the voice of the Methodist Church; it was begun in 1829 by Egerton Ryerson and continued under that name until 1925. The wide range of letters to the editor included in most of these periodicals suggest both their circulation and their vitality.

If rural Canadians had access to considerable information, they were also surprisingly able to get together socially with each other. The

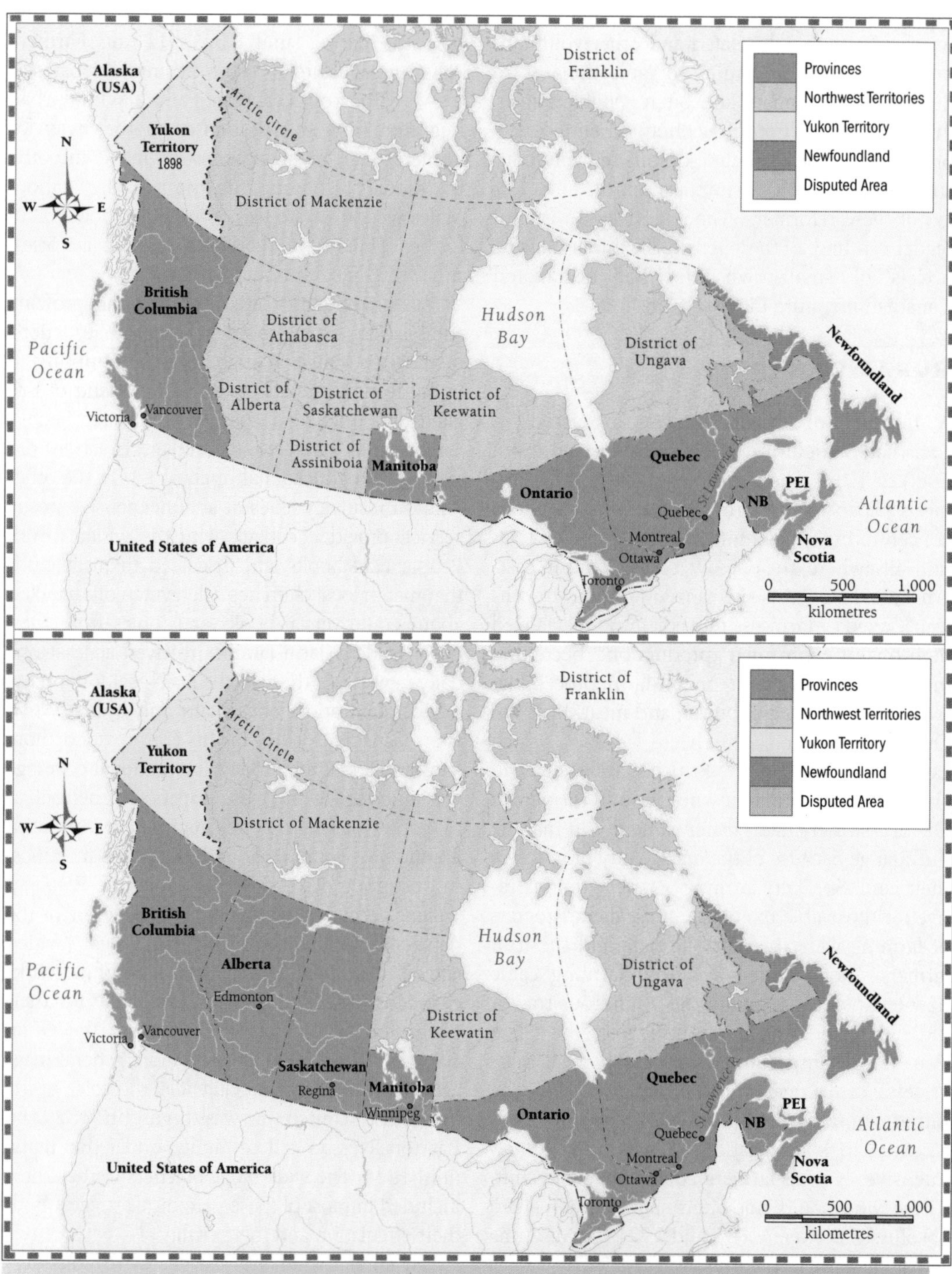

Canada in 1898 and 1905.

school and the church were two local institutions that served other functions besides providing formal education and worship services. School districts were usually the only sign of public organization in vast regions of rural Canada that were otherwise politically unorganized. The community jealously guarded its schoolhouse, which was from coast to coast typically of one room. The most common Quebec school in the 1913 census had one room, built at a cost of $1,200. Whether Protestant or Catholic, francophone or anglophone, rural Canadians took their religion seriously. Sermons provided topics for daily conversation. The activities of various auxiliary groups connected with any church, particularly the picnics and socials, were very popular. Winter did not shut down social life in rural areas, but permitted it to flower. The demands of the farm were much lighter in winter, while snow and ice provided a decent surface for horse-drawn sleighs and carrioles to travel about the countryside. 'A working day . . . was from about 4:30 a.m. to 11 o'clock at night,' reported one western farmer, 'but this was only in seeding and harvesting time. In the winter we used to really have fun' (quoted in Voisey 1988:158). A number of diaries and journals kept by rural Canadians in this period have recently appeared in print. They provide two revelations for the modern reader. The first is the sheer volume of social interchange, especially among the young, that actually occurred. The

'A BASKET SOCIAL IN P.E. ISLAND'

'Preserve me from "pie socials",' wrote Lucy Maud Montgomery in her journal on 4 April 1899. 'They are the abomination of desolation.' The following more positive view was expressed by 'Welland Strong' (presumably a nom de plume) in a 1901 issue of the *Prince Edward Island Magazine*. Whoever the author may have been, he or she was quite right in thinking that the social was not distinctive to the Island, but appeared everywhere in rural Canada.

A Basket Social in P.E. Island

by Welland Strong

Basket socials may not be a form of amusement peculiar to Prince Edward Island, but in all events, I have never seen a place where they attained to such prominence, among the various schemes for getting money, as in this province. . . .

Often it happens that in country villages a debt is to be paid by a congregation, either a balance due on their church or perhaps for a new organ. Instead of raising the necessary amount by private subscription, the people decide upon a basket social, and word is sent to everyone. Upon hearing this the young ladies all begin to prepare baskets containing ample lunch for two people. These they carry, carefully wrapped in many sheets of paper, to the hall on the night of the social, and hand over to the committee in charge. The baskets are sold by auction, and the purchaser of each must share its contents with the young lady who brought it. Of course every young men is anxious to get the basket prepared by his 'best girl': but as the names are not announced until after the baskets are sold, many mistakes are made, and the remarks sometimes uttered, by fond lovers who have paid a high price for the wrong one, look much better in print when expressed by a dash.

Let us try to imagine ourselves in a hall in almost any country settlement on the evening devoted to one of these popular meetings. . . . The committee, composed of elders of the church, were kept busy finding seats for the ladies; taking care of the baskets handed to them, and doing the many little things necessary at all such entertainments. Now, however, we see them placing a row of chairs on the platform, and pushing the organ into a more convenient position. Hardly had this been done when there enter from a side door a number of ladies and gentlemen, who proceed to occupy the chairs. This is the village choir, and during the past week they have been practicing pieces to be sung to-night. . . .

Cheers, whistles and stamping of feet greeted the choir, who arose and, to the accompaniment of a hard-breathing organ, sang 'Jingle Bells'. The first verse was sung amid perfect silence, but in the second the crowd caught the rhythm of the piece and kept time to it with their feet, especially in the chorus, when a string of sleigh bells was used to make the effect more realistic. A recitation, 'Curfew shall not ring to-night,' given by a young lady, followed the chorus, but as most of the audience knew the piece by heart, very little attention was paid, and the greater portion of the piece remained almost unheard. But amid the din the speaker's voice could be heard every now and then, and bravely she struggled through until, with the saving of the lover, the piece ended and the 'Amen corner' burst into thundrous applause. Then came a fine-looking soloist—tenor in the choir and local auctioneer. He began 'Ten thousand leaves are falling,' but having pitched the song in too high a key, his voice broke and he stopped, his failure being greeted by frantic howls and advice from one of the small boys to 'start her at five thousand.' The programme went on; chorus following reading, and solo, chorus, the last few numbers being rendered 'midst an almost deafening noise and shouts of 'Bring on the baskets.'

When it ended the choir moved to one side of the platform, the schoolmaster who was to act as secretary and treasurer took his place at the table, and the auctioneer stepped forward holding in his hand the first basket, now unwrapped and decorated in a most fantastic manner with flags, flowers and coloured tissue paper. . . . After all the baskets have been sold, the names of the purchasers and ladies are read off by the secretary, and the baskets opened by them. Usually besides various kinds of cake and pie, the basket contains glasses and a bottle of home-made wine; but in case this has been left out, and also for the benefit of the older people, the committee furnish plenty of tea. When the lunch has been disposed of, the men go to the nearest stables for their horses, which have been left there, while the young ladies gather their belongings, get muffled up ready for the drive home and, while waiting for their friends, sing a verse of 'God save the King.'

Sleigh after sleigh drives up to the door, the women and girls depart, and in a very few minutes no one remains in the hall save the members of the committee—counting over the money they have made and writing a report of the social to be published in the papers next day.

SOURCE: *The Island Magazine* 46 (Fall/Winter 1999), 7-12.

second is the extent to which Canadians of this era actively participated in their own entertainment rather than being amused as passive spectators by the activities of others. Canadians of both sexes and all ages routinely spent social evenings singing hymns and other songs. They created and performed their own skits and joined together in active games such as charades.

Rural life was not all bucolic pleasure, of course. The real reason for the rural exodus was not isolation but exploitation and lack of economic opportunity. The underside of life on the family farm was the exploitation of those who would not in the end inherit a substantial share in the property. The system was particularly hard on women, who usually did not share in the ownership of the farm and who seldom received remuneration for their labour. Western farmers especially were hostile to 'anachronistic' legal concepts such as dower rights. The homesteading system was generally unsympathetic to the rights of women to set up as independent farmers. For many women everywhere in Canada, the daily routine was even more continually demanding than it was for men. Women's responsibilities included not only the kitchen garden and the small livestock but care of the family itself. One consequence of the shift into specialized farming was that parts of the farm operation previously consigned to women that provided them with a small income ('egg money') were taken over by the males. Canadian rural society continued to be inherently patriarchal in its organization. Men owned the land and usually made the decisions, including when to uproot and resettle, often against the wishes of their wives. The figure of the rural patriarch as an intensely self-righteous, land-hungry, materialistic tyrant became a common motif in Canadian fiction of this and a slightly later period.

Despite the darker side, a vast majority of Canadians continued to hold rural values and to think of the nation largely in pastoral terms. Those who read Canadian poetry or looked at Canadian art found little but Canadian nature. Foreigners inevitably saw Canada as a completely undeveloped country and Canadians as an agricultural people. In the hands of the poets, Canadian nature was chiefly benign. Writers of prose sometimes depicted nature differently, often in terms of the victory of hardy settlers over the harsh landscape and climate. Many Canadian writers and painters of this period romanticized the farm and farming, none more so than Lucy Maud Montgomery. *Anne of Green Gables* summed up a major conflict of the era: the problem of reconciling the bucolic beauty and tranquillity of the rural landscape with the need to leave it in order to fulfil one's ambitions. For large numbers of Canadians of this era, growing up meant leaving the farm.

Another form of romanticization of rural life was the collection of its folklore and folk songs. Marius Barbeau (1883–1969) was the first great Canadian collector of folk traditions, beginning in 1911 when he was appointed an anthropologist at the Museum Branch of the Geological Survey of Canada (now the National Museum of Canada). There were thousands of publications, texts, and songs that Barbeau recorded and preserved in archives that document not only the folk traditions of rural Quebec but also those of the Aboriginal peoples in British Columbia. The folkways and songs that Barbeau and others collected were part of the traditional rural experience of Canada. They preserved almost nothing of urban origin. The collectors desperately gathered up dialects, riddles, tall tales, children's rhymes, all of which told more of the daily life of the people than most other historical evidence. Underlying the desperation was the fear that these traditions would disappear in the rapidly changing society of the period.

The dominance in Canada of the myth of agriculture carried over into the various efforts of the period to turn Aboriginal peoples into 'peaceable agricultural labourers'. Agrarian ideology had the advantage of both justifying the dispossession of the Native peoples of their hunting grounds and providing them with an alternate way of life. Before the Great War most Canadians regarded agriculture as 'the mainspring of national greatness' and farming as a way of life that uplifted one 'morally and emotionally' (Carter 1990:20). Scientists saw agriculture as a crucial step in the ladder of progress. They perceived other ways of using the land, such as mining or lumbering, as tainted and inferior. The government displaced Aboriginals by treaties, then removed them to reserves and encouraged them to farm. Exhortation was not the same as useful practical assistance. Native Canadians needed a good deal of help to shift from a nomadic hunt-

Lucy Maud Montgomery. Prince Edward Island Public Archives and Record office 3110-1.

ing/gathering existence to a settled agricultural one, and they did not consistently receive assistance. Government aid was sporadic, cheese-paring, and patronizing. After 1885 coercion replaced subsidization as the federal government's major weapon to impose agriculturalism on the reserves. Not surprisingly, the policy failed.

A final illustration of nature's appeal for Canadians came in the various back-to-nature movements. One form involved mounting crusades to preserve Canada's natural environment in the face of encroaching civilization. The fight for the conservation of Canadian wildlife involved the establishment of game reserves and legislation to curb indiscriminate hunting. The crusade's major victories came with the establishment of large numbers of national and provincial parks across Canada in the years before the Great War. Another expression of the back-to-nature movement was the summer cottage, which flourished among urbanites who could afford one by the early years of the twentieth century. Many refugees from the farm resolved their ambivalences through the summer cottage or summer travel, often into the wilderness. Thus alongside the burgeoning Canadian cities came the growth of summer cottages and resort hotels, located at lakeside or seaside, and frequently directly served by rail. Weekend train services poured middle-class Canadians by the thousands into the Laurentians of Quebec, the Muskoka, Algonquin Park, and Haliburton districts of Ontario, and from Winnipeg into the Lake of the Woods district. The Canadian fascination with the summer cottage had taken firm hold before the Great War.

While some Canadians settled temporarily into cottage or tourist hotel, others became fascinated with the recreational possibilities of wilderness travel. The waterways of Ontario and Quebec grew crowded with weekend canoeists enjoying a brief respite from the pressures of the city. Ernest Thompson Seton (1860–1946), who founded an organization called Woodcraft Indians in 1902, promoted a junior version of this outdoor activity. Some of the best publicists for the canoe and the wilderness were painters, especially those who eventually formed the Group of Seven in 1920. Its members, mainly English-born Torontonians making a living as commercial artists, had begun travelling north into the Georgian Bay and Algonquin wildernesses as early as 1911. This group captured the iconographic essence of wilderness Canada: a bleak and sombre but nonetheless curiously beautiful landscape of jack pines, rock outcroppings, and storm-driven lakes, totally uninhabited by people.

CULTURE

In the years 1870–1914, most Canadians continued to amuse themselves at home, often performing imported theatrical works. Outside the home, the amateur tradition remained strong. In most fields of artistic endeavour, Britain and the United States remained the dominant influences. Perhaps the outstanding achievements in Canadian cultural production in this period occurred in fiction. Three developments stand out. One was the creation of the Canadian social novel. A second was the rise of a major figure in Canadian humour to carry on the earlier tradition of Haliburton and McCulloch. The third development, related to the previous two, was the emergence of several Canadian authors as international bestsellers. Some of these authors were women. All the successful authors were at their best in writing about the values of rural and small town Canada at the end of the nineteenth century.

The best example of the social novel—also a novel of ideas—was *The Imperialist* by Sara Jeannette Duncan (1862–1912). Duncan had been born in Brantford and educated at the Toronto Normal School. She then became a pioneering female journalist, working for a long list of newspapers in the United States and Canada. In 1888 she and a female friend began a trip around the world, which she subsequently fictionalized. In 1904 she produced *The Imperialist*, a novel intended to describe the Imperial Question from the vantage point of the 'average Canadian of the average small town . . . whose views in the end [counted] for more than the opinions of the political leaders' (quoted in Klinck, 1965:316.) Duncan drew on her childhood experiences in Brantford to describe conditions in Elgin, a 'thriving manufacturing town, with a collegiate institute, eleven churches, two newspapers, and an asylum for the deaf and dumb, to say nothing of a fire department unsurpassed for organization and achievement in the Province of Ontario' (Duncan, 1968:25). The opening chapter began with an account of the celebrations in Elgin on 24 May, the Queen's Birthday. Duncan interwove the issue of imperialism with the social values of late Victorian Canada. For her protagonist, young politician Lorne Murchison, Canada's continuation as a British nation was of moral rather than strategic importance.

Duncan was perhaps the first Canadian writer to recognize the literary potential of small-town Canada, especially for satirical purposes, but she was not the greatest. Stephen Leacock (1869–1944) had been born in England, but grew up on a farm near Lake Simcoe. Educated at Upper Canada College, the University of Toronto, and the University of Chicago, Leacock published a successful college textbook, *Elements of Political Science,* in 1906. He produced his first volume of humorous sketches, *Literary Lapses,* in 1910, and two years later published *Sunshine Sketches of a Little Town*. This was an affectionate satirical look at life in Mariposa, a fictionalized version of Orillia, the nearest town to his boyhood home. Leacock perfectly captured the hypocrisy, materialism, and inflated notions of importance possessed by Mariposa's residents. He followed this triumph with a much more savage satire of a North American city, obviously the Montreal in which he lived and taught (at McGill University). The work was entitled *Arcadian Adventures with the Idle Rich* (1914). In this work, which he pretended to set somewhere in the United States, Leacock began the transference of his satire from Canada to North America. He moved on from these early works to produce a volume of humorous sketches virtually every year, increasingly set in an international milieu. His books were very popular in Britain and the United States. Many critics feel that Leacock's best work was his early Canadian satire, in which he scourged Canadian pretensions.

Duncan and Leacock both achieved international reputations as writers of fiction, and they were joined by several other Canadians in the years between 1900 and 1914. One was the Presbyterian clergyman Charles W. Gordon (1860–1937), who under the pseudonym 'Ralph Connor' was probably the best-selling writer in English between 1899 and the Great War. Born in Glengarry County, Canada West, and educated at the University of Toronto and Edinburgh University, Gordon became minister of a Presbyterian church in

Prof. Stephen B. Leacock, Montreal, 1914. II-202933 Notman Photographic Archives, McCord Museum of Canadian History, Montreal.

Winnipeg, where he lived for the remainder of his life. Ralph Connor's first three books, published between 1899 and 1902, sold over five million copies. One of these, *Glengarry School Days: A Story of Early Days in Glengarry* (1902) was probably the best book he ever wrote. Like Duncan and Leacock, Connor excelled at the evocation of small-town life and mores, drawing from his personal experiences as a boy. He was not a great writer but knew how to sustain a narrative and to frame a moral crisis. Some of his work—including novels in which clerical examples of muscular Christianity faced a variety of frontier challenges—obviously struck a respondent chord in an international audience. Connor's heroes triumphed over sin, anarchy, and unregenerate people by sheer force of character, Christian conviction, goodness, and even physical strength; they represented what his generation saw as the forces of civilization and progress. Fellow Presbyterian Nelly McClung (1873–1951) also had great success with similar material, even less artfully rendered, in books such as *Sowing Seeds in Danny* (1908). A much superior artist was Lucy Maud Montgomery (1874–1942), whose *Anne of Green Gables* also first appeared in 1908. Montgomery's books lovingly described rural life and presented some of the standard dilemmas faced by her readers, ranging from growing up to having to leave the farm.

IMPERIALISM, RACISM, AND REFORM

Contemporaries often characterized Canadian political life in this era in terms of its lack of ideology and its predilection for what the French observer André Siegfried called the 'question of collective or individual interests for the candidates to exploit to their own advantage' (Siegfried 1907:142). Lurking only just beneath the surface, however, were some serious and profound issues. First was the so-called Canadian question, which bore in various ways upon the very future of the new nation. It often appeared to be a debate between those who sought to keep Canada within the British empire and those who wanted it to assume full sovereignty. Into this discussion other matters merged subtly, including the 'race' question and the reform question. The former involved the future of French Canada within an evolving Anglo-American nation. The latter concerned the institution of political and social change through public policy. Debate and disagreement over the three loosely linked issues—imperialism, Anglo–French antagonisms, and reform—kept political Canada bubbling with scarcely suppressed excitement from the 1880s to the beginning of the Great War. Canada's involvement in the military conflict of Europe would bring those issues together, although it would not resolve them.

IMPERIALISM

The period from 1880 to 1914 saw a resurgence of imperial development around the world. The French, the Germans, even the Americans, took up what Rudolph Kipling called the 'White man's burden' in underdeveloped sectors of the world. About the same time, Great Britain began to shed its 'Little England' free trade sentiments. The world's shopkeeper discovered that substantial windfall profits came from exploiting the economies of Asia, Latin America, and Africa, especially the last. Canada first faced the implications of the resurgence of Britain's imperial pretensions in 1884 when the mother country asked it to contribute to an expedition to relieve General Charles Gordon, besieged by thousands of Muslim fundamentalists at Khartoum in the Egyptian Sudan. Sir John A. Macdonald's immediate response was negative, but he ultimately found it politic to allow Canadian civilian volunteers to assist the British army. By the end of the century Joseph Chamberlain at the Colonial Office was advocating that Britain's old settlement colonies be joined together in some political and economic union, the so-called Imperial Federation.

Encouraged by a new infusion of immigrants from Britain—nearly half a million between 1870 and 1896 and a million between 1896 and 1914—many anglophone Canadians began openly advocating Canada's active participation in the new British empire. Their sense of imperial destiny was not necessarily antinationalistic. They saw no inconsistency between the promotion of a sense of Canadian unity and a larger British empire. 'I am an Imperialist,' argued Stephen Leacock in 1907, 'because I will not be a Colonial.' Leacock sought 'something other than mere colonial stagnation, something sounder than independence, nobler than annexation, greater in purpose than a Little Canada' (quoted in Bumsted 1969, II: 78). Such pan-Britannic nationalism came to express itself concretely in demands for Imperial Federation. It was most prevalent in the province of Ontario.

Unfortunately for the imperialists, not all Canadians agreed with their arguments. Several strands of anti-imperial sentiment had emerged by the turn of the century. One strand, most closely identified with the political journalist Goldwin Smith (1823–1910), insisted that the geography of North America worked against Canadian national-

ON IMPERIALISM AND NATIONALISM

One of the opponents of Canadian imperialism was Henri Bourassa (1868-1952). In 1912 he explained his position in an address to the Canadian Club.

We speak of 'our Empire'. Have you ever considered how little we Canadians count in that Empire, the most wonderful fabric of human organization that has ever existed. Of course, as far as land is concerned, and water, and rocks, and mines, and forests, we occupy a large portion of the Empire. As to population we are only seven millions out of over four hundred millions. As to imperial powers, we have none. The people of the British Kingdom, forty millions in number, possess as their sole property the rest of that Empire. Suppose you except Canada with her seven millions, Australia with her four millions and a half, New Zealand with one million, and South Africa, with a little over one million of white people: apart from those semi-free states, the whole empire of India, the hundreds of

Crown colonies, and those immense protectorates in Africa or Asia, no more belong to us than they belong to the Emperor of Germany, or to the President of the French Republic. We have no more to say as regards the government, the legislation, the administration, the revenue and the expenditure, and the defence of that territory, comprising four-fifths of the total population of the Empire, than have the coolies of India or the Zulus of Matabeleland! I am not saying this in disparagement of the system; I am simply putting our position as it is. At the present time, the seven millions of people in Canada have less voice, in law and in fact, in the ruling of that Empire, than one single sweeper in the streets of Liverpool, or one cab-driver on Fleet Street in London; he at least has one vote to give for or against the administration of that Empire, but we, the seven million Canadians, have no vote and no say whatever.

When I hear splendid phrases, magnificent orations, sounding sentences, about that 'Empire of ours', I am forcibly reminded of the pretension of a good fellow whom I had hired to look after the furnace of a building of which I had the management in Montreal. Every year, when the time came to purchase the coal for the winter, he used to exclaim, with a deep sense of his responsibilities: 'How dear it costs us to keep up our building!' Our right of ownership, of tutelage, of legislation, in the British Empire is exactly what the right of partnership of that stoker was in that building.

. . . [A]t the sixth Imperial Conference, the delegates from Australia, representing a courageous, intelligent, progressive British community, with a high sea trade amounting in imports and exports to $650,000,000 a year, asked the representatives of the British Government why the British authorities, without even thinking of asking the opinion of Canada, of Australia, of South Africa, and of New Zealand, had concluded with the great maritime powers the international treaty known as the Declaration of London, which may affect beneficially or otherwise the trade of the world in future naval wars. They enquired also if it would be possible to have at least one representative from the self-governing British colonies on the Board of Arbitration, eventually to be constituted, under the terms of that treaty, to adjudicate upon the seizures of trade and ships in times of war. Sir Edward Grey, undoubtedly one of the ablest men in British public life to-day, showed there, I think, his great tact and his extraordinary command of words and of diplomatic means. But, when all the courteous terms and all the frills were taken off, his answer amounted to this: On that board the negro President of Hayti could sit, the negro President of Liberia could sit, but the Prime Minister of Canada or of Australia could not sit, simply because Hayti and Liberia are nations, whilst Canada or Australia are not nations. He explained that the colonies were not consulted because they exist only through Great Britain, and that the moment Great Britain accepted that treaty it applied to us as to her. Undoubtedly true and another evidence, I think, to show that in the 'imperial partnership', in the enjoyment of that imperial citizenship of which we hear so much, there still remains a *slight* difference between the British citizen in England, Scotland and Ireland, and the British citizen of Canada: one is a member of a sovereign community, the other is the inhabitant of a subjected colony.

SOURCE: H. Bourassa, *Canadian Club Addresses 1912* (Toronto: Warwick Bros & Rutter, 1912): 78–80.

ism. Smith advocated Canadian absorption into the United States. Fear of this development led many Canadians to oppose a new reciprocity agreement with the United States in 1911. Another strand, led by John S. Ewart (1849–1933) insisted on Canada's assumption of full sovereignty. Ewart argued that 'Colony implies inferiority—inferiority in culture, inferiority in wealth, inferiority in government, inferiority in foreign relations, inferiority and subordination' (Ewart 1908: 6). Yet another perspective was enunciated by Henri Bourassa (1868–1912), who advocated a fully articulated bicultural Canadian nationalism. He wrote, 'My native land is all of Canada, a federation of separate races and autonomous provinces. The nation I wish to see grow up is the Canadian nation, made up of French Canadians and English Canadians' (quoted in Monière 1981: 190). The Bourassa version of nationalism was considerably larger than the still prevalent traditional nationalism of French Canada. As the newspaper *La Vérité* put it in 1904, 'what we want to see flourish is French-Canadian patriotism; our people are the French-Canadian people; we will not say that our homeland is limited to the Province of Quebec, but it is French Canada. . . .'

The most common confrontations over the role of Canada within the empire occurred in the context of imperial defence. At Queen Victoria's Jubilee celebration in June 1897, Laurier had fended off a regularization of colonial contributions to the British military. The question arose again in July 1899 when the mother country requested Canadian troops for the forthcoming war in South Africa against the Boers. When the shooting began on 11 October 1899, the popular press of English Canada responded with enthusiasm to the idea of an official Canadian contingent. But newspapers in French Canada opposed involvement. As *La Presse* editorialized, 'We French Canadians belong to one country, Canada: Canada is for us the whole world, but the English Canadians have two countries, one here and one across the sea.' The government compromised by sending volunteers, nearly 5,000 before the conflict was over. The defence issue emerged again in 1909, this time over naval policy. Under imperial pressure, Canada finally agreed to produce a naval unit of five cruisers and six destroyers. Both sides attacked Laurier's compromise Naval Service Bill of January 1910. The anglophone Tories insisted it did not provide enough assistance for the British, while in Quebec nationalists and Conservatives joined forces to fight for its repeal.

THE AMERICANIZATION OF CANADA, 1907

In 1907 the American journalist Samuel E. Moffatt published a book entitled *The Americanization of Canada*, which extended Goldwin Smith's earlier arguments about the extent of Canadian integration into the United States.

In 1850, 147,711 persons of Canadian birth were living south of the border—about one-sixteenth of the number of people living in the British possessions at the same time. In 1860 the Canadian-born population of the United States had increased to 249,970, a gain of 76 per cent, while the general population of the Union was increasing at the rate of 35.6 per cent, and that of the British provinces at about 33.6. In 1870 there were 493,464 Canadians in the United States, an increase of 97.4 per cent for the decade against 22.6 per cent for that of the population of the Republic as a whole, and 16.2 per cent for that of the British colonies, now united in the Dominion of Canada. . . . While the population of the Republic was a little more than tripling in fifty years, and that of Canada was being multiplied by less than two and a half, the little Canada south of the boundary line saw the number of its inhabitants multiplied by eight. Of all the living persons of Canadian birth in 1900, more than one-fifth were settled in the United States. But if the statement stopped there it would be incomplete. In addition to the native Canadians in the United States in 1900, there were 527,301 persons of American birth but with both parents Canadian. There were also 425,617 with Canadian fathers and American mothers, and 344,470 with Canadian mothers and American fathers. Thus there were in all 2,480,613 persons in the United States of at least half Canadian blood, which is more than half the number of similar stock in Canada. . . .

In density of Canadian population, ignoring all other elements, Massachusetts stands first, exceeding any province of Canada, and Rhode Island second. The relative rank of the various Provinces and States previously named on this basis is:

Canadian population per square mile

1	Massachusetts	64.2
2	Rhode Island	64.0
3	Prince Edward Island	45.36
4	Nova Scotia	20.6
5	New Brunswick	11.2
6	Connecticut	10.9
7	New Hampshire	10.8
8	Ontario	8.4
9	Michigan	7.1
10	Vermont	6.8 . . .

Classified in the same way, the principal Canadian cities in 1900–1 were:

1	Montreal	267,730
2	Toronto	208,040
3	Boston	84,336
4	Quebec	66, 231
5	Chicago	64,615
6	Ottawa	49,718
7	Detroit	44,592
8	New York	40,400 . . .

SOURCE: Samuel E. Moffatt, *The Americanization of Canada*, with an Introduction by Allan Smith (Toronto: University of Toronto Press, 1972), 10-13.

RACISM

Racialist thinking was at its height during this period. Part of the 'race question' in Canada was not about 'race' at all but about the conflict between French and English Canada. While there was no racial barrier between French and English, contemporaries accepted race-based arguments and analyses as 'scientific'. Many imperialists regarded the historical progress of the United States, Great Britain, and Canada as evidence of the special genius of the 'Anglo-Saxon race'. The French were acceptable partners because they too were a northern people. Out of the scientific theories of Charles Darwin came the conviction that inheritance was the key to

'A FRIENDLY REPLY TO MR BOURASSA'

In April 1904, the editor of *La Vérité*, J.-P. Tardivel, opened a debate with Henri Bourassa by announcing in an anonymous article the nature of his disagreement with Bourassa's Nationalist League. Bourassa sought development of 'a Canadian feeling that is not concerned with questions of origin, language, or religion', wrote Tardivel, while *La Vérité* believed in French-Canadian nationalism. In the course of the subsequent exchange, the following piece appeared in the newspaper.

Those who cherish the idea of creating a great, unified Canada, homogeneous, stretching from Atlantic to Pacific, and taking in all the British possessions in North America, are also proposing an aim that has attractive aspects. However, this plan frightens and terrifies us, because, as we see all too clearly, it will come about only to the detriment of the French-Canadian nationality.

Mr. Bourassa distrusts colonial ties because the imperialists make use of them to build up the empire they dream of. We agree with this distrust, but does he agree with the distrust we feel for the interprovincial ties that serve as instruments in the hands of those who dream of creating a great, unified Canada by slowly strangling the autonomy of the French-Canadian nationality? We dare not answer this question, but we do feel the need of clearly defining our position and feelings . . . .

We are neither revolutionaries nor dreamers. We do not want to resort to violence in any way to break these interprovincial ties; the danger that we see for our nationality in the existence of these ties is very real; we wish these ties had never been formed, yet we know they exist and we must take them into account in all our dealings.

But it is only to prevent them from harming us French Canadians that we must take them into account. And we must know how to proclaim at the top of our voices: may these interprovincial ties perish rather than allow the French-Canadian nationality to be injured by them! . . .

This plan [Bourassa's plan for a 'duality of the races']—or should we say this dream—could have perhaps been put into effect if we had confined ourselves to the original plan of federation; that is, if we had been content to unite the four provinces of Quebec, Ontario, New Brunswick, and Nova Scotia under one federal government. Such a confederation would have had a certain geographical symmetry and sufficient uniformity of general material interests to keep itself going. Moreover, the two races would have been sufficiently equal in power to preserve the desired equilibrium and keep the governmental machine in good working order, based on 'the duality of the races and the special traditions this duality imposes'.

But from the beginning, megalomania and the mania for constant growth have laid hold of our politicians, and they introduced Prince Edward Island into the confederation—which could have been tolerated if really necessary—and then British Columbia and all the Northwest.

This was obviously too much; and wishing to erect a colossal edifice, we sinned against the laws of stability.

SOURCE: *La Vérité*, 15 May 1904, as quoted and translated in Ramsay Cook, ed., *French-Canadian Nationalism: An Anthology* (Toronto: Macmillan, 1969), 150–1.

evolution. Races were formed by natural selection, exhibiting quite unequal characteristics. In almost everyone's hierarchy, the present Canadian population was at the progressive top of the racial scale. Newcomers who could not or would not assimilate would inevitably lower the Canadian 'standard of civilization'.

Canadians saw the new immigration after 1896 as particularly troubling. Even that secular saint J.S. Woodsworth associated criminality with the newcomers. Many feared the potential degeneracy of the 'great northern race' through commingling with lesser stocks. Others concentrated on the campaigns for social purity, mixing restrictions on the consumption of alcoholic beverages with hostility to prostitution, venereal disease, and sexual exploitation. The first serious efforts at large-scale immigration restriction, designed mainly to keep out the 'degenerates', began in the early years of the century. Campaigns for social purity, immigration restriction, and exclusion of Asians all came out of the same stock of assumptions about heredity and environment that informed many reform movements of the period. The reformers often emphasized social and moral aspects, directing their efforts chiefly against newcomers.

REFORM

The reform movement of this period was rich and varied in its interests. It ranged from the women's suffrage movement to various efforts at social and humanitarian change. Mainstream Canadian reform movements had some features in common, however. Their leaders were members of the middle and professional classes who shared assumptions of the age about regeneration and social purity. Those of Protestant backgrounds tended to predominate, particularly in temperance/prohibition, public health, education, and women's suffrage. Women, because of their general nurturing role in society, played a major role in most reform movements. These women were often less concerned with restructuring gender roles in society than with the need for inculcating middle-class virtues or with helping the poor. French-Canadian women were significantly underrepresented in most national reform movements, partly because of the political isolation of Quebec, and partly because the ideology of the traditional society greatly limited the place of women in that province.

The suffrage movement did emphasize the gender question. It addressed women's political powerlessness by attempting to win for them the right to vote. The movement was chiefly an urban one, dominated by well-educated women who saw political power as necessary to bring about other legislative change. The suffragist leaders were almost exclusively Canadian or British-born and belonged to the main-line Protestant churches. Well over half of these women were gainfully employed, mostly in journalism and writing. The suffragists gradually lost contact with working-class women, who were suspicious of the class biases in both the suffrage and reform movements. They also failed to gain the support of farm women because they did not understand rural issues, especially the concern over rural depopulation. Many rural women became involved in their own organizations designed to deal with their own problems, such as the Women's Institutes. Adelaide Hoodless (1857–1910) founded the first Institute at Stoney Creek, Ontario in 1897. (In Henry James Morgan's biographical compilation *The Canadian Men and Women of the Time*, 2nd ed., 1912, she is listed under the entry for her husband John, who was an obscure furniture manufacturer in Hamilton.) Women's Institutes promoted appreciation of rural living, as well as encouraging better education for all women for motherhood and home-making. In 1919 the Federated Women's Institutes of Canada organized with its motto 'For Home and Country.'

One female reform organization, the Woman's Christian Temperance Union, had both rural and urban memberships. Founded in 1874 in Owen Sound, Ontario, the WCTU claimed 10,000 members by 1900, and had an influence

CARRIE DAVIES

Carrie Davies was born in Bedfordshire in 1897. She immigrated to Toronto in 1913 to join her married sister, and soon found work as a servant in the house of Charles Massey. She started to repay her relations for the cost of her passage and sent part of her pay packet home to her mother. In early February 1915, she appeared in Toronto Police Court, charged with shooting and killing her master. According to her story, Massey had become drunk and had made unseemly advances to Davies, pinning her to a bed and asking her to wear his wife's undergarments. She had brooded over this attack, waited for her employer to come home from work, and summarily shot him on the doorstep. 'I really shot him in self defence,' she told police, 'he took advantage of me yesterday and I thought he was going to do the same today.' A fundraising campaign by the Toronto Local Council of Women (the TLCW, whose members had attended the police court) provided funds for Davies' defence. The TLCW hoped to portray the case as a women's issue. A number of working girls also contributed to Davies' defence. At the same time, the Bedfordshire Fraternal Association (BFA), an organization of emigrants from Davies' home county, also raised funds and provided a lawyer. The BFA saw the case more as a matter of British patriotism in the midst of the Great War than of master–servant sexual abuse .

In the hands of defence lawyer Hartley Dewart, Davies became a symbol of the female innocence that British soldiers were fighting to defend against the barbarian Germans. Witnesses testified that she was a virgin and that she was concerned for her virtue. Her lawyer presented her as guarding her virtue from 'a fate she felt would be worse than death'. She was easily acquitted, and a large crowd of spectators approved. Davies' case was only one of a number of sensational court cases of the time in which female defendants claimed to have defended themselves against the unwanted sexual advances of men. In these cases, public sympathy could be enlisted on behalf of the woman much more easily than in ordinary cases of rape and violence, because there was no male defendant.

far beyond that number. Despite its name, the WCTU wanted prohibition, soon seeing the elimination of alcoholic beverages as a panacea for many of the ills currently besetting Canadian society, such as crime, the abuse of women and children, political corruption, and general immorality. The WCTU was only one of several members of the Dominion Alliance for the Total Suppression of the Liquor Traffic. Like most Canadian reform movements, prohibition required state intervention to be effective, and this eventually led some of its supporters to women's suffrage. Laurier held a national referendum on prohibition in 1898. Although its supporters won a narrow victory, the prime minister refused to implement national legislation because only 20 per cent of the total electorate had supported the principle. The prohibitionists turned to the provinces, succeeding in getting legislation passed in Prince Edward Island in 1900 and in Nova Scotia in 1910. The local option was even more effective, since it involved

CLARA BRETT MARTIN

The pioneering woman in the Canadian legal profession was Clara Brett Martin (1874–1923), who graduated with high honours in mathematics from Trinity College, Toronto, in 1890. In 1891 she petitioned the Law Society of Upper Canada to be registered as a student. The petition was denied, and she was advised to 'remove to the United States', where more than twenty states admitted women to the bar. Instead of leaving the country, Martin found an Ontario legislator willing to introduce a bill into the provincial legislature that would explicitly define the word 'person' in the Law Society's statutes as including females. This initiative was supported by Dr Emily Stowe, leader of the Dominion Woman's Enfranchisement Association, who gained the approval of Premier Oliver Mowat for the new legislation. By the time it was passed in 1892, the legislation was emasculated so that women could only become solicitors (not barristers), and then only at the discretion of the law society.

The Law Society subsequently again refused admission to Martin, and Oliver Mowat himself attended the next Law Society Convocation to move her admission. The Law Society agreed by the narrowest of margins, and Clara Martin became a student-at-law, accepted as an articling student by one of the most prestigious law firms in Toronto. Martin met much disapproval from within her law firm and was forced to change firms in 1893. She was also harassed in the lecture halls of Osgoode Hall, and missed as many lectures as she possibly could. She eventually completed her degree and easily passed the bar examinations. Martin also pressed for revision of the legislation that allowed women to act only as solicitors, not barristers. She won this battle too, and then had to face the Law Society again. A final controversy came over the dress code for female barristers, when women were required to wear their gowns over a black dress. Martin was finally admitted as a barrister and solicitor on 2 February 1897, the first woman in the British Empire entered into the legal profession. She practised for most of her legal career in her own firm in Toronto.

local communities where prohibitionist sentiment could be strong. Prohibitionism exemplified both the best and the worst features of reform. It had little Catholic or urban working-class support. Moreover, it tended to clothe its single-minded arguments with intense moral fervour, often of the social purity variety.

Humanitarian reform, usually of urban abuses, often focused on the human victims of disastrous industrial social conditions. One of the main spearheads of such reform was the Social Gospel. Beginning in the Methodist Church and expanding to all Protestant denominations in Canada, the Social Gospel saw Christ as a social reformer and the institution of the Kingdom of God on earth as its (and his) mission. The growth of city missions and church settlement houses led to the establishment of the Social Services Council of Canada in 1912. The most prominent Social Gospeller was James Shaver Woodsworth (1874–1942). Another branch of humanitarian reform involved various professionals who became concerned with social problems through their professional practices. Thus doctors, for example, were active in promoting a public health system and in recommending ways of improving public health care. Among the medical professional's public health recommendations was compulsory medical inspection of schoolchildren.

Schools and members of the teaching profession were also in the front lines of humanitarian reform. In this period educators pushed not only for improved schooling but for the schools to assume much of the burden of social services for the young by acting *in loco parentis* for the children of slum and ghetto dwellers. The pressure for compulsory school attendance legislation, extended on a province-by-province basis across the nation by 1914, was partly reformist in nature. Regular school attendance would provide a more suitable environment for children than roaming the streets or working in factories. The children might learn skills that would lift them out of their poverty, and (in the case of immigrants) would become assimilated to the values of Canadian society. Educators clearly believed that using schools for reform purposes was in the best interests of Canadian society. It was also in their own best interest. Compulsory education opened more employment and introduced the educator as social expert, a professional who knew more about what was important for children than parents, particularly the parents of the disadvantaged. Compulsory education, medical examinations, school nurses, lunch programs, all were part of a new form of social engineering that would only increase in emphasis over the century.

In the course of time, many of the private agencies of reform became conscripted as quasi-public ones under provincial legislation. They served as arms of the state in the intermediate period before the establishment of permanent government bureaucracies. Thus private child welfare programs became officially responsible for abandoned, abused, and delinquent children. Despite this trend towards a public approach, the framework remained that of individual morality. The humanitarian reformers commonly linked vice, crime, and poverty. Even those who focused on poverty tended to attribute it to almost every other cause than the failure of the economic system to distribute wealth equitably. The concept of a basic minimum standard of living as the right of all members of society was slow to develop in Canada. Attacks on poverty in this period retained a certain class overtone, with a 'superior' class helping an 'inferior' one.

Another whole category of reformers sought structural alteration within the Canadian system. Their model was often sound business practice, for the leaders of this movement were usually successful businessmen. They sought the elimination of wasteful graft and corruption through political reform, the creation of publicly operated (and profitable) utilities to reduce unnecessary taxation, and the introduction of public planning. They tended to focus on the big city, although they spilled over in various directions. These reforms, which in the United States were associated with the Progressive movement, all found allies within associated middle-class and professional groups. The City Beautiful Movement, for example, received much of its support from an expanding community of professional architects, who combined an urge to plan the city as a whole with aesthetic considerations of coherence, visual variety, and civic grandeur. Like Americans, many Canadians saw cities as the culmination of civilization, and many grand plans made their appearance on paper. Cities settled for a few monumental new buildings, such as the imposing legislative structures completed in many provinces before the war. Political reform of municipal government concentrated on 'throwing the rascals out', combined with structural changes to reduce the damage they could do when they were in. The changes often included the replacement of elective councils with more professional government by commission. Businessmen reformers also fought fierce battles over the question of the ownership of util-

J.L. MacDonald's class in School District No. 3, Glenelg, Ontario, 1910. Fred W. Kelsey/NAC, C-15490.

ities. While the utilities barons complained of the attack on private enterprise, the corporate reformers countered by arguing that utilities were intrinsic monopolies that should be operated in the public interest.

Much of the impulse behind reform of all sorts came from fear of class warfare and moral degeneration. The reformers did for the poor rather than with the poor. The result was a vast increase in the public concerns of the state, and the beginning of the growth of a public bureaucracy to deal with social matters. As with many other aspects of Canadian life, the Great War would have a profound impact on reform.

THE GREAT WAR

The entrance of Canada into the First World War marked a triumph of sorts for Canadian imperialism. Canada did not make its own declaration of war, but simply joined the British war effort. Before it ended, the war would inflict extremely heavy Canadian casualties: 60,661 killed in action and 172,000 wounded out of some 620,000 Canadians in uniform drawn from a population of only 8 million. The war gradually isolated French Canada and made possible sweeping national reforms on several fronts. Reform had always implied an interventionist state, and wartime conditions encouraged the Canadian government's intrusion into many new areas of life and work. The government's expenditures were enormous, but it managed to find the money to keep going, mainly through extensive borrowing. One of the new developments was a business profits tax, retroactive to the beginning of the war, introduced in 1916. Another was an income tax, first levied in 1917. Yet another was the nationalization of the railways. The war also accelerated and distorted virtually every economic development that Canada had experienced during the previous forty years.

Canadians entered the war with no idea of its ultimate length, intensity, or futile savagery. The initial enthusiasm of English-speaking Canadians assumed a short and swift defeat of Germany and its allies. By 1917 support for the war effort emphasized the extent of the sacrifices already made. Canada's military contribution was substantial. Nevertheless, Canadians who fought in Europe were almost exclusively volunteers. Serving as the shock troops of the British empire, Canadians achieved an enviable reputation for bravery and fierceness. Their commanders continually placed them in the most difficult situations, and they performed well. The list of battles at which they fought heroically (and at heavy cost) was a long one, beginning at Ypres in 1915 and continuing through to the Belgian town of Mons, where fighting ended for the Canadians at 11 a.m. on 11 November 1918.

Life in the trenches—which was the main battle experience of most Canadian soldiers in World War One—was a nightmare, so hard to describe that most returning veterans did not really try. Loved ones at home seldom heard accounts of the trench experience, either in letters from the front or after the war. The social world of the trenches was a bizarre, surrealistic experience like no other to be found anywhere in the world. It is true that troops were rotated in and out of the front lines, but almost all experienced the danger and discomfort of life in the trenches at some point. Artillery shelling was constant, and reserves in the secondary and tertiary lines of fortifications were if anything shelled more heavily by large guns than those in the front lines; artillery crews always fired at longer-range targets for fear of hitting their own men. Periods of rotation were not standardized, and during times of crisis the stay in the front line could seem a lifetime. Actual attacks and offensives were relatively rare, but life in the trenches was extremely wearing; men faced not only the shelling and continual risk of sniper fire but difficulties in sleeping, bad food, and the ubiquitous mud, in which many men drowned. The worst thing about the mud was having to move through it. Most Canadian soldiers carried more than sixty pounds (27 kg) of equipment, and a mud-soaked greatcoat could weigh another fifty pounds (23 kg).

While in the front trenches, soldiers had to be constantly on the alert. They were regularly employed on 'fatigues', moving rations, stores, and wounded men, and repairing the trenches. Sleep deprivation was common. Soldiers suffered from the heat in summer and the cold in winter, and from rain virtually year-round. Corpses lay everywhere in the trenches and outside them, attracting rats and lice in great numbers. One Canadian remembered, 'Huge rats. So big they would eat a wounded man if he couldn't defend himself' (quoted in Ellis 1975: 54.) The trenches also stank of chloride of lime (a disinfectant), creosol (for the flies), human excrement and human sweat, and the putrefaction of decomposing bodies. Most soldiers were conscious not only of the stench but of the noise, especially the sounds of various sorts of artillery fire that were part of the continual bombardment in the trenches, particularly during offensives. Some could distinguish the various weapons by the noises they made. Dr Andrew Macphail, who served at the front with the 7th Canadian Field Ambulance, commented in his diary:

> I amuse myself finding words to describe the sounds made by the various classes of guns. The 18 pounders thud, thud. The 4.7s bark like an infinite dachshund. The howitzers

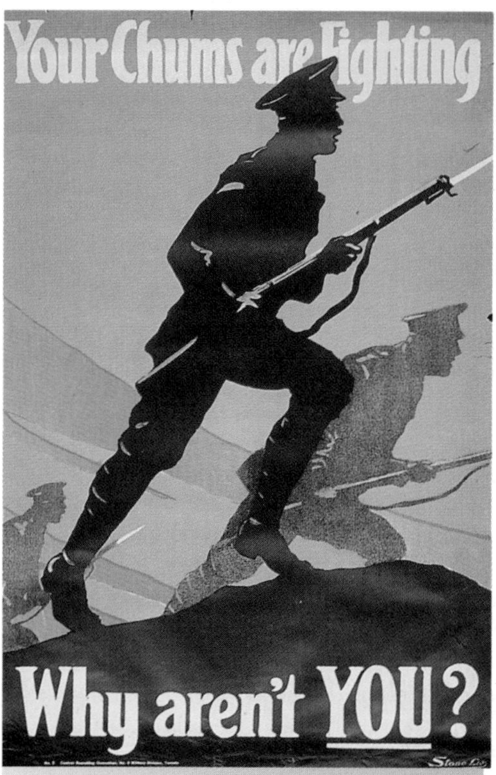
Your Chums are Fighting
Why aren't YOU?

A recruitment poster, lithograph, 1914-18. NAC, C-147822

> smash. The machine-guns rat-tat like the wood-pecker or the knocker of a door. A single rifle snaps like a dry twig when it is broken. Rapid rifle fire has a desolating sound; it is as if a load of small stones was being dumped from a Scotch cart. A large shell sounds exactly like a railway train; and shrapnel bursts as if boiler-plate were being torn into fragments, or as if the sky were made of sheet-iron, and had been riven by a thunderbolt. The whistle of the passing rifle bullet is unmistakable (Macphail 1915).

Many thought the worst things about the guns were the vibrations and the 'solid ceiling of sound'. By 1918 soldiers were also exposed to aerial attacks and bombardments. The Great War produced a new form of nervous illness, which came to be called 'shell shock', but which was really a combination of various assaults on the human nervous system.

Given the conditions under which the men operated, it becomes easier to understand how they could, from time to time, be led 'over the top' in open mass assaults or in raids in small parties—either way to risk death. Sleep-deprived and in a constant state of shock, most troops who actually engaged in battle were numb to virtually everything going on around them. They fought in a zombie-like state, and those who managed to return were totally exhausted. High command never really understood what the war was like in the trenches. The generals never appreciated that defensive firepower from a dug-in enemy meant that most attacks were nothing but human carnage. Field officers believed in the mystical value of intestinal fortitude. In April 1915, a Canadian regiment at Ypres withstood one of the first poison gas attacks, using for protection nothing but handkerchiefs soaked in urine. After beating back the enemy at great human cost and with other units retreating all around them, the regiment's colonel, supported by those remaining of his junior officers, volunteered to hold the line. He telephoned divisional headquarters and reported modestly, 'The 90th Rifles can hold their bit.' And they did. The casualties in this one unit in this one battle ran at 20 officers and 550 men killed, wounded, missing, or gassed—out of a total complement of 900.

While dispatches spoke reassuringly of the value of the assaults and the heroism, the soldiers knew perfectly well that their sacrifices were achieving very little. Canadian casualties, like those of other settlement colonies, tended to run considerably higher than those of the armies of the European allies. Whether the colonials had less experience as soldiers, or were placed in the most dangerous places, or simply fought more savagely, is not entirely clear. On one horrible day in 1916 at Ypres, 684 Newfoundlanders were trapped by barbed wire and mowed down by German machine guns; three hundred and ten died. While it was

The Newfoundland Regiment, D Company, near St John's, 1915. On 1 July 1916 the Newfoundlanders would see their first action in France. Of the 801 who fought that day at Beaumont-Hamel, in the first engagement of the battle of the Somme, more than 700 were killed, wounded, or reported missing. Provincial Archives of Newfoundland and Labrador, E 22-45.

possible to be invalided back to Britain ('Blighty') or even Canada with a serious enough wound (often called 'a blighty'), most of the Canadian soldiers sent to Europe either died on the battlefield or remained on the lines until the Armistice.

Despite these sacrifices, the Canadian government had to fight hard for a voice in imperial war policy. It also worked hard to maintain separate Canadian unit and command structures. The arguments for autonomy—and the manpower necessary to sustain them—dragged the government ever deeper into the quagmire. By the time of Vimy in April 1917, Canada could no longer recruit new volunteers to replace the mounting casualties. The government saw conscription as the only solution. Conscription was a policy intensely opposed by many French Canadians. From the standpoint of Anglo-Canadians, French Canada had not borne its fair share of the burden of war. English Canada argued that less than 5 per cent of the Canadian volunteers had come from French Canada. On the other hand, French Canadians came to feel increasingly under attack by English Canada. As a symbol of their position they focused on the plight of francophones in Ontario, where in 1915 Regulation 17 had seemingly imposed unilingualism on the elementary school system. Virtually all French-Canadian members of Parliament opposed the Military Service Act, which became law in August 1917. In its wake, and with a federal election coming, a Union government was formed out of the Conservatives and those Anglo members of the

☐ A Canadian battalion going 'over the top', October 1916. NAC PA-648.

Liberal party who had broken with Laurier over his opposition to conscription.

French Canada was not alone in becoming isolated by the war. Members of Canada's other ethnic minorities, many of them originating in parts of Germany and the Austro-Hungarian empire, found themselves under attack. The government became increasingly repressive as the war continued. It interned 'aliens' by Order-in-Council and suppressed much of the foreign-language press. The Wartime Elections Act of September 1917 ruthlessly disenfranchised Canadians of enemy origin. Organized labour found itself shackled. The government introduced compulsory arbitration into all war industries in 1916. In the crisis year of 1917, the government announced its intention to outlaw all strikes and lockouts.

The Union government was simultaneously bipartisan and sectional. It was able to implement several national reforms favoured by its Anglo-Canadian supporters. Many provinces had allowed women the vote earlier in the war. The Wartime Elections Act in 1917 granted the federal electoral franchise to women with close relatives in the war. In 1918 all women got the vote federally. Prohibition also triumphed nationally in 1918, not only to keep the soldiers pure and to ensure that the country to which they returned would be a better place to live but also to prevent waste and inefficiency. Previous arguments about infringing personal liberty lost their cogency during wartime.

Canadian industry—at least in central Canada and industrial Nova Scotia—benefited directly from the war. By March 1915 over 200 firms had converted to munitions manufacture. Later in 1915 the government set up the Imperial Munitions Board, chaired by businessman Joseph Flavelle (1858–1939). Canadian munitions production increased dramatically, raising the export of iron and steel products from $68.5 million in 1915 to $441.1 million only two years later. The Canadian munitions industry employed 200,000 workers in 673 factories. By 1917 the Imperial Munitions Board alone had an annual budget three times that of the federal government in 1914. In the latter years of the war nearly 40 per cent of Canadian manufacturing products found export markets. The high point came in 1918 when Canadian manufacturing exports reached $636 million, and total exports peaked at $1,540,000.

As for Canadian agriculture, it could not produce enough in the short run. From 1914 to 1919 in Canada as a whole, agricultural acreage under cultivation doubled. Wheat prices trebled, and western farmers expanded the size and number of their farms. The federal government created a national Wheat Board in 1917 to facilitate marketing. The number of prairie farms actually increased by 28 per cent between 1911 and 1921. Although the sons of Canadian farmers could gain exemption from conscription, by the time the draft was introduced in 1917 there were few young men left on the farms. Rural Canada, especially in the west, had outdone the remainder of the country in volunteer enlistment. The result was an increase in labour costs, which forced farmers to buy more agricultural equipment. Increased production also pushed up the price of land. Farmers therefore increased production by borrowing money at high rates of interest. Farm debt increased substantially. High prices also encouraged farmers to move cultivation onto marginal land while abandoning most of the tested techniques of soil and moisture conservation hitherto practised. The result of all this expansion would be an inevitable disaster when the price of grain and other crops ultimately fell on the international market.

CONCLUSION

The Great War had a profound impact on Canada in almost all aspects of life. Its rhetorical side was one of present sacrifice for future benefits. This war-to-end-all-wars would make the world safe for democracy. An era of full social justice would follow the great victory. That the Canadian government had ignored democratic civil liberties in fighting the war was an irony that escaped most contemporaries. The war's conclusion amounted to a triumph for Protestant Anglo-Canada, with little thought given to the tomorrows that would follow the coming of peace. A nation that had drawn heavily on its resources was really not ready to deal with the negative legacies of its efforts.

HOW HISTORY HAS CHANGED

THE GREAT WAR

As one might have expected, the traditional view of the period surrounding the First World War—which focused on European military troop movements and the political divisions that resulted from them, particularly the Conscription Crisis of 1917—has in recent years been replaced by a much broader view of the war and of the nation at war.

The military history of the war has been expanded in several senses. First, it has become clear that not all Canadians who served did so in the

Canadian Expeditionary Force (CEF). Many were in other branches: the navy, the air force, and the medical service, to name but the most prominent. Second, historians have concentrated on the experiences of CEF soldiers in the trenches, in effect writing a social history of trench warfare (which has had no equivalent in other wars) during the Great War. Finally, there has been an attempt at revisionism in terms of the reputations of the icons and heroes of the war. The person perhaps most affected here has been Billy Bishop, around whom a considerable controversy developed in the 1980s. This began with an iconoclastic television program aired on CBC in 1984 that charged Bishop with greatly exaggerating his wartime accomplishments. The outcome of this controversy was, at the very least, a downward revision of the number of Bishop's aerial victories, as well as some recognition of the difficulties surrounding the creation of heroes for home consumption.

The history of the war on the homefront has also been expanded substantially. Historians have realized that more was going on politically than the struggle between English Canada and French Canada, especially with respect to the treatment of ethnic minorities and the activities of labour leaders. A whole literature has emerged on the passage of the War Measures Act and the curtailment of civil liberties that resulted. A number of studies have explored the implications of war for social reform, women's issues (including suffrage), and women themselves. An increased appreciation of the strengths and weaknesses of the single-minded pursuit of war by national governments has also developed. This new assessment has been particularly evident in the economic analysis of western agriculture, but it has extended to other areas as well.

SHORT BIBLIOGRAPHY

Berger, Carl. *The Sense of Power: Studies in the Ideas of Canadian Imperialism, 1867–1914*. Toronto, 1970. The pioneer study of these ideas in Canada, and still easily the best.

Bacchi, Carole. *Liberation Deferred? The Ideas of the English-Canadian Suffragists, 1877–1918*. Toronto, 1983. An analysis of English-Canadian suffragism, emphasizing the distinction between maternal and radical feminism.

Bliss, J.M. *A Living Profit: Studies in the Social History of Canadian Business, 1883–1911*. Toronto, 1974. A collection of stimulating essays on Canadian business in a critical period.

Bradbury, Bettina. *Working Families: Age, Gender, and Daily Survival in Industrializing Montreal*. Toronto, 1993. A recent study on the effect of industrialization on the family and its strategies.

Carbert, Louise. *Agrarian Feminism: The Politics of Ontario Farm Women*. Toronto, 1995. The first full-length analysis of what farm women were up to before 1914.

Carter, Sarah. *Lost Harvests: Prairie Indian Reserve Farmers and Government Policy*. Montreal and Kingston, 1997. A fascinating account of federal policy towards the First Nations, focusing on the attempt to turn Aboriginals into farmers.

Christie, Nancy. *Engendering the State: Family, Work, and Welfare in Canada*. Toronto, 2000. A recent and controversial work that locates the origins of the Canadian welfare state in the quest for stability for the family.

Copp, Terry. *The Anatomy of Poverty: The Condition of the Working Class in Montreal 1897–1929*. Toronto, 1974. An early study of the urban working class in Montreal, probably still the best analysis available.

Courville, Serge, and Normand Séguin. *Rural Life in Nineteenth-century Quebec*. Ottawa, 1989. A synthesis of a good deal of secondary literature, which emphasizes how similar rural French Canada was to English Canada.

English, John. *The Decline of Politics: The Conservatives and the Party System, 1901–20*. Toronto, 1977. The best study of politics before the Great War.

Heron, Craig. *Working in Steel: The Early Years in Canada, 1883–1935*. Toronto, 1988. A brilliant account of the origins of steelmaking in Canada, especially strong on labour issues.

Linteau, Paul-André. *The Promoters' City: Building the Industrial Town of Maisonneuve, 1883–1918*. Toronto, 1985. A wonderful study of the creation of an industrial suburb in French Canada.

McCormack, A.R. *Reformers, Rebels, and Revolutionaries: The Western Canadian Radical Movement, 1899–1919*. Toronto, 1977. A work that resurrects and brings to life a collection of radicals previously neglected in the traditional literature.

McDonald, R.J. *Making Vancouver: Class, Status, and Social Boundaries, 1863–1913*. Vancouver, 1996. Urban social history that takes advantage of all the latest conceptualizations.

Miller, Carman. *Painting the Map Red: Canada and the South African War, 1899–1902*. Montreal, 1993. The best study of Canada and the Boer War.

Morton, Desmond. *When Your Number's Up: The Canadian Soldier in the First World War*. Toronto, 1993. A social history of the Canadian soldier.

Sager, Eric, with Gerald Panting. *Maritime Capital: The Shipping Industry in Atlantic Canada, 1820–1914*. Montreal, 1990. A study, based on quantitative data, of an important industry.

Valverde, Mariana. *The Age of Light, Soap, and Water: Moral Reform in English Canada, 1885–1925*. Toronto, 1991. One of the few overall syntheses of the reform movement, focusing particularly on its moral dimensions.

Voisey, Paul. *Vulcan: The Making of a Prairie Community*. Toronto, 1988. Probably the best historical community study ever executed in Canada.

Walden, Keith. *Becoming Modern in Toronto: The Industrial Exhibition and the Shaping of a Late Victorian Culture* (Toronto, 1997). A recent work in cultural studies, deconstructing the Toronto Industrial Exhibition.

STUDY QUESTIONS

1. What role did the patronage system play in Canadian political parties in the years before the Great War?
2. How did the industrialization of the period 1885-1914 differ from that of the 1850s and 1860s?
3. Compare the major problems of urban and rural life in Canada in the early years of the twentieth century.
4. What does the poem 'Town Directory' tell us about Treherne, Manitoba, in 1895?
5. Discuss the relationship between the small town and the development of Canadian fiction, 1890-1914.
6. What were the linkages between imperialism, racism, and reform before the Great War?
7. Imagine you are a soldier serving in the trenches of the Great War. Explain why you would find trench warfare difficult to describe to someone back home.

CHAPTER EIGHT

☐ Deferring Expectations, 1919–1945

■ Once the Great War had ended, Canadians did their best to put the conflict behind them. Many hoped for the emergence of a more just society. Stephen Leacock well expressed the ambivalence of the postwar period in *The Unsolved Riddle of Social Justice* (1919). Recognizing that industrial society did not normally employ its full potential, Leacock could only hope that the destructive energy of war could be harnessed for peacetime reform. The unsolved riddle was simply stated: 'With all our wealth, we are still poor.' Every child, Leacock insisted, should have 'adequate food, clothing, education and an opportunity in life'. Unemployment should become a 'social crime' (Bowker 1973: 74–80). Leacock did not offer specific solutions. Such a collective transformation would not be easy to accomplish. There were too many unresolved economic, constitutional, and social problems. The development of Canada over the next quarter-century demonstrated that at least in peacetime, Canadians still had great trouble coming to terms with the paradox Leacock had identified in 1919. During the Great Depression especially, the state seemed impotent to improve conditions. The politicians blamed the Constitution. Beginning in 1939, however, Canada would again demonstrate its capacity for waging total war within the constraints of the British North America Act.

Returning to 'Normalcy'

During demobilization Canada experienced one of the most devastating epidemics of modern times, the Spanish flu outbreak of 1918–19. The situation was so desperate in November 1918 that the government actually attempted, without success, to postpone public celebration of the Armistice for fear of spreading infection. Canadian deaths from the flu ultimately ran to 50,000—only some 10,000 thousand fewer than the number of Canadians who had died in battle. Fatalities had shifted from the trenches to the home front.

Yet another form of infectious epidemic made its appearance in 1919 with the great 'Red Scare'. The Bolshevik Revolution of 1917–18 in Russia provided the Canadian government and businessmen with an example of what might happen if popular unrest got out of hand. The Canadian authorities were quite ready to believe that large segments of Canadian society had been infiltrated by radical agitators, mostly of foreign origin. Political paranoia was as catching as the flu. Both the government and the business community became almost hysterical over the possibility that the revolution was nigh. The immediate focus of their concern was the Winnipeg General Strike of June 1919, but it had been preceded by the organization of the One Big Union, formed in Calgary in February amidst considerable anti-capitalistic rhetoric. As usual, the Canadian government responded to anything smacking of popular uprising with repression.

Most of the conditions and issues that initially produced labour unrest in Winnipeg in the spring of 1919 were traditional ones exacerbated

TIMELINE

1919
'Red Scare' begins. Government suppresses Winnipeg General Strike. First Congress of the League of Indians meets in Sault Ste Marie. *Canadian Bookman* is founded.

1920
Progressive Party is formed. First issues of *Canadian Forum, Canadian Historical Review* and *The Dalhousie Review* appear. The Group of Seven holds its first exhibition of paintings.

1921
In a federal election, the Progressive Party wins sixty-four seats. William Lyon Mackenzie King's Liberals form the government. The Maritime Rights Movement is organized.

1923
Famous Players' Canadian Corporation takes over Allen Theatres.

1924
William Aberhart begins the Prophetic Bible Institute broadcasts over Calgary's CFCN.

1925
United Church of Canada is formed. Pacific Coast Hockey League folds.

1926
Governor-General Byng refuses Prime Minister King a dissolution for a new election; a constitutional crisis ensues.

1929
Stock market collapses. Aird Commission report on public broadcasting favours nationalization of radio.

1930
Great Depression begins. R.B. Bennett's Conservatives are elected to power in Ottawa.

1931
Canadian government arrests and imprisons eight leaders of the Communist Party.

1932
Co-operative Commonwealth Federation is founded in Calgary. Bennett government forms the Canadian Radio Broadcasting Commission.

1933
Depression sees huge unemployment rolls. Regina Manifesto is adopted by the CCF. Maurice Duplessis becomes leader of the Conservative party of Quebec. T. Dufferin Pattullo wins election in British Columbia.

1935
R.B. Bennett announces a 'New Deal' for Canada, but is defeated by W.L.M. King in the election. Social Credit under William Aberhart sweeps to power in Alberta. Duplessis forms the Union Nationale. The On-to-Ottawa Trek is suppressed at Regina.

1936
Canadian Broadcasting Corporation is formed.

1937
General Motors strike in Oshawa. Royal Commission on Dominion–Provincial Relations is appointed. Lord Tweedsmuir creates the Governor-General's awards.

1939
Canada declares war on Germany. British Commonwealth Air Training Plan is founded.

1940
Royal Commission on Dominion–Provincial Relations recommends restructuring of public finances.

1941
Emily Carr wins Governor-General's award for *Klee Wyck*. Hong Kong surrenders to Japan. Pearl Harbor attacked.

1942
Dieppe raid sees 2,700 Canadians killed or captured. National plebiscite held to release government from non-conscription pledge.

1943	1944
Marsh report on social security is tabled in the House of Commons.	Family Allowances Act and National Housing Act are passed.

by the war: recognition of union rights to organize, higher wages, better working conditions. A walk-out by workers in the city's metal trades and building industries was quickly joined by other malcontents (as many as 50,000) in a general sympathy strike. On 15 May the strikers voted to close down the city's services. Much of the rhetoric of the strike sounded extremely radical. Some labour leaders hoped to use the general strike as a weapon to bring capitalism to its knees. Many demobilized servicemen supported the strikers. Worried businessmen saw the general strike as a breakdown of public authority. Workers in other cities, such as Toronto and Vancouver, responded with declarations of support and threats of their own strikes. The

The Winnipeg General Strike, 21 June 1919. Provincial Archives of Manitoba N2771, Foote Collection 1705.

Canadian government, represented locally by acting Minister of Justice Arthur Meighen (1874–1960), responded decisively. He supplemented the army with local militia, the Royal North-West Mounted Police, and 1,800 special constables. The Canadian Naturalization Act was hastily amended in early June 1919 to allow for the instant deportation of any foreign-born radicals who advocated revolution or who belonged to 'any organization entertaining or teaching disbelief in or opposition to organized government' (quoted in Avery 1986: 222).

Meighen effectively broke the strike on 17 June when he ordered the arrest of ten strike leaders on charges of sedition. On the 21st—'Black Saturday'—a public demonstration of strikers and returned soldiers, marching towards the Winnipeg city hall, was met by a charge of Mounties on horseback. The result was a violent mêlée that injured many, killed two strikers, and led to the arrest of a number of 'foreign rioters'. Black Saturday happened despite the best efforts of the strike leaders to prevent the demonstration from going forward. The Strike Committee subsequently agreed to call off the strike if a royal commission investigated it and its underlying causes. The royal commission, called by the province of Manitoba, found that much of the

HELEN JURY ARMSTRONG

Helen Armstrong (1875-1947) was born in Toronto and moved to Winnipeg from New York with her labour-leader husband George in 1905. She shared with her husband a firm belief in socialism and labour radicalism, and developed a considerable reputation as a feminist radical in Winnipeg during the Great War. She opposed the detention of 'aliens' and the introduction of conscription from numerous public platforms. In 1918 she was elected president of the Hotel and House Workers' Union in Winnipeg, and in February 1919 she resigned as president of the Women's Labour League when it supported the provincial Minimum Wage Board in recommendations that she felt were not in the best interests of female workers. Despite her break with the Women's Labour League, she ran the kitchen maintained by the League during the Winnipeg General Strike. It fed several hundred strikers every day. By this time she had acquired her nickname of 'Ma' Armstrong, and she would be subsequently dubbed by eastern newspapers 'the Wild Woman of the West'.

During the strike Armstrong was arrested on several occasions for 'disorderly conduct', usually the result of public demonstrations and agitations, often in support of female strikers. When her husband was arrested in June 1919 by the federal government for seditious libel, she became active in various campaigns to free him from arrest and, later, imprisonment. After George's incarceration in Stony Mountain Penetentiary, Helen organized concerts of children singing radical songs outside the prison. She ran unsuccessfully for the Winnipeg City Council in 1923, and subsequently departed Canada for Chicago with her husband. She died in California. Virtually forgotten for many years, she has recently been the subject of a major documentary film, *The Notorious Mrs. Armstrong* (2001).

labour unrest in Winnipeg was justified and that the strike's principal goal was to effect the introduction of collective bargaining. On the other hand, the Manitoba Court of Queen's Bench convicted most of the arrested leaders (who were either British- or Canadian-born) on charges of sedition. The Department of Immigration held deportation hearings for the 'foreigners' in camera. The use of the civil arm to suppress radicalism, long a part of the Canadian tradition, was given a new meaning in postwar Winnipeg. Perhaps most significantly, the strike and its handling by the government demonstrated the fragility of the postwar readjustment. The next decade would further emphasize the problems.

REGIONAL PROTEST IN THE 1920S

The decade of the 1920s is usually associated with prosperity, but in truth the period faced great economic difficulties. The boom did not begin until 1924 and it was quite limited in its influence. The depression of 1920–3 had seen world prices for resource products fall abruptly, while costs fell much more gradually. Prosperity finally came from substantial growth in new housing construction and a great wave of consumer spending, both understandable after the war and subsequent depression. There was a major expansion of consumer credit facilities to finance the new spending. An advertising industry quickly developed to promote consumerism. Speculative activities—in real estate, in the stock market, and in commodity futures—all flourished. So did gambling. However, much of the boom was at best internal, at worst artificial. International markets, except in the United States, were very soft. The traditional resource sectors of the economy had suffered most from the worldwide fall in prices, although they recovered somewhat in the latter years of the decade. Only Ontario's economy really prospered, chiefly on the strength of the manufacture of the motor car, both for domestic consumption and for export into a British empire protecting itself against the Americans. The economy of the Maritime provinces continued to decline precipitously, since both the power revolution and the new industrialization bypassed them while foreign markets (especially for fish) continued to decline.

Despite the government's brutal suppression of the Winnipeg General Strike, industrial unrest remained high through 1925. The One Big Union, a radical and militant industrial union, flourished briefly in western Canada. In 1921 labour representatives sat in seven of nine provincial legislatures. In the election of that year, more than thirty labour candidates contested federal constituencies, although only four were actually elected. Labour unrest after Winnipeg was most prevalent in the geographical extremes of the country. There were a number of notable strikes in Cape Breton, Alberta, and British Columbia. In the coalfields, 22,000 miners were on strike in August 1922. Several unions were broken in some of the most bitter labour violence that Canada had ever seen. Tactics in the mining communities made Winnipeg seem like a Sunday school picnic. A number of movements, mainly regionally based, sprang up to protest inequalities in the national system. Their collective inability to effect much change—though they tried a variety of approaches—was, and is, instructive.

Certainly nobody felt harder done by after the Great War than the farmer. The movement of farm protest reached its height in the 1921 election, before the final wheat market collapse and the spread of drought conditions. Farmers in Anglo-Canada disliked inflation and had two specific economic grievances beyond the wheat price collapse of 1920. First, the wartime wheat marketing system had been abandoned by the government in 1919. Second, the government had failed to introduce serious tariff reform to lower the costs of farming. Behind these complaints was a long-standing farmer conviction that the political system operated to the advantage of profiteering central Canadian capitalists.

The 'dust bowl': the prairies in the 1930s. Agriculture Canada, Research Branch, Research Station, Lethbridge.

Farmer discontent was national in scope, although western farmers were the most alienated. The new Progressive Party, formed in 1920, won sixty-four seats in the 1921 federal election in six provinces: thirty-seven on the prairies, twenty-four in Ontario, one in New Brunswick, and two in British Columbia. Joining fifty Conservatives and 117 Liberals, the Progressives broke the established two-party tradition.

Though they were entitled to become the official opposition, the Progressives were badly divided. Former Liberals wanted free trade, while the farm protesters sought more radical reform. The farm wing, led by Alberta's Henry Wise Wood (1860–1941), wanted to scrap the existing party system. It sought instead to focus on farmer grievances. The only actions the two wings could agree upon were negative. The Progressives would not become the official opposition, and they would not join in coalition with the Liberals, now led by William Lyon Mackenzie King (1874–1950). As a result, the inexperienced farmer MPs were unable to accomplish anything substantial in Ottawa when economic conditions in western Canada worsened. The King government provided token programs to gain the support of moderate Progressives. Meanwhile, drought and the worldwide collapse of wheat prices beginning in 1921 produced a widespread inability to meet mortgage payments. Much of the land in the dry-belt region reverted to the state for unpaid taxes. Its inhabitants went either to the cities or, in many cases, back to the United States. Surviving farmers became too disheartened to support a party

COAL MINING IN CAPE BRETON

In 1990 Earle Peach wrote a memoir of what he called his 'childhood', which included an account of his first days at Number 22 Colliery, Birch Grove. He began working in the mines at the age of 17.

Mother had filled another lunch can. At five-thirty in the morning I slung it over my shoulder and tramped with a few others over the familiar path along the washer drain, past the old wash plant, through the woods to Morrison Lake, and along the lake to No. 22 Colliery. In the wash house Newfoundlanders, Frenchmen, Poles, Hungarians, MacDonalds, MacRaes, and Smiths, bleary-eyed and sleepy, flailed a writhing mass of limbs in all directions as they wrestled on their pit clothes. Bearlike torsos, dirty backs (many miners washed only their faces), clear backs, bristly backs incredibly muscular, small retracted penises, huge flopping penises—obscene, good natured kidding in a dozen dialects—these were the men who worked in the coal mine, and I was to become one of them. . . .

When a week or so had passed, it no longer seemed strange to walk down out of the brilliant sunlight, out of the fresh air, into total darkness that took five or ten minutes before one's eyes adjusted to the reduced light of one's headlamp and one's nose accepted the fetid, mouldy air of decay common to a mine. Air from a huge compressor on the surface was driven down a carefully constructed air course, circulated slowly through all the work areas, and returned up the main haulage way, ensuring that no significant accumulation of deadly gasses could occur. Yet in most places you were unaware of any body change. When you were working, sweat streamed from your body, but when you sat down for five minutes, you were shivering. Add to this the fact that you could seldom stand up without stooping except where the 'roof' had been 'brushed'; the coal seam was five feet thick, but in the air course, the chief haulage areas, an extra foot of shale was taken down chiefly to ensure that it would not fall down and block traffic or slow air circulation. This left a roof of solid stone generally considered safe. As coal seams went, the Gowrie seam was of generous thickness; the harbour seam on which Glace Bay collieries nos. 11 and 24 operated was only three and a half feet thick and required a good deal more stooping. . . .

At No. 22 Colliery the coal seam emerged to the surface, and . . . the main slope had been driven down the seam. At one-thousand-foot intervals, landings or levels were broken off east and west from the slope; the term 'level' is a relative one, for convenient operation preferred a slight slope in the level. At similar intervals along the level, 'headways' were driven up and 'deeps' driven down the slope of the seam, each conforming to the twenty degree angle. This might be more easily visualized by picturing a level as a road built horizontally across the mid-slope of a mountain; roads going up the mountain from it are headways, those leading down from it are deeps. At one-hundred-foot intervals up the headways and down the deeps, 'rooms' were broken off, assigned numbers, and turned over to a pair of miners known at that time as 'butties'; these did the actual mining. The average headway or deep could employ thirty pairs of miners paid by the ton for the coal they mined. A miner at the 'face' could earn fifteen to twenty-five dollars per day, which in 1926 was a lot of money, considerably more than the mine manager earned. Within their room a pair of miners were the lords of creation, and God help anyone or anything that prevented them from 'getting their coal out'. This was free enterprise, indeed.

SOURCE: Earle Peach, *Memoirs of a Cape Breton Childhood* (Halifax: Nimbus, 1990), 112–13.

that had accomplished little in Ottawa, and the Progressives quickly disappeared.

A similar fate befell the major eastern expression of protest, the Maritime Rights Movement. Maritimers had difficulty joining western farmers in a common cause. The easterners sought not free trade but increased protectionism, as well as lower railway freight rates. The region was acutely conscious of its increasing impotency in Confederation, as its population base continued to decline proportionally to central Canada and the west. By the end of 1921, regional discontent found expression in the Maritime Rights Movement, which combined an insistence on equitable freight rates with a series of particular provincial demands. The result was a widespread, if brief, public agitation. Eschewing the third-party route of the Progressives, the Maritime Rights leaders decided in 1923 to appeal to the remainder of the country over the head of Ottawa. Although a major national advertising and public relations campaign on behalf of Maritime concerns had some success, it was not enough. When Maritimers started voting Conservative in 1923 by-elections, this merely annoyed the King government. After a royal commission investigated Maritime grievances, the Liberals bought off the region with concessions on freight rates, subsidies, and port development. None of these con-

ERNEST LAPOINTE

Ernest Lapointe (1876–1941) was born in St-Eloi, Quebec. He attended Rimouski College and then Laval University, being called to the bar in 1898. Six years later he became Kamouraska's Liberal MP. He was a staunch supporter of Wilfrid Laurier, but remained on the back benches for many years, although in Laurier's last days he was becoming more prominent, leading the Liberals in the debate over the Ontario Schools Question. In 1919 he was elected to Laurier's old riding in Quebec East. He came into his own under Mackenzie King, who appreciated his loyalty to the party and to the administration. King placed him in two patronage portfolios—marine and fisheries, 1921–24, and justice, 1924–30 and 1935–41—and treated Lapointe as his lieutenant in Quebec. As fisheries minister, he signed the Halibut Treaty with the United States in 1923, the first treaty signed by Canada itself rather than Britain.

Lapointe went with King to the Imperial Conferences of 1926 and 1931, supporting Canadian autonomy in international matters all the way. Domestically, Lapointe was in favour of tariff reduction and provincial rights, although he was the minister of justice who disallowed Social Credit's reformist legislation in Alberta because it infringed on federal rights. He was very cautious about federal interference in Quebec. But he also used federal patronage to great effect in the province, leading many to call Quebec a Liberal fiefdom. At the beginning of the Second World War, Lapointe promised Quebec there would be no conscription, and thus brought the voters of the province on side for the Liberals and the war. His death in 1941 left Mackenzie King without a French-Canadian lieutenant of stature during most of the war.

☐ Abbé Lionel Groulx. NAC, C-16657.

cessions touched fundamental economic problems. In the end, working through the two-party system achieved no more than the creation of a third party. The inability of regional protest in the Maritimes and the west to find common ground was palpable—and significant. Neither side could see beyond its regional interests. Clever federal politicians, like Mackenzie King, could play the game of divide and rule with impunity.

While the west and the Maritimes produced their ineffectual protests, Quebec turned increasingly inward. It pursued a nationalism that was at least partly a reaction against its increasing sense of isolation from the remainder of Canada. The chief outlet for this nationalism was the journal *L'Action Française*, founded on the eve of the Conscription Crisis by the Ligue des droits de français. This movement began with a crusade to save the French language, but gradually shifted into broader issues. Inspiration for both movement and journal came from the Abbé Lionel Groulx (1878–1967). Groulx worried about the survival of the traditional religion and culture in the face of an ever more materialistic environment. From the French-Canadian perspective, that environment was increasingly 'in the middle of an immense Anglo-Saxon ocean' (quoted in Cook 1969b: 193). In the 1920s Groulx denied that he was a separatist, although his arguments pointed in that direction. He called for a commitment to build the Quebec economy, preparing for a future in which Confederation would come to an end. By the late 1920s, Groulx had proved more successful at refashioning the history of French Canada than at gaining widespread public support.

The Depression and Responses To It

The stock market failed in October 1929, with Wall Street leading the way in a record collapse of stock prices everywhere in North America. Contrary to popular opinion, this disaster was fairly independent of the Depression that followed it. That Depression was really the cumulative result of the worldwide fall in prices, which had never readjusted from the inflation of wartime and the deflation of the postwar period. An international inability to buy left Canada and other resource producers, such as Argentina and Australia, with decreased orders for their products. Trade deficits quickly mounted. Nations that owed Canada money were unable to pay. The dollar fell, and in 1931 so did a number of major Canadian financial institutions, brokerage agencies, and insurance companies. The country would not recover until after the eruption of another war in 1939. For most Canadians, the 1930s depression was always the Great Depression. Canadians lived in its shadow for

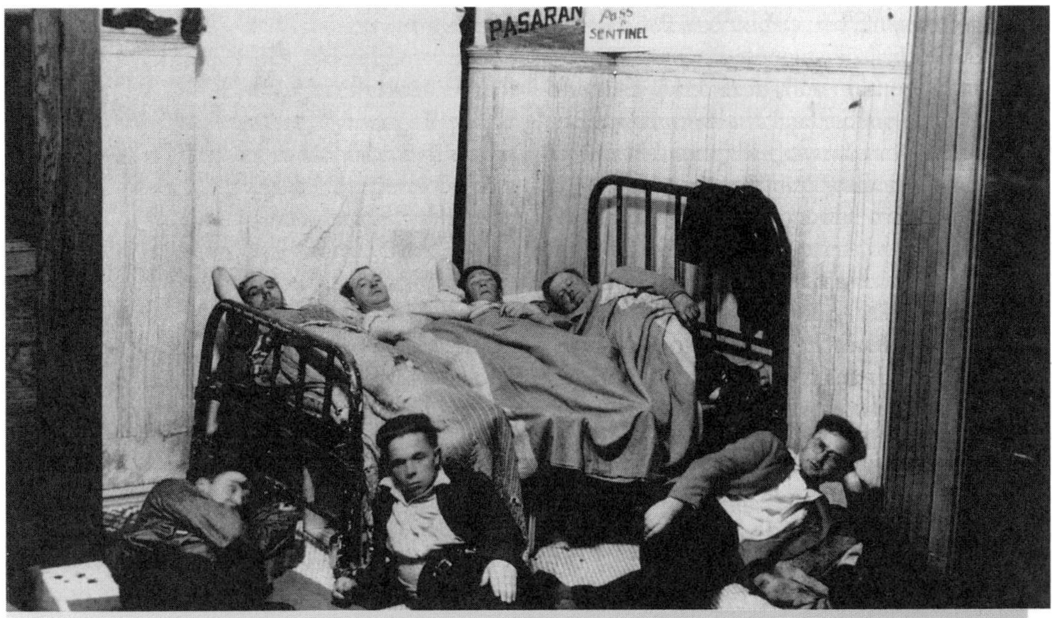

In this Depression-era photo (c. 1929–36), four men share a bed and three others sit on the floor. NAC, C-013236.

decades to come. Those generations who had experienced its effects were always sympathetic to calls for social justice.

What the Depression meant, first and foremost, was unemployment. Official statistics are totally meaningless as a measure of the extent of joblessness, much less its significance. According to the publication *Historical Statistics in Canada* (1983), reflecting contemporary government data, unemployment in Canada rose from 116,000 in 1929 to 741,000 in 1932 to 826,000 in 1933, ultimately declining to 411,000 in 1937 and increasing to 529,000 in 1939. These figures, while substantial enough in a nation of only 10 million, hardly reflected the reality. No farmers or fishermen, or their families, counted among the ranks of the unemployed at this time. The government regarded them as self-employed businessmen. Women out of work did not count either. Thus unemployment in the depths of the Depression, around 1933, ran to more than 27 per cent in the non-agricultural sector, but probably more than 50 per cent overall. At the same time, a farmer whose expenses exceeded his income was probably better off than a jobless city dweller whose expenses similarly exceeded his income. Farmers at least had some land on which food could be grown. Moreover, provincial governments tended to respond to the plight of the farmers, who made up a substantial proportion of the electorate in many provinces. The rural population actually grew in this decade as members of farm families returned from the city to the family farm.

The fall in prices meant that times were good for those with jobs, although almost everyone held their breath each time payday rolled around. As for Canadian business corporations, outside the financial sector there was little permanent damage. Most large corporations ruthlessly retrenched and waited for better times. Canadian business corporations actually suffered losses only in 1932 because they had been too slow to limit operations. In 1933, the lowest point on the economic curve, they ended collectively in the black.

The real victims of the Depression were the urban unemployed, who found that their relief became the great political football of the period. Traditionally Canadian municipalities and private charities had cared for the poor and jobless. The challenge in the 1930s was more than any city could handle, at least without the full cooperation and assistance of senior levels of government. R.B. Bennett (1870–1947), prime minister from 1930 to 1935, personally assisted from his own pocket many people who wrote him begging letters while he was in office, but Bennett had long opposed the dole system and insisted that the provinces were responsible for social welfare. The provinces, in turn, maintained that they lacked the appropriate taxing power. They passed the problem to the municipalities, which had to support the unemployed on declining revenue from property taxes that provided about 80 per cent of municipal revenue. Municipal assistance was grudging, almost always taking the form of credit vouchers to be redeemed at local stores rather than as cash, which might be spent on 'frivolities' or worse. The relief lines were not called 'the dole' for nothing. Cities often advised single unemployed men to go elsewhere and even paid their rail tickets out of town. The constitutional wrangling between the provinces and the federal government seemed quite irrelevant to Canadians looking for help.

Only in 1935, on the eve of a federal election, did R.B. Bennett become a convert to interventionist strategies. He announced his new policy, a 'New Deal' for Canada, in a live radio address to the nation early in January 1935, saying, 'I am for reform. I nail the flag of progress to the mast. I summon the power of the state to its support.' Bennett spoke of legislation regulating working conditions, insuring against unemployment, and extending credit to the farmer. Unfortunately for Bennett, his radio proclamations ran well ahead of the practical legislative program he and his cabinet had ready for Parliament. The Canadian electorate, moreover, was understandably suspicious of last-minute conversions. Instead, the voters brought back Mackenzie King's Liberals, who offered few promises but had the solid backing of Quebec.

R.B. Bennett's 'conversion' to New Dealism involved more than a desperate wish to return to office. It also represented a growing realization by large parts of the Canadian business and professional communities that stabilizing the nation's economy was necessary to prevent a more serious upheaval. Many leading businessmen and financiers were in favour of state intervention, not so much because they believed in social justice as because they wanted economic stability for capitalism. The prevailing political and economic system of Canada was under attack from many directions in the 1930s. Canadian politicians and businessmen did not need to look to Germany or Italy to find examples of radical responses to economic problems. What European experience did point out, however, was that radicalism was not necessarily confined to the traditional left, to be associated with organized labour, socialism, or communism. The great fear was that a demagogue of any political persuasion would emerge, offering simple but final solutions to a frustrated electorate. Canada had its share of prospective demagogues. Most of their success came on the provincial rather than on the federal level, however. All were advocates of provincial rights. This blunted their national effectiveness. Agreeing to bash Ottawa together was never a very creative strategy unless agreement could be reached on what to do next. About all these leaders had in common were their own curious mixtures of radical rhetoric and fundamentally conservative attitudes.

Perhaps the most successful radical response came in Alberta, where the Social Credit Party mobilized a population that had suffered heavily from drought and depression. The leader of Social Credit in Alberta was a Calgary radio preacher, William Aberhart (1878–1943), who since 1924 had used his Sunday broadcasts for the Prophetic Bible Institute over CFCN (Canada's most powerful radio station at the time) to build up a substantial personal following attracted to Protestant fundamentalism. In 1932 Aberhart added a secular dimension to his broadcasts, following his personal conversion to the economic ideas of a Scottish engineer named C.H. Douglas. An unconventional monetary theorist, Douglas claimed that capitalism's failure lay in its inability to translate its production into purchasing power for the mass of people. Douglas advocated distributing money—'social credit'—to bridge the gap between production and consumption. Neither Aberhart nor his Alberta audience ever truly understood Douglas's monetary theories, but both understood that the state would issue a social dividend, eventually set by Aberhart at $25 per month, to all citizens as part of their cultural heritage. With the assistance of Ernest Manning (1908–96), Aberhart organized the Social Credit Party early in 1935. The new party swept to success at the polls, taking fifty-six of sixty-three seats and winning 54 per cent of the popular vote. The federal government (and courts) opposed much of its original legislative program, particularly mortgage, debt, and banking legislation, eventually disallowing thirteen Alberta acts. Social Credit moved to more traditional fiscal practices, blaming Ottawa and eastern big business for its inability to enact its program. (Under Aberhart and, following his death in 1943, under Manning, Social Credit won nine successive elections in Alberta and governed the province until 1971.)

The emergent popular leader in Quebec was Maurice Duplessis (1890–1959). Duplessis came from a family of Conservatives. In 1933 he became leader of the highly fragmented Conservative Party of Quebec. He found allies in two burgeoning Quebec movements of the early 1930s: the Catholic social action of the École social populaire, and the Liberal radicalism of the Action libérale nationale (ALN). From Catholic social action Duplessis took a program of government intervention to redistribute wealth, protect farmers and workers, and regulate large corporations, all within the context of the Christian law of justice and charity. From the ALN he took an emphasis upon economic nationalism that called for liberation from colonial oppression through agrarian reform, new labour legislation, the promotion of small industry and commerce, and the destruction of the great financial establishments of the province. Duplessis negotiated the merger of the ALN with the Conservatives in 1935 to form the Union Nationale. The new party campaigned on the ALN's reform platform, winning an easy victory in the 1936 election of seventy-six seats and 58 per cent of the popular vote. Now 'prime minister' of Quebec, Duplessis quickly abandoned the reform program that had brought him to power. Instead, he concentrated power in his own hands. His considerable success in office relied on a nationalistic concern for provincial autonomy in federal–provincial relations, anticommunism, and calculated paternalistic grants and patronage for the disadvantaged. He carefully cultivated the Catholic hierarchy in the province. The Union Nationale's economic program consisted chiefly in giving American entrepreneurs a free hand to develop the province's resources.

Other provinces besides Quebec and Alberta also produced populist political leaders, although within the context of traditional party labels. In British Columbia, T. Dufferin (Duff) Pattullo (1873–1956) had led his Liberal Party to power in 1933 without sounding very radical. In office, however, Pattullo gradually became a convert to state activism of the New Deal variety. His government was arguably the most interventionist in Canada, held back only by the province's shortage of revenue. In Ontario, Mitchell Hepburn (1896–1953) led a Liberal government with a series of flamboyant political gestures designed chiefly as self-advertisement. He achieved national prominence in April 1937, in the midst of a strike at the General Motors plant in Oshawa, Ontario. More than 4,000 workers

THOMAS DUFFERIN PATTULLO

Thomas Dufferin Pattullo (1873–1956, usually known as 'Duff') was born in Woodstock, Ontario. He worked for Ontario newspapers before moving to the Yukon in 1897 as secretary to the commissioner of the Territory. He subsequently became acting assistant gold commissioner before leaving Dawson City in 1908 to open a brokerage firm. In Prince Rupert, he became a municipal political leader and then a member of the BC assembly (1916) and cabinet minister. He became provincial Liberal leader in 1928 and set about re-energizing the party and turning it from its previous conservative position to one of progressive liberalism far to the left of the federal Liberal party. In 1933 Pattullo's Liberals won a large majority in an election fought chiefly against the newly founded CCF party. The issue was socialism versus capitalism, and many voters failed to realize on how many points the Liberals and CCF were in agreement, with the CCF offering 'Humanity First' and the Liberals a 'New Deal' under the slogan 'Work and Wages'. Pattullo was something of a swashbuckler, and his insistence that the people were entitled to a decent standard of living guaranteed by government owed more to Franklin D. Roosevelt than to William Lyon Mackenzie King, the federal Liberal leader.

But the social reconstruction of British Columbia depended to a large extent on a new constitutional arrangement with the federal government, and Pattullo ended up fighting bitterly with Ottawa. He was unable to implement most of his ad hoc Keynesian views about pump-priming. In his early years in office, Pattullo was easily able to pass reform legislation which did not cost very much, but it was harder to find the money for social programs providing a decent standard of living. Pattullo settled for a program of public works. The defeat of the federal Tories in 1935 led Pattullo to hope for more assistance from Ottawa. Instead, Pattullo and King became involved in an unseemly struggle over provincial debts to Ottawa. British Columbia could not afford to implement Pattullo's cherished comprehensive health insurance scheme in 1937, the year the Liberals again faced the electorate. Although Pattullo's party was returned to office, he became more cautious and increasingly more hostile to the federal government. Standing foursquare for provincial rights, he was one of the chief critics of the Rowell-Sirois Commission when it recommended a transfer of functions to the federal government and a shift in taxation powers. Pattullo continued to advocate an enhanced role for government in the economy and in society, but by 'government' he meant the provincial, not the federal level. The only exception was the responsibility for unemployment, which he always saw as a national and federal matter.

struck for an eight-hour day, better wages and working conditions, and recognition of the new union of United Automobile Workers. This union was an affiliate of the recently formed Congress of Industrial Organization, which was organizing throughout the United States. Hepburn sided with General Motors and clashed publicly with the prime minister over Mackenzie

King's refusal to send RCMP reinforcements for the local police. The premier organized a volunteer force called Hepburn's Hussars. Both Pattullo and Hepburn got great political mileage out of their well-publicized clashes with Ottawa.

None of the prominent provincial political leaders of the 1930s had any serious socialist leanings. The most important alternative political response of the Depression years based in the socialist tradition came from the Co-operative Commonwealth Federation (CCF). A convention in Calgary in 1932 founded the CCF as a coalition of farmers' organizations, labour unions, and labour-socialist parties in the four western provinces. The League for Social Reconstruction (LSR) served as the CCF's midwife. The LSR, organized in 1931 by a number of prominent Canadian academics, believed in Fabian socialism. Like the Fabians, it was proudly non-Marxist and non-revolutionary, although vehemently committed to a welfare state and the state's take-over of key industries. At its first annual convention at Regina in 1933, the newly founded CCF adopted a political manifesto that promised a heady brew of political reform. The Regina Manifesto called for the nationalization (with compensation for the owners) of all industry 'essential to social planning'. It advocated a series of universal welfare measures for Canada—hospitalization, health care, unemployment insurance, and pensions—after amendments to the British North America Act to remove these areas from provincial jurisdiction.

The new party was an uneasy alliance of academics and public activists. It chose as leader the former Methodist minister James Shaver Woodsworth. Pacifist, idealist, and moralist, Woodsworth had since 1921 led a small cadre of labour-supported MPs in Ottawa. The new party attracted over 300,000 votes in the 1933 British Columbia provincial elections, more than 30 per cent of the popular vote. In the 1935 federal election it obtained 8.9 per cent of the popular vote, which translated into seven CCF seats. During the 1930s the party would flourish only in BC and Saskatchewan, however. It did not attract broad-based popular support, particularly east of Ontario.

The nation's politicians and businessmen grimly viewed the CCF as a threat from the radical left, failing to appreciate that the new party provided a far more restrained left-wing approach than the Communist Party of Canada (CP). At the outset of the Great Depression, only the CP had sought to organize popular discontent, especially among the unemployed. The Communists operated under several disadvantages, however. One was the charge that they were members of an international conspiracy. The other was the Canadian government's willingness to repress the party in any way possible. Ottawa used section 98 of the Criminal Code, introduced in 1919 at the time of the first 'Red Scare', to outlaw the advocacy of revolution. It arrested eight Communist leaders in August of 1931. The courts quickly convicted and sentenced them, although the government gradually released them from prison after continual public demonstrations on their behalf. Nevertheless, the repression checked the momentum of the party. After 1933 the CCF took away some CP support. By mid-decade the CP found itself caught up in rapidly changing orders from the USSR and by events in Europe. In 1937 many Canadian Communists entered the European struggle by joining the Mackenzie-Papineau Battalion to fight in the Spanish Civil War.

The CP took the credit for organizing, through the Workers' Unity League, a mass march on Ottawa in 1935 known as the On-to-Ottawa Trek. The marchers came out of the unemployment relief camps in BC, where unemployed young men found their only refuge. Conditions in the camps were degrading. Not even the Communists claimed that the discontent was anything but spontaneous. The trek began in Vancouver and ended in Regina. The RCMP allowed a delegation of eight marchers to take their grievances to Ottawa. The talks broke down and the delegation returned to Regina. At

Strikers from the BC relief camps heading east as part of the 'On to Ottawa' trek; Kamloops, June 1935. NAC, C-029399.

that point the Mounties moved in with baseball bat batons. The ensuing riot reduced downtown Regina to shambles and put 120 protesters in jail. Most of the remaining trekkers accepted offers of transportation back home. While the 1930s were punctuated from time to time by outbreaks of public discontent that turned to violence, as in Regina, two points must be emphasized about these incidents. The first is that with most of the spontaneous popular demonstrations, most of the damage to persons and property resulted from the authorities' efforts to break up what they regarded as ugly crowds. The second point is that much of the violence of the period resulted from confrontations between organized labour and the authorities. Clashes between police and strikers were common, as they always had been.

Canadian Society Between the Wars

For more than half a century before 1919, Canada had been making a gradual transition from frontier nation to modern industrial state. This process basically continued unabated between the wars. Most of the emerging social patterns were not very different from those that affected all heavily industrialized countries. Urbanization advanced while rural (and especially agricultural) society declined in importance. The traditional family unit seemed under attack. Technology rapidly altered communication and transportation. It also profoundly affected the ways in which Canadians entertained themselves.

Demographic Trends

Like all industrial countries, Canada experienced profound demographic changes. Some of these had been somewhat disguised by the federal government's failure, until 1921, to keep accurate national statistics beyond the census. Enormous infusions of new immigrants before 1914 also helped prevent the new demographic trends from becoming easily apparent, but they existed. By the 1941 census more Canadians lived in urban rather than rural places, a result of a substantial increase in urban residents, especially during the 1920s. Moreover, the 1941 census would be the last in which rural numbers and farm dwellers grew absolutely in number. Even before 1941, the impact of urbanization and industrialization was apparent.

First, mortality rates declined. In the critical area of infant mortality, the death rate had been steadily declining since the nineteenth century. Infant mortality took another major drop in the 1930s, while the overall death rate drifted perceptibly downward. By 1946 the median age at death was 63.1 for males and 65.3 for females. For the first time, Canadian society had begun to produce substantial numbers of people who would live beyond the age of productive labour; a rise in concern for old-age pensions in this period was hardly accidental. The main exception to the national trend was in the Aboriginal population. Their death rates ran to four times the national average; infant mortality was at least twice that of Canadian society as a whole. Large numbers of Native mothers died in childbirth. Moreover, Aboriginal people suffered up to three times more accidental deaths than Canada's population overall. They had a high suicide rate. Before 1940 most Aboriginal people died of communicable rather than chronic disease, with tuberculosis as the big killer. The decreasing death rate for Canadians in general resulted from an improved standard of living and better medical treatment. In 1921–6, 270 out of every 1,000 Canadian deaths came from pulmonary and communicable disease. By 1946 such fatalities dropped to just over sixty out of every 1,000 Canadian deaths. Cardiovascular problems, renal disease, and cancer—all afflictions of an aging population—became more important killers.

Then fertility rates declined. The extent to which the fall in the birth rate resulted from conscious decisions on the part of women is not entirely clear, but the two were plainly related. Increased urbanization made large families less desirable. As industrialization took more women out of the home and into the workforce, child care became a serious problem. More women, especially over thirty, began to limit the number of children they bore, practising some form of contraception. Birth rates had begun to fall in Canada before 1919 and continued to fall in the 1920s and 1930s. They recovered from an extremely low point in the middle of the Depression after 1941, increasing sharply after 1945. There were some significant internal differentials. One was between Quebec and the remainder of Canada. The birth rate in French Canada remained substantially higher than in the rest of the country, although it shared in the general decline. There was also a difference between urban and rural areas, with substantially higher birth rates in the latter. A third differential occurred between Catholics and Protestants, although certain Protestant subgroups, such as Mennonites and Mormons, had higher rates than the overall Catholic one. Finally, Aboriginal birth rates were at least twice the national average.

Among other demographic factors that

require consideration was immigration, which (despite the upheavals in Europe) did not return to its pre-1914 incidence after the Great War. Public opinion, as reflected in government policy, did not favour massive new immigration. Many Canadians felt that since most agricultural land was now settled, newcomers would compete for jobs while altering the ethnic make-up of the population. Immigration ran at around 125,000 per year in the 1920s and then fell to 20,000 per year during the 1930s when the government discouraged most immigration. Canadian immigration policy operated on a preferred-nation basis, discouraging new arrivals from outside northern Europe and demonstrating hostile indifference to immigrants from non-European nations. Canada was not at all officially receptive, moreover, to the plight of refugees, mainly Jewish, from Nazi persecution. The nation took only a relative handful (about 6,000) of these people.

Another important factor was divorce. The year 1918 saw 114 divorces in all of Canada, a rate of 1.4 per 100,000 people. By 1929 the divorce rate had reached 8.2 per 100,000, rising to 18.4 per 100,000 in 1939 and to 65.3 per 100,000 by 1947. Higher rates occurred partly because more Canadians gained access to divorce courts; Ontario courts obtained divorce jurisdiction in 1930. The increase also reflected changing attitudes, particularly among women, who instituted most divorce actions. Divorce statistics did not begin to measure the extent of marital dissolutions, however. Most dissolutions never reached a court. Especially during the Depression, husbands simply deserted their wives. Many contemporaries saw the increase in divorce as evidence of the disintegration of the Canadian family.

TECHNOLOGICAL CHANGE

Despite the nation's uneven economic record between 1919 and 1945, Canadians in these years experienced an increase in the rate and nature of technological change. The new technologies had enormous impact upon all aspects of Canadian life. On one level they forced governments to adopt a myriad of new policies. On another level they had tremendous psychological impact, particularly by militating against communalism in favour of the individual, family, or household.

One evident area of change was in the mass acceptance of the internal combustion engine in the form of the automobile and the tractor. Before 1920 automobile ownership had been almost entirely an urban phenomenon, but by 1920 it had become more general. In 1904 there were fewer than 5,000 motor vehicles in Canada. By 1920 there were 251,000, most of them built during the war. From 1918 to 1923 Canadian manufacturers, allied to US companies, were the second-largest car producers in the world. Canada was a major exporter, especially to the British empire. By 1930 only the United States had more automobiles per capita than did Canada. In that year Canada had 1,061,000 automobiles registered. Also significant was the increase in the number of tractors employed on the nation's farms after 1918.

The automobile was individually owned and operated as an extension of a household. It represented private rather than public transportation. No other single product operated so insidiously against communalism as the automobile. It also had tremendous spin-off consequences. Automobiles required roads, which were a provincial and municipal responsibility. More than one-quarter of the $650 million increase in provincial and municipal debt between 1913 and 1921 resulted from capital expenditures on highways, streets, and bridges. Road mileage in Canada expanded from 385,000 mi. (619,580 km) in 1922 to 565,000 mi. (909,254 km) in 1942. Motorists wanted not only roads but properly paved ones. Although in 1945 nearly two-thirds of Canadian roads were still of earth construction, the other third had been paved or gravelled at considerable expense. Automobiles ran on petroleum products. Not only did they

A Toronto traffic jam, 1924: motorists out for a Sunday drive on the newly built Lakeshore Boulevard. City of Toronto Archives, James Collection 2530.

encourage petroleum production, chiefly in Alberta, but they also created the gasoline station, the garage, the roadside restaurant, and the motel—new service industries to provide for a newly mobile population. Door-to-door rather than station-to-station mobility was one of the principal effects of the automobile revolution. Both the automobile and the truck competed with the railways, which began their decline in the 1920s. Although the automobile provided an important source of tax revenue for both federal and provincial governments, neither Ottawa nor the provinces made any serious effort to control the use or construction of motor vehicles, aside from some fairly minimal rules of the road and the issuance of drivers' licences to almost all comers. Despite its importance, the automobile and its 20,000 parts were produced entirely according to manufacturers' standards and consumers' desires, without government regulation. The car quickly became the symbol of North American independence and individuality. It also served as

HOUSEHOLD EQUIPMENT OWNERSHIP IN MONTREAL, 1941

Heating	
By stove	51.5%
Wood and coal	92.3
Cooking Fuel	
Wood and coal	17.7
Gas & electric	80.6
Bathtub	83.9
Refrigeration	
Mechanical	25.1
Icebox	65.0
None	5.1
Radio	85.5
Telephone	44.9
Vacuum cleaner	28.2
Automobile	15.7

SOURCE: Denyse Baillargeon, *Making Do: Women, Family, and Home in Montreal during the Great Depression* (Waterloo: Wilfrid Laurier University Press, 2000), 187.

Although this photo was staged, it conveys the avid interest that radio aroused in 1935. A receiver like this walnut-veneered Canadian General Electric model was a luxury that not many Depression-era Canadians could afford. NAC, C-80917.

a combined status and sex symbol, and according to some critics, as a 'portable den of iniquity'.

Unlike the automobile, radio was treated by the federal government as a public matter deserving of regulation. The programs broadcast, rather than the radio receiver itself, became the target of government control. The transmission and reception of sound via radio waves had initially been developed before the Great War as an aid to ships at sea. The 1920s saw the mass marketing of the radio receiver in North America. In order to sell radios, it was necessary to provide something to listen to. By 1929 eighty-five broadcasting stations were operating in Canada under various ownerships. Private radio broadcasting in Canada was not all bad, but it was uneven. A royal commission on broadcasting—the Aird Commission, appointed in 1928 and reporting in 1929—recommended the nationalization of radio. Its advice was not immediately taken. The Bennett government eventually introduced the Broadcasting Act of 1932, however, which led to the formation of the Canadian

Radio Broadcasting Commission to establish a national network and to supervise private stations. In 1936 this commission became the Canadian Broadcasting Corporation, with extensive English and French networks, and operated with federal financial support as an independent agency. No other Canadian cultural institution of its day was so closely associated with Canadian nationalism and Canadian culture than was the CBC. The CBC was not only pre-eminent but often unique in the fostering of Canadian culture. Often the battle seemed to be uphill, since Canadians usually preferred listening to the slick entertainment programming produced in the United States.

PROHIBITION AND CHURCH UNION

The impetus for social reform died after 1918. To some extent, the movement was a victim of its own successes. For many Canadians, the achievement of prohibition and women's suffrage—the two principal reform goals of the pre-war period—meant that the struggle had been won. To some extent, reform was a victim of the Great War. Reformers had exhausted themselves in a war effort that had produced devastation but no final victory. The war had been a disillusioning experience for many.

The failure of the prohibition experiment symbolized the decline of reform. Despite considerable evidence that the elimination of alcoholic beverages had made a social difference—the jails were emptied in most places, since they were usually filled with prisoners who had committed alcohol-related offences—the supporters of prohibition were unable to stem the tide. The Ontario Alliance for the Total Suppression of the Liquor Trade claimed in 1922 that the number of convictions for offences associated with drink had declined from 17,143 in 1914 to 5,413 in 1921, and drunkenness cases decreased in the province's major cities from 16,590 in 1915 to 6,766 in 1921. Nevertheless, various provinces went 'wet' between 1920 and 1924, and the Liquor Control Act replaced the Ontario Temperance Act in 1927. Opposition to prohibition after the war found a new argument to add to the old one that private conduct was being publicly regulated: attempts to enforce prohibition encouraged people to flout the law, and even created organized crime and vice. Too many people were prepared to ignore the law, said prohibition's opponents, who found more acceptable slogans of their own in 'Moderation' and 'Government Regulation'. In many provinces, the possibility of obtaining provincial revenue for tax-starved coffers led to the introduction of government control over the sale of alcohol. Taxing bad habits rather than forbidding them became part of the Canadian tradition.

While prohibition was dying, in 1925 the Methodist, Presbyterian, and Congregational churches (the first two were among Canada's largest denominations) merged as the United Church of Canada. As three of the most 'liberal' denominations in Canada, home of much of the Social Gospel commitment to Christian reform of secular society, they hoped to rejuvenate reform fervour through unification. Not all members of the three denominations were equally enthusiastic. Opposition to union was particularly strong among the Presbyterians. In the end, congregations could vote to stay out of the union. Thus 784 Presbyterian and eight Congregational congregations so declared, while 4,797 Methodist, 3,728 Presbyterian, and 166 Congregational congregations joined in the United Church of Canada. The new denomination became the most substantial Protestant communion of Canada, generally committed to liberal thinking and reform.

RACISM

Canadian society between the wars continued to be profoundly racist. That point was demonstrable in a variety of ways, although it must be emphasized that very few Canadians saw their exclusionary attitudes as either socially undesirable or dysfunctional.

Imported from the United States, the Ku Klux Klan flourished in Canada during the 1920s. In the United States the revived Klan spread anti-Black and anti-Catholic hate propaganda under the guise of a fraternal organization. In its secret rituals, fundamentalist Protestantism, and social operations, the Klan appeared to some Canadians to be little different from a host of other secret societies. The Klan assumed a Canadian face, posing as the defender of Britishness against the alien hordes and calling itself the 'Ku Klux Klan of the British empire'. Although the Klan had some success everywhere in Canada, it made particular headway in the late 1920s in Saskatchewan, where by 1929 there were over 125 chapters. In that province it found support from a number of Protestant ministers, who objected to the increasingly liberal leanings of the main-line Protestant churches. It also gained acceptance as a way of opposing the patronage-style politics of the provincial Liberal government. Few of its members associated it with American-style cross burning or midnight lynch mobs.

Canada's treatment of its Aboriginal population continued to reflect both belief in the superiority of non-Native culture and antagonism towards the Native peoples. The Department of Indian Affairs assumed that assimilation was the only possible policy. Deputy Minister Duncan Scott stated in 1920 that 'Our object is to continue until there is not a single Indian in Canada that has not been absorbed into the body politic, and there is no Indian question, and no Indian Department.' Indian Affairs employed a variety of policies. It forced Aboriginal children into schools, usually residential ones far removed from their families. It forbade and actively suppressed the practice of traditional Native rituals like the potlatch. It carried out the Canadian government's legislative provisions to enfranchise the Aboriginal people, thus in theory making them full citizens and no longer wards of the state. Most of the resistance to these measures was passive, although there was the beginning of organization. The first congress of the League of Indians convened at Sault Ste Marie, Ontario, in September 1919. The league's objectives were 'to claim and protect the rights of all Indians in Canada by legitimate and just means', and to assert 'absolute control in retaining possession or disposition of our lands' (quoted in Cuthand 1978: 31–2). The league and its successors met regularly thereafter.

In British Columbia, an anti-Oriental movement flourished during the interwar years. Much of the criticism of the 'menace' from Asia came from economic fears, although there was also a general concern for the racial integrity of the province as a White society. The general argument was that the newcomers would not assimilate, although there was considerable evidence that the Japanese, at least, were acculturating rapidly. Moving onto small holdings in the Fraser Valley and into salmon fishing along the coasts, the Japanese appeared to pose a potential military threat should their homeland—which was militarily aggressive in the Pacific from the beginning of the century—attempt to expand into Canada. If people from Asia were highly visible in some areas and in some industries, that fact was partly explained by their exclusion—in law and in practice—from so much of the life of the province.

In the later 1930s, the Canadian government showed little interest in accommodating refugees from the Nazi pogroms in Europe. Despite the Jewish community's continued efforts in Canada, the government refused to adopt a generous policy. Immigration officials systematically rejected highly skilled professionals and intellectuals (including doctors, scientists, and musicians) as inadmissible applicants. One government mandarin wrote, 'We don't want to take too many Jews, but, in the present circumstances particularly, we don't want to say so.' For a nation as deficient in world-renowned scientific, intellectual, and cultural talent as Canada, the result was a cruel, if totally deserved, shortfall. Other countries, particularly the United States, benefited greatly from immigrants in fields as diverse as physics, medicine, theatre, music, and education. Canada did not. Even in the most crass of non-humanitarian terms, Canadian policy was a disaster, but from a country that was constantly lecturing the world in moral terms, it was inexcusable.

WOMEN

Canadian women emerged from the Great War with the vote in hand. A few feminist critics had argued that the vote was no panacea for women's second-class position in Canadian society. It did not even assure a high level of political involvement. Between the wars women did not very often run for public office or constitute a recognizable voting bloc. The flapper, with her bobbed hair, short skirts, and spirit of independence, was the symbolic 'new woman' of the 1920s, but she was hardly typical. Most Canadian women did not smoke or sip cocktails or dance the Black Bottom. About all they had in common with the flapper was that, like her, they worked outside the home. Quebec women began moving into the workforce after 1918. More women worked in Canada in 1931 than in 1921, mostly in dead-end jobs. The Depression was particularly difficult for women. Public opinion turned against married women holding jobs that could be done by men. Most relief programs were geared to men, partly because it was not thought that women would threaten the social order by rioting and demonstrating.

In the gradual elaboration of unemployment insurance, many radicals opposed gender discrimination, but at the same time accepted the principle that married women should be supported by their husbands. Women's access to benefits was often limited without mention of gender. For example, traditionally female areas of employment—school teaching, nursing, domestic service performed in private homes—were excluded from UI coverage. Many husbands deserted their wives,

CHARLOTTE WHITTON

Charlotte Whitton (1896–1975) was born in Renfrew, Ontario, and was educated at Queen's University, where she had a spectacular academic record. In 1918 she was appointed assistant secretary to the Social Services Council of Canada. She was soon actively involved in social work and social work reform, and became first director of the Canadian Council on Child Welfare, which would become the Canadian Welfare Council, serving from 1926 to 1941. In this position she edited the journal *Social Welfare* and represented Canada on social issues at the League of Nations. She also campaigned courageously for improved standards in the care of children and juveniles, and insisted on the need for a more professional approach to social work. During her tenure as director of the Canadian Welfare Council she toured the nation, making frequent speeches and giving many lectures. Her major message during the 1930s was that while the Depression had made it impossible for private philanthropy to carry the social welfare load by itself, neither spending large sums of money on unemployment nor an active federal government was the answer to the problem. As an advisor to the Bennett government on federal unemployment relief, she offered the same opinions.

After her departure from the Welfare Council in 1941, Whitton became a private consultant on welfare matters. In 1943, in response to an invitation from new Progressive-Conservative leader John Bracken, she published *The Dawn of an Ampler Life*, obviously intended to serve as a background document for the new party's social policy. The reader would be hard pressed to decide exactly what Whitton was recommending, but it clearly was considerably less state interventionist than most of the competing visions of the time, and it had little impact on the welfare debate. Whitton subsequently became notorious for her opposition to liberal divorce laws and to married women who held jobs. In 1950 she was elected controller of the city of Ottawa, succeeding to the mayor's post on the death of the incumbent, thus becoming the first female mayor of a major Canadian city. She was re-elected in 1952 and 1954, then again in 1960 and 1962. When not mayor, Whitton served the city as an alderman. She was famous for her outspoken opinions and keen wit.

Charlotte Whitton (second from left) at the unveiling of commemorative bust of Agnes MacPhail in the House of Commons, Ottawa, 1955. With her are MP Margaret Aitken, Senator Cairine Wilson, and Secretary of State Ellen Fairclough. Duncan Cameron/ NAC, PA-121765

and even where the family remained together, the wife did most of the work to keep it functioning. In the House of Commons in 1935, J.S. Woodsworth cited the case of a child-murder and suicide in Winnipeg. The husband was unemployed, and came home to find his children and wife dead. His wife had left a suicide note that read, 'I owe the drug store 44 cents farewell' (quoted in Pierson 1990): 77–103).

CANADIAN CULTURE BETWEEN THE WARS

A resurgence of Canadian nationalism characterized the 1920s. The larger stories of the interwar period, however, were the blossoming of Canada's love affair with American popular culture and the simultaneous emergence of a number of substantial home-grown writers and artists. By the 1930s Canadians no longer had to be apologetic about their cultural achievements, although the number of individuals who could actually make a living from their creative work remained fairly small.

The Great War may have been fought for the British empire, but both its course and its outcome made Canadians more conscious of their nation's distinctiveness. In the 1920s Canadian nationalism wore a dual face. On the one hand, it had to reflect Canada's new international status. On the other, it felt it had to protect the country from being overwhelmed by foreign culture. The

'As for Me and My House'

In 1941 (James) Sinclair Ross (1908–96) published a novel in New York entitled *As for Me and My House*. Set in Horizon, Saskatchewan, in the 1930s, the story is told from the vantage point of Mrs Bentley, the wife of a local clergyman.

Sunday Evening, April 30.

The wind keeps on. It's less than a week since the snowstorm, and the land is already dry again. The dust goes reeling up the street in stinging little scuds. Over the fields this morning on our way to Partridge Hill there were dark, foreboding clouds of it.

Service was difficult this morning. They were listening to the wind, not Philip, the whimpering and strumming through the eaves,, and the dry hard crackle of sand against the windows. From the organ I could see their faces pinched and stiffened with anxiety. They sat in tense, bolt upright rows, most of the time their eyes on the ceiling, as if it were the sky and they were trying to read the weather. . . .

Philip and Paul and I stood on the school steps till the congregation were all gone. The horses pawed and stamped as if they, too, felt something ominous in the day. One after another the democrats and buggies rolled away with a whir of wheels like pebbly thunder. From the top of Partridge Hill where the schoolhouse stands we could see the prairie smoking with dust as if it had just been swept by fire. A frightening, wavering hum fled blind within the telephone wires. The wind struck in hard, clenched little blows; and even as we watched each other the dust formed in veins and wrinkles round our eyes. According to the signs, says Paul, it's going to be a dry and windy year all through. With the countryman's instincts for such things he was strangely depressed this morning. Not the history or derivation of a single word. . . .

I found it hard myself to believe in the town outside, houses, streets, and solid earth. Mile after mile the wind poured by, and we were immersed and lost in it. I sat breathing from my throat, my muscles tense. To relax, I felt, would be to let the walls round me crumple in. . . .

It's the most nerve-wracking wind I've ever listened to. Sometimes it sinks a little, as if spent and out of breath, then comes high, shrill and importunate again. Sometimes it's blustering and rough, sometimes silent and sustained. Sometimes it's wind, sometimes frightened hands that shake the doors and windows. Sometimes it makes the little room and its smug, familiar furniture a dramatic inconsistency, sometimes a relief. I sit thinking about the dust, the farmers and the crops, wondering what another dried-out year will mean for us.

We're pinched already. They gave us fifteen dollars this week, but ten had to go for a payment on the car. I'm running bills already at the butcher shop and Dawson's store. Philip needs shoes and a hat. His Sunday suit is going at the cuffs again, and it's shiny at the seat and knees. I sent for a new spring hat for myself the other day, but it was just a dollar forty-five, and won't be much.

SOURCE: Sinclair Ross, *As For Me and My House* (Toronto: McClelland and Stewart, 1970), 37–9.

Emily Carr in the Cariboo region of British Columbia, 1904.

painter Arthur Lismer (1885–1969) wrote, 'After 1919, most creative people, whether in painting, writing or music, began to have a guilty feeling that Canada was as yet unwritten, unpainted, unsung. . . . In 1920 there was a job to be done' (quoted in Thompson and Seager 1985: 158). That job was not simply to write books, paint pictures, and compose music that captured the true Canadian spirit. The task was also to organize national cultural organizations and institutions that would mobilize a new sense of national consciousness. A number of Canadian magazines and journals emerged to serve as vehicles for Canadian ideas. The *Canadian Bookman* appeared in 1919, and the *Canadian Forum*, the *Canadian Historical Review*, and *The Dalhousie Review* in 1920. The Canadian Authors' Association, founded in 1921, backed campaigns promoting Canadian writers. In 1937 it succeeded in persuading the governor general—the famous Scottish novelist John Buchan (1875–1940), Lord Tweedsmuir—to establish the prestigious Governor General's awards. In art, the Group of Seven consciously sought to create a Canadian mythology. According to their first exhibition catalogue, in 1920, their vision was simple: 'An Art must grow and flower in the land before the country will be a real home for its people' (quoted in Thompson and Seager 1985: 162).

Between 1920 and 1940 over 750 Canadian novels were published. While most of these works were escapist fiction, a number of Canadian novelists achieved national and even modest international reputations for their skill at their craft. Perhaps even more important, a small number of strong, confident, realistic novels appeared that formed the foundation of modern Canadian fiction. Not only was the move towards realism in line with international trends, but it responded to the nationalist demand for distinctively Canadian content. As for the visual arts, particularly during the Depression when most artists had to live at subsistence level, much work we now value highly was produced. Few visual artists in Canada could make a living from their work alone, but art schools were now sufficiently common in the larger Canadian cities to provide employment for painters and sculptors. British Columbia's Emily Carr (1871–1945) united art and literature in a highly original way. Combining French Post-Impressionism with Aboriginal form and colour, Carr gradually created a powerful and distinctive visual landscape. She also won a Governor-General's award for *Klee Wyck* (1941), a collection of stories based on her visits to Native villages. By the time of her death, Carr's paintings were probably the visual icons the average Canadian could most easily associate with an individual artist. She had triumphed not only over the disadvantages of Canadian geography but over the limitations faced by any woman who aspired to more than a genteel 'dabbling' in art.

During the interwar period, radio, motion pictures, and the great expansion of professional sports all represented major American influences on the Canadian consciousness. In popular culture Canada made little effort at national distinctiveness. The loudest critics of insidious Americanization usually had no alternatives to offer other than a somewhat outworn Britishness. At the same time, Canada and Canadians were hardly innocent victims of American cultural imperialism. As a nation Canada had choices it failed or refused to exercise. As a people Canadians were willing—indeed, active—collaborators in cultural production, both at home and in the United States itself. A closer examination of motion pictures and hockey in this period is instructive.

In the world of film, Hollywood's success was also Canada's, since there was no shortage of Canadian talent involved in the formative years of Tinseltown. Mack Sennett, Sidney Olcott, Louis B. Mayer, Jack Warner, Walter Huston, Mary Pickford, Norma Shearer, and Marie Dressler—some of Hollywood's biggest and most influential names at the time—were Canadian-born. Pickford, Warner, and Mayer founded three of the major Hollywood studios between 1919 and 1924. Canada itself had only the beginnings of a film industry, consisting mainly of the seven films produced by Ernest Shipman, of which *Back to God's Country* (1919) is a Canadian silent-film classic. Otherwise film making in Canada was confined chiefly to newsreels and documentaries, which were often appended to American features. By 1922 American studios were including Canadian receipts as part of domestic revenue, and in 1923 Famous Players' Canadian Corporation, a subsidiary of Pickford's studio, took over the leading Canadian cinema chain, Allen Theatres. At the height of the silent-film era, Hollywood succeeded in monopolizing the distribution of film in Canada; Canadian exhibitors and cinema owners were not much concerned about where the product had originated so long as it was profitable.

Other nations around the world took some sort of defensive action against the Hollywood juggernaut, either placing quotas on imported films or providing tax incentives for local productions. Canada did neither, partly because its citizens were so closely connected with the American film industry, partly because Canadians so clearly preferred Hollywood films to the alternatives. During the Great Depression, when the Dream Factory provided blessed release from the cares and woes of everyday life for millions of Canadians, that dream was plainly American. Canadians continued to love American movies despite the inaccuracy with which Hollywood persistently treated Canadian geography, society, and history. Symbolically, the successive and successful film portrayals of that quintessential American Abraham Lincoln by two Canadian actors, Walter Huston (1884–1950) and Raymond Massey (1896–1983), only solidified the close identification of Canadians and Americans in the popular mind on both sides of the border.

The situation with professional hockey was equally interesting. The National Hockey Association (NHA) was organized in 1909 in eastern Canada. On the West Coast, Frank and Lester Patrick, in 1911–12, formed the Pacific Coast Hockey League (PCHL), which defeated an NHA team for the Stanley Cup in 1915. In 1917 the National Hockey League (NHL) formed out of the NHA. The PCHL folded in 1925. That same year, the NHL granted a franchise lease to the Boston Bruins and became the top professional hockey league in North America. The New York Rangers and the Pittsburgh Pirates soon followed, and Chicago and Detroit received NHL franchises in 1927. Most of the American clubs were owned or

Radio Programming, 1939

Wednesday 2 August
Network Highlights

CBC

7:00 Songs of the World
7:30 Percy Faith's Music
8:00 Sunset Symphony
8:30 Nature Talk
9:15 Sunset Symphony
10:00 Everyman Theatre

NBC—BLUE

7:30 Idea Mart
8:00 Kay Kyser's Quiz
8:30 Fred Waring Orch.
10:30 Lights Out

CBS

9:00 Amos 'n' Andy
9:30 Paul Whiteman orch.

Station Programs

5:00 The Lone Ranger, sketch—CKY
5:00 Dinner Concert—CBC-CJRC, CBK
5:00 Fred Waring Orch—KFYR
5:30 Crackerjacks, songs—CBC-CJRC, CBK
5:30 Jimmy Allen, sketch—CKY
5:45 Howie Wing, sketch—CJRC
5:45 Waltz Time—CKY
5:45 Canadian Outdoor Days, Ozark Ripley—CBC-CBK . . .
7:00 Songs of the World, mixed choir, Montreal—CBC-CKY
7:00 Reports—CJRC
7:00 Horse and Buggy Days, songs of the 90s—KFYR
7:00 Percy Faith's Music; George Murray, Dorothy Alt, soloists, Toronto—CBC-CKY, CBK
7:30 Modern Music Maestros—CJRC
7:30 Idea Mart—KFYR
8:00 Interview from London, from BBC—CBC-CKY, CBK
8:00 Reports, Blaine Edwards, organ— CJRC
8:00 Kay Kyser's College, musical quiz—NBC—KFY until 9.
8:15 Teller of Curious Tales—CJRC
8:30 Dan McMurray's Nature Talk, Bank CBC-CKY, CBK
8:30 Five Esquires—CJRC
8:45 Lieder Recital—CBC-CKY, CBK
9:00 Canadian Press News—CBC-CKY, CBK
9:00 Reports; Piano Moods—CJRC
9:00 Amos 'n' Andy, sketch—CBS-WJR, WCCO, KMOX, KBL
9:00 Fred Waring Orch—NBC-KFTR, WHO, WLW
9:15 Summer Symphony, G. Waddington conducting from Walker Theatre, Winnipeg—CBC-CKY, CBK, CJRC, until 10.
9:30 Milt North Trio, WKNR
9:30 Tommy Dorsey Orch—NBC-KOR
9:30 Horace Heidt Orch—NBC-KFYR
9:30 Paul Whiteman Orch., guests—CBS-WCCO, KMOX, KSL.
9:45 Reports—CJRC

SOURCE: *Winnipeg Tribune* 2 August 1939: 2.

managed by Canadians, and the players were almost entirely Canadian. Indeed, the Patrick brothers had brought players from their PCHL teams to the American-based NHL teams they acquired in the 1920s. The Toronto Maple Leafs acquired a physical presence when Maple Leaf Gardens was built as their home. At the opening on 12 November 1931, Foster Hewitt (1902–85) broadcast his first 'Hockey Night in Canada', describing the game from a gondola overlooking the rink. For three decades thereafter, his high-pitched voice—and his excited refrain, 'He shoots! He scores!'—*was* hockey for most Canadians. 'Hockey Night in Canada' was the one and only Canadian-produced radio program on CBC that consistently outdrew American offerings with the Canadian listeners. Although the Depression benefited professional sports by creating a desperate need for escape, not all Canadians could afford to pay for admission. In Toronto, for example, ticket prices of 50¢ and $1.25 resulted in many empty seats. By 1939 the NHL had suffered the loss of all but two of its Canadian teams, the Maple Leafs and the Montreal Canadiens. The centre of professional hockey power shifted to the United States, although Canadians still knew that virtually all the players came from Canada, where hockey was still a way of life on the frozen rivers and lakes of the nation in the winter months.

While Canada's film and hockey successes were mainly in Hollywood and in American arenas, a vital grass-roots theatrical movement existed at home between the wars, almost entirely on the amateur level. It consisted of Little Theatre groups in most major cities and towns, hundreds of high school drama groups, dozens of university drama groups, and innumerable other drama and musical drama organizations sponsored by fraternal organizations, church groups, and labour unions. In most Canadian cities and towns, one group or another was rehearsing a play or a musical at any given time during the winter months. During the darkest days of the depression, Canadian theatre blossomed, providing relief for many from the grim conditions of their lives. Protracted hard times, while discouraging some artists, also energized others, particularly those who sought cultural directions that would encourage a new

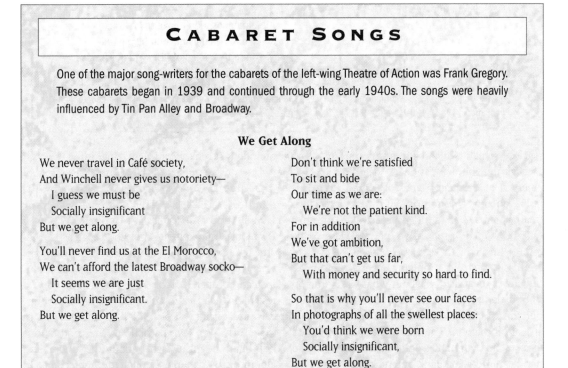

CABARET SONGS

One of the major song-writers for the cabarets of the left-wing Theatre of Action was Frank Gregory. These cabarets began in 1939 and continued through the early 1940s. The songs were heavily influenced by Tin Pan Alley and Broadway.

We Get Along

We never travel in Café society,
And Winchell never gives us notoriety—
  I guess we must be
  Socially insignificant
But we get along.

You'll never find us at the El Morocco,
We can't afford the latest Broadway socko—
  It seems we are just
  Socially insignificant.
But we get along.

Don't think we're satisfied
To sit and bide
Our time as we are:
  We're not the patient kind.
For in addition
We've got ambition,
But that can't get us far,
  With money and security so hard to find.

So that is why you'll never see our faces
In photographs of all the swellest places:
  You'd think we were born
  Socially insignificant,
But we get along.

The Syncopated Dictator

It's the Nineteen-Forties newest thrill,
You will have no peace of mind until
You get into the rhythm
And join in the crowd,
You start a-swingin' with 'em
And laughin' out loud—
When you're told.

In the Praha streets the abandoned Czechs
Wonder who Adolph will next annex;
They're tryin' like the devil
To swing to the left,
But with the help of Neville
They are always left
In the cold.
Under old Vesuvius
Though a little dubious,
They go to town;
Back in old Vienna
You'll see infant and duenna
who'll be bearin' it down—
wearin' it down—hey!

Chorus:
Clap your hands and clatter your heels,
Heil your partner, shiver like eels,
Syncopated Dictator's caught you—
Can't relax while the fascist's got you!

Point your toe and stiffen your knee,
Goosestep round and pivot with glee,
Mussolini's your latest hero,
Ghosts of Caesar and Shades of Nero!
But remember Nero fiddled while old Rome burned,
So don't trust your partner while your back is turned.

Now
On the boulevards of Baden-Baden
Start in shaggin' with a beg-your-podden,
Then as the music gets torrid and torrider
Truck on down along the Polish corridor!

All join hands, don't have to be urged;
Some day you may have to be purged—
You're the victim of—Heaven help you—
Syn-co-pated Dictator-ship!

SOURCE: Quoted in Toby Gordon Ryan, *Stage Left Canadian Theatre in the Thirties: A Memoir* (Toronto: CTR Publications, 1981), 189–91.

spirit of social involvement and commitment.

During the depression, a theatre of the left emerged in the major cities of Canada, particularly Vancouver, Toronto, Winnipeg, and Montreal, which spread to other places (like Timmins, Ontario) where 'progressive' people were to be found. In all of these places, there was a twin emphasis: first, on supplying theatre that spoke directly to its audiences about what was going on in Canada and the world; and second, on exemplifying the ideals of collective experience in theatrical production. The theatre of the left tended to exalt amateur values and participation. It also had far more Canadian content in its plays. The first tour of the Workers' Theatre, for example, included seven short plays, including *Eviction* (written by members of the Montreal Progressive Arts Club), *Farmers' Fight* (also written by the Montreal PAC), *Joe Derry* (written by Dorothy Livesay) and *War in the East* (written by Stanley Ryerson). Interestingly enough, progressive theatre groups did not shun the establishment-oriented Dominion Drama Festival (DDF), but instead competed frequently, seeking thereby to test their theatrical quality, apart from the political value of their work. The DDF adjudicators, in their turn, were sympathetic to the productions but often unenthusiastic about the doom and gloom of their themes, preferring lighter fare. In 1937, a four-person play entitled *Relief* written by

Minnie Evans Bicknell of Marshall, Saskatchewan, and performed by the Marshall Dramatic Club, was one of the finalists at the DDF. The play was a domestic tragedy performed in a naturalistic style in which the performers dealt with matters that were all too familiar in their daily lives, as the critics noted in their reviews. Toronto's Theatre of Action was particularly active in seeking out Canadian themes and Canadian playwrights. The thematic content of the drama preferred by the theatre of the left was undoubtedly one of the factors that limited its popular acceptance. Towards the end of the 1930s, however, influenced by the cabaret theatre of Kurt Weill and Bertolt Brecht as developed by left-wing American theatre groups, progressive theatre in Canada became more interested in musical theatre. Some of the cabaret productions actually featured songs that commented satirically upon Canadian politics. This topical humour offered a lighter alternative to the fare presented by the more earnest theatre companies.

THE SECOND WORLD WAR

Canada went back to war on 10 September 1939. This time the government waited a week after the British declaration of war against Germany to join the conflict, thus emphasizing Canada's 'independent' status. The nation's entry into the war helped complete the process of economic recovery. Unprepared militarily, as in the Great War, Canada proved capable of mobilizing resources remarkably swiftly when required. Canada quickly accepted the British Commonwealth Air Training Plan as its major war commitment. The details of the scheme were agreed upon by Britain and Canada on 17 December 1939. Within months the program's first graduates emerged from Camp Borden, Ontario. It eventually graduated 131,533 Commonwealth airmen, 72,835 of whom were Canadian, at a cost of $1.6 billion. A nation of less than 12 million people would eventually put over 1 million of them into uniform. Using the War Measures Act, Canada succeeded in mobilizing economic resources in a way that had seemed impossible during the Depression. Tax arrangements between the Dominion and the provinces were restructured during the emergency, with the federal government collecting most of the revenue and making grants to the provinces to recover their operating expenses.

The economy was totally managed and regulated, a process associated with Ottawa's wartime economic czar, Clarence Decatur Howe (1886–1960). By 1943 unemployment was well under 2 per cent, a figure regarded in most quarters as full employment. Federal spending rose from 3.4 per cent of the gross national product (GNP) in 1939 to 37.6 per cent of GNP by 1944, totalling a full $4.4 billion in the latter year. Industrial growth was better distributed across the regions than in 1914–18, inflation was controlled, and consumption was regulated by shortages and rationing. Canada's total GNP rose from $5.6 billion in 1939 to $11.9 billion in 1945. The nation became one of the world's industrial giants, producing 850,000 motorized vehicles and over 16,000 military aircraft during the war. The government borrowed heavily from its own citizens, partly in the form of war bonds. While the achievement was impressive, it suggested that the riddle of social justice remained unsolved. Canada appeared far more capable of efficient utilization of its productive capacity to fight destructive wars abroad than to battle domestically with poverty and unemployment.

As in the Great War, Canadians fought well whenever called upon. As in the previous conflict, they were often employed as shock troops. In the disastrous landing of the 2nd Canadian Division at Dieppe in August 1942, nearly 2,700 of the 5,000 Canadians who embarked were either killed or captured. The First Canadian Army, formed in 1942 under the command of General A.G.L. McNaughton (1887–1966), was composed of five divisions that were eventually split between Italy and northwest Europe. This army was independently commanded, although the Royal Canadian Air Force and the Royal Canadian Navy were mainly integrated with their British counterparts. Canadian flyers became noted for their work in bombers rather than in fighters, as in World War I. The RCN grew to 365 ships, spending the war mainly protecting convoys on the North Atlantic route and achieving such expertise in this duty that in May 1943 a Canadian, Admiral L.W. Murray (1896–1971), was given command of the Canadian Northwest Atlantic theatre. Many other Canadians and Newfoundlanders served in the Canadian merchant marine, a thankless task which kept them out of the loop for veterans' benefits for many years. Canada ultimately had the third largest navy among the Allied powers, the fourth largest air force, and the fourth largest army. Such a contribution ought to have made it something of a power in the world, although the major powers—Britain, the United States, and the USSR—routinely treated Canada as little different from Allied nations like Chile or Brazil, which had only token forces in the war. The superpowers

Life at Sea in a Canadian Corvette during the Second World War

One of Canada's major military functions during the war against Hitler was to provide escort service against Nazi submarines for convoys of ships plying the dangerous North Atlantic route. Much of this duty was carried out in small ships called corvettes. Built in Canadian shipyards and originally intended for coastal duty, the corvettes were manned by nearly 100,000 young Canadian sailors. Life aboard them was dangerous and uncomfortable, as the following account from Howard Cousins, leading signalman aboard HMCS *Algoma* in 1941–2, suggests.

The ship was your home and the weather had a direct effect on the degree of comfort that home provided. When the wind and seas built up, the comforts of your home were virtually non-existent. As the ship rolled and pitched, you were thrown around continuously, not daring to move without holding fast to something. The bridge was wet with spray, sometimes solid water.

The highly developed storm gear we have today was not available then. An oilskin coat worn over a duffel coat, a sou'wester on your head and sea-boots on your feet was the rig of the day. In theory, the oilskin coat overlapped the tops of the sea-boots. In practice, the wind whipping around the bridge caused the skirt of the coat to lift and flap. Before long water had seeped into your boots and soon your feet were wet and cold. Water also found its way down your neck. Some of us wore a towel around our neck, but before long the towel became soaked and water trickled down your chest and back.

A corvette on the crest of the wave could have one-third of the forward portion clear of the water. As the ship rolled and dropped down into the trough, it was almost a free fall. The poor blokes in the forecastle felt virtually weightless; anything on the lockers, shelves, and tables, including your meal, frequently floated off. When the ship smashed into the back of the next wave, it felt as if the ship had been dropped on concrete.

Drawing meals from the galley was awkward, to say the least. The galley was located aft of the wheelhouse and the duty messman had to collect the meals for his mess on a tray, then carry that tray along the open deck to the forecastle. With no hand available to hang on with, seas breaking over the side and down from the break of the forecastle, it was a perilous trip. Some meals did not make it.

I remember one occasion when the messman, having successfully made the trip, proudly stood at the head of the table as someone removed the oilskin protecting the food. The messman was starting to boast how good he was when the ship fell rapidly over the crest of a wave. When the ship was brought back up with the usual jolt, the messman and our food were thrown across the deck.

Bad weather also involved the laws of physics in the basic act of getting into your bed, which was a hammock suspended from steel rods on the deckhead. To get into your hammock, you grabbed the rod and swung yourself up and in. Timing was essential. If the ship was lifting to a sea, it was virtually impossible to push yourself off the deck, let along swing up into the hammock. On the other hand, if you waited until the ship was falling off the crest, a slight push of the toes was enough for you to float effortlessly up to the hammock.

Everyone's job became more difficult under bad weather conditions. . . . The cook often gave up and resorted to sandwiches. . . . No, home was not a place of comfort in bad weather, which did have one good thing going for it—there was very little chance that the convoy would be troubled with submarine attacks.

SOURCE: M. Johnston, *Corvettes Canada: Convoy Veterans of WWII Tell Their True Stories* (Toronto: McGraw-Hill Ryerson, 1994): 113–15.

admitted France to their council tables almost as soon as the nation was liberated, while ignoring Canada completely.

Canada fought chiefly in the European and North Atlantic theatres. Canadian assistance to American and British efforts in the Pacific and Southeast Asia was fairly minimal. In December 1941, however, two Canadian battalions were involved in the surrender of Hong Kong. The 1,421 men who returned home after years in Japanese prison camps had to fight for twenty-three years to win proper veteran's benefits from the Canadian government. As in the Great War, casualties in this conflict were heavy, with 42,642 Canadians giving up their lives. On the other hand, this was not a war of stalemate in the trenches. Instead, the establishment of beachheads was followed by a constant advance that involved liberating places held by the enemy. One innovation in this war was the active military service of women. As in 1914–18 large numbers of women were employed in the war industry, but by 1945 over 43,000 women were actually in uniform. A Gallup poll taken in 1944 indicated, however, that most Canadians, including 68 per cent of the women polled, believed that men should be given preference for employment in the postwar reconstruction. As a result, the machinery for women's participation in the work force, including day care centres, was dismantled with unseemly haste at the war's end.

As in the Great War, dissent was met with persecution. The Canadian government proved almost totally insensitive to pacifists' beliefs. It interned thousands of Canadians without trial, often for mere criticism of government policy. The most publicized abuse of the state's power was the treatment of the Japanese Canadians. Although the King government did not for a minute believe that Japanese Canadians represented any real military danger, it yielded to pressure from British Columbia and forcibly evacuated most Japanese Canadians from the West Coast. Many were sent to internment camps in the interior of BC, and others were scattered

Japanese Canadians being relocated to camps in the interior of British Columbia, 1942. NAC, C-046355.

EVACUATION FROM WOODFIBRE, BRITISH COLUMBIA, 1942

Takao Ujo Nakano published this account of his wartime experience in 1980.

Pearl Harbor, the opening strike of the Japan-U.S. conflict, shocked Woodfibre's inhabitants. The quiet town was completely transformed as rumours propagated rumours, fed by often conflicting reports. The Japanese community especially was in an uproar.

We Japanese, largely working-class immigrants, were, generally speaking, not given to sophisticated political thinking. Rather we had in common a blind faith in Japan's eventual victory. The extent of our reasoning, decidedly specious in retrospect, went something like this: The burst of energy at Pearl Harbor was exemplary. If the war were short, say of less than two years' duration,

Japan stood to win. If it were prolonged, Japan, weakened by over a decade of aggression in Manchuria and China, admittedly might lose. Meanwhile, we kept receiving reports of Japanese victories in the Far East. We therefore resolved to bear the present uneasiness patiently.

In the weeks that followed, life in Woodfibre was indeed changed. I remember especially the compulsory nightly blackout, meant to thwart the activity of Japanese bombers that might fly over British Columbia. With Canadians thus anxious, some drastic move was inevitable. By mid-January of 1942, some of us faced the prospect of evacuation. At that time it was said that if the Issei [Japanese-born] men aged eighteen to forty-five went to the road camps, then the Issei men over forty-five, the Issei women and children, and all Nisei [Canadian-born of Japanese descent] would be allowed to remain where they were. We Issei men accordingly received an order to depart on March 16.

As the day of departure drew nearer, tension mounted in the Japanese community. The lot of us Issei men was held to be a sorry one indeed. The Rockies were terribly cold in March; some of us would likely freeze to death in the twenty-below temperature. Again, the steep mountains were subject to avalanches; road work in them would be very dangerous. And again, deep in the mountains, men could easily become isolated by the snow and starve when provisions failed to get through to them. With such conjectures, the families of Issei men spent anxious days and sleepless nights. But the order to depart *was* a government order. To accept it as fate was our sorry resolve. . . .

SOURCE: Takao Ujo Nakano, *Within the Barbed Wire Fence: A Japanese Man's Account of his Internment in Canada* (Toronto: University of Toronto Press, 1980), 8–10.

across the country, their land seized and their property sold at auction. 'National emergency' was also used to justify the dissemination of propaganda, now called 'management of information'. Citizens needed to be educated in order to maintain faith and hope and to eliminate 'potential elements of disunity', a euphemism for criticism of the government. One major institution of information management was the National Film Board of Canada, under Scottish-born John Grierson (1898–1972), who believed in the integration of 'the loyalties and forces of the community in the name of positive and highly constructive ideas'. Grierson saw 'information services—propaganda if you like' as an inevitable consequence of the government's involvement in the crisis (quoted in Young 1978: 217–40).

Internally, wartime policies revolved around two major questions: conscription and postwar reconstruction. In a national plebiscite held on the question of conscription in the spring of 1942, the nation voted 2,945,514 to 1,643,006 to release the government from an earlier pledge not to conscript for overseas service. Quebec voted strongly in the negative. The conscription issue emerged again in 1944, when the military insisted (as in 1917) that it was necessary to ship overseas conscripts who had been drafted with the promise that they would not be required to serve abroad. In the end, although conscripts were sent to Europe, few served as combatants before the war ended in May 1945. For the King government, the increasing threat from the CCF became a problem as nagging as that of Quebec. As early as 1941 many Canadians had apparently come to realize that the failure to make a concerted assault on social injustice had been a result mainly of governments' refusal to act. Canada was now, in wartime, demonstrating how thoroughly the country could be mobilized if the will to do so was present. Public opinion in Anglo-Canada began turning to the social promises of the CCF. By the time of the

An anti-conscription rally organized by the Defence of Canada League at the Maisonneuve Market in Montreal, March 1942. NAC, PA-108258.

September 1943 federal election, the CCF received the support of 29 per cent of the electorate at the polls. In 1944 the Saskatchewan CCF wiped out a long-standing Liberal government in an election fought over social services.

King's Liberals had dragged their heels over social welfare reform. Federal unemployment insurance had been introduced in 1940, but other progressive legislation remained on hold. Now, in 1944, King declared in the House of Commons 'a wholly new conception of industry as being in the nature of social service for the benefit of all, not as something existing only for the benefit of a favoured few'. The introduction of social reform was necessary not only to deal with the threat from the CCF but also to prevent possible public disorder at the conclusion of the war and to assert the authority of the federal government. Once the political decision was made to implement social reform, there were plenty of schemes available, including a package in the 'Report on Social Security for Canada' tabled in the House of Commons Special Committee on Social Security by economist Leonard Marsh (1906–82) in 1943. In the end, a full program of progressive legislation was never actually enacted before the end of the war. The Liberal government did introduce the Family Allowances Act of 1944, Canada's first social insurance program with universal coverage. It provided benefits to

'W.L.M.K.'

In 1950 the poet and political activist Frank Scott responded to the death of William Lyon Mackenzie King with the following poem.

W.L.M.K.

How shall we speak of Canada,
Mackenzie King dead?
The Mother's boy in the lonely room
With his dog, his medium and his ruins?
He blunted us.

We had no shape
Because he never took sides,
And no sides
Because he never allowed them to take shape

He skillfully avoided what was wrong
Without saying what was right
And never let his on the one hand
Know what his on the other hand was doing.

The height of his ambition
Was to pile a Parliamentary Committee on a Royal
  Commission.
To have 'conscription if necessary
But not necessarily conscription'.
To let Parliament decide—
Later.
Postpone, postpone, abstain.

Only one thread was certain:
After World War I
Business as usual.
After World War II
Orderly decontrol.
Always he led us back to where we were before.

He seemed to be in the centre
Because we had no centre,
No vision
To pierce the smoke-screen of his politics.

Truly he will be remembered
Wherever men honour ingenuity,
Ambiguity, inactivity, and political longevity.

Let us raise up a temple
To the cult of mediocrity;
Do nothing by halves
Which can be done by quarters.

SOURCE: F.R. Scott and A.J.M. Smith, eds, *The Blasted Pine* (Toronto: Macmillan, 1962), 27-8.

mothers of children under age sixteen. In 1944 the Liberals also passed the National Housing Act, described as 'An Act to Promote the Construction of New Houses, the Repair and Modernization of Existing Houses, the Improvement of Housing and Living Conditions and the Expansion of Employment in the Postwar Period'. The King government turned to the postwar period, however, with intentions of attacking the problem of social justice and the constitutional limitations of the British North America Act simultaneously.

CONCLUSION

Despite war fatalities, injustices, and some deprivation, the Second World War was, on balance, a unifying and positive experience for most Canadians. Full employment helped a good deal. Rationing provided a better balanced diet.

Limited leisure time and the absence of big-ticket consumer items, such as automobiles and household appliances, forced many Canadians to save, often by purchasing war bonds and savings stamps. By war's end, a fifteen-year deferral of expectations had built up a powerful urge among Canadians to enjoy material comforts, free from concern over life's vagaries and hazards. This population was fully conscious of the dangers of assuming that social protection could be left to the private individual. It was equally aware that the state could intervene in the process, if it so desired.

HOW HISTORY HAS CHANGED

THE WINNIPEG GENERAL STRIKE

The historical interpretation of the Winnipeg General Strike of 1919 illustrates several different ways in which history changes. In the case of the Winnipeg General Strike, not only has one of the contemporary interpretations of its origins and meaning come to dominate, but its very importance in the nation's history has altered over time.

In 1919, there were two competing interpretations of the Winnipeg General Strike, both of them extreme. A conspiratorial one, propounded by its opponents, saw the strike as a daring attempt to overthrow the existing industrial and political system. The strikers themselves insisted that the strike was a legitimate, peaceful demonstration by labour to demand the right to organize and earn a living wage. Neither of these interpretations gained dominance at the time, and the strike—after a brief period in the national eye—was well-remembered only as a local issue for many years. Only J.S. Woodsworth's prominence in Ottawa kept it before the larger Canadian public in the 1930s and 1940s. Textbooks written in the 1940s made little or no mention of the strike. This limited profile began to change in 1950 with the publication of Donald C. Masters' *The Winnipeg General Strike*. The strike gained in importance during the expansion of Canadian textbook publishing in the 1960s, as authors discovered that it was one of Canada's most highly polarized historical events, ideal for 'conflicting interpretations' approaches. The strike's historical importance also benefitted from an increased popularity of history 'from the bottom up' and from a new sympathy towards radical movements.

Since 1970 a number of serious, full-length academic studies have been published. Most have accepted the strikers' own interpretation, seeing the strikers as moderate gradualists, victimized by their opposition through the law and the courts. No one could be found to defend seriously the role or policy of the federal government in the strike, which was seen not as an incipient revolution but merely as a modest attempt to win collective bargaining. New studies have examined other aspects of the strike, such as the role of women, the role of the 'alien' and racism, and socialist ideology, but the strikers' own interpretation has now been clearly established as the dominant one.

SHORT BIBLIOGRAPHY

Abella, Irving, and Harold Troper. *None is Too Many: Canada and the Jews of Europe, 1933–1948*. Toronto, 1982. The standard work on the subject, judicious, fair, and scathing in its critique of Canadian policy.

Baillargeon, Denyse. *Making Do: Women, Family, and Home in Montreal during the Great Depression*. Waterloo, 2000. A recent work exploring the role of women during the Depression.

Baum, Gregory. *Catholics and Canadian Socialism: Political Thought in the Thirties and Forties*. Toronto, 1980. A stimulating book emphasizing that not all Catholics were unsympathetic to social reform and socialism.

Berton, Pierre. *Hollywood's Canada: The Americanization of Our National Image*. Toronto, 1975. Perhaps Berton's best work, this one explores the ways in which Hollywood has dealt with Canada and Canadian subjects.

Bumsted, J.M. *The Winnipeg General Strike of 1919: An Illustrated History*. Winnipeg, 1994. Makes the history of the strike accessible to the general audience.

Finkel, Alvin. *Business and Social Reform in the Thirties*. Toronto, 1979. A useful analysis of the relationship between business and social reform in the Depression, emphasizing that many businessmen saw reform as the only alternative to the destruction of capitalism.

Forbes, Ernest R. *The Maritime Rights Movement 1919–1927: A Study in Canadian Regionalism*. Montreal, 1979. A fascinating study of one movement of regional protest that failed.

Lévesque, Andrée. *Making and Breaking the Rules: Women in Quebec, 1919–1939*. Toronto, 1994. An important study of women in Quebec between the wars.

Morton, W.L. *The Progressive Party of Canada*. Toronto, 1950. The classic account, still generally valid.

Owram, Doug. *The Government Generation: Canadian Intellectuals and the State 1900–1945*. Toronto, 1986. A synthesis of secondary literature on the subject to the mid-1980s.

Peers, Frank. *The Politics of Canadian Broadcasting 1920–1951*. Toronto, 1969. A first-hand history of the development of Canadian broadcasting before television.

Safarian, A.E. *The Canadian Economy in the Great Depression*. Toronto, 1959. The standard account of the performance of the Canadian economy in the 1930s.

Stacey, C.P. *Arms, Men and Governments: The War Policies of Canada 1939–1945* (Ottawa, 1970). A useful survey of the military policy of the second World War in Canada.

Strong-Boag, Veronica, *The New Day Recalled: Lives of Girls and Women in English Canada 1919–1939*. Toronto, 1988. A survey of the changing (or unchanging) role of women in English Canada between the wars.

Sunahara, Ann. *The Politics of Racism: The Uprooting of Japanese Canadians during the Second World Wari*. Toronto, 1981. A sober and unsentimental account that does not hesitate to call this part of Canadian war policy racist.

Thompson, John Herd, with Allan Seager. *Canada 1922–1939: Decades of Discord*. Toronto, 1985. The best synthesis of the interwar years, rich in detail.

Tippett, Maria. *Making Culture: English-Canadian Institutions and the Arts before the Massey Commission*. Toronto, 1990. Perhaps the only overview of the cultural infrastructure of any part of Canada before 1951.

Trofimenkoff, Susan Mann. *Action Française: French-Canadian Nationalism in the Twenties*. Toronto, 1975. An analysis of nationalism, mainly in Quebec, in the 1920s, focusing on the Abbé Groulx and his circle.

STUDY QUESTIONS

1. What was Stephen Leacock's 'unsolved riddle of social justice'? How did Canadians address this riddle in the interwar period?
2. Identify three causes of labour unrest in Canada after the Great War.
3. Explain why the Depression was a devastating experience for many Canadians.
4. What social and economic impacts did the automobile have on the Canadian public during this period?
5. Did gaining the vote substantially increase the political power of Canadian women? Explain.
6. Why was the 'theatre of the left' more active than the mainstream theatre in presenting Canadian themes during the 1930s?
7. For Canadians, in what ways was the Second World War a replay of the First? In what ways was it different?

CHAPTER NINE

Prospering Together, 1945–1959

The post-Second World War era, particularly before 1960, was a period of unparalleled economic growth and prosperity for Canada. Production and consumption moved steadily upward. Employment rose almost continuously. Canada substantially increased its workforce. Inflation was steady but almost never excessive. Interest rates were relatively low. The nation was in the midst of an uncharacteristic natural increase in its population growth rate that would become known as the baby boom. At the same time that many Canadians took advantage of the good times by conceiving children and moving to new homes in the suburbs, both the federal and provincial governments became active in providing new programs of social protection for their citizens. That network was not created without controversy, particularly of the constitutional variety, although the debate was still relatively muted until the 1960s. By that time, however, Canadian governments at all levels had become interventionist in a variety of areas, including culture.

Affluence

At the base of all developments from 1946 to 1960 (and beyond) was economic prosperity and growth. Almost all aspects of planning in both the public and private sectors were based on assumptions of constant growth, and such thinking seemed to work. Between 1946 and 1960, per capita income in Canada nearly doubled, thus increasing the Canadian standard of living. Canadians could be forgiven for believing that there were no limits to growth. Great Depressions were disasters of the past, and the standard of living could continue to rise. Both politicians and their expert advisers argued that governments could now manage economies. They could correct for negative movements soon after they began. The operative economic wisdom was Keynesianism, named after the English economist John Maynard Keynes, whose writings provided much of the theoretical underpinning of affluence.

Quebec's Tremblay Commission on Constitutional Problems well described the prevailing wisdom in 1953:

> The objective envisaged was the maintenance of economic stability and full employment. . . . Both expenditures and investments, by individuals as well as by companies, should, therefore, be encouraged. Moreover, the government should take a part in this, and co-operate in stabilizing the economy and in ensuring full employment by its own expenditures and investments. This would demand from it an appropriate fiscal and monetary policy, as well as a programme of carefully planned public works. . . . The new policy necessarily entailed a considerable number of social security measures regarded as indispensable for the correction of variations in the economic cycle (Kwavnick 1973: 183–4).

In truth, the overall pattern of affluence was neither solely attributable to government man-

TIMELINE

1945
Liberal government is re-elected. Dominion-Provincial Conference on Reconstruction is convened. United Nations is founded in San Francisco.

1947
Imperial Oil brings in Leduc, Alberta, oilfield. Prime Minister King acknowledges Canada's 'moral obligation' to refugees and displaced persons in Europe.

1948
Mackenzie King resigns and is replaced by Louis St Laurent. Newfoundland holds two plebiscites on its future, choosing to join Canada.

1949
Asbestos strike in Quebec. Newfoundland joins Confederation. Royal Commission on National Development in the Arts, Letters, and Sciences (Massey Commission) is appointed. North Atlantic Treaty Organization is formed.

1950
Canada joins Korean 'police action'. Interprovincial oil pipeline is built from Edmonton to Superior, Ontario.

1951
Old Age Security Act passed by Ottawa. Employees strike at Eaton's department stores. Aluminum Company of Canada begins the Kitimat project in British Columbia.

1952
First CBC television stations are opened.

1953
Quebec's Tremblay Commission on Constitutional Problems makes its report. Mackenzie Highway is completed to Northwest Territories. Transmountain oil pipeline is built from Edmonton to Vancouver.

1954
British Empire Games in Vancouver sees first mile run in less than four minutes by both Roger Bannister and John Landy. St Lawrence Seaway opens. First iron ore leaves Ungava, Quebec.

1955
Canso Causeway is opened in Nova Scotia, linking Cape Breton to the mainland.

1956
Canadian Labour Congress is formed from a merger of the Canadian Congress of Labour and the Trades and Labor Congress of Canada. The Unemployment Assistance Act is passed by Parliament. Trans-Canada Pipeline debate weakens the Liberal government. First transatlantic telephone cable is completed between Newfoundland and Scotland.

1957
Liberal government passes the Hospital Insurance Diagnostic Services Act. Diefenbaker's Tories win a minority government; St Laurent steps down. Lester B. Pearson wins the Nobel Peace Prize. The Canada Council is created.

1958
Inco strike. Lester B. Pearson is chosen Liberal leader. Diefenbaker Tories sweep the nation, including Quebec. Great Slave Railway is begun.

1959
Diefenbaker government decides to scrap the Avro Arrow. Maurice Duplessis dies.

1960
Royal Commission on Government Reorganization is appointed.

agement nor distinctive to Canada. It was general across the Western industrial world. It started, in part, with the rebuilding of the war-torn economies of Europe and Asia. It continued with heavy expenditures on military defence during the cold war. Filling consumer wants after a generation's deferral of expectations helped. Then prosperity continued on its own momentum for a time, aided by the baby boom.

Foreign trade was an important component of Canadian affluence. The volume of both imports and exports increased substantially. Canada became integrated into the American trading market as Great Britain decreased in importance as a trading partner. The government set the value of the Canadian dollar in relation to the American dollar, and attempted to control Canadian foreign exchange and Canadian domestic banking through the Bank of Canada. After 1954 banks were allowed to move into consumer credit and mortgage loans, although before 1967 they were limited in the interest they could charge. Canada's monetary policy was to increase the supply of money in circulation, producing inflation that would eventually run out of control.

The relative importance of various sectors of the domestic economy shifted. Agriculture declined from 25 per cent of the total workforce in 1946 to 11 per cent in 1961. The real growth areas were in the public sector, particularly public administration and the services necessary to manage the new state. In 1946 just over 15 per cent of Canadians were employed in the public sector, but by 1961 that figure had increased to just over 25 per cent. Many of the public-service employees were highly educated white-collar workers, and by 1960 over half of Canadians held white-collar jobs. In manufacturing, regional disparities continued and even grew. Central Canada, especially Ontario, experienced most of the gains in manufacturing. Ontario produced over 50 per cent of total manufacturing value added in the nation. Ontario dominated the manufacture of durable goods and big-ticket consumer items in many industries. In 1957, for example, Ontario turned out 98.8 per cent of Canada's motor vehicles, 90.7 per cent of its heavy industrial goods, 90 per cent of its agricultural implements, and 80.7 per cent of its major household appliances. Canadian manufacturing served two principal markets. One was the domestic consumer market, which exploded after fifteen years of doing without. The other was a huge market for military hardware to equip Canada's armed forces, which greatly increased in number after 1950. Canada had a natural ambition to produce homegrown equipment, but had to settle for subcontracting parts of Canadian orders through American branch plants. The Diefenbaker government's decision to scrap the Avro Arrow in 1959 marked the last serious Canadian venture in the independent development of military hardware.

The resource economy did reasonably well. Beginning in 1947, when Imperial Oil brought in the major oilfield at Leduc, in southern Alberta, there was significant expansion in western Canadian oil and gas. Most of the risk was assumed by Americans, and the Alberta oil industry was quickly taken over by multinational firms. Oil and gas began to be transported by pipeline from the west into the major centres of population and industry. Potash provided a major new resource for Saskatchewan, and uranium was a short-lived bonanza for northern Ontario. The burning of fossil fuels and the development of nuclear power were the growth areas in the energy industry. Hydroelectric generation, which accounted for almost 95 per cent of Canada's electrical capacity in 1946, had dropped to just over 75 per cent by 1960 and would be down to only half that by the 1970s, despite massive hydroelectric projects in many provinces, especially Quebec and British Columbia.

In this period of growth, nobody paid much attention to environmental issues. Affluence rather than effluence was the watchword. Canadians before 1960 were only dimly aware

THE AVRO ARROW

The CF-105 Avro Arrow (1953–59) was born when specifications were set for a Canadian-built interceptor aircraft to defend the nation's northern frontier. Prototypes were finally authorized by the Liberal government in December 1953, to be built by A.V. Roe of Canada. This airplane would have a crew of two, a supersonic combat radius of 200 nautical miles, a combat ceiling of not less than 60,000 feet, a maximum speed of Mach 2, a climb rate of not more than six minutes to 50,000 feet, a large internal weapons package, state-of-the-art weapons and control systems, twin engines, all-weather capabilities, and manoeuvrability of 2g at Mach 1.5 at 50,000 feet without loss of speed or altitude. Few of these specifications were found singly in any contemporary military aircraft, much less in combination. Because so many of the components did not exist, Canada was forced to do a good deal of development from scratch, especially of engine and control systems. Costs rapidly escalated. Ironically enough, neither the special Orenda engine nor the control system on which so much money was spent were ever installed in the aircraft.

After John Diefenbaker's Tories took office in 1957, the costs of the Arrow became an increasingly important political consideration. The government knew that the Americans and the British would never buy an aircraft built outside their respective countries, and it was unable to find other buyers for the Arrow, although a number of countries were interested in its various component parts. In 1957 the Arrow passed its first full test flight with flying colours—on the same day that the Russians put a capsule into space for the first time. This Soviet achievement provided ammunition for those who argued that missiles were the way of the future and that manned aircraft were obsolescent. The Diefenbaker administration cancelled the project on 20 February 1959 without being completely candid or sensible about its reasons. A.V. Roe fired all its workers, and many professional personnel headed off for other nations. The prototype and the plans were trashed immediately, without anyone taking responsibility for this action. Within a year, Canada was buying inferior interceptor aircraft from the Americans, thus accepting its subordinate function under the American defence umbrella. At the same time, Diefenbaker refused to allow the missiles installed on Canadian soil to be armed with nuclear warheads, rendering them useless in the event of an all-out Russian attack.

of the dangers of 'pollution', a word that had only just come into common usage. Nuclear experts insisted that nuclear accidents were extremely unlikely, and did not worry about the disposal of long-life nuclear wastes. Petrochemical plants dumped waste into surrounding waters, and paper-processing plants dumped poisonous mercury into rivers and lakes. Solid industrial waste was usually buried, often used as landfill to create new housing estates near large urban centres, such as the Love Canal area near Niagara Falls. Many inland rivers and lakes deteriorated into veritable cesspools of industrial waste and human sewage. Acid rain spread unrecognized as an international problem. Farmers dumped chemical fertilizers and weedkillers into the soil, where they eventually ended up in underground aquifers. Economic growth and development were the measures of all things, and the handful of Canadians preaching caution were often regarded as a lunatic fringe of troublemakers.

An artist's drawing of the CF 105 Avro Arrow. NAC, PA-111546.

The boom of the postwar years encouraged the growth of American direct investment in Canada and the rise of the multinational corporation, which usually had headquarters in the United States and a branch-plant operation in Canada. By 1950 more than three-quarters of total foreign investment in the country was American, chiefly in mining, manufacturing, and petroleum. In 1959 foreign-owned companies controlled nearly 60 per cent of assets in Canadian mining, over 60 per cent of the oil and gas industry, and over 50 per cent of Canadian manufacturing. The extent of foreign ownership of all major Canadian industries in 1959 was 34 per cent, of which 26 per cent was owned by United States residents. American ownership was especially prevalent in the highly profitable consumer area, where production flourished on the backs of American technology and American promotion of goods and brand names. American advertising and cultural values created consumer demand on a continental basis, and Canadian subsidiaries fulfilled this demand for the Canadian market. Not until 1957, however, did American investment and the growth of multinationals become important public issues. As late as 1956, one of the leading textbooks in Canadian economic history referred to foreign investment as 'one of the mainsprings of progress' without mentioning its less desirable aspects (Easterbrook and Aitken 1956: 402). The foreign investment issue was first brought to the public's attention by the Royal Commission on Canada's Economic Prospects, chaired by Walter Gordon. The report of the commission, released after the Liberal government that had appointed it was defeated in 1957, observed that 'No other nation as highly industrialized as Canada has such a large proportion of industry controlled by non-resident concerns' (*Royal Commission on Canada's Economic Prospects* 1958: 384). The commission's concern was not immediately shared by the public, however.

Part of the critique of American multinationalism was related to Canada's scientific research and development policy. Critics noted that Canada spent a far smaller proportion of its science dollar on the development side of research and development. They added that industry in Canada contributed a far smaller share of scientific activity than in any other highly industrialized nation. The reasons for these lags, many insisted, were to be found in

Canada's ability as a branch-plant economy to import technology developed elsewhere. In 1959, for example, industry was responsible for only 39 per cent of scientific research in Canada, as opposed to 58 per cent in Britain and 78 per cent in the United States. By this time the federal government's outlays in scientific activity were in excess of $200 million per year, while in 1959 Canadian industry spent only $96.7 million on research and development at home. Research money for the Avro Arrow was supplied not by A.V. Roe, but by the Canadian federal government. Between 1957 and 1961, moreover, 95 per cent of all Canadian patents involved foreign applicants, nearly 70 per cent of them American. Clearly Canada spent large sums of public money on scientific research, but was not getting much industrial advantage from the expenditures. Canadian scientists had co-operated with American counterparts to produce the IBM 101 electronic statistical machine in time for it to analyse the 1951 Canadian census data. But before long the new technology became American, and Canadians were never in the front lines of the microchip revolution of later years. In 1962 expenditure on research and development as a proportion of sales averaged 0.7 per cent by all Canadian manufacturers, as opposed to 2 per cent by American ones and even larger proportions in Germany and Japan.

An increased role for organized labour accompanied other economic trends of the affluent society. Union membership increased and unions were organized in a number of new

☐ The 1949 Asbestos Strike in Quebec. Metropolitan Toronto Reference Library.

industries. The Second World War had marked a major turning-point for Canadian labour, which had fought any number of bitter strikes during the Depression in search of an unfettered right to bargain collectively with employers. It received precious little support from government in this effort. The percentage of union members in the total civilian labour force had actually declined slightly between 1929 and 1939. During the war, however, the federal government had decided to co-opt labour into the war effort. Both Ottawa and the provinces began the slow process of altering labour legislation to recognize and protect the rights to organization and collective bargaining. The key breakthrough came in 1944 when the federal government, by wartime Order-in-Council, introduced PCO 1003. This order introduced recently adopted American principles of compulsory recognition and collective bargaining, creating the machinery necessary to protect both management and labour in contested cases. By 1946, 17.1 per cent of all workers and 27.9 per cent of non-agricultural workers belonged to unions.

With bargaining rights achieved, labour unions went on to hammer out working relationships with most of Canada's traditional industries. Improved working conditions and higher wages were the result. The process of coming to terms with employers was hardly a painless one. Throughout the 1950s there were never fewer than 159 strikes per year across Canada, involving between 49,000 and 112,000 workers annually. Important strikes that achieved national prominence included the great asbestos strike of 1949 in Quebec, the Eaton's strike of 1951, and the Inco strike of 1958 in Sudbury. A major breakthrough for public-sector unionism came at the very end of the 1950s when the postal employees organized and began demanding the right of collective bargaining. In 1956 the two largest Canadian umbrella organizations for labour—the Trades and Labor Congress of Canada and the Canadian Congress of Labour—merged as one consolidated body called the Canadian Labour Congress (CLC). This merger reduced jurisdictional disputes at the top of Canada's table of labour organization, although it did not deal with the question of the domination of so-called 'international' unions by their American members.

The Baby Boom and the Suburban Society

Canadians emerged from the Second World War with twenty years of disruption behind them. Normal expectations for family life had been interrupted in various ways. During the Depression, marriage and birth rates had decreased and the average age at marriage had risen. Between 1939 and 1952 the marriage rate jumped substantially, especially among the young. More family units were formed each year, while both the birth rate and the annual immigration intake rose. Birth rates rose because women who had married early tended to begin bearing children early as well—and to continue expanding their families while remaining at home. The result was a substantial increase in the total numbers of children in Canada between 1941 and 1961. This was the baby boom. These children went through each stage of life in waves, and their sheer numbers put heavy pressure on the facilities that had to deal with them. The phenomenon hit primary education in the 1940s and then rolled progressively through Canadian society as the baby boomers got older. Secondary schools were affected in the 1950s, universities in the 1960s, employment needs in the later 1960s, and so on.

We do not entirely understand why this demographic blip occurred. Pent-up deferral of expectations before the early 1940s is part of the answer. The fulfilment of deferred expectations, however, does not explain why an entire nation should suddenly decide to marry earlier and raise larger families. A better explanation is probably to be found in the fantasy package of a better life for postwar Canadians, fuelled by postwar affluence. The urge affected Quebecers as well as anglophone Canadians. Pierre Vallières described his father's postwar dream: 'We'll be at peace. The children will have all the room they need to play. We'll be masters in our own house. There will be no more stairs to go up and down. . . . Pierre won't hang around the alleys and sheds any more. . . . The owner was prepared to stretch the payments out over many years. . . . Life would become easier. . . . He would enlarge the house. A few years from now, Madeline and the "little ones" would have peace and comfort' (Vallières 1971: 98). In 1945 the Vallières family moved to Longueuil-Annexe, one of the 'mushroom cities' that grew up around Montreal.

What Canadians thought they wanted—and what the media told them was desirable—was a detached bungalow, preferably in a nice suburban neighbourhood, surrounded by green grass and inhabited by a traditional nuclear family. This fantasy included a wife who stayed at home and a houseful of perfect children. Suburbia was always less a geographical reality than a mental and emotional space. It is a convenient term that can be used to describe the fantasy world of the postwar period. After the war there was a popular domesticization of values that extended well into the ranks of the lower-middle and traditional working classes. Postwar suburbia was not only highly traditional in its gender roles but tended to be retrogressive in its emphasis on the role of the female as child bearer and nurturer. In its consumer orientation, as well as in its child centredness, it was a powerful force.

Houses became homes, easily the most expensive physical object possessed by their family-owners. So much time and emotional energy could be devoted to the edifice that it often seemed to possess its owners. The house focused the life of the nuclear family, while at the same time permitting individual members to have their own private space. Ideally each child got a bedroom, for example, and a large recreation room in the basement provided a place for the children to play and gather. The kitchen was often too small for gathering, and the living-room was, increasingly after 1950, the home of the television set. Advertising and articles in the media both exalted the roles of housewife and mother as the epicentre of this world. Radio, television, and the record-player all made it possible for popular culture to be consumed without ever leaving the house.

Central to any postwar middle-class household were its children, around whose upbringing the parents' lives increasingly revolved. The baby-boom generation grew up in a child-centred atmosphere in both home and school. Older standards of discipline and toughness in the parent–child relationship were replaced by permissiveness. New child-rearing attitudes found their popular expression in *The Pocket Book of Baby and Child Care* by the American pediatrician Benjamin Spock, which outsold the Bible in Canada after the war. Spock replaced more austere Canadian manuals. Many Canadian mothers referred to him as 'God'. The book was one of the earliest mass-market paperbacks, sold over the counter at drugstores and supermarkets for less than 50¢. In its pages the reader could find continual reassurance. Use your common sense, said Spock; almost anything reasonable is okay. 'Trust Yourself' was his first injunction. The good doctor came down hard against the use of coercion of any sort. In toilet training, for example, he insisted that 'Practically all those children who regularly go on soiling after 2 are those whose mothers have made a big issue of it and those who have become frightened by painful movements.' Spock explained that children passed through stages. Once parents recognized what stage of development their child had reached, they could understand otherwise incomprehensible behaviour, and recognize that seemingly exceptional problems were really quite common.

The baby boom combined with the attitudes of the permissively raised Spock generation the new affluence to produce a category of adolescence segmented from and sandwiched

☐ In the middle of the prairie outside Calgary, a billboard announces the new 'engineered' suburb of Glendale Meadows in August 1958. Photo Rosetti's Studio. Glenbow NA-5093-558.

between childhood and adult society. More and more young people were encouraged to remain in school longer. Progressive-minded educators treated them as a distinct social phenomenon. The authors of *Crestwood Heights*, a study of a wealthy Toronto suburb (1956), found a central theme in the 'difficulties experienced by the child in living up to the expectations of both parents and the school for "responsibility" and "independence".' They labelled the age group sixteen to nineteen as one of 'Dependent Independence'. The loss of community through urbanization and suburbanization provided a real challenge for social control. Kept out of the workforce, teenagers did not become full adults. Law and custom combined to prevent them from enjoying full adult privileges. These kids had considerable spending power. Encouraged to live at home, the youngsters were not often required to contribute their earnings (if any) to family maintenance. Instead, their parents gave them pocket money or allowances. Canadian teenagers rapidly became avid consumers, providing a market for fast food, clothing fads, acne medicine, cosmetics, and popular music. Melinda McCracken has explained that 'to be a real teenager you had to drink Cokes, eat hamburgers [known as nips in Winnipeg because the local Salisbury House chain sold them as such], French fries [known in Winnipeg as chips, in the English fashion], go to the Dairy Queen, listen to the Top Forty and neck' (McCracken 1975: 72).

Between 1946 and 1960 Canadian education, responding partly to the baby boom, partly to changing social expectations, transformed itself entirely. Canadians had long accepted the concept of universal education in the primary grades. In the 1940s and 1950s education for all was extended to secondary levels by raising the school-leaving age to sixteen. In 1945 there were 1,741,000 children in provincially controlled schools. By 1960–1 that figure had risen to 3,993,125. The expenditure per pupil in public schools nearly tripled between 1945 and 1958. Thousands of new schools had to be built to accommodate the increased student population. Teachers, who before 1946 had needed only a year or two of teacher-training college, now had to have a university degree. In 1956 the authors of *Crestwood Heights* observed that the flagship suburban community they had studied was 'literally, built around its schools'. In Crestwood Heights, education was 'aimed primarily at preparing pupils for a middle-class vocation in a highly-industrialized culture' (Seeley, Sim, and Loosley 1972: 224). Such was the goal of baby-boomer education all across Canada by the early 1960s.

Before the mid-1950s no one anticipated the arrival of a serious educational crisis, for in the decade after the war, classes in existing schools simply got larger while a few extra teachers were hired. But finally the problem of overcrowding became too obvious to ignore. Shortage of space was only partly a result of the baby boom. The new insistence on high school diplomas for everyone represented a profound social revolution and created a need for more room at the universities. Canadians saw more education as the key to dealing with modern industrial conditions. Curiously, however, Canada lagged badly behind other countries in terms of vocational and practical education, preferring instead to force the vast majority of its students into traditional academic endeavours. Much of the thinking that justified expanded education was imported from the United States, but these ideas were increasingly accepted by Canadian parents and taxpayers—particularly after 1957, when the Russians put Sputnik into orbit and inadvertently gave rise to a concerted campaign for educational reform throughout North America.

Not all the nation's population growth came from natural increase. Immigration also played its part. After the Second World War, European wives of Canadian soldiers (the war brides) were admitted virtually without question. Beginning in 1946, Canadian residents were allowed to sponsor relatives for immigration purposes; this was the first sponsorship provision in Canadian immigration policy. In 1947 Prime Minister King announced a characteristic one step forward, one step backward immigration strategy. On the one hand, immigration into Canada would be governed by the nation's absorptive capacity, which many Canadians took to mean that economic and ethnic considerations would control admission. On the other hand, King for the first time recognized Canada's moral obligation to refugees and displaced persons from war-torn Europe. Over the ensuing decade, a substantial number of refugees of European origin were allowed to come to Canada, more than 1,200,000 in total. Of that number, 34.1 per cent originated in the British Isles, 30.2 per cent in northwestern Europe, 15.1 per cent in central and eastern Europe, and 15.3 per cent in southeastern and southern Europe. Another 3.5 per cent were of Jewish origin, leaving only 1.7 per cent of 'other origin'. Old patterns died hard, however. Despite the formation of the Department of Citizenship and Immigration in 1950, immigrants received very little assistance from the Canadian government beyond employment placement once they entered Canada; no effort was made to sensitize Canadian society to their needs. The goal of the government and the many volunteer organizations that assisted immigrants, proclaimed the official Canadian yearbook in 1959, was to see the immigrant 'develop a sense of belonging to the Canadian community' (*Canada Year Book* 1959: 177). The onus was on the immigrant to make the adjustment.

Immigration was a privilege, and the government felt no obligation to explain its choices. By the late 1950s immigration department statistics indicated that most sponsored immigrants (the vast majority of newcomers) would not have otherwise qualified for admission. Between 1946 and 1952, Canada took nearly 165,000 displaced persons, while the United States took 329,000 and Australia 172,000. In 1956 a Canadian mission selected thirty-nine families for admission to the country from among some 900,000 refugees from the Arab–Israeli conflict, using discretionary powers allowed the minister of immigration under the 1952 immigration act. That same year, 1956, nearly 20,000 refugees from the Hungarian Revolution were admitted into Canada, the largest single intake of exiles since the Loyalists. The disparity between Middle Eastern and Hungarian admissions was obvious.

As in earlier periods, one group that did not fully benefit from affluence and growth was the Aboriginal population. Improvements in First Nations medical care began in 1945 when responsibility for it was transferred from Indian Affairs to the Department of National Health and Welfare. This shift helped close gaps but did not eliminate them, chiefly because improved health care was not a panacea; it treated only the symptoms, not the causes of First Nations problems. At this time, infant mortality rates among Native peoples were greatly reduced during the first twenty-eight days of life, but these rates continued to run four to five times the national average for the remainder of infants' first year. A change in major causes of death from infectious to chronic diseases also occurred, but overall Indian and Inuit mortality rates still ran at more than twice the national average, and the incidence of death from accidental causes and suicide only increased. Accidental and violent death was third on the list of killers for all Canadians, but first for First Nations—and this although automobile accidents were not common in most Native communities. Alcohol was probably the major health hazard, less from long-term effects than from accidents and violence, neither of which could be dealt with effectively by improvements in medical service. Native people drank for the same reasons that other socio-culturally dislocated and economically disadvantaged people around the world did: out of frustration and a desire to escape. The First Nations were slow to organize to improve their conditions. A number of Saskatchewan groups merged into the Federation of Saskatchewan Indians at the end of the 1950s, however, and in 1961 the National Indian Council was formed 'to promote unity among Indian people, the betterment of people of Indian ancestry in Canada, and to create a better understanding of Indian and non-Indian relationship' (quoted in Patterson 1972: 177).

THE GROWTH OF THE STATE

Government at all levels—federal, provincial, and municipal—grew extremely rapidly after the war. For the Dominion government, the extension of its power and authority represented a continuation of wartime momentum. For provincial governments, extensions of power were necessary to counter federal incursions in areas traditionally reserved for the provinces. All levels of government found the Canadian public responsive to the introduction of new social services, even if it was piecemeal. The emergence of a much more powerful and costly public sector was fuelled partly by increased social programs, partly by the growth of a Canadian public-enterprise system after the war.

While the Canadian public-enterprise system went back to the nineteenth century, the development of Crown corporations greatly accelerated during and especially after the Second World War. Both federal and provincial governments created Crown corporations, publicly owned and operated. They modelled management structures on private enterprise and usually administered the corporation on a hands-off basis. Many Crown corporations came into existence to provide important services that could not be profitably offered by private enterprise. There was a tendency for public enterprise, almost by definition, to risk unprofitability. The CCF government of Saskatchewan created many Crown corporations from the time of its election in 1944. One of the largest public enterprises of the 1950s, the St Lawrence Seaway, was a Crown corporation. For many rural Canadians the extension of electricity into all but the most remote corners of the country was a great development of the post-war period. Many provinces consolidated electric utilities in Crown corporations after the war to extend services. The federal government had hoped to expand Canada's social services after the Second World War, at least partly to justify continuing control of the major tax fields it had acquired under wartime emergency conditions. At the Dominion–Provincial Conference on Reconstruction, which began on 6 August 1945 (the day the first atomic bomb was dropped on Japan), Ottawa discovered that not all the provinces were willing to withdraw permanently from the fields of personal and corporate income tax. Quebec and Ontario, particularly, were equally unenthusiastic about surrendering their constitutional rights to social services. The provincial rebuff to Ottawa in 1945 did not mean that the Dominion gave up on social security measures. Both funding and constitutional haggling, however, would be continuing problems.

While we often talk about the Canadian welfare state, there is little evidence that many people in Canada, much less in the federal government, had any notion of a truly comprehensive and integrated national social security system that would include full employment, housing, and education as social rights of all Canadians. Social protection in Canada would instead grow on a piecemeal basis through the activities of all levels of government. Sometimes new programs responded to overt public demand, sometimes they met obvious public need. Frequently job creation was the immediate rationale for a social program. Oftimes a particular program of social protection was intended to provide a platform on which a government or political party could campaign. Political proponents of such programs hoped that the opposition would demur, thus providing a convenient election issue. Oppositions frequently failed to take the bait, accepting the programs and avoiding electoral battles. A patchwork of social programs thus emerged in fits and starts.

Canada ended the war with a limited federal pension program, a universal family allowance scheme, and a housing act designed chiefly to provide employment. In 1945 Ottawa had also proposed to the provinces a national universal pension scheme for Canadians over seventy (with a means test provincially administered for those sixty-five to sixty-nine), a national public assistance scheme for the unemployed, and a health insurance scheme to be shared by the provinces and the federal government. The almost inevitable demise of the Dominion–Provincial Conference on Reconstruction meant that federal progress on social protection moved ahead extremely slowly. Apart from the creation of the Central Mortgage and Housing Corporation to assist in providing low-cost mortgage loans to Canadian families and a limited home-building program (10,000 houses per year), little happened on the housing front in the fifteen years after 1945. On the health-care front, the government in 1948 established a fund for health research and hospital construction, but did little else on health until 1957 when it passed the Hospital Insurance and

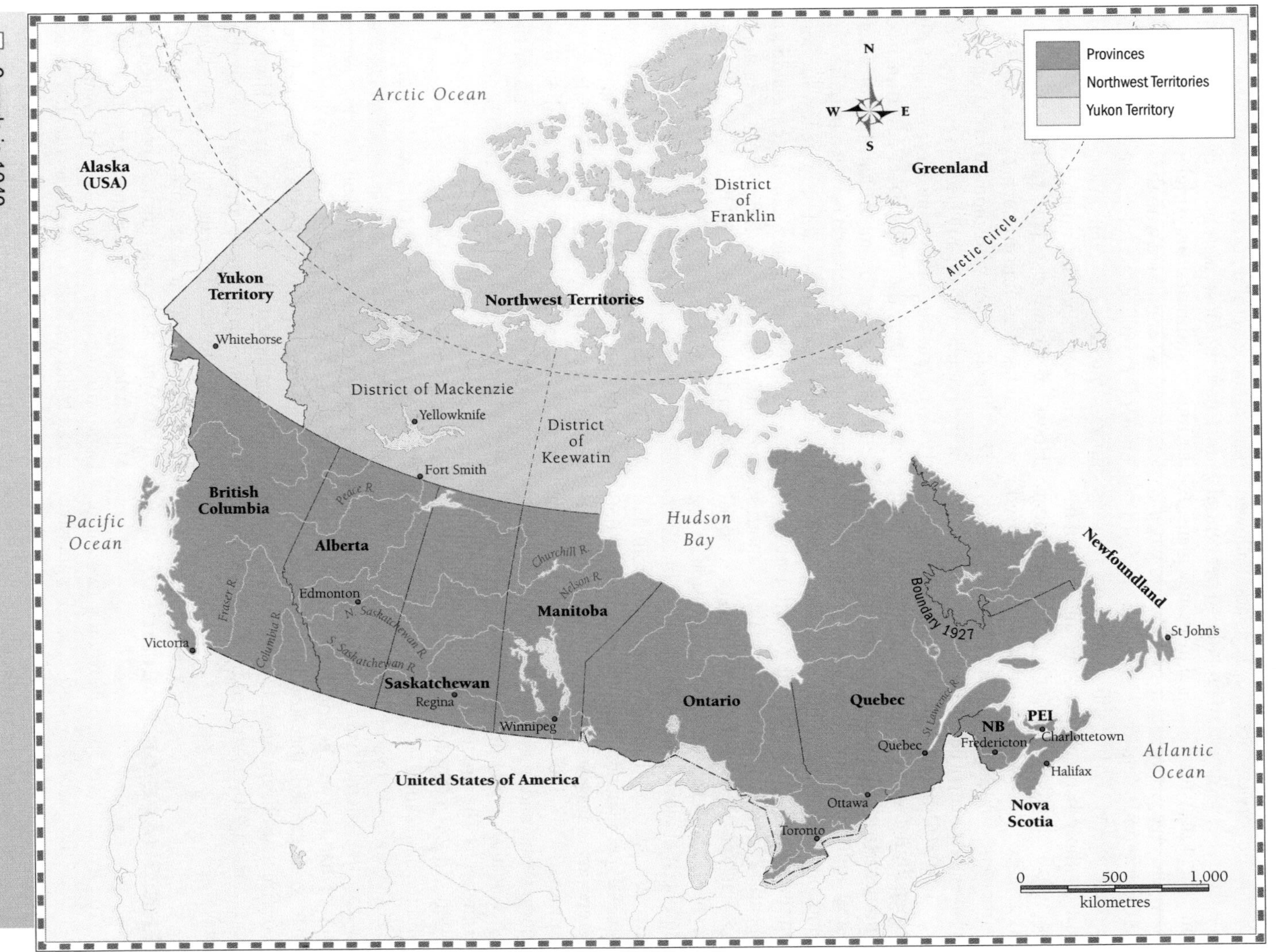

Provinces
Northwest Territories
Yukon Territory
N
W
E
S
Arctic Ocean
Alaska (USA)
Greenland
District of Franklin
Arctic Circle
Yukon Territory
Whitehorse
Northwest Territories
District of Mackenzie
Yellowknife
District of Keewatin
Fort Smith
British Columbia
Pacific Ocean
Peace R.
Alberta
Hudson Bay
Churchill R.
Nelson R.
Edmonton
N. Saskatchewan R.
S. Saskatchewan R.
Fraser R.
Columbia R.
Manitoba
Victoria
Saskatchewan
Regina
Winnipeg
Ontario
Quebec
Boundary 1927
Newfoundland
St John's
St Lawrence R.
Quebec
NB
Fredericton
PEI
Charlottetown
Halifax
Atlantic Ocean
Nova Scotia
United States of America
Ottawa
Toronto
0
500
1,000
kilometres

Canada in 1949.

Diagnostic Services Act. This legislation allowed the federal government to provide 50 per cent of the cost of provincial hospital insurance plans. A new Old Age Security Act of 1951 provided a $40-per-month pension to all Canadians over the age of seventy, but still insisted on a means test for those between sixty-five and sixty-nine. In 1956 a limited federal Unemployment Assistance Act with a means test passed Parliament. Education remained almost entirely a provincial matter before 1960.

In 1945, the last year of the war, federal expenditure was just over $5 billion, with another $451 million spent by the provinces and $250 million by municipalities. In 1960 the Dominion still spent $5 billion, although far less on the military, but provincial governments now spent $2.5 billion and municipalities another $1.7 billion. Much of the increase went to social services. The result was a vast expansion in the numbers of government employees. In 1945, the last year of the war, the Dominion had 30,240 permanent civil servants and 85,668 temporary ones. At the beginning of 1961, it employed 337,416 Canadians, most of them 'permanent' and many of them female. Both provincial and municipal employment grew even faster. The provinces employed 50,000 in 1946 and 257,000 twenty years later, while the municipalities increased from 56,000 in 1946 to 224,000 in 1966. By 1960 there was a sense (on at least the federal level) that matters could get out of hand. The Diefenbaker government in that year created the Royal Commission on Government Organization to improve efficiency and economy. It was chaired by J. Grant Glassco (1905–68).

THE SHAPE OF POLITICS

At the federal level there were only two major parties, the Liberals and the Progressive Conservatives. In this period there were a variety of other federal parties as well, chiefly the CCF and Social Credit. The nature of the Canadian electoral system—particularly the 'first past the post' method of determining victorious candidates in single-member constituencies—combined with the continued presence of a multiplicity of parties to reduce to inconsequence the relationship between the popular vote and the number of seats in the House of Commons. True political mandates were difficult to find in such electoral results. The Liberals never won more than 50 per cent of the popular vote in any election in the period 1945–60, although they came close to it in 1949 and 1954. Only the Diefenbaker government of 1958 was elected by more than half of actual votes cast. The correlation between popular vote and number of seats could be quite low for both major and minor parties. The system tended to translate any edge in the popular vote for a major party into considerably larger numbers of seats, and to dissipate votes for other parties. Third parties were much better off if their support was concentrated in a few ridings (as was true for Social Credit) and not spread widely across the country (as was the case for the CCF). In 1953, for example, the Liberals had 48.8 per cent of the popular vote to 31 per cent for the PCs, 11.3 per cent for the CCF, and 5.4 per cent for the Social Credit Party. These percentages translated into 171 Liberal seats, fifty-one PC, twenty-three CCF, and fifteen Social Credit.

The Liberals had a number of advantages in the pursuit of continued federal power, of which two were absolutely critical. Above all they had the ongoing support of Quebec, which elected one of the largest blocks of seats in the House of Commons. Support from francophone Quebec had come to the Liberals in the 1890s, was solidified during the Conscription Crisis of the Great War, and was further confirmed by Mackenzie King's management of that same issue during the Second World War. The Liberals did not lose a federal election in Quebec between 1896 and 1958, usually winning more than three-quarters of the available seats. To triumph nationally without Quebec's support, an opposition party needed to win the vast majority of seats in the remainder of the country, including Ontario (in which the two major parties were always fairly evenly matched). The Tories did win anglophone Canada in 1957. Such a victory could produce only a minority government, however. The Diefenbaker sweep of 1958 was the exception that proved the rule. In other elections the Liberals were able to persuade Quebec's francophone voters that the competing parties were unsympathetic to French Canada.

The apparent Liberal stranglehold on Quebec had its impact on the other parties, particularly in terms of choice of leaders and electoral strategies. During this period, neither the Progressive Conservatives nor the CCF ever seriously considered selecting a leader from Quebec—not even a unilingual English-speaker, let alone a French Canadian. Nor did the other parties make much of an effort to campaign in French Canada, except in 1958. The Liberal Party, therefore, continued its historic collaboration with francophone Quebec. It alternated its leaders between anglophones and francophones, following Mackenzie King (1919–48) with Louis St Laurent (1948–57) and Lester B. Pearson (1958–68). This association tended to polarize Canadian federal politics. The Liberals also did well with other francophone voters, particularly the Acadians of New Brunswick.

But the Liberal political advantage was not confined to support from francophones. While national political parties needed to appeal to a broad spectrum of voters across the nation in order to gain power, only the Liberals consistently succeeded in this appeal, chiefly by staking out their political ground outside French Canada slightly to the left of centre. Mackenzie King had specialized in adopting the most popular goals of the welfare state, often lifting them shamelessly from the platform of the CCF, a practice his successors continued. The Liberals preferred to find urbane, well-educated leaders from the professional middle classes, oriented to federal service and politics. Each man had his own expertise. Mackenzie King was a professional labour consultant and negotiator who had studied economics at Chicago and Harvard and had written a well-known book entitled *Industry and Humanity* (1918). St Laurent was a former law professor at Laval, who became a highly successful corporation lawyer and president of the Canadian Bar Association. Pearson had begun as a history professor at the University of Toronto before joining the Department of External Affairs as a mandarin and professional diplomat. None of these men had earned a doctorate, but all held appointments that in our own time would probably require one.

The Progressive Conservative Party also had three leaders in this period: John Bracken (1942–8), George Drew (1948–56), and John Diefenbaker (1956–67). Bracken and Drew had been successful provincial premiers with little federal experience, while Diefenbaker had been an opposition spokesman in the House of Commons from 1940. Bracken had been a university professor (of field husbandry) and administrator before entering politics. The other two had been small-town lawyers. All three were regarded as being to the left of their parties, and the PC party platforms of these years looked decidedly progressive. Diefenbaker was *sui generis*, a brilliant if old-fashioned public orator and genuine western populist. All the PC leaders had strong sympathies for the ordinary underprivileged Canadian, although only Diefenbaker managed to convince the public of his concerns. None of these men spoke French comfortably, and they left what campaigning was done in Quebec to others.

The Co-operative Commonwealth Federation had emerged from the war with high hopes, gaining 15.6 per cent of the popular vote and twenty-eight Members of Parliament in the 1945 federal election. Its popularity decreased regularly thereafter, however. By 1958 it was reduced to eight MPs and 9.5 per cent of the popular vote. This erosion of support came about partly because the CCF was mistakenly thought by some to be associated with international communism, and partly because much of the Canadian electorate regarded it as both too radical and too doctrinaire. The CCF showed no strength east of Ontario and was not a credible national alternative to the two major parties. After its 1958 defeat, the CCF remobilized through an alliance with organized labour (the Canadian Labour Congress), which in 1961 would produce the New Democratic Party under the leadership of former Saskatchewan premier T.C. (Tommy) Douglas. The Social Credit Party won some scattered seats in Alberta and Saskatchewan after the war, but would achieve prominence only after Robert Thompson (b. 1914) became president of the Social Credit Association of Canada in 1960 and party leader in 1961.

Liberal dominance before 1957 was moderated less by the opposition parties than by other factors. One was the increased size and scope of the apparatus of bureaucracy, including a 'mandarinate' at the top of the civil service. Powerful senior civil servants stayed in their posts despite changes of minister or government. They provided most of the policy initiatives for the government. Another important limitation was the force of public opinion, which often restrained policy initiatives and provided a public sense of

THOMAS CLEMENT DOUGLAS

T.C. (Tommy) Douglas at the founding convention of the New Democratic Party in July 1961, when he was selected as its first leader. NAC, C-36219.

'Tommy' Douglas (1904–86) was born in Scotland, and his family immigrated to Winnipeg in 1919, just in time for the Winnipeg General Strike. After working in the printing trade, he began studying for the ministry at Brandon College in 1924, acquiring a commitment to the social gospel in the process. He moved to Saskatchewan upon ordination in 1930, where he founded a local branch of the Independent Labour Party and participated in the creation of the CCF. He ran successfully for the CCF in the federal election of 1935, and served two terms in Ottawa, where he became highly skilled at supporting unpopular issues, such as civil liberties during wartime. In 1944 he led the CCF provincial party to overwhelming victory in Saskatchewan by campaigning on the need for social reconstruction after the efforts of the war. Douglas formed the CCF's first provincial government and then served as premier of the province for seventeen years.

His time in office demonstrated that the party could not only run an effective government but successfully implement an innovative social services program.

Academics within and without Canada were fascinated by the Saskatchewan experiment, since an agricultural province was the last place where political theory would have predicted success for a socialist party. Douglas began with expanding the province's health care services, and moved quickly to labour legislation, farm security, and school consolidation. The government also entered the insurance business in 1944, and in 1945 passed the Crown Corporations Act, which allowed it to establish a wide spectrum of government business enterprises. The recommendations of a royal commission on the management of northern resources were accepted; they emphasized conservation and sustainable development. Not all government initiatives, particularly in business enterprise, were successful, but the public takeover of Saskatchewan Government Telephones in 1947 and the Saskatchewan Power Commission in 1949 were generally popular. In 1948, the government established an extremely successful Arts Council. Many observers expected Douglas and the CCF to be a one-term wonder, but they managed to survive the first election in 1948 and several thereafter. The province became accustomed to the CCF approach, and it was not until the proposed introduction of medicare in 1960 that a well-organized opposition—led by the province's physicians, who entered into a bitter strike—appeared. Douglas stepped down in 1961 as provincial leader and re-entered federal politics, where he became the first leader of the NDP. Although he was unable to increase appreciably national support for the NDP, in the 1960s the party held the balance of power in several parliaments and pushed Liberal governments to the left. He left the leadership in 1971 and retired in 1979.

fair play. The Liberals under St Laurent lost the 1957 election for many reasons, but one of the most critical was a public sense that they had become too arrogant. Government closure of debate over the Trans-Canada Pipeline in 1956 served as a symbol for Liberal contempt of the democratic process. As the new leader in 1958, Lester Pearson blundered in challenging the minority government of John Diefenbaker to resign in his favour without offering any compelling reasons for so doing.

At the provincial level, few provinces enjoyed genuine two-party politics. Long-governing parties with near monopolies were common, and even in Atlantic Canada, where there was a long tradition of trying to keep provincial and federal governments of the same party, the party in power was not necessarily Liberal. The Tories, under Robert Stanfield, took over Nova Scotia in 1956; Tories ran New Brunswick from 1951 to 1961. Quebec was controlled by Maurice Duplessis's Union Nationale. The 'Big Blue Machine' ran Ontario, while Alberta (1935–72) and British Columbia (beginning in 1952) were governed by Social Credit. In British Columbia, W.A.C. Bennett (1900–79) took advantage of an electoral change (the preferential ballot), designed by a warring coalition to keep the socialists out of power, to win enough seats to form a minority government in 1952. Continuing to exploit brilliantly the social polarities of a province divided into free enterprisers and socialists, Bennett never looked back. The CCF governed Saskatchewan. There

☐ Prime Minister Louis St Laurent, December 1953. NAC, PA-144069.

was no provincial Liberal government west of Quebec between 1945 and 1960, although the coalition government of Manitoba was usually headed by a Liberal.

Liberal success in Newfoundland was a product chiefly of unusual local circumstances. Joseph R. Smallwood (1900–91) parlayed strong Liberal support for Confederation with Canada into an unbroken tenure as first premier from 1949 to 1971. After a somewhat complicated journey, Newfoundland joined Canada in 1949. Effectively bankrupt, the province had surrendered its elective government to Great Britain in 1933. It was governed until 1949 by an appointed commission, which balanced the budget but was not very popular. After 1945 the British government sought to get rid of its colonial obligations, and ordered a national convention elected in 1946 to decide Newfoundland's future. In a preliminary referendum in 1948 69,400 voters (44.5 per cent) voted for a return to the pre-1933 situation, 64,066 (41.1 per cent) voted for Confederation with Canada, and 22,311 (14.3 per cent) voted for the continuation of commission government. A second ballot held on 22 July 1948, which had an 84.9 per cent turnout, saw 78,323 Newfoundlanders (52.3 per cent) vote for Canada, and 71,344 (47.66 per cent) for the resumption of Crown colony status. Confederation did best outside the Avalon Peninsula and St John's. The Canadian cabinet accepted the decision on 27 July 1948, allowing Smallwood, now leader of the Liberal party, to head an interim government that easily won the province's first election in many years.

FRENCH CANADA AFTER THE SECOND WORLD WAR

The scope of social and economic change in French Canada, especially after 1939, went largely unheralded in the remainder of the nation until the 1960s. Pierre Elliott Trudeau began his editorial introduction to his book on the asbestos strike of 1949—entitled 'The Province of Quebec at the Time of the Strike'—with the words, 'I surely do not have to belabour the point that in the half century preceding the asbestos strike, the material basis of Canadian society in general, and of Quebec society in particular, was radically altered' (Trudeau 1974: 1). But in English Canada before 1960, the popular press was fascinated by Maurice Duplessis and his conservative Union Nationale; by ignoring the changes that were actually occurring, journalists presented a distorted picture of Quebec society. Duplessis mixed heavy-handed attacks on civil liberties and trade unions with traditional nationalism and laissez-faire economic policy, while ignoring the underlying social changes and debates occurring within Quebec. For many English-speaking Canadians, Quebec remained stereotyped as a priest-ridden rural society inhabited by a simple people. That Quebec had been lagging in the socio-economic aspects of modern industrialism made its rapid catch-up more internally unsettling and externally bewildering. As Trudeau had pointed out, by the 1950s Quebec was no longer behind the remainder of Canada in most social and economic indicators.

Many Canadian commentators outside Quebec who were aware of the province's transformation assumed that the continued electoral success of Duplessis and the Union Nationale represented confusion on the part of many French Canadians. Since social and economic modernization should in the long run lead to French-Canadian assimilation into the majority society of North America, said external observers, in the short run it must be causing internal chaos. Neither of the standard postwar assumptions about Quebec's modernization—that it meant short-term confusion and long-term loss of distinctiveness—was particularly valid. The socio-economic transformation was accompanied by a series of profound ideological shifts within Quebec society that shook its very foundations. The patterns of that development ought to have been comprehensible to anyone familiar with what was happening elsewhere in developing societies. The power and authority of defenders of traditional Quebec nationalism, including the Roman Catholic Church, were being swept away by a new secular nationalism that had become fully articulated under Duplessis. The main opposition to the new nationalism came less from the old nationalism than from a renewed current of nineteenth-century liberalism adapted to twentieth-century Quebec conditions. In the 1960s these two competing ideologies would find popular labels as 'separatism' and 'federalism'.

The new nationalism was profoundly different from the old in its intellectual assumptions, however similar the two versions could sound in rhetorical manifestos. In the first place, while often espousing Catholic values, the new nationalism was profoundly anticlerical. It opposed the entrenched role of the Church in Quebec society. In the second place, the new nationalism had no desire to return to a golden age of agricultural ruralism, but instead celebrated the new industrial and urban realities of modern Quebec. It insisted that Quebec nationalism had to be based on the aspirations of the newly emerging French-Canadian working class, which meant that nationalists had to lead in the battle for socio-economic change. While scorning international socialism because it would not pay sufficient attention to the particular cultural dimensions of French Canada, the new nationalists pre-empted much of the vocabulary and economic analysis of Marxism, including the essential concept of proletarian class solidarity. In their insistence on nationalism, they were hardly traditional Marxists. The postwar world, however, saw many examples of similar movements that combined Marxist analysis with national aspirations. The new nationalists—particularly the younger, more militant ones—were able to find intellectual allies and models everywhere. The external neo-Marxism most commonly cited came from the French ex-colonial world or from Latin America. The new nationalists had long insisted that the key to their program was an active and modern state. The homogeneous secular state represented the highest articulation of the nation, and was the best means of liberating humanity. Traditionalist forces in Quebec had historically collaborated with forces in Canada to keep French Canadians in their place. The active state envisioned by the nationalists was Quebec, not Canada.

Opposition to the new nationalism came from a tiny but influential group of small-l liberal intellectuals centred on the journal *Cité libre*. This publication was founded by Pierre Elliott Trudeau (b. 1919) and Gérard Pelletier (b. 1919), among others, at the height of the Duplessis regime, to which it was a reaction. These liberals were as revisionist in spirit as the new nationalists, but simultaneously suspicious of what they regarded as simplistic doctrinaire thinking. They were committed to the new rationalism of the new social sciences. As Trudeau wrote in an oft-quoted manifesto:

We must systematically question all political categories bequeathed to us by the intervening generation. . . . The time has arrived for us to borrow from architecture the discipline called 'functional', to cast aside the thousands of past prejudices which encumber the present, and to build for the new man. Overthrow all totems, transgress all taboos. Better still, consider them as dead ends. Without passion, let us be intelligent [quoted in Behiels 1985: 69].

Trudeau's small group was even more fiercely anticlerical than the new nationalists, perhaps

REFUS GLOBAL

In 1948, in Montreal, the painter Paul-Émile Borduas (1905–60) released a manifesto signed by himself and a number of other Quebec artists and intellectuals. An excerpt follows.

The magical harvest magically reaped from the field of the Unknown lies ready for use. All the true poets have worked at gathering it in. Its powers of transformation are as great as the violent reactions it originally provoked, and as remarkable as its later unavailability (after more than two centuries, there is not a single copy of Sade to be found in our bookshops; Isidore Ducasse, dead for over a century, a century of revolution and slaughter, is still, despite our having become inured to filth and corruption, too powerful for the queasy contemporary conscience).

All the elements of this treasure as yet remain inaccessible to our present-day society. Every precious part of it will be preserved intact for future use. It was built up with spontaneous enthusiasm, in spite of, and outside, the framework of civilization. And its social effects will only be felt once society's present needs are recognized.

Meanwhile our duty is plain.

The ways of society must be abandoned once and for all; we must free ourselves from its utilitarian spirit. We must not tolerate our mental or physical faculties' being wittingly left undeveloped. We must refuse to close our eyes to vice, to deceit perpetuated under the cloak of imparted knowledge, of services rendered, of payment due. We must refuse to be trapped within the walls of the common mould—a strong citadel, but easy enough to escape. We must avoid silence (do with us what you will, but hear us you must), avoid fame, avoid privileges (except that of being heeded)—avoid them all as the stigma of evil, indifference, servility. We must refuse to serve, or to be used for, such despicable ends. We must avoid DELIBERATE DESIGN as the harmful weapon of REASON. Down with them both! Back they go!

MAKE WAY FOR MAGIC! MAKE WAY FOR OBJECTIVE MYSTERY!

MAKE WAY FOR LOVE!

MAKE WAY FOR WHAT IS NEEDED!

We accept full responsibility for the consequences of our refusal.

Self-interested plans are nothing but the stillborn product of their author.

While passionate action is animated with a life of its own.

We shall gladly take full responsibility for the future. Deliberate, rational effect can only fashion the present from the ashes of the past.

Our passions must necessarily, spontaneously, unpredictably forge the future. . . .

We need not worry about the future until we come to it.

SOURCE: Ramsay Cook, ed., *French-Canadian Nationalism: An Anthology* (Toronto: Macmillan of Canada, 1969): 280–1.

because its members still believed in the need for a revitalized Catholic humanism and criticized the Church from within. It was equally critical of traditional French-Canadian nationalism, which it regarded as outdated, inadequate, and oppressive. *Cité libre* preferred to locate French Canada within an open multicultural and multinational state and society. Not only traditional nationalism but all nationalism was unprogressive and undemocratic.

At the end of the 1950s most Quebec intellectuals had arrived at some similar conclusions, however different the routes. The traditional nationalism in Quebec—of Catholicism, of the Union Nationale—led nowhere. The dead hand of the Church had to be removed. A modern state, secular and interventionist, was needed to complete Quebec's modernization. There was some disagreement over the nature of this modern state. The new nationalists were inclined to see it as a liberating embodiment of French-Canadian collectivities, while the *Cité libre* people saw it more as a regulating mechanism. It only remained to persuade the general populace of the province of the need for change.

Signs of the profound changes that had occurred and were still occurring in Quebec could be seen in the province's intellectual and artistic communities. In 1948 Paul-Emile Borduas released his famous manifesto, written originally in 1947. *Refus global* was a rambling series of passionate, almost poetic utterances attacking virtually everything in Quebec society at the time. Some young painters were not satisfied with the combination of spontaneity and traditional spatial perspectives advocated by Borduas. Led by Fernand Leduc, they produced a manifesto in 1955—signed 'Les Plasticiens'—that was less inflammatory than *Refus global*, but that also insisted on artistic freedom. It said that its subscribers were drawn to 'plastic qualities: tone, texture, forms, lines, and the final unity between elements' (quoted in Davis1979: 18.) Abstractionism quickly ceased to be regarded as particularly avant-garde in Quebec. In the theatre, some attempt was made to break out of the constraints imposed by realism. One particularly striking example was *Le Marcheur* (The Walker) by Yves Thériault, which was presented in 1950. It featured a dominant father (never seen on stage), who controlled the lives of everyone around him at the same time that he united them in their hatred for him. The father could be seen as the traditional French-Canadian paternal tyrant, or Premier Duplessis, or the Church.

FEDERAL–PROVINCIAL RELATIONS

The 1945–6 Dominion–Provincial Conference on Reconstruction had served as the arena for the renewal after the war of constitutional conflict between the Dominion and its provinces. In August 1945 the federal government tabled a comprehensive program for an extended welfare state based on the tax collection and economic policy of a strong central government. It sought the cooperation of the provinces to implement its plans. Ottawa wanted agreement that it could keep the emergency powers it had acquired to fight the war, especially the power to collect all major taxes. The conference adjourned for study, finally meeting again in April 1946. At this point Quebec and Ontario in tandem simultaneously denounced centralization while insisting on a return to provincial autonomy. Ontario had some social programs of its own in the planning stages. Quebec, led by Duplessis, wanted to keep control of social powers in order not to have them implemented. In the wake of this meeting, the federal government offered a 'tax rental' scheme to the provinces, whereby it would collect certain taxes (on incomes, corporations, and inheritances) and distribute payment to the provinces. Ontario and Quebec went their own ways, but the remaining provinces (and Newfoundland after 1949) accepted tax rental, which (along with suitable constitutional amendment) had been recommended by the Rowell–Sirois commission in 1940.

Constitutional revision was no easy matter to contemplate. As we have seen, conflict had been literally built into Confederation by the British North America Act. The Dominion of Canada was a federal state, with a central government in Ottawa and local governments in the provinces. While the intention of the Fathers of Confederation had been to produce a strong central government, they had been forced by the provinces (especially what would become Quebec) to guarantee them separate identities. These identities were protected through an explicit division of powers between federal and provincial governments in sections 91 and 92 of the British North America Act of 1867. The division thus created reflected the state of political thinking in the 1860s. It gave the federal arm the authority to create a viable national economy. It gave the provinces the power to protect what at the time were regarded as local and cultural matters. Some of the provincial powers, such as those over education, were acquired because the provinces demanded them. Others, such as the powers over the health and welfare of provincial inhabitants, were not regarded by the Fathers as critical for a national government. Lighthouses and post offices were more important than public medical care in the 1860s.

Over time the division of powers gave the provinces the responsibility, in whole or in part, for many of the expensive aspects of government, including health, education, and welfare. Provincial ability to raise a commensurate revenue was limited, however. Many important aspects came to be shared among governments. The BNA Act's division of powers was clearly dated, ambiguous, and contentious. Despite the miracle of Canada's survival, the Constitution was constantly strained. Then, as now, critics of the existing system stressed its tensions, while its defenders lauded its capacity for survival.

One of the key problems was the settling of disputes over interpretation of the BNA Act itself. The act provided for a judicature modelled on British arrangements, with a Supreme Court at the top. This court, established in 1875, was not always the court of final recourse on constitutional matters. Until 1949 constitutional questions could be finally appealed to a British imperial court, the Judicial Committee of the Privy Council of the United Kingdom. In the years after Confederation, this committee had interpreted the Constitution in ways highly favourable to the provinces. Even with the successful elimination, after the war, of this example of continued colonialism, amendment of the Constitution was extremely difficult. Amending procedures were not spelled out in the act itself. The convention had grown up that amendment required the consent of all provinces, which was not easy to obtain. Moreover, such amendment could ultimately be achieved only by an act of the British Parliament.

By the mid-twentieth century, Canadian political leaders had worked out a variety of informal means for dealing with matters of constitutional disagreement. One of the most important was the federal–provincial conference, which was employed regularly after 1945 to deal with financial business and gradually came to address constitutional matters as well. So long as the Union Nationale government of Maurice Duplessis represented Quebec at these gatherings, Quebec stood by a traditional view of the 1867 arrangement. The province protected its existing powers fiercely, but did not particularly seek to expand them. Another dimension was added to the postwar constitutional situation through John Diefenbaker's insistence on the introduction of a Canadian Bill of Rights, however. The Americans had produced their Bill of Rights (the first ten amendments to their 1787 Constitution) as part of the process of ratifying the Constitution. In Canada, the British constitutional tradition insisted that Parliament was supreme, while the courts automatically protected against the abuse of power. The BNA Act had protected some minority rights, but had displayed little interest in the rights of the individual, which were crucial to the American approach. This notion of spelling out rights—for individuals or collective groups—was a potentially profound change in the Canadian Constitution. Diefenbaker's Bill for the Recognition and Protection of Human Rights and Fundamental Freedoms, fulfilling campaign promises of 1957 and 1958, passed the federal Parliament in 1960. As it was limited to the federal level, and the rights it protected could be overridden by national emergencies, it had little immediate impact. A full ten years would go by before the Canadian Supreme Court would hear a case based upon the Bill of Rights, but its implications for constitutional reform—particularly when combined with the growth of new and politically conscious minorities in the 1960s—were substantial.

At the end of the 1950s the Canadian Constitution stood on the cusp of great change. Canadians ought to have recognized that neither constitutional nor federal–provincial problems were solely the product of the presence of Quebec in Confederation. Nevertheless, the issue of Quebec became inextricably bound up with increasing federal–provincial tensions. Constitutional reform would become the panacea for the nation's divisions.

THE RISE OF CANADIAN CULTURE

Culture in Canada and Canadian Culture (the two were never quite synonymous) after the Second World War emerged as major public issues. This was a major development of the postwar period. Culture had not been entirely ignored before 1945, but it had always taken a back seat to political and economic matters. Canada's cultural performance (or lack of it) was explained chiefly in terms of priorities. Culture was a luxury that would come only with political and economic maturity. Such maturity was now at hand. A number of parallel developments affecting culture occurred after 1945. One of the most obvious saw both federal and provincial governments attempt to articulate and implement public cultural policy. The policy initiatives were driven chiefly by concerns to protect indigenous culture from being overwhelmed by external influences. They helped create a variety of new cultural institutions in the postwar period. On the creative level, many contemporary artists began deliberately cultivating a naive or native style, with considerable public success, thus helping to breach the older boundaries of art and culture. Other artists enthusiastically joined international movements.

Canada was hardly alone in discovering that culture in its various forms was an important matter in the postwar world. Few nations, however, had a greater need for conscious cultural policy than Canada. It was a nation without a single unifying language and with at least two of what many after 1945 began to call founding cultures. At the same time, francophones and anglophones often meant something quite different when they talked about culture. While nobody doubted that French Canada's culture was distinctive, defining the culture of the rest of the nation was more problematic. More than most nations, Canada was exposed to external cultural influences, particularly from its behemoth neighbour to the south, the United States. The Americans purveyed to Canada and then to the world a profoundly American cultural style, anchored in popular culture.

In 1945 (or at any point earlier), Canada had considerably more cultural activity than most Canadians would have recognized at the time. One of the problems was that cultural commentators relied on highly restrictive critical canons and categories. Much of Canada's cultural life went on outside the boundaries of what critics and experts usually regarded as Culture with a capital C. Canadians became involved in culture on a non-professional basis for their own pleasure. The resultant culture came from folk traditions more than from high art. Moreover, it was not necessarily distinctly Canadian. By

GABRIELLE ROY

Gabrielle Roy (1909–83) was born in Saint-Boniface, Manitoba, a francophone suburb of Winnipeg. She was educated at Winnipeg Normal School and taught for many years in the province, mainly in isolated rural communities. Thoroughly bilingual, in 1937 she travelled to Europe, where she spent two years before the approach of World War II forced her to return to Canada. Roy settled in Montreal, where she worked as a journalist while beginning to write fiction. Her observations of the working-class district of Saint-Henri served as the background for her first novel, *Bonheur d'occasion*, which was published in 1945. This work introduced an international readership to the complexities of working-class life in urban Quebec in the first years of World War II. Her characters are divided by their desire to make the most of military service and military prosperity after a decade of unemployment, while still susceptible to the general hostility felt by French Canada to involvement in an overseas war.

Gabrielle Roy in the 1950s. NAC, C-18347.

The novel won a French Prix Fémina, and after translation into English as *The Tin Flute*, it garnered a major American award as well from the Literary Guild of America. In typical Canadian fashion, the novel was initially far more honoured outside the nation than within, although it did win the Governor General's award for fiction in 1947. Roy was invited to join the Royal Society of Canada that same year, which also saw her marriage to Dr Marcel Carbotte. Roy was far less regionally focused than most Quebec writers, and this was key to her popular success outside French Canada. Much of her later work was in the form of short stories or memoirs and was set in Manitoba or in the Arctic. She never returned to Manitoba to live, however, spending the remainder of her life in Europe and in Quebec. Roy wrote about the trials of ordinary people in a plain, accessible style. She was one of the first writers to depict Inuit characters in her fiction, and to employ them as protagonists. Unusual among francophone writers in Canada, Roy saw virtually all of her work skilfully translated into English.

1945, Canadian government—particularly at the federal level with the Public Archives, the National Gallery, the National Film Board, and the Canadian Broadcasting Corporation—already had a substantial if largely unrecognized role in culture. Prime Minister St Laurent was told during the 1949 elections that the Liberals might lose votes to the CCF from 'those Canadians who have a distinct national consciousness and feel that more should be done to encourage national culture and strengthen national feeling'. As a result, St Laurent appointed the Royal Commission on National Development in the Arts, Letters, and Sciences, usually known as the Massey Commission after its chairman, Vincent Massey.

The Massey Commission existed because its time had come. It did not invent a cultural policy but merely publicized it. While its recommendations were crucial in increasing government involvement in the arts, they were precisely the ones envisioned in the commission's terms of reference, which were in turn a product of considerable lobbying by well-established arts groups. The commission held extensive public meetings, receiving 462 briefs and listening to 1,200 witnesses. The witnesses, reported its chairperson, represented '13 Federal Government institutions, 7 Provincial Governments, 87 national organizations, 262 local bodies and 35 private commercial radio stations' (*Report of the Royal Commission on National Development in the Arts, Letters and Sciences* 1951: 8). In most respects the Massey Commission looked backward instead of forward. It attempted to promote a Victorian vision of culture. It may have established most of the agenda of federal cultural policy for at least a generation to follow, but that agenda was narrowly conceived.

Despite its mandate to articulate a national cultural policy, especially in radio and television broadcasting, the commission was chiefly interested in élite culture and élitist ways of dealing with it. What needed to be preserved was a culture of excellence that was 'resolutely Canadian'. In 1952 it recommended the creation of a national television service as quickly as possible. It also wanted both radio and television broadcasting to be 'vested in the Canadian Broadcasting Corporation'. This monopoly would help 'to avoid excessive commercialism and to encourage Canadian content and the use of Canadian talent' (*Report of the Royal Commission on National Development in the Arts, Letters and Sciences* 1951: 305). It supported the expansion of the National Film Board, the National Gallery, the National Museum, the Public Archives, the Library of Parliament, and the Historic Sites and Monuments Board of the National Parks Service. It also recommended the extension of the concept of the National Research Council (for scientific research) into the humanities and social sciences through the creation of a Council for the Arts, Letters, Humanities, and Social Sciences. Much of its agenda would be implemented in piecemeal fashion by federal governments over the next decade. The Canada Council, for example, was established in 1957.

Another royal commission on television appeared in 1955, chaired by Robert Fowler (1901–80) of Montreal. It made its final report in 1957. The Fowler Commission had to deal with the shift from radio to television and the prevalence of American-produced records, movies, and shows in both media. It insisted that the century-old Canadian answer to Americanization was for the government to provide 'conscious stimulation' through financial assistance, an approach it clearly favoured. In addition to subsidies and protective measures, the Fowler Commission recommended another cultural strategy: regulated competition with a 'mixed system of public and private ownership'. The Diefenbaker government translated Fowler's recommendations into its Broadcasting Act of 1958, creating the Board of Broadcast Governors to monitor broadcasting to ensure that the service would be 'basically Canadian in content and character' (*Report of the Royal Commission on Broadcasting* 1957: 8–11).

THE MASSEY COMMISSION REPORT, 1951

The Massey Commission was set up in 1949 to study and report on Canadian 'activities generally which are designed to enrich our national life, and to increase our own consciousness of our national heritage and knowledge of Canada abroad'. It made its report in 1951.

In writing this Report we have been forced to turn again and again to the dangerous neglect of the humanities and social sciences, studies essential to the maintenance of civilized life. It was suggested to us that the success of the National Research Council in the encouragement of scientific studies offered an example that should perhaps be followed in the establishment of a National Council for the Humanities and Social Sciences. We believe, however, that the implied parallel is misleading, that the essential nature and value of these studies makes it undesirable to isolate them in a separate body, that their present 'plight' may be partly explained, as we have previously suggested, by an effort to subject them too rigidly to scientific techniques and methods of organization. Moreover, we are convinced that, in our country particularly, encouragement of these studies must be carried on to a considerable extent through international exchanges, and through closer contacts with France, Great Britain and with other European countries where traditionally they are held in great respect. We think that the very important responsibility of encouraging these studies through a flexible scheme of scholarships and grants can best be carried out by an organization which will be obliged by its other responsibilities to keep in the closest touch with cultural affairs at home and abroad, and with universities, particularly with Canadian universities which, as we have seen, are the focal point for so many of our cultural activities.

We therefore recommend:

a. That a body be created to be known as the Canada Council for the Encouragement of the Arts, Letters, Humanities and Social Sciences to stimulate and to help voluntary organizations within these fields to foster Canada's cultural relations abroad, to perform the functions of a national commission for UNESCO, and to devise and administer a system of scholarships as recommended in Chapter XXII. . . .

SOURCE: *Report Royal Commission on National Development in the Arts, Letters and Sciences 1949–1951* (Ottawa: King's Printer, 1951): 376–7.

In September 1952, the Canadian Broadcasting Corporation opened the nation's first two television stations in Toronto and Montreal, and over the next two years it extended its television coverage to seven other metropolitan areas. At the time, only 146,000 Canadians owned television receivers (or 'sets' as they were usually called). They tuned their sets to American border stations and used increasingly elaborate antenna systems to draw in distant signals. Most Canadians thus missed entirely the first generation of American television programming, broadcast live from the studio, and tuned in only as US television moved from live to filmed programs and from New York to Hollywood. By 1952, 'I Love Lucy' had been running in the States for over a year. But if Canada's love affair with the tube was slightly belated, the country rapidly caught up. By December 1954 there were nine stations and 1,200,000 sets; by June 1955

ROBERT FARNON

Robert Farnon was born in Toronto in 1917 and studied trumpet from his childhood. In the early 1930s he became active in the Toronto dance band scene and later joined orchestras at the CBC led by Percy Faith and Geoffrey Waddington. He was best known publicly in Canada for his participation in CBC's 'Happy Gang' shows from 1937 to the early 1940s. At the same time, he developed a considerable reputation among musicians as a trumpet player, composer, and arranger. In 1943 he headed for Britain to become the conductor of the Canadian Band of the Allied Expeditionary Force. Many regarded this Canadian aggregation as superior to the UK band led by George Melachrino and the American band led by Glenn Miller because of Farnon's superior arrangements of tunes he copied off the short-wave radio. After the war Farnon became associated with the BBC, for which he wrote a succession of short program-signature tunes (including 'Jumping Bean' and 'Portrait of a Flirt') that made him one of the most listened-to composers in the world, albeit with little public recognition. He also became known among his peers as the leading figure in what the British called 'light music'. He wrote over thirty movie soundtracks, did arrangements for most of the leading British bands, and settled in Guernsey in 1959. In the 1960s and 1970s he had a highly successful British recording career, leading his own orchestra, and was still winning awards, including a Grammy, in the 1990s. Farnon occasionally wrote music with Canadian associations, but he never returned to Canada on a permanent basis. He is a perfect example of a highly successful Canadian performer and artist who is virtually unknown in Canada because most of a distinguished career was spent outside it.

there were twenty-six stations and 1,400,000 sets, and by December 1957 there were forty-four stations and nearly three million sets.

Television's popularity has been an international phenomenon transcending national circumstances and socio-economic conditions. Nevertheless, for Canadian society in the post-war years, television was the ideal technology. It fitted perfectly into the overall social and cultural dynamics of the time. Perhaps even more than the automobile, or the detached bungalow on its carefully manicured plot of green grass, television symbolized the aspirations and emergent lifestyles of the new suburban generation of Canadians. Unlike other leisure-time activities that required 'going out', television was a completely domesticated entertainment package that drew Canadian families *into* their homes. Until the late 1960s, most families owned only one television set, located in the living room. Particularly on weekend evenings during the long Canadian winter, the only sign of life on entire blocks of residential neighbourhoods was the dull, flickering glow of black-and-white television sets coming from otherwise darkened houses. The family could entertain friends who enjoyed the same popular programs, and everyone could enjoy snacks served on small metal 'TV tables' or even a meal taken from the freezer and heated (the 'TV dinner'). Some of what people watched was Canadian-produced, but most prime-time shows came from the Hollywood

The Impact of Science on Cultural Development

In 1948 the Canadian social scientist and economic history Harold Innis (1894–1952) delivered a paper to the Conference of Commonwealth Universities in Oxford. A part of that paper follows.

The impact of science on cultural development has been evident in its contribution to technological advance, notably in communication and in the dissemination of knowledge. In turn it has been evident in the types of knowledge disseminated; that is to say, science lives its own life not only in the mechanism which is provided to distribute knowledge but also in the sort of knowledge which will be distributed. As information has been disseminated the demand for the miraculous, which has been one of the great contributions of science, has increased. To supply this demand for the miraculous has been a highly remunerative task, as evidenced by the publications of firms concerned with scientific works. Bury described the rapidly growing demand in England for books and lectures, making the results of science accessible and interesting to the lay public, as a remarkable feature of the second half of the nineteenth century. Popular literature explained the wonders of the physical world and at the same time flushed the imaginations of men with the consciousness that they were living in the era 'which, in itself vastly superior to any age of the past, need be burdened by no fear of decline or catastrophe but, trusting in the boundless resources of science, might surely defy fate.' 'Progress itself suggests that its value as a doctrine is only relative, corresponding to a certain not very advanced stage of civilization, just as Providence in its day was an idea of relative value, corresponding to a stage somewhat less advanced.' The average reader has been impressed by the miraculous, and the high priests of science, or perhaps it would be fair to say the pseudo-priests of science, have been extremely effective in developing all sorts of fantastic things, with great emphasis, of course, on the atomic bomb. I hoped to get through this paper without mentioning the atomic bomb, but found it impossible. . . .

The effects of obsession with science have become serious for the position of science itself. It has been held that the scientific mind can adapt itself more easily to tyranny than the literary mind, since 'art is individualism and science seeks the subjection of the individual to absolute laws', but Casaubon was probably right in saying that 'the encouragement of science and letters is almost always a personal influence.' The concept of the state in the Anglo-Saxon world has been favourable to the suppression or distortion of culture, particularly through its influence on science. Under the influence of the state, communication among themselves has become more difficult for scientists with the same political background and practically impossible for those with a different political background, because of the importance attached to war. Mathematics and music have been regarded as universal languages, particularly with the decline of Latin, but even mathematics is a tool and has become ineffective for purposes of communication in a highly technical civilization concerned with war.

SOURCE: Harold Innis, 'A Critical Review', in Innis, *The Bias of Communication* (Toronto: University of Toronto Press, 1951): 192–3.

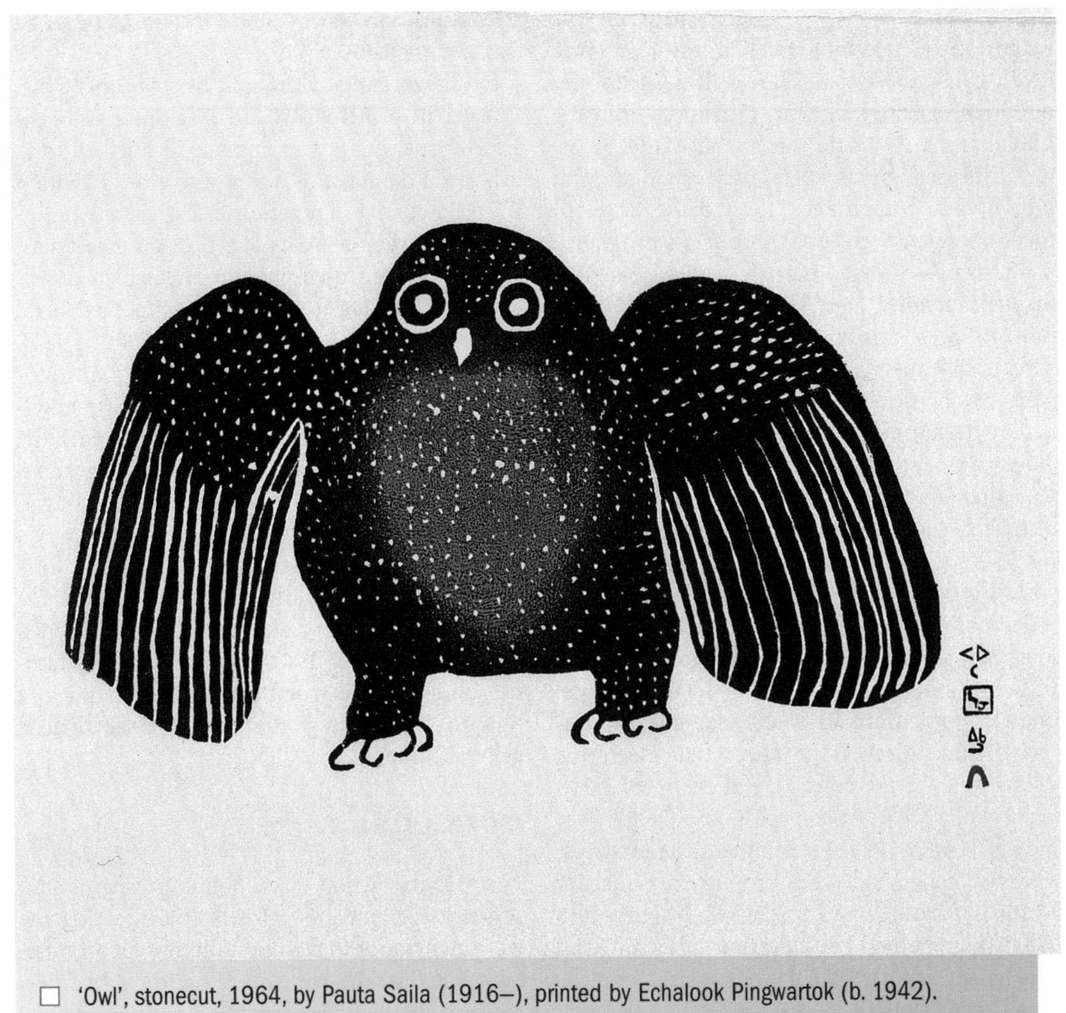

'Owl', stonecut, 1964, by Pauta Saila (1916–), printed by Echalook Pingwartok (b. 1942). Collection of the West Baffin Eskimo Co-operative Ltd, on loan to the McMichael Canadian Art Collection.

dream factory. Despite the popularity of Saturday evening's 'Hockey Night in Canada', first telecast in 1954, television served to draw Canadians ever deeper into the seductive world of American popular culture.

The post-war years were critical ones for popular culture in Canada. While governments wrestled with aspects of a cultural policy intended to protect Canadian culture and the Canadian identify from 'foreign' (read American) influence, their focus before 1960 was almost entirely on high culture. Few Canadians appreciated that the Americans were undergoing a cosmic shift of their own in cultural terms, particularly in the way they marshalled the media and their entire entertainment industry as delivery systems of American culture. One American scholar has described what happened as the shift from popular to mass culture. The secret of American success was an extraordinarily prosperous home economy, based partly on the extension of technological innovation into nearly every household. The result was a domesticization of entertainment, moving it from the public arena to inside the home. Many of the new consumer goods, such as television sets and high-fidelity equipment, required the development of related cultural products—programs, recordings—to make the new gadgets essential to every family. The American entertainment industry was clearly up to the challenge. All aspects of American culture, including sports, were systematically brought into the web of the new entertainment industry. The effect this would have on Canada would be profound.

After the war a handful of Canadian intellectuals became fascinated by the media's role in modern society. Given Canada's long history of wrestling with communications, this was perhaps not surprising. The Canadian scholar Marshall McLuhan (1911–80) would become the chief international guru of media culture, one of the first thinkers to arrive at and communicate some idea of the effect that electronic media were having on culture at every level. His first book, *The Mechanical Bride: Folklore of Industrial Man* (1951), examined comic strips, advertisements, and other promotional imagery of the American press to convey insights into 'that very common condition of industrial man in which he lives amid a great flowering of technical and mechanical imagery of whose rich human symbolism he is mainly unconscious' (McLuhan 1951: 4). Like his mentor, Harold Adams Innis (1894–1947), McLuhan took the media seriously. Unlike Innis, however, McLuhan was not prepared to condemn the mechanization process and its introduction of a 'mass' dimension.

Categorizing culture has never been simple. One of the principal artistic developments of the postwar period—the commercialization of Inuit art—well demonstrates the problems. The Inuit of the Arctic had for centuries carved a complex image world in ivory and other materials, mainly for their own pleasure. In the late 1940s several Canadian artists working in the north, led by James Archibald Houston (b. 1921), encouraged the Inuit to offer their carvings for sale in the south through co-operative marketing. Later in the 1950s Houston would teach the Inuit how to translate their striking images into prints. The federal government encouraged commercialization, with the assistance of the Canadian Handicrafts Guild and the Hudson's Bay Company. Inuit art quickly produced some of Canada's most distinctive images, known around the world. Its combination of folk tradition and deliberate commercialization, while not unique in this or any other period, resisted facile generalizations.

CONCLUSION

Against a backdrop of economic prosperity and substantial population growth, Canada after the war finally appeared to be fulfilling its promise. Substantial strides were made on fronts as different as social welfare and cultural policy. 'Progress' was everywhere. Quebec's place within the Constitution had not yet emerged as a serious problem for the federal government, which by 1959 appeared to have established itself as a typical twentieth-century centralized state.

HOW HISTORY HAS CHANGED

INTERPRETATIONS OF THE ARROW DEBACLE

The decision of the Diefenbaker government in 1959 to cancel the Avro Arrow provoked a contemporary storm, although much opinion at the time agreed with what has come to be the conventional mainstream historical wisdom: the Arrow was a great product, but it was simply not cost-effective, especially given that Canada's allies—the United States and Great Britain—did not wish to purchase it. The aircraft was so complex that it could not be flown by pilots in the reserves, which cut down considerably on even Canadian demand. Expenditures on the Arrow warped not only the military budget, but the entire federal budget. Once the government had established the plane's unmarketability, it was really a statesmanlike decision to pull the plug quickly, rather than allow the manufacturers to hang around for years hoping for a political change of heart. Canada had discovered one of the realities of postwar defence production: the smaller nations might get a piece of the action making component parts, but they could hardly expect to develop and produce independently their own hardware.

Despite the political realities of 1959, a cult of Avro Arrow supporters began almost immediately to write about the aircraft and the decision to cancel without much reference to the total context. In some ways they were quite right. The Arrow was a superb aircraft, years ahead of its time and superior to anything the Americans or the Brits had available at the time. It was a Canadian technological triumph, although technology never exists in a vacuum. But instead of setting out the full context, the Arrow supporters in book after book demonized the Diefenbaker administration and mythologized the aircraft's potential for success had the decision to cancel the program not been made. These authors concentrated on the fact that the Arrow had been terminated even before it was fully tested or put into production, suggesting that its admitted superiorities would ultimately have won over its critics in other nations. These writers showed no understanding of the *realpolitik* of the defence business, preferring to elaborate conspiracy theories about why and how the prototype and the plans had been 'mysteriously' destroyed. In 1999, the CBC distilled all of this paranoid literature into a television docudrama starring Dan Ackroyd, which further popularized the Arrow and strongly suggested that a terrible mistake had been made forty years earlier. Popular history has a way of changing historical attitudes, but not necessarily for the better.

SHORT BIBLIOGRAPHY

Abella, Irving. *Nationalism, Communism, and Canadian Labour*. Toronto, 1973. A well-balanced analysis of the conceptual and practical problems besetting Canadian labour.

Bashevkin, Sylvia. *True Patriot Love: The Politics of Canadian Nationalism*. Toronto, 1991. A thoughtful study of the ways politicians and the state have attempted to harness Canadian nationalism to their own purposes.

Behiels, Michael. *Prelude to Quebec's Quiet Revolution: Liberalism versus Neo-Nationalism 1945–1960*. Montreal and Kingston, 1985. A fascinating treatment of the intellectual battle in Quebec in the years before the Quiet Revolution.

Bothwell, Robert, Ian Drummond, and John

English. *Canada since 1945: Power, Politics, and Provincialism*, 2nd ed. Toronto, 1989. The best general account of the post-1945 period, somewhat dated, pro-federalist, and very Ontario-oriented.

Bryden, Kenneth, *Old Age Pensions and Policy-Making in Canada*. Montreal and London, 1984. A judicious study of a critical component of the welfare state.

Clark. S.D. *The Suburban Society*. Toronto, 1964. A study of the suburban phenomenon by the leading historical sociologist of his generation.

Doern, G. Bruce. *Science and Politics in Canada*. Montreal and London, 1972. A trenchant account of the history of Canadian science policy.

Guindon, Herbert. *Quebec Society: Tradition, Modernity, Nationhood*. Toronto, 1988. A useful overview of the recent history of Quebec.

Kostash, Myrna. *Long Way from Home: The Story of the Sixties Generation in Canada*. Toronto, 1980. A popular account of the 1960s, particularly useful for its take on the young.

Kwavnick, David, ed. *The Tremblay Report*. Toronto, 1972. An edited translation of the vital Quebec commission on constitutional problems of the early 1950s.

Litt, Paul. *The Muses, the Masseys and the Massey Commission*. Toronto, 1992. A revisionist study of the Massey Commission, which argues it was elitist and ineffective.

Owram, Doug. *Born at the Right Time: A History of the Baby Boom Generation*. Toronto, 1996. A scholarly attempt to understand the Baby Boomers.

Porter, John. *The Vertical Mosaic: An Analysis of Social Class and Power in Canada*. Toronto, 1968. The classic study, which argued that a social hierarchy existed among Canadians based on ethnic origins.

Rea, K.J. *The Prosperous Years: The Economic History of Ontario, 1939–1975*. Toronto, 1985. A useful analysis of the period of affluence in Canada's largest province and of the centre of its industrial growth.

Rutherford, Paul. *When Television Was Young: Primetime Canada 1952–1967*. Toronto, 1990. A scholarly treatment of the early history of the medium.

Safarian, A.E. *Foreign Ownership of Canadian Industry*. Toronto, 1966. A calm and dispassionate analysis of the hotly debated economic topic of the 1960s.

Seeley, John R., et al. *Crestwood Heights: A North American Suburb*. Toronto, 1956. A richly nuanced contemporary study of the Canadian suburban phenomenon, focusing on what was perhaps not a typical suburb.

Simeon, Richard, and Ian Robertson. *State, Society and the Development of Canadian Federalism*. Toronto, 1990. A useful overview of the recent historical development of federalism in Canada.

Stewart, Craig. *Arrow through the Heart: The Life and Times of Crawford Gordon & the Avro Arrow*. Toronto, 1998. Perhaps the best of the Arrow books, this one focuses on the man in charge of the project.

Trudeau, Pierre Elliott, ed. *The Asbestos Strike*. 1951, trans. Toronto, 1974. A fascinating study of one of the key events of the 1950s in Quebec.

STUDY QUESTIONS

1. After World War I, there was a three-year economic depression in Canada. World War II was followed by a prolonged economic boom. Identify and explain three changed conditions that might account for Canadian prosperity after the Second World War.
2. Explain why the Diefenbaker administration decided to scrap the Avro Arrow.
3. What was the main factor that made it possible for Canada to spend less than other developed nations on research and development while still benefiting from the latest technological advances?
4. What effects did the baby boom have on public education in Canada?
5. To what extent was suburbia an imagined world? How did this imagined world affect consumer spending patterns?
6. Give two reasons to account for rapid growth in the public sector of the economy between 1945 and 1960.
7. What were the chief factors that accounted for the Liberal Party's predominance at the federal level during this period?
8. Describe the main tenets of the 'new nationalism' that developed in Quebec after 1939.
9. What was the most important reason anglophone Canadians had so much trouble understanding the distinctiveness of their own culture?

CHAPTER TEN

Edging Towards the Abyss, 1958–1972

Periods in history are seldom neat and tidy. Decades and centuries have a nasty tendency to spill over their technical dates. The era from 1958 to 1972 in Canada will always be labelled 'the sixties'. Life in those years was a bit like riding on a roller-coaster. Revolution was in the air, but it never quite arrived. Everything seemed to be happening at roller-coaster speed. Although the ride was frequently quite exhilarating, the view from the front seemed to open into a bottomless abyss. Almost every positive development had its downside. The Canadian economy continued to grow, but the unpleasant side-effects became more evident. Government sought to reform the legal system regarding divorce while the rates of marital breakdown reached epidemic proportions. The Roman Catholic Church internationally introduced a series of unprecedented reforms, but Canadians stopped attending all churches in record numbers. An increasing number of students at Canadian universities became concerned about American influence in Canada, only to be influenced themselves by American student reaction to the war in Vietnam. A variety of collective minorities began insisting on their rights, the acceptance of which would require the complete remaking of social justice—and indeed society—in Canada. The nation celebrated its Centennial in 1967, the most memorable event of which was an off-the-cuff public exclamation by French President Charles De Gaulle.

The usual picture of Canada after the Second World War shows a naive and complacent society that, with the aid of imported American ideas, suddenly questioned virtually all its values. There are a number of important qualifications to make to such a view. There was more ferment under the surface in postwar Canada than was recognized at the time. In many respects, ideas and behaviour that had previously been underground suddenly shifted into the public arena. Discontent was a product of the rising expectations caused by economic affluence. As is so often the case, much confrontation occurred because institutions did not change rapidly enough. Canadians were able to take over much of the American critical vocabulary because of their profound suspicions of the American system. Social critics in the United States struck a chord with Canadians who had similar feelings about the contradictions of American society and culture.

THE 'RADICAL SIXTIES'

The era 1958–72 involved complex currents and countercurrents. Discussion of even the most major movements can only scratch the surface. Nonetheless, any account of the sixties must begin by considering three of the period's most striking developments: a broad societal shift towards liberalization; the appearance of a youth-centred counterculture; and the emergence of newly energized collective minorities in Canadian society. Sixties rhetoric was able to find

TIMELINE

1960
Introduction of Enovid. Royal Commission on Government Organization is created. Jean Lesage and the Liberals defeat Duplessis in Quebec. Bill of Rights passes federal Parliament.

1961
National Indian Council is founded. Canadian content regulations are introduced for television. CTV is formed. New Democratic Party is organized.

1962
Federal election returns a Diefenbaker minority government. Hydro-Quebec is formed. Lesage government wins again with the slogan 'Maîtres chez nous'.

1963
Lester Pearson becomes prime minister at the head of a Liberal minority government. Parent Commission reports on education in Quebec. Royal Commission on Bilingualism and Biculturalism is formed.

1964
Family allowances are expanded. Brock University is founded. New Canadian flag is adopted.

1965
Student Union for Peace Action is founded. National Pension Plan is introduced, with a separate plan for Quebec. War on Poverty begins. Simon Fraser University and York University are opened.

1966
Federal Medical Act of 1966 is passed. Union Nationale defeats Liberals in Quebec.

1967
Canadian Centennial Year celebrations (including Expo 67). Official national anthem is adopted. Royal Commission on the Status of Women is appointed. National Hockey League is expanded, with no new Canadian teams. René Lévesque resigns from the Quebec Liberal Party.

1968
Michel Tremblay's play *Les Belle-Soeurs* is produced. Federal divorce reform is introduced. Canadian Métis Society and the National Indian Brotherhood are formed. Special Senate Committee on Poverty is established.

1969
Criminal Code amendments dealing with abortion and homosexuality are introduced. Sir George Williams University Computer Centre is occupied by protesting students. Montreal Expos begin play. White Paper on Indian Affairs is published. Pierre Trudeau's Liberals are elected with large majority. Official Languages Act is passed.

1970
Ledain Commission on non-medical use of drugs reports. Robert Bourassa's Liberals win over the Union Nationale in Quebec. October Crisis of 1970.

1971
New federal Unemployment Insurance Plan.

1972
'Waffle' purged from Ontario NDP. Bobby Hull signs with Winnipeg Jets of the World Hockey Association.

a venue on radio and television. The reformers were the first radicals ever to have access to colour television. Only a few contemporaries ever managed to get beneath the rhetoric to understand the substance of the critique.

THE EMANCIPATION OF MANNERS

The sixties have been credited with (or blamed for) a revolution in morality in which the traditional values of our Victorian ancestors were overturned virtually overnight. Firmly held moral beliefs do not collapse quite so rapidly or easily, of course. Rather, a belief system that was already in a state of decay and profoundly out of step with how people actually behaved in their daily lives was finally questioned and found wanting. A previous Canadian reluctance to examine morality ended. The brief upsurge of formal Christianity that had characterized the postwar era suddenly terminated. Canadians ceased attending church in droves. The phenomenon was especially evident in Catholic Quebec. The shifts involved were international ones that went much further elsewhere in the industrialized world than in Canada. By comparison with Sweden or California, for example, Canadian manners appear in retrospect to have remained quite old fashioned.

The liberation of manners occurred simultaneously on several visible levels. The old media taboos against sexual explicitness, obscenity, and graphic depiction of violence virtually disappeared. Television attempted to maintain the traditional standards, but TV news itself constantly undermined that self-restraint with its coverage of what was happening in the world. The sixties were probably no more violent than any other period in human history. However, constant television coverage of the decade's more brutal events, increasingly in 'living' colour, brought them into everyone's living-room. The memories of any Canadian who lived through the period include a veritable kaleidoscope of violent images: the assassinations of John F. Kennedy, his brother Robert, and Martin Luther King; the Paris and Chicago student riots of 1968; scenes in Vietnam (including the My Lai murders of innocent civilians and the defoliation of an entire ecosystem). Closer to home, there was the October Crisis of 1970. Canadians liked to believe that violence happened outside Canada, especially in the United States. Canadians somehow were nicer. On the eve of the October Crisis, the Guess Who, a Canadian rock group, had a monster hit, the lyrics of which pursued some of the most common metaphors of the time. 'American Woman' identified the United States with violence and Canada's relationship with its southern neighbour in sexual terms, a common conceit of the time.

As for sexuality, it became more explicit. Canadians began to talk and write openly about sexual intercourse, contraception, abortion, premarital sex, and homosexual behaviour. In place of the winks and nudges that had always accompanied certain 'unmentionable' topics, a refreshing frankness appeared. Many of the issues of sexuality revolved around women's ambition (hardly new) to gain control of their own bodies and reproductive functions. Part of the new development was the rapid spread of the use of Enovid, the oral contraceptive widely known as 'the pill' after its introduction in 1960. The pill seemed to offer an easier and more secure method of controlling conception. Its use became quite general before some of its unpleasant side-effects came to light. One of the pill's advantages was that the woman herself was responsible for its proper administration. The birth rate had already begun declining in 1959, and probably would have continued to decline without the pill. Enovid symbolized a new sexual freedom—some said promiscuity—for women that gradually made its way into the media. By the mid-1960s, popular magazines that had previously preached marriage, fidelity, and domesticity were now featuring lead articles on premarital sex, marital affairs, and cohabitation before marriage.

Language, at least as the media used it, was equally rapidly liberated. Canadian writers—whether in fiction, poetry, drama, film, or history—had usually employed a sanitized and almost unrecognizable version of spoken French or English. Earle Birney's comic war novel *Turvey* (1949) suggested the use of profanities by Canada's soldiers by means of dashes in the text. But *Turvey* only hinted at the larger reality. In everyday life many ordinary Canadians used not only profanities but a rich vocabulary of vulgar slang that could be found in few dictionaries of the day. In French Canada, that everyday language was called 'joual'. While earlier writers like Gabrielle Roy and Roger Lemelin had suggested its use, later writers such as Michel Tremblay (b. 1942) actually began to employ it. Tremblay's play *Les Belles-Soeurs*, written in 1965 but not produced until 1968 because of concerns about its language, cast its dialogue in joual. His later plays added sexually explicit themes, including transvestism and homosexuality. By 1970 both language and themes previously considered unsuitable became public across the country.

The state played its own part in the reformation of manners. Pierre Elliott Trudeau (b. 1919) achieved a reputation that helped make him prime minister by presiding over a reformist Department of Justice from 1967 to 1968. He became associated with the federal reform of divorce in 1968, as well as with amendments (in 1969) to Canada's Criminal Code dealing with abortion and homosexuality. Trudeau's remark that the state had no place in the bedrooms of the nation struck a responsive chord. He was prime minister in 1969 when a commission was appointed to investigate the non-medical use of drugs. While its report, published in 1970, did not openly advocate the legalization of soft drugs, such as marijuana, its general arguments about the relationship of law and morality were symptomatic of the age. The commission maintained that the state had the right to limit the availability of potentially harmful substances through the Criminal Code. At the same time it added that it was not necessarily 'appropriate to use the criminal law to enforce morality, regardless of the potential for harm to the individual or society' (Addiction Research Foundation 1970: 503–26).

The concept that it was not the state's function to enforce morality flew in the face of the Canadian tradition, which had always embodied morality in the Criminal Code. The new liberalism informed many of the legal reforms of the later 1960s. A number of Roman Catholic bishops, in a brief to a special joint committee of the legislature on divorce in 1967, stated that the legislator's goal should not be 'primarily the good of any religious group but the good of all society' (*Proceedings of the Special Joint Committee of the Senate and House of Commons on Divorce* 1967: 1515–16). Such liberated thinking not only paved the way for a thorough reform of federal divorce legislation, making divorce easier and quicker to obtain, but also for amendments to the Criminal Code in 1969 regarding abortion. Termination of pregnancy became legal if carried out by physicians in proper facilities, and following a certification by a special panel of doctors that 'the continuation of the pregnancy of such female person would or would be likely to

☐ Earle Birney, winner of the 1950 Leacock Medal. NAC, C-31956.

THE USE OF DRUGS

In 1969 the newly-elected Trudeau government appointed a commission of inquiry into the non-medical use of drugs. That commission made its interim report in 1970. It included a number of transcriptions from testimony before it.

From a university professor in Eastern Canada

I have enjoyed smoking marijuana and hashish several times, and I feel that if they are made legal, we have far more to gain than lose. I think they can be easily incorporated with our way of life in Canada without eroding any but purely materialistic or exploitative values. Marijuana does not provide an escape from reality any more than alcohol, sex or a drive in the country: we know we cannot be high all the time; we enjoy taking a trip (in both senses of the word) and we remember it with pleasure, but we know that we have to come back home again and go to work, and continue our everyday life. I have so often heard the argument that pot or hashish lead to hard drugs. For the vast majority of pot smokers, this is rubbish. It is the argument that temperance societies use against alcohol: social drinking leads to alcoholism. I have never had the slightest desire to shoot anything into my arm, nor do I want to try speed in any of its forms. There will always be a few disturbed people in our world, and I don't think that laws should be made for that tiny minority. . . .

I wrote to John Turner last winter deploring the persecution of young long-hairs by the police and the RCMP. As many people have observed, this leads not to a lessening of pot and hash smoking, but to a disrespect for the police. I would like to see the force more respected, because, as we all know, police need public support and sympathy in order to perform efficiently. What sympathy can they expect when they disguise themselves as hippies in order to infiltrate and arrest them? Hippies are not communists circa 1947, and this police tactic only degrades the officer who undertakes it, as well as the force in general. The hippies feel that the RCMP is acting out of ignorance and fear; they believe that pot-smoking is good, and there is no reason why they should change their minds: they are working from experience, and RCMP actions, no matter how 'legal', spring from institutionalized paranoia.

I am not underestimating the temporary upheaval which legalizing marijuana and hashish might cause in certain sectors—police, puritans, all those who wish to force their own limits of freedom and pleasure on the country as a whole. I think we should have the right to choose for ourselves whether we want to smoke or not. I think we have far more to gain than to lose by legalizing pot . . . .

SOURCE: *Interim Report of the Commission of Inquiry into the Non-Medical Use of Drugs* (Ottawa: Queen's Printer, 1970): 292-3.

endanger her life or health'. The Criminal Code was also amended in 1969 to exempt from prosecution 'indecent actions' by consenting couples over the age of twenty-one who performed such acts in private.

The reformation of manners, if not morals, based on the twin concepts that the state had no place in enforcing morality and that individuals were entitled to decide on the ways in which they harmed themselves, was largely in place by 1969. There were clear limits to liberalization, however. Since 1969 Canada has witnessed a resurgence of demands for state intervention in areas where liberalization was held to produce adverse consequences. Thus many women's groups have come to advocate stricter legislation on obscenity and indecency, particularly in the media, in order to protect women and children from sexual abuse.

☐ Justice Minister Pierre Elliot Trudeau with Prime Minister Lester B. Pearson at the federal-provincial conference of February 1968. NAC, C-25001.

THE COUNTERCULTURE

One of the most obvious manifestations of the ferment of the sixties was the rebellious reaction of young baby boomers against the values of their elders, a movement that came to be known as the counterculture. Many Canadian rebels of the period took much of the style and content of their protest from the Americans, although they had their own home-grown concerns, especially in Quebec. As in the United States, youthful rebellion in Canada had two wings, never mutually exclusive: a highly politicized movement of active revolution, often centred in the universities and occasionally tending to violence; and a less overtly political one of personal self-reformation and self-realization, centred in the 'hippies'. Student activists and hippies were often the same people. Even when different personnel were involved, the culture was usually much the same, anchored by sex, dope, and rock music. The participants in the two Canadian branches of youthful protest also had in common distinctly middle-class backgrounds, for these were movements of affluence, not marginality.

The United States was the spiritual home of the sixties' counterculture in English Canada. Americans had gone further than anyone else both in suburbanizing their culture and in universalizing education. The rapidly expanding university campus provided an ideal spawning ground for youthful rebellion. The campus had helped generate, in the civil rights movement, a protest crusade that served as a model for subsequent agitation. Civil rights as a public concern focused attention on the rhetorical contradictions of mainstream American society, which preached equality for all while denying it to Blacks. It also mobilized youthful idealism and demonstrated the techniques of the protest march and civil disobedience, as well as the symbolic values of popular song. When some American Blacks left the civil rights movement, convinced that only violence could truly alter the status quo, they provided models for urban guerrilla activity, including the growing terrorist campaign in Quebec that was associated with separatism. (French-Canadian youths could identify with Pierre Vallières's *White Niggers of America*.)

In English Canada, what really ignited the revolt of youth was the war in Vietnam. In retrospect, the extent to which Vietnam dominated the period becomes even clearer to us than it was to people at the time. The war became the perfect

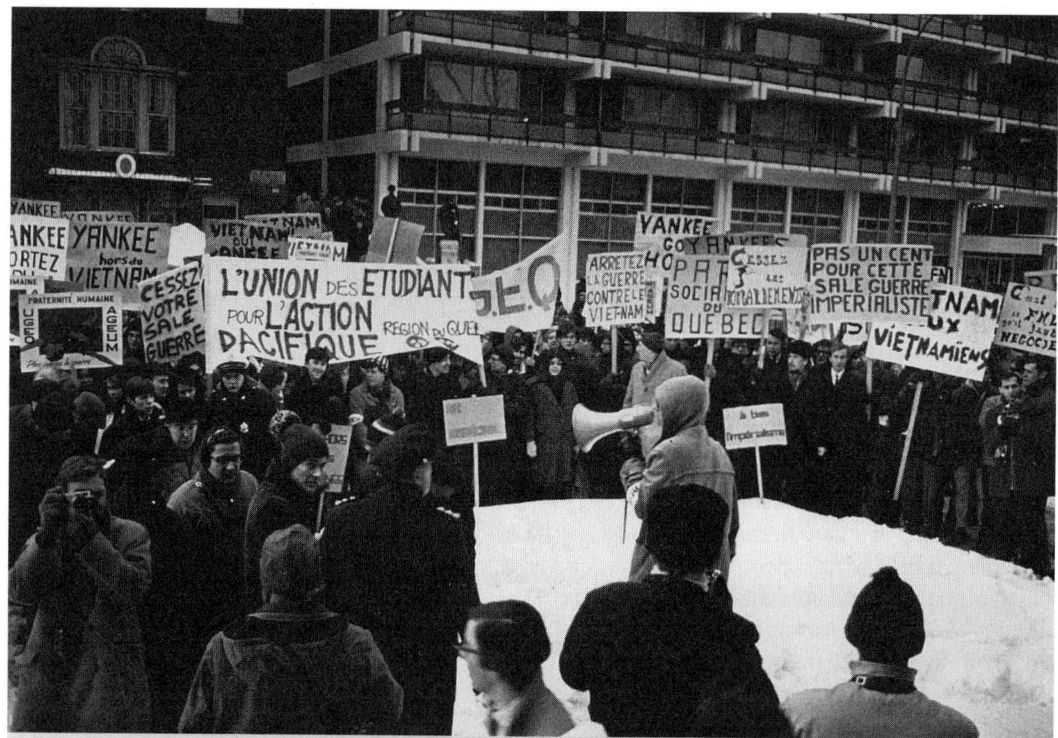

Anti-Vietnam War protesters make their way to the US Consulate in Montreal, 19 February 1966. NAC, PA-173623.

symbol for the sixties generation of everything that was wrong with mainstream American society. It was equally exportable as an emblem of American Evil, representing everything that the rest of the world hated about the United States, including its arrogant assumption that it was always morally superior. For these reasons, Vietnam was central to the Canadian counterculture in a variety of ways. Hostility to American policy in Vietnam fuelled Canadian anti-Americanism, as a paperback book about the United States entitled *The New Romans: Candid Canadian Opinions of the U.S.* demonstrated in 1967. This hostility also connected young Canadians with the burgeoning American protest movements. Many Canadian university faculty members recruited during the decade were Americans, most of them recent graduate students critical of American policy. They were joined in their sympathies by an uncounted number of American war resisters (some said as many as 100,000 at the height of the war), the majority of whom sought refuge in communities of university students or hippies in large Canadian cities.

The youthful reaction advocated an eclectic kind of socialism—Marxist-influenced, democratically oriented, and idealistically verging on romanticism—that is usually referred to as the New Left. The movement was much better at explaining what was wrong with the present system than at proposing workable alternatives. It had no example of a large-scale society that operated on its principles. Nevertheless, Canadian student activists rose to positions of power in their universities, establishing several national

CANADIAN WRITERS VIEW THE UNITED STATES

In 1968 the Canadian poet Al Purdy asked a number of his fellow writers in Canada to contribute their views of the United States to a collection he intended to publish. The following two poems came from George Jonas and Robin Mathews respectively.

American Girl: A Canadian View

It is reassuring
To spend part of a night
With an American girl.

Chances are she will not resemble
The leaders of her nation
In speech, figure, or stance:

If she has imperialistic designs
She may draw you without a struggle
Into her sphere of influence.

Then you'll find her battledress
Fit for her private battles,
See not her battleships but hear her battlecries,
And melt (perhaps with a wistful smile)
Before the native napalm of her eyes.

But she'll seem to be prepared
To give as well as to accept
Some foreign aid

And by midnight or so
While the fires of her manifest destiny smoulder
You'll be all ready to slip across
The world's longest undefended border.

—George Jonas

Centennial Song

Canada, my beauty,
everybody's love,
white flower of diamond-studded North,
let me tell you that
a tired prostitute beyond her prime,
dejected, hungry,
full of malice and uncertain fear
would throw her charms away less openly,
would exercise more choice
than you have ever done,
would charge at least a reasonable rate,
would try to be
(within the perils of the trade)
a self-respecting whore;
And What Is More
even in her wildest state
of drunken self-delusion,
howling at a corner
where the newsies thrive,
she wouldn't let you see her
stopping people —
friends and neighbours,
even relatives,
shouting with paranoid insistence
upon decency and moral strength,
that she is living better now than ever,
friends with everyone, and that
despite all rumour, not a shred
of proof has ever been produced
to show that she
(as gossips say)
is being regularly screwed.

—Robin Mathews

SOURCE: Al Purdy, ed., *The New Romans: Candid Canadian Opinions of the U.S.* (Edmonton: Hurtig, 1968): 53, 74.

organizations, such as the Student Union for Peace Action (1965). Student radicalism flourished at a few universities, such as Simon Fraser, York, and the Université de Montréal. Many of the less extreme student activists joined the Waffle wing of the NDP, which attempted to radicalize that party in the direction of economic nationalism and social reform. Perhaps the most publicized student protest in Canada occurred in February 1969 when the computer centre at Sir George Williams University (now Concordia) in Montreal was occupied for two weeks to protest racial intolerance and the 'military, imperialistic ambitions of Canada in the West Indies' (quoted in Forsythe 1971: 9). The student protesters ended their occupation on 11 February by smashing the computers and damaging university equipment and records estimated to be worth millions of dollars. Ninety occupiers were arrested, including forty-one Blacks, many of whom came from the Caribbean region.

Despite the incident at Sir George Williams, youthful protest was not quite the same in Quebec as in Anglo-Canada. While Quebec's

George Grant on 'Canadian Fate and Imperialism'

In 1969 the Canadian philosopher George Grant published a book of essays entitled *Technology and Empire*. An unrepentant Tory and classicist, Grant was a most unlikely guru for the radical generation of the time, but he was extremely popular in such circles.

To use the language of fate is to assert that all human beings come into a world they did not choose and live their lives within a universe they did not make. If one speaks in this way, one is often accused either of being pessimistic or of holding a tragic view of life. Neither of these accusations is correct. To say that one holds a tragic view of life would be to follow Nietzsche in thinking that Dionysian tragedy was a higher stance than that in Socrates; I do not think this. And the words optimistic and pessimistic are surely most accurately used, following Leibniz, to describe what one thinks about the nature of things, whether the world is good or not. It is quite possible to use the word 'fate', and to think that 'nature' is good, and not contradict oneself. It is in my opinion a sensible way to talk about events, though obviously it is far from the liberal dogmas within which most people are taught to think.

A central aspect of the fate of being a Canadian is that our very existing has at all times been bound up with the interplay of various world empires. One can better understand what it is to be Canadian if one understands that interplay. As no serious person is interested in history simply as antiquarianism but only as it illumines one's search for the good in the here and now, let me set the problem in its most contemporary form—Vietnam. What our fate is today becomes most evident in the light of Vietnam. It is clear that in that country the American empire has been demolishing a people, rather than allowing them to live outside the American orbit.

The Americans are forced to that ferocious demolition because they have chosen to draw the line against the Chinese empire in a country where nationalism and communism have been in large measure identified. How does this affect Canadians? On the one hand, many Canadians, whether their moral traditions come from Judaism, Christianity, the liberal enlightenment or a mixture, are not yet so empty that they can take lightly the destruction of a people—even in the case of Asians. On the other hand, the vast majority of Canadians are a product of western civilization and live entirely within the forms and assumptions of that enterprise. Today the enterprise of western civilization finds its spearhead in the American empire. In that sense our very lives are inevitably bound up in the meeting of that empire with the rest of the world, and the movements of war which draw the limits in that meeting. The depth of that common destiny with the Americans is shown in the fact that many Canadians who are forced to admit the sheer evil of what is being done in Vietnam say at the same time that we have no choice but to stand with the Americans as the pillar of western civilization. Beyond this kind of talk is of course the fact that this society is above all a machine for greed, and our branch plant industry is making a packet out of the demolition of Vietnam.

Our involvement is much deeper than the immediate profits of particular wars. Our very form of life depends on our membership in the western industrial empire which is centred in the USA and which stretches out its hegemony into parts of western Europe and which controls South America and much of Africa and Asia. Somewhere in the minds of nearly all Canadians there is the recognition that our present form of life depends on our place as second-class members of that system. By 'second class' I do not imply a low status, because there are a large number of classes within it. It is much nicer to be a Canadian than a Brazilian or a Venezuelan, or for that matter an Englishman. . . .

SOURCE: George Grant, *Technology and Empire: Perspectives on North America* (Toronto: Anansi, 1969): 63–5.

young were no less alienated than their anglophone compatriots, their anger found an outlet in opposition to Canadian federalism's colonial oppression of their own province. Young people of university age (although seldom at university) formed most of the active cells of the Front de libération du Québec (FLQ), including the one that provoked the October Crisis of 1970. The FLQ'S rhetoric and tactics during the crisis were clearly modelled on extreme movements of protest in the United States and Europe. English-speaking Canadian students talked of the 'student as nigger', but French Canadians saw their entire society as comparable with that of the Blacks in the US or an oppressed Third World nation (quoted in Kostash 1980: 250). Radical young Quebecers were able to become part of a larger movement of protest and reform that cut across the age structure of Quebec society. Unlike their counterparts in English Canada, young protesters in Quebec were not cut off from the mainstream of adult society.

'The bureaucratic forms of organization shared by communism and capitalism', wrote one American activist, 'were embodiments of insult to the ideals of individualism, spontaneity, mutual trust and generosity that are the dominant themes of the new sensibility' (quoted in Kostash 1980: 250). Such ideals motivated the hippies, who accordingly dropped out of mainstream society. Earlier generations of middle-class Canadians had dutifully struggled up the ladder of success. Many of the sixties generation lacked such ambition or direction. They were their parents' children, searching for personal self-fulfilment through any possible means. For some, the quest led to vulgarized versions of Eastern mystical religions. For others, it led to communes close to nature, often on remote islands. For the vast majority, it certainly meant experimenting with hallucinogenic drugs, particularly cannabis, and a sexual freedom bordering on promiscuity in an age when sexually transmitted diseases seemed easily treatable with antibiotics. Such experiments, together with a revolution in popular music, were the core of the sixties for participants and onlookers alike. Rock music was almost impossible to define, incorporating as it did so many musical styles ranging from Black rhythm and blues to traditional folk music to Indian ragas to medieval Gregorian chant. Nevertheless, rock served as the symbol that both united the young and separated them from their parents.

It is impossible to define a precise moment at which the bubble of the sixties' youth energy burst. Many of the characteristics and tendencies of the period continued in fragmented fashion into the succeeding decades. But at the end of the sixties the naive beliefs of the young received a series of shocks when American student activists were ruthlessly suppressed at Chicago (1968) and Kent State (1970). At the same time, the central rallying point—American involvement in Vietnam—was gradually removed. In Canada, the founding of the Parti Québécois in 1968 provided a place within the system for many Quebec student activists. Two years later the October Crisis demonstrated how far some activists were prepared to go in the use of violence, and how far the Canadian state was prepared to go in suppressing it. The purging of the NDP's Waffle movement in 1972 perhaps completed the process of neutralizing activism, at least in Anglo-Canada. Some observers explained the collapse of the sixties youth movements in terms of demography. Young people got older and acquired jobs. Perhaps. In any event, by 1973 only memories of the 'good old days', often in the form of the lyrics of rock songs, were left for most of the sixties generation.

THE RISE OF MILITANT COLLECTIVITIES

While much youthful protest disappeared at the end of the decade, the baby boomers had joined in some movements that outlasted the era. The sixties saw a number of previously disadvantaged groups in Canadian society emerge with articulated positions and demands. These included, among others, Aboriginal peoples, Blacks, women, and homosexuals. To some extent, all these groups shared a common sense of liberation and heightened consciousness during the heady days of the sixties, as well as some common models and rhetoric. The several Black movements in the United States, especially civil rights and Black power, were generally influential. It was no accident that almost every group, including French Canadians, compared itself with American Blacks. While on one level other emerging collectivities could hardly avoid sympathizing with French Canada, on another level the arguments and aspirations of Quebec often seriously conflicted with those of other groups. Many collectivities sought to mobilize federal power to achieve their goals, often seeing the provinces and provincial rights as part of their problem.

As with so many other long-standing Canadian problems, that of the Aboriginal peoples moved into a new activist phase in the 1960s. Native activists built partly on their own traditions of constructing organizations to speak for First Nations and Inuit concerns. In 1961 the National Indian Council (NIC) was founded 'to promote unity among Indian people, the betterment of people of Indian ancestry in Canada, and to create a better understanding of Indian and non-Indian relationships' (quoted in Patterson 1972: 177). This organization was formed by Native people—many of whom had recently moved to the city—who hoped to combine the concerns of status and non-status Indians. Métis were also involved in the NIC. In 1968 political incompatibility led to the dissolution of the National Indian Council and the formation of two new groups: the Canadian Métis Society (which in 1970 renamed itself the Native Council of Canada) representing Métis and non-status Indians, and the National Indian Brotherhood (which would become the Assembly of First Nations) representing status Indians. Activists were also able to take advantage of American models and Canadian federal policy, particularly the 1960 Bill of Rights. The search for new sources of raw materials for exploitation in the Canadian north threatened Aboriginal ways of life, forcing them into the political mainstream. By the end of the decade, an emerging Native militancy was able to marshal its forces to confront the federal government when it tried to rethink the Aboriginal problem.

In 1969 the Department of Indian Affairs, under Jean Chrétien (b. 1934), published a White Paper on federal policy. All-encompassing in its reassessment, the document had three controversial recommendations: the abolition of the Indian Act (and the Department of Indian Affairs), which would eliminate status Indians; the transfer of First Nations lands from Crown trust into the hands of the First Nations; and the devolution of responsibility for Aboriginal people to the provinces. The White Paper touched off bitter criticism in all quarters, not least because it had been generated with little prior consultation with Native groups. It produced the first popular man-

HAROLD CARDINAL

Harold Cardinal (b. 1945) was a member of the Sucker Creek Reserve band who became president of the Indian Association of Alberta at the young age of twenty-three. He had read widely in the American rhetorical literature of the 1960s regarding Aboriginal peoples, and he responded to the federal government's 1969 White Paper on Indian Affairs—which called for the advancement of the individual rights of Aboriginals rather than their collective rights—with an angry, best-selling book entitled *The Unjust Society*, an obvious reference to Pierre Trudeau's 'Just Society'. Cardinal described the White Paper as a 'thinly disguised programme of extermination through assimilation', adding that the federal government, 'instead of acknowledging its legal and moral responsibilities to the Indians of Canada and honouring the treaties that the Indians signed in good faith, now proposes to wash its hands of Indians entirely, passing the buck to the provincial governments.'

Cardinal coined the term 'the Buckskin Curtain' to describe the separation between Europeans and First Nations in Canada, observing that while 'Canadian urbanites have walked blisters on their feet and fat off their rumps to raise money for underdeveloped countries outside Canada', Canadians generally did not 'give a damn' about the plight of their own Native people. He also attacked 'Uncle Tomahawks' among his own people who continually apologized for being Aboriginal. He noted with some irony that Native people who wore their normal clothing risked being confused with hippies. Cardinal was also a critic of Canada's 'two founding peoples' concept, pointing out that it did not recognize 'the role played by the Indian even before the founding of a nation state known as Canada'. He insisted that the First Nations were not separatists; they merely wanted their treaty and Aboriginal rights recognized so that they could take their place 'with the other cultural identities of Canada'. He subsequently helped write the 'Red Paper' in 1970, and in 1977 published *The Rebirth of Canada's Indians*, which attempted to outline a positive program for his people. He served briefly as director general of Indian affairs in Alberta, but spent much of his career in Native politics at both the provincial and national levels. In later life he took up an appointment at the University of Alberta.

ifesto for Canadian Aboriginals in Harold Cardinal's *The Unjust Society: The Tragedy of Canada's Indians* (1969), which argued for the re-establishment of special rights within the strengthened contexts of treaties and the Indian Act.

The White Paper was consistent with federal policy towards all minorities, including French Canadians, at the end of the 1960s. It called for the advancement of the individual rather than the collective rights of Native peoples: 'The Government believes that its policies must lead to the full, free, and non-discriminatory participation of the Aboriginal people in Canadian society. Such a goal requires a break with the past. It requires that the Aboriginal people's role of dependence be replaced by a role of equal status, opportunity, and responsibility, a role they can share with all other Canadians' (*A Statement of the Government of Canada on Indian Policy* 1969: 5). An assimilationist document, the White Paper insisted that treaties between the Crown and Aboriginals had involved only 'limited and minimal promises' that had been greatly exceeded in terms of the 'economic, educational, health, and welfare needs of the Indian people' by subsequent government performance (*A Statement of the Government of Canada on Indian Policy* 1969: 5). Allowing Aboriginal people full access to Canadian social services (many of which were administered provincially) would mark an advance over existing paternalism. Ottawa seemed surprised that Native people responded so negatively to the White Paper, conveniently ignoring its implications for the concepts of treaty and Aboriginal rights. Prime Minister Trudeau defended the policy as an enlightened one, noting that 'the time is now to decide whether the Indians will be a race apart in Canada or whether they will be Canadians of full status'. He added, 'It's inconceivable, I think, that in a given society one section of the society have a treaty with the other section of the society. We must all be equal under the law' (Indian-Eskimo Association of Canada 1970: Appendix 8).

Like other collectivities that discovered a new voice in the 1960s, Canadian women had been quietly preparing for their emergence (or re-emergence) for many years. Whether or not one took a patient view of the lengthy period of quiescence from the enfranchisement of women to the blossoming of the women's liberation movement—and most modern feminists understandably did not—some things had changed, and some political experience had been acquired. The Committee on Equality for Women, which organized in 1966 to lobby for a royal commission on the status of women, consisted of experienced leaders from thirty-two existing women's organizations united by their feminism. Their first delegation to Ottawa was ignored. Laura Sabia (1916–96), president of the Canadian Federation of University Women and leader of the call for a national evaluation of women's status, responded with a classic sixties' threat: she would lead a women's protest march on the capital. The Pearson government behaved characteristically. Although not convinced that women had many legitimate grievances, it dodged trouble by agreeing to an investigation 'to inquire and report upon the status of women in Canada, and to recommend what steps might be taken by the federal government to ensure for women equal opportunities with men in all aspects of Canadian society' (*Report of the Royal Commission on the Status of Women in Canada* 1970: vii). The Royal Commission on the Status of Women, established in 1967, examined areas under provincial as well as federal jurisdiction and made its recommendations based on four operating assumptions: the right of women to choose to be employed outside the home; the obligation of parents and society to care for children; the special responsibilities of society to women because of maternity; and, perhaps most controversially, the need for positive action to overcome entrenched patterns of discrimination. The commission's report provided a program that would occupy mainstream feminism for decades to come.

Virtually simultaneous with the royal commission was the emergence of the movement usu-

REPORT OF THE ROYAL COMMISSION ON THE STATUS OF WOMEN

In September 1970 the Royal Commission on the Status of Women tabled its report, which began with a statement of 'Criteria and Principles'.

. . . 4. We have been asked to inquire into and report upon the status of women in Canada and we have done so in the light of certain principles. A general principle is that *everyone is entitled to the rights and freedoms proclaimed in the Universal Declaration of Human Rights*. We have examined the status of women to learn whether or not they really have these positive rights and freedoms both in principle and in practice. Some of our recommendations should establish a measure of equality that is now lacking for men as well as for women.

5. Explicit in the Terms of Reference given us by the Government is our duty to ensure for women equal opportunities with men. We have interpreted this to mean that equality of opportunity for everyone should be the goal of Canadian society. The right to an adequate standard of living is without value to the person who has no means of achieving it. Freedom to choose a career means little if the opportunity to enter some professions is restricted.

6. Our Terms of Reference also imply that *the full use of human resources is in the national interest*. We have explored the extent to which Canada develops and makes use of the skills and abilities of women.

7. Women and men, having the same rights and freedoms, share the same responsibilities. They should have an equal opportunity to fulfil this obligation. We have, therefore, examined the status of women and made recommendations in the belief that *there should be equality of opportunity to share the responsibilities to society as well as its privileges and prerogatives*.

8. In particular, the Commission adopted four principles: first, that *women should be free to choose whether or not to take employment outside their homes*. The circumstances which impede this free choice have been of specific interest to our inquiry. Where we have made recommendations to improve opportunities for women in the work world, our goal has not been to force married women to work for pay outside of the home but rather to eliminate the practical obstacles that prevent them from exercising this right. If a husband is willing to support his wife, or a wife her husband, the decision and responsibility belong to them.

9. The second is that *the care of children is a responsibility to be shared by the mother, the father and society*. Unless this shared responsibility is acknowledged and assumed, women cannot be accorded true equality.

10. The third principle specifically recognizes the child-bearing function of women. It is apparent that *society has a responsibility for women because of pregnancy and child-birth, and special treatment related to maternity will always be necessary*.

11. The fourth principle is that *in certain areas women will for an interim period require special treatment to overcome the adverse effects of discriminatory practices*. We consider such measures to be justified in a limited range of circumstances, and we anticipate that they should

quickly lead to actual equality which would make their continuance unnecessary. The needs or capacities of women have not always been understood. Discrimination against women has in many instances been unintentional and special treatment will no longer be required if a positive effort to remove it is made for a short period. . . .

SOURCE: *Report of the Royal Commission on the Status of Women* (Ottawa: Information Canada, 1970): xi–xii.

ally known as women's liberation. This articulate and militant branch of feminism had begun in the United States as an offshoot of the student movement, partly a product of the failure of male student leaders to take women seriously. Women's liberation shared much of its rhetoric with other leftist movements of decolonization. '[Woman] realizes in her subconscious what [Herbert] Marcuse says,' went one manifesto: 'Free election of masters does not abolish the masters or the slaves' (quoted in Kostash 1980: 169). Not surprisingly, the liberationists found their organizing principles in issues of sexuality, particularly in the concept that 'woman's body is used as a commodity or medium of exchange' (quoted in Kostash 1980: 196). True liberation would come only when women could control their own bodies, especially in sexual terms. Thus birth control and abortion became two central political questions, along with more mundane matters, such as day care and equal pay for equal work. Such concerns brought feminists into conflict with what became known as male chauvinism at all levels of society. At the beginning of the 1970s, the women's movement stood poised at the edge of what appeared to be yet another New Day.

The minority that was perhaps most closely linked to the women's liberationists was composed of homosexuals and lesbians. Like the libbers, the gays (a term they much preferred to other more pejorative ones) focused their political attention on sexuality, particularly the offences enshrined in the Canadian Criminal Code. By the late 1950s more advanced legal and medical thinking had come to recognize the value of decriminalizing homosexual activity, at least between consenting adults. The sixties would see the expansion of this view, partly because of public lobbying by a number of gay organizations, such as the Association for Social Knowledge (1964), that emerged in the period. An increasing number of gay newspapers and journals also made their appearance. Like other minority groups, homosexuals and lesbians began to concentrate on constructing a positive rather than a destructive self-identity. The 1969 revisions to the Criminal Code did not legalize homosexuality and lesbianism, but they did have a considerable effect on the gay community. It was now possible, if still courageous, to acknowledge one's homosexuality (the usual term was 'coming out of the closet'). The ranks of openly practising gays greatly expanded. It was also possible to become more aggressive in support of more homosexual rights, and the first gay liberation organizations were formed in Vancouver, Montreal, Toronto, and Ottawa in 1970 and 1971. These groups led the way in advocating the protection of sexual orientation in any human rights legislation adopted by the government.

By the early 1970s a number of collectivities were making new demands for constitutional reform and political change. The political and constitutional agenda of Canada was no longer confined to such matters as extending the welfare state, satisfying Quebec, or redefining the federal–provincial relationship. It now had to take into account a variety of organized and articulate subgroups of Canadian society—of which Aboriginal peoples, Blacks, women, and gays

JUDY LAMARSH

Julia Verlyn 'Judy' LaMarsh (1924–80) was born in Chatham, Ontario, and educated in Niagara Falls. After graduation from Hamilton Normal School, she served in the Canadian Woman's Army Corps from 1943 to 1946, translating Japanese documents. After the war she attended Victoria College and Osgoode Hall. In 1950 she joined her father's law firm. LaMarsh first ran for Parliament in 1960, winning a by-election in Niagara Falls. In 1962 she became part of the 'Truth Squad' that shadowed Prime Minister John Diefenbaker on his campaigns across the country, offering 'corrections' and 'constructive criticisms' to the prime minister's comments and speeches. This participation drew her to the attention of the media. A short, overweight woman, she took to wearing obvious wigs and knee-high leather boots. She was an extremely easy target for cartoonists to caricature, with increasing cruelty; and she was by her own account 'publicity prone', a situation hardly aided by her tendency to shoot from the lip. In 1963 she made a famous appearance at a benefit impersonating a Gold Rush prostitute.

Upon re-election in 1963, LaMarsh was made a member of the Pearson cabinet and became minister of Health and Welfare, a key portfolio and one that enabled her to capture many headlines. She personally helped draft the legislation for the Canada Pension Plan that was passed under her ministership. She was probably better known for having given up smoking while minister of Health and Welfare, however. LaMarsh subsequently became Secretary of State, in charge of Canada's Centennial year, travelling thousands of miles to participate in celebrations and helping to entertain visiting dignitaries, including the royal couple. She also was partly responsible for the creation of the Royal Commission on the Status of Women. Not a fan of Pierre Elliott Trudeau, she made a negative comment about him that was caught on tape at the 1968 leadership convention. She subsequently retired from politics, leaving the incoming Parliament extremely short of women members. In retirement Marsh wrote a notorious memoir of her years in politics, *Bird in a Gilded Cage*, which received a huge advance and sold many thousands of copies.

were only the most vocal—insisting that their needs also deserved attention.

A STILL BUOYANT ECONOMY

Behind all the reform sentiment of the sixties was a persistently prosperous economy. Inflation (which ran at an annual average rate of 2.1 per cent between 1959–68) and interest rates continued to be manageable. The nation continued to provide jobs for most of its expanding population, with unemployment rates under 6 per cent for most of the period. Critics might note that these rates were substantially higher than in other highly industrialized nations, where unemployment was under 2 per cent. But for the vast majority of Canadians, the performance of the economy seemed more than satisfactory, particularly after 1963, when a veritable explosion of construction projects began and foreign trade blossomed. Everywhere there were the visible signs of prosperity in the form of cranes and hard

TABLE 10.1
UNEMPLOYMENT RATES BY REGION, 1961–1970

Year	Atlantic	Quebec	Ontario	Prairies	BC	Canada
1961	11.3	9.3	5.5	4.6	8.5	7.2
1962	10.8	7.5	4.3	3.9	6.6	5.9
1963	9.6	7.4	3.8	3.7	6.4	5.5
1964	8.2	6.3	3.3	3.1	5.3	4.7
1965	7.4	5.4	2.5	2.6	4.2	3.9
1966	6.4	4.7	2.5	2.1	4.6	3.6
1967	6.6	5.3	3.1	2.3	5.2	4.1
1968	7.3	6.5	3.6	2.9	6.0	4.8
1969	7.5	6.9	3.1	2.9	5.0	4.7
1970	7.6	6.9	4.3	4.4	7.7	5.9

SOURCE: Department of Regional Economic Expansion, *Major Economic Indicators, Provinces and Regions* (Ottawa: Queen's Printer, 1971): Table 2.4

TABLE 10.2
PERCENTAGE OF EMPLOYMENT IN MANUFACTURING BY REGION, 1961 AND 1969, AND AVERAGE WAGE IN MANUFACTURING, 1969

Region	Employment 000	1961 Share %	1969 Share %	Average Wage $
Atlantic	76.8	4.6	4.5	4,995
Quebec	527.0	33.6	31.2	5,542
Ontario	836.9	47.8	49.5	6,228
Prairies	119.8	6.9	7.1	5,888
BC	130.7	7.7	7.7	6,591

SOURCE: Department of Regional Economic Expansion, *Major Economic Indicators, Provinces and Regions* (Ottawa: Queen's Printer, 1971): tables 3.3, 3.1.

hats. Montreal and Toronto built subway systems. Large and small shopping malls sprouted up everywhere. Cultural facilities proliferated. Each province put up new university buildings. Less visible but equally important were a number of projects in the north, usually associated with hydroelectric expansion. The bellwether of the Canadian economy continued to be Ontario, still the only province with a mixed economy balanced between manufacturing and primary production. Ontario contained such a large proportion of the nation's people that its successes consistently raised national averages.

The averages disguised marked discrepancies and disparities. Some of them were regional. Overall, the most seriously disadvantaged area was the Atlantic region—the Maritime provinces plus Newfoundland. Per capita average income in this region was persistently more than 30 per cent below the figures for the other provinces, and a much larger proportion of the population than elsewhere worked in marginal primary resource extraction, which was often seasonal in nature. Even after taxes, Ontario's per capita income in 1970 was 70 per cent higher than Newfoundland's. Many commentators insisted, however, that the real regional disparity was between the industrial heartland of central Canada and the resource hinterland that constituted most of the remainder of the country. Canadians were naturally drawn to the more prosperous regions, while both the Atlantic region and Saskatchewan–Manitoba lost population in the 1960s through out-migration. A perception of disparity underlay much of the nation's political discontent. Some disparities were not regional at all, although they often had geographical overtones. Low wages, high unemployment, low labour force participation, and a limited tax base (constraining the financing of public services) together created higher incidences of inequality in some provinces. Young people under twenty-five were twice as likely to be unemployed as Canadians over that age, for example, and youth unemployment skyrocketed in marginal areas. Substantial evidence was advanced in this period showing that an individual's ethnic group, racial origin, and gender also affected economic success. And then there were the poor. What constituted real poverty in Canada remained a matter of continual debate. What was indisputable, however, was the inequality of national personal income in Canada. The wealthiest 20 per cent of Canadians earned over 40 per cent of the income, and the poorest 20 per cent earned less than 6 per cent. Most of those in the poorest 20 per cent, it should be added, were employed.

TABLE 10.3
AVERAGE INCOME OF SALARIED MALES IN FOURTEEN ETHNIC GROUPS, QUEBEC, 1961

Ethnic Group	In Dollars	Index
General Average	3,469	100.0
British	4,940	142.4
Scandinavian	4,939	142.4
Dutch	4,891	140.9
Jewish	4,851	139.8
Russians	4,828	139.1
Germans	4,245	122.6
Poles	3,984	114.8
Asians	3,734	107.6
Ukrainians	3,733	107.6
Other Europeans	3,547	102.4
Hungarians	3,537	101.9
French Canadians	3,185	91.8
Italians	2,938	84.6
Native Indians	2,112	60.8

SOURCE: Canadian Dimension 5, no. 8 (February 1969): 17.

Some of Canada's endemic economic problems were better publicized (if not better resolved) in the 1960s. There were a number of obvious weak points. One was in the food-producing sector. Canadian farmers continued to find that increased mechanization and use of fertilizers meant that fewer hands were needed to produce larger crops. Canadian farms became ever more capital intensive, marginal lands less attractive, yet returns to the farmer remained sluggish. Most increases in food costs to the consumer were caused by non-agricultural factors, such as transportation and processing, rather than by increased returns to the farmer. The farm population in Canada had been declining absolutely for decades, and this era was no exception. Between the 1961 and 1971 censuses, the number of farm residents fell from 2,072,785 to 1,419,795. Drops were especially marked in Prince Edward Island and Manitoba. As for the fishery, the admission of Newfoundland to Confederation in 1949 only increased the numbers of fishermen in serious difficulty. Experts' warnings about overfishing were ignored by governments eager to create programs to aid fishermen.

By the end of the period, a handful of environmentalists had begun pointing out the damage being done by those reaping resources without concern for conservation practices. Moreover, the issue of foreign ownership, first introduced by the Gordon Commission in 1958, took on a new life in the later 1960s when it became associated with American multinational corporations. Radical younger scholars such as Mel Watkins (b. 1932) called for the repatriation of the Canadian economy. Watkins headed the Task Force on the Structure of Canadian Industry, which in February 1968 released a report entitled *Foreign Ownership and the Structure of Canadian Industry* (the Watkins Report). Such critiques of American multinationalism merged with a widespread Canadian hostility to the policies of the United States, especially in Vietnam, as well as with the concerns of those worried about maintaining a distinctive Canadian identity. Public opinion shifted considerably between 1964 and 1972 over the question of further investment of US capital in Canada. According to a 1964 Gallup poll, only 46 per cent of Canadians thought there was already enough American investment, and 33 per cent wanted more. By 1972, 67 per cent said that was enough, and only 22 per cent wanted further amounts.

Canadian nationalism emerged in the labour movement as well in the 1960s. This issue combined with others, particularly discontent among younger workers with the traditional nature of union leadership and organization. The older union leaders were not much interested in broad reform issues. They tried to dampen the reactions against local branches of international (i.e., American-dominated) unions that were seen as collaborators with American multinationals in both the 'sell-out' of Canada and the maintenance of the 'military-industrial complex'. By the later 1960s many rank-and-file union members expressed discontent with American domination. The Americans took more money out of the country in dues than they returned in assistance; they failed to organize outside traditional industrial sectors; they often supported American military adventurism abroad; and, finally, they did not understand Canada and treated Canadian members with contempt. At least so went the complaints. Withdrawal from international unionism began seriously around 1970, and would increase over the next few years as wholly Canadian unions grew in numbers and membership. One of the major factors in the home-grown union movement was the success of public sector unionism in the 1960s. In 1963 the Canadian Union of Public Employees organized, and in 1967 thousands of civil servants repudiated staff associations and formed the Public Service Alliance of Canada. Outside the civil service, but within the public sector, unionization was particularly marked in the teaching and health-care professions. Strikes by postal workers, teachers, and even policemen irritated large sectors of the Canadian public. Anger at the interruption of what many Canadians saw as essential services would eventually help make the unions easy targets in the 1970s as scapegoats for Canada's newly emergent economic problems.

POLITICAL LEADERSHIP

For much of the period, the Liberal hegemony of the King–St Laurent years appeared to be broken or at least bending. Not until the arrival of Pierre

Trudeau did the Liberals get back on track, and that was at least partly because Trudeau represented a new style of political leadership, consonant with the age of television. John Diefenbaker, who became prime minister in 1957 and swept to a great victory in 1958, had a very old-fashioned political style. His bombastic speeches sounded as if they had been rhetorically crafted in the nineteenth century, and he revelled in being a House of Commons man, good in the specialized cut and thrust of debate in that legislative body. Diefenbaker inspired tremendous loyalty from some members of his party, but he seldom created confidence in his capacity to master public affairs. He was better at being the leader of the opposition than prime minister. Diefenbaker held a variety of contradictory positions; his latest biographer calls him a 'Rogue Tory'. He was a populist reformer at the head of a party that contained many genuine conservatives. He was simultaneously a Cold Warrior and a Canadian nationalist, holding both positions equally fervently. Despite his electoral successes in Quebec in 1957 and especially 1958, Diefenbaker was always associated (and associated himself) with English Canada.

☐ John Diefenbaker and Lester Pearson, 30 January 1958. Duncan Cameron/NAC, PA-117093.

During much of Diefenbaker's tour of leadership of the Progressive Conservative Party from 1956–67, his chief political opponent was Lester B. (Mike) Pearson. The contrast between the two men was instantly apparent, and the 'Dief and Mike' show (in the Commons and outside) was the joy of political cartoonists and satirists for that entire decade. Pearson was a soft-spoken former diplomat who had won a Nobel Peace Prize for conciliation in the Suez Crisis of 1956. Quietly ambitious, he had little House of Commons or domestic political experience. Apart from the 1958 election, the nation never gave either Pearson or Diefenbaker a mandate to govern, thus perhaps reflecting its suspicion of their qualifications. The voters preferred Diefenbaker in 1957, 1958, and 1962 (the first and the third elections producing minority governments), and Pearson in 1963 and 1965 (both times in a minority situation). Pearson was better able to govern with a minority, since his party could arrive at unofficial understandings with the CCF-NDP, something not possible for the Diefenbaker Tories. Pearson was no more able than Diefenbaker to rein in ambitious colleagues or provinces, however. The decade 1957–67 was one of constant federal political turmoil and federal–provincial hassles.

The victory of Pierre Trudeau in 1968 marked a new era, which by the early 1970s saw a return to Liberal hegemony. The Tories had chosen Robert Stanfield (b. 1914) to succeed Diefenbaker. The soft-spoken Stanfield seemed a good match for Lester Pearson, but could not compete with the trendy and articulate Trudeau. Like the pop stars he seemed to emulate, Trudeau was capable of repackaging his image (and his policies) to suit conditions changing so fast they seemed to be 'blowin' in the wind'. Not only was Trudeau a thoroughly bilingual French Canadian who was likely to appeal to Quebec, but he was continually able to convince the electorate that he was far more of a reformer than his subsequent policies would indicate. After years of apparently irresolute national leadership, Trudeau also seemed to be a strong figure. In some respects he was, as his behaviour in the October Crisis of 1970 demonstrated. The prime minister did not hesitate for a moment to invoke the War Measures Act and employ the military against the FLQ. Most of the nation appreciated his decisiveness.

The era was also characterized by a number of long-serving and highly visible provincial premiers, who provided considerable stability for the provincial cause in the regularly held Dominion–provincial conferences. While federal leadership had been ineffective for the ten years before Trudeau, almost all the provinces had seemingly strong leaders. There continued to be little genuine two-party politics anywhere in Canada. Instead, dominant parties were usually in control. In Newfoundland Joey Smallwood still governed virtually unopposed. In New Brunswick Louis Robichaud was in control from 1960 to 1970. Ontario had John Robarts, Manitoba had Duff Roblin, Saskatchewan had Ross Thatcher, while Alberta still had Ernest Manning and British Columbia was led by W.A.C. Bennett. Few of these governments were Liberal. Ross Thatcher (1917–71) headed the only provincial Liberal government west of Quebec between 1945 and 1972, and he was a vociferous critic of federal Liberalism. By the early 1970s the only provincial governments controlled by the Liberals were in Prince Edward Island and Quebec. Pierre Trudeau's conception of liberalism and federalism certainly did not accord with that of Quebec's Liberal premier, Robert Bourassa (1933–96).

No matter who was in charge and at what level, the size and scope of the apparatus of bureaucracy continually expanded. The scope of bureaucracy had political as well as economic implications. The larger it got, the harder it was to manage. A host of journalists and popular commentators attacked governments at all levels for mismanagement and waste, but as one commentator astutely pointed out, 'It is true that the initial motive for reforms may be the outsider's simple-minded belief that gigantic savings can be effected. But once set an investigation afoot and the economy motive gets quickly overlaid with the more subtle and difficult problems of improved service and efficiency' (Hodgetts 1968: 7–18). The Royal Commission on Government Organization, appointed by Diefenbaker in 1960, found itself unable to effect major changes in the bureaucracy, particularly in downscaling the scope of operations. All governments, including federal Liberal ones, increasingly found themselves entrapped by the actions of their predecessors and by the difficulties of dismantling systems once created. Government was becoming more difficult and the nation increasingly impossible to lead.

THE EXPANSION OF THE WELFARE STATE

Part of the reason for the continual expansion of government bureaucracy, of course, was continual (if uncoordinated) expansion of the Canadian welfare state. Politicians viewed expanded social services as popular vote-getters, and no political party strenuously opposed the principles of welfare democracy. Although the Diefenbaker government was not associated with any major program, it had initiated a number of reviews and royal commissions, the recommendations of which would pass into legislation under the Liberals. The minority Pearson government was pushed towards improved social insurance by the NDP, its own reforming wing, and competitive pressures from an ambitious Quebec and other provinces. Were Ottawa not to introduce new national programs, the federal government could well lose control of them to the wealthier and more aggressive provinces. The expansion in

1964 of family allowances to include children up to the age of eighteen who were still in school merely imitated something introduced by the Lesage government in 1961. In 1965 the federal government attempted to introduce a national contributory pension scheme, but settled for one that allowed Quebec its own plan.

The changing demography of Canada guaranteed that there would be continual pressures on the government to improve the pension system. Those who wanted improved benefits were able to make common ground with those who sought to control costs. Both could agree on the superiority of a contributory scheme. The Medical Care Act of 1966 built on provincial initiatives with a cost-sharing arrangement. By 1968 all provinces and territories had agreed on cost-sharing arrangements with Ottawa that produced a social minimum in health care. For most Canadians, access to medical service (doctors and hospitalization) would thereafter be without charge. Occasionally cynicism triumphed. Early in 1965 the prime minister wrote his cabinet ministers asking for suggestions of policy initiatives that would shift attention from political harassment by the opposition over mistakes and difficulties. The result was a Canadian variation of Lyndon Johnson's War on Poverty. Canada proposed a full utilization of human resources and an end to poverty. Actual reforms were not very significant.

The first Trudeau government, responding to the reform euphoria of the era, actually contemplated shifting the grounds of social protectionism in 'the Just Society'. To the late 1960s the emphasis of mainstream reform had been to carry out the agenda of the 1940s for the establishment of a 'social minimum' providing basic economic security for all Canadians. Now, at least briefly, the bureaucrats and politicians debated the possibility of expanding the welfare state to include some measure of income distribution. Poverty came to be seen as a serious problem worthy of public focus. The Economic Council of Canada in 1968 described the persistence of poverty in Canada as 'a disgrace'. Later that same year a Special Senate Committee on Poverty was established under Senator David Croll's chairmanship. In 1971 this committee produced a report, *Poverty in Canada*, which insisted that nearly 2 million people in Canada lived below the poverty line. More radical critics, in *The Real Poverty Report* that same year, put the figure much higher.

TABLE 10.4
EXPENDITURES ON PERSONAL HEALTH CARE AS A PERCENTAGE OF GROSS PROVINCIAL PRODUCT AND PERSONAL INCOME, ONTARIO, 1960–1975

Year	GPP	Personal Income
1960	3.76	4.62
1961	3.95	4.98
1962	4.04	5.04
1963	4.14	5.17
1964	4.15	5.40
1965	4.18	5.47
1966	4.08	5.35
1967	4.43	5.67
1968	4.69	5.99
1969	4.76	6.04
1970	5.06	6.32
1971	5.32	6.57
1972	5.17	6.18
1973	6.56	6.05
1974	6.38	8.23
1975	6.94	8.57

SOURCE: K.J. Rea, *The Prosperous Years: The Economic History of Ontario 1939–75* (Toronto: University of Toronto Press, 1985): 119.

Poverty not only characterized the lives of millions of Canadians, but it was structural, regional, and related to racial and sexual discrimination. A number of schemes were suggested, including a guaranteed income for low-income families as part of the family allowance package. The year 1970 had already seen the publication of a federal White Paper called 'Income Security for Canadians', which pointed out the escalating costs of social insurance and criticized the principle of universality that had previously governed Canadian policy. The ultimate result was the new Unemployment Insurance Plan of 1971, which extended and increased coverage without actually addressing the concept of a guaranteed minimum income for all Canadians. At about the same time, Ottawa eliminated a separate fund for Canada pension contributions and began considering them as part of the general revenue of the government.

Reformers had long insisted that access to education was one of the social rights to which all Canadians were entitled. Increasing access meant creating new facilities. The presence of the baby-boom generation gave urgency to that implication. Parents were much attracted to the practical benefits of education in providing future employment and a better life for their children. The results in the 1960s were enormous pressures on education budgets and increasing demand for the production of more and better teachers. School authorities attempted to ease some of their problems by consolidating rural education through use of the ubiquitous yellow school bus, a process that continued into the early 1970s. Teachers acquired more formal credentials, became better paid, and organized themselves into a powerful professional lobby that was sometimes even unionized. By the late 1950s virtually everyone could agree on the need for universal high school education, and by 1970 over 90 per cent of Canadian children of high school age were in school. Increasing numbers of high school graduates were entitled to a university education, and the decade of the 1960s was the golden age of university expansion in Canada. Not only were new facilities constructed, but 20,000 new faculty members were recruited, most of them from the United States. By 1970 public spending on education had risen to 9 per cent of the gross national product, and represented nearly 20 per cent of all taxes levied by all three levels of government.

Before 1970 the disagreement between the universalists and the means testers had been relatively muted. Both sides could agree that there had been an absence of overall integrated planning in the growth of the welfare state. Little attention had been paid to the long-range implications of any policy. Bureaucracies and programs had been allowed to expand with no thought for tomorrow. The later 1960s had introduced a new ingredient into the mix, however. Governments began routinely spending more money than they were receiving.

QUEBEC

The 1960s was the decade in which the average Anglo-Canadian discovered that Quebec was unhappy with Confederation. That discovery was part of the completion of Quebec's transformation into a secularized, urbanized, and industrialized region that differed little in many respects from its central Canadian neighbour, Ontario. The transformation was often associated with the Quiet Revolution in the first half of the decade, a term used by the media to describe the modernization of Quebec. The structural changes to French-Canadian society had already taken place before 1960, even though at the close of the 1950s traditional French-Canadian nationalism in church and state, symbolized by the Union Nationale, still seemed to prevail. The critique of tradition had already been elaborated and the program of reform for Quebec was well articulated. All that remained was to fit the government of Quebec and popular aspirations together. That task was begun by the provincial Liberal Party, led by Jean Lesage, which defeated the Union Nationale and came to power in 1960. The leading Liberal strategists did not realize at the time just how ready Quebec was for change, or how easily the traditional institutions and ways would crumble once they were confronted by an activist government composed of politicians drawn from Quebec's new middle and professional classes.

The first major step had to do with hydroelectricity. The tradition that had to be overcome was the long-standing Quebec fear, nurtured for decades by the Union Nationale, of anything resembling economic statism (or socialism or communism). *Anti-étatisme* in Quebec was not the same thing as a do-nothing government. Under Duplessis, the provincial government had spent a lot of money on public services, including many hydroelectric projects to assist rural electrification. What the minister of natural resources, René Lévesque, proposed on 12 February 1962, without consulting his col-

LESAGE ENDORSES HYDRO-QUÉBEC

In 1962 René Lévesque, as Quebec's minister of natural resources, publicly committed himself to the nationalization of private hydroelectric companies in the province without gaining the support of his premier and party leader, Jean Lesage. In his memoirs, Lévesque recounted the resolution of the problem.

After having wished me in hell at one time because of my ideas on hydro, Lesage had curiously enough avoided opening the subject again. Since the others were thus prevented from expressing their opinions, I was left free to sell my wares. But certain ministers were growing more and more nervous, and others didn't hesitate to say I was taking up too much room and should be shut up or such talk would eventually put the government in danger. When the fall session came, then, suspense had built up even more. It was becoming urgent to put our cards on the table.

Thus, on September 3, cabinet was summoned to a special meeting in the chalet at Lac-à-l'épaule. Driving up there I reviewed all the elements to the dossier, including some last-minute figures that seemed to me to clinch the feasibility of our plan. But could one ever know? In politics so often there are reasons logic has nothing to do with.

The first night reinforced these doubts. The atmosphere was heavy. Most of my colleagues were in an ugly mood. Some really had it in for me, this nobody, this black sheep who was the cause of all their woes. Discussion seemed to start up, only to fizzle out again in back-room bickering. Some had taken a glass too many, and since Lesage was one of these, it soon became apparent that the evening was a write-off. It was so depressing I wondered if I hadn't better let the whole thing drop. But I had promised the team not to come back without a clear decision one way or another. So I stayed on and passed a very bad night.

Next morning things didn't look much better. Mornings after the nights before are always gloomy. At last, about eleven, Lesage decided to call the meeting to order and, to get the ball rolling, gave me the floor. After distributing copies of our memo, which certain members shoved disdainfully aside, I made a special effort to be as concise as possible, just hitting the highlights.

In rebuttal George Marler did his best to demolish me. . . . An old Liberal leader returning to

Montreal after a tour of duty in Ottawa, he had been named to that little provincial senate called the Legislative Council, and it was from here Lesage had invited him to join the cabinet as his right-hand man in financial matters. He was reputed to have a very tight grasp on the purse strings. . . . That day Marler was not the eminent and phlegmatic notary who never raised his voice. . . . Insisting on the cost of the operation, on the danger of isolation Quebec might be exposed to, and on the opposition that was being manifested, particularly by the Chambers of Commerce, Marler had the bad idea to conclude by suggesting he might possibly resign. Lesage sat bolt upright and indignantly adjourned the meeting for lunch. . . .

Then suddenly everything was back on track again when early in the afternoon Lesage reopened the session and, after briefly summarizing the proposition, turned to Georges-Émile Lapalme, whom we hadn't heard from yet. 'Well, George, haven't you got anything to say? What do you think of this business?

Lapalme took his time. As usual, behind those heavy glasses with their black frames that made him look like an evil owl, he stared long and without indulgence at the man who had taken his place. He had been leader of the opposition during the last Duplessis years until he was replaced by Lesage in 1958, just on the eve of that string of events that at long last brought the Liberals back to power. Although he had consented to remain in the government, he was serving under a successor who would always be a usurper for him. This visibly gnawed at his vitals, and even though he adored the Ministry of Cultural Affairs that had been expressly created for him, he was too sensitive and deeply embittered to carry on much longer. In a few months he would be gone. But for the time being he was saving a surprise for us.

'Well, yeah . . .' he said, stretching his pauses, '. . . is the project a good one? As for me, I'd say yes. . . . Is it feasible? . . . Yes, again. . . . But how should we go about it? That's the question . . .'

'Do you think,' Lesage continued, 'that we could make it an election issue?'

'Well, . . . it's a big deal. . . . Before we get involved in it, it wouldn't be a bad idea to go for a new mandate.'

'Good. Well, let's see now,' said Lesage, leafing through an agenda he had just pulled out of his pocket. 'How does November 14 strike you?'

SOURCE: R. Lévesque, *Memoirs*, translated by P. Stratford (Toronto: McClelland and Stewart, 1986): 174–6.

leagues, was the enforced government consolidation of all existing private hydroelectric companies into one massive Hydro-Québec. Hydroelectricity was an ideal place to fight the battle of nationalization, partly because electrical generation and supply was a public enterprise right across North America, partly because it directly touched the pocketbook of the rural Quebecer, who was most likely to oppose state action. Despite a famous 'Jamais!' from Premier Lesage, nationalization was quickly accepted by the Liberal cabinet as a winning campaign issue, and the Liberals took it to the province in 1962 with the slogan 'Maîtres chez nous'. Led by Lesage and a compelling Lévesque, the Liberals managed to turn Hydro-Québec into a symbol of the economic liberation of Quebec from its colonial status, thus co-opting the new nationalism with a vengeance. Liberal expenditures on welfare state reform and public enterprise tripled the provincial budget in the early 1960s, which saw provincial government involvement in almost every economic, industrial, and social activity in Quebec.

The other great symbolic reform of Lesage's Quiet Revolution was the secularization and modernization of Quebec's educational system. Since before Confederation, education had been in the hands of the Catholic Church, which staffed its schools chiefly with priests and nuns teaching a curriculum slow to change from the nineteenth-century classical one. By 1960 the Church itself was in trouble, not just in Quebec but around the world. Criticism of Quebec education was led by a Catholic clergyman, Brother Jean-Paul Desbiens (b. 1927), who published the best-selling *Les Insolences de Frère Untel* (translated in 1962 as *The Impertinences of Brother Anonymous*), based on a series of letters he had written to *Le Devoir* in 1959. The spate of responses to *Frère Untel*, many of them in the form of letters to editors of newspapers, demonstrated that he had struck a chord in the province. Lesage responded with a provincial commission of enquiry into education, chaired by the vice-rector of Laval University, Monseigneur Alphonse-Marie Parent. The commission's hearings produced a battery of complaints and indictments of the Quebec system, most of which the commission endorsed in its 1963 report. The Parent Commission called not only for modernization along North American lines but for administration by a unitary secular authority. Armed with this endorsement, in 1964 the Lesage government passed Bill 60, which for the first time placed education in Quebec under provincial administration. Quebec education was thereafter rapidly brought up to national standards.

The Lesage government also sensed the importance of Frère Untel's call for the preservation and extension of French-Canadian culture and the French language. It had already created the Ministry of Cultural Affairs in 1961, which presided happily—with grants and other forms of support—over a veritable explosion of French-Canadian art and writing in the 1960s. The Ministry of Cultural Affairs in many ways typified the Quiet Revolution. The Lesage government was not so much the agent of change in Quebec as its *animateur*. As such it was the beneficiary of years of preparation by others. What the Liberals did was to identify some of the key problems, thus liberating the new-found aspirations of Quebec. Nevertheless, Lesage's government was defeated in 1966 by a rejuvenated Union Nationale under Daniel Johnson (1915–68), chiefly because it had failed to follow to its nationalist conclusion the logic of the revolution over which it had presided. The Union Nationale continued the Lesage program with louder nationalist rhetoric. In 1970 the party in turn was defeated by the Liberals under the new party leader, Robert Bourassa, partly because too many of its leaders had suffered fatal heart attacks, partly because it was squeezed between the Liberals and the PQ.

Quebec's attitude towards Confederation changed perceptibly during the 1960s. Under Duplessis, Quebec supported provincial rights to prevent Ottawa from taking control of them. Under Lesage and his successors, provincial powers were something to be exercised positively as Quebec built its own welfare state and accompanying bureaucracy. Quebec's newly empowered middle class became increasingly conscious of the powers beyond their reach. A substantial separatist movement developed in the province, its most visible example the FLQ. This organization, founded in March 1963, soon began a terrorist campaign to publicize its views. In November 1967, René Lévesque took a more traditional path towards political change when he resigned from the Quebec Liberal Party and began organizing the Parti Québécois, which was devoted to some form of independence. Along with increased constitutional militancy came increased fears for the future of the French language, with many French Canadians turning a suspicious eye on the immigrant groups in Quebec who were still educating their children in English. By 1970 no Quebec politician wanted to be publicly associated with anything less than provincial autonomy. The first round of separatist agitation came to a climax in October 1970 when two cells of the FLQ kidnapped a British diplomat (Trade Commissioner James Cross) and a Quebec cabinet minister (Pierre Laporte), murdering the latter.

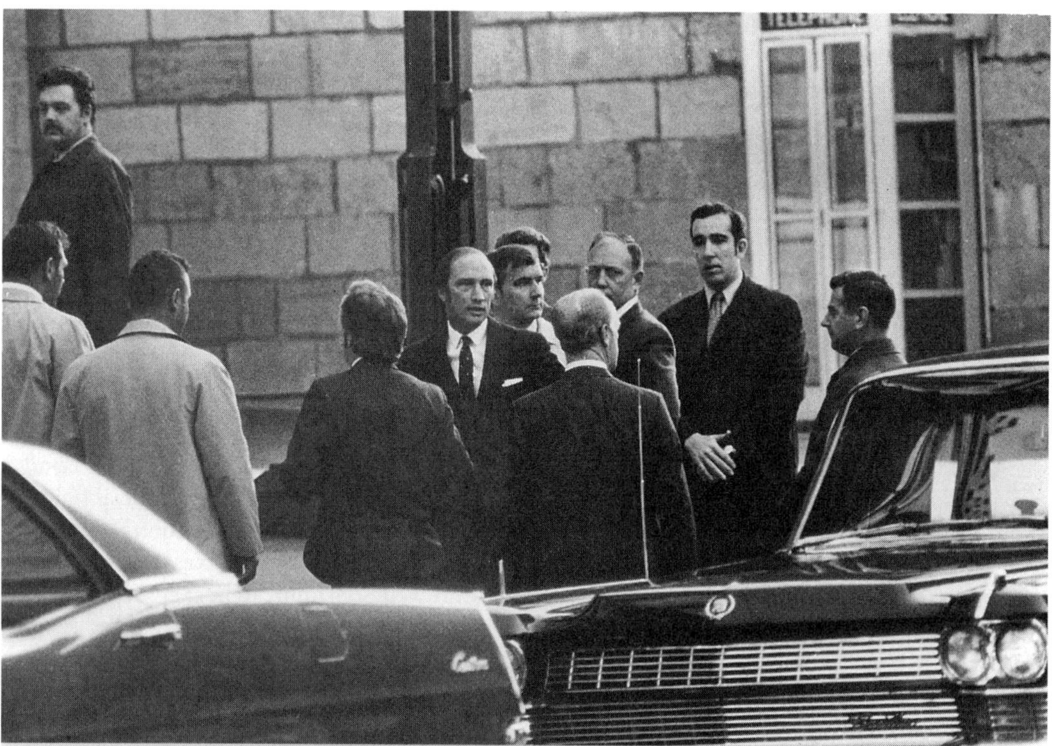

☐ Prime Minister Pierre Trudeau arriving at the Notre-Dame basilica in Montreal for the funeral of Pierre Laporte, 20 October 1970. An FLQ cell had seized Laporte on 10 October, and his body was found a week later in the trunk of a car at the St-Hubert airport. His murder helped to justify the federal government in its imposition of the War Measures Act. NAC, PA-113490.

THE IDEOLOGY OF THE FLQ

On 5 October 1970 two armed men kidnapped British Trade Commissioner James Cross from his home in Montreal. A few hours later a communiqué from the abductors, a cell of the Front de libération du Québec, was received. It was later broadcast as demanded by the abductors. Sandwiched in the middle of the document, between specific demands, the FLQ summarized its ideology.

. . . Through this move, the Front de libération du Québec wants to draw the attention of the world to the fate of French-speaking Québécois, a majority of which is jeered at and crushed on its own territory by a faulty political system (Canadian federalism) and by an economy dominated by the interests of American high finance, the racist and imperialist 'big bosses'.

When you examine the origins of Confederation you are in a better position to understand what were the true interests ($$$) which inspired those who were called the Fathers of Confederation. Besides, in 1867, the Quebec people (Lower Canada) were not consulted as to the possibility of creating a Confederation of existing provinces. It was a question of big money and these questions are only sorted out by interested parties, the capitalists, those who possess and amass capital and the means of production and who, according to their sole needs and requirements decide on our whole lives as well as those of a race of people.

Thousand of Québécois have understood, as did our ancestors of 1837–38, that the only way to ensure our national as well as economic survival is total independence.

The Front de libération du Québec supports unconditionally the American blacks and those of Africa, the liberation movements of Latin America, of Palestine, and of Asia, the revolutionary Catholics of Northern Ireland and all those who fight for their freedom, their independence, and their dignity.

The Front de libération du Québec wants to salute the Cuban and Algerian people who are heroically fighting against imperialism and colonialism in all its forms, for a just society where man's exploitation by man is banished.

However, we believe that the only true support we can give these people moving towards their liberations is to liberate ourselves first. During and after our struggle we shall offer much more than the usual sympathy of shocked intellectuals confronted with pictures showing aggression in a peaceful and blissful setting. . . .

WE SHALL OVERCOME. . . .

SOURCE: Quoted in J. Saywell, *Quebec 70: A Documentary Narrative* (Toronto: University of Toronto Press, 1971): 37-8.

THE NATION AND QUEBEC

Although John Diefenbaker had come to power with the assistance of the Quebec voter, neither 'the Chief' nor his English-Canadian supporters ever really attempted to understand Quebec's aspirations. It was left to the Liberal minority ministries of Lester Pearson to respond to what was obviously a more feisty Quebec. To some extent, most Canadians were prepared to be sympathetic with Quebec, since few could conceive of a nation without its francophone province. Pearson adopted three strategies. One was cooperative federalism, a concept exemplified in a series of agreements (1963–5) between Ottawa and the provinces, which accepted the need for consultation and flexibility, chiefly by having Ottawa give up many of the constitutional pretensions it had been insisting upon since the 1940s. This strategy ran aground because, as one political scientist put it, 'Quebec's demands for autonomy appeared to be insatiable' (Smiley 1970: 48–66). Later critics would regard Ottawa's concessions as the beginning of the end for a strong federal state.

A second strategy dealt with the symbols of sovereignty, with the government looking towards reform before 1967 and the Centennial Year of Confederation. A new Canadian flag was adopted by Parliament in 1964 after the Liberals ended the debate through closure; a new national anthem was approved in 1967. Centennial Year gave everyone a chance to display the new flag and sing the new anthem. Substantial amounts of money were spent on the celebration, with its centrepiece the Canadian Universal and International Exhibition at Montreal, familiarly known as Expo 67. The show was attended by millions of Canadians.

That summer an event occurred that shares an almost equal place in the history of the period. The occasion was the visit of French President Charles De Gaulle. From the outset, Ottawa and Quebec had jostled over protocol for

The Canadian pavilion at Expo 67, dominated by a huge inverted pyramid. The dome beside it was clad with enlarged photos of Canada.

the visit. On 24 July De Gaulle stood on the balcony of a Montreal hotel with open arms, receiving the tumultuous applause of half a million Quebecers. It was an emotional moment. He spoke of cherished memories such as the Liberation of France in 1944. Then, before the huge crowd and a television audience of millions, he concluded: 'Vive Montréal! Vive le Québec! Vive le Québec libre!' Whether De Gaulle had deliberately insulted the Canadian government and people (the official Pearson position) or had merely referred to Quebec's efforts to affirm its identity (the Johnson position) was irrelevant. The exclamation had been vociferously cheered, and the nation had been given yet another reminder of its deep division.

The final policy initiative of the Pearson Liberals was the concept of equal partnership, including the notions of cultural dualism and 'two founding races'. The Royal Commission on Bilingualism and Biculturalism was set up in 1963 to implement equal partnership. The commission discovered, to its surprise, that not all Canadians believed in cultural dualism. It ended up recommending some acceptance of multiculturalism as well as an official bilingualism that was implemented by the Official Languages Act of 1969. By the time bilingualism was formally adopted, Quebec had passed well beyond the stage of accepting its implications. Many political leaders were calling for a policy of unilingualism within the province. After the earlier entrance of Quebec's 'Three Wise Men' (Jean Marchand, Gérard Pelletier, and Pierre Trudeau) into Parliament and the cabinet in 1965, Pearson's resistance to Quebec had stiffened, however.

Quebec was not the home of all French Canadians, for there were hundreds of thousands of francophones living outside that province. The need to provide continuing protection for this outlying population was a principal argument of the federalists within Quebec. Francophones outside Quebec were understandably ardent federalists, and they were the chief beneficiaries of bilingualism and biculturalism. Only in New Brunswick were the francophones (the Acadians) sufficiently concentrated geographically and sufficiently numerous to regard themselves as a distinct people. The 1960s saw a renaissance of Acadian culture and a new political awareness that Acadian interests had to be served. Thus both major New Brunswick parties supported bilingualism, French-language education (including a university at Moncton), and the entrenchment of Acadian culture in the province. Bilingualism and biculturalism helped rejuvenate francophones elsewhere in Canada, most of whom were fluently bilingual. Not only did they gain advantages in obtaining federal employment in their regions, but their educational and cultural facilities came to receive a good deal of financial assistance from the federal government as well.

CANADIAN CULTURE

In some senses, Canadian culture came of age in the 1960s. Years of development of cultural infrastructure within the private sector, combined with a new government recognition of the need for conscious cultural policy and an enormous expansion of the Canadian university system, brought at least élite culture to a flowering. A national cultural policy, first articulated by the Massey Commission, was actually implemented under Diefenbaker and Pearson. Intended to foster a distinctive Canadian identity in the face of the ubiquitous Americans, it employed all possible cultural strategies, ranging from subsidies (the Canada Council) to protectionism (periodical policy and Canadian content regulations for television introduced in 1961) to regulated competition (the Board of Broadcast Governors, established in 1958, licensed new television stations, which came together as a new television network in 1961 called CTV). Within the realm of 'serious' culture, Canadian governments at all levels were prepared to spend large amounts of money to produce works that would meet international standards. To a considerable extent they succeeded. Whether the culture that resulted was Canadian Culture was, of course, another matter entirely.

Perhaps the greatest success story was in Canadian literature. Before the 1960s the market for, and interest in, works of literature by Canadian writers was not strong. There was no tradition of indigenous literary criticism, only a handful of literary periodicals, and almost no sense of a literary community anywhere outside Quebec. In 1976 critic Northrop Frye noted 'the colossal verbal explosion that has taken place in Canada since 1960' (Frye 1976: 849). That explosion saw a number of Canadian writers achieve international critical recognition. *The Apprenticeship of Duddy Kravitz* by Mordecai Richler (1931–2001), published in 1959, met with great popular success and established Richler as a major writer. Duddy Kravitz entered Canadian folklore as an ethnic wheeler-dealer desperate for the security of land. Richler was not the first novelist to mine the rich vein of ethnicity in Canada, but he was the first to mythologize the urban ghetto, its inhabitants, and way of life. In 1966 he confessed: 'No matter how long I continue to live abroad, I do feel forever rooted in Montreal's St Urbain Street. This was my time, my place, and I have elected to get it exactly right' (quoted in Woodcock 1979: 27).

Margaret Laurence (1926–89) was another Canadian novelist who created a mythologized

Canadian space. Having lived with her husband in Somalia and Ghana from 1950 to 1957, she was residing in Jordan when her African novel *This Side of Jordan* (1960) appeared. Soon afterward, she completed the first of her four 'Manawaka' novels, which brought her international acclaim. *The Stone Angel* (1961), *A Jest of God* (1966), *The Fire-Dwellers* (1969), and *The Diviners* (1974) could be read on many levels and were easily the most richly textured fiction ever produced by a Canadian writer. Laurence's setting may have been as far removed from urban Montreal as it was possible to get, but like Richler, she created a place out of what she knew. The mythical town of Manawaka, set somewhere on the Canadian prairies, was a strongly conceived and living entity, linking some powerful female protagonists struggling against hypocritical Scots-Canadian constrictions and their own pasts. Noting that she was not much aware that her 'so-called Canadian writing' was Canadian, Laurence once commented that 'this seems a good thing to me, for it suggests that one has been writing out of a background so closely known that no explanatory tags are necessary' (quoted in Woodcock 1969: 9).

With a smaller readership than fiction commanded, poetry not only held its own but acquired a substantial audience. Irving Layton (b. 1912), Earle Birney (1904–95) and Al Purdy (1918–2001) were sent on reading tours by their publisher, and became almost as adept in performance as in writing. Performance of a different kind marked the career of Leonard Cohen (b. 1934), who straddled the worlds of high and popular culture when he set some of his poems to music, wrote new songs, and sang them to his own guitar accompaniment. Cohen had played in a band in his teens and published his first book of poetry, *Let Us Compare Mythologies*, in 1956 at the age of 22. It was followed in the sixties by two novels, including his haunting classic *Beautiful Losers* (1966), and by several poetry collections that were exceptionally appealing to the younger generation in their imagery and themes. In 1968, he refused a Governor General's Award for his *Selected Poems*. In the same year his first record album, *Songs of Leonard Cohen*, appeared, soon to be followed by *Songs from a Room* (1969). A few of his songs had already been performed by Joan Baez and Judy Collins, but Cohen's own liturgical baritone was the perfect vehicle for popularizing them. By 1970 he was competing successfully with other poet-singers like Bob Dylan, Donovan Leitch, and Paul McCartney. Such songs as 'Suzanne', 'Bird on a Wire', 'It Seems so Long Ago, Nancy', and 'The Story of Isaac'—with its repeated image of an eagle becoming a vulture—entered the consciousness of the counterculture. Cohen captured perfectly youth's scorn for hypocrisy. His songs counselled survival by withdrawal from the contests of life into a private world of the spirit, not in triumph or failure but in endurance through ceremony and self-understanding. These were powerful messages for the Woodstock generation. Ironically, while Cohen's songs contained almost no specific Canadian references, his sense of self-deprecation and self-abegnation was generally accepted as quintessentially Canadian.

The sixties also saw the creation of a number of small presses across the nation, and the emergence of 'Can Lit' as an acceptable field of study. By 1970 virtually every Canadian university offered an undergraduate course in Canadian literature, and a critical canon had more or less been established, which naturally emphasized the distinctly Canadian qualities of Canadian writing. Without a new breed of scholarly critics who were prepared to take Canadian writing seriously—and without the subsidies that helped sustain author, critic, teacher, and journals—that writing would have developed more slowly. McClelland and Stewart's enduring New Canadian Library series began in 1958, offering during the sixties mainly reprints of classic and long out-of-print novels. *Canadian Literature*, 'the first review devoted only to the study of Canadian writers and writing', was founded in 1959 by George Woodcock (b. 1912). The col-

POEMS BY MARGARET ATWOOD

In 1971 Margaret Atwood published a small book of poems entitled *Power Politics*. The first selection below appeared on the opening page, as an epigraph.

you fit into me
like a hook into an eye

a fish hook
an open eye

*****

After the agony in the guest
bedroom, you lying by the
overturned bed
your face uplifted, neck propped
against the windowsill, my arm
under you, cool moon
shining down through the window

wine mist rising
around you, an almost-invisible halo

You say, Do you
love me, do you love me

I answer you:
I stretch your arms out
one to either side
your head slumps forward.

Later I take you home
in a taxi, and you
are sick in the bathtub.

SOURCE: Margaret Atwood, *Power Politics* (Toronto: Anansi, 1971): 1, 6.

lectively written *Literary History of Canada* was published by the University of Toronto Press in 1965. At the beginning of his 'Conclusion' to the first edition of this work, Northrop Frye (1912–91) wrote:

> This book is a tribute to the maturity of Canadian literary scholarship and criticism, whatever one thinks of the literature. Its authors have completely outgrown the view that evaluation is the end of criticism, instead of its incidental by-product. Had evaluation been their guiding principle, this book would, if written at all, have been only a huge debunking project, leaving Canadian literature a poor naked *alouette* plucked of every feather of decency and dignity. True, the book gives evidence on practically every one of its eight hundred odd pages, that what is really remarkable is not how little but how much good writing has been produced in Canada (Klinck 1965: 821).

For many critics, the challenge was to reveal quintessential Canadian-ness in the imaginative elements of the literature. Québécois fiction shared in the cultural flowering, with the anger and violence of language and subject matter, and with radical changes in syntax and formal structure, not only mirroring but fostering the spirit of liberation and the new goals of Quebec society.

The coming of age of Canadian writing was not matched by a similar maturation in Canadian book publishing, which found itself subject to several disturbing market trends, most notably an inability to make money in a retail climate

☐ Northrop Frye, c. 1967. Brigdens Limited.

dominated by foreign publishers. Ryerson Press, the oldest major publisher in Canada and supported by the United Church of Canada, was so much in debt that it was sold in 1970 to the American firm McGraw-Hill. In the same year, the Ontario government appointed a Royal Commission on Book Publishing (1970), and had to rescue McClelland and Stewart from an American takeover. Even though the federal government established a policy of giving support to Canadian-controlled publishing firms through such agencies as the Canadian Book Publishing Development Program and the Canada Council—as did provincial governments in various ways, including through the Ontario Arts Council—Canadian publishing had entered an era of chronic precariousness that the quality of the writing available to be published only served to emphasize. The relatively small market for English-language books in Canada, the enormous volume of foreign books available, the dominance of foreign-owned publishers, and the self-defeating policy of allowing full return of unsold books—all of these factors put Canadian-owned publishers at a competitive disadvantage. For authors even to be successfully published in the United States had its disadvantages, since the American publishers would sell their left-over books (known as 'remainders') in Canada at a fraction of the price the Canadian publisher was still asking for the same book. Publishers in Quebec experienced less difficulty than those in the rest of Canada, despite the small market. Apparently the people of Quebec were more willing to buy books about themselves and their culture from local publishers.

The effect of the socio-economic changes in Quebec on writing in that province was considerable. The influence was reciprocal: one fuelled the other. The literary transformation began in the late 1950s with *La Belle Bête* (1959) by the 20-year old Marie-Claire Blais (b. 1939). This novel astonished the reading public (no less in its English translation, *Mad Shadows*) and scandalized the clergy with its portrayal of characters representing various kinds of moral and physical ugliness, and for its powerful impressionistic scenes of betrayal, disfigurement, pyromania, murder, and suicide. Blais was discovered outside Quebec by the American critic Edmund Wilson, who observed that she showed herself 'incapable of allowing life in French Canada to appear in a genial light or to seem to embody any sort of ideal' (Wilson 1964: 147). The literary transformation that began in the late 1950s continued throughout the next decades. The anger and violence of language and subject matter, radical changes in syntax and formal structure, the freeing of style and content from the constraints of tradition, not only mirrored but fostered the spirit of liberation and the new goals of Quebec society. This work was no longer called French-Canadian but 'Québécois' fiction. The journal *parti pris* (1963–8), founded just after the first wave of FLQ bombings with an *indépendantiste*

MARIE-CLAIRE BLAIS

☐ Marie-Claire Blais.

Marie-Claire Blais was born in Quebec City in 1939. She received her early education from Catholic nuns, but soon became disillusioned with academic subjects, leaving school at age fifteen to work in a factory. She subsequently attended Laval University and began writing. Her earliest novels, *La Belle Bête* and *Tête Blanche*, brought her to the attention of the distinguished literary critic Edmond Wilson, who described her in a *New Yorker* article on Canadian literature as the most promising young author in the country. As a result, she was able to study in Paris on a Guggenheim Fellowship. From the beginning, Blais's fiction had been experimental in language, form, and thematic content. She was one of the first Quebec novelists to break with realism, in favour of a surreal world of street dialogue and menacing sexuality.

In her work, Blais reflected major tensions in Quebec society. She was extremely conscious of the ways in which Quebec had oppressed its women. *Une saison dans la vie d'Emmanuel*, published in 1965, explores the life of a farm family during the months following the birth of the sixteenth child, Emmanuel, and emphasizes the brutality with which society responded to the older children's yearnings for something better. It won the Prix France-Canada and the Prix Médicis, and became a favourite topic for literary critics. Three semi-autobiographical novels about Pauline Archange, published between 1968 and 1970, echoed the critique of their parents by the younger generation in the 1960s.

In the 1970s Blais wrote about homosexuality. *Les nuits d'underground* (1978) was an evocative study of the everyday life of a lesbian frequenter of gay bars in Montreal. The later novels became increasingly characterized by stream-of-consciousness third-person narrative. Blais also published poetry and drama. For many readers, Blais became the epitome of the alienated artist and intellectual in modern Quebec society. Like the books of Gabrielle Roy, Blais's novels have all been translated into English, and she is one of a handful of Quebec novelists fully accessible to anglophones in Canada and beyond.

and Marxist perspective, published in January 1965 a special issue entitled *Pour une littérature québécoise*—giving a name, quickly adopted, to the current and future works of francophone writers in Quebec. That issue also promoted the use of joual in creative writing. The poet Paul Chamberland (b. 1939), one of the founding editors, wrote, '. . . any language must be shaken to its very foundations through the disfigurement inherent in our common speech, and in the lives of all of us.' Most of this literary explosion went unheeded in English-speaking Canada, partly because of the scarcity (and difficulty) of translations, but also, one suspects, because of the uncongenial spirit behind it.

Canadian scholarship, like other areas of élite culture, expanded and was strengthened in the 1960s. A combination of grants from the Canada Council, the Social Sciences and Humanities Research Council of Canada (SSHRCC), the National Research Council), together with an increase in the number of Canadian universities, vastly added to the numbers of academics and research students. Canadian scholarship grew not only in volume but in reputation, achieving international recognition in many disciplines. One field that had great difficulty coming to terms with the rapidly changing world of scholarship was Canadian history. Canadian historians almost by definition could not aspire to international repute, since in the broader scheme of things the history of Canada was of little interest to anyone outside the country. For most historians of Canada working within the English-speaking tradition, Canadian history was National History. The focus was unremittingly progressive. The country was settled, adopted representative government, turned responsible government into the union of the provinces, and with union moved gradually but inexorably towards full nationhood. Quebec, of course, had its own paradigm, equally nationalistic and political in nature. This comfortable mindset was overturned when younger historians began asking new questions about race, class, ethnicity, and gender that emerged out of the political turmoil of the late 1960s. These younger scholars also questioned the glaring neglect in the traditional approach towards Aboriginals, women, the working classes, and racial minorities. To these changes, Quebec historians added their own, often influenced by new European schools of analysis. Research and writing in Canadian economic and social history began to ask implicitly whether the old paradigm of nation-building was flexible and capacious enough to integrate the new methodologies and theories. By 1970 it was increasingly clear that the old fabric would not hold, although neither mainstream Canadian historians nor the revisionists had any idea of how to reweave it. Although the traditional synthesis had broken down, a new history had not yet appeared.

A new maturity and international acceptance of culture produced in Canada was to be found everywhere. We can see one major shift in the performing arts, where an amateur tradition of the 1950s was transformed quite swiftly into a full-fledged professional system operating from coast to coast. For example, Winnipeg—a middle-sized, geographically isolated urban centre with no particular tradition of cultural patronage—by 1970 was supporting a fully professional symphony orchestra; the Royal Winnipeg Ballet and other dance companies; an opera association mounting several works each year; the Manitoba Theatre Centre, an acclaimed model for regional theatre, whose impressive mainstage opened in 1970; an active art gallery; and a major concert hall. Thanks to various centennials, similar facilities and institutions soon existed in every major urban centre across Canada. By 1970 no important Canadian city or region was without its own professional theatre company, art gallery, and symphony orchestra.

Created with substantial public monies in the form of block grants from all levels of government, new arts institutions initially relied heavily on recent immigrants to Canada for professional expertise. Many of these professionals became teachers and sponsors of spin-off activities. It was not long before highly qualified younger Canadians were ready to step into these companies and organizations, and a substantial local audience had been developed. One of the secrets of public success in music and theatre was the introduction of annual subscription campaigns. Unlike audiences in New York, London, Paris, or Berlin, where tickets were sold for individual events, patrons of Canada's performing arts were asked to buy blocks of tickets in advance to guarantee an audience. If by 1970 the personnel in the performing and exhibitory arts were mainly Canadian, the repertoire on display tended to be largely an international one, both in origin and in style. Canadian artists, playwrights, composers, and choreographers still had trouble finding their own place and audience within the standard repertoire regardless of their style. How their art could be distinctly Canadian was an open question that ate away at the hearts of many Canadian creative people throughout the period.

The 1960s was also a critical decade for popular culture, particularly that valiant effort to keep the Canadian identity from being totally submerged by American influences. The record was mixed, as developments in Canadian sports well demonstrate. Nothing could be more quintessentially Canadian, for example, than hockey. But that sport entered the postwar period in the hands of the American entertainment industry, and the situation never really altered. By the 1960s only at the NHL level did Canadian teams have any real representation (two of six teams, in Toronto and Montreal). At the minor-league level only Vancouver had a professional team. The NHL finally expanded in 1967, adding six new American franchises in hockey hotbeds like St Louis and Philadelphia. Not even Vancouver, to its chagrin, could get a look-in. The chief argument against new Canadian teams was related to television. American TV viewers would not watch professional sports played by 'foreign' teams, said the experts, and the secret of expansion's success was a US national television contract. In 1969, on the other hand, the National Baseball League granted a franchise to a Montreal team to be called the Expos, demonstrating that if the local markets were big enough, the moguls could be won over. As for the Canadian Football League, it entered its most successful decade to date. Teams became totally professional and drew considerable crowds. The fans appeared quite satisfied with the Canadian game and its differences from the American one—the size of the field, the number of downs, the 'rouge'—and with the large number of Canadians who, thanks to a quota system on imports, played it.

In September 1961 the federal government finally took some initiative on the problem of sports in Canada. Bill C-131, intended to 'encourage, promote and develop fitness and amateur sport in Canada', passed both Houses of Parliament unanimously. Much of the bill's bipartisan political support was a result of public outcry over Canada's poor performance in international competitions, including hockey, and was part of the country's cold war posturing. Speaking about amateur sports at that time, Opposition leader Lester Pearson (who had played lacrosse and hockey while at Oxford) said: 'all the publicity attached to international sport and the fact that certain societies use international sport, as they use everything else, for the advancement of prestige and political purposes, it is a matter of some consequence that we in Canada should do what we can to develop and regain the prestige we once had, to a greater extent than we now have in international competition' (quoted in Morrow 1989: 328). Although the act was deliberately vague, it allowed the government to subsidize amateur coaches and teams, particularly in national and international competitions. In 1968 the National Advisory Council, set up under the act to recommend policy and oversee its implementation, was shunted to one side in favour of professional bureaucrats within the Ministry of National Health and Welfare. Amateur sports in Canada had been taken under the wing of the welfare state. In that same year Pierre Trudeau promised in the election

BOBBY HULL

Robert Marvin Hull, Jr (a.k.a. 'the Golden Jet') was born in 1939 in Pointe Anne, Ontario. He began playing hockey at an early age and joined the Chicago Black Hawks of the National Hockey League in 1957. A left-winger, he was an intimidating presence on the ice, noted for his development of the 'slap shot', a technique for shooting the puck at the goalie at much increased speeds. He scored fifty or more goals five times, and led the Black Hawks to the Stanley Cup in 1961. He was first in the NHL in goals scored seven times and in total points scored three times.

In 1972 Hull signed a lucrative contract with the Winnipeg Jets of the upstart World Hockey Association, a league formed largely of Canadian teams that were unable to get NHL franchises. The NHL responded to this action by refusing to allow Hull to play for its team in the Canada-Russia hockey series of 1972. But Hull's signing gave the WHA considerable credibility. He won the WHA's most valuable player award in 1972–3 and led his team to several post-season championships in the 1970s. In 1980 he signed with the Hartford Whalers of the NHL, and finished his career there. By his retirement, Hull had amassed in the NHL a total of 609 goals, 555 assists, and 1,164 points, and in the WHA 303 goals, 335 assists, and 639 total points. Whether those totals should be added together is the subject of continued controversy among hockey historians. After his retirement he maintained his public persona as television spokesman for several commercial products. He was elected to the Hockey Hall of Fame in 1983.

campaign a new study of sports in Canada. The 'Report of the Task Force on Sports for Canadians' was published in 1969. Despite the increased government involvement in and subsidization of amateur sports, in 1976 Canada acquired the dubious distinction of becoming the first (and so far only) nation to host the Olympic Games without winning a gold medal.

CONCLUSION

On the whole, the developments in sports were remarkably similar to those in other cultural sectors, and indeed the nation in general. By the early 1970s sports had been thoroughly drawn into the net of federal and provincial government policy, turned over to the bureaucrats and bean-counters. It had not yet answered the question of whether excellence and Canadian-ness were truly compatible, although the sense was that a sufficient expenditure of money would in the end resolve all problems. Unbeknownst to its participants, however, sports in Canada was about to share with other aspects of the Canadian experience a new sense of existing on the edge of some kind of precipice, about to free fall into new and unknown territory. What consequences the fall would have were anybody's guess, although there were increasingly loud mutterings about the limits of growth. After 1972 Canadians would have to explore together the implications of a world in which not all things were possible. They would discover, as money and resources became more limited, that the infighting could be extremely fierce.

HOW HISTORY HAS CHANGED

PERSPECTIVES ON SEX

Like everything else in Canadian society and culture, historical writing has been subject to censorship and taboos, often self-imposed. The student will still look in vain in any textbook on Canadian history for any detailed examination of sexual activity or the excretory functions. It was acceptable to mention bathrooms, toilets, outhouses, and toilet paper (including the use of newspapers and department store catalogues in earlier eras), so long as there was no detailed discussion of what Canadians did in them or with them. Toilet behaviour is universal enough to be describable, but its very universality means that there is probably no need for explicitness; we can take such things pretty much for granted. As historians we could describe a sexual act only if one of our historical characters provided us with a documentable account of it, and most such personalities were amazingly reticent, even in their most revealing memoirs, about the existence of relationships, much less behaviour. Canadians were as astounded as Americans in the 1940s by the revelations of Dr Alfred Kinsey regarding sexuality in America. But even aside from explicit description of particular acts, the larger issues of sexuality have only very gradually become available as topics for public scrutiny. Modern historians have not themselves taken the lead in discussing sexuality, but have only responded to distinct shifts in public perceptions.

Although 'unnatural' sexual acts had been taboo in society for centuries, and could be severely punished by the authorities when they were found, sexual deviancy emerged as an important social matter only in the later nineteenth century. In many cases, same-sex sexual activity was overlooked or regarded as tolerable in places where females were in short supply. Those concerned with social purity and 'race suicide' eventually attempted to preserve procreation from the evils of masturbation and other forms of perversion. The newly emerging social sciences began to study deviancy, and various specific meanings of it became enshrined in the Canadian Criminal Code. A homosexual 'type' gradually began to emerge, and 'gross indecency' was first introduced to the Criminal Code in 1890. In general, Canada followed the United States and Great Britain in their understandings of what was permissible sexual practice. By the end of the 1890s, the concern of Canadians was with the immorality and degeneracy of what they regarded as deviant sexual activities. At the same time, the increasing social sophistication of Canadian society apparently led to an increase in organized underground behaviour of a deviant sort.

Unlike Britain and the United States, where historians began to study and write openly about both sexual activity and sexual deviancy by the 1950s, Canada had to wait until the 1980s for similar work to appear. Elsa Gidrow's autobiographical account of her lesbian experiences in Montreal during World War I appeared in print in 1986 (published in the United States), and Gary Kinsman's *The Regulation of Desire: Sexuality in Canada*–a thorough historical examination of the question–was first published only in 1987. Two factors led to a new openness of discussion. One was pressure from the gay community for a new Canadian attitude towards sexuality, including what Kinsman calls 'a more historically grounded perspective on gay and lesbian liberation: a view which understands the social forces that have both organized our oppression and made it possible for us to resist' (Kinsman 1987: 15). Political pressure was evident in open protests by thousands of gays on the streets of Toronto in 1981 in response to police raids on bathhouses. The second factor was probably the emergence of AIDS, a disease which was from the outset associated with the homosexual community and which could not be discussed and analyzed apart from that community. In recent years 'Queer Studies' have become an acceptable approach for postmodern discourse. This is not surprising, since one major point of revisionist historians depends on the postmodern insistence on the social construction of everything, including 'deviancy'.

SHORT BIBLIOGRAPHY

Axelrod, Paul. *Scholars and Dollars: Politics, Economics and the Universities of Ontario 1945–80*. Toronto, 1982. An excellent study of the postwar universities in Ontario, emphasizing the expansion of existing universities and the creation of new ones, as well distinct shifts in the justifications for higher education.

Behiels, Michael, ed. *Quebec since 1945*. Toronto, 1987. An admirable and comprehensive collection of articles on postwar Quebec.

Bergeron, Léandre. *The History of Quebec: A Patriote's Handbook*. Toronto, 1971. A translation of a radical 'people's' history of Quebec, strongly separatist in tone.

Cardinal, Harold. *The Unjust Society: The Tragedy of Canada's Indians*. Edmonton, 1969. The first attempt to tell the First Nations' story from the Native standpoint.

Clairmont, Donald, and Dennis Magill. *Africville: The Life and Death of a Canadian Black Community*. Rev. ed., Toronto, 1987. A work which documents the destruction of Africville and insists it was improper and unnecessary.

Desbiens, Jean-Paul. *The Impertinences of Brother Anonymous*. Toronto, 1962. The famous critique of Quebec politics and culture that caused a furor when first published.

Forsyth, Dennis, ed. *Let the Niggers Burn: The Sir George Williams University Affair and its Caribbean Aftermath*. Montreal, 1971. An account of the most famous Canadian incident of student protest.

Handler, Richard. *Nationalism and the Politics of Culture in Quebec*. Madison, 1981. A detailed analysis of the manifold ways in which Quebec nationalism has influenced Quebec culture and cultural policy.

Kinsman, Gary. *The Regulation of Desire: Sexuality in Canada*. Montreal, 1987. A pioneering study of sexuality and its treatment by the state.

Levitt, Kari. *Silent Surrender: The Multinational Corporation in Canada*. Toronto, 1970. The most notorious statement of the nationalist critique of foreign investment and the multicultural corporation in Canada.

Morton, W. L. *The Canadian Identity*. Toronto, 1961. An effort to discover the essence of Canada by one of its leading historians.

Saywell, John. *Quebec 70: A Documentary Narrative*. Toronto, 1971. A useful account of the FLQ crisis of 1970.

Simeon, Richard. *Federal-Provincial Diplomacy: The Making of Recent Policy in Canada*. Toronto, 1972. A fascinating study of the international implications.

Vallières, Pierre. *White Niggers of America*. Toronto, 1971. A brilliant polemical memoir about living as a French Canadian.

Weaver, Sally M. *Making Canada's Indian Policy: The Hidden Agenda 1968–1970*. Toronto, 1981. A sober account of Canadian Aboriginal policy in a crucial period of re-evaluation.

STUDY QUESTIONS

1. Identify at least one way in which Canadian manners were emancipated during the 1960s in each of the following areas: religion, the media, literature, sexuality, and the law.
2. Explain why the 'counterculture' was mainly a youthful phenomenon.
3. Canada was never directly involved in the Vietnam war. Why did this war have such a strong impact on Canadian society?
4. Identify four militant collectivities that arose in the 1960s. For each, summarize briefly their goals.
5. What do Tables 10.1 and 10.2 (p. 384) tell us about unemployment in the 1960s?
6. In what ways did the 'Quiet Revolution' change Quebec society?
7. What three policies did the Pearson government develop to deal with Quebec's aspirations? Comment on the effectiveness of these policies.

CHAPTER ELEVEN

Coming Apart, 1972–1992

After a quarter-century of optimism, the years after 1972 presented Canadians with a different picture. Everything, from the economy to the very nation itself, suddenly seemed to be in a state of confusion bordering on disintegration.

The Problems of Liberal Federalist Nationalism

Until the early 1970s the postwar era had been for most Canadians one of affluence and optimism. It was characterized by a nationalism anchored by strong central federal government. This relatively positive climate had been achieved by policies dominated by twentieth-century small-l 'liberalism', a delicate balancing act that accepted an economic system based on private enterprise and corporate capitalism while also attempting to provide a social welfare safety net for the nation's citizens. Not all the resulting policies were influenced by Keynesian economics, but many of them were. Such policies were the operative ones for governments throughout the Western industrialized world. They were non-partisan. All major Canadian political parties, for example, at all levels of government—ranging provincially from the Socreds of the west to the separatists of Quebec—were essentially exponents of variants of liberalism with a small 'l'.

If the political consensus sought by all democratic governments in this period was formally dominated by liberal economics, the constitutional framework in which the liberalism was to operate increasingly produced conflict. For much of the period before 1970, the Liberal Party had combined liberal economics with a constitutionally centralized federalism. Although the Progressive Conservatives, in their six years of power between 1957 and 1963, had demonstrated different emphases, even they had not seriously contemplated overturning the broad framework. As we have seen, the Liberal consensus had come under attack in the 1960s, mainly from the left. It began seriously unravelling in the 1970s, and was in tatters by the beginning of the 1990s.

The Canadian political arena seemed incapable of dealing with both economic problems and constitutional problems simultaneously, at least at the same level of intensity. The period after 1972 saw an alternation of focus between the Constitution and the economy. The two questions were not entirely divorced, of course. One of the major arguments of the federalists was that only strong national policies could deal with the problems of the economy, and with the demands of minorities not geographically embodied into provinces and regions. Moreover, while constitutional matters were largely under the control of Canadians, economic ones were chiefly international. After the election of a Tory government under Brian Mulroney in 1984, both nationalism and federalism were jettisoned for free trade and Meech Lake, while the principles of liberal economics were replaced by privatization, claw-backs, and deregulation.

No single factor or event can possibly be iso-

TIMELINE

1972
Canada–Russia hockey series. Trudeau Liberals win in close election. NDP defeats W.A.C. Bennett in British Columbia.

1973
OPEC raises price of oil. Robert Bourassa's Liberals are elected in Quebec, but the Parti Québécois finishes strong.

1974
Trudeau Liberals win another close election. Trudeau imposes wage and price controls.

1976
Canadian Airline Pilots Association strike. Montreal Olympics are held. Parti Québécois wins power in Quebec. Joe Clark is chosen leader of the Tories.

1977
Quebec government passes Bill 101.

1978
Task Force on National Unity tours Canada.

1979
Antonine Maillet publishes *Pélagie-la-Charette*. Joe Clark's Tories win minority government.

1980
Quebec referendum results in 60 per cent *Non* and 40 per cent *Oui* on question of sovereignty association. The Clark government falls, and Trudeau's Liberals are swept back to power. Trudeau proposes constitutional reform.

1981
Supreme Court rules on federal constitutional initiative. The PQ is re-elected in Quebec. The 'Gang of Nine' cuts a deal on the Constitution. Revised constitutional package passes Parliament.

1982
A revised Constitution is approved by the British Parliament.

1983
Brian Mulroney replaces Joe Clark as Tory leader.

1984
Trudeau retires and is succeeded by John Turner. Brian Mulroney leads Progressive Conservatives to a federal sweep. The Cirque du Soleil is formed.

1985
PQ defeated by Robert Bourassa's Liberals.

1986
Mulroney government negotiates Free Trade Agreement with the US.

1987
Meech Lake agreement is reached.

1988
Mulroney's Tories win again. Mulroney signs redress agreement with National Association of Japanese Canadians. Ben Johnson wins a gold medal at Seoul Olympics, which is later revoked because of a positive steroid text.

1989
Fourteen female engineering students are gunned down in Montreal.

1990
Meech Lake accord fails. Lucien Bouchard forms the Bloc Québécois. Mohawks confront Quebec government at Oka. Audrey McLaughlin is chosen as first female party leader in Canada.

1991
GST officially introduced. Jean Chrétien becomes Liberal leader.

1992
Charlottetown Accord is reached. Toronto Blue Jays win World Series. National referendum rejects the Charlottetown Accord.

lated as responsible for the collapse of the liberal federalist-nationalist consensus in Canada. Instead, a cumulation of what Marxist analysts would call 'contradictions'—matters that simply could not be resolved within the consensus—would eventually defy attempts at management, compromise, or hopeful neglect. The contradictions would come together at centre-stage to produce a series of what the media liked to call 'crises'. Many of the pressures were not really of Canada's own making but were part of international trends over which no Canadian government had very much control. Increasingly both politicians and the public came to feel that all political responses were defensive reactions to unmanageable situations, and that all policies were merely band-aids placed over festering wounds. Public trust in the nation's political leaders declined as the consensus disintegrated and was not replaced by a new paradigm. Cynicism became entrenched at the core of the Canadian national psyche. To some imponderable extent, the increase in cynicism and the gradual emergence of ever more unalloyed self-interest as the mainspring of human action contributed to the further deterioration of the old consensus. The Second World War had been fought on the basic principles of the deferral of expectations and the need for national sacrifice for the greatest good of the greatest number—a classic liberal utilitarianism. Canadians, whether as private individuals or as voting citizens, became increasingly less willing to buy such arguments. They became ever more prepared to accept the calls of leaders who, by implication or open assertion, opposed either waiting or sharing.

In 1973 a cease-fire agreement allowed the United States to withdraw from Vietnam, and the American process of national disillusionment continued with the Watergate affair, in which an apparently successful president was eventually forced to resign on 9 August 1974 rather than risk removal from office by impeachment for years of lying to the public. In Canada, Vietnam seemed less important than the October Crisis, bringing to the fore the Parti Québécois, which succeeded in electing seven candidates in the 1970 Quebec election. Then on 6 October 1973—the Jewish holy day of Yom Kippur—the Arabs and Israelis went to war, as they had done periodically for many years. On this occasion, however, events in the Middle East had an immediate impact on the world and on Canada. The Arab oil exporters (who dominated the world market) embargoed shipments of oil to nations supporting Israel. Shortly thereafter, the Organization of Petroleum-Exporting Countries (OPEC), which for thirteen years had been a toothless cartel, managed to agree on another price increase, more substantial than the modest one announced before the Yom Kippur War. The price of oil more than tripled in 1973, and all Western industrialized nations suddenly realized how much their economies had depended on a constant supply of cheap oil.

Perhaps more than any other single commodity of the postwar era, oil symbolized the economics of the age of affluence as well as its North American problems. Cheap oil made possible the development of large, powerful, and comfortable automobiles—the 'Yank Tanks' as they were called in Canada before they briefly became the 'Detroit Dinosaurs'—that sat in every suburban driveway and clogged every freeway. Those freeways, of course, had been paved with materials conjured out of petroleum derivatives. The manufacture and sale of instantly obsolescent, gas-guzzling automobiles, as well as the construction of roads that connected thousands of new suburban developments and shopping malls, were major components of postwar economic prosperity in both the United States and Canada. Some saw the car as a symbol of postwar progress, while others saw it as a sex symbol. Either way, a 20-horsepower electric engine could hardly provide the same effect. The typical Detroit automobile not only consumed gas and oil as if there were no tomorrow, but discharged harmful hydrocarbons—serious contributors to the air pollution that increasingly affected everyone's health. Detroit engineering—never renowned for its flexibility—was slow to respond to the need for fuel efficiency brought about by significantly higher oil prices. By the time it had moved to smaller vehicles, the Japanese had taken command of the North American automobile market, a fact that strongly suggested a new world trading order.

If petroleum—literally as well as symbolically—fuelled the contradictions of the North American economy, it also exposed Canadians to a number of distinctly home-grown problems. Many of these matters had already been newsworthy before OPEC pulled the plug, but they seemed more urgent and apparent as the nation searched for a viable energy policy to respond to the 'crisis'. The Canadian petroleum industry, located chiefly in Alberta, was almost entirely owned and operated by multinational corporations, most (though not all) of them American-based. Oil, indeed, was one of those resources that most obviously epitomized the problems of foreign ownership that were addressed by a series of governments and task forces in the early 1970s. Moreover, although the petroleum still in the ground was a Crown resource, the Crown involved was the province and not the federal state. When the problems of jurisdiction over offshore oil were added to provincial control of oil as an internal natural resource, the result was a key item of potential dispute in federal–provincial relations. Most oil consumption in Canada occurred in the industrialized east, while most of the raw material was in the resource-rich west, a discrepancy that exacerbated regional tensions. Finally, increased petroleum prices had a ripple effect throughout both the Canadian and world economies. Prices rose overnight, and an already steady inflation soared to new highs at a time when Canadian labour unions had only recently succeeded in establishing themselves in many key industries, especially in the public sector. Having achieved full recognition of collective bargaining, union organizers next moved for improved working conditions and higher wages to match the cost of living. OPEC's price increases, with promises of more to come, thus affected Canada in several vulnerable areas: foreign ownership, federal–provincial relations, regional conflicts, and labour relations.

Virtually the only long-standing problem that oil did not seem to affect directly was Quebec. On 29 October 1973, only three weeks after the start of the Yom Kippur War, Quebecers went to the polls to elect a new provincial government. From the outset of the contest between the Liberals of Robert Bourassa and the Parti Québécois headed by René Lévesque, the chief issue had been the desirability of a separate Quebec. Both parties had worked to polarize the electorate on this simple issue. The result, on the surface, was a resounding victory for the Liberals: 1,600,000 votes (54.8 per cent of the total votes cast) to 897,000 for the PQ, and 102 seats in the legislature to six for the PQ. Nonetheless, the Péquistes had improved their performance over the 1970 election in almost every riding, and did exceptionally well among younger voters in Montreal. Post-election studies suggested that the majority of Liberal supporters had favoured federalism and a majority of PQ supporters wanted independence for Quebec. The anglophone voters were much more staunchly federalist than the francophones. In any event, separatism had suddenly become respectable. While no other province was prepared to join the PQ in the front lines of the quest for a new constitutional arrangement for Canada, resource-rich provinces like Alberta certainly favoured new guarantees of constitutional autonomy for the provinces.

The relationship between Quebec separatism and Canada's economic problems after 1973 was difficult to determine. In 1976 the PQ won a somewhat surprising victory, not necessarily to be interpreted as a mandate for separatism or sovereignty association, although one of its pre-election platform planks was the promise of a referendum on sovereignty association. When the referendum was held in May 1980, the

ROBERT BOURASSA

Robert Bourassa was born 14 July 1933 on Parthenais Street in Montreal's East End. His father, Aubert Bourassa, was a documents clerk for the National Harbours Board, where he was made to work in English. His mother, Adrienne Courville, did not demand that Robert do household chores, permitting him to study instead. He attended the local St Pierre Claver parish school, then the Collège Brébeuf, then the Université de Montréal, where he was president of the French-Canada Association while studying law. He also wrote for the university newspaper, mostly advocating solidarity for the francophone minority. His first article for *Le Quartier latin* was an interview with Maurice Duplessis. Bourassa had excellent grades and received many scholarships and bursaries. He won the Mackenzie King scholarship of the Royal Society, the Governor General's medal, and a Ford Foundation bursary.

At the university Bourassa met Andrée Simard, who came from a family of rich industrialists in Sorel. They married in August 1958 and then went to London for further study. He got a job as financial advisor with the federal revenue department in 1960 and taught economics at the University of Ottawa. He first ran for elected office in 1966, winning his seat in the Mercier riding while the Liberals lost their majority. Bourassa joined the nationalist wing of the provincial Liberals, attempting to keep pace with Daniel Johnson, now premier. He accompanied René Lévesque as part of the Montreal VIP delegation when de Gaulle made his famous speech. He was uncomfortable with de Gaulle's declaration, and told the St Laurent Kiwanis Club in November 1967, 'the economic aspect of a completely independent Quebec always leads to a stumbling block, no matter how you look at it, when it comes to the problem of suddenly instituting a Quebec currency.' Bourassa won on the first ballot at the Liberal leadership convention of 17 January 1970 and would begin his leadership career positioned ideologically halfway between Pierre Trudeau and Réne Lévesque. Bourassa as leadership candidate promised '100,000 jobs' and was elected premier on 29 April 1970 on this same platform. Instead of creating jobs, he would spend the next five years passively resisting Trudeau's 'patriation' campaign and searching for 'social peace'. He tried to emphasize foreign investment, but got caught up in the October Crisis, in which he often appeared a weakling.

The FLQ manifesto which had to be read over Radio-Canada referred to 'Bourassa, the Simard canary, Trudeau the faggot'. After the Laporte kidnapping, it was Bourassa who wanted the War Measures Act invoked. 'If that's what you want,' Trudeau told Bourassa, 'you'll have to ask me formally and say that you are faced with a state of potential insurrection.' The October Crisis, the subsequent constitutional negotiations which bypassed Quebec, and the increased popularity of separatism, all weakened Bourassa's power base. Although his government was easily re-elected in 1973, it collapsed in 1976 amidst charges of scandal and corruption connected with the Olympic Games that same year. Bourassa retreated into private life, but re-emerged in 1983 as leader of the Liberals after the failure of Claude Ryan to provide a viable opposition to the Parti Québécois.

In 1985 Bourassa led his party back to power, despite his personal defeat in the riding of Bertrand. Bourassa initially seemed to benefit from Prime Minister Mulroney's attempts to bring Quebec onside constitutionally at Meech Lake, but in the end the failure of Meech Lake and the subsequent defeat in a national referendum of the Charlottetown Accord damaged his reputation inside and outside Quebec. He resigned in 1994 after treatment for skin cancer and died in 1996.

Nons—those opposed to sovereignty association—won 60 per cent to 40 per cent. The PQ, however, were re-elected the next year. Especially after the referendum, the federal government under Pierre Trudeau turned its attention from the economy to the Constitution. Trudeau himself was not only a federalist Quebecer but a constitutional lawyer far more comfortable with the intricacies of the British North America Act than with oil-price equalization or economic planning. Oil and the Constitution were scarcely the only issues after 1973, but they were certainly front and centre for many years. The various attempts to resolve the problems they helped to create (as well as the ones they obscured) precipitated the deterioration of the postwar consensus.

Pressure for continual expansion of the welfare state came from many directions before 1980, because income security became essential to the federal government's power, representing as it did the main link between Ottawa and the people. After 1980, however, contrary tendencies became evident and eventually dominant. Canada's involved economic and social problems would continue to produce demands for expansion of social insurance, but with the erosion of revenue and intense international competition, the federal government increasingly focused on restraint and privatization. Before 1992, no major element of the existing welfare net had actually been eliminated, however. Pension benefits for the elderly even improved. But the government cumulatively reduced the universality of the system of family benefits through the income tax system. In unemployment compensation, revised regulations increased the waiting period, making it more difficult to use unemployment funds as income supplements. The notorious goods and services tax (GST) was a thoroughly regressive tax that hit hardest at the poor. Still, the greatest irony of government policy towards social welfare remained unchanged from the earlier part of the century. The government of Brian Mulroney was continually concerned about spending and the deficit, but had no trouble finding funds to support its military cooperation in the Gulf War of 1990. The unsolved riddle of social justice was still a challenge.

THE SHAPE OF FEDERAL POLITICS

The Ottawa scene from 1972 to 1992 divides into two periods, with the break coming in 1984. During most of the first period the Liberals under Trudeau clung tenaciously to power in a series of very close elections (1972, 1974, 1979, and 1980), although they were replaced in office briefly, in 1979, by a minority Tory administration headed by Joe Clark. This period was one of a gradual Liberal Party deterioration paralleling the unravelling of the small-l liberal consensus of the postwar era. In 1984 the Tories under Brian Mulroney swept to power in the most decisive election since 1945, exceeding even the

Diefenbaker sweep of 1958 in percentage of popular votes and number of seats. As with most decisive electoral shifts in Canada, the one in 1984 involved a massive reorientation of votes in Quebec and Ontario. The change in Quebec was particularly critical, although it was not clear whether Quebec's party shift was a long-term one, or precisely what it meant. At the end of their tenures of office, both Trudeau and Mulroney engendered enormous currents of fierce voter hostility in a general atmosphere of public mistrust of politicians.

Whether Mulroney's Tories actually represented a different political vision that could serve as the basis for a new consensus was always an open question. Certainly they sought to move to the consensual centre, which public opinion polls and voting behaviour suggested had become dubious about many of the old assumptions, but there was no clear evidence that a new political paradigm was emerging from the shards of the old liberal one. Instead, the events of his second administration suggested that Mulroney, like Diefenbaker a generation earlier, was simply perplexed and confounded by the chaos of the disintegration of federalism. The problem of Quebec, which came to dominate public attention across Canada in the late 1980s and early 1990s, contributed to further confusion.

THE LIBERALS

The fortunes of the federal Liberal Party between 1968 and 1984 became increasingly associated with Pierre Elliott Trudeau, its leader for most of that period. The identification was partly due to television's relentless search for visual images and Trudeau's brilliant mastery of the medium. But it was also a result of Trudeau's operating as a loner, not encouraging strong colleagues to emerge around him. Trudeau's 'arrogance', the term most often used to describe his behaviour, was personal, not political. As a French Canadian who had always firmly opposed Quebec separatism, he had little scope for manoeuvre when public opinion polarized in that province. As an equally strong federalist, he had no more time for western expressions of provincial or regional autonomy than he did for for Quebec's. A central-Canadian urban intellectual, he could not empathize with the problems of either the Atlantic region or western Canada. The east never deserted him, but by 1980 'western alienation' had reduced the number of Liberal MPs west of Ontario to two (both from Manitoba).

Never a fervent party man, Trudeau did not cultivate the grassroots. The powerful Liberal political organizations that had flourished before 1970 were allowed to wither away in most provinces, surfacing when federal patronage was to be dispensed but not at federal election time. Trudeau distressed many Canadians with forthrightness ('Just watch me'), vulgarity bordering on obscenity (one four-letter word in the House of Commons was transcribed as 'fuddle duddle', a raised-finger gesture to a western crowd appeared in newspapers across the nation), and personal unconventionality. Perhaps most damaging of all was an increasing tendency to treat almost everyone (members of his own caucus, the opposition, reporters, the voters) as ill-informed and irrational. Trudeau's public persona oscillated between that of a genial swinger (who could date Barbra Streisand) and that of a university professor facing a particularly stupid class.

Trudeau had announced his intention of retiring in 1979 following the Liberals' unexpected electoral defeat. But the Clark minority government fell before his replacement could be chosen. The Liberal caucus persuaded him to lead the party into the unanticipated election of 1980, and he remained in power for four more years. In 1984 Trudeau made his retirement stick. He was succeeded by John Turner (b. 1929), who had waited in the wings for years. Chosen on 16 June 1984 as Liberal leader and becoming prime minister two weeks later, Turner dissolved Parliament on 9 July for the fateful 1984 election. Turner was born in England, but was thoroughly bilingual. His decision regarding

☐ Prime Minister Trudeau and the newly elected premier of Quebec, Robert Bourassa, at the federal-provincial conference of September 1970, in Ottawa. Duncan Cameron/NAC, PA-117468.

the election was a difficult one. He chose to run as a fresh face, on the momentum of his selection as leader, rather than remaining in office to attempt to improve the government's image. He had no new policies. Instead he was encumbered by the twin albatrosses of Trudeau's mounting unpopularity and the growing collapse of the liberal consensus. To everyone's surprise, he also proved utterly inept on television. The weak Liberal showing of 1984 (forty seats in Ottawa) was hardly unexpected. Something better was expected in 1988, however. In that election the Liberals did even worse in Quebec than in 1984, and Turner was a lame duck on election night. He was finally replaced in the summer of 1990 by Jean Chrétien (b. 1934), another veteran of earlier Liberal governments. Chrétien was a loyal party man and a proven campaigner. His leadership opponents had labelled him 'Yesterday's Man' with some justification, but lacked sufficient credibility or charisma to beat him.

THE PROGRESSIVE CONSERVATIVES

Robert Stanfield led the Tories to three successive defeats at the hands of the Trudeau Liberals. He was too low-key and uncompelling. Stanfield spoke French badly and his party did poorly in Quebec during his leadership (four seats in 1968, two in 1972, and three in 1974). He was followed as Tory leader by Alberta MP Joe

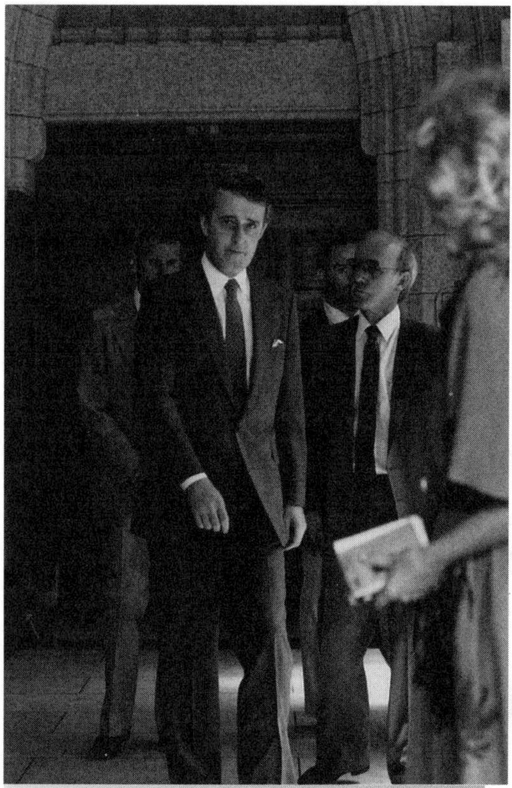

Brian Mulroney in 1983, the year before he became leader of the Progressive Conservative party, MP for Central Nova, and leader of the Opposition. He was elected prime minister the following year. Ed McGibbon/NAC, PA-146485.

(Charles Joseph) Clark (b. 1939), who emerged from nowhere as the compromise 'progressive' candidate at the 1976 leadership convention. 'Joe Who?' never did establish a distinct personality with the voters, except as a man who was accident-prone. In 1979 his Tories received 136 seats to 114 for the Liberals. Clark formed a minority government despite having won only two seats in Quebec (to sixty-seven for the Liberals). He tried to govern as if he had a majority, mistakenly assuming either that other parties would support him in Parliament rather than face another election or that the nation would rally to his banner in a new election. Neither assumption was true. The NDP refused to support Clark, especially over the privatization of Petro-Canada. His government fell on a motion of non-confidence about the budget, involving gasoline pricing. Clark remained party leader after the disastrous election of 1980, but in June 1983 was replaced by 'the Boy from Baie Comeau', Brian Mulroney (b. 1939).

Brian Mulroney entered Canadian politics at the highest level without ever having held public or elected office, although he had been active in the political back rooms for years. Unlike Clark, whose public utterances were unpolished and delivered in a boyish tenor (he reportedly took elocution lessons to lower his voice), Mulroney was a fluent speaker, perfectly bilingual, and possessed of one of the richest and most mellifluous voices ever heard in Canadian politics. He was an experienced labour lawyer and corporation executive, at his best at behind-the-scenes conciliation. Mulroney understood the need for Tory success in Quebec, and he brought a number of new faces into the campaign, some of whom were refugees from the old Union Nationale. In 1984 he successfully captured the centre of the new Canadian political spectrum. Although Mulroney's Tories promised they would not dismantle the existing welfare state, they put an ominous emphasis on 'fiscal responsibility'. They were equally committed to better relations between Canada and the United States, which meant less economic nationalism, as well as improved relations between Ottawa and the provinces (especially Quebec), which meant surrendering federalist pretensions.

Once in office with an enormous majority, including fifty-eight seats from Quebec, Mulroney succeeded in 1986 in negotiating a free trade agreement with the United States and the Meech Lake constitutional accord with the provinces. On the coat-tails of these successes the Tories won again in 1988, with sixty-three of their 169 seats coming from Quebec. Mulroney's second term was an unmitigated disaster. Given the amount of public support he had enjoyed in 1984 and 1988, the rapid growth of hostility to Mulroney in the early 1990s was quite remarkable. A variety of things went wrong. Government spending got quite out of hand. What was supposed to be a progressive tax reform, the GST, proved to be the most unpopular tax ever introduced in Canadian history, doubly resented for the way the Tories stacked the Senate to ensure its passage. The GST replaced previously hidden levies with an all-too visible tax computed at the cash register. Unlike provincial sales taxes, it was applied to everything without exception. With the provincial taxes, the GST meant a surcharge of nearly 20 per cent in several provinces on most consumer spending. Meech Lake failed, and in a national referendum in October 1992 the nation rejected its successor, the Charlottetown Accord. Much of Canada came to believe that the Tory constitutional deals, especially with Quebec, not only made too many concessions but had actually stirred up unnecessary trouble.

Other National Parties

Throughout this period the New Democratic Party remained the constant third party. Its continuity was exemplified by the steadiness of its popular vote in federal elections, which ran between 15 and 20 per cent, and by the steadiness of its policies, which were indisputably federalist, nationalist, and liberal. Some complained that the party was not sufficiently socialist. It had certainly purged its socialist wing, the Waffle, in the early 1970s. But it was still unable to make inroads east of Ontario, consistently the big loser when the popular vote was translated into parliamentary seats. From 1971 to 1975 the NDP was led by David Lewis (1909–81), the son of Russian immigrants to Canada and a Rhodes scholar who had spent a lifetime associated with the CCF-NDP. His selection as leader followed a bitter fight with the radical caucus within the party. From 1972 to 1974 the Lewis-led NDP propped up the minority Liberal government, arguably turning it to the left, but paying for the collaboration at the polls in 1974.

In 1975 Ed Broadbent (b. 1936), a former political science professor at York University, succeeded Lewis. Broadbent's national position in Canada in the 1980s was a peculiar one. He consistently headed the polls as the most popular and trustworthy national leader, but his party was never able to increase its public support. In 1990 Broadbent was replaced by Audrey McLaughlin (b. 1936), a former social worker from the Yukon Territories who spoke halting French and had no appeal in Quebec. Her selection as the first female party leader in Canada, however, marked the NDP as yet again in advance of the other parties, for feminist issues were part of the unresolved agenda of Canadian politics in the 1990s.

The Provinces, the Constitution, and the Charter of Rights

The Shape of Provincial Politics

The provinces continued to have difficulty generating truly viable two-party or multiparty systems. Instead, most provinces operated through a single dominant party (often outside the two major federal ones) that remained in office in election after election, producing what C.B. Macpherson described for Alberta as a 'quasi-party' system. A single dominant party, Macpherson argued, satisfied voters and mediated local conflict by insisting that the important battle was against external forces symbolized by the Canadian federal government. Conflict with Ottawa had been an endemic feature of provincial politics and government since Confederation. Offers to outbash the opposition regarding Ottawa were standard fare in provincial elections, particularly highly contested ones. Party identification with government in Ottawa was always extremely dangerous when provincial rights issues were on the table.

In some ways the 1970s were hard on dominant parties in the provinces. Four long-dominant provincial parties went down to defeat: the Liberals in Newfoundland and Quebec, and the Socreds in Alberta and British Columbia. It was never clear whether the coincidence of these defeats was part of a much larger political shift, the product of changing economic circumstances, or mere accident. In any event, political veterans like Joey Smallwood, Ernest Manning, and W.A.C. Bennett were replaced by younger leaders such as Peter Lougheed (b. 1928) in Alberta, Brian Peckford (b. 1942) in Newfoundland, and Bill Bennett (b. 1932) in British Columbia. For the younger men, Dominion–provincial relations were not conditioned by depression, war, or postwar prosperity so much as by provincial self-interest ruthlessly pursued.

FEDERAL–PROVINCIAL RELATIONS

The 1970s

Throughout the 1970s federal–provincial relations were dominated by oil, Quebec, and abortive constitutional reform. In June 1971, at the premiers' conference held in Victoria, the Trudeau administration made another effort to agree on a formula for constitutional repatriation that would satisfy Quebec's aspirations. Three points are worth noting about the 1971 discussions: first, entrenching rights in a charter was regarded as one way to reassure those who feared losing British constitutional protection; second, Quebec did not achieve a sufficiently distinctive place in Confederation to suit its demands; and finally, only Quebec and Ontario were given perpetual vetoes (other provinces could together mount a veto only using complicated cooperative formulas). The question of constitutional reform was not picked up again until 1980, by which time much had changed for both Canada and its provinces. Oil and the whole question of resource management had become subjects of continual tension between some of the provinces (led by Alberta) and the federal government after 1973. Before OPEC pulled the plug, Alberta had often singlehandedly opposed Ottawa over resource management. With non-renewable resources now hot commodities, more provinces recognized the advantages of provincial autonomy. Only PEI, Manitoba, and New Brunswick were left to visualize their provincial self-interest as best served by a strong federal government. By 1980 the rich provinces, usually led by hard-headed businessmen who insisted that they put balance sheets ahead of sentiment, were ready to help dismantle Ottawa's centralized arrangements, especially in the area of social insurance programs.

The Parti Québécois and the Constitution

The occasion for a new round of constitutional discussions was provided by the Parti Québécois, not through its electoral victory of 1976 but through its referendum on sovereignty association of 1980. The PQ victory came as a shock to English-speaking Canada, although it was really quite predictable. The Bourassa government in Quebec had been badly shaken by charges of scandal and corruption on top of its seeming inability to deal expeditiously with either the separatists or Pierre Trudeau. It had lost considerable face when the Canadian Airline Pilots Association went on strike in June 1976, ostensibly over safety but really over bilingualism, an issue that only the federal government could resolve. Rumours of cost overruns and construction disasters in the preparations for the 1976 summer Olympics in Montreal had been rife for years. Bourassa's government was not directly involved in the problems, which were primarily the responsibility of Jean Drapeau's Montreal government, but Drapeau was a Liberal ally and Bourassa had waffled over intervening. The province took over the Olympics construction only at the last minute. There were similar concerns over the control of the James Bay hydro-

René Lévesque on provincial election night, 29 October 1973. Duncan Cameron/NAC, PA-115039.

electric development, but in the summer of 1976 these were not so immediately visible in Montreal as the Olympics fiasco. A resurgent Parti Québécois won over many voters who did not normally support it, as the electorate simultaneously rejected Bourassa's Liberals and embraced Lévesque's party.

Issues are never tidy in any election. No evidence suggested that the PQ, despite its resounding victory, had received any mandate for its well-publicized sovereignty association. The Parti Québécois had insisted that they would not act unilaterally on separation without a provincial referendum. Voters could thus support the reformist social-democratic zeal of the PQ without signing on to its extremist constitutional position. English-speaking Canada, however, responded to the Quebec election by assuming that separatism had triumphed in Quebec. The nation had to be saved at any cost. Had Lévesque sought to renegotiate the constitutional issues in the immediate wake of the victory, he might have been offered some sort of two-nations formula, but the PQ was committed both to internal Quebec reform and to a democratic approach to separation.

In office Lévesque's PQ successfully pursued policies of economic and linguistic nationalism. Its most controversial legislation was Bill 101, which went well beyond an earlier piece of Bourassa legislation (known as Bill 22) in its effort to turn Quebec into a unilingual francophone province. Bill 101 made it necessary for most Quebecers, regardless of their background or preference, to be educated in French-language schools. Only those temporarily resident in Quebec or whose parents had been educated in English-speaking schools in the province were exempted. The bill also insisted that French was the only legal medium in business and government, requiring the elimination of virtually all English-language signs in the province. In 1979 the Quebec government produced a White Paper detailing what it meant by sovereignty association. It wanted 'a free, proud and adult national existence' within the context of a series of joint Quebec–Canada institutions, including a court of justice and a monetary authority (Parti Québécois 1979). A totally independent Quebec, it insisted, would still have access to Canada and its economy. Outside the ranks of the converted, the scheme seemed far too lopsided in Quebec's favour. The proposal was a unilateral Quebec initiative.

As had been promised, there was a referendum, eventually scheduled for 20 May 1980. Referendums are notoriously tricky political instruments. They often encourage No votes. Certainly the non-francophone population of Quebec (less than 20 per cent of the whole), although vehemently opposed to a *Oui* vote, were not by themselves numerous enough to reject sovereignty association, but in the end almost 60 per cent of the province's voters and even a bare majority (52 per cent) of its francophones voted *Non*. This fairly decisive result left 40.5 per cent of the Quebec population, and just under half of its francophones, in favour of sovereignty association. Nevertheless, Quebec had publicly rejected separation from Canada. The nation responded by breathing a collective sigh of relief and calling for a new federalism. Forgotten for the moment was the simple truth that pressure for change of the fundamental sort represented by separatism does not go away because of one set-back at the ballot-box.

The First Round of Constitutional Revisions

Canadians had discussed and debated both national unity and constitutional change since the PQ victory in 1976. More than enough proposals

CHRONOLOGY OF QUEBEC SEPARATISM

March 1963	Front de libération du Québec is founded.
November 1967	René Lévesque resigns from the Quebec Liberal party and begins organizing the Parti Québécois.
25 June 1968	Pierre Trudeau is elected with a large Liberal majority.
7 July 1969	Canada becomes officially bilingual through the Official Languages Act.
October 1970	Kidnapping of James Cross and Pierre Laporte. War Measures Act is invoked.
29 Oct. 1973	PQ wins six seats in the Quebec election and becomes the official opposition.
15 Nov. 1976	PQ wins majority in Quebec election and takes over government.
26 Aug. 1977	Bill 101 makes French the official language of Quebec.
15 April 1980	Sovereignty referendum campaign begins.
14 May 1980	Trudeau promises constitutional reform.
20 May 1980	Sovereignty association is defeated by 60–40 per cent.
2 Oct. 1980	Trudeau announces that the Constitution will be repatriated.
13 April 1981	PQ wins a majority in the Quebec election.
2–5 Nov. 1981	Ottawa and nine anglophone provinces reach a deal on the

	Constitution. Lévesque claims he has been stabbed in the back.
1 July 1982	Queen gives royal consent to a new Constitution.
21 July 1985	René Lévesque retires.
3 October 1985	Pierre-Marc Johnson, new leader of the PQ, becomes Quebec premier.
2 Dec. 1985	Liberals under Bourassa defeat Johnson's PQ and form a new government.
3 June 1987	Meech Lake Accord is negotiated.
1 Nov. 1987	Death of René Lévesque.
17 March 1988	Jacques Parizeau is elected new leader of the PQ.
2 June 1990	Meech Lake Accord fails when Manitoba and Newfoundland fail to ratify within deadline. Quebec says it will not take part in further constitutional deals.
25 June 1990	Seven independent Quebec MPs, led by Lucien Bouchard, form the Bloc Québécois.
28 Jan. 1991	Quebec Liberal Party calls for a decentralized Canada.
27 March 1991	Bélanger–Campeau Commission recommends a referendum on sovereignty by November 1992 if there is no deal with Canada.
24 Sept. 1991	Ottawa proposes recognition of Quebec as a distinct society, Senate reform, Aboriginal self-government, economic union, and adjustments to federal–provincial powers to give provinces more control.
12 March 1992	First formal federal–provincial meeting since the failure of Meech Lake.
7 July 1992	Federal government, nine provincial premiers (all but Quebec's), and Aboriginal leaders agree on a new formula for reform.
4 August 1992	Bourassa meets with other premiers and PM Mulroney.
19–23 Aug. 1992	Charlottetown Accord is negotiated, including Senate reform, Aboriginal self-government, an expanded House of Commons, some new power arrangements, and a provincial veto over future change to federal institutions.
18 Sept. 1992	National referendum campaign on Charlottetown begins.
26 Oct. 1992	Canadian voters reject Charlottetown 54–45 per cent.
25 Oct. 1993	Federal Liberals under Chrétien demolish the Tories and NDP; Bouchard's BQ forms the official opposition in Commons with 55 seats.
11 Jan. 1994	Bourassa resigns and is succeeded by Daniel Johnson.
12 Sept. 1994	PQ elected in Quebec and promises referendum on sovereignty.
12 June 1995	Parizeau, Bouchard, and Action Démocratique (ADQ) leader Mario Dumont form a coalition to fight for *Oui* on referendum.
30 Oct. 1995	Sovereignty rejected by 50.7–49.3 per cent; turnout for the referendum is an astonishing 93.5 per cent of eligible voters.
31 Oct. 1995	Parizeau resigns as PQ leader.
11 Jan. 1996	Lucien Bouchard is chosen PQ leader and Quebec premier.
18 Jan. 1996	Bouchard resigns as BQ leader.
17 Feb. 1996	Michel Gauthier is chosen as head of BQ.
Sept. 1996	Quebec nationalist Guy Bertrand wins right in Quebec Superior Court to seek a court injunction against a new sovereignty referendum.

for reform floated about the country. Many surfaced in the travelling road show (known as the Task Force on National Unity) sent across Canada in 1978. Out of the flurry of activity and the myriad suggestions, several points were clear. One was that many Canadians—including a fair proportion of academics and lawyers, if not historians—were prepared to make relatively major alterations in the British North America Act, the document that served as the nation's Constitution. A second was that the vast majority of anglophone Canadians were prepared to make substantial concessions to keep Quebec within Confederation. A third point, perhaps less well understood by the public, was that the anglophone provinces of Canada—led by the western provinces of Alberta, British Columbia, and Saskatchewan, and strongly supported by Nova Scotia and Newfoundland—had developed their own agenda for constitutional reform. These provinces saw Ottawa's federalism as operating almost exclusively in the interests of central Canada. They were quite prepared to take advantage of Quebec's moves towards greater autonomy, particularly if these pressures reduced Quebec's influence within Confederation and allowed for constitutional change in the best interests of other provinces. What the other provinces wanted most was unrestricted control over their own natural resources and reform of some of Ottawa's governing institutions, notably the Senate and the Supreme Court, to reflect regional interests. The Trudeau government had seemed on the verge of conceding much of the provincial program when it was defeated in 1979. The Clark government had not dealt with the issue when it too failed at the polls.

The opportunity presented to Prime Minister Trudeau by the Quebec referendum, when he called a first ministers' conference for early June 1980, was real, if dangerous. Once the box of constitutional revision was opened, it might never be closed. From the federalist perspective, it was necessary to deal with Quebec's aspirations without conceding too much to the other provinces, none of which was controlled by a Liberal government and all of which had their own visions of change. Ottawa's most consistent ally was Ontario, confirming regional charges that it had been the chief beneficiary of the old federalism. Quebec did not participate in the new discussions, but it could not be churlish about them. Its best strategy was to allow the anglophone provinces to initiate the dismantling of Confederation. Indeed, one of the principal characteristics of this round of constitutional discussion was that Quebec's concerns were not front and centre. General consensus was developed on economic issues, balancing provincial resource control against federal economic planning. But other questions remained difficult to resolve. Ottawa wanted to entrench a Charter of Rights in any new constitutional document, chiefly to guarantee francophone linguistic rights across the nation, but the majority of the provinces (including Quebec) objected to such a Charter as threatening their own rights. The provinces, for their part, wanted an amending formula that would allow all provinces the right of veto and the right to opt out of any amendments that they regarded as threatening their powers. This round of discussions broke down in September 1980. As Prime Minister Trudeau had been threatening for months, Ottawa prepared to take unilateral action.

Politically the federal constitutional package developed in Ottawa was carefully calculated. As an ardent federalist, a trained constitutional lawyer, and an exponent of realpolitik, Pierre Trudeau was clearly in his element. The new proposal called for the elimination of recourse to the British Parliament for amendment of the British North America Act ('repatriation'). It also contained a Charter of Rights, which by establishing the rights of other collective minorities was intended to prevent the French Canadians from being treated as an exceptional case. The package also provided for a new method of amendment— through national referendum initiated in Ottawa—to be used in the event of provincial obstructionism. The Trudeau government was prepared to pass the package through the federal Parliament and send it to Britain for approval without recourse to either the Supreme Court of Canada or the provinces, although it clearly infringed on the informal 'right' of the provinces to consent to constitutional change. Not surprisingly, the federal NDP supported this position, leaving the Progressive Conservative minority in Parliament to oppose it and voice the objections of nearly all the provinces except (again not surprisingly) Ontario.

Parliamentary amendments eliminated some of the least saleable features of the original proposal and introduced some new wrinkles, including the specific affirmation of 'aboriginal and treaty rights of the aboriginal peoples of Canada' (McWhinney 1982: 176). The Liberal

CANADIAN CHARTER OF RIGHTS AND FREEDOMS

RIGHTS AND FREEDOMS IN CANADA.

1. The Canadian Charter of Rights and Freedoms guarantees the rights and freedoms set out in it subject only to such reasonable limits prescribed by law as can be demonstrably justified in a free and democratic society.

FUNDAMENTAL FREEDOMS.

2. Everyone has the following fundamental freedoms:

(a) freedom of conscience and religion;
(b) freedom of thought, belief, opinion and expression, including freedom of the press and other media of communication;
(c) freedom of peaceful assembly; and
(d) freedom of association.

DEMOCRATIC RIGHTS OF CITIZENS.

3. Every citizen of Canada has the right to vote in an election of members of the House of Commons or of a legislative assembly and to be qualified for membership therein.

MAXIMUM DURATION OF LEGISLATIVE BODIES / CONTINUATION IN SPECIAL CIRCUMSTANCES.

4. (1) No House of Commons and no legislative assembly shall continue for longer than five years from the date fixed for the return of the writs at a general election of its members.

(2) In time of real or apprehended war, invasion or insurrection, a House of Commons may be continued by Parliament and a legislative assembly may be continued by the legislature beyond five years if such continuation is not opposed by the votes of more than one-third of the members of the House of Commons or the legislative assembly, as the case may be.

ANNUAL SITTING OF LEGISLATIVE BODIES.

5. There shall be a sitting of Parliament and of each legislature at least once every twelve months.

MOBILITY RIGHTS OF CITIZENS / RIGHT TO MOVE AND GAIN LIVELIHOOD / LIMITATION / AFFIRMATIVE ACTION PROGRAMS.

6. (1) Every citizen of Canada has the right to enter, remain in and leave Canada.

(2) Every citizen of Canada and every person who has the status of a permanent resident of Canada has the right

(a) to move to and take up residence in any province; and
(b) to pursue the gaining of a livelihood in any province.

(3) The rights specified in subsection (2) are subject to
(a) any laws or practices of general application in force in a province other than those that discriminate among persons primarily on the basis of province of present or previous residence; and
(b) any laws providing for reasonable residency requirements as a qualification for the receipt of publicly provided social services.

(4) Subsections (2) and (3) do not preclude any law, program or activity that has as its object the amelioration in a province of conditions of individuals in that province who were socially or economically disadvantaged if the rate of employment in that province is below the rate of employment in Canada. . . .

LIFE, LIBERTY AND SECURITY OF PERSON.

7. Everyone has the right to life, liberty and security of the person and the right not to be deprived thereof except in accordance with the principles of fundamental justice.

. . .

TREATMENT OR PUNISHMENT.

12. Everyone has the right not to be subjected to any cruel and unusual treatment or punishment.

SELF-INCRIMINATION.

13. A witness who testifies in any proceedings has the right not to have any incriminating evidence so given used to incriminate that witness in any other proceedings, except in a prosecution for perjury or for the giving of contradictory evidence.

INTERPRETER.

14. A party or witness in any proceedings who does not understand or speak the language in which the proceedings are conducted or who is deaf has the right to the assistance of an interpreter.

EQUALITY BEFORE AND UNDER LAW AND EQUAL PROTECTION AND BENEFIT OF LAW / AFFIRMATIVE ACTION PROGRAMS.

15. (1) Every individual is equal before and under the law and has the right to the equal protection and equal benefit of the law without discrimination and, in particular, without discrimination based on race, national or ethnic origin, colour, religion, sex, age or mental or physical disability.

(2) Subsection (1) does not preclude any law, program or activity that has as its object the amelioration of conditions of disadvantaged individuals or groups including those that are disadvantaged because of race, national or ethnic origin, colour, religion, sex, age or mental or physical disability.

OFFICIAL LANGUAGES OF CANADA / OFFICIAL LANGUAGES OF NEW BRUNSWICK / ADVANCEMENT OF STATUS AND USE.

16. (1) English and French are the official languages of Canada and have equality of status and equal rights and privileges as to their use in all institutions of the Parliament and government of Canada.

(2) English and French are the official languages of New Brunswick and have equality of status and equal rights and privileges as to their use in all institutions of the legislature and government of New Brunswick.

(3) Nothing in this Charter limits the authority of Parliament or a legislature to advance the equality of status or use of English and French. . . .

SOURCE: The Queen's Printer, 1982.

government had neatly set against each other two sets of rights, one the human rights protected in the entrenched Charter and the other the provincial rights ignored in both the amending process and the Charter itself. Eight of the provinces (excluding Ontario and New Brunswick), often unsympathetically referred to in the media as 'the Gang of Eight', organized as the leading opponents of unilateral repatriation, although Quebec and the English-speaking premiers had quite different views on positive reform.

The first major hurdle for the federal initiative was the Supreme Court of Canada, to which constitutional opinions from several provincial courts had gone on appeal. If the federal government won support from the Supreme Court, it would render untenable the provincial claim that the package was unconstitutional. While the Supreme Court deliberated, René Lévesque and the PQ won a resounding electoral victory in Quebec. The win did not, of course, resolve the deep contradiction that the PQ represented as a separatist party committed to non-separatist action, but it did reactivate Quebec on constitutional matters. Although the British government had refused to deal officially with the provincial premiers (much as it had in 1867 when Nova Scotia sent Joe Howe to London), Canada's Native peoples set up their own lobbying office in London. They had some claim to direct treaty connections with the British Crown, and a decent legal case. The Supreme Court of Canada handed down its ruling on 28 September 1981. Many Canadians had trouble comprehending both the process and the decision, since neither the constitutional nor the political role of the Canadian court was as well understood as that of its American equivalent.

As one constitutional expert commented, the decision was in legal terms 'complex and baffling and technically unsatisfactory' (McWhinney 1982: 80). In political terms, such complexity was doubtless exactly what the Supreme Court intended. Essentially, by a decision of seven to two, it declared the federal patriation process legal, since custom could not be enforced in courts. It then opined, by a decision of six to three, that federal patriation was unconventional. Since most of the legal arguments against the process revolved around violations of constitutional 'convention' (or custom), these two opinions were mutually contradictory, although in law Ottawa had won. What the politicians could make of a result that said, in effect, that the federal package of repatriation was strictly speaking legal but at the same time improper was another matter.

In the end the nine English-speaking premiers, including seven of the original Gang of Eight, worked out a deal with Prime Minister Trudeau on 5 November 1981. Trudeau made substantial concessions—for example, abandoning the provision for a referendum. Ontario joined Quebec in agreeing to drop its right of veto in favour of a complex formula that ensured that either one or the other (but not both) would have to agree to any amendment. This represented less of a loss for Ottawa than for the central provinces, especially Quebec. At the same time, provinces that had refused to concur with constitutional change had the right to remain outside its provisions until they chose to opt in, a considerable move from Trudeau's earlier positions. Trudeau's greatest concessions were in the Charter of Rights, particularly the so-called 'notwithstanding' clause, which allowed any province to opt out of clauses in the Charter covering fundamental freedoms and legal and equality rights, although not other categories of rights, including language rights. There was disagreement over the intention of the negotiations regarding Native peoples, resulting in a temporary omission of the clause guaranteeing Aboriginal treaty rights, which subsequently had to be restored by Parliament. As for a definition of those rights themselves, there was to be a constitutional conference to identify them.

The final compromise satisfied the nine anglophone premiers. It certainly strengthened in theory the rights of the provinces to opt out of the Charter on critical issues, including both

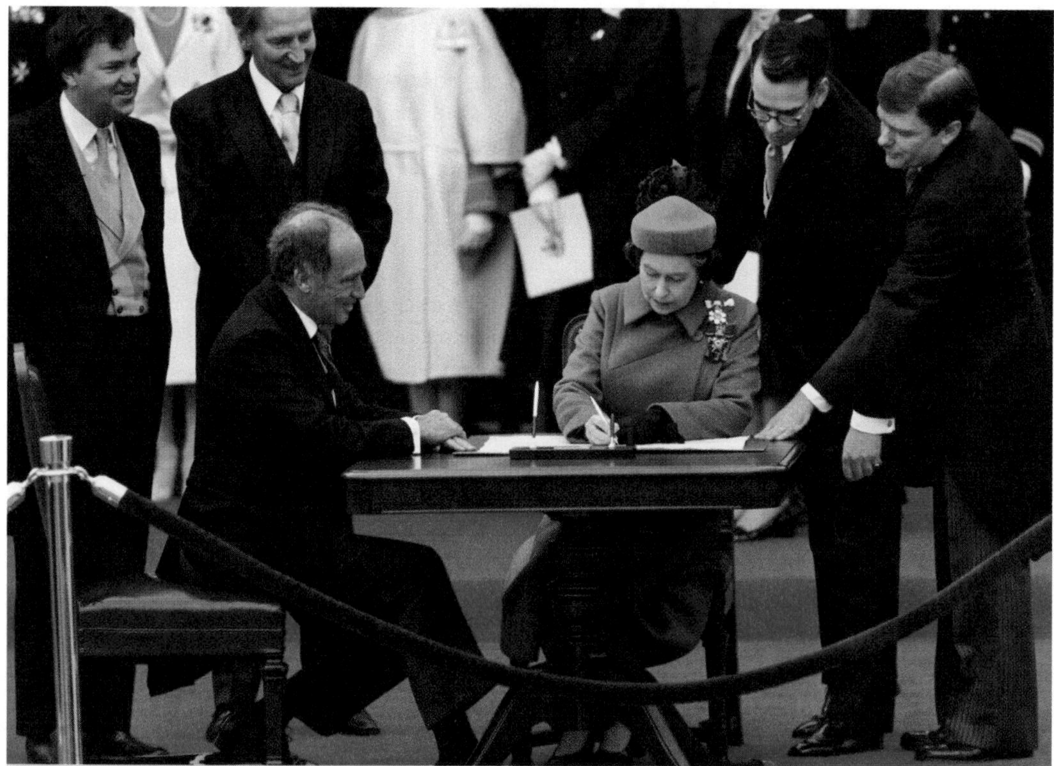

Prime Minister Trudeau looks on as Queen Elizabeth II signs Canada's constitutional proclamation in Ottawa, 17 April 1982. CP/Ron Poling.

Native rights and women's rights, through use of the 'notwithstanding' clause. Perhaps understandably, both Native groups and women's groups vowed to fight on in opposition to the package as revised. As for Quebec, all it had lost was some of its self-perceived distinctive status in Confederation. That loss would prove fairly crucial, however, for Quebec would consistently refuse to accept the constitutional reforms on the grounds that one of Canada's two 'national wills' had not been consulted. That position would lead to another attempt at provincial unanimity at Meech Lake in 1987.

The revised constitutional package passed the Canadian Parliament in December 1981 and the British Parliament early in 1982. The latter had resolutely refused to become involved in the various protests against the new agreement, thus surrendering its role as court of last resort against unconstitutional actions within Canada. Canadians did not at the time fully appreciate what had happened constitutionally, or what the changes would mean. The principle of patriation had been purchased at considerable expense by the Trudeau government. The Charter of Rights did reflect the principle that collective and individual rights transcending the current British North America Act (and its conception of relevant players) had to be carefully guarded. But in place of the earlier British constitutional position that the legislature (federal and provincial) was the source of protection, the Charter established the American constitutional notion that the court system would enforce fundamental rights over the legislature and the government responsible to it. In place of the earlier concept that Parliament was supreme, it introduced a whole new series of formal checks and balances limiting parliamentary supremacy.

A good example of the Charter principles in action would come in 1988, when Prime Miniser Brian Mulroney signed a Redress Agreement between the National Association of Japanese Canadians and the Canadian government regarding the handling of Japanese Canadians during and after the Second World War. In letters to 20,000 Japanese Canadians in 1990, the prime minister acknowledged that the wartime treatment 'was unjust and violated principles of human rights as they are understood today'.(This subject is discussed in more detail on p. 493.)

The new Constitution not only gave new powers to the provinces, it also recognized new and rather amorphous political collectivities in the Charter of Rights, which was somewhat less concerned than the American Bill of Rights with defining the rights of individuals and somewhat more concerned with delineating collective rights. Thus, in addition to providing equality before the law for individuals facing discrimination 'based on race, national or ethnic origin, colour, religion, sex, age or mental or physical disability' (section 15.1), the Charter also specifically permitted in section 15.2 'any law, program, or activity that has as its object the amelioration of conditions of disadvantaged individuals or groups', including (but not limited to) those disadvantaged by discrimination as in section 15.1. Moreover, Aboriginal and treaty rights of the Aboriginal peoples, although deliberately not defined, were entrenched, as were sexual equality and multiculturalism. Although at first glance these Charter provisions seemed to represent the ultimate triumph of liberalism, in several respects they did not. In the first place, the liberal Charter provisions were balanced by the increased power given to the provinces to control their own resources and to call their own shots about the applicability of the Charter and any constitutional amendments. In the second place, the constitutional introduction of a whole series of new collectivities created further complications for an already overloaded political process. In the end this would help stifle the liberal impulse itself. Finally, the well-publicized antics of the politicians over the Constitution contributed to a further reduction in the esteem with which those politicians were held by an increasingly cynical Canadian public.

Constitutional Revision: Rounds Two and Three

The 1982 Charter, with its explicit and implicit recognition of both collective and individual rights, was hardly the last word on the subject. A body of case-law would have to be developed by the courts, especially the Supreme Court of Canada, which became the ultimate arbiter charged with interpreting the vague terminology of the document. Governments offered no clarification. The Charter simply became a wild card exercised by the Supreme Court of Canada on behalf of Canadians, arguably more amenable to change than the parliamentary system.

In 1987 the Mulroney government fastened on one of the loose ends of the 1982 constitutional process, Quebec's refusal to accept the 1982 Constitution. By this time René Lévesque had retired (in June 1985) and the PQ had been defeated in December 1985 by the Liberals under a rehabilitated Robert Bourassa. Once again in power, Bourassa offered to compromise. Mulroney summoned a new 'Gang of Ten' to a closed-door session on 30 April 1987 at Meech Lake, where a revised constitutional arrangement acceptable to Quebec was worked out. While Quebec was to be constitutionally recognized as a 'distinct society' and given further concessions, including a veto over most amendments to the Constitution, there were also inducements to the other provinces, which would also enjoy some gains in autonomy. The federal government would compensate all provinces for programs they refused to join. Each province was given a veto over further amendments. There was to be

NDP MLA Elijah Harper sits in the Manitoba legislature holding an eagle feather for spiritual strength as he continues to delay debate on the Meech Lake Accord, 19 June 1990. CP/Wayne Glowacki.

regular discussion of Senate reform, although no particular formula was agreed upon. Nevertheless, there was a consensus among participants that the federal Parliament, and the legislatures of all ten provinces, would have to approve the agreement by early June 1990, the lengthy time frame allowed for public hearings and feedback, or the arrangement was dead.

The three years permitted between the Meech Lake meeting and the deadline for approval created many difficulties. While the Mulroney government understandably insisted that no changes could be made in the agreement until it had been formally approved, not every provincial government felt bound by the particular terms accepted by whoever happened to be premier in April 1987. The subsequent public debate made clear that not all Canadians agreed with what was perceived as a further dismantling of central authority in favour not merely of Quebec but of all the provinces. The poorer have-not provinces—led by Manitoba, New Brunswick, and eventually Newfoundland—were concerned that few new federal programs would be mounted if the richer provinces had the option of receiving federal funds for their own programs. Other collectivities, such as Aboriginal peoples and women, worried that their rights were being bartered away to the provinces. Across the country, suggested revisions sprung up almost like grass, many of them offering structural panaceas, such as a reformed and more effective Senate.

As the deadline for acceptance loomed, only Manitoba and Newfoundland held out, the latter having rescinded an earlier legislative endorsement after Brian Peckford's Tories were defeated by the Liberals under Clyde Wells (b. 1937). Prime Minister Mulroney, drawing on his experience as a private-sector negotiator, called the premiers into closed-door sessions designed to shame them into support on the eve of the deadline. This tactic appeared to work, but in Manitoba, Cree leader and NDP MLA Elijah Harper (b. 1949) objected to the Accord on the grounds that it neglected Aboriginal people. Harper delayed debate on the Accord, preventing the legislature from voting to ratify it before the deadline. Since Manitoba was not going to approve, Newfoundland's Wells backed off from a previous commitment to gain his province's legislative endorsement. In the end, the two provinces refused endorsement and Meech Lake failed. Ominously, in the last days before the deadline, several Conservative MPs from Quebec, led by Minister of the Environment Lucien Bouchard (b. 1938), left the government to form a pro-separatist Bloc Québécois.

In the post-mortems on Meech Lake, a number of points stood out. One was that after 1987 the popular support for Brian Mulroney (and the

1987 CONSTITUTIONAL ACCORD (THE MEECH LAKE ACCORD)

June 3, 1987

WHEREAS first ministers, assembled in Ottawa, have arrived at a unanimous accord on constitutional amendments that would bring about the full and active participation of Quebec in Canada's constitutional evolution, would recognize the principle of equality of all provinces, would provide new arrangements to foster greater harmony and cooperation between the Government of Canada and the governments of the provinces and would require that annual constitutional conferences composed of first ministers be convened not later than December 31, 1988; AND WHEREAS first ministers have also reached unanimous agreement on certain additional commitments in relation to some of those amendments; NOW THEREFORE the Prime Minister of Canada and the first ministers of the provinces commit themselves and the governments they represent to the following:

1. The Prime Minister of Canada will lay or cause to be laid before the Senate and House of Commons, and the first ministers of the provinces will lay or cause to be laid before the legislative assemblies, as soon as possible, a resolution, in the form appended hereto, to authorize a proclamation to be issued by the Governor General under the Great Seal of Canada to amend the Constitution of Canada.

2. The Government of Canada will, as soon as possible, conclude an agreement with the Government of Quebec that would

(a) incorporate the principles of the Cullen–Couture agreement on the selection abroad and in Canada of independent immigrants, visitors for medical treatment, students and temporary workers, and on the selection of refugees abroad and economic criteria for family reunification and assisted relatives,

(b) guarantee that Quebec will receive a number of immigrants, including refugees, within the annual total established by the federal government for all of Canada proportionate to its share of the population of Canada, with the right to exceed that figure by per cent for demographic reasons, and

(c) provide an undertaking by Canada to withdraw services (except citizenship services) for the reception and integration (including linguistic and cultural) of all foreign nationals wishing to settle in Quebec where services are to be provided by Quebec, with such withdrawal to be accompanied by reasonable compensation, and the Government of Canada and the Government of Quebec will take the necessary steps to give the agreement the force of law under the proposed amendment relating to such agreements.

3. Nothing in the Accord should be construed as preventing the negotiation of similar agreements with other provinces relating to immigration and the temporary admission of aliens.

4. Until the proposed amendment relating to the appointments to the Senate comes into force, any person summoned to fill a vacancy in the Senate shall be chosen from among persons whose names have been submitted by the Government of the province to which the vacancy relates and must be acceptable to the Queen's Privy Council for Canada.

Motion for a Resolution to Authorize an Amendment to the Constitution of Canada

WHEREAS the Constitution Act, 1982 came into force on April 17, 1982, following an agreement between Canada and the provinces except Quebec; AND WHEREAS the Government of Quebec has established a set of five proposals for constitutional change and has stated that amendments to give effect to those proposals would enable Quebec to resume a full role in the constitutional councils of Canada; AND WHEREAS the amendment proposed in the schedule hereto sets out the basis on which Quebec's five constitutional proposals may be met; AND WHEREAS the amendment proposed in the schedule hereto also recognizes the principles of equality of all the provinces, provides new arrangements to foster greater harmony and co-operation between the Government of Canada and the governments of the provinces and requires that conferences be convened to consider important constitutional, economic and other issues; AND WHEREAS certain portions of the amendment proposed in the schedule hereto relate to matters referred to in section 41 of the Constitution Act, 1982; AND WHEREAS section 41 of the Constitution Act, 1982 provides that an amendment to the Constitution of Canada may be made by proclamation issued by the Governor General under the Great Seal of Canada where so authorized by resolutions of the Senate and the House of Commons and of the legislative assembly of each province; NOW THEREFORE the (Senate) (House of Commons) (legislative assembly) resolves that an amendment to the Constitution of Canada be authorized to be made by proclamation issued by Her Excellency the Governor General under the Great Seal of Canada in accordance with the schedule hereto.

SCHEDULE

CONSTITUTIONAL AMENDMENT, 1987

Constitution Act, 1867

1. The Constitution Act, 1867 is amended by adding thereto, immediately after section 1 thereof, the following section:

2. (1) The Constitution of Canada shall be interpreted in a manner consistent with

(a) the recognition that the existence of French-speaking Canadians, centred in Quebec but also present elsewhere in Canada, and English-speaking Canadians, concentrated outside Quebec but also present in Quebec, constitutes a fundamental characteristic of Canada; and

(b) the recognition that Quebec constitutes within Canada a distinct society.

(2) The role of the Parliament of Canada and the provincial legislatures to preserve the fundamental characteristic of Canada referred to in paragraph (1) (a) is affirmed.

(3) The role of the legislature and Government of Quebec to preserve and promote the distinct identity of Quebec referred to in paragraph (1)(b) is affirmed.

(4) Nothing in this section derogates from the powers, rights or privileges of Parliament or the Government of Canada, or of the legislatures or governments of the provinces, including any powers, rights or privileges relating to language. . . .

federal PCs) and Meech Lake had declined together. Quebec understandably interpreted the mounting hostility to Meech Lake in English-speaking Canada as directed specifically against the 'distinct society', but the fact was that most Canadians appeared to be prepared to allow Quebec its autonomy. What people objected to was the extension of that autonomy to the other provinces, a process that would balkanize the nation. Moreover, Elijah Harper's action called attention to Meech Lake's incompatibility with the collective rights recognized by the Canadian Charter. During the summer of 1990 the failure of Meech Lake was followed by an extremely nasty confrontation between Aboriginal peoples in Quebec, led by the Mohawks of Oka, and the Bourassa government. Bourassa called in the federal armed forces, as he had done in the October Crisis of 1970.

The crushing defeat in early September 1990 of one of the main supporters of Meech Lake, Premier David Peterson of Ontario, by the NDP led by Bob Rae (b. 1948) was perhaps another straw in the wind. Certainly the NDP's achievement of power (for the first time) in Ontario suggested that there might be a resurgence of the left. The NDP's victory proved illusory, based chiefly on hostility to Peterson's government. Subsequent 1991 NDP victories in British Columbia and Saskatchewan only demonstrated the electorate's discontent and the NDP's inability to establish a new political paradigm.

The federal government spent most of 1991 attempting to figure out how to allow for 'democratic input' into the process of constitutional revision. The Mulroney administration was far too unpopular simply to force through legislation. Public hearings were followed by weekend conferences, none of which provided much direction. Canada had no tradition of consultative reform. In the end, another series of closed-door meetings between Ottawa and the anglophone provinces, subsequently joined by Quebec in August 1992 at Charlottetown, produced a revised package. This one offered Quebec a distinct society, the provinces a veto, the Aboriginal peoples self-government, and the country reform of both the Supreme Court and the Senate. The nation voted on the package in a referendum on 26 October 1992, the day after the Toronto Blue Jays won the World Series. (The World Series was named after the New York newspaper the *World* and had no international implications.) To the simultaneous amusement and consternation of Canadians, in the opening ceremonies, the United States Marine Corps had inadvertently carried the Canadian flag upside down. The eventual victory sparked an outpouring of Canadian nationalism across the country.

Table 11.1
Results by Province of the 26 October 1992 Referendum on the Charlottetown Accord

Province	Percentage Yes	Percentage No
Newfoundland	62.9	36.5
Nova Scotia	48.5	51.1
Prince Edward Island	73.6	25.9
New Brunswick	61.3	38.0
Quebec	42.4	55.4
Ontario	49.8	49.6
Manitoba	37.9	61.7
Saskatchewan	45.5	55.1
Alberta	39.6	60.2
British Columbia	31.9	67.8
Northwest Territories	60.2	39.0
Yukon	43.4	56.1
National	44.8	54.2

Some commentators openly feared for a country that could find togetherness only by celebrating the success of a collection of highly paid foreign athletes. How the win factored into the referendum is not known.

Six provinces (including Quebec) voted No. The national totals were 44.8 per cent in favour of the agreement and 54.2 against. Polls indicated that Charlottetown failed because the majority of Canadians regarded the agreement as a bad one. Poorer provinces favoured Charlottetown, while poorer, younger, and less well-educated Canadians opposed it. According to one poll, household income of $60,000 per year was the economic cut-off between Yes and No, while a university degree was the educational one. Most of those who voted

No believed that their vote would have no negative consequences for the nation. Perhaps.

THE ECONOMY

One of the many reasons for the failure of Keynesian economics was that after 1972 the system no longer worked according to its rules. Government management, even wage and price controls, could not prevent runaway inflation, high interest rates, high levels of unemployment, and substantial poverty. With the manufacturing economies of the industrialized world fully recovered and new competition from the industrializing world emerging daily, Canadian manufacturing was in serious structural trouble. So too were the farmer and the fisherman. Symptomatically, the government's complex attempt, after 1973, to create a new national energy policy—based on a federally owned petroleum company to be called Petro-Canada—created only controversy.

As usual, Canadians had trouble understanding the intersection of international and domestic economic problems. They sought a reassuring way of comprehending their difficulties, for the notion that the country was internationally uncompetitive could not be seriously entertained. There were several potential scapegoats at hand. The bankers could have been blamed for the interest rates, or the businessmen for the unemployment. Instead, the country chose to fasten on the most visible and immediate of the trinity of troublesome indicators—inflation—and on a single factor to explain it. Polls taken in 1975 indicated that Canadians were willing to believe that the chief culprits on the inflation front were too-powerful labour unions demanding unreasonable wage settlements. Labour unions were understandably attempting to protect their members in the context of the new economic situation. They wanted wage increases to keep pace with inflation, and opposed management efforts to rationalize or modernize their workforces through lay-offs or redundancies. Strikes in many industries, including a much-publicized postal strike in the summer of 1975, made the demands of labour appear unreasonable. When policemen, firemen, nurses, and teachers began taking similar steps, Canadians became alarmed. Not only were key public services threatened with interruption, but wage settlements in the public sector would have to be financed either with higher taxes or with deficit spending.

Although the extent of government deficits would not become a major public issue until later, by the early 1970s all levels of Canadian government were well into deficit financing. High interest rates made the government debt much more expensive to service. The economic problems of the period set into motion a series of automatic mechanisms, built into the social services safety net, that greatly increased public expenditures. Even without those economic problems, spending on social services constantly escalated according to some mysterious law of increased demand and expectation. The propensity to expand the civil service had its own logic. A variety of conservative economists now appeared to criticize the government's spending principles. Like the public, Pierre Trudeau's federal Liberals talked about the need for structural reform of the economy, but they were unable to confront the problems before the dangers posed by the PQ victory led to a renewed concern with the Constitution. Like all other governments around the world, Ottawa continued to spend more than it collected in taxes and revenue. In 1970 the per-capita debt figure of the Canadian government was $795. By 1990 it was $14,317. Between 1981 and 1990, the total debt of the federal government soared from $100 billion to $380 billion. The last budget surplus had been in fiscal 1972–3.

Not surprisingly, the deficit was used as a weapon by conservatives opposed to the continued expansion of social assistance. These critics—headed by spokesmen for the business community—insisted that increases in social assistance programs were largely responsible for the problem, and they maintained that a balanced budget

TABLE 11.2
FEDERAL GOVERNMENT DEBT (MILLION DOLLARS)

Dates	Net Federal Debt	Gross Federal Debt	*Components of the Gross Debt* Marketable Bonds	Treasury Bills	Savings Bonds	Other Securities	Pension Plans	Other Liabilities
1866-7	76	93	69	–	–	–	–	24
1917-18	1,192	1,863	1,428	75	–	–	5	355
1949-50	11,645	16,723	12,882	450	891	850	175	1,475
1974-5	23,958	55,289	14,490	5,360	12,915	51	12,378	9,825
1983-4	162,250	210,841	58,994	41,700	38,204	3,228	37,988	30,727
1990-1	385,047	443,278	147,104	139,150	34,444	4,514	74,807	43,259

SOURCE: *Canada Year Book 1994* (Ottawa: Statistics Canada, 1994): 304.

could be achieved only by making deep cuts in such programs. In reality, the deficit was caused mainly by the same people who worried most about it. Concern about deficits was accompanied by fear of runaway inflation, and the war against inflation was waged chiefly by the Bank of Canada, through its control of interest rates. High interest rates created substantial unemployment, which in turn meant reductions in income tax revenues and increased expenditures on unemployment insurance and welfare. According to one economist, almost two-thirds of the 1992 deficit was caused by lost tax revenues from unemployment and increased costs of social assistance; the remainder was the result of high interest payments to creditors. A team of economists at the University of Toronto examined the reasons for the 1989–92 recession in Canada. They concluded that the chief factor was the Bank of Canada's consistent anti-inflationary/high interest policies. Many Canadians remained convinced, however, that dismantling the welfare state was the only way to deal with huge budgetary deficits. At the same time, most public opinion polls indicated that the vast majority of the electorate were not eager to surrender their social benefits.

Like the government, the Canadian consumer lived increasingly in Tomorrowland. Canadian consumer debt more than doubled in the 1980s, increasing in small but steady stages from 18.7 per cent of personal income to over 20 per cent. Much of that debt was incurred through the medium of plastic credit cards. In the last year of the decade alone, the number of bank credit-card transactions increased from just over 100 billion to 150 billion. Residential mortage debt nearly tripled. Over ten years Canadian personal consumer debt (including mortgages) increased from 54.1 per cent of disposable personal income to 71.7 per cent, despite heavier taxes and truly debilitating interest rates. One popular automobile bumper sticker proclaimed, 'We're spending our children's inheritance.'

Despite its talk of privatization, such as selling the assets of the Canada Development Investment Corporation, the Mulroney government backed away from an open confrontation with the welfare system. Instead, it took back benefits (such as the mothers' allowance) from those with higher incomes and concentrated on increasing revenue through improving economic prosperity. The main vehicle for this increased prosperity was to be a new economic relationship with Canada's largest trading partner, the United States. The eventual Free Trade Agreement, characteristically negotiated in secret during 1986 and 1987, ran to 3,000 pages of legal technicalities. Tariffs would gradually be removed, leaving Canadians astonished to discover that tariffs were not much responsible for the disparity between what goods cost in American and Canadian stores. Canadians were equally surprised to find that 'free trade' did *not* apply to ordinary people shopping in the United States and returning to Canada with their purchases. The national debate over the deal generated little useful information. Not even the economic experts could safely predict the ultimate effects of the treaty, although most favoured it in principle. Some critics complained that the Canadian negotiators had gained less-than-useful access to the American market in return for continental economic integration. This was a futile argument, since most of that integration had already occurred. Only a fraction of total Canadian–American trade was actually affected by the treaty.

The most telling criticism was that the Free Trade Agreement did *not* revolutionize Canadian–American economic relations. Instead, the FTA was merely a cosmetic overhaul of the existing continental arrangement. Including the Mexicans in the North American Free Trade Agreement in the early 1990s was potentially more significant, but many observers could see few advantages to Canada in an economic partnership with a nation possessing a lower standard of living and cheaper labour.

After 1975 the Canadian economy more or less settled down to rates of unemployment, inflation, interest charges, housing costs, and taxation that would have previously been regarded as disastrous. Only food costs remained unaffected, which was not good news for the farmer. Indeed, agriculture re-emerged as a major economic problem for the nation. Despite quotas and marketing boards, the Canadian farmer continued to produce more than the market could consume, especially when that market was also being supplied by American farmers. No Canadian doubted that farmers were part of the backbone of Canadian society, but it was also obvious that farmers were leaving their farms in droves, both because they could not make a decent living and because of the continued attractions of the city's amenities. The government preferred financial assistance for farmers to higher food prices. The problem was that not all farmers would be supported. In 1986 Agriculture Canada admitted that its solution to the 'farm problem' was to encourage thousands of marginal farmers—perhaps up to 20 per cent of the total—to leave the business. To state openly that there were too many farmers was to play with political dynamite. That the government did so was a graphic illustration of how much the nation had changed since Confederation, which had been conceived in part to allow Canada to open a new agricultural frontier.

Although the opposition in Parliament wanted to know how the 'one-in-five' farmer would be chosen for elimination, there was no mystery about who was most at risk: younger entrant farmers, any farmer heavily in debt, and any 'inefficient' farmer. These categories were often mutually reinforcing. Young farmers often had to buy their land at inflated prices. To be efficient they needed to borrow money at high rates of interest in order to buy expensive equipment and machinery. When farm commodity prices turned downward, many farmers were in serious trouble, although it must be added that the costs of modern farming increasingly made it an uneconomic proposition for most farmers. The solution—significantly higher prices for farm crops—was simply not popular. Canadians were willing to pay increasing sums for more convenient packaging and marketing of the food they ate but were not prepared to put more money into the pocket of the farmer.

There were economic slow-downs in the early 1980s and early 1990s. From the standpoint of its conservative intentions, the welfare state worked. In both slow-downs the social protection apparatus clicked in, and while more families fell below the poverty line, there were few demonstrations in the streets. Canadians became conscious that jobs were harder to get and harder to keep. The young responded to the lack of jobs by seeking further education in courses that promised some immediate economic pay-off, but they did not become radicalized. Perhaps they were too busy working to keep up the payments on their credit cards.

CANADIAN SOCIETY

A number of social trends characterized Canadian society in the 1970s and 1980s. One was a constant increase in the traditional indicators of 'instability'—divorce, suicide, rape, crime, and sexually transmitted diseases. Canada seemed to be coming apart socially as well as constitutionally and economically. Another trend was an increase in abuse (often violent) of others and extreme self-indulgence, both products of alienation. These trends were also linked to the power of the media, which on the one hand publicized what had long been occurring beneath the surface, and on the other hand produced new consumer fads, fashions, and even needs. A third trend involved the baby-boom generation, which was coming up to early retirement in the 1990s, at which point they would aggravate a fourth trend, the increasingly rapid growth in numbers

THE GREAT CANADIAN BRAIN ROBBERY

In 1984 Canadian historians (and university professors) David Bercuson, Robert Bothwell, and Jack Granatstein published a controversial critique of contemporary higher education in Canada entitled *The Great Brain Robbery*. The following is an excerpt from that work.

Students still fail at Canadian universities, but not as much as they used to, and they get A and B grades far more frequently than they did in the past. We not only let more students into university who are not truly qualified, we let more of them pass and give a larger number of them better grades. A student who graduates with a B average today would likely have received a C+ twenty years ago. (Teachers, amusingly enough, point to this phenomenon to prove that the new grading system turns out better students.) Professors and university administrators love to point self-righteously to the grade inflation that has undermined the value of a high school education, but they are themselves guilty of causing or acquiescing in a grade inflation in the universities that is steadily eroding the real value of a university degree.

Once upon a time, there was the bell curve. It was a guide to the distribution of grades at universities and was based on the axiom that few of us are outstanding, few of us are very poor, and the great bulk of us lie somewhere in between. If a bell curve is applied to the performance of students in a given class, a small number of students at the very top will be awarded A grades and a small (but somewhat larger) number at the bottom of the class will fail. The majority will earn a grade slightly better than C. It was and is a patently unfair system of grading because students who deserve high grades on the basis of their actual performance in a class may not receive those grades if there are too many excellent students in one class, and students who should be failed may not be failed if there are too many poor students. In its heyday it was applied rigorously in some classes (usually science courses where a large number of multiple choice exams were and are used) and totally ignored in others. Even though it is an unfair system, however, it serves as a constant reminder to the professor that all students are not as excellent as others, and it forces professors to protect the value of higher grades. Students who constantly receive A grades under a bell curve system are truly and without question the best of their class. The bell curve ensured that grading standards remained the same from year to year; if a professor was unduly harsh in grading in one year and very generous in the next, the same percentage of A grades would emerge from the class.

The bell curve is gone (good riddance!) but nothing has replaced it. From year to year average grades awarded at Canadian universities creep higher and higher. Figures to prove this are almost impossible to obtain from universities—they are aware that grade inflation is a serious matter and do not want to draw attention to it—but statistics are available from the University of Calgary and the University of Alberta, and these are disturbing indeed. At the University of Calgary grades awarded across the university in 1982 were more than 9 per cent higher in 1982 than in 1970! At the University of Alberta there has been almost no grade inflation across the university as a whole since 1970—the average grade there was a generous *B or better even then*—but there has been significant inflation in faculties such as Business and especially in upper-level courses. At both universities it is clear that some faculties and disciplines are now awarding high grades far more frequently than they did a decade and a half ago.

SOURCE: David J. Bercuson, Robert Bothwell, and J.L. Granatstein, *The Great Brain Robbery: Canada's Universities on the Road to Ruin* (Toronto: McClelland and Stuart, 1984), 77–9.

of elderly Canadians. A final development of the era was the increased visibility of racial minorities, resulting in new social problems.

In 1974 a study found that suicide had become Canada's fifth-ranked cause of 'early death' (i.e., death between the ages of one and seventy). Suicide rates continued to rise, and were especially serious among young males in general and young Aboriginal males in particular, reaching epidemic proportions in some communities. A 1984 National Task Force on Suicide in Canada indicated that the causes were 'complex and multifactorial', adding that 'inter-provincial studies appear to show that there has been a change in the contemporary fabric of society with lessened self-restraints and lowered morals (anomie). This coincides with a period of expanding economy, greater affluence as a whole, high-technology industrialization, and increased unemployment' (National Task Force on Suicide in Canada 1984: 9). A similar explanation could have been advanced for many of Canada's 'morbidities'. Another set of rising statistics related to crimes of violence against the person. From 1982 to 1987 crimes against property increased 0.1 per cent, while crimes of violence increased 30.1 per cent. From 1987 to 1991 violent offences increased another 29.8 per cent, while total criminal offences increased by only 11.5 per cent. On 6 December 1989 a lone gunman, apparently a misogynist, killed fourteen female engineering students at the École Polytechnique in Montreal. This horrifying event occurred near the close of a year in which, according to one estimate, over 32,000 Canadian women had been raped. The number of divorces had been 32,389 in 1972, rising to 90,985 in 1987 before beginning to decline slightly in numbers. By the late 1980s it was estimated that well over half of all Canadian children born after 1980 would at

TABLE 11.3
OFFENCES BY TYPE, 1987–1991

Type	1987	1988	1989	1990	1991	Percentage change, rate/100,000, 1987-91
Violent offences	219,381	232,606	248,579	269,381	196,680	+29.8%
Property offences	1,468,591	1,457,361	1,443,048	1,551,278	1,726,226	+12.8%
Other offences	1,276,036	1,265,861	1,300,005	1,343,397	1,470,454	+10%
Total	2,960,908	2,955,828	2,992,632	3,164,056	3,440,671	+11.5%

SOURCE: *Canada Year Book 1994* (Ottawa: Statistics Canada, 1994): 222.

some point experience life in a broken home. As divorce increased, marriage declined. Moreover, the number of common-law relationships more than doubled between 1981 and 1991.

The incidence of racial and sexual abuses of various kinds appeared to increase dramatically. The general professional consensus was that abuse had not become more common but that it was more likely to be reported. Racial and sexual abuses that might have gone unrecorded in previous generations were now openly publicized. Wife-beating—for decades the most common domestic crime on the police blotter—became a matter of public concern. Not surprisingly, much of the abuse was directed against the less powerful—children, women, Aboriginal peoples, and visible minorities—by traditional authority figures ranging from fathers to pastors to teachers to policemen and judges. On one level it was possible to take solace in the fact that such improper behaviour was now being addressed. On another it was possible to argue that what had changed was not so much the behaviour of people in authority as society's willingness to tolerate the excesses of this type of behaviour. Both the extent of the abuse and the undermining of authority to which it contributed were distressing. Canadians could no longer believe that they were all good guys living in the Peaceable Kingdom, nor could they continue to believe in the inherent beneficence of authority figures or in the fairness of the Canadian judicial system.

The revelations of the post-1972 period, particularly in the 1980s, could only contribute to a growing national mood of sullen cynicism with regard to authority, which was hardly appeased by the unimaginative and self-seeking behaviour of the politicians. No institution proved itself above reproach, and all institutions demonstrated their willingness to cover up their inadequacies and failures. Some of the most shocking revelations came from Newfoundland, where a provincial inquiry in 1989 brought to light evidence of the sexual abuse of children by priests and brothers of the Roman Catholic Church at the Mount Cashel Orphanage. Such evidence was soon augmented by material indicating that the clergy of all the major denominations had been abusing Aboriginal children for years in residential schools and orphanages. The situation was not improved by the discovery that the Canadian system of justice was hardly very just, at least when it came to Aboriginal people or accused murderers. The ways in which the system failed Donald Marshall, who served eleven years in prison for a murder he did not commit,

DONALD MARSHALL, JR

Donald Marshall, Jr, was born at Sydney, Nova Scotia, in 1953. In late May 1971 he was arrested after a Black companion named Sandy Seale was fatally stabbed while the two youths crossed a park late at night. A Mi'kmaq, Marshall had a reputation as a troublemaker. The Sydney police ignored contradictory evidence and testimony, and defence counsel did not bring them out at the trial. Marshall was convicted of murder and sentenced to life imprisonment. The police subsequently ignored evidence that a man named Roy Ebsary had committed the crime, and the Department of the Attorney General of Nova Scotia ignored evidence of judicial error because the defence had not raised the question. Marshall spent eleven years in prison, during which his case was re-examined on three separate occasions, before he was finally released on bail by the Nova Scotia Court of Appeal. Marshall was subsequently forced to prove his innocence (not simply the lack of real evidence of his guilt) in court. The Court of Appeal in its acquittal insisted that 'any miscarriage of justice' was 'more apparent than real' because Marshall had told a variety of stories under police interrogation.

Marshall understandably did not feel fully exonerated, and with his lawyer's assistance pressed for a public inquiry into the affair. Eventually Roy Ebsary was convicted of the death of Sandy Seale, and in 1986 the Nova Scotia government launched a royal commission to examine the Marshall case. The commission heard from more than one hundred witnesses during hearings in Sydney and Halifax in 1987. Witnesses testified to a pattern of incompetence and cover-up extending over many years. The commission concluded that Marshall had been let down by the criminal justice system at virtually every turn. The miscarriage of justice—which would have been easily correctable by proper and professional behaviour on the part of those involved—was in part due to the fact that Marshall was Aboriginal. The royal commission's 1989 report was itself criticized for refusing to single out those most responsible for the cover-up. Like most victims of judicial abuse, Marshall attempted to keep a low profile following his complete exoneration. But in 1993 he was arrested and prosecuted on three charges under the Fisheries Act for catching eels during the closed season in Pomquet Harbour, Nova Scotia. His lawyers argued that Marshall believed he was exempt from the fishery regulations because of treaties between the Crown and the Mi'kmaq in 1760 and 1761. Marshall was found guilty, a verdict subsequently affirmed by the Nova Scotia Supreme Court. But in 1999, the Supreme Court of Canada acquitted him on appeal, ruling that Marshall had a treaty right to a 'moderate livelihood' from the natural resources of his region.

were particularly instructive in this regard.

Even the Red Cross, previously a model of institutional altruism, proved susceptible to incompetence and coverup. The Canadian Red Cross had managed Canada's blood supply service since 1947, but the relationship between the government and the Red Cross had never been clearly defined. It remained unclear what government agency was responsible for assuring the safety of the blood supply, and for this reason it was difficult for the government to respond to problems when they emerged. In the late 1970s and early 1980s there were blood shortages in some parts of Canada, and this made the Red Cross reluctant to introduce screening measures that might further reduce the supply. As a consequence, the Canadian blood transfusion service in the early 1980s was sometimes (if infrequently) using blood infected both with the HI virus and with infectious hepatitis C. Much of the infected blood was given to hemophiliacs, who because of their medical condition require a constant series of transfusions. Approximately 1200 people were infected with HIV and 12,000 with hepatitis C through blood transfusions before the Red Cross introduced security measures to test for these viruses in 1985. Even after bringing the system back under control, it would take another dozen years to establish why the problem had occurred in the first place, as both government and Red Cross officials attempted to avoid the possible imputations of responsibility.

Other forms of abuse were self-inflicted, often related to short-term gratification without regard for long-term consequences. The availability of drugs continued to increase steadily. Alcohol abuse continued unabated, along with substance abuse of many descriptions, including gasoline sniffing; and the use of steroids by athletes became common. Canada's most notorious substance abuser was the Olympic sprinter Ben Johnson (b. 1961), whose gold medal at Seoul in 1988 was ignominiously stripped from him for using steroids. Johnson initially denied the charge but eventually had to acknowledge his guilt at a well-publicized public enquiry. The most dangerous drug of all was tobacco. Canadian adults, reflecting the health consciousness of the baby boomers, led the way internationally in quitting smoking during the late 1980s. The young, however, remained undeterred by cigarette prices, which were often in excess of $6 per pack. One calculation revealed that tobacco would ultimately kill eight times as many fifteen-year-olds as automobile accidents, suicide, murder, AIDS, and drug abuse combined. Self-inflicted abuse was part of the new world of self-indulgence. Those who made their way to the top could reward themselves with luxuries and expensive toys. Sniffing cocaine became an indulgence of choice among the affluent. As for the poor, they had access to little pleasure that was not addictive and physically harmful.

Because AIDS is mainly a sexually transmitted disease, with a high incidence among homosexuals and the sexually adventurous, it became a favourite target for moralists in the 1980s. Many concerns were expressed that AIDS would encourage a judgmental response from Canadians with regard to both homosexuality and sexual freedom, but these concerns were not borne out in the available survey literature. While surveys indicated that relatively few Canadians were morally judgmental, they also demonstrated much ignorance about AIDS and its prevention. Moreover, Canadians responded far less vigorously to the fear of infection than one might have expected, given the media attention AIDS received. In one Canadian study in 1989, for example, 63 per cent of those questioned knew that sexual intercourse was the most common way of becoming infected with AIDS, and about half identified homosexuals as the people most likely to become infected. Virtually everybody (90 per cent) believed that the best prevention was safe sex. Eighty-one per cent of those surveyed regarded having sex with one partner in a long-term relationship as a 'very effective' means of prevention, while 78 per cent considered complete sexual abstinence 'very effective'. Only 41 per cent rated condoms a 'very effective' method of protection against AIDS. At the same time, however, only 54 per cent of male and 41 per cent of female respondents said they had changed their sexual behaviour because of the risk of AIDS infection; truly safe sex was far from the Canadian norm. Not only did large numbers of respondents take no precautions, but the study suggested a tendency, particularly among males, for people with more knowledge of AIDS

ROBERTA BONDAR

Roberta Bondar was born at Sault Ste Marie, Ontario, in 1945. She took science and mathematics courses in high school, learned to pilot an airplane, and dreamed of the possibility of space flight. Bondar studied zoology and biology at the University of Guelph, from which she graduated in 1968. After taking an M.Sc. at the University of Western Ontario (1971), she studied for her Ph.D. at the University of Toronto. She then attended medical school at McMaster University, specializing in neuro-ophthamalogy (the study of the way the brain interacts with the eye). She did post-graduate work in neurology at several institutions, including the New England Medical Centre in Boston. At the time of her acceptance into the Canadian space program in 1983, she was assistant professor of neurology at McMaster University. Her research on the relationship between the nervous system and the eye was of particular importance to space flight.

One of six candidates selected by Canada in 1983 from thousands of applicants, Bondar soon after began formal training as an astronaut and joined the faculty of medicine at the University of Ottawa in 1984. Early in 1990, she was designated a prime Payload Specialist for the first International Microgravity Laboratory, which led directly to her flight as the first Canadian woman in space on the space shuttle *Discovery* in January 1992. On this flight she performed a number of experiments in the spacelab and at middeck that were designed to prolong space flight in the future. Both before and after her space flight, Bondar conducted research on the Transcranial Doppler Ultrasound, with particular reference to astronauts. Since 1992 she has held a number of distinguished appointments at a variety of medical schools in the United States and Canada, and has become an extremely popular speaker and role model for young women, especially in Canada. Her book recounting her space experiences was published as *Touching the Earth* in 1994.

to take greater risks. Other studies suggested that only about half of Canadians between 15 and 19 years of age thought they were at risk from sexually transmitted disease, and thus about half of this age group presumably took no precautions. Chlamydia became far more common than AIDS among the young.

In many ways the post-1970 era was dominated by the baby-boom generation. Before 1970 the boomers had their chief impact on the educational system. Now they put pressure on the employment system not only by their sheer numbers but by their educational qualifications. Not all were able to get the jobs for which they had prepared. The tightness of the job market, combined with the increased consumer requirements of the boom generation, produced more childless working couples and further lowered fertility rates. By the 1980s the baby boomers' demand for detached housing drove up housing prices in most of the nation's larger cities. Even after the inevitable bust, prices could never return to previous levels. In cities of premium-priced housing (such as Toronto and Vancouver), it was estimated that less than a quarter of those seeking to purchase their first house could qualify for a mortgage. Many boomers had money to spend on nice things: 'My Tastes Are Simple', read one popular bumper sticker, 'I Like the Best.' Marketing strategies to reach these consumers included slick magazines distributed free to homes in neighbourhoods with the appropriate demographics. Articles on various aspects of affluent lifestyles—home (re)decorating, gourmet foods eaten at home or in restaurants, and luxury travel—were some of the subjects featured. The boomers continued their fascination with the 1950s and 1960s pop and rock music of their youth. The music nostalgia industry thrived. Radio stations that for decades had tried to appeal to the kids suddenly shifted their programming to the 'Golden Oldies' in a blatant attempt to capture the largest single audience segment: middle-aged baby boomers.

The progressive aging of the Canadian population was neither a new development of the post-1970 period nor a distinctly Canadian one. By 1991 life expectancy for Canadian men had reached seventy-four years, and over eighty years for women. The leading causes of death in

☐ Dr Roberta Bondar. Canadian Space Agency photo.

Table 11.4
Leading Causes of Death, 1990

	Male		Female	
	No.	Rate	No.	Rate
Diseases of the circulatory system	38,823	296.3	36,266	269.0
Cancer	28,865	220.3	23,560	174.8
Respiratory diseases	9,351	71.4	6,921	51.3
Accidents and adverse effects	9,064	69.2	3,993	29.6
Diseases of the digestive system	3,961	28.2	3,303	24.5
Endocrine diseases, etc.	2,533	19.3	2,939	21.8
Diseases of the nervous system	2,275	17.4	2,580	19.1
All other causes	9,358	71.2	8,434	62.7
Total, causes	104,230	793.3	87,996	652.8

Canada were all diseases of the old. The emerging conception of a 'crisis' was primarily connected with what seemed to be the increased costs associated with the elderly—pensions and health care—in the welfare states of the advanced world. Part of the problem was that the proportion of the population who were productive members of the workforce able to finance the care of the aging was constantly declining. In 1983 in Canada there were eighteen people over sixty-five for every 100 between eighteen and sixty-four. One prediction suggested that there would be fifty-two people over sixty-five for every 100 between eighteen and sixty-four by 2031.

Pensions had always been based on the notion that the working generation would support the retired one. One study in the mid-1980s argued that by the year 2021 the funds required for public pensions would be three and one-half times greater than in 1976, given the continuation of the 1976 level of payments. Without a high level of pension support, the elderly would become an even greater proportion of Canadians below the poverty line. In 1986, 46.1 per cent of unattached females over the age of sixty-five were below that level. Longer life obviously meant more demands on the health care system, culminating in the potential need for expensive nursing home facilities. In 1986, only 9 per cent of Canada's elderly could be accommodated in nursing homes. Studies demonstrated that the cost of medical care for the last year of life was substantially greater than for the entire earlier lifespan. The problem was to decide when the last year had come, and what medical strategy to adopt.

The increased visibility of racial minorities was especially evident in the nation's larger cities, where they tended to congregate. This concentration only encouraged racism. Despite higher levels of media attention, government expenditure, and Aboriginal self-consciousness, the demographic realities of Native life, while improving, continued to recall conditions in

TABLE 11.5

IMMIGRANTS ARRIVING BY PLACE OF BIRTH, 1981–1990

Place	Number	Percentage
Europe	351,511	26.4
Great Britain	81,460	6.1
Portugal	38,630	2.9
France	15,256	1.1
Greece	6,884	0.5
Italy	11,196	0.8
Poland	81,361	6.1
Other	116,724	8.8
Africa	72,941	5.5
Asia	619,089	46.5
Philippines	67,682	5.1
India	90,050	6.8
Hong Kong	96,982	7.3
China	74,235	5.6
Middle East	90,965	6.8
Other	199,175	15.0
North & Central America	114,073	8.6
US	63,106	4.7
Other	50,967	3.8
Caribbean & Bermuda	89,908	6.7
Australasia	5,877	0.4
South America	67,936	5.1
Oceania	10,040	0.8
Other	375	
Total	2,416,423	

SOURCE: *Canada Year Book 1994* (Ottawa: Statistics Canada, 1994): 116.

nations generally regarded as the most backward on the planet. Infant mortality and overall death rates ran high. Conditions on many remote reserves continued to be absolutely deplorable. It was not surprising that many Aboriginals migrated to cities like Winnipeg, where they met considerable social disapproval. After 1973 new immigrants to Canada came chiefly from the non-European Third World. In that year, Hong Kong, the Philippines, Jamaica, Trinidad, and India appeared among the top ten countries of origin for Canadian immigrants. Reform of immigration legislation in 1976, 1978, and 1987 further encouraged immigration from non-traditional sources. Beginning in 1986, individuals with substantial amounts of capital could invest this money in approved projects and thereby gain access to Canada. People of Third World origin, who represented less than 1 per cent of the Canadian population in 1967, represented 4.6 per cent by 1986. In that year, Canadian residents from the Third World totalled 30 per cent of all foreign-born.

CANADIAN CULTURE

After 1972 Canadians discovered that culture had not only moral, intellectual, and aesthetic dimensions but powerful economic implications as well. Canadian bureaucrats began to talk about 'cultural industries' instead of just culture, measuring jobs and spin-offs as well as enlightenment. At about the same time, governments began to discover how much money they had been putting into various aspects of culture since the halcyon days of the 1950s and 1960s. An additional debate over cultural policy focused on how both to limit and to supplement the vast public expenditures on activities ranging from university research to art events. To the extent that it was regarded as a non-essential, culture was extremely vulnerable to budget cutting. Not only limitation but pay-off became a lively issue. Canadian cultural policy was hotly debated, particularly since the politicians sought to use cultural policy to other ends, notably in the area of multiculturalism. The always artificial distinction between commercial and non-commercial culture had now been partially overcome by the inclusion of cultural enterprise in the economy. Thus popular culture (including sports) came to be more frequently recognized as a legitimate part of culture.

Certainly one of the defining events of a lifetime for many Canadians was the Canada–Russia hockey series of 1972. The largest television audience ever assembled in Canada was glued to the TV, mesmerized by an unofficial sporting event, played for no historical trophy or recognized world title. Paul Henderson of the Toronto Maple Leafs scored the game- (and series-) winning goal with thirty-four seconds remaining in regulation time. Despite this moment of national togetherness, the schism between francophone and anglophone cultures was constantly widening, and all levels of government continued to jostle for advantage. The result was a strong sense of diffusion and decentralization—some would say regionalization (although not merely geography was involved)—of what had once been perceived as a monolithic cultural establishment. Such developments parallelled and reinforced the retreat of centralism in the political and constitutional area, while contributing to the sense that Canadian society was unravelling.

By 1990 the *Canada Year Book* could call the cultural sector 'the fourth largest employer in Canada' (*Canada Year Book* 1990). A few years earlier, a 1985 Statistics Canada compendium entitled *Arts and Culture: A Statistical Profile* had estimated that in 1982 culture's share of the gross domestic product was $8 billion, calculated that there were 280,000 Canadian arts-related jobs in the 1981 census, and insisted that arts jobs were growing more quickly than the total labour force in all provinces. The 1986 Task Force on Funding in the Arts revised the economic dimensions of the cultural sector upwards to $12 billion and the job numbers to 415,000. Despite the billions of dollars of public support, however, government spending on arts-related culture

TABLE 11.6
PERCENTAGE OF TELEVISION VIEWING TIME DEVOTED TO CANADIAN AND FOREIGN PROGRAMMING IN PRIME TIME (7 P.M.–11 P.M.)

	English			
	1984–5		1992–3	
	Canadian	Foreign	Canadian	Foreign
CBC	62.0	38.0	81.7	18.3
CTV	20.8	79.2	17.3	82.7
Global	7.9	92.1	17.4	82.6
Independent	16.4	83.6	17.9	82.1
	French			
SRC (Radio-Canada)	72.1	27.9	90.9	9.1
TVA	46.2	53.8	66.3	33.7
TOS	54.8	45.2	47.6	52.4

SOURCE: *Globe and Mail* (1 February 1996): A21.

represented only about 2 per cent of the total of government expenditure at all levels. Moreover, little of the vast sum spent on culture trickled down to the primary producers—the writers, painters, actors, and composers. Government surveys of artists from 1978 to 1984 indicated that very few Canadians could make a living from the sale of their work or talents. Most held other employment, often in teaching. At the same time, the fact that even a few thousand Canadians could conceive of making a living as professional producers of culture certainly distinguished the post-1970 period from earlier times.

Little enough changed in terms of the distinctive Canadian content of culture in Canada, still seen by many observers as a major problem. The statistics were revealing. In book publishing, for example, titles published in Canada in 1984 (most written by Canadian authors) accounted for only 25 per cent of books sold. Nearly half the books sold to Canadians came directly from foreign sources. Twelve foreign-controlled firms in 1984 had 89 per cent of the sound-recording market in Canada, most for recordings made outside Canada. In one week in 1986 the top seven TV shows in English-speaking Canada were all American. The situation was quite different in French Canada, where all seven top shows were locally produced. In the 1980s there was great hope for satellite and cable technology, but while these improved access for many Canadian viewers, they did little for actual Canadian content.

Government support for High Culture further aided a respectable Canadian showing in areas of traditional activity, such as painting and literature. But at the very time Canadian High Culture was achieving international recognition, the idea of High Culture was breaking down. In addition, tensions were developing between what came to be labelled 'national' and 'regional' cultures, not to mention between French and English Canada. Before the late 1960s, a major problem for Canadian creators was receiving public exposure outside Toronto and Montreal.

SUMMARY OF GAME EIGHT, CANADA-USSR HOCKEY SERIES, 1972

CANADA 6 USSR 5

FIRST PERIOD

1. 3:34 USSR, Yakushev (Liapkin, Maltsev)
2. 6:45 Canada, P. Esposito (Park)
3. 13:10 USSR, Lutchenko (Kharlamov)
4. 16:59 Canada, Park (Ratelle, D. Hull)

Penalties

2:25 White (holding)
3:44 Petrov (hooking)
3:44 Petrov (holding)
4:10 Parisé (interference, 10 min., misconduct and game misconduct)
9:27 Ellis (interference)
9:27 Tzigankov (interference)
9:46 Petrov (interference)
12:51 Cournoyer (interference)

SECOND PERIOD

5. 0:21 USSR, Shadrin
6. 10:32 Canada, White (Gilbert, Ratelle)
7. 11:43 USSR, Yakushev
8. 16:44 USSR, Vasiliev (Shadrin)

Penalties

14:58 Stapleton (crosschecking)
18:06 Kuzkin (elbowing)

THIRD PERIOD

9. 2:27 Canada, P. Esposito (P. Mahovlich)
10. 12:56 Canada, Cournoyer (P. Esposito, Park)
11. 19:26 Canada, Henderson (P. Esposito)

Penalties

3:41 Mishakov (major, fighting)
3:41 Gilbert (major, fighting)
4:27 Vasiliev (tripping)
15:24 D. Hull (highsticking)
15:24 Petrov (elbowing)

SHOTS ON GOAL

Canada	14	8	14	36
USSR	12	10	5	27

SOURCE: Jack Ludwig, *Hockey Night in Moscow* (Toronto: McClelland and Stewart, 1972), 192–3.

The small presses and galleries that cropped up in the country, especially after 1970, became possible for several reasons. One was the allocation of new provincial funding for the arts, often from the revenues of publicly authorized gambling activities. In Quebec, cultural subsidies were a matter of high politics. Another was the emergence of local cultural entrepreneurs in what was now a large enough market for culture in second-tier cities such as Quebec, Halifax, and Winnipeg. Almost inevitably the new publishers and galleries tended to stress local themes and settings. Cultural regionalism grew to match political regionalism. It began to appear that the

ANTONINE MAILLET

☐ Antonine Maillet, December 1984. Harry Palmer/NAC, PA-182393.

Antonine Maillet was born in Bouctouche, New Brunswick, in 1929, and was educated at the Université de Moncton. She first came to public attention in 1958, when her play *Poire-Acre* won the best Canadian play award at the Dominion Drama Festival. Maillet spearheaded a cultural renaissance in her home region of Acadia, by focusing on stories about the Acadian people. Most of her protagonists are poor and semi-literate women who still find reasons for celebrating life. Much of her work employs the old-fashioned French of the Acadian people, with its direct links to the seventeenth and eighteenth centuries, a dialect deliberately coarsened by the author.

Maillet made it big in 1971, with the publication and first staging of *La Sagouine* (The Slattern), a series of sixteen monologues originally starring Viola Léger. The title character was a talkative, matter-of-fact, and long-suffering old charwoman and former prostitute. The wife of an Acadian fisherman, she recalls her past in the salty Acadian dialect while scrubbing the floor throughout the performance. She comments on a gamut of events from the perspective of Bouctouche in a manner that is uncultured but quite sensible. A subsequent television series in Quebec introduced large numbers of French-Canadians to the eastern shore of New Brunswick, which in the hands of the tourist industry became known as 'la Sagouine country'.

Maillet's greatest achievement was her epic novel *Pélagie-la-Charette*, published in 1979. In it an old woman recalls the return of her family and other exiles to Acadia after the expulsion by the British in 1755. Unlike the nineteenth-century poet Longfellow, who turned the expulsion into a romanticized tragedy in his poem *Evangeline*, Maillet focused on the renewal of the Acadian people as they returned to their traditional homeland. *Pélagie* won the Prix Goncourt in 1979, Maillet being the first non-French citizen and non-native of France to be awarded that prestigious prize. A few critics complained that Maillet dealt too much in a folklorized past, but most were happy to accept her characters as symbols of Acadian courage, survival, and regeneration. The first Acadian writer to establish an international reputation, Maillet has received nearly thirty honorary degrees.

very concept of a Canadian National Culture was an artificial one, impossible for most Canadian artists to realize in a fragmented nation. Precious few books published in Quebec were ever translated into English, for example.

One exception to all generalizations about culture in Canada began in 1984, when a group of young street performers in Montreal organized a festival that toured Quebec in celebration of the 450th anniversary of the landing of Jacques Cartier. The organizers built on a long tradition of the burlesque in Quebec and incorporated the more recent expression of avant-garde theatre in the province. The show toured in a large blue-and-yellow tent. It was a circus without animals or freaks, featuring acrobatic performances, brilliant costumes and imaginative choreography with rock music accompaniment. This 'Cirque du Soleil', as it came to be called, was a huge success at Expo 86 in Vancouver. It took California by storm in 1987. The company toured the United States in 1988, went to Europe in 1990, and Japan in 1992. It established permanent circus shows in Las Vegas in 1992 and later at Walt Disney World in Florida. By the late 1980s it was recruiting performers around the world, and began touring a number of different productions, with accompanying music composed by René Dupéré. Over the 1990s, the Cirque du Soleil became Canada's (or Quebec's) best-known cultural export, providing evidence that Canada could take the lead in the imaginative creation of culture that crossed all sorts of boundaries.

In early 1991, when the Quebec government of Robert Bourassa finally responded to the collapse of Meech Lake, it listed immigration, health and manpower, and cultural matters as the key areas in which it would demand increased constitutional powers. 'As far as culture is concerned, yes we should be in charge', announced Liberal Minister of Cultural Affairs Liza Frulla-Hebert in January 1991. 'We have to work toward being the one and only one giving the pulse of Quebec culture. Listen, culture belongs to Quebec' (*Winnipeg Free Press*, 25 January 1991). No Canadian could doubt that in Quebec, culture was lively and distinctive, certainly better able to withstand American influence than elsewhere in Canada. Whether Quebec Culture was a National Culture became, in the end, a question more susceptible to political than intellectual answers.

CONCLUSION

For many Canadians, especially those in English-speaking Canada, the years after 1972 were characterized by considerably less optimism and buoyancy than the previous quarter century had been. In historical development, disparate events often come together in surprising ways to weave a complex web. This was the case with such seemingly unrelated trends as the rise of Quebec separatism; the growing power of the provinces; the international oil crisis; the shift away from trade protectionism and a managed economy; the weakening of Christian belief; and the passage through life of the baby boomers. The result was a Canadian society concerned mainly with hedonism and anxiety, displaying all the morbid symptoms that might have been expected.

HOW HISTORY HAS CHANGED

ECONOMIC THEORY

Differing historical interpretations often result from conflicting theories about how the world works. This has been particularly true of the Canadian economy. Between the end of World War II and the early 1970s, the dominant economic theory in Canada was associated with the English economist John Maynard Keynes. His theory had been developed in reaction to the economic conditions of the Great Depression. Keynes insisted that the best way to tackle the big economic problems—which he identified as stagnant economic growth and high unemployment rates—was by employing the taxing and spending powers of the state. When the economy slowed down, the pump needed to be primed, often through governmental spending on public works projects.

Like their predecessors the liberal-democrats, Keynesians believed in market capitalism, properly regulated. Canada's civil servants were more willing than the country's politicians to accept that full employment and an end to poverty required a thoroughly interventionist state. For the most part, the Keynesians were also proponents of the welfare state. Keynesianism went hand-in-hand with protectionist economies, and understandably dominated economic thinking in an age of economic growth and expansion. The most influential Keynesian in North America was the Canadian-born John Kenneth Galbraith. In a series of influential books, Galbraith insisted on pushing the new liberalism in a social democratic direction. Ironically, Galbraith's views were enthusiastically received by the Kennedy and Johnson administrations in the United States but more or less ignored in Canada.

Increasingly, after 1970, Keynes's interventionist views were challenged by another group of economic thinkers, often called Friedmanites after the American economist Milton Friedman. Friedman rejected state intervention in the economy, insisting that Keynesians exaggerated the utility of government taxing and spending in determining the level of national income and gross national product. The best policy (which came to be known as monetarism) was to control the stock of money in order to reduce inflation, and otherwise to leave the economy to regulate itself. Warring on inflation benefited the creditor class more than the debtor class, and also worked to the advantage of foreign investors who were able to profit from an artificially favourable exchange rate. Many Friedmanites, including the master himself, opposed the welfare state. Friedman's most famous phrase was 'There is no such thing as a free lunch.' On the other hand, the monetarists, as part of their attitude toward the self-regulation of the market, also believed in free trade. In many ways the worst feature of the debate over economic and social policy was the presumption on all sides that what was being purveyed was hard scientific truth rather than socio-political ideology.

Monetarism gained support from the business community as governments of the 1970s and 1980s went increasingly deeper into debt. Much of the debt was blamed on expensive social programs, although the federal and provincial budgets had been balanced during the years of the greatest expansion of social policy. In turn, the Keynesians insisted that government deficits were caused by anti-inflationary policies at the Bank of Canada. They charged these policies also caused unemployment, cut back on income-tax revenues, and increased expenditures on unemployment compensation and welfare assistance.

SHORT BIBLIOGRAPHY

Bashevkin, Sylvia. *True Patriot Love: The Politics of Canadian Nationalism*. Toronto, 1991. An important study of the way politicians have bent Canadian nationalism to their own purposes.

Bibby, Reginald. *Fragmented Gods: The Poverty and Potential of Religion in Canada*. Toronto, 1987. A perceptive account of the state of religion in Canada as of the mid-1980s, based on specially conducted national surveys and standard public opinion polls.

Cairns, Alan. *Disruption: Constitutional Struggles, from the Charter to Meech Lake*. Toronto, 1991. An analysis of the constitutional problems of the 1980s by one of Canada's leading constitutional specialists.

Corse, Sarah. *Nationalism and Literature: The Politics of Culture in Canada and the United States*. Cambridge, 1997. A stimulating comparative study of recent cultural policy in the field of literature in the United States and Canada.

Frazer, William. *The Legacy of Keynes and Friedman: Economic Analysis, Money, and Ideology*. Westport, CT, 1994. An intellectual history of one of the major ideological disagreements in North America in the late 20th century.

Giangrande, Carole. *Down to Earth: The Crisis in Canadian Farming*. Toronto, 1985. A discussion of the reasons Canadian farmers were in serious financial trouble in the 1980s.

Gwyn, Richard. *The Northern Magus*. Toronto, 1980. Arguably the best biography of that complex Canadian Pierre Elliott Trudeau.

Harris, Michael. *Unholy Orders: Tragedy at Mount Cashel*. Markham, ON, 1990. An exposé of one of the first of Canada's sexual abuse scandals within a major religious denomination.

Jenish, D'Arcy. *Money to Burn: Trudeau, Mulroney, and the Bankruptcy of Canada*. Toronto, 1996. A partisan analysis of the 'crisis' of the deficit, presenting it as the major challenge to the present generation of Canadians.

McQuaig, Linda. *Shooting the Hippo: Death by Default and Other Canadian Myths*. Toronto, 1995. A study by a leading radical economic and social analyst who insists that the deficit was an invented crisis, easily soluble.

McWhinney, Edward. *Canada and the Constitution, 1979–82*. Toronto, 1982. A well-balanced contemporary narrative.

Magder, Ted. *Canada's Hollywood: The Canadian State and Feature Films*. Toronto, 1993. A study of Canadian cultural policy with particular reference to the film industry.

Morgan, Nicole. *Implosion: An Analysis of the Growth of the Federal Public Service in Canada, 1945–1985*. Montreal, 1986. An explanation of the growth of Canada's federal bureaucracy.

Parsons, Vic. *Bad Blood: The Tragedy of the Canadian Tainted Blood Scandal*. Toronto, 1995. An angry look at one of the worst examples of the failure of public policy in the arena of public health.

Savoie, Donald. *The Politics of Public Spending in Canada*. Toronto, 1990. A dispassionate discussion of the financial crisis in Canada as of 1990.

STUDY QUESTIONS

1. What roles did the economy and the Constitution play in the disintegration of the liberal federalist-nationalist consensus during the 1970s?
2. In what ways did oil illustrate the excesses and weaknesses of the age of affluence?
3. After winning a second enormous majority for the Progressive Conservative Party in 1988, Brian Mulroney quickly became one of the most unpopular prime ministers in Canadian history. Identify and explain three reasons for his fall from grace.
4. If you think of the attempts at constitutional reform from 1980 to 1992 as a battle between the federal government and the provinces, who would you say won? Explain your answer.
5. What provisions did the Meech Lake Accord make regarding immigrants to Quebec? Why do you think Quebec wanted these provisions?
6. 'The bell curve ensured that grading standards remained the same for year to year,' according to Professors Bercuson, Bothwell, and Granatstein. Explain why you agree or disagree with this statement.
7. What did the Donald Marshall case reveal about the status of Aboriginal people in the Canadian justice system?
8. In about ten years, the Cirque du Soleil grew from a ragtag band of street performers to an international cultural institution. What factors led to the Cirque's success?

CHAPTER TWELVE

Facing the World, 1900–2001

As a result of both its geographical position and its colonial situation, Canada before 1914 was able to enjoy relative isolation from the turmoil of international politics, concentrating on its own domestic development. Like Americans, most Canadians were relatively inward-looking, even isolationist, in their attitudes towards the wider world. Most French Canadians saw themselves as an autonomous people without close European or international connections, while Canadians of British origin felt varying degrees of loyalty to Great Britain, which looked after most international affairs in the name of the British empire. Canada's corps of diplomats was tiny, confined to Washington, London, and Paris. After 1909 a small Department of External Affairs supervised and coordinated the nation's sporadic formal relations with the world. While most Canadians felt no need to be citizens of the world before 1914, they were not necessarily ignorant of it. The larger daily newspapers covered foreign affairs far more assiduously than their modern equivalents, for example.

After the Great War, Canada's international position changed rapidly. In the interwar period, Canada broke its imperial ties and began to construct its own foreign policy and diplomatic apparatus. Before 1939–40, direct American influence over Canadian foreign and defence policy was minimal; as late as the 1920s the Canadian military still thought of the United States as a potential enemy rather than as an ally. The Second World War completed the process of withdrawal from the British umbrella and initiated the process of Canada's integration into an informal American empire. Canada's scope for genuinely autonomous action in the world was never very great, but most Canadians were reasonably content with the nation's situation as they understood it. Until the late 1980s, Canada stood as a junior partner of the United States in the international struggle with communism known as the cold war. Then suddenly the USSR collapsed. The cold war ended. What would replace it was an open question.

The 1920s and 1930s

Even before the First World War, many Canadians appreciated that Canada had no voice in the affairs of the British empire. The war brought the point home in increasingly graphic fashion, however. Prime Minister Borden took the lead in pressing for change. He argued privately in 1916 that 'it can hardly be expected that we shall put 400,000 or 500,000 men in the field and willingly accept the position of having no more voice and receiving no more consideration than if we were toy automata' (quoted in Stacey 1981: 192). The British eventually invited Dominion ministers to sit in imperial councils as a token gesture. The Dominions insisted on full representation as participants in the Paris Peace Conference of 1919, but in the end settled for being part of the British empire delegation. Nevertheless, Borden himself led a strong

TIMELINE

1871
Sir John A. Macdonald signs Treaty of Washington.

1884
Canadian volunteers go to Sudan.

1899
Canada sends volunteers to South Africa.

1903
Alaska Boundary Dispute between Canada and the United States is handed over to a joint commission of six 'impartial jurists of repute'.

1909
Department of External Affairs is created.

1914
Canada joins the Allies in the Great War.

1917
Canada joins the Imperial War Council.

1919
Canada attends Paris Peace Conference at part of the British Empire delegation.

1920
Canada becomes member of the League of Nations.

1925
O.D. Skelton appointed to External Affairs.

1926
First Canadian minister to Washington appointed.

1930
Westminster Conference.

1931
Statute of Westminster makes Canada legislatively independent of Great Britain.

1932
World Trade Conference at Ottawa.

1935
Most-favoured-nation treaty signed with the US.

1939
Canada declares war on Germany.

1940
Ogdensburg meeting between Canada and the US. Lend-lease program exchanges destroyers for Newfoundland bases.

1941
Hyde Park Declaration.

1945
Canada helps found United Nations.

1946
Gouzenko Affair. Cold War begins.

1948
Canada becomes part of the Marshall Plan.

1949
North Atlantic Treaty Organization is created.

1950
Canada joins UN force in Korea.

1954
Canada joins a joint commission on Vietnam.

1956
Distant Early Warning line is established.

1957
Lester B. Pearson wins Nobel Peace Prize. Canada joins NORAD.

1959
Avro Arrow is cancelled.

1963
Cuban Missile Crisis.

1964
Canada sends a peacekeeping force to Cypress.

1972
Trudeau proposes 'Third Option'.

1989
Berlin Wall is torn down.

1990
Canada participates in Gulf War.

1992
Canada sends first peacekeepers to Bosnia.

1993
Canada agrees to peacekeeping in Somalia. Canada closes last two military bases on German soil. Canada withdraws peacekeepers from Cypress.

1994
NAFTA takes effect. Last troops withdrawn from Lahr, Germany.

1996
Fisheries crisis with Spain.

1997
Commission of Inquiry reports on Somalia Affair.

2001
Canada sends troops to Afghanistan.

Canadian delegation to Paris, pressing successfully for full membership in the League of Nations and various collateral League bodies.

Once Canada was admitted to the League of Nations as a full member, it became a regular (if uninfluential) participant, occasionally surfacing to lecture the world on its failures. During the 1920s the major energy of external relations was spent redefining the nation's role in the British empire. The ultimate result was the Westminster Conference of 1930, attended by Mackenzie King's successor, R.B. Bennett. The resulting Statute of Westminster (1931) made six Dominions—Canada, Australia, New Zealand, the Irish Free State, South Africa, and Newfoundland—legislatively independent. As Bennett himself said at the time, with the adoption of the Statute of Westminster 'the old political Empire disappears'. But, he went on to add, he hoped that it would be replaced by 'the foundations of a new economic Empire' (quoted in Stacey 1981: 135). The 1920s also saw the expansion of the Department of External Affairs, initially under undersecretary O.D. Skelton (1878–1941). Skelton recruited a number of young men of talent, albeit from a fairly narrow male, upper middle-class spectrum of Canadian society, who served the nation abroad until the 1950s. Under Skelton's tutelage, external affairs expanded abroad. A Canadian minister to Washington was appointed in 1926. Similar legations opened in Paris and Tokyo in 1928. A few foreign embassies opened in Ottawa.

The decade of the 1930s, in terms of foreign affairs, divides at 1935. Between 1930 and 1935, foreign relations were dominated almost exclusively by economic considerations. Even at the Westminster Conference, Canada was really more interested in economic than constitutional matters. The result was a conference in Ottawa in 1932 intended to re-examine imperial economic policy. The meeting was not a success, beyond a bit of tariff reform. Canada set the tone by bargaining almost exclusively in terms of its own immediate advantage. As for Canadian–American relations, the two neighbours had imposed high protective tariffs on one another in 1930. Gradually they resumed more normal cooperative relations. Mackenzie King made American negotiations one of the first points on the government's agenda after his electoral success in 1935. The result was a most-favoured-nation treaty with the United States signed on 15 November 1935. By this time, the Italian invasion of Ethiopia had made all the nations of the world realize the dangers of the military rearmament undertaken by Germany, Italy, and Japan. Canada clearly needed friends, for the Canadian military was in no position to defend it in an age of renewed aggression. The nation spent only pennies per capita on its military. A regular force of 3,000 and the militia were maintained to provide domestic security, but the country had no modern anti-aircraft guns, not a single operational aircraft, and only enough artillery ammunition for ninety minutes of firing 'at normal rates'.

After 1935 international events moved inexorably towards another conflagration. Canadians displayed an increased interest in external affairs and in foreign policy. In 1937 the first serious debate over external affairs in years occurred in Parliament. The pacifist J.S. Woodsworth moved a resolution of strict Canadian neutrality 'regardless of who the belligerents might be' (quoted in

OSCAR DOUGLAS SKELTON

Oscar Douglas (O.D.) Skelton was born in Orangeville, Ontario on 13 July 1878. His father was a schoolteacher. The Skeltons later moved to Cornwall, and in 1896 he won a scholarship to Queen's University, where he was an excellent student, winning prizes in classical languages. He enrolled for graduate work in Greek at the University of Chicago in 1901, but went to England in the summer of that year to sit the open examinations for the British civil service. He qualified for the highly regarded Indian service, but did not pursue the matter further. Instead he became assistant editor of *The Booklovers Magazine* and married in 1904. In the autumn of 1905 he returned to Chicago to finish his Ph.D. Three years later, he succeeded Adam Shortt as John A. Macdonald Professor of Political Science and Economics at Queen's University in Kingston. His doctoral dissertation, revised, was published in 1911 as *Socialism: A Critical Analysis*. Skelton took on Marxism as well as socialism in this work. He soon began writing on reciprocity for the Liberal government.

In 1913 Skelton was named Sir Wilfrid Laurier's official biographer, and he worked on the biography throughout the war. It appeared as the two-volume *Life and Letters of Sir Wilfrid Laurier* in 1921, a year after the publication of his study of Sir Alexander Tilloch Galt. Early in 1922 Skelton addressed the Ottawa Canadian Club on imperial policy, arguing for an independent Canadian policy, and a year later he was invited to accompany Prime Minister King to the Imperial Conference in London. In 1924 Skelton took a leave-of-absence from Queen's to join the Department of External Affairs, and when Sir Joseph Pope resigned in 1925, Skelton became External's Under-Secretary of State, with Mackenzie King himself as Secretary of State. Skelton's tenure in Ottawa coincided with the elaboration of civil service reform including the introduction of competitive examinations in place of purely political appointments. Over the next few years Skelton helped recruit a number of young Canadians to the department. Without exception, these recruits were bright generalists rather than specialists, drawn from a fairly narrow spectrum of Canadian society. Qualifications for External Affairs included a university degree and special training in political economy and international law, as well as skill in a foreign language. (This last requirement was sometimes overlooked.) The young men of External were 'affable' males, most from a middle-class WASP background, who had been educated at Canada's major universities and had done postgraduate work at Oxford, Cambridge, or the London School of Economics. They did not always agree with one another, but they shared a substantial number of assumptions about how the world ought to operate. By the time Skelton died in 1941, External Affairs had expanded abroad and was prepared to enter its 'golden age', the period between 1940 and 1960 in which Canada became a 'middle power' of considerable influence in the world.

Stacey 1970: 195–6). The government's response was that its hands should not be tied. At the 1937 Imperial Conference connected with the coronation of George VI, Mackenzie King refused publicly to make commitments, but privately admitted to British leaders that Canada would again support Britain in a war against European aggressors. In a meeting with Adolph Hitler early in the summer of 1937, King was mesmerized by the Nazi leader's personality and persuaded by his assertions that Germany did not want a war. Fully understanding the threat of war, Canada quietly supported the British policy of appeasement. Such a policy was arguably necessary since Canada was even more ill-prepared than other Western democracies to resume a shooting conflict. Less defensible was Canadian policy towards the victims of the Nazi pogroms in Europe, especially the Jews, as discussed in Chapter 8.

Canadian External Relations in Wartime, 1939–1945

The greatest value of appeasement, apart from buying a bit of time for reinvigorating long-neglected military establishments, was that it delayed war until only the most ardent pacifist or isolationist could deny its necessity. By the summer of 1939 no informed observer could doubt that the next German aggression would be met firmly by the allied governments. On 10 September Canada responded to the German invasion of Poland by joining Britain and France in its own separate declaration of war against Germany. The Canadian government had no intention of rushing troops overseas. Instead, it emphasized a Canadian air training program, economic assistance, and an intermediary's role with the United States, which did not join the Allies until December 1941. Despite official American neutrality, Canada found the Roosevelt administration receptive to mutual defence undertakings. When France fell to the Germans in 1940 and Britain stood virtually alone in Europe against the Nazi war machine, Canada simultaneously supported the British while creeping quietly under the American military umbrella.

From the outset of war, it was obvious that Canada's connections with Britain would be reduced as a consequence of it. After Dunkirk, the Americans sought desperately to prop up the tottering British. Washington's friendship with its northern neighbour made it possible to use Canada to channel assistance to the British while still remaining officially neutral. In August 1940 Franklin Roosevelt on his own initiative invited Mackenzie King to Ogdensburg, New York, where the two leaders, according to their joint press statement, 'agreed that a Permanent Joint Board on Defence shall be set up at once by the two countries'. Canada could serve not only as a conduit to Britain, but with its economy legally able to gear up for wartime production, could assist in American rearmament. Shortly after Ogdensburg, the Americans sent the British fifty destroyers in return for long leases on military bases within the British empire, including Newfoundland. Since that island had surrendered its Dominion status in 1933 as an alternative to bankruptcy and was now technically a British colony, its government was not consulted about the deal. In April 1941 Canadian–American co-operation was advanced by the Hyde Park Declaration, which consisted of a statement that 'each country should provide the other with defence articles which it is best able to produce, and above all, produce quickly, and that production programmes should be coordinated to this end' (Cuff and Granatstein 1977: Appendix A). The Americans ordered military equipment made in Canada under a program using American technology and money. Until the Americans were legally at war and even beyond that date, the Canadian production would prove quite useful.

As in the Great War, Canadians fought well whenever called upon, and, as in the previous conflict, they were often employed as shock troops, sustaining heavy losses. In the disastrous landing of the 2nd Canadian Division at Dieppe in August 1942, of the 5,000 Canadians who embarked nearly 2,700 were killed or captured. The Dieppe raid became a classic example of military bungling because the Canadian troops were sent into combat under circumstances that almost guaranteed failure. On the other hand,

CHARLES PERRY STACEY

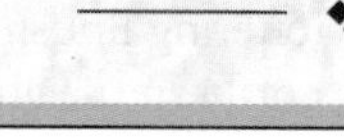

Charles Perry (C.P.) Stacey was born in Toronto in 1906, the son of a physician. He attended the Normal Model School, the University of Toronto Schools, and University College at the University of Toronto, where he took honours in English and History and enrolled in the Canadian Officers' Training Corps, later joining the militia. He attended Corpus Christi College at Oxford University on a Parkin fellowship (1927–9), and then Princeton University. While at Princeton he discovered American history, which led him in turn to Canadian history. Stacey taught as an instructor at Princeton and published his dissertation (*Canada and the British Army*) in London in 1936. His next project was for the Carnegie Endowment for International Peace on armament and disarmament in North America. It was completed but never published because the Endowment ran out of funds. In 1940 he was appointed a historical officer at Canadian Military Headquarters in London, and like other Canadian soldiers he said goodbye to his wife for the duration of the war to head off for England.

In 1942 Stacey drafted a report on Canadian participation at Dieppe, which was not initially well received. It was rewritten by an American officer whose literary experience had been in Hollywood, and Stacey was then ordered to return it to its original state. After many cuts of details the report was duly released. Stacey then turned to doing careful research on the Dieppe raid itself, in the process becoming the Canadian 'expert' on the raid. As well as discharging his official responsibilities, Stacey later co-authored a booklet entitled *The Canadians in Britain*, which was eventually published as *The Canadians in Britain, 1939–1944* by the Department of National Defence (DND). The book sold nearly 100,000 copies in both official languages.

Stacey returned to Canada late in 1944 and drafted a proposal for an official history of the Canadian Army in the war, a non-technical work aimed at the 'intelligent general reader'. He subsequently served as chief army historian between 1945 and 1959. Despite considerable difficulty with the Ottawa mandarins over the accessibility, contents, and interpretation of documents, *The Canadian Army 1939–45*—an overall sketch of the final version—was published in 1948. The detailed history was not completed until 1960. The preparation of this history provided Stacey with some difficult problems of interpretation, including what to do when eyewitnesses remembered things wrong. In 1959 he retired from the military to take up an appointment as professor of history at the University of Toronto, briefly serving (1965–6) as director of the DND's directorate of history. He retired from the university in 1976. Stacey's influence was important in developing professional standards for Canadian military history during the critically formative period of World War II and afterwards. A memoir of his life was published in 1983 as *A Date with History*.

the eagerness of Canada's armed forces in Britain to get into the thick of things contributed to the failure of their leading officers to protest effectively against the British planning for Dieppe. Apart from the Dieppe adventure, most Canadian troops remained in Britain from their arrival (beginning in 1941) until early 1944, when they were deployed, first in Italy and then in Northwest Europe.

Prime Minister King and his advisers seemed reasonably satisfied—most of the time—with Canada's role as a secondary power under the tutelage of Winston Churchill's Britain and Franklin Roosevelt's United States. Canada had difficulty gaining information about many high-level decisions, but never pushed for access to the inner corridors of power. It did try for representation on middle-level coordinating bodies, such as the Munitions Assignment Board, the Combined Production and Resources Board, and the Combined Food Board. It also insisted that it deserved to be fully represented on any formal international organizations, such as the United Nations Relief and Rehabilitation Administration, which was formed in 1943. A Canadian rationale for these efforts was developed at the Department of External Affairs in the spring of that year. Called 'functionalism', it expressed a Canadian stance regarding international organizations that continued well into the 1960s. Canada insisted that authority in world affairs be neither concentrated solely in the hands of a few superpowers nor distributed equally among states regardless of size. Instead, 'representation on international bodies should be determined on a functional basis so as to permit the participation of those countries which have the greatest stake in the particular subject under examination.' Along with functionalism went multilateralism, another governing principle of Canadian diplomacy for generations. Multilateralism insisted on Canadian involvement in multinational arrangements rather than bilateral partnerships with nations that would inevitably seek to dominate it. Both functionalism and multilateralism led to Canada's interest in the United Nations. The Canadian delegation at the 1945 San Francisco Conference, which drafted the UN charter, consisted of a veritable Who's Who of Canadian mandarins and diplomats. The Canadians made some major contributions to the Charter's ultimate acceptance as an international document. Most important, they fully supported the notion that security issues were no more critical than economic and social ones in establishing any new basis for world peace.

☐ Prime Minister Mackenzie King at the San Francisco conference, April-June 1945. NAC, PA-23272.

Canada had hoped to claim an appropriate voice in postwar deliberations for Europe, based on its military contributions. Such was not to be. Mackenzie King recognized that the Great Powers would make the major decisions, but on the basis of functionalism he hoped to be allowed some share of influence on those decisions. Canada was the largest and most deserving

MACKENZIE KING AND WINSTON CHURCHILL, 1944

In September 1944 Prime Minister King had his last conversation with Winston Churchill, at the time of the second Quebec Conference. What follows is from King's diary.

At the table in the evening . . . Churchill had spoken eloquently. . . of our not desiring an acre of land, of not wishing anything in the way of additional power, but fighting simply for the maintenance of our honour and the preservation of freedom.

As we were driving through the narrow gateway of the Citadel, between the guardrooms and the gate, I said to him that while this [his impression of Canada's altruism] was true, I believed it had been due to the recognition of the complete position of each of the Dominions acting on its own; the absence of any centralization. Said that any attempts at centralization would do great harm. Churchill to my great surprise said I agree 100 percent with you, you are perfectly right. Each part of the Empire must direct completely its own affairs. The relationship must be one of co-operation not centralization. What Churchill said was not expressed just in those words but that was the meaning. What came to me as a surprise was the emphatic way in which he spoke. . . . We then spoke of the mistake it would have been to have tried to form an Empire Cabinet to run affairs during the war. He said, you remember Menzies [Robert Menzies, Prime Minister of Australia to August 1941], he wanted to put me out; he wanted to have the war run by himself and others . . . . I said I remembered very well what Menzies had said to me on his arrival in Canada from Britain [in May 1941]. That he wanted to speak to me very seriously about the need of having myself, himself and others control the policy of the war. I said that my last words to him at Ottawa had been that he would find when he got back to Australia that he had lost . . . the leadership of his country, also that the place of all of us as leaders of the Dominions was in our own Dominions and not in London. Churchill said you were perfectly right. He then went on to say you have been so fine about letting England lead, not making it difficult for us by insisting always on several having direction. I said it had been difficult to maintain my position at times but that as long as I knew we were being consulted and getting informed on new policies and were able to speak about them before they were settled, I thought it was much better before the world to leave the matter of leadership in the hands of the President and himself. He said that had meant everything in the effecting of needed co-operation.

SOURCE: J.M. Pickersgill and D.F. Forster, eds, *The Mackenzie King Record*, II (Toronto: University of Toronto Press, 1968): 90–1.

of the 'lesser powers', however, and to involve this country would set a precedent that would open the door to others; so argued the Great Powers. They adopted an exclusive approach to settling postwar peace questions. The USSR objected to the Commonwealth nations having an independent voice in negotiations unless Soviet republics were similarly recognized. Britain wanted Commonwealth assistance, but only under the British umbrella; during the Berlin airlift London went so far as to offer to put British insignia on Canadian planes. Some nations—Australia for one—complained bitterly and publicly about this sort of treatment. The

Canadian government was resentful but silent, partly because it was committed to facilitating international reconstruction, and partly because it felt that any public discussion might divide the nation. The main reason for Canada's rapid unilateral withdrawal from Europe was that King and his government felt Canada was being exploited.

THE COLD WAR

By 1945, Canada was probably already too deeply enmeshed in its linkages with the United States ever to cast them aside. Great Britain, financially strapped, was not likely to provide much of a counterweight. Canadian involvement in the cold war was almost inescapable. There were numerous signs in the latter years of the war that the Russians and the Americans were the emergent world superpowers, eager to carve up the world into respective spheres of influence. Countries like Canada found themselves virtually excluded from the process of peacemaking with the defeated enemies, as well as from most of the significant diplomatic manoeuvring of the postwar period. As a result of the war, Canada substantially increased its overseas diplomatic contacts, with twenty-five posts abroad in 1944 and thirty-six by 1947, but it hardly improved its international position. Towards the close of the war Canada tried to create some diplomatic distance from the Americans in their continual arm-wrestling with the Russians, but the notorious Gouzenko affair made it difficult for Ottawa to remain on sympathetic terms with the Russians.

Igor Gouzenko (1919–82) was an obscure cipher clerk in the Russian Embassy in Ottawa. In September 1945 he brought to the RCMP material that demonstrated how the Russians had organized a spy ring in Canada during the war. Nowadays spying is taken for granted, but at the time, Gouzenko's information and the subsequent arrests of Canadian citizens (including one member of Parliament) were absolutely shocking. Canada did not exchange ambassadors again with the Russians until after 1953. In public opinion polls in 1946, Canadians proved far more willing than people in other nations to believe that Russia sought to dominate the world. The Gouzenko business would also send shock waves across the Western world, for loose ends from the files made it apparent that the Russians had suborned not only Canadians but their allies. Moreover, it became evident that the tight security connected with research on atomic energy carried on in Montreal had been breached. The Russians had received secret information that may have aided them in developing their own atomic bomb in 1949. With the two superpowers both possessing nuclear capability, the stand-off that characterized the cold war began in earnest. Unlike the British and French, the Canadian government declared its refusal to use nuclear power for military purposes.

Economic considerations impelled Canada in the same inevitable direction as the nuclear stand-off. Prime Minister King was leery of a complete economic integration proposed by the Americans late in the war—and supported by many of his own civil servants—but Canada and the United States became closer trading partners than ever before. Moreover, when the American Congress approved the Marshall Plan early in 1948—by which the United States proposed to rebuild war-torn Europe with unrestricted gifts of money and goods—Canada was forced to do something. If European reconstruction was limited solely to American goods, Canadian trade would shrink to nothing. Canada needed market access into the American program, that is, permission for Europe to use American money to buy Canadian goods. The US readily agreed. King used North Atlantic security as a way out of continental free trade. A security treaty would not only deflect reciprocity but, as a multilateral arrangement, might provide a much-needed international counterbalance against American military domination. The Americans were not enthusiastic about a multilateral arrangement for North Atlantic security, but the Canadians

IGOR GOUZENKO

☐ Igor Gouzenko with a copy of his novel *The Fall of a Titan*, 15 October 1954. NAC, PA-129625

Igor Gouzenko was born in Rogachov, USSR on 13 January 1919, amid the turmoil of the aftermath of the Russian Revolution. In 1943 he was posted with his wife and son to Canada, officially serving as a secretary and interpreter at the Russian embassy in Ottawa. His superior was the Russian military attaché and head of Soviet military intelligence in Canada; Gouzenko was his cipher clerk, with access to much specialized information. In September 1945, Gouzenko was recalled to the Soviet Union, and he and his wife determined to defect rather than return home. Gouzenko was sensible enough to realize that his reception by the Canadian authorities would be greatly smoothed if he could provide secret documentation of some value to the West. On 5 September 1945, he returned in the evening to his office at the embassy, and removed a collection of 109 documents that he had previously taken from the files. Arranging the documents around his body, he managed to leave the embassy building without being detected.

Gouzenko took the documents to the night editor at the *Ottawa Journal*, who recommended that he take them to the RCMP. He did so, and was told to come back in the morning. The entire Gouzenko family appeared at the Justice Building in Ottawa on 6 September but were turned away. They tried again at the *Ottawa Journal*, but were told politely, 'Nobody wants to say anything but nice things about Stalin these days.' Gouzenko went again to the Justice Building, then tried the Crown Attorney's office, where the family was met with sympathy but no assistance. They eventually returned to their apartment, where Gouzenko climbed a railing and spoke to an RCMP sergeant who was a neighbour. The Gouzenkos were sheltered in an adjacent apartment when a party from the Russian embassy broke into their apartment, where the RCMP discovered them searching for something. Gouzenko was then taken to RCMP headquarters.

Meanwhile, Gouzenko's visit to the Justice Building was brought to Prime Minister Mackenzie King's attention, but King refused to deal with the matter because it might jeopardize Canadian–Soviet relations. Gouzenko's interrogation by the RCMP indicated that his incredible stories were true. A Soviet spy ring was operating in Canada. Prime Minister King hesitated for five months before appointing a royal commission on 13 February 1946 to take evidence from Gouzenko, whose testimony was detailed and totally credible. Canadian authorities accepted that Gouzenko would have to be given a new identity, and he only appeared in public with a hood covering his face. His revelations did not always lead to successful prosecutions, for the RCMP was clumsy in its investigations.

Gouzenko received little or no money from the Canadian government, but his disclosures in *Cosmopolitan Magazine* (February 1947) and his autobiography *This Was My Choice* (1948) made him a rich man. Despite the establishment of a trust fund, Gouzenko was not able to hold on to his money and was subsequently reduced to soliciting interviews from the media. In 1954 he was interviewed by an American Congressional subcommittee, an occasion that led to the publication of a novel under Gouzenko's name entitled *The Fall of Titan*. This book won the Governor General's award for literature in 1954. A subsequent government investigation demonstrated Gouzenko was incapable of living within his means. The former spy spent his later years living on a tax-free pension of just over $1,000 a month. He died in 1982, apparently of natural causes.

pressed hard. Some Canadian diplomats even wanted non-Atlantic Commonwealth countries admitted, and Escott Reid (b. 1905), the deputy undersecretary of state for external affairs, sought a treaty that encompassed social and economic issues as well. The Americans ultimately accepted the North Atlantic Treaty's military and security provisions, particularly the centralization of command under what would inevitably be an American general. They quietly scuttled other aspects of the alliance.

The Search for Middle-Power Status

By the time NATO was established in 1949, the cold war had extended beyond Europe into Asia, where a communist government headed by Chou En-lai had taken over China. Communism made gains in other places like Indochina and Korea, which had been partitioned after the war. The United States always saw these communist governments as mere extensions of international communism rather than as movements of legitimate national liberation. In 1950 North Korea invaded American-supported South Korea. The Americans took advantage of a temporary Soviet boycott of the Security Council of the United Nations to invoke universal collective security. The Canadian government was in a quandary. It had no peacetime military of its own to send, nor was it enthusiastic about participating in collective security under the American aegis. Eventually a Canadian Army Special Force of 20,000 volunteers served in Korea, suffering 1,557 casualties and 312 fatalities. Most of the Canadians were involved after the Chinese had intervened on behalf of North Korea. Canada was more eager than the United States for an armistice, but usually supported the Americans in public.

The Korean War increased the pressure for a military build-up. By 1953 the defence budget stood at nearly $2 billion, up tenfold since 1947. Public opinion in the 1950s consistently supported rearmament. The policy makers at the Department of External Affairs did their best to give Canada an autonomous international presence, developing a Canadian reputation for send-

THE NORTH ATLANTIC TREATY, 1949

The North Atlantic Treaty was signed at Washington on 4 April 1949. The preamble and the first five articles are reprinted below.

The Parties to this Treaty reaffirm their faith in the purposes and principles of the Charter of the United Nations and their desire to live in peace with all peoples and all governments.

They are determined to safeguard the freedom, common heritage and civilization of their peoples, founded on the principles of democracy, individual liberty and the rule of law.

They work to promote stability and well-being in the North Atlantic area.

They are resolved to unite their efforts for collective defense and for the preservation of peace and security.

They therefore agree to this North Atlantic Treaty:

ARTICLE 1. The Parties undertake, as set forth in the Charter of the United Nations, to settle any international disputes in which they may be involved by peaceful means in such a manner that international peace and security, and justice, are not endangered, and to refrain in their international relations from the threat or use of force in any manner inconsistent with the purposes of the United Nations.

ARTICLE 2. The Parties will contribute toward the further development of peaceful and friendly international relations by strengthening their free institutions, by bringing about a better understanding of the principles upon which these institutions are founded, and by promoting conditions of stability and well-being. They will seek to eliminate conflict in their international economic policies and will encourage economic collaboration between any or all of them.

ARTICLE 3. In order more effectively to achieve the objectives of this Treaty, the Parties, separately and jointly, by means of continuous and effective self-help and mutual aid, will maintain and develop their individual and collective capacity to resist armed attack.

ARTICLE 4. The Parties will consult together whenever, in the opinion of any of them, the territorial integrity, political independence or security of any of the Parties is threatened.

ARTICLE 5. The Parties agree that an armed attack against one or more of them in Europe or North America shall be considered an attack against them all; and consequently they agree that, if such an armed attack occurs, each of them, in exercise of the right of individual or collective self-defense recognized by Article 51 of the Charter of the United Nations, will assist the Party or Parties so attacked by taking forthwith, individually and in concert with the other Parties, such action as it deems necessary, including the use of armed force, to restore and maintain the security of the North Atlantic area.

Any such armed attack and all measures taken as a result thereof shall immediately be reported to the Security Council. Such measures shall be terminated when the Security Council has taken the measures necessary to restore and maintain international peace and security.

SOURCE: National Defence Headquarters, Department of National Defence, *The North Atlantic Treaty* (Ottawa: Queen's Printer, 1995) [includes a facsimile of the original treaty signed at Washington].

ing small numbers of soldiers to trouble spots to supervise international agencies and monitor local conditions. Peacekeeping operations were carried out in Indochina and the Middle East, especially Cyprus. The nation's standing reached its high point in 1957 when Lester B. Pearson won the Nobel Peace Prize for his efforts to end the 1956 hostilities in Suez. Pearson, with American support, found a way for Britain and France to back out of an impossible situation created by their ill-conceived invasion of Egypt to protect the Suez Canal. Canada had earned its place among the 'middle powers', a characterization that became popular with Canada's international-relations specialists at the same time that it flattered the nation's pretensions. But the world changed rapidly after Suez, and middle-power status altered with events.

THE RETREAT FROM INTERNATIONALISM

Part of the gradual change in Canada's place in the world was a result of technology. When, in 1953, the USSR added a hydrogen bomb to its nuclear arsenal, Canadians became even more conscious than before that their nation sat uneasily between the two nuclear giants. Everyone's attention turned to air defence. Canada expanded the RCAF and began development of the famed CF-105 (the Avro Arrow). The United States pushed for increased electronic surveillance in the Arctic. In 1955 Canada agreed to allow the Americans to construct at their own expense a series of northern radar posts called the Distant Early Warning (or DEW) line. The Americans also pressed for an integrated bilateral air-defence system, the North American Air Defense Command (NORAD), which was agreed to by the Diefenbaker government soon after it took office in 1957. Diefenbaker's administration gave way to the Americans on the big principles while balking over the unpleasant consequences and details. Diefenbaker, moreover, was thoroughly detested by American President John F. Kennedy, who referred to 'the Chief' as one of the few men he had ever totally despised. Three related issues—the decision to scrap the Avro Arrow, the acceptance of American Bomarc-B missiles on Canadian soil, and the government's reaction to the Cuban Missile Crisis of 1962—illustrate the government's problems.

When Diefenbaker terminated the Avro Arrow project early in 1959, he did so for sound fiscal reasons. The plane had no prospective international market and would be inordinately expensive to build only for Canadian needs. The prime minister justified his decision in terms of changing military technology and strategy. An aircraft to intercept bombers would soon be obsolete, said Dief, and what Canada needed were missiles obtainable from the Friendly Giant. It turned out that Canada still needed fighters, however, and the country had to buy some very old F-101 Voodoos from the Americans. By cancelling Canada's principal technological breakthrough into the world of big military hardware in return for an agreement whereby parts of equipment purchased by Canada from the American defence industry would be assembled in Canada, Diefenbaker probably accepted reality. But the Bomarc-B missile was armed with a nuclear warhead, and Canada had a non-nuclear policy. Diefenbaker thus refused to allow the Bomarcs to be properly armed, erroneously insisting that they could be effective with non-nuclear warheads. The question took on new urgency in 1962 after President Kennedy confronted the USSR over the installation of Russian missile bases in Cuba. As Soviet ships carrying the missiles cruised westward towards Cuba and Kennedy threatened war if they did not turn back, NORAD automatically ordered DEFCON 3, the state of readiness just short of war. Neither Diefenbaker nor his ministers were consulted—much less informed—about this decision. The prime minister was furious that a megalomaniac American president could, in effect, push the button that would destroy Canada.

In the end Nikita Khrushchev backed down

in the fearsome game of nuclear chicken, but Cuba changed Canadian public opinion, which had tended to be against nuclear armament. The crisis provoked considerable media discussion of the government's prevarications and inconsistencies over nuclear and defence policy. NATO made it quite clear that Canada was part of the nuclear system. Liberal leader Lester Pearson announced that the Liberals would stand by the nation's nuclear commitments even if the government that had made them would not. There was no point in housing nuclear weapons on Canadian soil if they could not be instantly deployed in the event of a crisis. Such defence blunders did Diefenbaker no good in the 1962 election. By January 1963 defence issues had reduced his cabinet to conflicting factions. The minority government fell shortly afterwards. Traditional Canadian nationalism as practised by John Diefenbaker was simply not compatible with the missile age.

The returning Liberals, who regained power in 1963 under Pearson, spent most of the 1960s attempting to implement the integration of Canada's armed forces, mainly on the grounds that duplication of resources and command structures was an expensive luxury the nation could not afford. A unified Canadian military would be both leaner and meaner, capable of remaining within acceptable budget figures. A *White Paper* to this effect was released in March of 1964, and Bill C-90, which amended the National Defence Act by creating a single Chief of Defence Staff, was introduced into the House of Commons on 10 April 1964. The amendments producing a fully integrated military headquarters with a single chain of command received Royal Assent on 16 July 1964. The country and its politicians, however, continued to hold schizophrenic attitudes towards the Canadian military, its foreign obligations, and Canada's overseas role. Canada wanted to control its own destiny, which probably required a neutral stance internationally. Neutrality in international affairs would cost even more than the American and NATO alliances, however, so everyone pretended that Canada could hold the line on military spending and still honour its commitments through administrative reform. At the same time, Canada began a long, slow, gradual process of reducing its armed forces, a process that was still underway in the twenty-first century.

Despite Prime Minister Pearson's high profile as a successful world diplomat, his governments were not distinguished for their triumphs in the international arena. In fairness to Pearson, the world was changing in other ways not sympathetic to Canada's self-proclaimed role as a middle power. After 1960 the United Nations General Assembly opened its doors to dozens of Third World countries, most of them recently emerged from colonial status and quite hostile to the Western democracies. The new complexities of politics and expectations at the assembly, and in the various collateral UN organizations, worked against a highly developed and industrialized nation such as Canada—populated chiefly by the descendants of White Europeans—which also happened to be a junior partner of the United States. In UN bodies Canadian diplomats found themselves in the embarrassing position of defending the country's internal policy, particularly towards Aboriginal peoples, in the face of criticisms of racism and insensitivity to human rights. Canada was not in the same league as South Africa, perhaps, but its record on human rights was a hard one to explain internationally. At the same time, the success of the European Economic Community (first established in 1958) made western European nations more important international players, while Japan had succeeded in restoring its industrial position. As a result, Canada became less important among the industrial nations at the same time that it became less credible in the Third World.

It was not only the configuration of world politics that had altered by the 1960s. So had the policy of the United States. President Kennedy and his successor, Lyndon B. Johnson, were actually more hard-bitten and confrontational Cold

WHITE PAPER ON DEFENCE, 1964

The *White Paper on Defence* was issued by the Pearson government in March 1964. This excerpt is from that document.

In the opinion of the government this solution [the gradual transfer of executive control of common requirements to the Chairman, Chiefs of Staff] does not adequately resolve the basic issues. If a single command structure is not established, co-ordination by the committee system will remain with all of its inevitable delays and frustrations.

The fundamental considerations are operational control and effectiveness, the streamlining of procedures and, in particular, the decision-making process, and the reduction of overhead. To the extent that operational control is exercised by Canada, it is the view of the government that it can be most effectively exercised by a single command.

The question of duplication and unnecessary overhead, too, cannot be ignored. The present headquarters organization of the Department of National Defence is far too large. The fact that our field forces are modest creates a serious imbalance between the field and headquarters branches of the service. As it appears that we will have to maintain modest forces in being for many years to come, it is apparent that a re-organization is required.

Following the most careful and thoughtful consideration, the government has decided that there is only one adequate solution. It is the integration of the Armed Forces of Canada under a single Chief of Defence Staff and a single Defence Staff. This will be the first step toward a single unified defence force for Canada. The integrated control of all aspects of planning and operations should not only produce a more effective and co-ordinated defence posture for Canada, but should also result in considerable savings. Thus, integration will result in a substantial reduction of manpower strengths in headquarters, training and related establishments, along with other operating and maintenance costs. The total savings to be effected as a result of such reductions will make available funds for capital equipment purchases, and eventually make possible more equitable distribution of the defence dollar between equipment and housekeeping costs. Sufficient savings should accrue from unification to permit a goal of 25 per cent of the budget to be devoted to capital equipment being realized in the years ahead.

Two objections are given as reasons why integration should not be undertaken. First, that morale or 'esprit de corps' is weakened, and second, that competition is diminished. Neither of these objections will stand against careful scrutiny. 'Esprit de corps' by nature is associated with ship, or corps, or regiment, or squadron, as well as with the service. There is no thought of eliminating worthwhile traditions and there is no reason why morale should not be high—a direct result of effectiveness. Similarly, there will be no lack of competition. The sailors will press for more ships, the soldiers for more tanks and the airmen for more planes. This is as natural as breathing. Competition will not be lost but it will be contained at the service level.

SOURCE: *White Paper on Defence*, March 1964 (Ottawa: Queen's Printer, 1964): 18–19.

PAUL HELLYER

Paul Hellyer was born at Waterford, Ontario, on 6 August 1923. His family operated a ginseng farm. Hellyer graduated in aeronautical engineering at the Curtiss-Wright Technical Institute of Aeronautics in Glendale, California. He worked briefly at Fleet Aircraft in Fort Erie, Ontario, and then enlisted in the RCAF in the spring of 1944. As a result of an administrative decision to release surplus airmen, he ended up in the Royal Canadian Artillery. Hellyer married Ellen Ralph in June 1945 and, after his discharge, enrolled at University College at the University of Toronto. He financed his education by running a ladies ready-to-wear store on Bloor Street West that he purchased with the assistance of his family.

He ran successfully for Parliament in 1949 in the strongly Tory riding of Davenport, and was subsequently forced in the early 1950s to take charge of a building firm (Curran Hall) he had purchased when it was on the verge of bankruptcy. He was appointed Associate Minister of National Defence in 1957, but soon became another victim of the Diefenbaker sweep of that year. Now he was thankful that Curran Hall provided him with a non-governmental career. Lester B. Pearson encouraged Hellyer to run again in 1958. He was again defeated, but returned to Parliament through a by-election in December 1958. One of his first jobs was to speak for the opposition in the debate over the cancellation of the Avro Arrow. He was subsequently named to the 1960 Canada–United States parliamentary–congressional group. As a result of briefings he attended as a member of that group he wrote a new defence policy for the Liberals, which, foreseeing the shift from bombers to missiles, called for Canada to abandon the Bomarc system, cancel the F-104, and bow out of the nuclear strike force. He argued that Canada should accept nuclear weapons while concentrating on the provision of conventional ones. Pearson adopted this stance, and Hellyer became one of the bright young men of the party.

When the Liberals formed the government in 1963, Hellyer became Minister of National Defence. He soon perceived that each of the services was preparing for a different sort of war, and that reform of defence policy was a priority item. The result was the *White Paper on Defence* issued in March 1964, calling for a unified armed forces under a single chief of staff. Hellyer succeeded in implementing the main lines of the *White Paper*'s unification proposal, but in the process alienated many in his own party. In 1968 he ran for the leadership of the Liberal Party, but was easily defeated by Pierre Elliott Trudeau. Given responsibility for housing policy, Hellyer headed a Task Force on Housing and Urban Development, but when its recommendations were rejected by the Cabinet in 1969, he left the government and eventually the Liberal Party. He ran successfully for Parliament as a Conservative in 1972, but gradually drifted away from politics in favour of a role as an independent political commentator. He wrote several books and for many years was a syndicated newspaper columnist.

Warriors than their predecessors, Truman and Eisenhower. The latter had been extremely embarrassed in 1960 when the Russians shot down an American U-2 spy plane and captured its pilot, Francis Gary Powers. Kennedy, on the other hand, authorized dirty tricks by the CIA in foreign countries, and he made no apology when they were exposed. His only regret about the abortive 1961 Bay of Pigs invasion of Cuba by US-backed Cuban exiles, for example, was that it had failed. Most important, however, both Kennedy and Johnson permitted their governments to become ever more deeply involved in the quagmire of Southeast Asia. In 1945, Ho Chi Minh declared the Democratic Republic of Vietnam, with Hanoi as its capital, to be independent of French colonial control. When the French government proved incapable of defeating the armed 'insurgents', Canada in 1954 became involved in attempts at international control. It served as one of three members, with Poland and India, of a joint commission. Canada was actually eager to participate to bolster its middle-power pretensions in the world. The 1954 commission set the pattern for the next twenty years: one Iron Curtain nation, one Western ally of the United States, one neutral power, with votes often going against Canada as the American supporter. From the outset Canada had deceived itself into believing that it had a free hand to carry out its work without either upsetting the Americans or appearing to act merely as a lackey of the United States.

When the American administration gradually escalated both US involvement and the shooting war in Vietnam after 1963, Canada's position became increasingly anomalous, both on the commission and outside it. Lester Pearson was still hoping to mediate in April 1965 when he used the occasion of a speech in Philadelphia to suggest that the American government might pause in its bombing of North Vietnam to see if a negotiated settlement was possible. He was soon shown the error of his ways in no uncertain

The Heeney–Merchant Report on Canadian–American Relations, 1965

In 1965 a report entitled Canada and the United States, *Principles for Partnership*—authored by a former American ambassador to Ottawa, Livingston T. Merchant, and a former Canadian ambassador to Washington, Arnold D.P. Heeney—was published as the United States was escalating its involvement in Vietnam. The following excerpt is taken from that report.

The current concern in Canada—determined as ever upon its independent North American future—has its roots in history, in its struggle to achieve its own destiny, and in the disparity of size and power. The present preoccupations of Canadians, however, relate primarily to social and economic developments of more recent date—the massive influence of American cultural expression upon Canadian life, the extent of American ownership of Canadian industry and resources, and the prevailing attractions south of the border for Canadian scientists, engineers and professional men and women. Such phenomena must be seen by Americans as well as Canadians within the context of history and national aspirations. If in their dealings, public and private, there is to be the mutual confidence that both desire and need, there must be conscious effort on both sides to appreciate the historical as well as the current factors which tend to divide them.

The mutual involvement of the two countries and peoples has also complicated, on both sides, the problems arising from the disparity in power. In most—though not all—of their bilateral affairs the capacity of the United States to benefit or harm Canadian interests is greater than that of Canada to affect the prosperity and security of the United States. Canadians are more conscious than Americans of this element in their dealings with the United States. On the other hand, the United States, preoccupied with the responsibilities of world power, may sometimes be inhibited in its bilateral dealings by considerations which do not operate directly on Canadian attitudes. Here restraint is required of both sides.

Canadians sometimes feel that, because they are so close, so 'American', there is a disposition on the part of the United States to expect more of Canada than of other allies—as in setting other countries a good example—reflecting a tendency to apply to Canada a kind of 'double standard' of international conduct. The result is sometimes to tempt Canadians into demonstrating their independence by adopting positions divergent from those of the United States. In a quite different sense, Americans are inclined sometimes to suspect the application of a 'double standard' on the part of Canada when, for example, in an international negotiation, the United States is urged to be 'reasonable,' to make unilateral concessions to break a logjam which has been created by the intransigence of others. For Canadians cannot but be disturbingly aware that, despite their underlying confidence in the basic motives of the United States, Canada could be involved inevitably in the consequence of United States' decisions in circumstances over which Canadians had little influence or control. Such tendencies, on each side, arising from mutual involvement, inequality and the facts of international life, should be recognized but not exaggerated.

SOURCE: A.D.P. Heeney and Livingston T. Merchant, *Canada and the United States, Principles for Partnership* (Ottawa: Queen's Printer, 1965): 16–18.

terms. In a private meeting with Lyndon Johnson shortly thereafter, the American president shook Pearson by his lapels and criticized Canadian presumptuousness with Texas profanity. Vietnam certainly contributed to a new Canadian mood in the later 1960s, both in Ottawa and on the main streets of the nation. Canadians now sought to distance themselves from the policies of the 'Ugly Americans', although never by open withdrawal from the American defence umbrella.

After Pierre Trudeau succeeded Pearson in April 1968, an undeclared and never coordinated policy of retreat from middle-power pretensions was accelerated. Trudeau had long been critical of Canada's foreign and defence policies. Soon after his accession to office, he initiated formal reviews, which the departments of national defence and external affairs found most threatening. The prime minister was particularly eager to raise 'fundamental questions', such as whether there was really a Russian threat to world order, or whether the US '[would] sacrifice Europe and NATO before blowing up the world' (quoted in Granatstein and Bothwell 1990: 17). The bureaucrats were not comfortable with such questions, nor were several of Trudeau's cabinet colleagues. Trudeau had a reputation as an internationalist, but he disliked the military, and ultimately proved much more comfortable with domestic matters than external ones. For Trudeau, protecting the sovereignty of Canadian territory was far more important than international peacekeeping. Defence budgets continued to be cut and active Canadian involvement in NATO was pared to the lowest limits of allied acceptability. The best-known armed action by the Canadian military was its occupation of Quebec during the October Crisis of 1970. In 1973 Canada sent a large military mission to Vietnam to serve on a revised International Commission for Control and Supervision. Its purpose was to allow the Americans to withdraw from that troubled corner of the world, but the commission was not able to act effectively. The Trudeau government called it home in mid-1973. Canada was no longer a self-defined middle power. It had no clear conception of its place or role in world affairs.

INTERNATIONAL DRIFTING

Canada's problem in the world was basically simple. Its economic indicators entitled it to major-league status, but its population was small and its close relationship with the United States inevitably consigned it to being a minor-league subsidiary player. The Canadian image abroad was as perplexing as its policies. On the one hand, the country continued its irritating habit of preaching from on high to nations that did not regard themselves as morally inferior. Catching Canada in hypocritical moral contradictions became a favourite international game. Canada's multilateral involvements limited its abilities to provide practical support for human rights issues, despite some internal pressures to adopt a more interventionist human rights position. On the other hand, Canada continued to be one of the most favoured destinations for immigrants from around the world. Ordinary people accepted that life was better in Canada. Indeed, surveys regularly listed Canada at the top of the international standard-of-living table.

Whatever the Department of External Affairs was or was not doing, Canadians themselves became citizens of the world in a way that would have been incomprehensible to earlier generations. By the early 1970s, relatively cheap airplane tickets to go anywhere in the world had become an accepted part of life. In the 1960s kids had travelled the world, carrying backpacks festooned with the Canadian flag and sleeping in youth hostels. Now their parents followed them, staying in hotels that were just like those at home. Almost every Canadian family had at least one member with photographs of a major overseas expedition. Cheap air fares also brought relatives from abroad to Canada. All this travel combined with new immigration to make Canada an increasingly cosmopolitan place to live. Canadians drank less beer and more wine, much of it imported. They ate in restaurants with exotic cuisines, learned to cook similar food at home, and insisted that this type of food be available at their local supermarkets.

Pierre Trudeau's attempt to reorient Canadian foreign policy met with limited success. He managed to reduce Canada's military commitment to NATO and to reduce the size of Canada's armed forces. In 1972 the government produced a policy document that recommended a 'Third Option': less dependence upon the Americans. But if Canada moved away from the Americans, where would it go? The obvious answer was to Europe. Canada had waited too long and had become too closely identified with (not to mention integrated in) the American economy. The fizzle of the European initiative was followed by a similar effort in Asia, with perhaps slightly better success. After 1975, however, Canada returned to closer ties with the United States. Aside from perennial concern over trade figures and the occasional international conference attended by the prime minister, Canada's relations outside North America assumed a very low profile during the 1980s. Canadians expected precious little from foreign policy initiatives. The Free Trade Agreement with the Americans merely confirmed what everyone knew.

The key international developments of the 1980s were totally beyond Canada's control. The

Peacekeeping in Cambodia: Corporal Corena Letandre of the Canadian Forces' 2 Service Battalion comforts a hospitalized child. Department of National Defence/Canadian Forces photo.

first was *glasnost*, the process of liberation from the repression of communism in the Soviet Union. The Soviet regime had been opening up for decades, but no one was prepared for the rapid changes of the later 1980s when the Russians made it clear that they were no longer prepared to prop up unpopular governments in eastern Europe and wanted to shift their own internal priorities in what appeared to be capitalistic and democratic directions. The most obvious symbol of collapse was the razing of the Berlin Wall, which was demolished, along with the government of East Germany, in November 1989, clearing the way for German reunification in late 1990. This event ultimately permitted Canada to close its last two bases on German soil in 1993. The demise of communism did not occur without difficulty. In many of the Iron Curtain nations, it turned out that the communist regime had been the only force supporting unity and stability, whatever the price. Movements of national liberation tore apart the USSR itself, as well as other ethnically complex constructions, such as Yugoslavia. Civil war among Serbs, Croats, and Muslims in Bosnia became an international concern. The transition to a capitalistic economy was so painful that many citizens of the old Soviet bloc began voting in free elections for their former communist masters. By the mid-1990s it was clear that the cold war was indeed dead. What would replace it as a principal of international dynamics was not so clear.

The elimination of communist repression did not necessarily save the world for democracy. As if to demonstrate the fragility of international peace, in the summer of 1990 the Iraqi army invaded Kuwait, one of the small independent oil-rich principalities on the Persian Gulf. The world witnessed the unusual spectacle of American–Russian cooperation at the United Nations, and elsewhere, in opposition to Saddam Hussein's move. With Russian approval, President George Bush sent American forces to the Persian Gulf. Canada contributed three ancient destroyers to the international force. For the first time, Canada's military involvement abroad did not feature the army, but rather regular naval and air force units. Paradoxically, despite earlier military unification, the Canadian services did not act jointly as a national force in this conflict, at least partly because the forces of other nations (especially the United States) were still organized more conventionally. The Canadians did co-operate very successfully with their allies. The Canadian Navy considered its work in the Gulf War highly successful, particularly given the equipment with which it had to operate. The Canadian government got just what it wanted: an active, limited, and relatively inexpensive (about $1 billion) operation within a coalition in which Canadians served apart from direct American control.

In some ways the collapse of the cold war temporarily opened up new ways for Canadians to offer their services to the world. Canadian peacekeepers were in constant demand around the world, ultimately serving in trouble spots like Somalia and Bosnia with a singular lack of effectiveness. Canada also flirted with the dangers of diplomatic isolation in 1995, as its attempts to enforce limits on offshore fishing led to an open confrontation with the Spaniards. Fortunately, there was enough support for the Canadian position behind the scenes to discourage Spanish militancy. The crisis was resolved peacefully.

Canadian involvement in the United Nations' Balkan peacekeeping was suggested by

THE SOMALIA AFFAIR, 1997

In 1997 a Commission of Inquiry made its final report on the behaviour of Canadian troops in Somalia in 1993. The following extract explains the background to the inquiry.

In the spring, summer, and fall of 1992, the United Nations, concerned about the breakdown of national government in Somalia and the spectre of famine there, sought international help to restore some semblance of law and order in Somalia and feed its starving citizens. Canada, among other nations, was asked to help. After months of planning and training, and after a change in the nature of the United Nations mission from a peacekeeping mission to a peace enforcement mission, Canadian Forces personnel, as part of a coalition of forces led by the United States, were deployed for service to Somalia, mainly in December 1992. Many of the Canadian personnel involved in the deployment belonged to the Canadian Airborne Regiment Battle Group (CARBG), itself made up largely of soldiers from the Canadian Airborne Regiment (a paratroop battalion), with other army personnel added to it, including A Squadron, an armoured car squadron from the Royal Canadian Dragoons, a mortar platoon from 1st Battalion, the Royal Canadian Regiment, and an engineer squadron from 2 Combat Engineer Regiment.

On the night of March 16–17, 1993, near the city of Belet Huen, Somalia, soldiers of the Canadian Airborne Regiment beat to death a bound 16-year-old Somali youth, Shidane Arone. Canadians were shocked, and they began to ask hard questions. How could Canadian soldiers beat to death a young man held in their custody? Was the Canadian Airborne Regiment suitable or operationally ready to go to Somalia? Was racism a factor in improper conduct within the Regiment? Before long, Canadian media began to publicize accounts of other incidents involving questionable conduct by Canadian soldiers in Somalia. Major Barry Armstrong, surgeon to the Canadian Airborne Regiment, acting in fulfilment of his military duties, alleged that an earlier incident on March 4, 1993, where an intruder was shot dead and another was wounded by Canadian Airborne soldiers, appeared to have been an execution-style killing. And so, other questions arose: Were incidents in Somalia covered up, and, if so, how far up the chain of command did the cover-up extend? Did the Canadian Forces and the Department of National Defence respond appropriately to the allegations of cover-up? And perhaps most problematic of all, were the mistreatment of Shidane Arone and other incidents of misconduct caused by a few 'bad apples', or were they symptomatic of deeper institutional problems in the Canadian military at the time—problems relating to command and control, accountability, leadership, or training? If so, did these problems still exist?

The Canadian Forces responded in many ways to the death of Shidane Arone and other incidents that occurred in Somalia. Several courts martial, arising mostly though not exclusively from misconduct relating to the death of Shidane Arone, were launched and concluded. A court martial trial began against Master Corporal Clayton Matchee, the person who allegedly beat Shidane Arone to death. The trial did not proceed, however, because injuries resulting from an apparent suicide attempt rendered MCpl Matchee unfit to stand trial. The most prominent court martial was arguably that of Private Kyle Brown, who was convicted of manslaughter and torture in the death of Mr. Arone. In some cases, appeals of the courts martial arising from the Somalia operation were launched. Other individuals involved suffered sanctions less severe than imprisonment upon conviction.

But perhaps more important, the Canadian Forces recognized the need for additional measures to respond to public concern about what happened in Somalia. Accordingly, the Chief of the Defence Staff of the Canadian Forces appointed an internal board of inquiry under section 45 of the National Defence Act to look into issues arising from the Somalia operation. The board conducted the first phase of its work from April to July 1993. The board's final report made several recommendations for change. However, its terms of reference were restricted in two ways. First, to avoid challenges to its jurisdiction under the *Canadian Charter of Rights and Freedoms*, it was essentially precluded from looking into incidents that could give rise to court martial proceedings. . . . Second, its focus was on issues such as leadership and discipline relating to the CARBG, which included the antecedents of the CARBG in Canada and higher headquarters in Somalia before and during its deployment there. Thus, it had no authority to look into the actions or missions of persons at the highest levels of the chain of command within the Canadian Forces. As well, the hearings were not open to the public. It was intended that there would be a second phase of the inquiry to address issues not addressed in its first phase.

Critics argued that an open inquiry was needed to get to the truth of what happened and why. Representatives of the Liberal Party of Canada, the official opposition at the time the board of inquiry was established, argued for an open public inquiry under the *National Defence Act*. When the Liberals gained power after the 1993 federal election, they continued to express this view. However, as more revelations suggesting possible cover-up and other disclosures were made, the Government eventually decided to establish a public inquiry independent of the military that would have the power to subpoena witnesses not belonging to the military. As a result, on March 20, 1995, this Commission of Inquiry, governed by the federal Inquiries Act, was created. This act sets out the statutory powers and responsibilities of inquiries, generally giving us broad powers to summon and enforce the attendance of witnesses and to require the production of documents.

SOURCE: *Dishonoured Legacy: The Lessons of the Somalia Affair; Report of the Commission of Inquiry into the Deployment of Canadian Forces to Somalia* (Ottawa: Minister of Public Works and Government Services, 1997): I, 1-3.

the Mulroney government as early as 1990 and reiterated in 1991, but the Mulroney initiative was not popular with Canada's allies. The British foreign secretary told Mulroney, 'Trouble with you Canadians is you think there is a solution to every problem' (quoted in Gammer, 2001: 81). Nevertheless Canada persisted in driving the United Nations and NATO forward on the Balkan peacekeeping front, and it could hardly avoid contributing to a peacekeeping force for Bosnia in 1993 despite recognition of the difficulties of the situation. To a considerable extent, Canadian commanders on the scene were if anything more aggressive than the government had intended, and the military did its best to adapt to Canada's doctrines of interventionism in the early 1990s.

Lack of success, lack of funding, and some nasty scandals reduced the credibility of Canada's military to the point that by 1996 the nation could fully anticipate that Canada's armed forces would no longer be serving anywhere in the world but at home. A total withdrawal from Europe had been delayed by peacekeeping in Yugoslavia, but in early 1996 Canada announced it was acting unilaterally to bring its forces home. Somalia and Bosnia were both public-relations disasters that marked an end to a new Canadian willingness to intervene in local disputes. In the former, supposedly highly disciplined Canadian soldiers brutalized the locals. In the latter, Canadian peacekeepers seemed unable to accomplish anything positive, and were often held as impotent hostages by the warring factions.

In the end, the Chrétien government chose to return to a more traditional interpretation of peacekeeping, in which Canada served as a neutral arbitrator rather than an interventionist peacekeeper. To a considerable extent the withdrawal to neutral peacekeeping was a product of the failure of the military to be successful, complicated by the military insistence that success required better hardware and increased expenditures. Chrétien cancelled several large orders for new hardware the military commanders deemed necessary to keep the forces competitive. Public exposure of Canadian soldiers' racism and brutality towards one another did little for either image or morale. One battalion of paratroopers, the Canadian Airborne, was totally disbanded. Canadian troops did yeoman duty in two domestic emergencies, a major flood in Manitoba in May 1997, and a devastating ice storm in Quebec in January 1998. Both actions served to refurbish the military's public image and self-confidence.

The disarray of the military and the withdrawal from an active peacekeeping role seemed symptomatic of Canada's international posture. The idealism of earlier days was now replaced by incompetence and impotence. Public opinion polls by the end of the century routinely reported that Canadians no longer expected to be defended from foreign aggression by their own military.

CONCLUSION

The post-Cold War world was both menacing and confusing. Ethnic and religious conflict was on the rise in many quarters. An increasing number of developing nations acquired nuclear capabilities, and began threatening employ them against their neighbours. International terrorism continued to be a serious threat. Canadians had great difficulty in identifying their friends and allies, particularly since Canada was indisputably one of a handful of rich nations in a world in which most nations and people were poor. Virtually the only possible response for many Canadians seemed to be a retreat from international involvement into relative isolationism under the American defence umbrella.

HOW HISTORY HAS CHANGED

MILITARY AND FOREIGN POLICY

Canadian history has experienced very few major controversies. What usually happens is that new perspectives overtake older ones as new dimensions are added to existing interpretations. The history of Canadian military and foreign policy has experienced fewer debates than most subjects, particularly over the fundamental shape of these policies as they developed over time. This agreement results partly from the leading historians of these subjects sharing a common experience of service in the Canadian government, either in External Affairs or in the directorate of history in the Department of National Defence. These historians were often professional insiders who were hardly likely to be critical of policies and decisions in which they themselves participated. But beyond the commonality of experience resides a more important tempering factor: the limited nature of the options available to Canada in either military or international policy and, consequently, the relative absence of partisan disagreements about either subject among the nation's political leaders. Canada's military and foreign policies have since 1939 been carried on with a minimum of debate on anybody's part. Canada joined the British in World War II because the nation's leaders could see little choice. The historian Frank Underhill got into trouble with his administration at the University of Toronto in the early days of the war because he publicly insisted that Canada would end up sheltering under the American umbrella, becoming an American dependent rather than a British one. This prediction proved to be quite accurate, and at least since 1945 no major Canadian political leader has seen any alternative to American dependency. Only occasionally have historians raised the question of how much dependency there should be, and then never very seriously.

There has been a substantial consensus on the shape of Canadian foreign and military policy since World War II. Before the 1960s Canada attempted to play the role of a middle power, but was forced to abandon these pretensions both because of changing world circumstances and because of the cost of maintaining a large military establishment. Briefly in the 1970s Canada made an effort to escape the American umbrella, but without success. It then fell back into a position of a junior ally of the United States, distinguished only by its utilization of a small but well-trained military in peacekeeping exercises around the world. Even peacekeeping ultimately failed, however. As the century ended, Canada was in no position to step out on its own either diplomatically or militarily, and it fell once again into its familiar role of dependency after 11 September 2001.

SHORT BIBLIOGRAPHY

Bercuson, David. *Significant Incident: Canada's Army, the Airborne and the Murder in Somalia*. Toronto, 1996. A historian's account of the Somalia affair, emphasizing deep-rooted problems.

Eayrs, James. *In Defence of Canada*, vol. 4: *Growing Up Allied*. Toronto, 1980. Perhaps the best volume of a multi-volumed classic, dealing with postwar defence matters.

Gammer, Nicholas. *From Peacekeeping to Peacemaking: Canada's Response to the Yugoslav Crisis*. Toronto, 2001. A monograph analysing the attempt of the Mulroney government in the early 1990s to take a more active role in world peacekeeping.

Granatstein, J.L. *The Ottawa Men: The Civil Service*

Mandarins 1935–1957. Toronto, 1982. A very useful study of the men who ran the Canadian government—on the domestic as well as the external side—before, during, and after World War II.

Granatstein, J.L., and Robert Bothwell. *Pirouette: Pierre Trudeau and Canadian Foreign Policy*. Toronto, 1990. A surprisingly sympathetic study of the efforts of Pierre Elliott Trudeau to remake Canadian foreign policy in the 1970s.

Hellyer, Paul. *Damn the Torpedoes: My Fight to Unify Canada's Armed Forces*. Toronto, 1990. A bit self-serving, this memoir offers an insider's look at the unification of the armed forces in the 1960s.

Holmes, John. *The Shaping of Peace: Canada and the Search for World Order, 1943–1957*. Toronto, 1979. Another classic, part of a multi-volumed study of Canadian foreign policy during and after World War II.

Keating, Tom. *Canada and World Order: The Multilateralist Tradition in Canadian Foreign Policy*. Toronto, 1993. An important study emphasizing the importance of multilateralism to postwar Canadian policy.

Nash, Knowlton. *Kennedy and Diefenbaker: Fear and Loathing across the Undefended Border*. Toronto, 1990. A journalist's account of the Canadian–American relationship at the leadership level in the early 1960s.

Reid, Escott. *Time of Fear and Hope: The Making of the North Atlantic Treaty 1947–1949*. Toronto, 1977. A cross between a monograph and a memoir by one of the participants in the NATO business.

Stacey, C.P. *Canada and the Age of Conflict: A History of Canadian External Policy*. 2 vols. Toronto, 1984. A classic account of Canadian external policy by one of Canada's greatest military and international historians.

Stairs, Denis. *The Diplomacy of Constraint: Canada, the Korean War, and the United States*. Toronto, 1974. A wonderful account of the problems faced by Canada in the Korean War.

Veatch, Richard. *Canada and the League of Nations*. Toronto, 1975. An excellent survey of Canada's participation in the League, emphasizing its difficulty in making itself heard.

STUDY QUESTIONS

1. Identify three ways in which Canada's international relations changed between the end of the First World War and the beginning of the second.
2. What were Canada's three most important contributions to the war effort in the early days of World War II?
3. Explain the meaning of the term 'functionalism' as it was used in a foreign policy sense after World War II.
4. Who was Igor Gouzenko? What role did he play in the development of the cold war between the West and the Soviet Union?
5. Explain why, between 1959 and 1963, issues of military defence gradually eroded Prime Minister Diefenbaker's support base in his own cabinet.
6. What is Canada's most fundamental problem in developing an independent foreign policy?
7. Argue the case for or against Canada's developing an increased military presence in the twenty-first century.

CHAPTER THIRTEEN

Freefalling into the Twenty-first Century, 1992–2001

If one listened to the journalists and the media pundits, Canada and Canadians lived in a constant state of crisis and turmoil in the 1990s, lurching from one emergency to the next without any road-map to the future. While such may have been the case, in this view there is little perspective. The 'news' almost by definition has no sense of history. Certainly Canada was not unique in its problems, which almost without exception were occurring in many other places around the world. Even the potential disintegration of the Canadian Confederation was hardly unique. Movements of national liberation were everywhere, and contrary to the situations in Bosnia, the USSR, and Sri Lanka—to name but a few troubled nations—at least in Canada the conflicting sides were not yet armed camps. Moreover, despite the nation's well-publicized problems, most of the population of the remainder of the world would have probably traded their situation for that of the average Canadian. Canada continued to rank at or near the top of everyone's world standard-of-living table. As for the claim that Canada lacked direction, it would have been equally true at any time in the past. With hindsight, historians can offer some notion of what the direction was and what the ultimate outcome would be. We can see an inexorable line from the Great Depression through the Second World War to the social service state, for example. Those who live in the midst of the maelstrom, however, can have little sense of how the issues and paradoxes of the moment will eventually be resolved. Nor can the participants in the chaos of the moment tell whether the resolution will be progressive or retrogressive, apocalyptic or gradual. About all we can say with assurance is that the future is—as it always has been—uncertain. That fact is not in itself a crisis.

Politics

At the federal level, the most important political development of the mid-1990s was probably the triumph of the Liberal Party in the 1993 election, combined with the absolute collapse of the Progressive Conservative Party and its replacement by two openly antagonistic regional parties. National political parties had failed abysmally at the polls before (the Liberals in 1918, the Tories in 1940). Regional parties (such as the Progressive Party) had temporarily risen to prominence. What was new about the election of 1993, of course, was the emergence in the House of Commons of two regional parties of equal strength, the Reform Party and the Bloc Québécois, each committed to irreconcilable policies and their combined seats unequal to the large Liberal majority. These two regional parties both tended to draw their strength from voters who had previously supported the Tories. At the same time, the Liberals did win a major victory, but without any evidence of new policies.

By the close of 1992 it was clear that Prime Minister Brian Mulroney's popularity ratings, consistently lower than any other Canadian

TIMELINE

1990
Japanese-Canadians get apology from Canadian government. Lucien Bouchard leaves PC party, forms Bloc Québécois.

1991
Royal Commission on Aboriginal Peoples formed.

1992
Referendum on Charlottetown Accord.

1993
Kim Campbell is chosen leader of the Progressive Conservative Party and becomes prime minister of Canada in June. In October the Liberals win a great victory. Jean Charest becomes PC leader.

1994
NAFTA proclaimed. PQ victory in Quebec.

1995
Mike Harris's Tories demolish the NDP in Ontario. Separatism defeated in Quebec in close referendum vote. Quebec Nordiques leave for new home in Colorado.

1996
Sheldon Kennedy accuses his former hockey coach of sexual abuse.

1997
Liberals win another federal victory, PQ a victory in Quebec. Asia-Pacific Economic Co-operation (APEC) meeting held in Vancouver. Canada agrees to Kyoto Accord on greenhouse gasses. Supreme Court hands down judgment on Delgamuukw case.

1998
Jean Charest steps down as federal PC leader to lead Quebec's provincial Liberal Party. Joe Clark becomes PC leader. United Church apologizes to Aboriginal people for residential school abuse.

1999
United Alternative Convention held. Adrienne Clarkson becomes governor-general of Canada.

2000
Molson's 'I am Canadian' advertising campaign begins. In July Stockwell Day is chosen over Preston Manning to lead the Canadian Alliance. In November the Liberals win their third term in office.

2001
Terrorists destroy the World Trade Centre in New York City.

prime minister had ever previously experienced, were not likely to improve with time. At the leadership convention that ensued in June 1993, Kim Campbell (b. 1947) was chosen to lead the party on the second ballot. Campbell, a British Columbian who had originally been associated with the Social Credit party in that province, thus became Canada's first female prime minister. Although a relative newcomer to federal politics, she had more experience than Brian Mulroney at the time of selection. She had held two major cabinet portfolios beginning in 1989. The Tories apparently hoped that her gender and her refreshing 'candour' would lead the country to see Campbell as a fresh face, although her credentials in French Canada were hardly up to those of the man she had beaten out (Jean Charest of Quebec). Some observers, particularly among feminists, argued that Campbell had been chosen as a 'sacrificial lamb' to bear the brunt of the inevitable election defeat about to occur. In any case, like John Turner a decade earlier, Campbell inherited the enormous unpopularity of her predecessor. She had little time to

KIM CAMPBELL

Kim Campbell was born on 10 March 1947 in Port Alberni, British Columbia, as Avril Phaedra Douglas Campbell. She changed her given name to Kim soon after her mother left the family in 1959. She attended the University of British Columbia and received a BA in Political Science in 1969 and subsequently attended the London School of Economics, 1970–3, leaving with her thesis incomplete. In 1972 she married Nathan Divinsky, whom she divorced in 1983; a second marriage ended in divorce in 1993. From 1975 to 1981 Campbell taught political science and history at UBC and Vancouver Community College. In 1980 she entered politics and was elected to the Vancouver School Board, becoming chairman in 1983. Also in 1983 she received her LL.B. from the University of British Columbia and by 1985 she was serving as a political advisor to Bill Bennett's Social Credit government. In 1986 she was elected a Social Credit MLA, and only two years later accepted an invitation from the federal Progressive Conservative Party to run in the riding of Vancouver Centre, where she was elected to Parliament in 1988.

Campbell was fast-tracked by the Tories from her first appearance in Ottawa. She was made minister of state for Indian and Northern Affairs, a prominent portfolio, in 1989, and a year later became the first female minister of Justice and Attorney General. In this post she introduced into Parliament a Criminal Code amendment for firearms control and another amendment for sexual assault, both in the wake of the Montreal Massacre of 1989. She became minister of National Defence in 1993 at the time of the Somalia debacle. When Brian Mulroney announced his retirement, she entered the competition to succeed him, beating her closest rival, Jean Charest, at a leadership convention in June. She thereupon became Canada's first female prime minister. Given the unpopularity of the Tories, who would have to face an election within a few months, the victory was in many ways deceptive. Many commentators believed that Campbell was made a sacrificial lamb by a party that knew it had no chance of victory thanks to the unpopularity of NAFTA, the GST, and various constitutional fiascos. The Tories could expect little support from Quebec and were under attack in the west from the Reform Party. An economic recession completed the list of liabilities. Campbell herself contributed to the defeat by running an inconsistent campaign in which slurs against the Liberal leader Jean Chrétien were at first encouraged and then retracted. The Tories were virtually wiped out in the election, their seats in Parliament reduced to two. Campbell could not even save her own riding. Few historians hold her responsible for the Tory debacle of 1993, attributing it instead to the unpopularity of the Mulroney government and structural shifts in the political makeup of Canada's national parties. Her refusal to continue in politics encouraged the return of Joe Clark. Campbell returned to the academy with a fellowship at Harvard before accepting in 1996 a ceremonial post as Canada's Consul General in Los Angeles. She published her memoirs in 1996 as *Time and Chance: The Political Memoirs of Canada's First Woman Prime Minister*, a relatively innocuous volume.

establish a new government image before having to call an election.

Jean Chrétien's Liberals were in some ways well prepared for the contest, certainly financially, although the party platform was somewhat schizophrenic, committed to carrying on the welfare state while balancing the budget and reducing the deficit. Chrétien was hardly a brilliant campaigner, but he proved adequate to the task, much aided by a series of blunders by Campbell and her advisers. The worst occurred shortly before the end of the campaign, when Campbell was unable to distance herself quickly enough from a negative political ad campaign suggesting that Chrétien was handicapped. Negative campaigning in the media had become common in the United States, but this one backfired by generating popular sympathy for the Liberal leader. Submerged under the national media attention given to Campbell and Chrétien were a series of fascinating local races featuring a variety of conservative third parties, of which the Reform Party and the Bloc Québécois proved on election day to be the most attractive to the voters. The Liberals did not so much receive a mandate as triumph over an otherwise badly divided field headed by the singularly inept Tories.

☐ Prime Minister designate Kim Campbell with Brian Mulroney outside the official residence at 24 Sussex Drive, Ottawa, 14 June 1993. CP/Tom Hanson.

The Reform Party had been organized in October of 1987 by (Ernest) Preston Manning, son of the great Alberta Social Credit leader Ernest Manning. Its backbone was in traditional Alberta and British Columbia Socred constituencies, but it had some appeal as far east as Ontario among retired Canadians and first-time young voters. Manning was a professional management consultant. He was a colourless speaker, but his lack of charisma was somewhat redeemed by a self-deprecating humour seldom seen among major political leaders. The Reform Party stood four-square for the traditional, often populist, values of the Anglo-Canadian west. It wanted to cut federal spending, to reform Parliament to make it more responsive to the popular will, and to provide for the equal treatment of provinces and citizens alike. The party had no time for the sovereignist pretensions of Quebec or for French-Canadian culture. Reform liked multiculturalism little better than biculturalism. Manning indicated his willingness to contemplate new limitations on immigration to Canada, although he was not pressed hard on the issue.

As for the Bloc Québécois , it was associated both within and without Quebec with its major campaign issue, the separation of that province from the Canadian Confederation, and with its leader, Lucien Bouchard. Born in St-Coeur-de-Marie in 1938, Bouchard had been a lawyer in Chicoutimi before his appointment as Canadian ambassador to France in 1985 by the Mulroney government. In the election of 1988 he had run as a successful PC candidate, but he had left the

Opposition leader Preston Manning at a post-election news conference in Calgary, 3 June 1997. CP/Frank Gunn.

party before the 1992 referendum on the Charlottetown Accord to sit as an independent committed to a sovereign Quebec. The responses to Bouchard pointed to some interesting cultural differences between francophone Québécois and other Canadians. While many of the former found Bouchard compelling and charismatic in the traditional pattern of *le chef* (the best example of which had been Maurice Duplessis), anglophones inside and outside the province were not attracted to him in the slightest.

Not only were the PCs—soon led by Jean Charest (b. 1958)— reduced to a mere two seats on 25 October 1993, but both they and the NDP (with nine seats) lost official standing in the House of Commons. The loss of standing was particularly serious for the NDP, which had relied heavily on Commons financial support for its Ottawa infrastructure. With fifty-four seats to Reform's fifty-three, the Bloc Québécois became the official opposition, offering the somewhat anomalous spectacle of 'Her Majesty's Loyal Opposition' committed to the destruction of the institution in which it was participating. The Liberals had a pretty easy time in most respects, since the opposition was unable to agree on very much and lacked numerical strength anyway. In power, the Chrétien government continued to exhibit the schizophrenia of its campaign platform, trying to reduce federal expenditure and the deficit without doing serious damage to any of the major social programs—or its image. A major review of the entire welfare and unemployment system, headed by Lloyd Axworthy (b. 1939), ended up making essentially cosmetic changes to the system designed to make it more difficult to remain for long periods on social assistance or to use welfare to subsidize seasonal employment. The government predictably sought to save money by cutting deeply into cultural programs and the military, and by reducing the amount of transfer payments to the provinces for health and higher education. As the time for another election approached, the Liberals had precious little in positive accomplishment to take to the nation, however.

Despite the many weaknesses of Chrétien's government, the Liberals won easily in 1997. This victory was less the result of Liberal success than of opposition failure. The conservative forces were still divided regionally, with Bouchard's Bloc Québécois dominating in Quebec, and Manning's Reform and Charest's Progressive Conservatives dividing the vote outside Quebec. While the PCs did best outside the west, Reform got all its 60 seats from the four western provinces, especially Alberta and British Columbia, where western alienation continued to be strong. The NDP still could not mount an eastern breakthrough, and was hampered by its lack of a strong or imaginative platform; the party was badly divided between those who wanted to make it the radical alternative and those who thought such a stance would be the kiss of death. The Liberals collected 155 seats to 145 for the combined opposition, despite gathering only 38.4 per cent of the total vote.

The nation's most obvious political need was for a unified conservative opposition. This was far more difficult to obtain than might have been expected, given the potential prize of national political power were it accomplished. In April 1998, Jean Charest stepped down as leader of the national PCs to become leader of the Quebec Liberal Party. This shift of allegiance probably bothered the voters outside Quebec less than those within the province. Into the national gap stepped Joe Clark, the leader and ex-prime minister earlier dismissed from the leadership in favour of Brian Mulroney. Clark was popular with backroom Tories in eastern Canada, but hardly anybody else. In early 1999, 1,500 delegates assembled in Ottawa at a United Alternative Convention, which hoped to lay the framework for a new political party of the right. Most of these delegates were members of the Reform Party, and there was little enthusiasm for this initiative from either the BQ or the Tories. The United Alternative turned into the Alliance party. Most Reform members shifted their allegiance, but Joe Clark resolutely remained outside the new umbrella. Preston Manning attempted unsuccessfully to become the Alliance's new leader, but was thwarted by a relative newcomer named Stockwell Day. Day was selected, in July 2000, probably because he seemed the only viable alternative to Manning, who graciously stepped aside as leader of the opposition in Day's favour. Manning had been rejected because he was perceived to be unacceptable outside western Canada. Unfortunately, Day proved to be less than compelling as a political leader. His first appearance in the role saw him don a wetsuit and ride a jet ski to meet the media. There was also the lingering problem of a lawsuit filed against him by a lawyer whom Day had criticized for defending a pedophile; the legal costs were assumed by the province of Alberta. Day was forced to lead the Alliance (officially the Canadian Reform Conservative Alliance) into an election within a few months of his selection and before he was able either to put his mark on the party platform or to develop any popular new initiatives.

In the 2000 federal election, the Liberals actually gained both in seats and in percentage of the popular vote. The number of Liberal seats increased to 172 and the party's percentage of the popular vote grew to 40.8 per cent. Some of the increase was at the expense of the Bloc Québécois, which dropped from 44 to 38 seats, although a number of seats were also taken from both the Progressive Conservatives and the NDP. The Alliance actually gained in seats over the Reform total in 1997, winning in 66 ridings, although still exclusively in western Canada. As leader of the opposition, Stockwell Day proved ineffective. Before long, leading members of his caucus like Deborah Grey and house leader Chuck Strahl were publicly criticizing Day's leadership. By April 2001, most of the caucus had turned against him and 13 walked out; six of the thirteen subsequently returned.

Meanwhile, Prime Minister Chrétien came under attack in the House of Commons, in the media, and in his own caucus over his involvement with developers in his riding for whom he solicited government support. As well, there were a number of other ethically dubious interventions. The government's newly appointed ethics advisor ruled in all cases brought before him that Chrétien had broken no guidelines, but neither the opposition nor the public were entirely convinced. One of the chief issues in the Liberal caucus involved succession politics. Chrétien was widely expected to step down soon after his 2000 victory, and every potential leadership candidate tried to build up a financial war chest and support against the day the prime minister either announced his departure or authorized open campaigning for his successor.

Developments at the provincial level confirmed the split personality of the electorate. The public was concerned about the size of the deficits and was generally opposed to higher taxes, but at the same time was not at all enthusiastic about deep cuts in social programs. Whether these sentiments were held by the same people or by different groups of voters was not entirely clear. In Alberta, the Tory government of Ralph Klein (b. 1942) won a big election victory

MARIO DUMONT

Mario Dumont was born on 19 May 1970 in Cacouna, Quebec, a small town not far from Rivière-du-Loup. He first entered politics at the age of 16, when he became a member of the youth commission of the Quebec Liberal Party, subsequently serving on the executive of the Liberal youth commission. In 1991 he was elected chairman of the youth commission during the Liberal convention that adopted the Allaire report as party policy on the Constitution, and he was one of the leaders of the young people's wing of the Liberal Party in 1992. He campaigned against the Charlottetown Accord as co-chairman of the Network of Liberals, voting No. In 1993 Dumont received his BA in economics from Concordia University in Quebec, and six months later (in January 1994) he was one of the founding members of the *Action Démocratique du Québec*. He was elected party president in March 1994 and became leader of the party at the age of 24 in April, when Jean Allaire resigned from the post. In September he led the ADQ in the general election and emerged as MNA for the riding of Rivière-du-Loup.

As leader of the ADQ, in June 1995 Dumont was a signatory (along with Jacques Parizeau and Lucien Bouchard) to the well-known tripartite pact on the campaign for Quebec sovereignty. His appearance in connection with this agreement was probably the first time most of Canada (or even Quebec) ever heard of him, and Dumont campaigned actively for sovereignty in the Quebec referendum of October 1995. Indeed, he was probably one of the few winners in the defeat of the referendum, since the campaign gave him an opportunity to become better known as one of the province's 'fresh faces' on the political front. He acquired his nickname of 'Super Mario' in emulation of the great hockey player Mario Lemieux. Re-elected from Rivière-du-Loup as MNA in 1998, Dumont helped lead his party to a stunning victory in the by-election in Saguenay in April 2002, taking advantage of the PQ's reputation as a reform party to stake out ground on the right and possibly make his party the logical successor to the Union Nationale.

in 1993 on a platform of realistic government budgeting. Klein carried through with major budget cuts, although because of Alberta's relative wealth, these probably hurt less than they would have in a province like Nova Scotia. In Ontario, the NDP government of Bob Rae (b. 1948), which had not succeeded in controlling finances and had run afoul of the province's trade union movement in its attempts to cut the costs of its civil service, was demolished in 1995 by the Tories led by Mike Harris (b. 1945). The chief campaign issue was government spending. When Harris actually began to cut spending, however, the cries of wounded outrage were deafening. In Ontario, as elsewhere, there was some evidence from the polls that Canadians were actually prepared to pay higher taxes to preserve some of their social benefits, particularly in the health care sector.

The reasons for the 1994 electoral victory of the Parti Québécois—or the mood of the electorate in that province—were, as usual, clouded by the sovereignty issue. The Bourassa government had not controlled spending, but the PQ did not present itself in the campaign as the party of fiscal restraint. In 1997 Bouchard's PQ easily won re-election over Jean Charest's Liberals by campaigning chiefly on a platform of preserving a 'zero deficit', which obviously meant deep cuts to education, social services, and health care. The party kept a low profile on separatism, and this probably only confused the electorate. The big winner in the 1997 election was the Action Démocratique du Quebec (ADQ), led by an articulate young former Liberal named Mario Dumont (b. 1970) who advocated sovereignty association. The ADQ presented a right-wing alternative to the two major parties, and picked up much support from those who in earlier days would have supported the Union Nationale. Although the NDP was wiped out in 1995 in Ontario and in 2001 in British Columbia, in both cases standing accused of fiscal irresponsibility, it came to power in Manitoba in 1999 to replace a Tory government that had come to grief over mismanagement of health care. What was evident everywhere in Canada was that no politician or political party had any fresh ideas for resolving the fiscal dilemma.

THE CONSTITUTION

Any hope that the referendum defeat of the Charlottetown Accord had put a lid on constitutional matters was ended by the 1994 PQ victory in Quebec. Led by Jacques Parizeau (b. 1930), the PQ moved inexorably towards another Quebec referendum on sovereignty. Parizeau had initially opposed sovereignty association, but gradually came to see it as a way to satisfy some soft nationalists. Realizing that one of the major problems with the 1980 referendum had been the uncertainty regarding both the question and any consequent action, Parizeau sought to tie down the new question. He had legislation passed defining the terms. In June 1995 he and the two other separatist leaders, the BQ's Bouchard and the ADQ's Dumont, agreed on a plan. Quebecers would be asked to authorize the Quebec government to open negotiations with Ottawa on sovereignty association. If the province gave a mandate and if an agreement with Canada was not reached within a year, Quebec would unilaterally declare sovereignty. By joining forces, the three leaders hoped to allay fears that the Quebec government would, in Parizeau's words, 'jump the gun' on a declaration of sovereignty. The vote was soon set for 30 October 1995. The official question was 'Do you agree that Quebec should become sovereign, after having made a formal offer to Canada for a new Economic and Political Partnership, within the scope of the Bill respecting the future of Quebec and of the agreement signed on June 12, 1995?'

In the beginning the federalist (*Non*) forces seemed to be well in control of the situation. Experts expected the usual ballot bonus for the federalists, who would turn out a higher proportion of their supporters. They also anticipated the usual conservative response to uncertainty. For the most part, Ottawa kept its distance from the campaign, allowing Liberal leader Daniel Johnson to carry the *Non* message to the electorate. The federal strategy was to do as little as possible to fuel the sovereignist position. Then, with polls showing a marked advantage for the *Non* side, Lucien Bouchard actively entered the fray. Bouchard had only recently recovered from a rare bacterial infection that cost him a leg and nearly his life. He had not been originally expected to be an important campaigner, but the province was clearly not excited by Parizeau and Dumont. Bouchard introduced a new level of emotion into the campaign, simplifying the issues considerably. For many Quebecers, the need to move forward on the constitutional front became the key question in the referendum. When the need for constitutional change rather than the need for sovereignty became the real referendum question, the situation rapidly deteriorated for the federalist forces. What had earlier been a ho-hum campaign suddenly turned into a real barn-burner. At the last minute, Prime Minister Chrétien revealed the panic in Ottawa

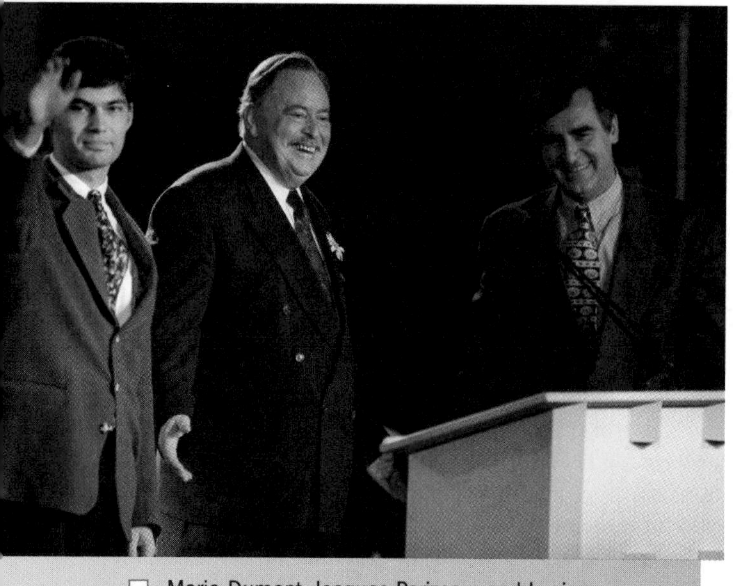

Mario Dumont, Jacques Parizeau, and Lucien Bouchard at a rally for Yes supporters in Longueuil, Quebec, 29 October 1995. The referendum vote was held the following day. CP/Paul Chiasson.

by offering Quebec concessions, including yet another 'distinct society' constitutional proposal.

The vote turned into a cliff-hanger as virtually every eligible resident of Quebec cast his or her ballot. The final turnout—over 94 per cent of the total electorate—has seldom been matched except in police states with compulsory voting. Millions of Canadians remained tuned to their television sets until late in the evening, waiting for the decisive result. Finally, it became clear that the *Non* forces had won a narrow victory. In the end, 2,362,355 Quebecers (or 50.6 per cent) of the total voted *Non*, while 2,308,054 (or 49.4 per cent) voted *Oui*. The young, the francophone, and the Quebecer outside Montreal led the way in voting *Oui*. There were many informal complaints about voting irregularities, but the vote was allowed to stand. Premier Parizeau had prepared a gracious speech of conciliation to accompany a sovereignist victory. In his bitter acknowledgement of failure on national radio and television, he was less gracious, blaming anglophones and ethnics for thwarting the aspirations of francophone Quebec. As Parizeau spoke, the cameras panned around the crowd of people gathered at *Oui* headquarters. Many were in tears. Parizeau's impulsive attack turned much public opinion against him, even within his own party. Within hours he announced his resignation. In February 1996 he would be officially replaced by Lucien Bouchard.

In the wake of the referendum, the Chrétien government passed a unilateral declaration in the Canadian Parliament that recognized Quebec as a distinct society, but as virtually everyone had come to appreciate, this gesture was too little too late. French Canadians in Quebec had made clear their desire for a new constitutional relationship with Canada. Virtually the only question remaining was whether or not a sovereign Quebec would remain within some sort of Canadian Confederation. Post-referendum polls continued to emphasize that Quebecers wanted to remain within Canada, but not under its present Constitution. Canadians turned to debate the next step in the ongoing constitutional process. One of the most difficult parts of this debate was trying to figure out a process for generating a new constitutional arrangement, since most of the previous approaches appeared discredited.

Any new constitutional arrangement would have to deal with more than merely the aspirations of Quebec. One of the most important additional items on the agenda for constitutional reform was the First Nations, who wanted the constitutional entrenchment of their conception of Aboriginal self-government. Although in many ways this position parallels Quebec's own position with respect to Canada, the province rejects Aboriginal claims to sovereignty within its jurisdiction. This refusal helps explain the insistence of the Quebec government in early 1996 that 'Quebec is indivisible.' The Constitution Act of 1982, while entrenching the existing Aboriginal and treaty rights of the First Nations, had not really come to terms with Aboriginal self-government, chiefly because the First Nations and Ottawa were so far apart on the subject. The Aboriginal peoples have insisted that their government should be based on inherent jurisdiction as a historic right. For many Aboriginals this involves sovereign jurisdiction and the independent right to make laws and institutions for their people and their territory, since these rights were not surrendered with treaties. The militants object to the concept of Aboriginal self-government as an equivalent of municipal government, delegated to the First Nations by those jurisdictions (Ottawa and the provinces) that claim the sovereignty under the Crown and Constitution of Canada. As sovereign governments, First Nations would deal only as equals with Ottawa, which the Native people insist still owes them a heavy debt of financial responsibility. As municipal governments, they would become the agents of the senior governments, with only those powers allowed them by those governments. To recognize the First Nations (more than 500 bands) as sovereign would certainly be more possible in a Constitution that so accepted Quebec. For many Canadians, however, such recognition would not only further balkanize the country but would create independent jurisdictions within Canada that benefited from their Canadian affiliation but held no concurrent responsibilities under it. As the new millennium began, Quebec became more concerned with economic problems than with sovereignty issues, but all observers recognized that separatism could very easily slip back into the spotlight.

THE ECONOMY

The Canadian economy had now been running for a long time without correcting itself. In the 1990s some of the traditional indicators were positive for economic growth. Inflation was low, interest rates were low and constantly falling, and the Canadian dollar was lower against other world currencies. The resulting economic growth rate was slow, but constantly upward. Foreign trade continued to be buoyant, although mainly in the resource sector and associated industries. On the other hand, construction starts were stagnant and sales of new cars were lower than had been the case since the early 1980s. The Americans chipped ominously away at the Free Trade Agreement whenever doing so worked to their advantage. The buoyant real estate market of the 1980s was no more, even in the still overheated British Columbia economy. Household debt was up to 89 per cent of disposable income. Most important, official unemployment rates were over 10 per cent nationally, while some of the regional figures were alarming, with rates above the national average east of Ontario and below it from Ontario westward. Official unemployment in Newfoundland in 1994 was 20.4 per cent, and in Quebec 12.2 per cent. These figures, of course, included only the people still looking for work. Many of those previously employed in dead industries like the Atlantic fishery had simply given up, as had quite a few of the young.

Finding a job was not easy. Keeping one was equally difficult. Downsizing continued to be the order of the day. Governments at all levels were attempting to reduce their work forces, and almost every private enterprise was trying (with some success) to make do with less. Even those who still had their jobs lived in constant fear of the next round of rationalization. As for the rationalizers, there was growing evidence that downsizing was no more self-correcting than other economic strategies. According to hopeful economic theory, once business profits went up substantially, excess profits would be reinvested in expansion. This was at least partly the thinking behind the practice of keeping business taxes low in what came to be known as 'Reaganomics', after the American president who had campaigned on this view. What often seemed to be happening in the 1990s, however, was that the increasing profits were simply distributed to the shareholders. Nonetheless, governments hesitated to increase the tax rates.

Perhaps as disturbing as the nagging fear of the chop for those who still had jobs was the absence of recognizable new career growth areas for those seeking to prepare themselves for employment. The education counsellors had virtually run out of suggestions for viable careers. There were still plenty of jobs in the part-time, semi-skilled (and low-paid) end of the workforce. 'Working at McDonald's' became the catchphrase encompassing all such employment, which had no attractive future whatsoever and provided few or no fringe benefits. The younger generation faced with such employment prospects came to label itself Generation X. The post-baby boomers who, through no fault of their own, had arrived at adulthood after all the decent jobs were taken had little to look forward to. Generation X was both hedonistic and bitter, a volatile combination. The creation of new jobs was high on the wish list for most Canadians, but particularly for the young.

One economic growth area continued in household appliances and equipment. What had once been luxury items now became necessities, and new gadgets were being introduced every day. As had been the case for over a century with household equipment, constant reductions in price through technological innovation made mass marketing possible. In 1980 few homes had microwave ovens. By the mid-1990s over 80 per cent of households owned them. By 1994 more than half of Canadian households possessed a gas barbeque, and over 25 per cent of Canadian homes had some kind of air conditioning. Compact-disc players and home computers had exploded from a standing start in the late 1980s, and by 1995 were in over 50 per cent of households. Much of the electronic household gadgetry was assembled abroad, providing jobs only on the retail sales and highly technical service ends. At the same time, there was obviously room for employment in computers. Canadians established some reputation for software development. Connected to the enormous expansion of the home computer was the growth of e-mail and the use of computer networks for both business and personal communication. By 1996 the Internet—another communications medium in which Canadians had taken the lead, especially in terms of usage—had become so popular and overloaded that it no longer worked very well. Never designed for mass participation, the Internet had grown without any regulation whatsoever, which was part of its attraction and would increasingly become part of its problem. While there was a future in the computer and the microchip, this was a highly technical business that required special skills and special aptitudes. Business publications were full of stories of successful Canadian initiatives involving the glitzy new technologies, but they never explained how this would translate into large-scale employment for the average Canadian.

The high-tech industries collapsed into chaos on 11 September 2001, the day a group of terrorists succeeded in orchestrating an air attack on the United States involving four hijacked airliners. This 'meltdown' might have occurred differently under other circumstances, but there was plenty of evidence that the technological sector had expanded far too rapidly and with far too little attention being paid to proper management and accounting practices. What was collapsing was a typical overheated boom. Osama bin Laden and his conspirators were allowed to take entirely too much credit for the economic chaos that followed '9–11'.

The private enterprise philosophy associated with the growth of schools of management at the universities had, by the 1990s, been operative for nearly twenty years. There was precious little evidence, however, that the economic thinking of the free enterprisers had produced a more satisfactory economy for most Canadians than had Keynesianism. Unemployment remained high nationally and was even higher in certain regions and among certain age groups. Like earlier economic pundits, the private enterprisers insisted that their theories had not yet been given a fair chance, but few Canadians wanted to take the gamble. As for the free trade agreements made with the Americans, the jury remained undecided, although there was increasing evidence that the they were not unqualified successes. The North American Free Trade Agreement (NAFTA), which extended the earlier Free Trade Agreement (FTA) to include Mexico, took effect on 1 January 1994, with very little controversy and even less publicity. Subsequently, a number of well-publicized incidents suggested that there was little in NAFTA to protect Canadian business from American vested interests, if those interests sought to exercise their power. Thus the American softwood lumber industry, in the most highly publicized case, successfully argued that their Canadian counterparts were competing unfairly by pursuing policies that were perfectly acceptable under NAFTA. The result was the introduction of heavy surcharges on imports of Canadian lumber into the United States. As for Mexico, it became a haven for automobile manufacturers seeking to escape the high wages paid in Ontario. By the beginning of the new century, moreover, even the financial press in Canada—always sympathetic to free trade—began to run stories about the hollowing out of Canadian business. This process, by which management and executive power is taken out of the country and placed at head office, usually in the United States, had long been one of the major concerns of the opponents of free trade.

GLOBALIZATION

Scholarly studies in the 1970s and 1980s had often called into question the market view of industrial development, but regional economic integration gave a new boost to convergence theories. These theories predicted the gradual spread across the globe of similar patterns of economic life once constraints were removed. While the academic economists were careful to confine their theories to the economic realm, the business press and other popularizers quickly applied such thinking to a variety of forces, such as new communications technologies and the mobility of capital, and identified something that came to be labelled 'globalization'. The term first appeared sometime in the late 1980s. Kenichi Omae's *The Borderless World: Power and Strategy in the Interlinked Economy* (1990) was probably the key text. The globalizers argued that international flows of capital, services, and goods, in a world of instant communications and liberal trade policies were not being controlled—indeed, could not be controlled—by traditional national agencies.

The proposed Multilateral Agreement on Investment (MAI) became the epitome of the new order in which a rampant international capitalism would sweep everything before it. This global treaty on investment aligned the capital-exporting nations of the industrial West against the less developed nations. The Organization for Economic Co-operation and Development (OECD), which consisted of the twenty-nine most highly developed nations of the world (including Canada), set a target date of 1997 for the introduction of the new world order. MAI generated an enormous amount of opposition, not just from the Third World, but from the developed nations as well. Much of the consciousness raising and organization behind this opposition was made possible by the Internet, which thus demonstrated that it could be a force of resistance as well as of liberalization. In this case, the Internet publicized an international arrangement that the bankers and politicians had deliberately kept out of the public eye as much as possible. The critics argued that MAI gave to multinational corporations a series of political powers that had for several centuries been regulated by the nation-state. Under MAI, international corporations could be treated no differently than domestic ones, and the nation-state could impose no unusual performance requirements upon them. While the introduction of MAI was quietly abandoned in the face of considerable opposition and criticism, the threat of some form of multilateral agreement by the rich nations of the West remained very much in place. Such a spectre fuelled many of the fierce public demonstrations at various economic summit meetings held by the leading industrial nations in the late twentieth and early twenty-first centuries.

Perhaps the most publicized Canadian reaction occurred at the Asia–Pacific Economic Cooperation (APEC) meeting in Vancouver in November 1997. APEC was a meeting of eighteen nations proposing a free trade zone in the Asian region of the globe. Demonstrators were alarmed by this example of globalization (one group of UBC opponents argued, 'if you thought NAFTA was scary, wait until you hear about APEC.'). But the APEC meetings provoked other concerns as well. Many demonstrators were upset that Canada was hosting several heads of state whose record on human rights was undistinguished, including Jiang Zemin of China and General Suharto of Indonesia. UBC students were unhappy that the meeting was being held on their campus (at the Museum of Anthropology) without their consent. Student demonstrators were doused by the RCMP with pepper spray when they did not move aside quickly enough, resulting in what came to be called 'Peppergate'. The RCMP insisted that it was only responding to orders from the Canadian government, while Prime Minister Chrétien's response was: 'Pepper? I put that on my plate.' A formal investigation was held to get to the bottom of the matter. It did not really resolve the question of who was responsible for the pepper spray, although in the process the reputation of the Prime Minister's Office was probably damaged by its failure to fully co-operate in releasing top secret government files. The Canadian public became increasingly sensitized to the dangers of secrecy and stonewalling.

The MAI and its various offshoots posed a somewhat different problem for Canada than did North American free trade. Both were held by their critics to threaten the Canadian nation-state, but free trade encouraged mainly a North American economic integration, while globalization went much further. A number of pundits saw continental economic integration as leading inevitably to political and social integration (or 'convergence', as it came to be called), although most theories dealt with the economic arena. In the late 1990s, Conrad Black's new newspaper, *The National Post,* became a vocal advocate of total North American integration, although the paper softened its stance after being purchased by the Asper family early in the new millennium. Convergence theory is not monolithic. Instead, a number of alternative scenarios have been advanced by various convergence theorists. One scenario emphasizes strong market forces and weakened governments. Another talks about imitation of the best way to operate—the mimicking of 'best practices'—as a consequence of institutional competition. A third scenario speaks of convergence through enforced international agreement, as in the European Economic Community or in NAFTA. A minority of theorists would insist that not just external forces but concomitant internal ones are necessary to bring about convergence. And not all economists agree that convergence is necessarily the way of the future. Most of those who disagree emphasize the continued ability of the nation-state to resist and adjust to new pressures. In the jargon of the economist, the 'border effect' continues to be a silent but powerful retardant to convergence. Moreover, there is now an explicit backlash within many nations to integration and globalization, and this is producing new political alliances and new ways of preserving the power of the nation state.

A related economic problem for Canada involved the extent to which the nation could afford to be pressured by the international community on environmental concerns. In 1997 an international summit meeting at Kyoto, Japan, had agreed on a world protocol for environmental improvement, most notably through reducing the emission of hydrocarbon gasses that many scientists blamed for the so-called 'greenhouse effect' and other pollution. The extent of the greenhouse effect was still being debated by the scientific community. But the larger question involved the economic costs of complying with Kyoto. The lead in the creation of the Kyoto Accord had been taken by the nations of industrialized Europe, which for a variety of reasons had managed to go much further in reducing industrial pollution than had North America. Europe was supported by a Third World community that either had little polluting industry or did not intend to observe the protocol. The Americans bowed out of the Kyoto Accord, calling it too expensive to implement. As one of the few nations in the world seriously affected, Canada continued to debate the question, although in typically Canadian fashion Kyoto got tied up in constitutional hassles between the federal and provincial governments over jurisdiction.

CANADIAN SOCIETY

THE AGED

While all the symptoms of social morbidity continued their alarming progress, perhaps the most disturbing trends occurred at the opposite ends of the life cycle, particularly among the aging. The first of the baby boomers were coming up to (early) retirement, soon to be followed by the deluge. That the system was really not ready for this event became increasingly clear. In 1995 the Canadian Institute of Actuaries (CIA) reported that in 1992 retired Canadians (numbering 19 per cent of the working-age population) had paid $9 billion in taxes and received $54.4 billion in public funds in a variety of forms, including medical treatment. By 2030 the percentage of retired Canadians would be up to 39 per cent of those eligible to work. The payout at 1992 rates

KYOTO PROTOCOL TO THE UNITED NATIONS FRAMEWORK CONVENTION ON CLIMATE CHANGE

The Kyoto Accord of 1997 has been one of the most controversial international agreements that Canada has ever signed. The opening pages of this document, reprinted below, illustrate the complexity of the issues with which the Canadian public must now deal on a routine basis.

The Parties to this Protocol, Being Parties to the United Nations Framework Convention on Climate Change, hereinafter referred to as 'the Convention', In pursuit of the ultimate objective of the Convention as stated in its Article 2, Recalling the provisions of the Convention, Being guided by Article 3 of the Convention, Pursuant to the Berlin Mandate adopted by decision 1/CP.1 of the Conference of the Parties to the Convention at its first session, Have agreed as follows:

Article 1

For the purposes of this Protocol, the definitions contained in Article 1 of the Convention shall apply. In addition:

1. 'Conference of the Parties' means the Conference of the Parties to the Convention.

2. 'Convention' means the United Nations

Framework Convention on Climate Change, adopted in New York on 9 May 1992.

3. 'Intergovernmental Panel on Climate Change' means the Intergovernmental Panel on Climate Change established in 1988 jointly by the World Meteorological Organization and the United Nations Environment Programme.

4. 'Montreal Protocol' means the Montreal Protocol on Substances that Deplete the Ozone Layer, adopted in Montreal on 16 September 1987 and as subsequently adjusted and amended.

5. 'Parties present and voting' means Parties present and casting an affirmative or negative vote.

6. 'Party' means, unless the context otherwise indicates, a Party to this Protocol.

7. 'Party included in Annex I' means a Party included in Annex I to the Convention, as may be amended, or a Party which has made a notification under Article 4, paragraph 2(g), of the Convention.

Article 2

Each Party included in Annex I in achieving its quantified emission limitation and reduction commitments under Article 3, in order to promote sustainable development, shall:

(a) Implement and/or further elaborate policies and measures in accordance with its national circumstances, such as: (i) Enhancement of energy efficiency in relevant sectors of the national economy; (ii) Protection and enhancement of sinks and reservoirs of greenhouse gases not controlled by the Montreal Protocol, taking into account its commitments under relevant international environmental agreements; promotion of sustainable forest management practices, afforestation and reforestation; (iii) Promotion of sustainable forms of agriculture in light of climate change considerations; (iv) Promotion, research, development and increased use of new and renewable forms of energy, of carbon dioxide sequestration technologies and of advanced and innovative environmentally sound technologies; FCCC/CP/1997/L.7/Add.1 (v) Progressive reduction or phasing out of market imperfections, fiscal incentives, tax and duty exemptions and subsidies in all greenhouse gas emitting sectors that run counter to the objective of the Convention and apply market instruments; (vi) Encouragement of appropriate reforms in relevant sectors aimed at promoting policies and measures which limit or reduce emissions of greenhouse gases not controlled by the Montreal Protocol; (vii) Measures to limit and/or reduce emissions of greenhouse gases not controlled by the Montreal Protocol in the transport sector; (viii) Limitation and/or reduction of methane through recovery and use in waste management, as well as in the production, transport and distribution of energy;

(b) Cooperate with other such Parties to enhance the individual and combined effectiveness of their policies and measures adopted under this Article, pursuant to Article 4, paragraph 2(e)(i), of the Convention. To this end, these Parties shall take steps to share their experience and exchange information on such policies and measures, including developing ways of improving their comparability, transparency and effectiveness. The Conference of the Parties serving as the meeting of the Parties to this Protocol shall, at its first session or as soon as practicable thereafter, consider ways to facilitate such cooperation, taking into account all relevant information. 2. The Parties included in Annex I shall pursue limitation or reduction of emissions of greenhouse gases not controlled by the Montreal Protocol from aviation and marine bunker fuels, working through the International Civil Aviation Organization and the International Maritime Organization, respectively. 3. The Parties included in Annex I shall strive to implement policies and measures under this Article in such a way as to minimize adverse effects, including the adverse effects of climate change, effects on international trade, and social, environmental and economic impacts on other Parties, especially developing country Parties and in particular those identified in Article 4, paragraphs 8 and 9 of the Convention, taking into account Article 3 of the Convention. The Conference of the Parties serving as the meeting of the Parties to this Protocol may take further action, as appropriate, to promote the implementation of the provisions of this paragraph. 4. The Conference of the Parties serving as the meeting of the Parties to this Protocol, if it decides that it would be beneficial to coordinate any of the policies and measures in paragraph 1(a) above, taking into account different national circumstances and potential effects, shall consider ways and means to elaborate the coordination of such policies and measures.

Article 3

The Parties included in Annex I shall, individually or jointly, ensure that their aggregate anthropogenic carbon dioxide equivalent emissions of the greenhouse gases listed in Annex A do not exceed their assigned amounts, calculated pursuant to their quantified emission limitation and reduction commitments inscribed in Annex B and in accordance with the provisions of this Article, with a view to reducing their overall emissions of such gases by at least 5 per cent below 1990 levels in the commitment period 2008 to 2012.

2. Each Party included in Annex I shall, by 2005, have made demonstrable progress in achieving its commitments under this Protocol.

3. The net changes in greenhouse gas emissions from sources and removals by sinks resulting from direct human-induced land use change and forestry activities, limited to afforestation, reforestation, and deforestation since 1990, measured as verifiable changes in stocks in each commitment period shall be used to meet the commitments in this Article of each Party included in Annex I. The greenhouse gas emissions from sources and removals by sinks associated with those activities shall be reported in a transparent and verifiable manner and reviewed in accordance with Articles 7 and 8.

4. Prior to the first session of the Conference of the Parties serving as the meeting of the Parties to this Protocol, each Party included in Annex I shall provide for consideration by the Subsidiary Body for Scientific and Technological Advice data to establish its level of carbon stocks in 1990 and to enable an estimate to be made of its changes in carbon stocks in subsequent years. The Conference of the Parties serving as the meeting of the Parties to this Protocol shall, at its first session or as soon as practicable thereafter, decide upon modalities, rules and guidelines as to how and which additional human-induced activities related to changes in greenhouse gas emissions and removals in the agricultural soil and land use change and forestry categories, shall be added to, or subtracted from, the assigned amount for Parties included in Annex I, taking into account uncertainties, transparency in reporting, verifiability, the methodological work of the Intergovernmental Panel on Climate Change, the advice provided by the Subsidiary Body for Scientific and Technological Advice in accordance with Article 5 and the decisions of the Conference of the Parties. Such a decision shall apply in the second and subsequent commitment periods. A Party may choose to apply such a decision on these additional human-induced activities for its first commitment period, provided that these activities have taken place since 1990. . . .

SOURCE: See website: www.cnn.com/SPECIALS/1997/globalwarming/stories/treaty.

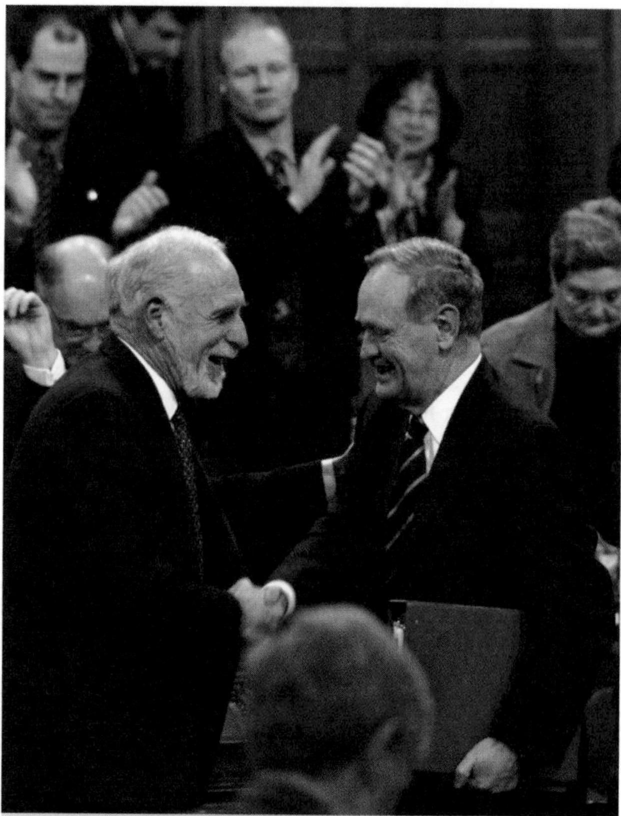

☐ Prime Minister Jean Chrétien and Environment Minister David Anderson shake hands following the House of Commons' vote on ratification of the Kyoto Agreement, 10 December 2002. CP/Tom Hanson.

would be well beyond the capacity of the system to absorb. The present system worked only because the demand upon it had not yet grown sufficiently. The CIA concluded that the present system of social insurance payments was not 'sustainable in [its] current form. Contributions will rise. Benefits will be cut; retirement ages deferred; universality curtailed.' Surveys suggested that many Canadians had begun to appreciate the difficulties, although most were still confused and few had any solutions. According to one survey, most Canadians feared that the Canada Pension Plan would be unable to look after their retirement, but fewer than 15 per cent had more than $10,000 put away somewhere apart from their CPP pensions. The age at which most Canadians still expected to retire was fifty-nine, although the experts and the politicians were now suggesting that such an age was simply a pipe dream for most people.

Retirement pensions were only part of the problem. The other major concern was health care, the cost of which continued to spiral upward despite desperate efforts by provincial governments to bring it under control through cost cutting and privatization. Per capita health care expenditure (in constant 1986 dollars) had progressively and annually increased from $1,257.25 in 1975 to $1,896.27 in 1993. The proportion of gross domestic product devoted to health care had gone up from 7.1 per cent in 1975 to 10.1 per cent in 1993. Although these Canadian figures were not as alarming as the corresponding American ones—the proportion of GDP given to health care in the US had increased from 8.4 per cent in 1975 to 14.4 per cent in 1993—they pointed to a financial crisis if they were not capped somehow. Much of the increasing cost involved care for the elderly, and life expectancy continued to advance. The baby boom and increased life expectancy together produced the demographic prospect of ever larger numbers of elderly people making increasing demands on the health care system.

While provincial governments closed hospitals and reduced the numbers of beds available within those remaining, Canadians began to debate hard questions, such as the extent to which the terminally ill should be offered the expensive treatment that medical science now had at its disposal. Even if the elderly were not given expensive treatment, their increasing numbers produced a housing problem. Only one out of every four Canadians expected to have to look after his or her parents in old age, which was far too low an estimate of future realities. But even if all Canadians took in their still functioning elderly, the numbers of those requiring extensive care beyond the home were bound to increase enormously. Dealing with seniors was clearly the most important problem facing the social insurance system, particularly given the national sense that deficit financing was already too high. One could only sympathize with the younger generation, unable to establish themselves in careers, but still being asked to finance the post-retirement years of their elders. According to one study by the Research for Public Policy group, younger Canadians would have to pay increasingly more in taxes than they would ever receive in social benefits to maintain the present structure, which was not only 'unsustainable' but 'immoral'. But this was not the only morality question surrounding health care. Much of the cost of the health care system continued to be absorbed in looking after seniors in their last months of life. Few Canadians wished to do less, whatever the cost. Despite all the rhetoric, health care was still more of an ideological issue than a practical one for most Canadians. While some might want the opportunity to jump queues to get their needs looked after more quickly, not many Canadians really sought to cut into the basic principle of universal health care available to all. For many, access to free health care had become one of the major factors of the Canadian identity. According to one oft-quoted comedian, a Canadian was an unarmed American with free and universal health care coverage.

Redress for Historic Abuse

Early in 1990, thousands of Canadians received from the Minister of State for Multiculturalism and Citizenship a letter enclosing a substantial cheque and an 'acknowledgement signed by the Prime Minister'. The recipients of this material were Japanese Canadians who had been uprooted from their homes in 1942 by the Canadian government. The cheque was for 'redress' (or compensation, as it was usually called), and the document from the prime minister acknowledged that 'the treatment of Japanese Canadians during and after World War II was unjust and violated principles of human rights as they are understood today.' Japanese Canadians had first organized to seek redress in 1977, at the time of the centennial of the first arrival of Japanese in Canada. The government of Pierre Trudeau had refused to consider action on this issue, but the leader of the opposition, Brian Mulroney, was more sympathetic. After Mulroney's Progressive Conservatives swept to power in 1984, the Japanese renewed their efforts, which led finally on 22 September 1988 to the signature of the prime minister on a Redress Agreement between the National Association of Japanese Canadians and the Canadian government (Miki and Kobayashi 1991). This agreement symbolized the changed attitudes towards both ethnicity and redress at the end of the twentieth century. The government's action with respect to the Japanese encouraged a variety of other groups to apply for redress, including the Ukrainian aliens interned by Canada during the Great War and the Acadians deported from Nova Scotia in the 1750s.

When the unsinkable ship the *Titanic* went down in the Atlantic Ocean in 1912, it took with it over 100 Canadian victims. The literature on the *Titanic* demonstrates quite clearly that the tragedy could have been prevented, and that responsibility for the disaster was systemic and widely distributed. But what is perhaps often forgotten is that most of the survivors and the families of the victims never seriously considered demanding a public inquiry or government compensation. Nor did they engage in class-action litigation in the courts to the same end. Disasters in Canada were traditionally regarded as acts of God. The federal government did supply compensation for victims of the Halifax Explosion of 1917, but that was because the disaster was regarded as a war matter. When the notion of public assistance for disaster losses began to take hold in Canada after World War II, compensation was not initially regarded as a matter of right or of reparation. Rather it was one of relief and generosity, which meant that it was not really compensation at all. Victims of the Manitoba Flood of 1950 received assistance from the federal and provincial governments, as well as from a privately raised relief fund. We do not understand just how disaster relief gradually became translated into a right of compensation, but by the 1990s that concept was clearly well in place.

Part of the shift was doubtless associated with the rise of insurance to cover various sorts of damage, including malpractice and accidental injury to property and person, and the increasing insistence on dealing with such matters in the courts. Seeking damages for injury through the courts is, of course, something that has been with us as long as there have been civil courts. The practice was greatly escalated in the United States after World War II, with juries awarding ever larger damage amounts, often exceeding the defendant's ability to pay them. In the process, the concept of liability was transformed by the courts. In recent years, simple damage suits have grown into class actions, in which a large, amorphous body of victims engages in litigation. Prime examples of such actions, of course, are the cases that have been introduced against various tobacco companies for illnesses resulting from smoking. We may not understand the way this trend developed, but it is perfectly clear that one of the major social issues in Canada in the last third of the twentieth century was the appearance of the idea that someone must be held responsible for every negative consequence. (A related concept is that every victim is entitled to compensation for his or her injury). In the context of Canada's Aboriginal peoples this clearly was the outstanding social issue in Canada at the end of the century.

ABORIGINAL PEOPLES

In 1996 there were some 554,000 status Indians in Canada. Two-thirds of them lived on about 2,300 reserves in nearly 600 registered bands, and the remainder resided chiefly in larger southern cities such as Winnipeg. In addition, there were 41,000 Inuit. The numbers of non-status Indians and Métis are harder to estimate. The number accepted by the government is 210,000, but the total across Canada is probably at least 500,000. Despite increased levels of media attention, government expenditures, and Aboriginal self-awareness, the realities of Native life—while improving—continue to recall conditions in Third World countries. In the 1990s, the First Nations for the first time were popularly perceived as an important Canadian political 'problem', perhaps the most important and controversial one of the decade. The immediate crisis was not over the demographics of Native life, although particular cases of violence and abuse continued to make newspaper headlines. The problem was really three related issues that came to prominence in the nineties. The first was how to deal with the land rights of the indigenous peoples. The second was how to deal with Native administration and the Aboriginal insistence on the right to self-government. The third was how to make reparations for earlier mistreatment of Aboriginals, particularly in the residential school system of Canada.

Land Rights

The Aboriginal peoples had long attempted to claim their land rights. Those claims came under three headings. First were the claims resulting from agreements or treaties made with the Crown, whether before Confederation, between 1871 and 1877 (the so-called Numbered Treaties, 1–11; see p. 215), or in modern times. Second were claims based on continuing Aboriginal title (established historically). Finally, there were specific claims, usually involving either improper seizure of land or government failure to pay proper compensation for lands seized legally. In 1969, the Trudeau government established the Indian Claims Commission to deal with land claims, but the slow pace of negotiations soon led the Aboriginal peoples to turn to the courts for redress. A series of landmark court decisions, many of them in the Supreme Court of Canada, gradually produced new policies from the federal and provincial governments. Over the ensuing years, a number of historic agreements would be reached with Aboriginal peoples, although the settlement of claims was a slow, labyrinthian process. Literally hundreds of land claims have been raised, and not all have been dealt with, either through negotiations or through the courts. By and large, the courts have not so much settled land claims as maintained the Aboriginal right to hold them and to negotiate them with the government.

In 1973, the Supreme Court of Canada ruled in the *Calder* case that the Nisga'a of British Columbia had Aboriginal title to their land that had never been extinguished. Mr Justice Wilfred Judson concluded: 'The fact is that when the settlers came the Indians were there, organized in societies and occupying the land as their forefathers had done for centuries. This is what Indian title means. What they are asserting in this action is that they had a right to continue to live on their lands as their forefathers had lived and that this right has never been lawfully extinguished.' Mr Justice Emmett Hall added, 'What emerges from the . . . evidence is that the Nishgas in fact are and were from time immemorial a distinctive cultural entity with concepts of ownership indigenous to their culture and capable of articulation under the common law. . . .' In August 1973, Minister of Indian Affairs Jean Chrétien stated publicly that the federal government was committed to settling Aboriginal land claims.

A Supreme Court ruling in 1973 that the Quebec government could not continue with its James Bay hydroelectric project until it had resolved Aboriginal claims led to a historic agreement in 1975 between the province and the James Bay Cree and Inuit. It provided for $225 million in financial compensation, as well as establishing land ownership and usage in the region of Northern Quebec. Aboriginal rights and treaty rights were recognized in the 1982 Constitution Act, although individual cases would have to be decided by the courts. In 1984, in a final ruling in *Guerin* v. *the Queen* (a case brought in 1975 by the Musqueam Indian Band), the Supreme Court of Canada recognized that Aboriginal rights in Canada predated Confederation.

In 1984 a suit filed in the Supreme Court of British Columbia by thirty-five Gitksan and thirteen Wet'suwet'en chiefs contested 58,000 square kilometres of land in the province. The case (known as the *Delgamuukw* case) was heard from 1987 to 1990, and a decision was brought down on 8 March 1991. Before this decision, the Supreme Court of Canada had ruled in 1990 in *Sparrow* v. *the Queen* that section 35 of the Constitution Act protected Aboriginal rights, which it insisted must be dealt with by the courts in a generous manner. In his decision in the *Delgamuukw* case, Chief Justice Allan McEachern denied the plaintiffs the right to exclusive land ownership and self-government, in large measure because he rejected the oral history on which the claims had been based. He did rule, however, that the plaintiffs had 'unextinguished non-exclusive aboriginal rights, other than right of ownership.' As a result of this case, the government of British Columbia and the First Nations agreed to a treaty-making process. The plaintiffs in *Delgamuukw* appealed, however, and were rejected again on their major points in 1993. Another appeal was heard by the Supreme Court of Canada, with a decision handed down on 11 December 1997. The Supreme Court did not rule on title, indicating that the case would be better resolved through negotiations. But it did indicate that the courts must 'come to terms with the oral histories of Aboriginal societies, which for many Aboriginal Nations, are the only record of their past' (Chief Justice Lamer; in *Delgamuukw* v. *British Columbia, 3 S.C.R., 1997*).

On 16 July 1998, the federal and British Columbia governments signed a final agreement with the Nisga'a people, which granted them 1,930 kilometres of land, self-government, and a large amount of cash.

Aboriginal Self-Government

Aboriginal self-government was another longstanding question in Canada (Engelstad and Bird 1992). The First Nations insisted that the assertion of ultimate sovereignty over the land by the Crown interfered with neither Aboriginal land rights nor the rights of Aboriginals to govern themselves according to their own laws in their traditional territories. Considerable historical evidence exists to indicate that historically the Crown did not usually attempt to assert its direct political authority over Aboriginal land. Exactly how the government or the courts viewed the legal relationship between the Crown and the First Nations was and is another matter entirely. In most instances, Aboriginal self-government follows the municipal model, with local councils ultimately responsible to the Crown, although several First Nations organizations insist that it must become something more (Royal Commission on Aboriginal Peoples 1993).

In May 1993, the federal government agreed not only to settle the Inuit land claims to the eastern Arctic, but to establish a new territory (to be called Nunavut) with a form of Aboriginal self-government. This arrangement came after agreement in principle had been reached in 1990. The demand for self-government originated with the Inuit, who had refused to surrender it in the years of discussion over land rights. The new territory, which was hived off from the Northwest Territories, came into existence on 1

DELGAMUUKW V. BRITISH COLUMBIA, DECEMBER 1997

Late in 1997 the Supreme Court of Canada handed down a judgment on appeal from the Court of Appeal of British Columbia. The case had been brought to the Supreme Court by Delgamuukw (a.k.a. Earl Muldoe) on behalf of a number of Gitksan and Wet'suwet'en 'houses' upon the earlier rejection of their Aboriginal claims by the British Columbia court. A portion of the judgment follows, specifically some of the dissenting opinion of justices La Forest and L'Heureux-Dubé. This indicates the complexity of the reasoning involved.

The reasons of La Forest and L'Heureux-Dubé JJ. were delivered by

187 LA FOREST J.—I have read the reasons of the Chief Justice, and while I agree with his conclusion, I disagree with various aspects of his reasons and in particular, with the methodology he uses to prove that aboriginal peoples have a general right of occupation of certain lands (often referred to as 'aboriginal title').

188 I begin by considering why a new trial is necessary in this case. It is true, as the Chief Justice points out, that the amalgamation of the appellants' individual claims represents a defect in the pleadings and, technically speaking, this prevents us from considering the merits of the case. However, in my view, there is a more substantive problem with the pleadings in this case. Before this Court, the appellants sought a declaration of 'aboriginal title' but attempted, in essence, to prove that they

had complete control over the territory in question. The appellants effectively argued on appeal, as they did at trial, that by virtue of their social and land tenure systems—consisting of Chief authority, Houses, feasts, crests, and totem poles—they acquired an absolute interest in the claimed territory, including ownership of and jurisdiction over the land. The problem with this approach is that it requires proof of governance and control as opposed to proof of general occupation of the affected land. Only the latter is the *sine qua non* of 'aboriginal title'. It follows that what the appellants sought by way of declaration from this Court and what they set out to prove by way of the evidence were two different matters. In light of this substantive defect in the pleadings, a new trial should be ordered to permit a reassessment of the matter on the basis of these reasons.

189 In my view, the foundation of 'aboriginal title' was succinctly described by Judson J. in *Calder* v. *Attorney-General of British Columbia*, [1973] S.C.R. 313, where, at p. 328, he stated: 'the fact is that when the settlers came, the Indians were there, organized in societies and occupying the land as their forefathers had done for centuries. This is what Indian title means . . . .' Relying in part on Judson J.'s remarks, Dickson J. (as he then was) wrote in *Guerin* v. *The Queen*, [1984] 2 S.C.R. 335, at p. 382, that aboriginal peoples have a 'legal right to occupy and possess certain lands, the ultimate title to which is in the Crown'. As well, in *Canadian Pacific Ltd.* v. *Paul*, [1988] 2 S.C.R. 654, this Court stated, at p. 678: 'The inescapable conclusion from the Court's analysis of Indian title up to this point is that the Indian interest in land is truly *sui generis*. It is more than the right to enjoyment and occupancy although . . . it is difficult to describe what more in traditional property law terminology'. More recently, Judson J.'s views were reiterated in *R.* v. *Van der Peet*, [1996] 2 S.C.R. 507. There Lamer C.J. wrote for the majority, at para. 30, that the doctrine of aboriginal rights (one aspect of which is 'aboriginal title') arises from 'one simple fact: when Europeans arrived in North America, aboriginal peoples *were already here*, living in communities on the land, and participating in distinctive cultures, as they had done for centuries' (emphasis in original).

190 It follows from these cases that the aboriginal right of possession is derived from the historic occupation and use of ancestral lands by aboriginal peoples. Put another way, 'aboriginal title' is based on the continued occupation and use of the land as part of the aboriginal peoples' traditional way of life. This *sui generis* interest is not equated with fee simple ownership; nor can it be described with reference to traditional property law concepts. The best description of 'aboriginal title', as set out above, is a broad and general one derived from Judson J.'s pronouncements in *Calder, supra.* Adopting the same approach, Dickson J. wrote in *Guerin, supra*, that the aboriginal right of occupancy is further characterized by two principal features. First, this *sui generis* interest in the land is personal in that it is generally inalienable except to the Crown. Second, in dealing with this interest, the Crown is subject to a fiduciary obligation to treat aboriginal peoples fairly. Dickson J. went on to conclude, at p. 382, that '[a]ny description of Indian title which goes beyond these two features is both unnecessary and potentially misleading'. I share his views and am therefore reluctant to define more precisely the 'right [of aboriginal peoples] to continue to live on their lands as their forefathers had lived'; see *Calder*, at p. 328.

191 The approach I adopt, in defining the aboriginal right of occupancy, is also a highly contextual one. More specifically, I find it necessary to make a distinction between: (1) the recognition of a general right to occupy and possess ancestral lands; and (2) the recognition of a discrete right to engage in an aboriginal activity in a particular area. I defined the latter in *R.* v. *Côté*, [1996] 3 S.C.R. 139, at para. 97, as

'the traditional use, by a tribe of Indians, that has continued from pre-contact times of a particular area for a particular purpose'. The issue in *Côté*, as in *Van der Peet*, was whether the use of a particular fishing spot was really an aspect of the aboriginal peoples' way of life in pre-contact times; see also in the *Van der Peet trilogy R.* v. *Gladstone*, [1996] 2 S.C.R. 723, and *R* v. *N.T.C. Smokehouse Ltd.*, [1996] 2 S.C.R. 672. In all those cases, the fishing rights asserted by the aboriginal claimants were not associated with a more general occupancy of the affected land. By contrast, the present case deals with a general claim to occupy and possess vast tracts of territory (58,000 square kilometres). This type of generalized land claim is not merely a bundle of discrete aboriginal rights to engage in specific activities. Rather, it is, as the Chief Justice states, at para. 111, the 'right to use land for a variety of activities, not all of which need be aspects of practices, customs and traditions which are integral to the distinctive cultures of aboriginal societies'. These land-based activities are, of course, related to the aboriginal society's habits and mode of life.

192 I note, as well, that in defining the nature of 'aboriginal title', one should generally not be concerned with statutory provisions and regulations dealing with reserve lands. In *Guerin, supra*, this Court held that the interest of an Indian band in a reserve is derived from, and is of the same nature as, the interest of an aboriginal society in its traditional tribal lands. Accordingly, the Court treated the aboriginal interest in reserve lands as one of occupation and possession while recognizing that the underlying title to those lands was in the Crown. It was not decided in *Guerin, supra*, and it by no means follows, that specific statutory provisions governing reserve lands should automatically apply to traditional tribal lands. For this reason, I am unable to assume that specific 'reserve' provisions of the *Indian Act*, R.S.C., 1985, c. I-5, and the *Indian Oil and Gas Act*, R.S.C., 1985, c. I-7, apply to huge tracts of land which are subject to an aboriginal right of occupancy.

SOURCE: *Delgamuukw* v. *British Columbia*, [1997] 3 S.C.R. 1010.

April 1999. In Nunavut's legislative assembly, Inuktitut and English are the two official languages. Some observers have argued that Nunavut is not really run by the Inuit, since the federal government continues to have a strong presence through its agencies, co-management boards, and financial dealings with the territory. Instead, they say, Nunavut has something more like a highly traditional colonial government (Wall 2000: 143–67).

Residential Schools

The beginnings of the residential school system long predated Confederation. In the seventeenth century, schools were usually part of the missionary work of the churches, designed both to educate Aboriginal people and to assimilate them into European society. Residential schools came in a variety of forms, although in the twentieth century the most common were the so-called industrial schools. They were located in almost every province and territory. The government of Canada shared in the administration of these schools from at least 1874. By the end of the nineteenth century, the schools had shifted from being church institutions partly funded by the government to being government institutions operated by the churches. Their purpose also shifted, from assimilating students into European society to preparing them for life on controlled reserves. From an early date, there was an undercurrent of abuse and intimidation connected with the schools, for their rationale was based upon the (often forcible) removal of children from their families in order to 'civilize' them and convert them to Christianity. In most of the

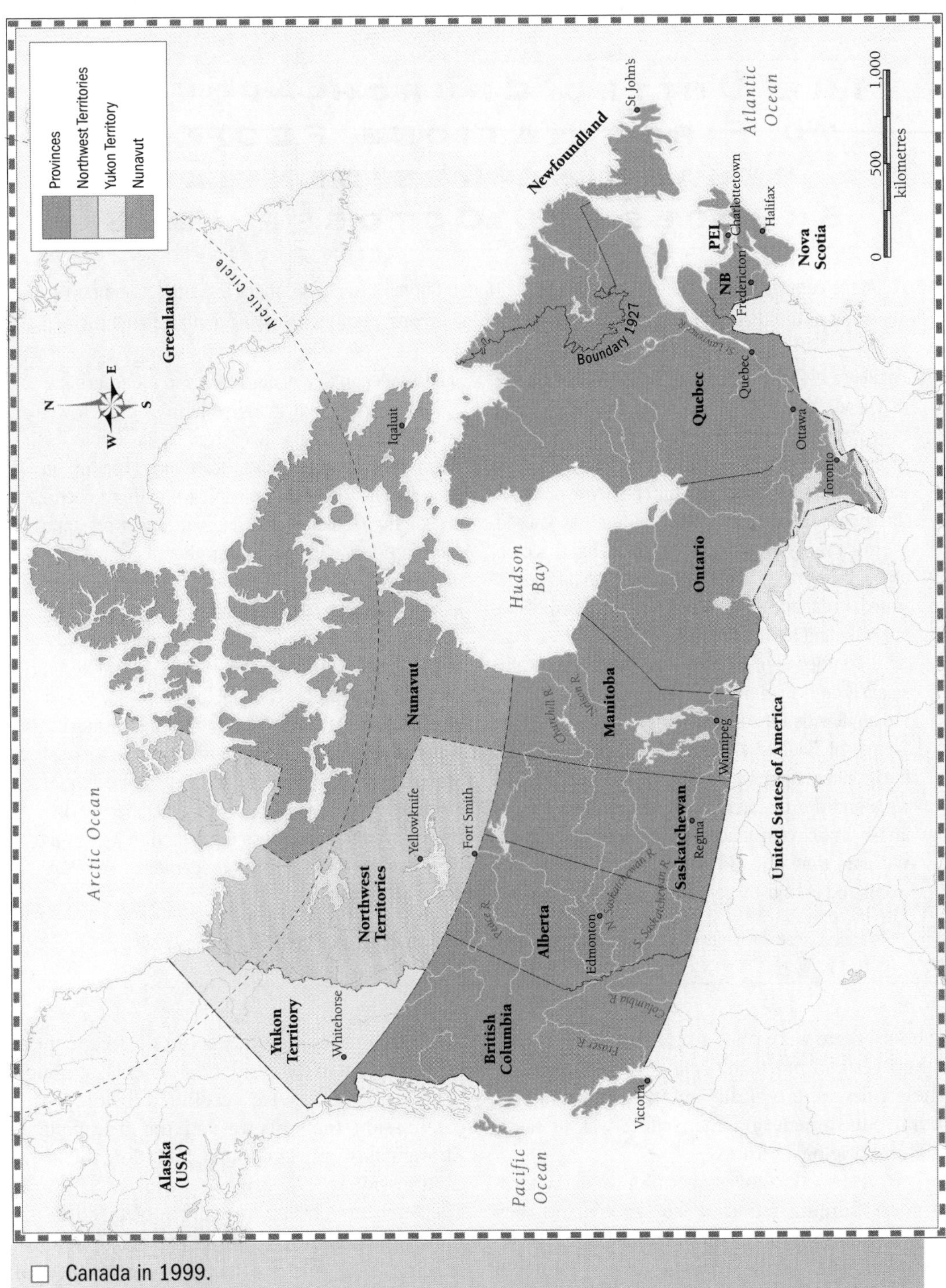
Provinces
Northwest Territories
Yukon Territory
Nunavut
Arctic Ocean
Greenland
Arctic Circle
Alaska (USA)
Pacific Ocean
Atlantic Ocean
Hudson Bay
Yukon Territory
Whitehorse
Northwest Territories
Yellowknife
Fort Smith
Nunavut
Iqaluit
British Columbia
Victoria
Fraser R.
Columbia R.
Alberta
Edmonton
Peace R.
N. Saskatchewan R.
S. Saskatchewan R.
Saskatchewan
Regina
Manitoba
Winnipeg
Churchill R.
Nelson R.
Ontario
Toronto
Ottawa
Quebec
Quebec
St Lawrence R.
Boundary 1927
Newfoundland
St John's
NB
Fredericton
PEI
Charlottetown
Nova Scotia
Halifax
United States of America
0 500 1,000
kilometres
N E S W

Canada in 1999.

THE UNITED CHURCH APOLOGY TO FIRST NATIONS PEOPLES REGARDING RESIDENTIAL SCHOOLS, 26 OCTOBER 1998

At the conclusion of a four-day meeting of the United Church's General Council Executive, the moderator of the United Church, the Right Reverend Bill Phipps, read the following announcement.

I am here today as Moderator of the United Church of Canada to speak the words that many people have wanted to hear for a very long time. On behalf of the United Church of Canada I apologize for the pain and suffering that our church's involvement in the Indian Residential School system has caused. We are aware of some of the damage that this cruel and ill-conceived system of assimilation has perpetrated on Canada's First Nations people. For this we are truly and most humbly sorry.

To those individuals who were physically, sexually and mentally abused as students of the Indian Residential Schools in which the United Church of Canada was involved, I offer you our most sincere apology. You did nothing wrong. You were and are the victims of evil acts that cannot under any circumstances be justified or excused. We pray that you will hear the sincerity of our words today and that you will witness the living out of this apology in our actions in the future.

We know that many within our church will still not understand why each of us must bear the scar, the blame for this horrendous period in Canadian history. But the truth is we are the bearers of many blessings from our ancestors, and therefore we must also bear their burdens. We must now seek ways of healing ourselves, as well as our relationships with First Nations peoples. This apology is not an end in itself. We are in the midst of a long and painful journey. A journey that began with the United Church's Apology of 1986, to our Statement of Repentance in 1997 and now moving with this apology with regard to Indian Residential Schools. As Moderator of the United Church of Canada I urge each and every member of the church, to reflect on these issues and to join us as we travel this difficult road of repentance, reconciliation and healing.

SOURCE: United Church of Canada website, http://www.rockies.net/-spirit/united/articles/9810news.html.

schools, there were rules against speaking Native languages and practising Native religious beliefs; these rules were typically enforced through corporal punishment and their effect was to denigrate Aboriginal cultures.

In 1969, the government of Canada took over the administration of the schools and they gradually disappeared, the last closing in 1996. Both churches and government were slow to respond formally to the tide of complaints from the Aboriginal community about the treatment of their children in the residential schools, although stories of abuse were recounted before every commission that investigated the treatment of Aboriginal people in Canada, including the Royal Commission on Aboriginal Peoples (1991–6). The Anglican Church formally apologized to the Aboriginal community for its part in the schools only in 1993, and the federal government and the United Church in 1998.

Beginning in the 1990s, Aboriginal victims of the residential schools began taking the federal government to court over their treatment. The government in its turn insisted on involving the various churches as co-defendants, in the process virtually bankrupting at least the Anglican Church of Canada and a number of its dioceses. By the end of the decade there were more than 8,000 such cases pending. Early in January 1998, the government of Canada announced a program ('Gathering Strength—Canada's Aboriginal Action Plan') to deal with past injustices, based on reconciliation and concrete action for the future. The government issued a statement of reconciliation acknowledging its part in the residential schools and apologizing for its actions. It offered $350 million to help heal the injuries, but was not able to come to terms with the litigants. As of this writing, the federal government has stated that it did not intend to destroy the churches by involving them in the lawsuits, but it has not offered any solution to the problem. Many churches, dioceses, and religious orders have been bankrupted by legal fees. Some Aboriginal spokesmen have maintained that the churches caused their own problems by attempting to use the courts to protect themselves from liability.

Contemporary Abuse

Charges of sexual abuse were not confined to incidents far in Canada's past. In September 1996, the National Hockey League's Sheldon Kennedy (b. 1969) told the Calgary police that between the ages of 14 and 19, he had been sexually abused more than 350 times by his nationally known hockey coach. The coach admitted the offences and was sentenced to prison early in 1997. After the sentencing, Kennedy's interviews with the press created a considerable controversy. One question that was asked repeatedly was whether the whistle should have been blown much earlier on the abusive coach. The main question, however, centred on extent to which Kennedy's experience was an aberration. Kennedy did his best to help others, particularly in a campaign to raise funds for a home for sexual abuse victims. Despite his well-publicized in-line skate across Canada in 1998, this venture foundered under the burden of bad management.

Other cases of abuse continued to surface in the media, usually involving authority figures who took advantage of their positions. Understandably, such cases always involved a concern that the good reputation of the vast majority of authority figures would be sullied by the behaviour of a few bad actors. Much evidence suggested that abusive behaviour was not common, but attempts on the part of higher authorities to deny it or sweep it under the carpet were all too frequent. The problem was not confined to Canada. In 2002, the international furor over abusive behaviour by priests of the Roman Catholic Church forced the Vatican for the first time to deal publicly with the issue.

Canadian Culture

Economic restraint hit hard at Canada's cultural industries, almost all of which had relied heavily on public subsidies. Cut-backs were inevitably accompanied by exhortations to financial responsibility and efforts to seek assistance from the private rather than the public sector. To the mid-1990s, much of the slack was taken up by cost-cutting and private fund-raising. Ways of raising money became increasingly imaginative and required far more attention from cultural administrators. Too much of the increased revenue, said some critics, came from state-run gambling and privately run lotteries. Public involvement in fund-raising was not necessarily a bad thing, for those in the community who helped raise money developed close ties with the enterprise. Few of the main-line establishment organizations in dance, classical music, and the theatre were actually forced out of existence, although everyone complained that there was no room for experimentation and risk-taking in the

ADRIENNE CLARKSON

☐ Adrienne Clarkson and her husband, John Ralston Saul, at a news conference following her appointment as governor general, Ottawa, 8 September 1999. CP/Fred Chartrand.

Adrienne Clarkson was born in Hong Kong in 1939; her father, William Poy, was an employee of the Canadian Trade Commission there. In 1942, Japan and the United States negotiated a prisoner exchange program after the Japanese occupation of Hong Kong. Not many Americans were available for exchange, so the Canadian Trade Commission was able to send some of its employees to Canada under the program's auspices. The Poys arrived in Montreal, where Canadian immigration officials attempted unsuccessfully to invoke 1923 exclusionist legislation against them. They ended up in Ottawa, where Adrienne attended school. She was later educated at the University of Toronto, and then at the Sorbonne, where she polished her French. She began a television career with the CBC in the mid-1960s, serving as host for a number of popular interview programs, including the 'Fifth Estate' and 'Adrienne at Large'. Her marriage to Stephen Clarkson ended in 1975. Clarkson parleyed her television exposure into a career in journalism and the arts. She wrote a regular column for *Chatelaine Magazine*, and between 1982 and 1987 she served as agent-general for Ontario in Paris, then as publisher of McClelland and Stewart from 1987 to 1988. In 1999 she was installed as the second female governor general of Canada, and the first Canadian citizen to serve as governor general who had not been born in Canada. She was also the first governor general whose consort was well-known in his own right; Clarkson had married the Canadian philosopher and author John Ralston Saul in 1999. As governor general, Clarkson served as an articulate spokesman for Canadian multiculturalism.

new financial climate. A few specialized operations bit the dust, and several symphony orchestras were threatened with extinction by militant musicians' unions. Nevertheless, despite the constant cries of crisis, the private sector did seem able to fill most of the gaps in the establishment world of haute culture.

Curiously enough, popular culture seemed

more genuinely affected by fiscal restraint than did haute culture. The long decline of the Canadian Broadcasting Corporation continued unabated, and Parliament carried on with annual cuts to the corporation's operating budget. Across the corporation as a whole, regional production was the first to suffer. The CBC's problems were many. Not all services ought to have been in equal trouble, however. The radio services were generally acknowledged to be the best in the world. Radio-Canada's television operation in French consistently outdrew the opposition, producing almost all of the most-watched television programs in Quebec. The sink-hole was English-language television, which had never been able to carve out a satisfactory niche for itself in an increasingly complex viewing world. The introduction of a variety of new Canadian-based cable networks in 1994 further eroded the CBC's position as a showcase for Canadian programming. Few seemed willing to scrap the television service, however. Another government commission, this one chaired by Pierre Juneau, recommended an increase in Canadian content, an end to commercial advertising, and additional revenue from taxes on the competing services. CBC-TV would no longer have to compete in the world of commercial television, but would instead become a Canadian version of America's Public Broadcasting Corporation, appealing to the higher instincts of the viewing public. There was no certainty that these recommendations would be accepted. What was definite was that the corporation would have to make do with less. Huge staff cuts were announced, with more to follow. Like employees of almost every other enterprise in Canada, those at the CBC could only look forward to further downsizing.

The prospects for Canadian content were improved to some extent by the expansion of specialty cable channels on television, although much of the new production came in the form of cooking shows and competitive sports channels. No shortage of Canadian talent existed in the field of comedy. 'Saturday Night Live' and 'SCTV' were both successful comedy programs of the late 1980s featuring a number of Canadian comedians who subsequently had major careers in the United States. 'The Kids in the Hall'—with an all-Canadian line-up—flourished in the early 1990s. Most of the humour on these shows was generically North American in content, but the McKenzie brothers were an exception: two small-town Canadians—'hosers'—who swilled beer, sported toques, talked incessantly about hockey, and struck a chord in their considerable audience. 'The Red Green Show' satirized the same kind of rural Canada. It was particularly subtle in its approach, superficially accepting the masculine values of the hunting-and-fishing set while constantly poking fun at them as well. Several of the show's catch phrases, including 'Keep your stick on the ice' passed into the larger national vocabulary. More directly political was the 'Royal Canadian Air Farce'. Its 'chicken cannon' regularly blasted a Canadian prominent in the current news.

One of the most powerful examples of Canadian content came in television commercials produced by the Molson Brewing Company, the makers of the beer labelled 'Canadian'. Molson released a number of ads with subtly anti-American themes, and in March 2000 produced a nationalist 'rant' entitled 'I Am Canadian', which was the talk of the nation for many months. The rant was very simple. An ordinary Joe stands before a slide display of Canadian backgrounds while he recites his litany. According to one account, high school students chanted the rant spontaneously in the corridors of their schools (*Calgary Herald*, 30 April 2000). Many commentators wondered why it was a beer company and not the government that was involved in promoting Canadian pride. Characteristically, the Americans did not seem to notice the commercial at all.

It wasn't perfectly clear whether the problems of professional sports in Canada were caused by budgetary restraint in the public sector, although it *was* clear that sports teams in

THE 'I AM CANADIAN' RANT

In late March 2000, the Molson brewing company unveiled a new commercial, in which a male actor recited the following lines against a background of Canadian images and the music of British composer Sir Edward Elgar.

Hey. I'm not a lumberjack or a fur trader.

And I don't live in an igloo, or eat blubber, or own a dogsled.

And I don't know Jimmy, Sally or Suzy from Canada, although I'm certain they're really, really nice.

I have a Prime Minister, not a President.

I speak English and French, not American, and I pronounce it 'about,' not 'a boot.'

I can proudly sew my country's flag on my backpack. I believe in peace keeping, not policing, diversity, not assimilation, and that the beaver is a truly proud and noble animal.

A toque is a hat, a chesterfield is a couch, and it is pronounced 'zed' not 'zee.' Zed!!!

Canada is the second largest landmass! The first nation of hockey! And the best part of North America!

My name is Joe! And I am Canadian!!!

Thank you.

SOURCE: Molson Canada.

Canada could no longer be sustained by massive infusions of indirect aid from the public purse, often in the form of arena facilities. This changing attitude combined with other factors to cause a number of disasters. One was an international market in player salaries with which Canadian teams could not successfully compete. The Canadian Football League, faced with escalating costs and declining attendance in the later 1980s and early 1990s, responded aggressively to its problems by expanding directly into the United States. This strategy proved absolutely disastrous. The new American franchises all folded after a season or two, leaving behind nothing but confusion and a trail of debt. The CFL regrouped and actually achieved some success as an acknowledged minor league protected by the National Football League. As for hockey, American integration finally caught up with it. The Quebec Nordiques left Canada for Colorado in 1995, and the Winnipeg Jets announced their departure for Phoenix, Arizona, early in 1996. Many experts calculated that the Edmonton Oilers, Calgary Flames, and Ottawa Senators could not be far behind, although all three teams continued to hang on into 2003 despite claims of financial losses. The National Hockey League, now run by high-powered American business executives, decided that Canadian franchises in smaller cities were not sufficiently profitable. The League refused to share television revenue equally and made impossible demands in terms of the facilities and financing of arenas, thus literally forcing the franchises to move to greener pastures. A similar situation prevailed in baseball. The Montreal Expos had responded to years of money-losing seasons in 1994 by dismantling a team that might have won the World Series had not a players' strike led to cancellation of the post-season activities. Eventually, the American executives decided to eliminate the team altogether, and were only prevented from doing so for reasons that had nothing to do with baseball in Montreal. In professional basketball, the Vancouver Grizzlies moved to Charlotte, North Carolina, in 2001, the team's unsuccessful finan-

CELINE DION

Celine Dion was born in Charlemagne, Quebec, in 1968, the fourteenth child in a French-Canadian family. Her parents operated a local night club, in which Celine began performing at the age of five. In 1980, she recorded with her family on a demo tape a song that she had composed many years earlier. This tape greatly impressed the talent agent René Angelil, who financed Celine's first record album by mortgaging his house. Success came quickly. In 1982 Dion won the Gold Medal for top song and the Musicians' Award for top performer at the Yamaha World Song Festival in Tokyo, and a year later she was the first Canadian to produce a gold record in France. Dion spent the mid-1980s becoming Quebec's best-selling recording performer, and then had another leap forward in 1988 when she won the Eurovision Song Contest in Dublin, performing her song live in front of a huge television audience.

A year later Dion burst onto the American scene with the title track to the Disney movie *Beauty and the Beast*. The song was awarded an Academy Award and a Grammy, and reached number one on the American charts. Thanks to several Canadian platinum albums, she literally owned the Juno awards in the early 1990s, and her song 'Think Twice' also reached the top of the British charts. She became one of the few female performers ever to sell a million singles in the United Kingdom. In 1994 she married Angelil. Dion followed her British success with a series of North American best-selling albums, one of which, *Falling into You*, was on the top of the charts in eleven different nations with total sales of over 25 million copies. Dion songs were featured on a number of Hollywood soundtracks, and in 1997 one of her songs on the soundtrack for Titanic won a second Oscar.

Dion retired from most public performances at the end of the decade, announcing her intention of becoming a mother and undertaking a highly publicized *in vitro* process of fertilization. By this time she had become the best-selling pop music recording artist anywhere in the world. In the process she had significantly raised the profile of Canadian, and especially Quebec, popular music on the international scene.

cial record since the establishment of the franchise in 1994 aggravated by a series of bad management decisions.

A full generation ago, one team of sports historians insisted, 'If we cannot save hockey, we cannot save Canada'. In recent years the federal government has indicated its willingness to add NHL hockey to the list of items that it is committed to protecting. Exactly where hockey fits into the overall cultural picture is as difficult to assess as the nature of its problems. The very extent of the integration of hockey into the American entertainment industry is one of the difficulties—as the agonized discussion over the transfer of hockey icon Wayne Gretzky from Edmonton to Los Angeles demonstrated in August 1988. But globalization is just as serious a problem. Since the 1980s the number of Canadian-born hockey players in the NHL has steadily declined, and the number of Canadian-born superstars has declined even more precipitously. Since the professionals now stock the teams in international

☐ Members of the Canadian women's hockey team pose with their coach, Danielle Sauvageau, and their gold medals after defeating the US team 3-2 at the Salt Lake City Winter Olympics, 21 February 2002. CP/Mike Ridewood.

hockey, Canadian teams have not been able to dominate the annual world championships or (with the exception of the 2002 games) the Winter Olympics. Many critics have suggested that the Canadian system has failed to produce large numbers of highly skilled players because it is not sufficiently committed to élite development. But it is also worth noting that the Canadian national women's hockey team won seven consecutive world titles without consoling many Canadians about the situation in men's hockey. Canadian women's hockey at the international level was one of the great sports success stories of the 1990s—not to mention the 2002 Olympics—but it was still unable to make many inroads into a sport dominated by the ethos of the male professionals.

CONCLUSION

While in the larger scheme of things one pattern of historical development has always been cyclical, few analysts think that Canada can ever return to the optimistic prosperity of the 1950s. Instead, the road ahead seems at best to consist of a series of hard choices. How Canadians and their political leaders will come to terms with such decisions is an open question. Although Canadians are having some trouble living with the new uncertainties, we should not conclude on a negative note. Today most Canadians live longer, earn more, are better educated, travel more, and possess more consumer goods than they did in the 1950s. Few would wish to return to the period in which there were no life-saving drugs, little family planning, and a minimal welfare and health care system. Fewer still would want to go further back, to the time when only men could vote, ballots were open, and unabashed sexism and racism were taken for granted. On every international indicator of quality of life—health standards, cultural achievement, environmental protection, infrastructure, gross national product per capita, political rights and civil liberties, and per capita purchasing power—Canada continues to rank at or near the top. The statistics only confirm what Canadians themselves instinctively know: Canada is a great country and a good place to live.

HOW HISTORY HAS CHANGED

THEORETICAL DEVELOPMENTS

The period since 1990 has been characterized by two seemingly contradictory developments in the writing of Canadian history. One has been a remarkable resurgence of what is usually called 'popular history', written or produced to be accessible to a larger audience. Popular history has not been confined to books, but has increasingly found a place in the media, particularly on television, where separate specialty channels devoted exclusively to history serve up a 24-hour-a-day menu of documentaries, historical films, and historical 'reality' television programming. The concentration on biography in many of the documentaries has become a major trend. This trend has not been confined to Canada. An American magazine recently argued that 'Pop culture has become the salvation of interest in history' (*Vanity Fair,* May 2002). Evidence of the new financial stakes involved in popular history has included the reports of large-scale plagiarism by some of the most successful practitioners. Pop history is part of a general international movement caused in large part by the other new development, also an international one: the emergence of cultural studies and new social theory as influences on the discourse of younger academic historians in Canada. Much of the new academic writing draws heavily on linguistic and epistemological theory, and its arcane style can make it almost entirely incomprehensible to the average reader.

A large part of the new body of theory was developed in post-war Europe. Structuralism (derived from the linguistic theories of Ferdinand de Saussure) uses the rules of language to provide the basis for a collection of laws to govern analysis. It tends to operate without much reference to time or chronology, and is hostile to inductive analysis and human agency. Semiotics (associated with the work of Roland Barthes and Louis Althusser) is a subset of structuralism that looks for meaning in human communication by analyzing its variations as signs. Post-structuralism (associated with Jacques Derrida and Michel Foucault) exists most commonly in the form of deconstructionism, in which a text is broken down and stripped of all its mystifications. These theorists believe that texts do not necessarily say what their authors intended, but have subtexts which are never constant and are always changing in meaning. For them, language has no permanence of meaning and hence all knowledge is arbitrary and relative. There is no truth, only the interpretation of the moment. Postmodernism builds on the philosophical ideas of Friedrich Nietzsche and Martin Heidegger, both critics of modern rationalist thought. Like the linguistic theorists, these philosophers (both of whom were extremely popular in Nazi Germany) argued there were no facts, only interpretations, and no objective truth or truths, but only perceptions that depend entirely on the point of view of individuals and groups. Obviously the new history seeks in large measure to undermine the old history, developed in the Renaissance and refined by the Enlightenment, which tended to see historical study as analogous to science in its accumulation of objective and 'provable' knowledge. Popular history flourishes in the face of the new history partly because it avoids any confrontation with theory. It presents narratives that are not treated as problematic but as factual.

The underlying problems of epistemology and methodology currently debated in some historical circles do not often intrude on survey courses in Canadian history, but students need to be aware of their existence.

Short Bibliography

Bibby, Reginald. *The Bibby Report: Social Trends Canadian Style*. Toronto, 1995. A useful survey of material about Canadian society in the 1990s.

Clarke, Tony. *MAI: The Multilateral Agreement on Investment and the Threat to Canadian Sovereignty*. Toronto, 1997. An impassioned defence of Canadian sovereignty in the age of globalization.

Driedger, Leo. *Multi-Ethnic Canada: Identities & Inequalities*. Toronto.1996. A careful scholarly study of ethnicity in modern Canada.

Engelstad, Diane, and John Bird, eds. *Nation to Nation: Aboriginal Sovereignty and the Future of Canada*. Toronto, 1992. A collection of essays on Aboriginal governance.

Magder, Ted. *Canada's Hollywood: The Canadian State and Feature Films*. Toronto, 1993. An important analysis of the failures of Canadian cultural policy, particularly in the area of film.

Magosci, Paul Robert, ed. *Encyclopedia of Canada's Peoples*. Toronto, 1999. A monument to the scholarship of the 1990s in Canada.

Miki, Roy, and Cassandra Kobayashi. *Justice in Our Time: The Japanese Canadian Redress Settlement*. Vancouver, 1991. An account of the redress process involving the Japanese, written by one of the participants.

Long, David, and Olive Patricia Dickason, eds. *Visions of the Heart: Canadian Aboriginal Issues*. 2nd ed. Toronto, 2000. An important collection of essays that serves as an introduction to the First Nations and their problems at century's end.

Randall, Stephen, and Herman W. Konrad, eds. *Nafta in Transition*. Calgary, 1995. A collection of essays on NAFTA that includes an important study by John Thompson of Canadian cultural policy.

Report of the Sub-Committee on the Study of Sport in Canada. Ottawa, 1998. The first attempt by Parliament to study sport in Canada, chaired by David Mills. The report begins with the premise that professional sport is an important part of the fabric of sport in the nation.

Silver, Jim. *Thin Ice: Money, Politics, and the Demise of an NHL Franchise*. Halifax, 1995. A case study of the problems of professional sport in contemporary Canada.

Watson, William. *Globalization and the Meaning of Canadian Life*. Toronto, 1998. A relatively sanguine account of globalization and its Canadian impact.

Windshuttle, Keith. *The Killing of History: How Literary Critics and Social Theorists are Murdering Our Past*. New York: The Free Press, 1997. Despite its sensationalist title, this book is a responsible and intelligent critique of the relationship between historical study and new postmodern theories, written by an Australian historian.

STUDY QUESTIONS

1. List and explain three factors that contributed to the collapse of the Progressive Conservative Party in the federal election of 1993.
2. What was the main reason for the opposition's failure to mount a successful challenge to the Liberal domination of Parliament after 1993?
3. Define in your own words the term 'globalization'.
4. Explain why Canada's aging population created a crisis in health care.
5. Why did sexual abuse become an important social issue in the 1990s?
6. What significant gains did Canada's Aboriginal peoples make in regard to land rights in the 1990s?
7. In one sense the 'I am Canadian' rant was just another beer commercial. Why did it become such a popular phenomenon?

Into the New Millennium

History texts that carry the story up to the present day sometimes conclude with an observation to the effect that nobody can know what the future will bring. To some extent, such observations are perfectly true. History is hardly a predictive science. Yet many of the issues that fill the newspaper headlines today trigger a strong sense of *déjà vu*. Often the specific event or issue seems quite new, even unique, but as the story unfolds, we realize that it is actually an expression of some unresolved question that has been with us for a long time, and is not about to disappear in the immediate future. Today there are four areas in particular where important questions remain unresolved: relations with the United States, Canadian identity, national governance, and the environment.

Relations with the United States

In the spring of 2003, any Canadian newspaper reader would have to regard relations with the US as the most important unresolved question facing Canada. By the time this book is published, the international situation may appear less menacing, but the need to come to terms with Uncle Sam is not likely to go away. Canada's place as the nearest neighbour of a superpower has been at issue for well over a century, and Canadian policy-makers have been performing a balancing act—trying to preserve Canadian autonomy while sheltering under the American military and diplomatic umbrella—at least since 1939. Before September 11, 2001, few people in North America could have expected a small group of terrorists to breach the continent's security so easily, or with such devastating results. But once the United States felt genuinely threatened, it was bound to respond with some kind of international action, in which it was equally bound to expect full support from Canada, its long-time ally. Instead, Canada has ceded its position as 'best buddy' to the United Kingdom, and many Americans are doubting Canadians' reliability in times of crisis. Further complicating our situation, decades of relative neglect of our armed forces have left us particularly vulnerable and in need of American protection at the very time when we are attempting to stand apart from what many Canadians regard as the excesses of American imperialism. Because of the complexities of the relationship, increased American suspicions regarding Canada's friendship will undoubtedly be reflected in further conflict over matters ranging from trade to culture.

Canadian Identity

Another constellation of unresolved questions has to do with the way Canadians perceive themselves and their nation. One example is the problem of constitutional change, which was not settled by either the national referendum on the Charlottetown Accord (1992) or the Quebec referendum on sovereignty (1995). In 2003, constitutional issues do not seem particularly urgent, but we know they could re-emerge at any time, since the underlying causes of discontent have never been removed, particularly where Aboriginal people and Quebec are concerned. Moreover, as a federal state made up of widely disparate regions, Canada may well face challenges from disadvantaged areas such as Atlantic Canada, which continues to lose population to the more prosperous provinces.

Quite apart from the constitutional questions they pose, the First Nations represent another series of unresolved policy issues for the federal government, the provinces, and the Canadian people. Aboriginal land claims have not been settled, any more than have the issues surrounding residential schools, the treatment of First Nations people living in urban areas, and the manifold problems of Aboriginal people in the Canadian justice system.

By the end of the twentieth century, most Canadians appeared to have accepted the principles of multiculturalism. But this acceptance can hardly be regarded as final. On 4 July 2002, for example, Statistics Canada announced that the Canadian fertility rate had fallen to 1.5 children per mother—far below the 2.1 level required to replace the existing population. This low fertility will have several consequences for Canadian society in the future. For example, population maintenance—not to mention expansion—will depend on immigration, and high immigration from the Third World will increase the speed at which the existing ethnic stock (chiefly of European origin) is replaced. Low fertility also means that the average age of the Canadian population will continue to rise, and a relatively small number of working-age Canadians will be obliged to support growing numbers of people retired from the workforce. Inevitably, an aging population will also place greater demands on the health-care system.

On the cultural front, maintaining a distinctively Canadian character (especially with respect to the United States) has continued to be a difficult exercise. The world of communications technology is changing almost daily, and in theory this technology should be encouraging cultural convergence. No doubt it is doing so in certain areas, such as popular music. Yet research in the area of public opinion over the last several generations suggests there has been less convergence than might have been expected (see Perlin 1997; Nevitte 1996). As we have seen in this volume, the term 'culture' refers to a good many different matters, and this diversity probably encourages difference.

CANADIAN GOVERNANCE

A full ten years after the implosion of the national Conservative Party in 1993, Canada has still not managed to find another national party to oppose the Liberals, either in Parliament or at the polls. While Canada's party system has never been perfect, we have never before gone so long without an effective national opposition, and we do not fully understand what this lack, if it continues, will mean over the long haul. In the short run, the inability of the parliamentary opposition to hold the Liberal government to account clearly contributed to the recent gun-control fiasco, when the auditor-general of Canada—not the opposition—pointed out the escalating expenditures on implementation of the policy. How a single-party system of government at the national level will affect other areas of national concern, such as health care, is unknown. It may well be that in the future effective opposition to the government in Ottawa will come mainly from the provinces rather than the rival parties in the House of Commons. If so, such a shift will require a major rethinking of the nation's political process.

THE ENVIRONMENT

The debate over the ratification and implementation of the Kyoto Accord has already raised the question of whether Canada can afford to adopt policies favourable to the conservation of natural resources and the prevention of environmental disasters. Part of the problem is that Canada does not exist in a vacuum and must compete economically in a world where not all nations can afford to have very much concern for the future. We do not know the extent to which Canadians are prepared to tighten their belts on behalf of the environment, especially when other nations are not doing the same thing. What we do know is that eventually non-sustainable policies lead to disaster. One example is the Atlantic cod fishery.

CONCLUSION

The world is a far more complex place today than it was in 1900, or even 1950. The issues outlined in this epilogue may never be resolved—certainly not to everyone's satisfaction—and difficult new questions seem to arise almost every day. Yet history can help us to face these uncertainties, and not only by telling us 'facts' about past events that we can use to guide our present actions. In addition, history can help us to appreciate points of view quite different from our own. It can also give us the perspective we need to cultivate a healthy skepticism about current 'crises', as well as an essential faith in the fact that change is constant—and life, in one form or another, does go on.

REFERENCES

Addiction Research Foundation. 1970. *Summary with Comments on the Interim Report of the Commission of Inquiry into the Non-Medical Use of Drugs*. Toronto: Addiction Research Foundation.

Akins, T.B., ed. 1869. *Selections from the Public Documents of the Province of Nova Scotia*. Halifax: n.p.

Allen, Robert S. 1992. *His Majesty's Indian Allies: British Indian Policy in the Defence of Canada, 1774–1815*. Toronto and Oxford: Dundurn Press.

Arthur, E. 1986. *Toronto: No Mean City*. Toronto: University of Toronto Press.

Avery, D. 1986. 'The Radical Alien and the Winnipeg General Strike of 1919'. In *Interpreting Canada's Past*, vol. 2, edited by J.M. Bumsted, 222–39. Toronto: Oxford University Press.

Ballantyne, R. 1879. *Hudson's Bay: or, Everyday Life in the Wilds of North America*. London: T. Nelson and Sons.

Behiels, M.D. 1985. *Prelude to Quebec's Quiet Revolution: Liberalism Versus Neo-Nationalism, 1945–1960*. Montreal and Kingston: McGill-Queen's University Press.

Bell, W.P. 1990. *The 'Foreign Protestants' and the Settlement of Nova Scotia: The History of a Piece of Arrested British Colonial Policy in the 18th Century*. Fredericton: Acadiensis Press.

Benson, A.B., ed. 1937. *The America of 1750: Peter Kalm's Travel in North America*, 2 vols. New York: Dover Publications.

Berger, C. 1986. 'The True North Strong and Free'. In *Interpreting Canada's Past*, vol. 2, edited by J.M. Bumsted, 154–60. Toronto: Oxford University Press.

Binnie-Clark, G. 1914. *Wheat and Woman*. Toronto: Bell & Cockburn.

Bliss, M. 1972. 'Canadianizing American Business: The Roots of the Branch Plant'. In *Close the 49th Parallel: The Americanization of Canada*, edited by I. Lumsden, 38. Toronto: University of Toronto Press.

Bourassa, H. 1912. *Canadian Club Addresses 1912*. Toronto: Warwick Bros & Rutter Ltd.

Bowker, A., ed. 1973. *The Social Criticism of Stephen Leacock: The Unsolved Riddle of Social Justice and Other Essays*. Toronto: University of Toronto Press.

Brebner, J.B. 1927. *New England's Outpost: Acadia before the Conquest of Canada*. New York: Columbia University Press.

Brode, P. 1984. *Sir John Beverley Robinson*. Toronto: University of Toronto Press.

Bruce, V., trans. 1977. *Jean Rivard* by A. Gérin-Lajoie. Toronto: McClelland and Stewart.

Bumsted, J.M., 1971. *Henry Alline, 1748–1784*. Toronto: University of Toronto Press.

———, ed. 1969. *Documentary Problems in Canadian History*. Georgetown: Irwin-Dorsey.

———, ed. 1986. *Understanding the Loyalists*. Sackville: Mount Allison University Press.

Campbell, Patrick. 1937. *Travels in the Interior Inhabited Parts of North America in the Years 1791 and 1792*. Edited by H.H. Langton. Toronto: Champlain Society.

Canada Year Book. 1959. Ottawa: Queen's Printer.

———. 1990. Ottawa: Queen's Printer.

———. 1994. Ottawa: Statistics Canada.

Carr, E.H. 1964. *What Is History?* Harmondsworth: Penguin.

Carter, S. 1990. *Lost Harvests: Prairie Indian Reserve Farmers and Government Policy*. Montreal and Kingston: McGill-Queen's University Press.

Clark, C.S. 1898. *Of Toronto the Good: a Social Study*. Montreal: Toronto Publishing Co.

Clark, E.A. 1988. 'Cumberland Planters and the Aftermath of the Attack on Fort Cumberland'. In *They Planted Well: New England Planters in Maritime Canada*, edited by M. Conrad, 49. Fredericton: Acadiensis Press.

Commission of Inquiry into the Non-Medical Use of Drugs. 1970. *Interim Report*. Ottawa: Queen's Printer.

Conrad, Margaret, et al., eds. 1988. *No Place Like Home: Diaries and Letters of Nova Scotia Women 1771–1938*. Halifax: Formac.

Cook, R. 1969a. *Provincial Autonomy: Minority Rights and the Compact Theory, 1867–1921*. Ottawa: Queen's Printer.

———, ed. 1969b. *French-Canadian Nationalism: An Anthology*. Toronto: Macmillan.

Craig, G.M., ed. 1963. *Lord Durham's Report*. Toronto: McClelland and Stewart.

Cuff, R.D., and J.L. Granatstein. 1977. *The Ties That Bind:*

Canadian-American Relations in Wartime from the Great War to the Cold War. Toronto: Samuel Stevens Hakkert & Co.

Cuthand, S. 1978. 'The Native Peoples of the Prairie Provinces in the 1920s and 1930s'. In *One Century Later: Western Canadian Reserve Indians Since Treaty 7*, edited by I.A.L. Getty and D.B. Smith, 31–2. Vancouver: University of British Columbia Press.

Davis, Ann. 1979. *Frontiers of our Dreams: Quebec Painting in the 1940's and 1950's*. Winnipeg: Winnipeg Art Gallery.

Department of Regional Economic Expansion. 1971. *Major Economic Indicators, Provinces and Regions*. Ottawa: Queen's Printer.

Dollier de Casson, F. 1928. *A History of Montreal 1640–1672*, edited and translated by R. Flenley. London: J.M. Dent & Sons.

Duncan, S.J. 1990. *The Imperialist*. Toronto: McClelland and Stewart.

Durand, E. 1981. *Vignettes of Early Winnipeg*. Winnipeg: Frances McColl.

Dyer, G., and T. Viljoen. 1990. *The Defense of Canada: In the Arms of the Empire 1760–1939*. Toronto: McClelland and Stewart.

Easterbrook, W.T., and M.H. Watkins. 1962. *Approaches to Canadian Economic History*. Toronto: McClelland and Stewart.

———, and G.J. Aitken. 1956. *Canadian Economic History*. Toronto: Macmillan.

Eccles, W.J. 1983. *The Canadian Frontier 1534–1760*, rev. ed. Albuquerque: University of New Mexico Press.

Ellis, John. 1975. *Eye Deep in Hell: Trench Warfare in World War I*. Rep. Baltimore: Johns Hopkins University Press, 1989.

Engelstad, Diane, and John Bird, eds. 1992. *Nation to Nation: Aboriginal Sovereignty and the Future of Canada*. Toronto: Anansi.

Ewart, J.S. 1908. *The Kingdom of Canada: Imperial Federation, the Colonial Conferences, the Alaska Boundary and Other Essays*. Toronto: Morang.

Fairley, M., ed. 1960. *The Selected Writings of William Lyon Mackenzie*. Toronto: Oxford University Press.

Fingard, J. 1988. 'The Relief of the Unemployed Poor in Saint John, Halifax, and St John's, 1815–1860'. In *The Acadiensis Reader*, vol. 1, edited by P.A. Buckner and D. Frank. Fredericton: Acadiensis Press.

Fisher, R. 1977. *Contact and Conflict: Indian-European Relations in British Columbia 1774–1890*. Vancouver: University of BC Press.

Forsythe, D., ed. 1971. *Let the Niggers Burn: The Sir George University Affair and Its Caribbean Aftermath*. Montreal: Black Rose.

Frye, N. 1976. 'Conclusion'. In *Literary History of Canada*, rev. ed., edited by C.F. Klinck, 849. Toronto: University of Toronto Press.

Gage, Thomas, Papers. William Clements Library, University of Michigan.

Gammer, Nicholas. *From Peacekeeping to Peacemaking: Canada's Response to the Yugoslav Crisis*. Montreal: McGill-Queen's University Press, 2001.

Gerry, Thomas M.F. 1990/91. '"I Am Translated": Anna Jameson's Sketches and *Winter and Summer Rambles in Canada*', *Journal of Canadian Studies* 25: 4 (Winter).

Granatstein, J.L., and R. Bothwell. 1990. *Pirouette: Pierre Trudeau and Canadian Foreign Policy*. Toronto: University of Toronto Press.

Grant, G. 1965. *Lament for a Nation: The Defeat of Canadian Nationalism*. Toronto: Macmillan.

Grant, G.M. ed. 1876. *Picturesque Canada*. Toronto: Hunter, Rose & Co. Printers.

Gray, Charlotte. 1999. *Sisters in the Wilderness: The Lives of Susanna Moodie and Catharine Parr Traill*. Toronto: Viking.

Gray, J. 1966. *The Winter Years: The Depression on the Prairies*. Toronto: Macmillan.

Gunn, G.E. 1966. *The Political History of Newfoundland, 1832–1864*. Toronto: University of Toronto Press.

Haliburton, T.C. 1838. *The Clockmaker: or The Sayings and Doings of Samuel Slick, of Slickville*. London: Richard Bentley.

Halpenny, F.G., ed. 1976. *The Dictionary of Canadian Biography*, vol. IX. Toronto: University of Toronto Press.

Hatch, R. 1970. *Thrust for Canada*. Boston: Houghton-Mifflin.

Hind, H.Y. 1869. *The Dominion of Canada: Containing a Historical Sketch of the Preliminaries and Organization of Confederation*. Toronto: L. Stebbins.

Hodgetts, J.E. 1968. 'The Changing Nature of the Public Service'. In *The Changing Public Service*, edited by L.D. Musoff, 7–18. Berkeley: University of California Press.

Indian-Eskimo Association of Canada. 1970. *Native Rights in Canada*. Toronto: Indian-Eskimo Association of Canada.

Innis, H. 1948. *The Diary of Simeon Perkins, 1766–1780*, vol. 1. Toronto: Champlain Society.

Johnston, M. 1994. *Corvettes Canada: Convoy Veterans of WWII Tell Their True Stories*. Toronto: McGraw-Hill Ryerson.

Kealey, G., ed. 1973. *Canada Investigates Industrialism [The Royal Commission on the Relations of Labour and Capital, 1889*, abridged]. Toronto: University of Toronto Press.

Keefer, T.C. 1853. *Philosophy of Railroads, Published by Order of the Directors of the St Lawrence and Ottawa Grand Junction Railway Company*, 4th ed. Montreal: J. Lovell.

Kostash, M. 1980. *Long Way from Home: The Story of the Sixties Generation in Canada*. Toronto: J. Lorimer.

Kwavnick, D., ed. 1973. *The Tremblay Report*. Toronto: McClelland and Stewart.

Lévesque, R. 1986. *Memoirs*, translated by P. Stratford. Toronto: McClelland and Stewart.

Lucas, C.P., ed. 1912. *Lord Durham's Report*, 3 vols. Oxford: Clarendon Press.

McArthur, D.A. 1924. 'The Teaching of Canadian History'.

Ontario Historical Society Papers 21.

MacBeath, G. 1966. 'Charles de Saint-Étienne de La Tour'. In *Dictionary of Canadian Biography*, edited by G. Brown, 592–6. Toronto: University of Toronto Press.

McCracken, M. 1975. *Memories Are Made of This: What It Was Like to Grow Up in the Fifties*. Toronto: J. Lorimer.

MacDonell, Sister M. 1982. *The Emigrant Experience: Songs of Highland Emigrants in North America*. Toronto: University of Toronto Press.

McLuhan, M. 1951. *The Mechanical Bride: Folklore of Industrial Man*. New York: Vanguard Press.

Macphail, Andrew. 1915. Diary, vol. 1, 28 Dec. Macphail Papers, National Archives of Canada.

McWhinney, E. 1982. *Canada and the Constitution 1979–1982*. Toronto: University of Toronto Press.

Marshall, J., ed. 1967. *Word from New France: The Selected Letters of Marie de l'Incarnation*. Toronto: Oxford University Press.

Marwick, Arthur. 1970. *The Nature of History*. London and Basingstoke: Macmillan.

Masters, D.C. 1936. *The Reciprocity Treaty of 1854*. London: Longmans Green & Company.

Miki, Roy, and Cassandra Kobayashi. 1991. *Justice in Our Time: The Japanese Canadian Redress Settlement*. Vancouver: Talonbooks.

Monière, D. 1981. *Ideologies on Quebec: The Historical Development*. Toronto: University of Toronto Press.

Moodie, S. 1852. *Roughing It in the Bush, or, Life in Canada*, vol. 1. London: Richard Bentley, 1852.

Morrow, D. 1989. *A Concise History of Sport in Canada*. Toronto: Oxford University Press.

Morton, W.L., ed. 1970. *Monck Letters and Journals 1863–1868: Canada from Government House at Confederation*. Toronto: McClelland and Stewart.

National Archives of Canada. 1745. 'Representation of the State of His Majesty's Province of Nova Scotia' (8 November 1745).

National Task Force on Suicide in Canada. 1984. *Suicide in Canada*. Ottawa: Queen's Printer.

Naylor, R.T. 1975. *The History of Canadian Business, 1867–1914*, vol. 1. Toronto: J. Lorimer.

Neatby, H. 1972. *The Quebec Act: Protest and Policy*. Toronto: Prentice-Hall of Canada.

Nelles, H.V. 1974. *The Politics of Development: Forests, Mines & Hydro-Electric Power in Ontario, 1849–1941*. Toronto: Macmillan.

Nevitte, Neil. 1996. *The Decline of Deference: Canadian Value Change in Cross-National Perspective*. Peterborough, ON: Broadview Press.

Patterson, E.P. 1972. *The Canadian Indian: A History Since 1500*. Toronto: Collier-Macmillan.

Perlin, George. 1997. 'The Constraints of Public Opinion: Diverging or Converging Paths?' In Keith Banting, George Hoberg, and Richard Simeon, eds, *Degrees of Freedom: Canada and the United States in a Changing World*. Montreal and Kingston: McGill-Queen's University Press.

Pope, Sir J. 1930. *Memoirs of the Rt Hon. Sir John A. Macdonald*, vol. 1. Toronto: Oxford University Press.

Preston, R.A., ed. 1974. *For Friends at Home: A Scottish Emigrant's Letters from Canada, California and the Cariboo 1844–1864*. Montreal and London: McGill-Queen's University Press.

Proceedings of the Special Joint Committee of the Senate and House of Commons on Divorce. 1967. Ottawa: Queen's Printer.

Pryke, K.G. 1979. *Nova Scotia and Confederation, 1864–1874*. Toronto: University of Toronto Press.

Quaife, M.M., ed. 1962. *The Western Country in the 17th Century: The Memoirs of Antoine Lamothe Cadillac and Pierre Liette*. New York: The Citadel Press.

Québec conseil exécutif. 1979. *Québec-Canada, a New Deal: The Québec Government Proposal for a New Partnership between Equals, Sovereignty-Association*. Québec conseil exécutif.

Raspovich, A.W. 1969. 'National Awakening: Canada at Mid-Century'. In *Documentary Problems in Canadian History*, vol. 1, edited by J.M. Bumsted, 225. Georgetown: Irwin-Dorsey.

Rea, K.J. 1985. *The Prosperous Years: The Economic History of Ontario 1939–75*. Toronto: University of Toronto Press.

Recollections of the War of 1812. 1964. Toronto: Baxter Publishing Company.

Report of the Royal Commission on Broadcasting. 1957. Ottawa: King's Printer.

Report of the Royal Commission on National Development in the Arts, Letters and Sciences. 1951. Toronto: King's Printer.

Report of the Royal Commission on the Status of Women in Canada. 1970. Ottawa: Queen's Printer.

Robertson, J.R. 1911. *The Diary of Mrs John Graves Simcoe, Wife of the First Lieutenant-Governor of the Province of Upper Canada, 1792–1796*. Toronto: W. Briggs.

Royal Commission on Aboriginal Peoples. 1993. *Partners in Confederation: Aboriginal Peoples, Self-government, and the Constitution*. Ottawa: Queen's Printer.

Royal Commission on Canada's Economic Prospects. 1958. Ottawa: Queen's Printer.

Royal Commission on the Donald Marshall, Jr, Prosecution, vol. 1: Findings and Recommendations. 1989. Halifax: The Commission.

Royal Society of Canada. 1932. *Fifty Years' Retrospective 1882–1932*. Toronto: University of Toronto Press.

Rubio, M., and E. Waterston, eds. 1987. *The Selected Journals of L.M. Montgomery, vol. 2: 1910–1921*. Toronto: Oxford University Press.

Saywell, J. *Quebec 70: A Documentary Narrative*. Toronto: University of Toronto Press.

Seeley, J.R., R.A. Sim, and E. Loosley. 1972. *Crestwood Heights: A North American Suburb*. Toronto: University of

Toronto Press.

Siegfried, A. 1907. *The Race Question in Canada*. London: E. Nash.

Smiley, D. 1970. 'Canadian Federalism and the Resolution of Federal-Provincial Conflicts'. In *Contemporary Issues in Canadian Politics*, edited by F. Vaughan et al., 48–66. Toronto: Prentice-Hall.

Special Committee on Social Security. 1943. *Report on Social Security for Canada, Prepared by Dr L.C. Marsh for the Advisory Committee on Reconstruction*. Ottawa: King's Printer.

Stacey, C.P. 1970. *Arms, Man and Governments: The War Policies of Canada 1939–1945*. Ottawa: Queen's Printer.

———. 1981. *Canada and the Age of Conflict: A History of Canadian External Policies, vol. 2: 1921–1948*. Toronto: Macmillan.

Stanley, G.F.G. 1977. *Canada Invaded, 1775–1776*. Toronto: Canadian War Museum.

Statement of the Government of Canada on Indian Policy. 1969. Ottawa: Queen's Printer.

Statistics Canada. 1957. *Manufacturing Industries of Canada 1957*. Ottawa: Queen's Printer.

Steele, S. 1915. *Forty Years in Canada: Reminiscences of the Great North-West* . . . . Toronto: McClelland, Goodchild & Stewart.

Stephens, H.F. 1890. *Jacques Cartier and His Four Voyages to Canada: An Essay with Historical, Explanatory and Philological Notes*. Montreal: W. Drysdale & Co.

Sykes, E.C. 1912. *A Home-Help in Canada*. London: G. Bell & Sons Ltd.

Thompson, J.H., and A. Seager. 1985. *Canada, 1922–1939: Decades of Discord*. Toronto: McClelland and Stewart.

Traill, C.P. 1846. *The Backwoods of Canada*. London: M.A. Nattali.

Trudel, M. 1973. *The Beginnings of New France 1524–1663*. Toronto: McClelland and Stewart.

Vallières, P. 1971. *White Niggers of America*. Toronto: McClelland and Stewart.

Voisey, P. 1988. *Vulcan: The Making of a Prairie Community*. Toronto: University of Toronto Press.

Waite, P.B. 1962. *The Life and Times of Confederation, 1864–1867: Politics, Newspapers, Union of British North America*. Toronto: University of Toronto Press.

———, ed. 1963. *Confederation Debates in the Province of Canada*. Toronto: McClelland and Stewart.

Wall, Denis. 2000. 'Aboriginal Self-Government in Canada: The Cases of Nunavut and the Alberta Métis Settlements'. Pp. 143–67 in David Long and Olive Patricia Dickason, eds. *Visions of the Heart: Canadian Aboriginal Issues*. 2nd edn. Toronto: Harcourt Brace.

White, Richard. 1991. *The Middle Ground: Indians, Empires and Republics in the Great Lakes Region, 1650–1815*. New York: Cambridge University Press.

Williamson, J.A., ed. 1962. *The Cabot Voyages and British Discoveries under Henry VII*. Cambridge: Hakluyt Society of the University Press.

Williamson, M. 1970. *Robert Harris, 1849–1919: An Unconventional Biography*. Toronto: McClelland and Stewart.

Wilson, Edmund. 1964. *O Canada: An American's Notes on Canadian Culture*. New York: Farrar, Straus and Giroux..

Wright, E.C. 1955. *The Loyalists of New Brunswick*. Fredericton: University of New Brunswick Press.

Wynn, G. 1980. *Timber Colony: A Historical Geography of Early 19th Century New Brunswick*. Toronto: University of Toronto Press.

Young, W. 1978. 'Academics and Social Scientists *versus* the Press: The Policies of the Bureau of Public Information and the Wartime Information Board, 1939 to 1945'. In *CHA Historical Papers, a Selection from the Papers Presented at the Annual Meeting of the Canadian Historical Association* (1978).

INDEX

NOTE: page numbers in italic type refer to illustrations